Penguin Books

THE

Time Out

AMSTERDAM

GUIDE

The *Time Out Amsterdam Guide* is more than just a book for tourists. It covers all the major sights and attractions, and hundreds of lesser-known, unusual and fascinating places. We list the major museums and art collections as well where to find work by contemporary artists. We describe how to book a session with a personal philosopher and explain the hidden workings of the city's canals. We steer you round the major stores and help you find smaller, more specialist shops. Naturally, we've listed and reviewed all of Amsterdam's worthwhile places of entertainment – theatres, cinemas, music venues and clubs – but we've also given an insider's view of the current cultural scene. Every place listed in the Guide has been visited, assessed by residents, and given an honest review – what it's like, what to see and what to avoid. This is Amsterdam by Amsterdammers.

For the past 20 years, if you've wanted to know what's going on in London, you've consulted *Time Out*. We've now turned our expert eye on Amsterdam, to produce the definitive guide to this most welcoming of cities. Cafés and restaurants, shops, how to make your way around and surviving an emergency: all are covered, along with the city's history, sports facilities and business services.

It should be stressed that the information we give is impartial. No organization or enterprise has been listed in this guide because its owner or manager has advertised in our publications. Impartiality is the reason our guides are so successful and well respected. We hope you enjoy the *Time Out Amsterdam Guide* and that it helps you to enjoy your stay. But if you disagree with any of our reviews, let us know; your comments on places you have visited are welcome.

THE Time Out AMSTERDAM GUIDE

Penguin Books

PENGUIN BOOKS

Published by the Penguin Group
Penguin Books Ltd, 27 Wrights Lane, London W8 5TZ, England
Viking Penguin, a division of Penguin Books USA Inc.
375 Hudson Street, New York, New York 10014, USA
Penguin Books Australia Ltd, Ringwood, Victoria, Australia
Penguin Books Canada Ltd, 2801 John Street, Markham, Ontario, Canada L3R 1B4
Penguin Books (NZ) Ltd, 182–190 Wairau Road, Auckland 10, New Zealand

Penguin Books Ltd, Registered Offices: Harmondsworth, Middlesex, England

First published 1991
10 9 8 7 6 5 4 3 2 1

Copyright © Time Out Publications Limited, 1991
All rights reserved

Printed in England by Clays Ltd, St Ives plc

Except in the United States of America, this book is sold subject to
the condition that it shall not, by way of trade or otherwise, be lent,
re-sold, hired out, or otherwise circulated without the publisher's
prior consent in any form of binding or cover other than that in
which it is published and without a similar condition including this
condition being imposed on the subsequent purchaser

Contents

About the Guide

PRACTICAL GUIDE

The *Time Out Amsterdam Guide* will be updated every two years. As well as trying to make it an interesting read, we've attempted to make this book as useful as possible. Addresses, telephone numbers, transport details, opening times, admission prices and credit card details are all included in our listings. And, as far as possible, we've given details of facilities, services and events.

All the information was checked and correct when we went to press – but please remember that owners and managers can change their arrangements at any time. We urge you to phone, before you set out, to check opening times, the dates of exhibitions, admission fees and other important details. In particular, we have tried to include information on access for the disabled, but it is always wise to phone first to check your needs can be met.

AMSTERDAM'S AREAS

For every place listed in the Guide, we give an idea of its location: just after the address, and before the telephone number, are some letters which refer to areas of Amsterdam. These areas are highlighted on the map at the back of the Guide, but roughly speaking: **C** (*Central*) covers the area bounded by the River IJ in the north of the city and the Singel and Nieuwe Herengracht canals; **IE** (*Inner East*) is defined by the IJ, Nieuwe Herengracht, Binnenamstel and Singelgracht; **IS** (*Inner South*) by Binnenamstel, Singelgracht and Leidsegracht; **IW** (*Inner West*) by Leidsegracht, Singelgracht, Singel, and back again to the River IJ to the north. Beyond these inner areas are **OE** (*Outer East*), stretching east from Singelgracht and the River Amstel; **OS** (*Outer South*), south from Singelgracht between the River Amstel and Overtoom; and **OW** (*Outer West*) between Overtoom and the River IJ. With areas a long way from the centre of Amsterdam – and beyond the range of our map – we have tried to give a little more information by making the compass directions more specific. For instance, the Metro stations at the far end of the line are listed as **OSE** (*Outer South East*). Finally, **N** (*North*) indicates those areas north of the River IJ. The majority of the places listed within this Guide fall within the C, IE, IS and IW areas.

TELEPHONES

Many **Amsterdam phone numbers were changed** between February and April 1991. By March 1991 all six-digit numbers should have the figure '6' added in front of the number; all seven-digit numbers will remain the same. Throughout the Guide, we have printed the full seven-digit number; if, in Spring 1991, you dial a seven-digit number and do not get through, try re-dialling, omitting the first '6'.

PRICES

The prices we've listed throughout the Guide should be used as guide-lines. Fluctuating exchange rates and inflation can cause prices, in shops and restaurants especially, to change rapidly. If prices or services somewhere vary greatly from those we've quoted, ask whether there's a good reason. If not, go elsewhere. Then, please let us know. We try to give the best and most up-to-date advice, so we always want to hear if you've been overcharged or badly treated.

CREDIT CARDS

Throughout the Guide, the following abbreviations have been used for credit cards: **AmEx**: American Express; **CB**: Carte Bleue; **DC**: Diners' Club; **JCB**: Japanese credit cards; **MC**: MasterCard (linked to Access and Eurocard); **TC**: travellers' cheques in any currency; **f TC**, **£TC**, **$TC**, and so on: travellers' cheques in guilders, sterling, US dollars or other specified currencies; **V**: Visa (linked to Barclaycard).

Edited and designed by
Time Out Publications Limited,
134-146 Curtain Road,
London EC2A 3AR
(phone: 071 729 5959/
fax: 071 729 7266)

Publisher
Tony Elliott
Managing Director
Adele Carmichael
Financial Director
Kevin Ellis

Senior Managing Editor
Peter Fiennes
Managing Editor
Marion Moisy
Editor
Ruth Jarvis
Consultant Editor
Ann Campbell-Lord

Art Director
Kirk Teasdale
Designer
Iain Murray

Advertisement Director
Lesley Gill
Sales Director
Mark Phillips

Cover Illustration
Lo Cole

Introduction

Of all Europe's capital cities, Amsterdam is perhaps the least typical. It has a population of less than 800,000, covers an area only a fraction the size of London or Paris and it's not the seat of government, which is 50 kilometres (31 miles) away in The Hague. More than any other west European city, Amsterdam has developed an intriguing, ambiguous reputation: quaint, gabled backwater; archetypal melting-pot of cultures and a Mecca for non-conformists from all over the world; and modern, commercial city. Amsterdam is all these things, and its unique attraction lies in discovering for yourself how and why they manage to co-exist.

Part of the answer lies in a tradition of practical tolerance and liberal attitudes going back centuries, beginning with the city's open-door policy to seventeenth-century European Jews and culminating more recently when it became the unofficial capital of the hippy movement in the 1960s and the protest generation in the 1970s. It's no coincidence that John Lennon and Yoko Ono chose the Amsterdam Hilton for their 'sleep-in', nor that the present city council, run by a former student activist, has decided to paint the city's trams bright red with yellow spots.

The strange mix between Amsterdam's cosmopolitan outlook and its intimate, provincial charm has tended to obscure the fact that it is one of the most important business and financial centres in Europe. Its impressive communications links and proximity to Rotterdam, the world's largest port and distribution centre, mean that post-1992 Europe is an event the city is eagerly awaiting.

Amsterdam's late but explosive flowering as an international financial services centre in the eighties has had the side-effect of mellowing the appearance – and radical reputation – of the inner city. The construction of high-rise glass towers, conference centres and arts complexes is gradually bringing a more respectable, professional gloss to the picturesque cobbled streets.

With cultural and commercial development breathing new life into an already buzzing metropolis, Amsterdam in the run-up to 1992 has never been a more exciting place to visit. All the perennial advantages of the city are as much in evidence as ever: an open, welcoming population whose facility for English is virtually universal and often flawless; a picturesque, compact city centre; hundreds of restaurants and cafés close to major museums and galleries; and a perpetually youthful atmosphere. Unlike many capitals, Amsterdam does not close down after the summer, and you don't need to wait for a particular time of year to visit.

Ailsa Camm

AMSTERDAM

GET ON
YOUR BIKE FOR
LESS THAN
£70

INCLUDES YOUR FARE & HOTEL FOR **2 NIGHTS** DEPARTURES DAILY

Amsterdam TRAVEL SERVICE

Phone now to book this sensational offer

0920 467444

ABTA
10981

Essential Information

How do you get off a tram, find a taxi or just say 'Hello'? *Julie Sinclair-Day* shows how to get started: Amsterdam made easy.

Most visitors to Amsterdam are swiftly put at ease by the city's compact size, efficient transport system and the linguistic skills of its cosmopolitan inhabitants. A visitor's struggling attempts at Dutch will often be met with a smile, followed by a reply in perfect English. But, as with any city of character, Amsterdam has its own way of getting things done. The following list of essentials is designed to help you get your visit off to a good start. For more detailed advice on staying healthy and dealing with emergencies *see page 221* **Survival**, and for details of the abbreviations used within this guide *see page vi* **About the Guide**.

see page 221
see page vi

VISAS

A valid passport is all that is required for a stay of up to three months in The Netherlands if you are an EC national or from one of the following countries:
*Australia, Cyprus, Finland, Iceland, New Zealand, Norway, Sweden, Vatican City, Yugoslavia
*Africa: Botswana, Burkina-Faso, Lesotho, Malawi, Niger, Swaziland, Togo
*The Americas: Argentina, Bolivia, Brazil, Canada, Colombia, Costa Rica, Ecuador, Guatemala, Honduras Republic, Jamaica, Mexico, Nicaragua, Panama, Paraguay, Peru, El Salvador, Uruguay, USA, Venezuela

If you are unsure of visa requirements or know you need a visa, contact your nearest Dutch embassy or consulate at least three months before your departure. For stays of longer than three months EC citizens need an extension visa, available from the **Bureau Vreemdelingenpolitie** (Aliens' Police, *listed below*). For information on work and residence permits *see page 188* **Business**.

see page 188

Bureau Vreemdelingenpolitie (Aliens' Police)
Waterlooplein 9, C (general enquiries 559 9111/visa enquiries 559 3179). Tram 9, 14. **Open** 8.30am-12.30pm Mon-Fri.
An extension visa is free of charge and can normally be obtained on the day of application. Appointments are not required but queues start at around 7am and you can expect a wait of up to two hours. Once you are through the queue it takes literally minutes for the interviewer to process your application and grant you a visa. You will need to take ID and proof of an address in The Netherlands, such as the phone number of your hotel, as well as proof of sufficient funds for a longer stay.

CUSTOMS

EC citizens over the age of 17 may import the following goods for personal use, if bought tax-paid:
*300 cigarettes or 75 cigars or 400g (14oz) of tobacco
*1½ litres (2.64 pints) of spirits (over 22 per cent alcohol) or 3 litres (5.28 pints) of liqueur wine/ sparkling wine (under 22 per cent) or 5 litres (8.8 pints) of non-sparkling wine
*75g (2.65oz) of perfume
*1kg (2.2lb) of coffee
*200g (7.1oz) of tea
*Other goods to the value of f890 for non-commercial use
Citizens from non-EC countries or those importing goods duty-free may import:
*200 cigarettes or 50 cigars or 250g (8.82oz) of tobacco
*1 litre (1.76 pints) of spirits (over 22 per cent alcohol) or two litres (3.52 pints) of fortified wine (under 22 per cent) or two litres (3.52 pints) of non-sparkling wine
*50g (1.76oz) of perfume
*500g (1.1lb) of coffee
*100g (3.53oz) of tea
*Other goods to the value of f125
The import of meat, meat products, fruit, plants, flowers and protected animals is restricted or forbidden. There are no restrictions on the import and export of currency.

INSURANCE

EC countries have reciprocal medical treatment arrangements with The Netherlands. British citizens will need form E111, which can be obtained by filling in the application form in leaflet SA30, available in all Department of Social Security (DSS) offices. Make sure you read the small print on the back of form E111 and ensure that you know how to obtain medical or dental treatment at a reduced charge, since the chances are you'll have to explain this to the Dutch doctor or dentist who treats you. If you should need treatment, photocopy your insurance form and leave that with the doctor or dentist who treats you.

Citizens of other EC countries should make sure they have obtained one of forms E110, E111 or E112.

Citizens of the following **non-EC countries** can also receive medical treatment at reduced rates by producing the appropriate form: Austria form O/NL111 or O/NL112; Morocco MN111; Yugoslavia YN111; Tunisia TUN/N111; Turkey TUR/N111; Sweden SV/N111.

Citizens from **all other countries** should take out private medical insurance before their visit. Dutch medical treatment costs about half what it would in the USA, which is still more than enough to make travelling without insurance unwise.

As always when travelling abroad, visitors should take out insurance on personal belongings before leaving for Amsterdam. Such insurance is usually included in package holidays, but be sure to check.

MONEY

The unit of Dutch currency is the **guilder**, variously abbreviated as f, fl or Hfl. Throughout this guide the abbreviation 'f' is used. The guilder is divided into 100 cents, rather more obviously abbreviated to 'c'. Coins in use are 5c, 10c, 25c, f1, f2.50 and f5. The 5c coin is copper, 10c, 25c, f1 and f2.50 coins are silver and the f5 coin is gold. The 5c coin is also known as *stuiver*, the 10c coin *dubbeltje*, 25c *kwartje* and the f2.50 coin is called *rijksdaalder*. Notes come in f5, f10, f25, f50, f100, f250, f500 and f1,000 denominations. To make it easier to tell them apart, the f5 note is green, f10 blue, f25 pink, f50 yellow and f100 brown. Raised symbols give the denominations for blind people (*see page 221* **Survival: Disabled**).

Since the Dutch don't have 1c or 2c coins, prices are rounded up or down to the nearest 5 cents, so fl.53 will be charged as fl.55.

Amsterdammers prefer to use cash for most transactions, although the larger hotels, shops and most restaurants will accept one or more of the major credit cards (Access/Eurocard/Mastercard, American Express, Diners Club, Visa) and many will take Eurocheques with guarantee cards, and travellers' cheques with ID such as a passport.

BANKS

Banks and bureaux de change offer similar rates of exchange but banks tend to charge less commission. Most banks are open 9am to 4pm Monday to Friday, some staying open until 7pm on Thursdays. As yet no banks open on Saturdays but exchange facilities are available at the bureaux de change *listed below*. Dutch banks buy and sell foreign currency and exchange travellers' cheques and Eurocheques, but few give cash advances against credit cards. For this you'll need to go to a bureau de change (*see below*). For a full list of banks in Amsterdam *see page 188* **Business** or look in the Amsterdam *Yellow Pages* (*Gouden Gids*), under 'Banken'. *Gouden Gids* can be found in post offices, hotels and phone centres (*see page 221* **Survival**).

BUREAUX DE CHANGE

Bureaux de change can be found throughout the city centre, especially on Leidseplein, Damrak and Rokin. Those listed below give reasonable rates of exchange, although they charge more in commission than the banks. Try to avoid using hotel and tourist bureaux exchange facilities (*see below* **Tourist Information**) as these are generally more expensive.

American Express
Damrak 66, C (520 7777). Tram 4, 9, 16, 24, 25. **Open** 9am-5.30pm Mon-Fri; noon-5pm Sat. *Exchange facilities also available* 11am-4pm Sun, public holidays.
This office has a 24-hour cash machine for card holders and an automatic travellers' cheque refund service. Mail can also be sent poste restante if you are a cardholder; this service is free. It should be addressed, with your name, to *Customer Mail Service, American Express, Damrak 66, 1012 LM, Amsterdam*. When collecting mail you need to show ID and your AmEx card.

Change Express
Damrak 86, C (622 1425). Tram 1, 4, 9, 16, 24, 25. **Open** 8am-11.30pm daily. **Branch** *Leidsestraat 106, C (625 0922). Tram 1, 2, 5.* **Open** 8am-midnight daily.

GWK
Centraal Station, C (627 2731). Tram 1, 2, 4, 5, 9, 13, 16, 17, 24, 25. **Open** 24 hours daily. **Branch** *Amsterdam Schiphol Airport (in the railway station) (601 0507).* **Open** 24 hours daily.

Thomas Cook
Dam 23-25, C (625 0922). Tram 4, 9, 14, 16, 24, 25. **Open** 9am-6pm Mon-Sat; 9am-5pm Sun.

TRANSPORT

TO & FROM THE AIRPORT

Schiphol Airport Rail Service
Schiphol Airport/Centraal Station (information 06 899 1121). **Times** trains daily at15-minute intervals 5am-1am; then hourly 2am, 3am, 4am. **Tickets** *single* f4.75; under-12s with adult f1; under-4s free; *return* f8; under-12s with adult f2; under-4s free. **No credit cards**.
The journey to Centraal Station takes about 20 minutes.

KLM Hotel Bus Service
Main exit Schiphol Airport (664 9561/649 1393). **Times** buses at 30-minute intervals 6.25am-11.25pm daily. **Tickets** f15. **No credit cards**.
This service is available to anyone; you don't need to have travelled on the airline or be staying at one of the hotel stops. There are two routes, the *yellow line*, covering the Leidseplein area and stopping at the Ibis, Amsterdam Hilton, Barbizon Centre, Parkhotel and Amsterdam Apollo hotels, and the *orange line* going to the Dam Square area and stopping at the Pulitzer, Sonesta/Holiday Inn, Victoria, Krasnapolsky and Barbizon Palace hotels.

Taxis
There are always plenty of taxis outside the main exit. It's pricey, however: at the time of writing about f60 from the airport into central Amsterdam, and even more at night. For details of the car hire firms operating from Schiphol Airport *see p221* **Survival**. For more details about Amsterdam's taxi service, *see below* **Public Transport**.

The **yellow tram** (listed under **Transport: Trams & Buses***) is becoming as synonymous with Amsterdam as the red double-decker bus is with London. The vehicles are kept clean and – excepting traffic jams – make for fast and efficient travel, but other road-users be warned that they will stop only when absolutely necessary. Cyclists should listen out for the tram's distinctive warning bell and motorists should avoid blocking tramlines – cars are only allowed to venture on to them if they're turning right. It doesn't pay to argue with a tram. Those on bikes should cross tramlines with the front wheel at an angle in order to avoid getting stuck. It's easily done and can result in a painful and undignified tumble. To get on or off a tram, press the yellow button adjacent to the doors at the front, middle and rear of the vehicle, which will then open.*

AIRLINE INFORMATION

For general airport enquiries ring Schiphol airport on *601 0966*. The major airlines can be reached at the following addresses. Staff answering telephone enquiries will speak English.

British Airways

Stadhouderskade 4, OS (685 2211). Tram 1, 2, 5, 6, 7, 10. **Open** 9am-5pm Mon-Fri; 9am-noon Sat. **Credit** AmEx, DC, MC, V.

British Midland

Ticket desk Schiphol Airport (604 1459/freephone information 06 022 2426). **Open** 6am-10pm Mon-Fri; 6am-8pm Sat; 8am-10pm Sun. **Credit** AmEx, DC, MC, V.

Dan Air

Luchthaven Schiphol; ticket desk in arrival hall (601 0311). **Open** 9am-5.30pm Mon-Fri. **Credit** AmEx, DC, MC, V.

KLM

Leidseplein 1, IS (649 3633/24-hour information and reservations 674 7747). **Tram** 1, 2, 5, 6, 7, 10. **Open** 8.30am-5.30pm Mon-Fri; 10am-2pm Sat. **Credit** AmEx, DC, MC, V.

Pan Am

Leidseplein 31C, IS (626 2021). Tram 1, 2, 5, 6, 7, 10. **Open** 9am-5pm Mon-Fri. **Credit** AmEx, DC, MC, V.

TWA

Singel 540, C (626 2277). Tram 4, 9, 14, 16, 24, 25. **Open** 9am-5.30pm Mon-Fri. **Credit** AmEx, DC, MC, V.

CITY TRANSPORT

Getting around Amsterdam by public transport is easy. The city has an efficient, reasonably priced tram and bus system and, because of its compact size, it's possible to cycle or simply walk to most places of interest. Cycling is the method of transport preferred by many native Amsterdammers and, true to the cliché, the streets are busy with bicycle traffic all through the day. The canals are also well-used by pleasure boats, commercial barges and water taxis. If you are thinking of bringing a car to Amsterdam for a short stay – don't! Trams, bikes and buses jostle alarmingly at the larger junctions and jams are common on the narrow one-way systems around the canals. Parking places are elusive and expensive. However, public transport provision for those with disabilities is dire and, although there are lifts at all Metro stations apart from Waterlooplein, the staff can't help people in wheelchairs. So

One of the city's best-selling T-shirts has the legend I cycled in Amsterdam – and lived. *It's not really as bad as that, though the heavy tram, car and bike traffic in the centre does demand a certain strength of nerve. On warm days* **bikes** (listed under **Transport: Cycling**) *are everywhere and weave in and out of the pedestrians on the main streets. Shoppers should be on the alert and avoid stepping blindly into bike lanes. For both visitor and native, cycling is for many the cheapest and most fun way of getting around the city.*

if you can't do without a car *see page 221* **Survival** for information on car hire, parking and what to do if the car breaks down. For details of orientation and maps *see below* **Tourist Information;** for public transport maps see at the back of the Guide.

PUBLIC TRANSPORT

For information, tickets, maps and an English-language brochure explaining the city's ticket system, visit the **Municipal Transport Authority** *(listed below)*. But if all you need is information on Amsterdam's complicated ticketing system *see below* **Tickets.**

GVB (Amsterdam Municipal Transport Authority)

Stationsplein 15, C (627 2727 8am-11pm daily). Tram 1, 2, 4, 5, 9, 13, 16, 17, 24, 25. **Open** 7am-10.30pm Mon-Fri; 8am-10.30pm Sat; 8.30am-4.30pm Sun. **No credit cards.** The GVB runs Amsterdam's Metro, bus and tram services.
Branches *GVB Head Office, Prins Hendrikkade 108, C.* **Open** 8.30am-4.30pm Mon-Fri. **No credit cards.** *Amstel Railway*

Station, Julianaplein, OE. **Open** 7am-8.30pm Mon-Fri; 10.15am-5pm Sat, Sun. **No credit cards.**

METRO

The Metro (underground) system in Amsterdam uses the same ticketing system as trams and buses, (*see below* **Tickets**) but it mainly serves the eastern and south-eastern suburbs and so is mostly used by commuters. There are two lines, both terminating at Centraal Station. Trains run from 6am Mon-Fri (6.30am Sat; 7.30am Sun) to about 12.15am daily.

TRAMS & BUSES

As a visitor to Amsterdam you will find buses and particularly trams (*see page 4* **picture and caption**) a good way to get around the city centre. Tram services run from 6am Monday to Friday, 6.30am on Saturday and 7.30am on Sunday, with a special night bus service taking over after midnight. **Night buses**

GROUPS & INDIVIDUALS

Let me be your own personal guide.

- ● EXCURSIONS
- ● ARCHITECTURE
- ● MUSEUMS
- ● ART
- ● EDUCATION

NATIONAL TOURIST GUIDE
WALTER M.G. ALTENA

Pieter Lastmankade 34-1ᵉ
1075 KK Amsterdam - Holland
Telephone and Fax: (0)20 - 662 97 84

Globepost Ltd

AMSTERDAM from £85

DAILY FLIGHTS EX GATWICK

Dept 0840	Rtn 1150
Dept 1245	Rtn 1615
Dept 1700	Rtn 1945
Dept 2030	

EUROPEAN SPECIALISTS
071-587-0303
ABTA 90721 IATA

International telephone
Normal public telephone prices,
the cheapest in Amsterdam
All cabines are airconditioned.
Also collect and credit card calls.

and telefax-service
Confidential transmission.
Send and receive.
Costs: send fl. 5,- and telephone costs.
Receive fl. 3,50 per message
Fax number: (31.20)208559

Photocopy-service/Excursions

Leidsestraat 101 Amsterdam Phone: 020 - 208599
Open 7 days a week from 10.00 - 24.00 hours

are numbered from 71 to 77, with numbers 73 to 76 running through the city centre. Night bus stops are indicated by a black square at the stop with the bus number printed on it. However, even the night buses stop running between 2am and 4am Monday to Friday and 2.30am to 3.30am Saturday and Sunday, so between these times the only alternatives are walking or taxis (*see below* **Taxis**).

Yellow signs at tram and bus stops indicate the name of the stop and further destinations. There are usually maps of the entire network in the shelters and diagrams of routes on board the trams and buses. Amsterdam's bus and tram drivers are generally courteous and will happily give directions if asked.

In buses there is only one door. There are three doors on trams, all of which serve as both exits and entries. If you want to buy a ticket enter by the door nearest the driver.

TICKETS

Strip tickets (strippenkaart). In Amsterdam a strip ticket (*strippenkaart*) system operates on trams, buses and the Metro, which is initially confusing but ultimately good value for money. Prices range from f1.35 for a strip with two units to f9.05 for 15 units. Foreign pensioners and unemployed unfortunately aren't entitled to any reductions on ticket prices, but children under four travel free and older children pay reduced fares for two-day tickets (*see below*). Tickets can be bought in GVB offices (*see above* **Public Transport**), post offices (*see page 221* **Survival**), train stations and many tobacconists. The tickets must be stamped aboard a tram or bus and on entering a Metro station. The city is divided into five zones: Noord (north), West, Centrum, Oost (east) and Zuid (south); most of central Amsterdam falls, not surprisingly, within zone Centrum.

For travel in a single zone, two units must be stamped, while three are stamped for two zones, four for three zones and so on. In trams you can stamp your own tickets in the yellow box-like machines at the back. Just fold it so the unit you need to stamp is at the end. On buses, drivers stamp the tickets and on the Metro there are stamping machines in the entrance to stations. An unlimited number of people can travel on one card, but the appropriate number of units must be stamped for each person. The stamps are valid for an hour, during which time you can transfer to other buses and trams without having to stamp your card again. If your journey were to take more than an hour you would have to stamp more units, but no single tram journey in central Amsterdam is likely to take more than an hour. There is no time limit on the use of a *strippenkaart*.

Day ticket (dagkaarten). A cheaper option for unlimited travel in Amsterdam, a day ticket costs f9, two days cost f12.10 and three days f14.80, with each additional day costing an extra f2.80. Only Dutch pensioners and unwaged are eligible for cheaper travel, but for a child (aged 4 to 11) a two-day ticket costs f6.05 and three days f7.40, with each additional day costing a further f1.40. Child day tickets are not valid on night buses. A day ticket is valid on trams, buses and the Metro on the day it is stamped and throughout that night. Only the one-day ticket and the less economical hourly ticket can be bought on board trams and buses from their drivers. The hourly ticket is valid in all five zones for one hour and costs f2.70 for everybody.

Season tickets (sterabonnement). These can be bought from GVB offices and are valid for a week, a month or a year. A weekly pass for zone Centrum costs f12.50, a monthly one f41 and a yearly one f410. Children between the ages of 6 and 11 can get the weekly pass at half price. You will require a photograph and passport.

Beware of travelling on a bus or tram without a ticket. Uniformed inspectors make regular checks and those without a valid ticket – or an exceptionally good excuse – are liable to be fined f100 on the spot. Foreign visitors professing ignorance of the rules rarely escape penalty.

TAXIS

Generally Amsterdam's taxi drivers are an informed and friendly lot

One of Amsterdam's most imposing structures, the ornate **Centraal Station** *(listed under* **Transport: Trains***) gives a bustling first impression of the city. All conceivable needs of the newly-arrived visitor are catered for here, from shower facilities and restaurants inside the station to hotel, travel and entertainment booking services on the Stationsplein just outside. As most of the city's bus and tram services begin and end at the station it is also an ideal starting point for trips around the city. A year-round entourage of flower stalls, street entertainers and hippy buskers singing* Hey Joe *in front of the main entrance adds to its character, though beware of pickpockets and hustlers.*

WHEREVER YOU'RE BOUND, WE'RE BOUND TO HAVE BEEN.

At STA Travel, we're all seasoned travellers so we should know a thing or two about where you're headed. And because we know the travel business backwards, we can offer you the best deals on fares – even the flexibility to change your mind as you go, without having to pay over the top for the privilege. We operate from 120 offices worldwide. So call in soon.

North America 071 937 9971. Europe 071 937 9921. Rest of World 071 937 9962

74 & 86 Old Brompton Road, SW7
117 Euston Road, NW1
Manchester, Oxford, Cambridge, Bristol

99209

STA TRAVEL

Guidor is the organisation for professional tourist guides in the Netherlands

Office: P.O. Box 3351
1001 AD Amsterdam

Phone: (..31)20 624 60 72

Reservations for multilingual guide services   (..31)20 627 00 06
(..31)70 320 25 00

Fax: (..31)70 320 26 11

The VVV (listed under Tourist Information), The Netherlands' government-supported tourist information service, provides a welcoming and efficient service. There are two offices in Amsterdam and many more dotted around the country, all with well-trained and multi-lingual staff. Amsterdam's high tourist season starts at Easter and runs until September, during which time you can expect long queues, especially at the Stationsplein office in the mornings. On maps of The Netherlands, VVV offices are denoted by a white triangle on a blue square and can be found in most towns and places of interest.

though, as in every city, there is the odd rogue. Always check the meter is blank (aside from the minimum charge) and ask the driver for an estimate of how much the journey will cost before setting out. Keep an eye on the meter. Even short journeys are expensive, working out at f2.28 per kilometre (f3.67 per mile) between 6am and midnight and rising to f2.80 per kilometre (f4.51 per mile) at night and, particularly on the narrow streets around the main canals, you may get stuck behind an unloading lorry and end up paying a fortune for the privilege. If you feel you have been ripped off, ask for a receipt, which you are legally entitled to see before handing over any money. If the charge is extortionate, refer it to the central taxi office (*677 7777*), or the police. We stress that such rip-offs are rare – taxi drivers have too much to lose if they are caught.

You cannot hail a taxi in the street, but there are ranks dotted around the city. Places you are likely to find a taxi waiting in a rank include Centraal Station (C); next to the bus station at the junction of Kinkerstraat and Marnixstraat (OW); Rembrandtsplein (IS); and

Leidseplein (IS). You generally can't book a cab in advance, but if you call Amsterdam's 24-hour central taxi control on *677 7777* a taxi will arrive almost immediately. The line is busy on Friday and Saturday nights, but there's a telephone queuing system.

Taxis can only take **wheelchairs** if they are folded. If you need to travel in a wheelchair, phone the car transport service for wheelchair users on *613 4134*. The office is generally open between 9am and 6pm, Monday to Friday, although office hours are casual and you might well find someone there outside these times. You need to book one or two days in advance and it costs f2.50 per kilometre (f4 per mile).

WATER TAXIS

It would be rather extravagant to use this service as you would a regular taxi and so few Amsterdammers use water taxis for anything other than special occasions. However, it is possible to hire a taxi, with guides, food and drink provided by the company at extra charge, and use it for your own personal canal tour or mobile party. The boats are modern and well-maintained, with both covered and on-deck seating.

For details of canal tours *see page 13* **Sightseeing.**

Water Taxi Centrale
Stationsplein 8, C (622 2181). Tram 1, 2, 4, 5, 9, 13, 16, 17, 24, 25. **Open** *9am-1am daily.* **Cost** *8-person boat* f120 per hour; *15 and 30-person boats* f190 for 1st hour, then f180 per hour. **Credit** AmEx, DC, MC, TC, V.
Advance booking is advisable as the service is usually busy, particularly in high season. Water taxis can be hailed as they're sailing along a canal if they're free, but that's unlikely.

CANAL BUSES

Canal Bus
Nieuwekeizersgracht 8, IE (623 9886). Tram 9, 14. **Open** *9am-5pm Mon-Fri.* **Cost** *day ticket* f12.50; *under-12s* f10; *two-day ticket* f20; *under-12s* f15. **No credit cards.**
The 52-seater canal buses are the latest addition to Amsterdam's water transport system. They offer a regular service through the canals from the Rijksmuseum to Centraal Station, stopping at Leidseplein, Leidsestraat/Keizersgracht and Westerkerk/Anne Frank House. The service operates every day between 10am and 6pm at 45-minute intervals.

CYCLING

Cycling is widely considered the most pleasant, convenient – and Dutch – means of transport around the city (*see page 5* **picture and caption**). There are bike lanes everywhere, clearly marked with blue circles. At first, cycling on Amsterdam's busy roads may appear a hazardous exercise, but motorists are well-used to the abundance of cyclists and collisions are rare. Remember, however, that cycling two abreast is illegal, as is going without reflector bands on both front and back wheels. Never leave your bike unlocked, as there's a thriving and long-established trade in stolen bikes in Amsterdam. And be sure to use a sturdy lock; some thieves are equipped with powerful cutters which will make short work of thin chains. There's no shortage of bike hire firms where a good vehicle can be hired for about f8 a day. Below we list three reputable companies; others can be found in the Amsterdam *Yellow Pages* (*Gouden Gids*) under '*Fietsen en Bromfietsen Verhuur*', which translates as 'Bikes and Motorbikes for Hire'.

The Bulldog
Oudezijds Voorburgwal 126, C (624 8248). Tram 4, 9, 14, 16, 24, 25. **Open** *10am-6.30pm daily.* **Cost** f7.50 per day plus f100 deposit and passport. **No credit cards.**
See also p91 **Cafés & Bars.**

Make the most of your visit with the Amsterdam Visitors Guide

YELLOW PAGES
Visitors
Guide
AMSTERDAM

Ask for your **free** copy upon your arrival at Schiphol/Amsterdam Airport (information desk in the arrival hall).

Also available at selected business centres, hotels and shops in Amsterdam.

The Visitors Guide is an ITT (Yellow Pages) publication

Rent-A-Bike
Pieter Jacobsdwarsstraat 11, C (625 5029).
Tram 4, 9, 14, 16, 24, 25. **Open** 9am-6pm
daily. **Cost** f9 per day plus f50 deposit and
passport. **Credit** AmEx, DC, MC, TC, V.

Take-A-Bike
Centraal Station, Stationsplein 6, C (624
8391). Tram 1, 2, 4, 5, 9, 13, 16, 17, 24, 25.
Open 6am-11.30pm daily. **Cost** f7 per day
(8am-10pm) plus f200 deposit. **No credit**
cards.

TRAINS

From Centraal Station (*see page 7*
picture and caption), one of the
biggest stations in Europe, you can
get direct trains to many major cities
across the continent. But be warned,
you must obtain a reservation for
international trains and the reservations office gets very crowded
during the summer season. Tickets
can be reserved over the phone but
you must do this seven days in
advance. For more information on
rail travel *see page 200* **Beyond**
Amsterdam.

Centraal Station Information
Desk
Stationsplein 13, C (international
reservations 620 2266/national reservations
06 899 1121). Tram 1, 2, 4, 5, 9, 13, 16, 17,
24, 25. **Open** *information desk* 8am-10pm
Mon-Fri; 9am-8pm Sat, Sun; *reservations*
office 8am-8pm Mon-Fri; 9am-5pm Sat, Sun.
Credit MC, V.

TOURIST
INFORMATION

The national tourist information
organization is the VVV, which
stands for *Vereniging Voor*
Vreemdelingenverkeer – the
Association for Tourist Traffic – and
is pronounced 'Vay Vay Vay'. There
are two offices in Amsterdam and
about 450 throughout the rest of The
Netherlands, all offering services
similar to those listed below. In the
larger branches all the staff speak
English, German and French, and
English is spoken by almost all the
staff in the smaller offices.

Many phone centres (*see page 221*
Survival: Communications) run a
booking service for theatres, car
hire, hotels and excursions.

VVV
Stationsplein 10, C (626 6444). Tram 1, 2,
4, 5, 9, 13, 16, 17, 24, 25. **Open** *Easter-June,*
Sept 9am-11pm Mon-Sat; 9am-9pm Sun; *July,*
Aug 9am-11pm daily; *Oct-Easter* 9am-6pm
Mon-Fri; 9am-5pm Sat; 10am-1pm, 2-5pm,
Sun. **No credit cards.**

This is the main office of the VVV. Both
here and at the branch listed below
English-speaking staff can change money
and provide information on transport,
entertainment, exhibitions and day-out
ideas for the whole of The Netherlands.
The VVV can also arrange theatre and
hotel bookings for a fee of f3.50, and excursions and car hire for free. There is a
comprehensive range of brochures for sale
detailing walks, cycling tours, cassette
tours, maps and, for f2.50, the useful fortnightly English-language listings magazine
What's On. The VVV runs a general information line on **626 6444** which is open
9am-5pm Mon-Sat and features an English-
language service. *See also p9* **picture and**
caption.
Branch *Leidsestraat 106, IS. Tram 1, 2, 5, 6,*
7, 10. **Open** *Easter-June, Sept* 9am-11pm
Mon-Sat; 9am-9pm Sun; *July, Aug* 9am-11pm
daily; *Oct-Easter* 10.30am-5.30pm Mon-Fri;
10.30am-9pm Sat. **No credit cards.**

AUB Uitburo
Leidseplein 26, IS (621 1211). Tram 1, 2, 5,
6, 7, 10. **Open** 10am-6pm Mon-Sat. **No**
credit cards.
Information and advance tickets for theatre, concerts and other cultural events.
The reservation fee is f2. You can also get
the Cultureel Jongeren Passport (CJP)
here (f15), which is valid for a year from
September to August and entitles people
under 26 to discounts on museum
entrance fees and cultural events nationally. It has chatty and helpful staff, plus a
comfortable café area where visitors can
leaf through listings guides and brochures
at leisure.

MAPS

Almost every complimentary
brochure or leaflet that you will find
in hotels and some bars will provide a sketchy map. But if you
require more detail, the *Falk Pocket*
Book Map (f10) and the *Falk* fold-
out map (f7) are useful and
accurate, and have a full street
index. Cheaper and smaller, but
perfectly adequate is *Falk's* small
fold-out plan (f5.50). Steer clear of
the complicated *Falk* 'patent-folded'
map unless you're keen on origami.
All these can be bought from
newsagents and bookshops (*see*
page 221 **Survival**).

WHAT'S ON

Amsterdam's theatres, cafés, bars
and libraries supply Dutch-
language freesheets with general
entertainment information and
display a weekly cinema listing.
Such information is easy to follow
even without an understanding of
Dutch. The fortnightly English-
language listings magazine
What's On, f2.50, is available in
hotels, restaurants and information
offices.

Even in high summer, the smart traveller to Amsterdam will include an
umbrella in his or her luggage. The city vies with Manchester and Glasgow as the
rain capital of Europe, with sudden heavy downpours a speciality. The adaptable
Amsterdammers, however, are quick to make the most of good **weather** *(listed*
under **Climate**) *when it happens. At the merest hint of sunshine, tables and*
chairs crowd the city's terraces and pavements.

TIME

In spring and summer Amsterdam time is two hours ahead of Greenwich Mean Time (GMT); in the autumn and winter it's one hour ahead of GMT.

CLIMATE

Amsterdam's climate is very changeable (*see page 11* **picture and caption**). January and February are the coldest months, with icy winds whipping around the narrow streets from off the canals. It can be very humid in the summer, when mosquitoes thrive on the canals and in campsites. The average range of temperatures are: January-February 0.3°C to 4.6°C (32.5°F to 40.3°F); March-May 5.5°C to 12.1°C (41.9°F to 53.8°F); June-September 11.5°C to 19.4°C (52.7°F to 66.9°F); October-December 4.1°C to 10°C (39.4°F to 50°F).

PUBLIC HOLIDAYS

Called *Nationale Feestdag* in Dutch, they are: **New Year's Day; Good Friday** 29 March 1991, 17 April 1992; **Easter Sunday** and **Monday** 31 March, 1 April 1991 and 19 April, 20 April 1992; **30 April** (*Koninginnedag*, the former Queen Juliana's Birthday, *see page 76* **Amsterdam By Season**); **Ascension Day** 9 May 1991, 28 May 1992; **Whit (Pentecost) Sunday** and **Monday** 19, 20 May 1991 and 7, 8 June 1992; **Christmas Day** and **the day after Christmas**.

OPENING TIMES

For all our listings in this guide we give full opening times, but in general shops are open from 12.30pm to 6pm on Monday; 9am to 6pm on Tuesdays, Wednesdays and Fridays; 9am to 9pm on Thursdays; and 9am to 5pm on Saturdays. Smaller, specialist shops tend to open at varying times; if in doubt phone first. For shops that are open late *see page 144* **Early Hours**.

Bars close around 1am (2am on Fridays and Saturdays). Restaurants are generally open in the evening from 5pm to 11pm; some close on Sunday and Monday.

TIPPING & ETIQUETTE

Although by law a service charge is included in hotel, taxi, bar, café and restaurant bills, most Amsterdammers generally also round up the change to the nearest five guilders for large bills and to the nearest guilder for smaller. In taxis the most common tip is around 10 per cent on short journeys. Because of the compulsory service charge, never feel obliged to leave a tip; use your discretion and do so only when the service warrants it.

QUEUING

A ticketing system is widely used here cuts out the need for the traditional 'queue'. From supermarket delicatessen counters and information bureaux to doctors' surgeries, you tear off a numbered ticket from a small machine on entry and then wait until your number is either called or appears on an electronic screen. This allows you to seek somewhere comfortable to wait; you can wander off for a while, but beware, if you miss your turn it will take some persuasive arguments if you are to be served.

Any queues that you do come across, like those at tram stops, tend to be multinational, and so vary in character from tidy to non-existent, depending on who's in them. An example of the Dutch love of efficiency, this system is also catching on in the UK, though slowly.

VOCABULARY

The vast majority of Amsterdammers speak good English and are happy to show off their linguistic talents. However, some knowledge of the absolute basics of the language may be useful – and polite – particularly if you intend to venture out of the city. Pronunciations given are the nearest approximation we could find.

PRONUNCIATION
v – pronounced like 'f' in 'for'
w – like 'w' in 'which', with a hint of the 'v' in 'vet' thrown in
j – like 'y' in 'yes'
ch – like 'ch' in Scots pronunciation of 'loch'
g – similar to above (this has to be heard to be imitated)
oo – like 'o' in no
ou, au – like 'ow' in 'cow'
ui – similar to above (has to be heard to be imitated)
oe – like 'oo' in 'book'
ie – like 'ea' in 'lean'
ee – like 'ay' in 'hay'
ÿ – similar to above

USEFUL PHRASES
hello – *hallo* (hullo) or *dag* (darch)
goodbye – *tot ziens* (tot zeens)
yes – *ja* (yah)
no – *nee* (nay)
please – *alstublieft* (als – too – bleeft)
thank you – *dank u* (dank-oo)
excuse me – *pardon* (par – don)
I'm sorry, I don't speak Dutch – *Het spijt me, ik spreek geen Nederlands* (Het spate meh, ik spraykt hane nay – der – lants)
do you speak English? – *spreekt u Engels?* (spraykt oo engels)
sir – *meneer* (menayr)
madam – *mevrouw* (mevrow). NB: the progressive Amsterdammers rarely address anyone as 'Miss'
waiter – *meneer* or *mevrouw*
open – *open*
closed – *gesloten*
I want.... – *ik wil graag.....*
how much is...? – *kost...?*
could I have a receipt? – *mag ik een bonnetje alstublieft?*

how do I get to...? – *hoe kom ik in...?*
how far is it to...? – *hoe ver is het naar...?*
left – *links*
right – *rechts*
straight ahead – *rechtdoor gaan*
far – *ver*
near – *dichtbij*
street – *straat*
canal – *gracht*
square – *plein*
good – *goed*
bad – *slecht*
big – *groot*
small – *klein*

NUMBERS
0 *nul*; 1 *een*; 2 *twee*; 3 *drie*; 4 *vier*; 5 *vijf*; 6 *zes*; 7 *zeven*; 8 *acht*; 9 *negen*; 10 *tien*; 11 *elf*; 12 *twaalf*; 13 *dertien*; 14 *veertien*; 15 *vijftien*; 16 *zestien*; 17 *zeventien*; 18 *achttien*; 19 *negentien*; 20 *twintig*; 21 *eenentwintig*; 22 *tweeëntwintig*; 30 *dertig*; 31 *eenendertig*; 32 *tweeëndertig*; 40 *veertig*; 50 *vijftig*; 60 *zestig*; 70 *zeventig*; 80 *tachtig*; 90 *negentig*; 100 *honderd*; 101 *honderd een*; 110 *honderd tien*; 200 *tweehonderd*; 201 *tweehonderd een*; 1,000 *duizend*

Sightseeing

Fine buildings, ancient monuments and an informal mood are Amsterdam's greatest assets. *Abi Daruvalla* takes you on a tour of the prime sights.

Amsterdam is small enough to make sightseeing a pleasure rather than an endurance test. The major sights are easily accessible from the city centre, and many pleasant hours can be spent meandering from one to another, following a canal or stopping off in one of the numerous bars. Trying to adhere to a strict itinerary is inadvisable; the city's main asset is its spontaneous, relaxed atmosphere.

Entertainment is everywhere in Amsterdam, not only in the cinemas, clubs and theatres, but most of all on the streets. Tourist spots such as **Leidseplein** and the **Dam** (*both listed under* **Focal Points**) attract every kind of street performer, day and night, throughout the year; but buskers seem to play in every park and lurk on every street corner.

Amsterdam is breathtaking by night. Many of the magnificent canal-side buildings and most of the bridges are illuminated and the city is still alive and kicking at two in the morning (most bars close around two at the weekend, clubs usually later). Compared to other major cities, the streets are reasonably safe, provided you take sensible precautions (*see page 221* **Survival: Police & Security**).

Our Sightseeing chapter should be used as a quick reference to Amsterdam's major sights (and some of the less familiar ones as well). Most of the places listed below appear elsewhere in the Guide in greater detail; and the subjects covered (Amsterdam's history, its sights, transport and culture) are dealt with in depth in other chapters.

FOCAL POINTS

Like all cities, Amsterdam has several well-known areas where tourists tend to congregate. These have an international flavour – billboards, busking and pavement cafés – so don't expect to find the 'real' Amsterdam there.

Dam

C. Tram 1, 2, 4, 5, 9, 16, 24, 25.
Although tourists tend to cluster here, this square is one of the least atmospheric parts of the city, with few cafés and no worthwhile nightlife. Nevertheless, there are a number of important landmarks on and around it. The west side is flanked by the **Royal Palace** (*see below* **Heritage**) and **Nieuwekerk** (*see below* **Churches & Viewpoints**); in the middle of the eastern side is the **National Monument** (*see also page 64* **World War II**). This 22m (72ft) obelisk is dedicated to the Dutch servicemen who died in World War II. Designed by JJP Oud, with sculptures by John Rädecker, it incorporates 12 urns: 11 filled with earth collected from the then 11 Dutch provinces, the twelfth with soil from war cemeteries in Indonesia, which was a Dutch colony until 1945.

Leidseplein

IS. Tram 1, 2, 5, 6, 7, 10.
The area around Leidseplein probably has more cinemas, theatres, nightclubs and restaurants than any other part of the city. Several cafés border the square, dominating the pavements during the summer; the best of them is Eylders (*see p26* **Amsterdam by Area: Leidseplein**). You can also take a drink on the terrace of the Hotel Americain (*see p79* **Restaurants**), a prominent example of the Amsterdam School of architecture at the south of the square. Leidseplein itself is a stage for every kind of performer. During the city's street festivals (*see p36* **Amsterdam by Season**) fire-eaters, jugglers, acrobats, singers and small-time con-artists fill the square (watch out for pickpockets). In the winter, part of the Leidseplein is transformed into an open-air ice skating rink (*see p183* **Sport & Fitness**). The rapid development of the Leidseplein over the last few years and the invasion of 'McDonalds culture' (there's a branch of the burger chain here) has not been unreservedly welcomed by all of the locals, who feel the essential Dutch flavour of the district is being destroyed for a fast buck. Just off the square is the Adamant, a white pyramid-shaped sculpture given to Amsterdam by the city's diamond industry in 1986 to commemorate 400 years of the trade. Designed by Jacob van Saanten at a cost of f75,000, it uses light to create a rainbow hologram.

Red Light District

C. Tram 4, 9, 16, 24, 25.
The lure of Amsterdam's red light district, known colloquially as *de walletjes* because it's the area within the old city walls, proves irresistible to most visitors. Sex for money, the age-old trade, is on offer in and around one of Amsterdam's oldest streets, Warmoesstraat. Obviously the area attracts more than its fair share of crime, but if you stay away from Zeedijk, the red light district is safe enough. The prostitutes are mainly

concentrated along Oudezijds Voorburgwal, Oudezijds Achterburgwal and the small interconnecting alleyways. They take up their shop window positions at about 10am and are still there well into the small hours. While this area is the main tourist attraction, there are smaller red light districts in two other parts of town: along Spuistraat (between Centraal Station and Raadhuisstraat) and Singel by the Sonesta Hotel, and along Ruysdaelkade between Ferdinand Bolstraat and Ceintuurbaan. *See also p26* **Amsterdam by Area.**

Rembrandtplein

IS. Tram 4, 9, 14.
The gloriously tacky Rembrandtplein only comes alive at night. Offerings range from the faded fake elegance of traditional strip-tease parlours to seedy peep-show joints and nondescript cafés and restaurants. Nevertheless, there are a few exceptions to this exuberant display of trash (including the fantastic art deco Café Schiller, *see p91* **Cafés & Bars**, and Tuschinski Cinema, *see p122* **Film**). Just round the corner on the Amstel is a stretch of gay cafés (*see p169* **Gay Amsterdam**).

Waterlooplein

C. Tram 9, 14/Metro Waterlooplein.
This up-and-coming district is dominated by the ultra-modern **Stadhuis-Muziektheater** (*see below under* **Cultural Centres**). It opened in 1985 amid great controversy; protesters were furious that it had been sited on what had for centuries been an important open space (*see p68* **Post-war**). Also here is the Waterlooplein Flea Market (*see below* **Markets** and *p153* **Shopping**) and Rembrandthuis (*see p100* **Museums**). *See also p26* **Amsterdam by Area.**

HERITAGE

Anne Frankhuis (Anne Frank House)

Prinsengracht 263, IW (626 4533). Tram 13, 14, 17. **Open** *Sept-May* 9am-5pm Mon-Sat; 10am-5pm Sun, public holidays; *June-Aug* 9am-7pm Mon-Sat; 10am-7pm Sun, public holidays. **Admission** f5; f3 10-17s; free under-10s; group discount. **No credit cards.**
Every visitor to Amsterdam should pay a visit to this seventeenth-century canalside house where the young Jewish girl Anne Frank spent over two years in hiding during World War II. It is not a cosy re-creation of a family home; the Nazis destroyed the furniture and the interior has been left bare, although you can still see the diary and the bookcase which concealed the entrance to the annexe where the family hid. The Anne Frank Foundation was founded in 1957 to safeguard the house and combat fascism, racism and anti-Semitism. Regular exhibitions are held, but visit early to avoid the crowds. *See also p64* **World War II** and *p100* **Museums.**

Begijnhof

Spui, C. Tram 1, 2, 5.
A quiet backwater hidden behind a doorway just off Amsterdam's noisy main shopping area, the Begijnhof is a group of houses built around a secluded courtyard and garden. It was established in the fourteenth century to

provide modest homes for the Begijntjes, a religious sisterhood of unmarried women of good families who, although not nuns, lived together in a close community and often took vows of chastity. They did many charitable works, especially in education and nursing. The last sister died in 1974. Most of the neat little houses were 'modernized' in the seventeenth and eighteenth centuries. In the centre of the courtyard stands the English Reformed Church, built in about 1400 and a principal place of worship for Amsterdam's English community (*see p130* **Music: Classical & Opera** and *p221* **Survival**). The pulpit panels were designed by Mondrian. You can also see a Catholic church, built clandestinely out of two houses in 1665, following the banning of the Roman Catholic faith after the Reformation of 1587. The wooden house at number 34 is dated 1475 and is the oldest house standing in the city. This is the best known of the city's numerous hofjes; for details of others *see p23* **Hofjes**.

Munttoren (Mint Tower)

Muntplein, C. Tram 4, 9, 14, 16, 24, 25.
On Singel between the floating flower market (*see below* **Markets**) and the start of Kalverstraat (the pedestrianized shopping street), this medieval tower was the western corner of the Regulierspoort, a gate in the city walls in the 1480s. In 1620 a spire was added by Hendrik de Keyser, the foremost architect of the period. Its name, 'mint

tower', comes from the fact that the city authorities used it to mint coins for a short period in 1672 when Amsterdam was cut off from its money supply during a war with England, Munster and France. There's a shop on the ground floor selling fine Dutch porcelain (*see p161* **Specialist Shops: Gifts**), but the rest of the tower is closed to visitors. The Munttoren is prettiest at night, when it's floodlit; although day-time visitors may be able to hear its carillon, which often plays for 15 minutes at noon (*see p130* **Music: Classical & Opera: Carillons**).

Koninklijk Paleis (Royal Palace)

Dam, C (624 8698 ext 217). Tram 1, 2, 4, 9, 13, 14, 16, 17, 24, 25. **Open** *June-Sept only 12.30-5pm daily.*
The Royal Palace was designed by Jacob van Campens in the seventeenth century along standard classical lines and was originally intended to be the city hall (*see p55* **The Golden Age**). The exterior is not particularly impressive for a building of its stature and betrays its municipal origins. Inside it's a different story, with chimney pieces painted by artists such as Ferdinand Bol and Govert Flinck, both pupils of Rembrandt. The city hall was transformed into a royal palace in 1808 after Napoleon had made his brother, Louis, king of the Netherlands (*see p59* **Decline & Fall**). A fine collection of furniture from this period can be seen on a guided tour of the building.

The Palace is still used occasionally by the present royal family, based in The Hague (*see p208* **The Randstad**). *Guided tours June-Sept, 1.30pm Wed (f3.50, under-12s f1.50); group tours (min 10 people) can also be arranged Oct-May, phone for details.*

Schreierstoren (Weeping Tower)

Prins Hendrikkade, C. Tram 1, 2, 4, 5, 9, 13, 16, 17, 24, 25.
The most interesting relic of Amsterdam's medieval city wall is the Weeping Tower. Legend relates that the wives of sailors leaving on trade expeditions (*see p52* **Early History**) stood here and waved tearful farewells to their men. Of course, the Dutch have a more pragmatic explanation: *schreier* can also mean 'saddle' and the tower does indeed straddle two canals. Dating from 1487, it was successfully restored in 1966 and its most interesting feature is its gablestones (*see p61* **Between the Occupations: Gables & Gablestones**). In 1927, a bronze memorial plaque was added by the Greenwich Village Historical Society of New York: its English text states that it was from this point on 4 April 1609 that Henry Hudson departed in search of shorter trade routes to the Far East. He ended up colonizing a small island in the mouth of a river in North America. The river was later named after him and the colony was called New Amsterdam; only to have its name changed by the English to New York. And there's another, less grandiose, American connection. In 1956 some stones from the Schreierstoren were taken to Chicago and placed into the wall of the *Chicago Tribune* building alongside similar chunks from famous buildings from around world, including Athens's Parthenon, Paris's Notre Dame cathedral and the Great Wall of China. Visitors are not allowed inside the Schreierstoren.

Beurs van Berlage (Berlage Stock Exchange)

Damrak 277, C (626 5257/fax 620 4701). Tram 4, 9, 16, 24, 25. **Open** *office and enquiries* 9am-5pm Mon-Fri.
Designed in 1896 by Hendrik Petrus Berlage as the city's stock exchange, the Beurs represents an important break with nineteenth-century architecture and prepared the way for the modern lines of the Amsterdam School (*see p61* **Between the Occupations**). No longer used as a stock exchange, the building has been sensitively converted into a conference and exhibition centre (*see p188* **Business**) and two concert halls (*see p130* **Music: Classical & Opera**), with a café and restaurant (*see p79* **Restaurants**). Tours can be arranged by Archivise, *see below* **Tours**.

De Waag (Weigh House)

Nieuwmarkt, C. Tram 9, 14/Metro Nieuwmarkt.
The Waag, previously called St Antoniespoort, stands in the centre of the Nieuwmarkt and dates from 1488, when it was built as a gatehouse for the city defences. It's an odd, squat building with turrets protruding from unlikely places. Over the years it has housed various institutions: in 1617 the ground floor was a public weigh house while the first floor housed the trade

Amsterdam may attract fewer tourists than Paris, Madrid or London, but this hasn't stopped Europe's street performers and buskers from claiming the city as their own.

guilds of smiths, bricklayers, painters and surgeons. The surgeons' annual anatomy lectures were the inspiration of Rembrandt's 1656 painting, *The Anatomy Lecture of Dr Jan Deyman*, which hung here from 1691 until it was seriously damaged by fire in 1723. It now hangs in the Rijksmuseum (*see below* **Cultural Centres**). After 1819, the building was no longer used as a weigh house and has since been put to a variety of uses – it was the Jewish Historical Museum from 1932 to 1986 (*see p100* **Museums** and *p26* **Amsterdam by Area: Waterlooplein & The Plantage**). After ambitious plans to convert it into a cultural centre fell through it has fallen into disuse and was boarded up at time of writing.

ATTRACTIONS

Artis Zoo

Plantage Kerklaan 40, IE (523 3400). **Tram** *7, 9, 14.* **Open** *9am-5pm daily; last Planetarium show 4pm; children's farm 10am-1pm, 2-4.30pm, daily.* **Admission** *zoo, children's farm, Planetarium and Zoological Museum* f16; f9 *under-10s; group discount (min 20 people).* **No** credit cards.
Amsterdam Zoo – or Natura Artis Magistra (that's Latin for 'nature is the master of the arts'), as it is formally called – was established in 1838, making it the oldest zoo in The Netherlands. It's home to over 6,000 animals. Though popular, it is never too crowded to prevent enjoyment of the beautifully laid out gardens and broad range of exhibits. The liberal use of perspex allows generally unrestricted views, and the aquarium, one of the zoo's best features, boasts over 2,000 fish and a wide variety of species. Don't miss the seals being fed at 11.30am and 3.30pm; or the penguins at 3.30pm. Also recommended are the reptile house, the luxuriant tropical greenhouse, the young animals' section, a children's farm (*see p180* **Children & Parents**) and a spectacular planetarium (with Dutch commentary, but an English-language summary is available). Unfortunately, a few of the enclosures, particularly for the big cats, rhinos and hippos, appear cramped, which may be upsetting for some visitors. However, the zoo has plans for expansion in 1991, which we hope will solve this problem. Another drawback is that the guidebook is in Dutch. All in all, it's a very pleasant place to while away a few hours – with or without kids – and it's not far from the city centre.
Café and restaurant. Guided tours by prior arrangement (free). Schools' educational programme. Shop. Wheelchair access and toilets for the disabled.

Diamond workshops

Coster Diamonds *Paulus Potterstraat 2-6, OS (676 2222).* **Tram** *2, 3, 5, 12.* **Open** *9am-5pm daily.* **Tours** *throughout the day on request, free, duration approx 20 mins.*
Gassan Diamond House *Nieuwe Uilenburgerstraat 173-175, C (622 5333).* **Tram** *9, 14/Metro Nieuwmarkt.* **Open** *9am-5.30pm Mon-Fri.* **Tours** *throughout the day on request, duration 45 mins-1 hour, free soft drink at end of tour.*
Holshuysen-Stoeltie *Wagenstraat 13-17, C (623 7601).* **Tram** *9, 14.* **Open** *9am-5pm daily.* **Tours** *throughout the day on request,*

The **Oudekerk** (**Old Church**, see under **Churches & Viewpoints**), *first built in 1306, is dedicated to St Nicholas, the patron saint of sailors, and various types of ship are painted above the organs, on the stained glass and on the ceiling. The latter were painted over at the time of the Reformation, but rediscovered when the church was restored between 1955 and 1979. You can even see carvings of ships in the choir stalls, which were apparently etched by bored sailors attending Sunday services. Impressive views can be had from the top of the 72-metre/262-foot tower.*

free, duration 30 mins-1 hour, free soft drink at end of tour.
Van Moppes & Zoon *Albert Cuypstraat 2-6, OS (676 1242).* **Tram** *16, 24, 25.* **Open** *8.30am-5pm daily.* **Tours** *throughout the day on request, free, duration approx 30 mins.*
Amsterdam has a fascinating association with diamonds dating back to the sixteenth century (*see p61* **Between the Occupations**). The largest diamond ever found, the Cullinan, and the world-famous Koh-I-Noor, part of the British Crown Jewels, were cut by Amsterdam workers. The smallest 'brilliant cut' diamond (a brilliant cut has 57 facets) was also cut here, a tiny sliver of sparkle measuring just 0.0012 carat. There are about 24 diamond polishing factories in Amsterdam, and the four bigger ones listed above welcome visitors. All offer similar tours, lasting from around 20 minutes to an hour. The guides provide a brief history of the diamond industry and Amsterdam's strategic importance in it. You'll probably be shown a worker polishing or setting a diamond, but the real thrill (only offered to those in large groups) is when the guide nonchalantly pours diamonds from a black velvet bag onto a table for your inspection. **Gassan Diamond House**, built in 1879 as a diamond factory, offers one of the more enjoyable tours. There's not much to choose between the others, but be prepared for an unenthusiastic commentary and a very brisk walk around to the sales room if you're

not part of a group. Tours can be given in any European language.

Heineken Brewery

Stadhouderskade 78, IS (670 9111). **Tram** *6, 7, 10, 16, 24, 25.* **Information** *from VVV tourist offices, see p3* **Essential Information**.
Beer production here was stopped at the beginning of 1988 amid some outcry – after all, Heineken is virtually the national drink. In 1990 the famous tours of the old brewery – complete with the subsequent all-the-beer-you-can-drink hospitality – came to an end. Breweries elsewhere in The Netherlands can now turn out bottles at more than 12 times the speed of the old Amsterdam plant. But Heineken has remained public-spirited and is going to convert the site into a Brewery Museum. This new attraction is expected to open in 1991, but whether it will have the same atmosphere as the traditional white-tiled brewhouse, with its huge copper vats, is not yet known.

Madame Tussaud's

Kalverstraat 156, C (622 9949). **Tram** *4, 9, 14, 16, 24, 25.* **Open** *July, Aug 9am-7pm Mon-Sat; 10am-7pm Sun; Sept-June 10am-6pm daily.* **Admission** *f10; f7.50 under-14s; f28 family ticket (2 adults, 2 children).* **No credit cards.**
In its present cramped premises, Madame

Expand Your Mind...

thic Chic ❂ Eastern Eu
ice Sabotage ❂ The h
sound of Sheffield ❂ M
Mica Paris ❂ Suckerba
l II Soul ❂ Natural Uppe
erspace ❂ Legal Hig
at Jeans ❂ A deacad
-Deas ❂ Mancheste
of Fashion ❂ 808 Sta

Villiam Gibson ❂ Ice Hockey ❂ John Richmond ❂ Water sca
Tantric sex ❂ Chaos Theory ❂ Vic Reeves ❂ Duffer Of St George
frican Football ❂ Phil Ridley ❂ Hanif Kureishi ❂ Religious Cults
signer health foods ❂   Sport Psychology ❂ S
ys ❂ Clubs ❂ Gay Ac   ski ❂ John Godfrey
thlon ❂ Films   otball ❂ Water scares
one Roses ❂ Positively   lists ❂ Computer gar
n ❂ Positively   808 State ❂ Buggin
Chaos Theory ❂

...Once a Month with

i-D magazine

i-Deas, Fashion, Clubs, Music, People

Available from all good newsagents or contact i-D, 134-146 Curtain Road,
London EC2A 3AR. Tel: 071-729 7305/Fax: 071-729 7266

ROUTE
EUROPEAN RAIL **26** FOR UNDER 26's

DISCOVER EUROPE BY TRAIN

TICKET

100's Of Destinations

▶ Great discounts on standard rail fares for those under 26 yrs

▶ Tickets valid for two months

▶ Stop off anywhere along the way

▶ Hundreds of destinations

▶ Offices throughout Europe offering help along the way

▶ Fares available to all stations in the Netherlands

▼ WASTEELS

121 WILTON ROAD LONDON SW1V 1JZ Tel: 071-834 7066

THE DUTCH CONNECTION

DAILY & OVERNIGHT SERVICES

AMSTERDAM FROM **£43** YOUTH RETURN

Over 190 destinations all over Europe by coach

Book at Eurolines, 52 Grosvenor Gardens, Victoria SW1

or contact your local NATIONAL EXPRESS Agent.

Enquiries 071 730 0202 • Credit Cards 071 730 8235

euro lines
EUROPEAN EXPRESS COACHES

COACH YOUR WAY ACROSS EUROPE

Tussaud's is a crowded and dull experience. Visitors can plod past the often rather dubious likenesses of the famous, not so famous and embarrassingly *passé*. Boy George, David Bowie, Marilyn Monroe and Margaret Thatcher are some of the international figures among a broad selection of Dutch celebrities and politicians, such as Queen Beatrix and the Dutch Prime Minister (Ruud Lubbers at time of writing). An elaborate tableau of Rembrandt at work is one of the more impressive exhibits. At the end of your visit you'll probably be harassed by a tenacious character trying to sell you a poorly printed photo of you entering the premises – it's that kind of place. Things may change in mid-1991, when the museum is due to move to larger premises further along the street above the Peek & Clopenburg shop (Kalverstraat 114). There will be new exhibits (details of which are being kept secret until the opening), twice the space – and a higher admission charge.

Amsterdams Historisch Museum

Kalverstraat 92, C (523 1822). Tram 1, 2, 4, 5, 9, 14, 16, 24, 25. **Open** 11am-5pm daily. **Admission** f5; under-16s f2.50; f12.50 family ticket (2 adults, 2 children); free with Museum Card; group discounts (min 20 people). **No credit cards.**
The city's elegant historical museum is a wonderful cluster of buildings and courtyards, located on the site of St Lucy's Convent (which was built in 1414). The Museum used to house an orphanage and is one of the most underrated attractions of the city centre. Exhibits are well displayed but not interactive. *See also p100* **Museums.** *Restaurant.*

Concertgebouw

Concertgebouwplein 2-6, Van Baerlestraat, OS (ticket reservations 10am-3pm daily 671 8345/recorded information in Dutch 675 4411). Tram 3, 5, 12, 16. **Open** box office 10am-5pm Mon-Fri; 40 minutes before performance for ticket sales and collection. **Tickets** f25-f50; CJP card holders, students f15-f30. **Performances** 8.15pm. **Credit** AmEx, DC, MC.
Amsterdam's venerable Concertgebouw, known as one of the world's three most acoustically perfect concert halls (the others are in Boston and Vienna), was actually outside the city limits when it opened to much fanfare in April 1888. For the event, the 422 horse-drawn carriages bearing the city's élite to the first concert were lined up from Museumplein to the Amstel River. A century later, the hall celebrated its centenary with a face-lift that involved replacing the 100-year-old wooden piles with concrete ones, and the addition of a controversial glass side wing – the performers never missed a beat. Currently about 500 performances a year are given for some half million visitors. *See also p130* **Music: Classical & Opera.**
Wheelchair access by arrangement.

Rijksmuseum

Stadhouderskade 42, OS (673 2121). Tram 6, 7, 10. **Open** 10am-5pm Tue-Sat; 1-5pm Sun, public holidays. **Admission** f6.50; f3.50 under-17s; free with Museum Card; group discounts (min 20 people). **No credit cards.**

The Dutch national museum is an imposing sight on the otherwise boring Stadhouderskade. It's one of The Netherlands' most prestigious museums and houses a rich collection of paintings by the seventeenth-century greats, such as Rembrandt (including his world famous *Night Watch*, the object of several recent attacks), Vermeer and Frans Hals. Opened in 1885, the museum building itself came in for a lot of criticism. People felt it was too French, that it should not have been situated outside the city centre (it was well outside the municipal boundaries at that time) and that it looked too much like Centraal Station or a Gothic church in style. This is not really surprising as architect Paul Cuypers also designed Centraal Station and many churches. As well as paintings, the Rijksmuseum contains thousands of examples of other arts and crafts, including: sculptures, gold and silverware; glass, ivory and pottery artefacts; and Delft ware. There are also changing exhibitions in the Print Room and a huge collection of treasures in the **Museum of Asiatic Art**, which is also housed in the Rijksmuseum. Holding approximately seven million works of art, the Rijksmuseum should be visited in palatable time spans rather than in one exhausting day. *See also p100* **Museums.**

Stadhuis-Muziektheater

Waterlooplein 22, C (625 5455). Tram 9, 14/Metro Waterlooplein. **Open** box office 10am-6pm Mon-Sat; noon-6pm Sun. **Tickets** opera f20-f80; ballet f20-f45; reductions for CJP card holders, over-65s. **Performances** opera 8pm; ballet 8.15pm. **No credit cards.**
Dominating the Waterlooplein is the modern Music Hall/City Hall complex, home of the **Netherlands Opera** (*see p130* **Music: Classical & Opera**) and **Dutch National Ballet** (*see p118* **Dance**). Designed by Wilhelm Holzbauer and Cees Dam and opened in 1985, it occupies 30,000 sq m/35,900 sq ft and cost f300 million to construct. The project has had a troubled history ever since it was first mooted in the 1920s, although it was not until 1954 that the City Council selected Waterlooplein as the site and 1979 before the decision was made to combine the civic headquarters with an opera house. This decision was a controversial one – as was the project itself. Indeed, one of Holland's top composers called the proposed building 'a monument of deceit, mediocrity and lack of taste – a European scandal'. Amsterdammers showed their discontent by organizing demonstrations and continued to protest during construction (*see p68* **Post-war: Stopera!**). Finally, in

1982, a riot caused a million guilders' worth of damage to construction equipment. In the passage between the City Hall and the Muziektheater there is a display of geological information, the Amsterdam Ordnance Project. This includes a device showing the NAP (normal Amsterdam water level; *see p55* **The Golden Age**) and a cross-section of The Netherlands showing its geological structure.

Stedelijk Museum

Paulus Potterstraat 13, OS (573 2911/Dutch recorded information 573 2737). Tram 2, 3, 12, 15, 16. **Open** 11am-5pm daily; 11am-4pm public holidays. **Admission** f7; f3.50 under-17s, CJP card holders; under-7s free; free with Museum Card; group discounts (min 50 people). **No credit cards.**
This is probably the most lively of the trio of mighty institutions – the others are the Rijksmuseum (*see above*) and the Van Gogh Museum (*see below*) – that dominate Museumplein. A refreshingly light and airy building, it holds art from 1850 to the modern day and includes photographs, video arts, industrial design and posters. Most significant is its collection of the modern art classics by painters such as Cézanne, Chagall, Manet, Matisse, Mondrian, Monet and Picasso. Unfortunately, the Museum doesn't have the space to keep all of these on permanent display. Worth a mention is the excellent café and its courtyard terrace. *See also p100* **Museums.**

Van Gogh Museum

Paulus Potterstraat 7, OS (570 5200). Tram 2, 3, 5, 12, 16. **Open** 10am-5pm Tue-Sat; 1-5pm Sun, public holidays. **Admission** f10; f5 under-18s, CJP card holders; f3.50 with Museum Card; group discounts (min 20 people). **No credit cards.**
The Van Gogh Museum opened in 1973 to provide a permanent home for over 700 letters, 200 paintings and over 500 drawings by Van Gogh, including *Sunflowers* and several self-portraits. Also on display are works by contemporaries such as Gauguin and Toulouse-Lautrec. In 1990 the Dutch flung themselves into celebrating the centenary of Van Gogh's death with great vigour and everything from Van Gogh wine to Van Gogh potatoes were sold, while a whole Van Gogh village appeared on Museumplein. All of which would have been very gratifying to the great man himself, who suffered agonies of self-doubt and sold just one painting during his lifetime. *See also p100* **Museums.**

Lutheran Church

Kattengat, C (information from Sonesta Hotel, 621 2223). Tram 1, 2, 4, 5, 9, 13, 16, 17, 24, 25. **Concerts** 11am Sun; jazz concerts 3pm one Sun per month. **Admission** f7; f6 under-10s, CJP card holders; f14 family ticket (2 adults, 2 children); *jazz concerts* f25. **No credit cards.**
Extensive restoration of this seventeenth-century church was completed in the mid-1970s, financed by the national monuments committee, the city of Amsterdam and the Sonesta hotel (of which it is now part). Since then the

outer stairways, fencing and façade have all been restored or replaced in the original style. Its gloriously grand interior is perfect for today's use as a banqueting hall, conference venue and concert hall; original marble tombstones lie beneath the carpet. The church was deconsecrated in 1935 because of a dwindling congregation. The copper dome was replaced in 1950. The organ, still in use, was built in 1830 by the Batz brothers of Utrecht and has recently been restored; the Sunday morning coffee concerts are an inexpensive treat.

Nieuwekerk (New Church)

Dam, C (Nieuwekerk foundation 626 8168). Tram 1, 2, 4, 5, 9, 13, 14, 16, 17, 24, 25. **Open** 11am-5pm daily. **Admission** free.

While the Oudekerk (*below*) was built in 1306, the Nieuwekerk dates from 1408, hence the surprising name. It is not known how much damage was caused by the great fires of 1421 and 1452, or how much rebuilding took place, but most of the pillars and walls have been erected after that period. Iconoclasm in 1566 left the church intact, although statues and altars were removed in the Reformation (*see p53* **War & Reformation**). In 1645 the church was completely gutted by fire, hence the Renaissance furnishings, and the ornately carved oak pulpit and great organ are thought to have been constructed shortly after then. Among points of interest is the tomb of naval hero Admiral de Ruyter who died in 1676. A white marble relief depicting the sea battle where he died is behind his black marble tomb. Poets Pieter Cornelisz Hooft and Joost van den Vondel are also buried here. The Nieuwekerk is no longer used as a place of worship, but for exhibitions, organ recitals (*see p130* **Music: Classical & Opera**) and state occasions, such as the crowning of Queen Beatrix in 1980.

Oudekerk (Old Church)

Oudekerksplein 23, C (625 8284). Tram 4, 9, 16, 24, 25. **Open** *church* 15 Apr-15 Sept 11am-5pm Mon-Sat; *16 Sept-14 Apr* 1-3pm Mon-Sat; *tower June-mid Sept only,* 2-5pm Mon, Thur; 11am-3pm Tue, Wed. **Admission** *church* fl; *tower* fl. **No credit cards.**
Originally built in 1306 as a wooden chapel and constantly renovated and extended between 1330 and 1571, this is Amsterdam's

oldest and most interesting church. All furnishings were removed during the Reformation, but the church retains a wooden roof painted in the fifteenth century with figurative images, a Gothic and Renaissance façade above the northern portal, and stained glass windows, parts of which date from the sixteenth and seventeenth centuries. The church is also noted for its carillon and large organ built in 1738-42, which is still in use; *see p130* **Music: Classical & Opera**. Rembrandt's wife Saskia, who died in 1642, is buried under the small organ. *See also p15* **picture and caption.**

Westerkerk (West Church)

Prinsengracht 281, IW (624 7766). Tram 13, 14, 17. **Open** 10am-4pm Mon-Sat; *tower* June-Sept only, 2-5pm Mon, Thur, Sat. **Admission** *to tower* fl. **No credit cards.**
The neo-classical Westerkerk was built at the beginning of the seventeenth century by Hendrik de Keyser and its 83m/273ft tower, topped with a somewhat gaudy gold, blue and red crown, dominates the city skyline. The story goes that in about 1500, Maximilian, the Holy Roman emperor, granted the city the right to include this crown on the city arms as a sop to local merchants who had lent him money. An impressive exterior belies a rather featureless interior, which was undergoing extensive renovation at time of writing. Points of interest include Tuscan pillars and an organ built in 1680 by Duyschot with shutters painted by Gerard de Lairesse. It's worth climbing to the top of the tower for the superb view of Amsterdam – and while you recover from the exertion, ponder the fate of one of Amsterdam's most famous sons, Rembrandt van Rijn: it is thought that the painter is buried somewhere in the graveyard here, although no-one knows for certain which grave is his. Rembrandt died a pauper, and though his burial on 8 October 1669 was recorded in the church register, the actual spot was not specified. There's a good chance that he shares a grave with his son, Titus, who died a year earlier. The Dutch, however, redeemed themselves by erecting a monument in memory of the painter inside the church.

PARKS & GARDENS

Although the local council claims there are 28 parks in Amsterdam, the city really only has a few green spaces worth visiting: **Amsterdamse Bos, Beatrixpark, Hortus Botanicus** (Botanical Gardens), **Vondelpark** and **Amstelpark**. The rest are either small scraps of grass – for a very short period in the spring these are transformed into sheets of colour by beautiful displays of tulips and crocuses – or found in uninteresting residential neighbourhoods. For gardens outside Amsterdam, *see page 203* **Excursions in Holland**. Admission to all the parks listed below is free.

Amstelpark

OS. Bus 8, 48, 49, 60, 158, 173. **Open** dawn-dusk daily.
Created for Floriade 1972, a garden festival held in a different location every ten years (*see p203* **Excursions in Holland**), this major park offers recreation and respite in the suburb of Buitenveldert (near the RAI Congress and Convention Centre). A formal rose garden and rhododendron walk are among the seasonal floral spectacles. Art shows at the Glass House (Glazenhuis), pony rides, a children's farm, and tours aboard a miniature train are available. The Rosarium Restaurant serves expensive meals; its outdoor café is somewhat less pricey.

Amsterdamse Bos

OS. Bus 170, 171, 172. **Open** 24 hours daily.
Created in the thirties, partly as a job creation scheme to ease what was a chronic unemployment problem, the 2,000-acre (800 ha) Bos (Dutch for wood) is a favourite retreat for Amsterdam families, especially at weekends. The man-made Bosbaan (canal) is used for boating and swimming and other attractions include a horticultural museum (*see p100* **Museums**), play areas, jogging routes, a buffalo and bison reserve, a watersports centre, horse-riding stables and a picnic area. In the outdoor pancake restaurant, the peacocks have a habit of flapping noisily from table to table. Bicycles can be hired (March-October) at the main entrance.

Beatrixpark

OS. Tram 5. **Open** dawn-dusk daily.
A little off the beaten tourist track, though on the doorstep of the RAI business centre (*see p188* **Business**) in the elegant south of the city, this is one of Amsterdam's loveliest parks. There are no real amenities, but what is offered is peace and quiet and a pond complete with ducks, geese and herons. There's also a children's wading pool.

Hortus Botanicus

Plantage Middenlaan 2, IE (625 8411). Tram 7, 9, 14. **Open** *Oct-March* 9am-4pm Mon-Fri; 11am-4pm Sat, Sun, public holidays; *April-Sept* 9am-5pm Mon-Fri; 11am-5pm Sat, Sun, public holidays.
The University of Amsterdam has had its own medicinal plant garden since 1638, and it has been at this location since 1682, making it one of the oldest gardens in The Netherlands as well as one of the most beautiful. Best of all are the greenhouses, which are planted with tropical and subtropical plants: one is filled with various carnivorous plants, while the palm house (which includes a 400-year-old cycad, reputed to be the oldest potted plant in the world) also has several tanks of tropical fish. You can also seek out Van Gogh's favourite plants with the help of a special leaflet. Information and suggested route guides are available in English. There's another botanical garden, run by the Vrije University, *see p100* **Museums**.

Vondelpark

OS. Tram 1, 2, 3, 5, 6, 12. **Open** dawn-dusk daily.
Named after the city's most famous poet, Joost van den Vondel (1587-1679), this is the most central major park. It was designed in

the 'English style' by D Zocher, with the emphasis on natural landscaping. The original 10 acres were opened in 1865. It has several ponds and lakes (no boating), several cafés (the most pleasant being the terrace of the Filmmuseum, which backs onto the park; *see p100* **Museums** and *p122* **Film**), and children's play areas. This was once the Mecca of hippiedom and the famous Sunday afternoon pop concerts in the summer (*see p135* **Music: Rock, Folk & Jazz**) are still *de rigueur*, although they are now under threat. In 1989, they came under attack from some of the park's neighbours, with the result that only four gigs were held in 1990.

A stroll along any of Amsterdam's 160 canals is always pleasant – but be warned, driving along the narrow, one-way streets on either side of them is a nightmare. The four concentric city-centre canals – Singel, Herengracht, Keizersgracht and Prinsengracht – and the tiny streets that connect them (don't miss Reestraat, Hartenstraat, Berenstraat, Runstraat, . Huidenstraat, Wolvenstraat and Herenstraat) are the most interesting to wander round. Smaller, connecting canals to seek out for their charm include Leliegracht, Lauriergracht, Egelantiersgracht, Bloemgracht, Spiegelgracht and Brouwersgracht. But don't be too methodical in your approach or you'll be fighting the relaxed mood of the canals, which are the perfect antidote to inner-city stress.

Seeing Amsterdam from the water is an unforgettable experience. There are plenty of tours (*see below*), but if you prefer to drift at will, hire a pedal boat or, if money is no object, a water taxi. And don't forget to navigate on the right-hand side of the waterways. *See also page 33* **Canals**.

Canal Bike
Amstel 57, 1018 EG (626 5574). **Open** *office* 9am-6pm Mon-Fri. **Moorings** *Centraal Station; Leidsekade at Leidseplein, between Marriott and American Hotels; Stadhouderskade, opposite Rijksmuseum; Prinsengracht, by Westerkerk; Keizersgracht, on the corner of Leidsestraat.* **Hire** costs 2-person pedalo f18.50 per hour; 4-person pedalo f27.50 per hour. **Deposit** f50. **Credit** fTC.

Canal Bike has two- and four-seater pedalos for hire.

Roell
Mauritskade 1, by the Amstel, OE (692 9124). Tram 6, 7, 10. **Open** *Apr-Sept* 8am-10pm Tue-Sun; *Oct-Mar* 9am-6pm Wed-Sat. **Hire** costs 2-person pedalo f18 per hour; 4-person pedalo f26 per hour; 4-person motor boat f37.50 for one hour, f60 for two hours; 10-person boat with skipper f90 per hour. **Deposit** pedalo f50; 4-person motor boat f150. **No credit cards.**
Roell is a general watersport centre which has four-seater pedal and motor boats for hire. A 10-seater family boat, complete with skipper, costs f90 per hour, but can only be hired for a maximum of three hours.

While it is the sea that has been responsible for Amsterdam's development and prosperity, it has also been the city's greatest adversary. Most of Amsterdam is below sea level, making building extremely difficult. Although a system of dikes now protects the whole of the western Netherlands, the water which regularly flooded the Amsterdam area for hundreds of years has left a soft peat layer, preventing usual building methods. The visible evidence of this underground problem is the number of buildings that noticeably lean from the vertical.

During the Middle Ages, houses were made from wood to keep their weight to a minimum and prevent subsidence. After a number of huge fires had reduced parts of the city to ashes, wooden houses were banned in 1669. The use of brick and stone in buildings meant that foundations had to be laid on wooden pilings, which were driven about 11 metres/36 feet into the ground so they rested on a sturdy layer of sand – quite an achievement when done by hand. An incredible number of pilings were needed: the **Royal Palace**

This house on the corner of Leliedwarsstraat and Bloemgracht leans precariously over the street in true Amsterdam fashion.

on the Dam (*listed under* **Heritage**), for example, was built on 13,659 pilings. Amsterdam's buildings are still constructed on pilings, although concrete has replaced wood since World War II and the pilings are now sunk as deep as 60 metres/195 feet.

Despite the pilings, you won't have to walk far in Amsterdam before you encounter your first collapsing house. Windows have been re-cut to fit into crushed frames; while inside, floors slope, table legs are propped up by slabs of paper and furniture trundles from wall to wall. Any dip in the water table exposes the piles to the atmosphere. Wooden ones start to rot and subsidence sets in. The dry summer of 1990 is expected to have exacerbated the situation further.

Solutions to the problem vary. Many grand old houses suffer from little more than an elegant list (*see* **picture and caption**), and since they have inclined so for hundreds of years seem to need no special attention. Others, particularly in less wealthy areas, are propped up or girdered together with steel brackets and timbers. Eventually they will have to be restored or rebuilt.

Some of the decrepit buildings may be amusing, but they are inhabited – which illustrates the housing shortage that has been an expensive headache for Amsterdam Council for years.
Jon and Sara Henley.

Bank-Change -Cheques- Credit Cards

In Holland you'll always find a GWK office near at hand. At nearly all important border crossings and at 35 railway stations. GWK offices are open seven days a week, from early in the morning till late at night. The GWK offices at the railway station at Schiphol Airport and the Central Station of Amsterdam are even open 24 hours a day. For changing all currencies and cashing all traveller's cheques. You can also make use of the Western Union Money Transfer service and withdraw money against credit cards: American Express, Diners Club, Visa, Eurocard, Master-Card, Access, JCB and AirPlus Card. For information dial free: 06-0566.

GWK
De Grenswisselkantoren N.V.
Head office: P.O. Box 721, 1000 AS Amsterdam.

Roland Smit BV
NATIONAL HOUSING SERVICE

• Furnished and semi-furnished flats, houses and villas
• Rental prices from NLG 1,500 pm
• Minimum 6 month
• Licensed realty of V.V.W./ V.B.O. associations

ALSO SALES AND PROPERTY INVESTMENTS

FOR INFORMATION
(0)20 - 679 14 54 / 676 42 02
Fax (0)20 - 662 73 83; Apollolaan 197 - 1077 AW Amsterdam

Water Taxi Centrale

Stationsplein 8, C (622 2181). Tram 1, 2, 4, 5, 9, 13, 16, 17, 24, 25. **Open** *9am-1am daily.* **Cost** *8-person boat* f120 *per hour; 15 and 30-person-boats* f190 *for 1st hour, then* f180 *per hour.* **Credit** AmEx, DC, MC, TC, V.

You can't hail a taxi from this company – you have to book by phone. The boats can take up to 30 passengers and charge a tariff based on the duration of your trip (f2 per minute).

BRIDGES

With so many canals, it's logical that Amsterdam should also have a fair number of bridges – in fact there are over 1,200 of them. There's a point on Reguliersgracht, at the junction with Keizersgracht, where you can see seven parallel bridges, floodlit by night. One of Amsterdam's most unusual bridges is the Magerebrug, also known as the Skinny Bridge, which was originally built in the seventeenth century. Uniquely, it's made from wood and has to be repaired every 20 years. It's opened by hand whenever a boat needs to pass; which tends to be about every 20 minutes. It links Kerkstraat and Nieuwekerkstraat. You should also try to see the Blauwebrug, which was inspired by the elaborate Pont Alexandre III in Paris. *See also page 33* **Canals: picture and caption.**

Amsterdam's windmills

D'Admiraal *Noordhollandsch Kanaaldijk, near Jan Thoméepad, N. Bus 34, 37, 39.*
De Bloem *Haarlemmerweg, near Nieuwpoortkade, OW. Bus 18.*
De Rieker *Amsteldijk, near De Borcht, OS. Bus 148.*
1200 Roe *Haarlemmerweg, near Willem Molengraaffstraat, OW. Bus 85.*
De Gooyer *Zeeburgerstraat, IE. Tram 10/bus 22, 28.*
1100 Roe *Herman Bonpad, Sportpark Ookmeer, OW. Bus 19, 68.*

Amsterdam is not the best place to see windmills – go to nearby Zaanse Schans to see some more impressive examples in action (*see p203* **Excursions in Holland**); but if you are desperate there are six in the city. Unfortunately, none of them are open to the public, but no-one's going to stop you from having a look at the outside. All the mills are capable of working, or at the very least turning their sails, and do so on National Windmill Day (*see p36* **Amsterdam by Season**). With the exception of *D'Admiraal*, which was built in 1792 to grind chalk and is now empty, all are private homes or shops. The best example is *De Rieker*, situated on the banks of the Amstel, which can be reached by walking through Amstel Park. Built in 1636 to drain

the Rieker polder, it is beautifully preserved and is now a private home. This was a favourite spot of Rembrandt's and there is a small statue close by to commemorate the fact that he used to paint here. There are two mills on the Haarlemmerweg: *1200 Roe* (circa 1632) – a roe is an old-fashioned unit used to calculate the distance from the city centre – and the corn mill *De Bloem* (1768). The other mills are *De Gooyer* (1725) on Funenkade in the east of the city, which was another corn mill; and *1100 Roe*, an old water-mill in a western suburb.

Albert Cuyp Markt

Albert Cuypstraat, OS. Tram 2, 16, 24, 25. **Open** *9am-4.30pm Mon-Sat.*

This is the largest general street market in Amsterdam, and bargains can be picked up from stalls selling clothing, shoes, materials, jewellery, spices, fruit and vegetables. The fish and olive stalls are particularly fascinating, offering a staggering choice of varieties. It's best on a sunny Saturday, when the traders are on top form. *See also p26* **Amsterdam by Area: De Pijp** and *p153* **Shopping Around: Markets.**

Bloemenmarkt (Flower Market)

on Singel canal between Koningsplein and

Muntplein. Tram 1, 2, 4, 5, 9, 14, 16, 24, 25. **Open** *9am-6pm Mon-Sat.* *See* **picture and caption.** *See also p161* **Specialist Shopping: Classic Dutch.**

Noordermarkt

Noordermarkt, OW. Tram 3/bus 18, 22, 44. **Open** *9am-noon Mon.*

Bargain hunters come from far and wide to this Monday morning textile market with its vast selection of material, extending from PVC to fun fur.

Oudemanhuis Book Market

Oudemanhuispoort (off Oudezijds Achterburgwal), C. Tram 4, 9, 14, 16, 24, 25. **Open** *10am-4pm Mon-Sat.*

People have been buying and selling books, prints and sheet music along this charming arcade since the nineteenth century. English-language books appear from time to time. When the alley was first built, in 1601, it was the entrance to the homes for the elderly (one each for men and women); hence the strange name. *See also p53* **War & Reformation** and *p153* **Shopping Around: Books.**

Stamp & Coin Market

Pedestrian island in front of Nova Hotel, Nieuwezijds Voorburgwal 276, C. Tram 1, 2, 5, 13, 17. **Open** *11am-4pm Wed, Sat.*

A specialist market for collectors of stamps and coins, old postcards and commemorative medals.

You can find a lot more than tulips on Amsterdam's floating **Bloemenmarkt** *(Flower Market, see under* **Markets***), where the stalls are set out on barges. A riot of colour in all seasons, the market has an incredible variety of plants, bulbs and dried flowers as well as a stunning assortment of cut flowers. At night the floating greenhouses are lit with strings of fairy lights.*

IT'S
NEW,
THRILLING, EXCITING,
FANTASTIC, MOVING,
UNBELIEVABLE,
HOT, COLD,
ANCIENT, FUTURISTIC:

MADAME TUSSAUD
SCENERAMA
DAM SQUARE

(Opens June 1991)

Waterlooplein Flea Market

Waterlooplein, C. Tram 9, 14/Metro Waterlooplein. **Open** 10am-5pm Mon-Sat.
Situated alongside the smart new Muziektheater/City Hall complex (*see above* **Cultural Centres**), Amsterdam's flea market has a spectacular collection of curiosities, clothing, furniture, household articles and unadulterated junk. *See p153* **Shopping Around: Markets.**

TOURS

For advice on how to get around town under your own steam, *see above* **Canals** and *page 3* **Essential Information: Transport.**

WALKING

Amsterdam is compact enough to be a great city for walking around, but it probably isn't the world's best for stilettos, pushchairs or wheelchairs because of its uneven streets and tramlines. The tourist organization VVV (*see page 3* **Essential Information**) has a series of English-language brochures outlining eight easy-to-follow walks, including ones themed around Van Gogh, sculpture and the Amsterdam School of architecture. The following operate guided tours; English is spoken.

Amsterdam Gallery Guide

Laurierstraat 70, IW (625 2275). Tram 13, 14, 17. **Tours** 2pm, last 3-4 hours. **Cost** f35 per person. **No credit cards.**
A one-woman operation, offering tailor-made guided tours of up to six of Amsterdam's galleries or museums in a single afternoon. The maximum number of people per group is ten, the minimum is one. In July and August the tours tend to concentrate on ceramics, jewellery and interior design, as many of the painting and sculpture galleries are closed. The price of guided tours does not include admission to museums.

Archivise

PO Box 14603, 1001 LC Amsterdam (625 8908).
Archivise organizes tailor-made architectural tours, and runs regular theme tours. Phone for details of charges, which vary greatly.

Mee in Mokum

Hartenstraat 16, C (625 1390/3685). Tram 13, 14, 17. **Tours** 11am Tue-Fri, Sun; last 2-3 hours. **Cost** f3.50 per person. **No credit cards.**
Long-time residents of Amsterdam, all aged over 55, give highly personal and individual tours of the city and Jordaan areas (*see p26* **Amsterdam by Area**). Advance booking is necessary.

BOATS

If you've got just one hour in Amsterdam, spend it on a guided boat trip (*rondvaart*). It may sound predictable, but the best way to see the city is from the water. Don't be put off by the hordes of coach parties lining up to get on board. There are plenty of tour operators, most of them with embarkation points along Rokin opposite Centraal Station; we list the main ones below. Some of them offer night-time cruises, when many of the buildings and most of the bridges are illuminated. Some of the trips include a stop at 'a real Amsterdam

HOFJES

It is a little publicized fact that tucked behind certain Amsterdam green doors are courtyards rich in greenery and calm. These hofjes (pronounced 'hofyes') date from the seventeenth and eighteenth centuries, when many were built by wealthy tradesmen to house poor or marginalized groups. The **Begijnhof** (*listed under* **Heritage**) is the classic example, but those prepared to stray from the standard tourist routes will gain a behind-the-scenes glimpse at more intimate (and inhabited) sites. Hofje-spotting requires patience, the boldness to push open apparently closed doors and the discretion to avoid outstaying your welcome.

The highest concentration of small hofjes is around the Jordaan (*see page 26* **Amsterdam by Area**), although there are also some fine examples in Haarlem (*see page 208* **The Randstad**). People live and work in them; they are not signposted as sights and it is up to their residents to choose whether or not to leave doors open for public access – which means they are open irregularly. Visit in small groups (three's a crowd) and bear in mind that although residents don't usually mind you having a look, you are in fact standing in their garden.

Hofjes are usually liberally decorated with the gablestones that were used to identify homes until house numbers were introduced in 1796 (*see p59* **Decline & Fall**). Our listings cover a selection of Jordaan hofjes. Not all of the doors will open when you push them, but they are close together and the area itself is attractive and interesting enough to wander around if you can't get in.

All hofjes listed below are in the Jordaan (IW). *Tram 13, 14, 17.*

Bon's Hofje

Prinsengracht 171.
Newer, noisier and slightly less bijou than some of the more carefully preserved hofjes; but it's often open.

Claes Claeszhofje

Eerste Egelantiersdwarsstraat, white gate opposite No.4.
See **picture and caption.**

Hofje Venetia

Elandsstraat 106-138.
Partly restored in 1957, this hofje was originally built by a trader in Venetian goods in 1650. It has a beautiful garden.

Sint Andrieshofje

Egelantiersgracht 105-141.
Built in 1617 with the inheritance of cattle farmer Ivo Gerritszoon, this is one of the oldest hofjes in Amsterdam and it has been very well restored. The engraving above the inner entrance means 'peace be with you': 'silence please', ask the residents.

Suykerhofje

Lindengracht 147-165.
There's a beautifully overgrown garden here.
Jon and Sara Henley.

Claes Claeszhofje *is actually two hofjes (dating from the early seventeenth century) which were combined in 1945. There's an impressive wooden tower, which has what must be a back-breaking staircase. It's now inhabited by music students and is often open to the public.*

Amsterdam, City of Diamonds!!!

For over 400 years Amsterdam has maintened its well deserved reputation for polishing diamonds. While in Amsterdam, experience the thrill of seeing the famous diamond polishers at their craft, transferring rough diamonds into fascinating brilliants. The 5 members of the Diamond Foundation Amsterdam (D.F.A.) invite you to visit their factories, all situated in the very heart of the city.

While touring the factories, multilingual staff will give you an ample explanation as to where diamonds are found, how they are polished, graded and mounted. Large collections of loose stones as well as comprehensive jewelry collections are available, from modestly priced to extravagantly chosen.

Only after a visit to one of the five D.F.A. members, is your Amsterdam Tour complete.

❖ **Amsterdam Diamond Centre**
   Rokin 1-5, 1012 KK Amsterdam.
   Phone: (0)20-626 57 87.

❖ **Gassan Diamonds B.V.**
   Nwe Uilenburgerstr. 173-175,
   1011 LN Amsterdam.
   Phone: (0)20-622 53 33.

❖ **Van Moppes & Zoon B.V.**
   Albert Cuypstraat 2-6,
   1072 CT Amsterdam.
   Phone: (0)20-676 12 42.

❖ **Coster Diamonds**
   Paulus Potterstraat 2-4,
   1072 CZ Amsterdam.
   Phone: (0)20-676 22 22.

❖ **Holshuysen Stoeltie**
   Wagenstraat 13-17,
   1017 CZ Amsterdam.
   Phone: (0)20-623 76 01.

pub' and all evening tours offer cheese and wine, although the quality usually leaves much to be desired.

The Best of Holland
Depart from Rederij Lovers landing stage opposite Centraal Station, C (623 1539). Tram 4, 9, 16, 24, 25. **Cruises** approx every 30 mins, 9am-6pm daily; *night cruise* (reservation required) 9.30pm daily. **Duration** *day cruises* 1 hour, 1½ hours; *night cruise* 2 hours. **Tickets** *day cruises: 1-hour* f9; f4.50 under-13s; *1½-hour* f12; f6 under-13s; *night cruise* f35; f17.50 under-13s. **Credit** MC, V.

Holland International
Depart opposite Centraal Station, C (622 7788). Tram 1, 2, 4, 5, 9, 13, 16, 17, 24, 25. **Cruises** approx every 30 mins, 9am-6pm daily; *luncheon cruise* (reservation required) 10.30am Mon, Wed, Sat; *night cruise* (wine, cheese, stop-off at bar; reservation required) 9.30pm daily; *dinner cruise* (4-course dinner, reservation required) 8pm Tue, Thur-Sat. **Duration** *day cruises* about 1½ hours; *luncheon cruise* 3 hours; *night cruise* 2 hours; *dinner cruise* 3 hours. **Tickets** *day cruises* f9; f6 under-13s; *luncheon cruise* f52.50; f42.50 under-13s; *night cruise* f39; f22.50 under-13s; *dinner cruise* f135; f95 under-13s. **Credit** AmEx, MC, V.
One of the most commercial companies, which attracts coach parties by the score.

Lindenbergh
Damrak 26, C (622 2766). Tram 4, 9, 16, 24, 25. **Cruises** approx every 30 minutes; *March-Oct* 10am-6pm daily; *Nov-April* 9am-5pm daily; *night cruise* (wine, cheese) 9pm, 9.30pm, daily. **Duration** *day cruises* 1 hour; *night cruises* 2 hours. **Tickets** *day cruises* f8.50; f5.50 under-13s; *night cruises* f35; f17.50 under-13s. **Credit** MC, V.

Rondvaarten
Kooy BV Rokin (opposite 125) at the corner of Spui, C (623 3810). Tram 4, 9, 16, 24, 25. **Cruises** *Mar-mid Oct* every 30 minutes 9am-10pm; *mid Oct-Feb* every 30 minutes 10am-4pm. **Duration** 1 hour. **Tickets** f8.50; f5 under-13s. **No credit cards.**
A guide will point out the sights on these tours, which seem to attract fewer coach parties. The company also offers candlelight wine and cheese tours from April to mid October at 9.30pm. The tours last two hours and cost f35.

CYCLING

Rental of a bicycle for the duration of the tour is included in the prices below. For bicycle hire shops, *see page 3* **Essential Information**.

Ena's Bike Tour
PO Box 2807, 2601 CV, Delft (015 143797). **Open** 24-hour answerphone. **No credit cards.**
All tours cover about 35km (23 miles) and take about seven hours. The only ride individuals can join is the **Amsterdam Tour**, which leaves at 10am from Amstel Station

on Julianaplein (June-Sept only, f37.50); it's not in fact a tour of Amsterdam, but a ride through the countryside to the south of the city, with a stop to row on a lake (and swim if desired) and a visit to a cheese farm and a windmill. Lunch (picnic or restaurant) is not included in the price. Among the tours for groups is the **Tulip Tour** (April, May, min 15 people), which includes a visit to a tulip farm and a windmill. The tour costs from f30 per person (not including lunch), and the departure/pick-up point is arranged on request.

Yellow Bike
Twede Boomdwarstraat 4-6, C (620 7140). Tram 1, 2, 5, 13, 17. **Open** 9am-5pm Mon-Fri; 9.30am-noon Sat. **No credit cards.**
Glide past Amsterdam's main sights with Yellow Bike's **City Tour**; it takes 3½ hours, departs at 9am and 1pm every day from the Beurs van Berlage building (Damrak 247), and costs f25. The **Waterland Tour** takes you further afield and lasts about 7 hours; the trip includes a visit to a cheese factory and a clockmaker and a return or outward bus journey. Tours depart at 8.30am daily from the Beurs van Berlage or at noon from Centraal Station, and cost f30 (not including lunch).

HELICOPTER

KLM Helicopter Tours
(649 1088). **Open** 9am-5pm Mon-Fri.
If you're keen to get an aerial view of Amsterdam and its surroundings, you can charter a helicopter through KLM. Mind you, it'll cost a cool f5,000 per hour. Helicopters take a maximum of 25 people.

One of the statistics that the VVV provides at every opportunity is that Amsterdam has 2,400 houseboats; what is less well known is that the Council doesn't want any more. This seems to be because the bobbing metropolis of barges, sheds on concrete, converted lighters (flat-bottomed barges) and brightly daubed junk along some stretches of canal contradicts the image of a fast-moving, hyper-successful Euro-capital that the Council seeks to promote. Boats are widely used as bar terraces, suntraps, resting-places, rubbish dumps and to hold builders' paraphernalia (*see page 33* **Canals**) – but residents say it is becoming increasingly difficult to live on them.

Houseboats became popular in the fifties when a shortage of affordable housing coincided with a decline in inland waterway traffic – Amsterdammers bought them up from impoverished barge skippers and turned them into attractive homes. But a licence is required to

live on a houseboat and strict conditions are now enforced to enable newcomers to get one; the right kind of boat (known as an *ark*, really a chalet on concrete) is more likely to gain a licence. Residents also say that the fees they pay – harbour dues to include electricity, water and phone connections – have risen rapidly in recent years. It is not easy to use a houseboat to commute: if the boat has an engine it carries a 'P' on its licence plate, which means owners don't receive full houseboat rights (fully-fledged houseboat plates carry a 'G'). Neighbours have to help with basic amenities such as power and water.

Fortunately, houseboat residents have a lobby which takes action when their interests are under threat. Even though some of the dilapidated or abandoned floating homes can be an eyesore, it would be hard to replace the informal, friendly atmosphere generated by the many houseboat communities.

Houseboats are moored in certain areas throughout Amsterdam, with many quite a way from the centre. The best area for an introductory ramble is along Brouwersgracht and its junctions with the other main canals. Starting at its intersection with Prinsengracht – and following this right the way up to the Anne Frankhuis – gives an excellent impression (for an even better view, you can also follow this route on a 'canal bike' or pedalo (*see under* **Canals**), but peering in windows is strictly not done).

As well as the older boats, there are a couple of 'designer' *arks*: opposite Prinsengracht 149 (the view is particularly good from the other side of the canal) and Keizersgracht 109. Many more stately floating residences can be seen on the Amstel. And on Singel near the Lutheran Church there's even a houseboat for stray cats (*see page 221* **Survival: Pets**).

Jon and Sara Henley.

Amsterdam by Area

The best (and worst) of Amsterdam's street life: an introductory tour around the city's most famous areas.

Most visitors to Amsterdam will have no need to travel far beyond the *grachtengordel* (canal ring) that defines its centre, except for taking a short stroll south to the area around Museumplein where the major museums are concentrated. Roughly speaking, the further out you travel, the newer the areas are. In the centre are the few medieval buildings, the old port, the earliest and prettiest canals and the seventeenth-century merchants' houses. Slightly further out are quarters built to house the various waves of incoming workers, such as the **Jordaan** (*see below*), to the west; behind it is the Kinkerbuurt area, which, like the **Pijp** (*see below*), was built at the end of the nineteenth century to accommodate workers who moved to the city during the Industrial Revolution. To the south, the area around the museums (*see below* **The Museum Quarter**) also dates from the late 1800s, when it was built between two working class areas to house the rich and take pressure off the overcrowded centre.

After the war, new self-contained 'garden neighbourhoods' were built further out, including those to the west at Osdoorp and Slotermeer. Further building projects are also going on nearer the centre: in the east, formerly the port area (*see below* **The Waterfront**), new homes are being built to replace old housing and warehouses are being converted. Amsterdam Noord, across the River IJ behind Centraal Station, has always been considered to be out on a limb, but it has been opened up, traffic permitting, by the IJ tunnel (which can be walked through).

LEIDSEPLEIN

On the south-west edge of the *grachtengordel* (canal ring), Leidseplein is a lively centre, with pavement cafés and buskers. Although called a square, it is in fact on a dog-leg, running from the end of Leidsestraat to the bridge over Singelgracht. The address is also used very flexibly by businesses and tour operators.

In the current climate of city-centre traffic reduction schemes, this square is a reminder that such ideas are not new. During the Middle Ages, carts and wagons were banned from the centre of Amsterdam. People heading for the city had to leave their vehicles in *pleinen*, or squares. At the end of the road from Leiden was a 'cart park' surrounded by warehouses and establishments catering for this captive clientele.

Leidseplein has always been a centre for one reason or another. In the twenties and thirties artists and writers used to congregate here and it was the scene of pre-war clashes between political factions ranging from the communists to the Fascists. During the war it was a focus for protests which were ruthlessly broken up by the occupying Nazis; there's a commemorative plaque on nearby Kerkstraat where a number of people were killed. More recently, Leidseplein was the venue for celebrations after the 1988 Dutch victory in the European Cup and for Nelson Mandela's 1990 visit.

The café society associated with Leidseplein began in earnest with the city's first bar to incorporate a terrace: the Café du Théatre. It was demolished in 1877, twenty years before Kromhout's impressive Hotel Americain, now a prominent meeting place (*see page 79* **Restaurants**), was completed at the south-west end of the square. Opposite the Americain, and originally the showcase of top department store Hirsch and Cie (built in 1882), is a building which reflects Leidseplein's transformation into its current state of architectural billboard. The violet flashing Sony and Drum adverts add nothing to the building's former grandeur.

The overriding feature of the square is people (*see page 27* **picture and caption**). During the summer at least 1,000 seats are available on café terraces, and in winter (usually from November to early spring, depending on the weather) a skating rink becomes the centre of attention. There's always plenty going on: Leidseplein has become an open-air stage for street performers and a market for hawkers of trinkets.

Eylders
Korte Leidsedwarsstraat 47, IS (624 2704). Tram 1, 2, 5, 6, 7, 10. **Open** *bar* noon-1am Mon-Thur, Sun; noon-2am Fri, Sat; *kitchen* 5-10pm daily. **No credit cards.**
Just off the square itself, this stylish brown café has a curious interior including art deco-style wrought iron lamps-cum-hat-stands, a semi-circular bar and stained glass. It's relatively free of tourists for the area.

Hoopman Bodega
Leidseplein 4, IS (638 1408). Tram 1, 2, 5, 6, 7, 10. **Open** 9am-1am Mon-Thur, Sun; 9am-2am Fri, Sat. **No credit cards.**
The place to hire your skates for the miniature ice-rink during the winter. They cost around f6 per pair, and there's no time limit.

THE MUSEUM QUARTER

The Museum quarter is part of one of the wealthiest areas of the city, *Oude Zuid* (Old South). Its border runs along the Rijksmuseum and Vondelpark in the north, down Emmastraat to Reijnier Vinkeleskade and up along Hobbemakade in the east.

A little over a hundred years ago the area was still officially outside the city limits and consisted of little more than vegetable patches and summer resorts. There were seven windmills and a candle factory which, because of the horrible smell it spread, had been built far from the centre of Amsterdam. But towards the end of the century the city expanded rapidly, and the city fathers saw the need to build an upper class neighbourhood between two working class areas to the west and south.

Most of the beautiful mansions, with their characteristic *jugendstil* gateways and stained glass windows, were built around the turn of the century. The exclusive shopping streets PC Hooftstraat and Van Baerlestraat are frequented by the rich and famous and are known throughout the country. The centre of it all is Museumplein, the city's largest square and the cultural heart of The Netherlands. It is surrounded by the Rijksmuseum, the Stedelijk

Museum and the Van Gogh Museum (*see page 13* **Sightseeing** and *page 100* **Museums** for all three), and the Concertgebouw (*see page 13* **Sightseeing** and *page 130* **Music: Classical & Opera**).

Museumplein itself is better described as a green than as a proper square. Its irregular oblong shape has been causing the city problems since its development in 1872. It originally served as a location for the World Exhibition of 1883 and was then rented out to the Amsterdam ice-skating club from 1900 to 1936. During the Depression, the neglected field was put to use as a sporting ground, and during World War II the Germans built four bunkers and a concrete shelter on it, that remained until 1952. A year later Museumstraat, the large road that divides the square in two, was completed; it is now sadly known as the shortest motorway in the world.

But although Museumplein has not turned out to be the peaceful resting point it was once meant to be, it is of value for having been an important gathering place for massive demonstrations throughout its history. One of them, the 1981 peace demonstration in which 400,000 people protested against nuclear weapons, is commemorated by a monument; *see page 68* **Post-war**. In more recent years the square has been the site of cultural events such as the Vincent van Gogh Village and a rock concert by David Bowie for thousands of onlookers. And with its impressive view of the historical buildings that surround it, it is a place to remember.

Wildschut
Roelof Hartplein 1, OS (673 8622). Tram 3, 5, 12, 24, 25. **Open** *bar* 9am-2am daily; *kitchen* noon-5pm, 6-10pm, daily. **No credit cards.**
In recent years Wildschut, a so-called grand café, has become one of Amsterdam's hotspots, a place which people visit from all over the city to drink, chatter and be seen. In summer it is practically impossible to find a space on the overcrowded terrace that overlooks Roelof Hartplein, a square built in the typical style of the Amsterdam School. But not to worry, because the beautiful art deco interior is well worth a look. Unfortunately the Wurlitzer jukebox is not in use, and there is better food to be had elsewhere, but that doesn't stop people from crowding the place until owner Luuc Wildschut finally has to kick them out.

Rijksmuseum
Stadhouderskade 42, OS (673 2121). Tram 6, 7, 10. **Open** 10am-5pm Tue-Sat; 1-5pm Sun, public holidays. **Admission** f6.50; f3.50

Leidsestraat, the busiest pedestrian street in the city, acts as a funnel into **Leidseplein** *for the throngs of tourists and locals, especially at night. The sleaze factor has been heightened by the arrival of dozens of fast-food establishments in and around the square, but the essential character of the place prevails. With about 20 films showing within ten minutes' walk and live indoor entertainment ranging from the sordid to the sophisticated close by, it remains an area where both Amsterdammers and visitors congregate, communicate and watch each other go by.*

under-17s; free with Museum Card; group discounts (min 20 people). **No credit cards.**
The monumental neo-Gothic building was designed by PJH Cuypers and completed in 1885. The archway that runs through it was intended to be an easy connection with the city's centre, and at one time there were even plans to run a tramline through it – thankfully they have now been abandoned. Because of the great acoustics there are always young street musicians playing under the archway, which adds to its special atmosphere. The Rijksmuseum's garden, contrary to the Stedelijk's sadly neglected one, is an oasis of peace in the middle of the bustling city. Its entrance is at the back of the Museum on Hobbemastraat, and it is open from 10am to 5pm daily. For details of the Museum itself, *see p100* **Museums**.

Roemer Visscherstraat
OS. Tram 2, 3, 5, 12.
Roemer Visscherstraat is a quiet street leading into Vondelpark and one could easily pass it by. But for those interested in architecture it is worth taking a look at the houses from No.20 to No.30. Each represents a different country and was built in the appropriate style. Russia comes complete with a miniature dome, Italy has been painted pastel pink and Spain's candy stripes have made it one of the street's favourites.

Vondelpark
OS. Tram 2, 3, 5, 12.
A short walk away from Museumplein, Vondelpark holds many attractions for those who wish to escape the crowds (*see p13* **Sightseeing** and *p183* **Sport & Fitness**), not least the Filmmuseum's Café Vertigo (*see p122* **Film** and *p100* **Museums**), an excellent place to watch passers-by and, weather permitting, get a nice tan on the terrace. Throughout the park are statues and monu-

ments, including the statue of Joost van Vondel, the famous Golden Age poet after whom the park was named, on the south side.

THE RED LIGHT DISTRICT

Amsterdam's red light area is the oldest part of the city. Roughly speaking, it is bounded by Warmoesstraat to the west, Zeedijk to the north, Kloveniersburgwal to the east and Damstraat/Oude Doelen/Oude Hoogstraat to the south. Known as the Wallen (Walls) because it used to be enclosed by the old town walls, the red light area comprises a few pretty, tree-shaded canals lined with sixteenth- to eighteenth-century houses, criss-crossed by narrow alleys. Because it is the city's oldest quarter, some of the earliest buildings are within easy reach, including the Schreierstoren (Weeping Tower), Oudekerk (for both *see page 13* **Sightseeing**) and Oudemanhuispoort (*see page 53* **War & Reformation**). For a suggested stroll around the area, taking you past the sights, shops and cafés listed below, *see page 28* **A Walk on the Wild Side**. For the Cannabis Info Museum and the Sex Museum, *see page 100* **Museums**.

There have been prostitutes in this

part of town since the city began, attracted by the port, although the neat little windows with *kamer te huur* (room to let) signs are a more recent introduction. Prostitution is still technically illegal in The Netherlands, yet the window girls pay tax on their earnings and there are moves to set up a city council licensing scheme. Women work the windows in six-hour shifts, and windows in the more popular streets are in use 24 hours a day. Sex is strictly heterosexual, although some of the Thai 'girls' may well be 're-built' boys. Tourists are not advised to take photos, as there is usually a heavy hanging around for protection.

Despite the red light district's reputation as an area of high crime, full of muggers and junkies, most people who get into trouble there do so because they've been foolish. Following a dealer up a dark alley, waving wadges of money around, or being obviously drunk or stoned is asking for trouble. If you do get

attacked, report it to the Warmoesstraat police station and insist on making it official (the police have a tendency to discourage people from reporting muggings to keep the crime statistics down). That said, if you keep your wits about you, there is no reason to be worried walking around the area on a summer evening: there will be countless other people doing exactly the same thing.

Despite the 'sex and drugs', there is still ordinary life here: there are plumbers, grocers, launderettes and haberdashers. The fact is that flats with a view over a canal are extremely desirable – and expensive.

Casa Rosso
Oudezijds Achterburgwal 106-108, C (627 8954). Tram 4, 9, 14, 16, 24, 25/Metro Nieuwmarkt. **Open** 8pm-2am daily. **No credit cards.**
A respectable sex club with chandeliers, multi-lingual doormen and live floor shows.

Hanky Panky's
Oudezijds Voorburgwal 141, C (627 4848). Tram 4, 9, 14, 16, 24, 25/Metro

Nieuwmarkt. **Open** 11am-6pm Mon-Sat. **No credit cards.**
See p29 **picture and caption.**

Hooy & Co
Kloveniersburgwal 12, C (624 3041). Tram 4, 9, 14, 16, 24, 25/Metro Nieuwmarkt. **Open** 8.30am-6pm Mon-Fri; 8.30am-5pm Sat. **No credit cards.**
This old-fashioned herb and spice shop is full of wonderful smells, lotions and potions.

Het Karbeel
Warmoesstraat 58, C (627 4995). Tram 4, 9, 16, 24, 25. **Open** *bar* 10am-midnight daily; *kitchen* 6-10.30pm daily. **Average** f20. **No credit cards.**
Calm and quiet, this café restaurant on the bustling Warmoesstraat has a small pavement terrace. It has a wide range of sausages and cheeses, specializes in cheese fondue and stages live jazz on occasional Sundays.

De Pieter
Pieterspoortsteeg, C (623 6067). Tram 4, 9, 14, 16, 24, 25. **Open** midnight-dawn daily. **No credit cards.**
This scruffy late-night bar gets lively at around 2am. The ownership changes regularly and the clientele is an odd assortment of squatters, artists and night owls.

A WALK ON THE WILD SIDE

A good starting point for exploring the red light area on foot is the National Monument on the Dam. The Dam was once exactly that, a dam (*see page 52* **Early History**), and Damrak, which leads from Centraal Station, was once the River Amstel. As well as being the site of several Amsterdam landmarks (*see page 13* **Sightseeing**, the Dam is a favoured hang-out for dodgy street dealers.

Turn up Warmoesstraat (by the Hotel Krasnapolsky), which is one boundary of the oldest part of the city. The first section of the street, including a jewellery shop, the Condomerie (*see page 161* **Specialist Shops**) and the art gallery at number 151, is part of the Blaauwlakenblok, a block of houses which was once intended to be demolished to build a car park. The buildings (apart from the convent in the middle of the block) were first squatted, then bought by the council, and are now rented out (sometimes to the original squatters) for peppercorn rents. Warmoesstraat, once the city's vegetable market, has every kind of restaurant you can imagine, and several wonderful old-fashioned coffee wholesalers, remnants of

Amsterdam's colonial past. Past the police station turn down the Lange Niezel, which will take you to the heart of the Wallen and the window girls.

Turn to the right at Oudezijds Voorburgwal and you will pass a pretty cobbled square and the Oudekerk, the city's oldest church (*see page 13* **Sightseeing**). One bridge across is the Oudezijds Achterburgwal. These streets run along the two parallel canals that cut through the area, and are home to the sex shops and sex clubs, whose dinner-jacketed doormen attempt to attract custom.

Still heading east, connecting alleys lead to Zeedijk (once a sea wall), notorious for its junkie population and now one target of a failing clean-up campaign. In 1989 the city council began a major propaganda exercise to bring back normal shops and residents. Houses were renovated and low-rent shops were built to attract new blood. However, the lack of political will in tackling the junkie problem has lead to disillusionment on the part of many who invested in the idea. While the top end of the street looks better (and the shop which sold only silver

paper, spoons and lemons has finally been closed down) junkies and dealers, the majority of whom are not Dutch, still congregate here.

At the south end of Zeedijk you reach the Chinese area, with a few cheap, dragon-filled restaurants, although many of the Chinese who first settled here have gone on to bigger and better things. At the bottom of the street is Nieuwmarkt, a wide square dominated by the Waag (the old weigh house, *see page 13* **Sightseeing**), which at time of writing was being extensively redeveloped. Much of this area was demolished during the building of the Metro in the late seventies and early eighties (*see page 68* **Postwar**), but it is coming alive again, with café terraces and odd little shops.

Walk down Kloveniersburgwal, turn right along the Oude Hoogstraat and you will cross what the natives call the Pillenbrug (pill bridge), because of the number of junkies buying and selling pills. Continue down Damstraat, past the Old Man Head Supplies (featured in every British tabloid 'Amsterdam drugs' exposé) and you are back at the beginning again, on the Dam.

THE JORDAAN

Ask Amsterdammers to define the borders of the Jordaan and you'll never get the same answer. Everyone agrees on the first three: Singel to the east, Brouwersgracht to the north and Lijnbaansgracht to the west. Even the city authorities disagree about the fourth, some placing it at Elandsgracht and some as far as Leidsegracht. One thing all agree on: the Jordaan is magical. It has a distinctive subculture that may rival those of London's East End and New York's Greenwich Village. There are small streets that change name at every block, secret green courtyards and beautiful old buildings that are protected monuments. Weird and wonderful shops pepper the streets; typical are Purple Heron Gallerie Atelier and Annabelle (*see page 153* **Shopping Around: Handicrafts**).

Long-time residents of the area speak a slang Dutch as colourful as the English spoken in Brooklyn, have a distinctive kind of music (*see page 30* **Drinking to Music**) and their own style of home furnishings. In the evenings, a pink glow emanates from the windows of most of the houses: the people here love pink lampshades and lots of tassels. Above all, there is a spirit of camaraderie in this predominantly working class neighbourhood that has persisted over the centuries. Struggling artists are drawn to the area and show their work in their living-room windows or on pavement easels. Yuppies are here too, buying old houses on the canals, with an obligation to the city to maintain original features of architecture.

The area was originally established in the early seventeenth century, mostly by French Huguenot settlers in search of religious toleration, and to this day many of the residents have French surnames. Immigrants from many other cultures also influenced the language and habits of the district, and many Yiddish words found their way into the slang still spoken. The major industry in the Jordaan in the seventeenth century was tanning. Looiersgracht (Tanner's Canal) bears witness to this, and many of the surrounding streets are named for the animals whose pelts were used. To name a few: Hazenstraat (Hare Street), Reestraat (Deer Street), Elandsgracht (Elk Canal) and Wolvenstraat (Wolf

The owner of **Hanky Panky's**, *a highly respected and licensed tattoo parlour and museum (see under* **Red Light District**), *is Mr Hank Schiffmacher (above). He's more than just a needle man, although his clients include Motorhead and the Stray Cats. Go down to the basement and see for free the results of Mr Schiffmacher's research into the history of tattooing: a permanent exhibition of over 150 tattoo designs from all over the world and the machines that were used to create them. But the finest exhibit here is Hank himself. He has travelled the world, collecting tattoos on his skin. Those he received in Thailand are meant to increase fertility – at time of writing Mr Shiffmacher was due to be a father again. And in case you're wondering, the dog's name is Harry and he's a she.*

Street). Several streets were given names of trees and plants; they include Bloemstraat (Flower Street), Rozengracht (Rose Canal) and Laurierstraat (Laurel Street).

Many of the buildings in the Jordaan have been proclaimed monuments and restored to their original state. They are recognizable by a blue and white tile on the façade, which will often say much about the building's history (in Dutch, of course). Another kind of plaque that proliferates is the gablestone (*see page 60* **Gables & Gablestones**), a picture tile or hanging sign designed to inform even the illiterate on the nature of the building. At Tuinstraat 57 an illustration of warp and weft threads indicates a sheet maker's business; at 1e Egelantiersdwarsstraat 60 the gablestone portrays a group of singers. The premises used to be used by a 'musical newspaper'; people would make up songs about current events and render them around the neighbourhood in return for coins thrown down from windows. The houses at Lindengracht 206-218 bear a variety of gablestones.

Lijnbaansgracht was originally a

swamp, and much of the surrounding ground was swampy, making it cheap to purchase. Some successful merchants bought land and had it filled in, and when they built their elegant homes they also made an inner courtyard to be used as a *bleekveld* (bleaching field) for laying out clothing and linens to bleach in the sun. Sometimes the owners didn't live there themselves, using them instead to house their workers or underprivileged groups. Nowadays, these *hofjes* are usually planted with roses and wildflowers and serve as communal gardens, hidden from unsuspecting passers-by on the streets.

EXPLORING THE JORDAAN

You can walk into some of the *hofjes*, a selection of which are listed in **Sightseeing**, *page 13*, but people live in the surrounding houses and they value their privacy. One of the best ways to get an insider's view of Amsterdam past and present is through Mee in Mokum (Come Along in Amsterdam). Guides take small groups on informal, anecdotal walking tours, pointing out historical monuments and unusual sights, including hidden courtyards normally closed to the public. For details, *see page 13* **Sightseeing: Tours.**

Somewhat less tiring is a climb to the top of the Westertoren (Western Tower) of the Westerkerk on Prinsengracht, from where you can look down on the Jordaan's streets and canals. It's only open during the summer: for details of times *see page 13* **Sightseeing.** For a really lazy time, rent a pedalo from Canalbike, by the tower, and explore the Jordaan by water. Boats cost f18.50 per hour for two, f27.50 per hour for four. Pick up a sandwich from Wegewijs at Rosengrach 32, or moor the boat at Café 't Smalle, Egelantiersgracht 12 (*see page 91* **Cafés & Bars**), where you can order lunch from the café's small jetty. Don't leave the boat unattended or it may be towed away.

FESTIVE SEASON

Traditionally, many areas hold street festivals in September, usually during the second and third weeks. The most famous and most typically Dutch is in the Jordaan, when a stage is set up on Elandsgracht for local performers, including talented (or otherwise) children. There are various stalls and barbecues in many streets, parties in local bars (*see below* **Drinking to Music**), a fair with rides on Palmstraat and cabaret in the Palm building (Palmstraat 34). Shops stay open until 9pm and the streets are full of merry-makers day and night, including Sunday.

WATERLOOPLEIN & THE PLANTAGE

Waterlooplein, to the south-east of the red light area (*see above*), takes you out of the old and into the new: it's a crossroads with a mishmash of architectural styles and a clash of cultures. Indeed, stand on Mr Visserplein and you are surrounded by busy main roads: Weesperstraat goes past hideous concrete office blocks where most the newspapers are based; Walkenburgstraat leads up to the IJ tunnel, which goes under the old sea harbour (*see below* **The Waterfront**); and Plantage Middlenlaan goes past Artis Zoo and the Tropenmuseum. It is, frankly, a bit of a mess.

On Waterlooplein itself is the nineteenth-century Mozes en Aaronkerk church, which before the building of the Stadhuis-Muziektheater (*see page 13* **Sightseeing**) dominated the view over the Blauwbrug (Blue Bridge) and marked the way into the city from the east. The current bridge was built in 1873, but a plaque depicting the original (taken from a demolished house) has been placed at the entrance of the Muziektheater car park. The church, covered in political murals, has been used as a social and cultural centre since 1970. Squashed in between that and the Muziektheater complex is the flea-market (*see page 153* **Shopping Around**).

The area where the Muziektheater now stands was once a Jewish ghetto. Jews had been settling in Amsterdam from about 1600, when they came to escape persecutions throughout Europe, but little remains of Jewish Amsterdam now. There are a few synagogues clustered around the Joods Historisch Museum (Jewish Historical Museum, *see page 100* **Museums**), but demolition work to make room for the Muziektheater, the highways and the Metro destroyed the sixteenth- and seventeenth-century buildings. St Antoniesbreestraat, Jodenbreestraat and the surrounding areas have all been rebuilt with council housing, and a few chic clothes shops are springing up. The Jewish past is mostly visible through contemporary tributes: Nieuwmarkt Metro station features murals to the Jewish deportations of World War II and the Dokworker statue on Jonas Daniel Meijerplein is a memorial to the dock workers' strike in protest at these deportations (*see page 64* **World War II**).

Weesperstraat, leading to the highways out of the city, has little to recommend it, except as an example of how not to redevelop a city. One ambitious sixties' development, Hertzberger's student complex (*see page 196* **Students**), won architectural awards but is described as a 'nightmare' to work and live in.

The Plantage Middenlaan is a different matter, winding past Hortus Botanicus, Artis Zoo and the Tropenmuseum (*see page 100* **Museums** for all three), the last two built on land that was part of an eighteenth-century plan to create a

DRINKING TO MUSIC

The people of the Jordaan traditionally love music, whether it's opera, Dutch 'oom-pa-pa' carnival-type sing-alongs or the melancholy ballads peculiar to the area. The story goes that the origin of this fondness for tragic songs came about because French and (to a lesser degree) Italian settlers had a passion for opera. They would save their hard-earned cash to go see small local productions as often as possible and counter the monotony of the long working day by singing the most popular tunes. The contemporary ballads tell stories of bereavement, lost love and similarly cheery subjects. The music here is most often played on the organ or accordion and the best way for visitors to experience it is to visit one of the bars listed below, where patrons often sing along, sometimes with visible emotion. Cafés with a genuine Jordaanse clientèle are the epitome of *gezelligheid* – a word impossible to translate but implying cosiness, friendliness, comfort and happiness. If you go as a tourist to stare at the natives, you'll be given the cold shoulder. Go prepared to join in the spirit and you'll have the time of your life.

Some authentic Jordaan cafés are Willems Bar, Willemsstraat 16; Brouwer, Goudsbloemstraat 91; De Bel, Lindengracht 103; De Prins, Prinsengracht 124 (*see page 91* **Cafés & Bars**); and Het Bruine Paard, Prinsengracht 44; but two not to be missed are:

Café Nol
Westerstraat 109, IW (624 5380). Tram 10. **Open** *9am-3am Mon-Thur, Sun; 9am-4am Fri, Sat.* **No credit cards.**
See p31 picture and caption.

Twee Zwaantjes
Prinsengracht 114, IW (625 2729). Tram 13, 14, 17. **Open** *3pm-1am daily.* **No credit cards.**
Patrons sing solo or together – some are surprisingly good – to live organ music, covering every musical genre (including opera). If you visit only one café, make it this one. It's most fun at weekends, including Sundays.

garden city for those rich city dwellers who did not have a house on a canal. The Jews settled here too, and the area was redeveloped on nineteenth-century diamond money (diamond cutting was one of the few trades open to the Jews). The splendid headquarters of the diamond cutters' trade union still stands on Henri Polaklaan. The brightly coloured Van Eyck's Moedershuis, a mother and child refuge, is on Plantage Middenlaan and on the other side of the road is the Huize St Jacob, an old peoples' home, rebuilt on the site of an earlier one, using the same stone portal.

The Plantage is still wealthy, with a somewhat faded charm. Its graceful buildings and tree-lined streets are a much sought-after residential area for those who want to live centrally, but away from the tourists. The area has always undergone extensive redevelopment and the work is still continuing. Past the Muiderpoort city gate, the old army barracks and dockside warehouses are being turned into flats and houses for sale on the open market.

East of Eden
Linnaeusstraat 11, OE (665 0743). Tram 9, 10, 14. **Open** *11am-1am Mon-Thur, Sun; 11am-2am Fri, Sat.* **No credit cards.**
A pleasant, relaxed café on a corner overlooking the Tropenmuseum, with a sunny terrace.

Frankendael
Middenweg 72, OE. Tram 9. **Open** *Gardens only sunrise-sunset daily.* **Admission** free.
This is the area's only surviving example of an eighteenth-century mansion. The house cannot be visited, but the gardens are open to the public. *See also p59* Decline & Fall.

Portuguese Israelite Synagogue
Jonas Daniel Meijerplein, C (622 6188). Tram 9, 14. **Open** *10am-4pm Mon-Fri, Sun.* **Admission** *f2.50.* **No credit cards.**
One of a cluster of several seventeenth-century synagogues, many of which are now incorporated into the Jewish Historical Museum.
Guided tours by arrangement, f20 per person.

Zuiderkerkhof
Zuiderkerk foundation, Zuiderkerkhof, C (623 2334). Tram 9, 14/Metro Nieuwmarkt. **Open** *church by appointment; tower 1 June-15 Oct 2-5pm Wed; 11am-2pm Thur, Fri; 11am-4pm Sat.* **Admission** f1. **No credit cards.**
The skull-adorned gateway to this small courtyard off St Antoniesbreestraat is all that remains of the Zuiderkerk's cemetery. The early seventeenth-century church itself is now used for council exhibitions, but the tower can be climbed in summer. The courtyard's (council) housing complex was built after the demolition to build the metro.

The slogan at **Café Nol** *(see under* **The Jordaan: Drinking to Music***) is: 'Café Nol, altijd lol' (Café Nol, always fun). The décor is pure Jordaan kitsch – pink neon lights. It's another world in here, with a carnival atmosphere all year round. Unfortunately, patrons aren't too keen on strangers invading their haven. Wear a smile and hope you're accepted.*

DE PIJP

The colourful Pijp area (the pipe) is the best-known of the working-class quarters built in the late nineteenth century, when a population boom was bursting the city's seams. After four cholera epidemics, three eminent doctors (including Samual Sarphati, 1813-1866) diagnosed crisis and prescribed housing. New areas were built up at the rate of 600 houses per year, often without any municipal inspection. Many of the buildings collapsed, killing new residents; those that didn't formed the beginnings of the new *wijken* (districts), such the Pijp. It was officially titled 'Area YY', but the students who lived there soon gave it the more catchy name it retains today, probably because of the long, narrow and similar streets.

The main focus for the area is Albert Cuypstraat, site of Amsterdam's largest street market (*see page 32* **picture and caption** and *page 153* **Shopping Around**). It's the centre of the Pijp streetlife and generally spills into the adjoining roads: the junctions of Sweelinckstraat, Ferdinand Bolstraat and 1E Van der Helststraat, both northward into the often lively Gerard Douplein and south towards

Sarphatipark. This small but pleasant park was designed by Samual Sarphati as a 'Bois de Boulogne in miniature', and on a sunny day you can just about see what he meant.

Beyond the stalled area of Albert Cuypstraat, across Ferdinand Bolstraat, is the coach-party attraction of the Van Moppes Diamond factory (*see page 13* **Sightseeing**). This building is on the junction of the Ruysdaelkade, the Pijp's red light district.

Over 250 artists live in the vicinity of the Pijp and although it's no Greenwich Village, the area's creative community is highly active and gaining status in this district where most streets are named after their more illustrious forebears. The *Kunstroute de Pijp* is an exhibition of local work, displayed in the windows of shops, cafés and offices; the Heineken Brewery has in the past provided a major exhibition space, but whether this will continue after it becomes a museum (*see page 13* **Sightseeing**) is not confirmed. The *Kunstroute* is usually held during the first two weeks in September. A combined route map and catalogue can be obtained from the VVV. Fringe events are held concurrently in Sarphatipark

Beyond the market and its environs the Pijp is mostly residential, but a diverse range of coffee shops, cafés and small restaurants, usually very reasonable in both price and quality, characterize the area. Running parallel to Albert Cuypstraat, the Ceintuurbaan with its high-street shops has little of note for the visitor, with the exception of the building at Nos.251-255. There are certainly few houses in the city incorporating giant green gnomes with red hats in their wooden façades.

Albert Cuypstraat Market
Albert Cuypstraat, OS. Tram 4, 16, 24, 25.
Open 9.30am-6pm Mon-Sat.

Broodje van Popov
Van Woustraat 20, OS. Tram 4, 16, 24, 25.
Open 10am-5pm Tue-Sat. No credit cards.
A *broodje* (open roll) café that's very popular locally. The French sticks (*stookbrood*) and hamburgers are especially good.

Koffiehuis De Markt
Albert Cuypstraat 122B, OS (662 0105).
Tram 4, 16, 24, 25. Open 6am-6pm Mon-Fri; 6am-5pm Sat. No credit cards.
This difficult-to-find coffee bar is a genuine, traditional, smoky stallholders' card-playing joint. Rough and ready but friendly.

Peppino
1e Sweelinckstraat 16, OS (676 4910).
Tram 4. Open 11am-11pm daily. No credit cards.
An essential port of call for the connoisseur, this renowned Italian ice-cream parlour offers 19 flavours of *gelati* plus three that change according to which fruits are in season.

A late nineteenth-century housing development, the present-day **Pijp** *is a bustling daytime centre of commerce. Its effervescent and cosmopolitan community is epitomized by the area's backbone, the* **Albert Cuypstraat Market***. In 1860 this thoroughfare had 17 windmills and a canal running the length of it. Currently 20,000 people per day (50,000 on a busy Saturday) pass by the 300 stalls of Amsterdam's biggest market.*

THE WATERFRONT

While Rotterdam is by far the world's largest port, Amsterdam and the nearby North Sea Canal ports of Zaanstad, Beverwijk and IJmuiden together rank among the world's 15 largest ports, handling 45 million tonnes per year. Since 1876 access to the sea has been via the North Sea Canal, running west from Amsterdam, and because the working docks are also to the west, there is little activity on the IJ behind Centraal Station beyond a handful of passenger ships and the free ferry that runs across to Amsterdam Noord.

During Amsterdam's trading heyday in the seventeenth century (*see page 55* **The Golden Age**) most maritime activity was centred east of Centraal Station, along Prins Hendrikkade and on the artificial islands east of Kattenburgerstraat. The VOC's wharf was here; a small naval base still is and the Admiralty has been converted into the Scheepvaart Museum (maritime museum), which dominates the area. Nearby is another nautical museum, Werf 't Kromhout, a working nineteenth-century shipyard. For both, *see page 100* **Museums**. A ten-minute walk from the Scheepvaart Museum, Café Zeilvaart serves pub-type grub as well as drinks (including 37 types of

Beerenberg *jenever*, once touted as a cold cure).

The old harbour is now virtually disused and the generally run-down area is in need of regeneration. A very ambitious project, known as the IJ-Oever (IJ Bank) project, seeks to rival London's Docklands development. Although part will resemble New York's South Street Seaport (renovated historic buildings), most is more futuristic in design.

Moving westwards, the Havengebouw, just left of Centraal Station, houses the Port authority and several shipping companies. At only 13 storeys, it is a contender for the title of Amsterdam's only 'skyscraper'. On the twelfth floor, MartInn serves (pricey) food and has a superb view over the city.

The Westerlijk Eilands (Western Islands), north-west of Centraal Station, were created in the seventeenth century and used for shipping-related activities such as storage; there are consequently a number of old warehouses there. The Islands have become a separate little village favoured by artists, with (increasingly) trendy flats, converted warehouses and a yacht basin. The name reflects the Dutch capital city's trading traditions, and De Gouden (Golden) Reael is a pleasant port-side restaurant (*see page 79* **Restaurants**) in a lovingly restored seventeenth century building. It's an excellent starting (or stopping) point for a walk through this historic district. The working docks are further west still. They're not a particularly attractive sight, but they are thriving.

The best way to see Amsterdam is by glass-topped canal (*rondvaart*) boat cruises, and these always include part of the port. A more expensive option is hiring a water taxi. The VVV publishes an English-language walking tour guide (*A Journey of Discovery Through Maritime Amsterdam*, f2.50) covering much of the historic port area. For details of all the above, *see page 3* **Essential Information.**

Café Zeilvaart
De Ruijterkade 106, C (625 2237). Tram 1, 2, 4, 5, 9, 13, 16, 17, 24, 25. Open *bar* 9am-1am Mon-Thur, Sun; 9am-2am Fri, Sat; *kitchen* noon-10pm daily. No credit cards.

MartInn
De Ruijterkade 7, C (625 6277). Tram 1, 2, 4, 5, 9, 13, 16, 17, 24, 25. Open for groups only noon-2.30pm, 5.30-9.30pm, Mon-Fri. Average f70. Credit MC, V.
Children welcome. Booking preferred.

Canals

Once Amsterdam's commercial arteries, today's canals provide recreation – and a convenient dumping ground for anything from bikes to bodies. *Jon Henley* dredges up the facts.

Amsterdam owes a lot to Henrik Staets, Frans Oetgens, Lucas Sinck and Daniel Stalpaert. In 1607, these four men were commissioned to design the canal network which enabled the city to become a stronger trading force and one of the most attractive capitals in Europe. The plan was to develop the 541 hectares/1,336 acres set aside by the city council for expansion outside the crowded medieval town, then bounded by the Singel and Kloveniersburgwal canals, which dated from around 1426.

The four notables (respectively master carpenter, ex-mayor, surveyor and architect) had three main aims: to provide accommodation for the merchants, craftsmen and refugees then pouring into the town; to reflect the achievements and ambitions of the western world's commercial capital, and – perhaps most importantly – to create the best possible conditions for sea trade to continue to flourish.

Given that the land at their disposal was largely marsh, the plan drawn up by Staets, Oetgens, Sinck and Stalpaert was probably inspired less by any of these grandiose schemes than by sheer necessity: for drainage and transport, canals were both the best and the only solution. Barges, loaded from the ships moored in the harbour and horse- or man-drawn, would be able to travel the full length of the canals, which are some 3m/9ft 10ins deep. Nonetheless, their vision – of a cobweb or a concentric ring of three wide, imposing canals intersected by narrower, radial waterways – has created much of the city centre's intimacy and appeal.

The canals

Work originally began on what was to become **Herengracht** (named in honour of the gentlemen who held the city's purse strings) in 1585. Integrated into the master plan, which was approved in 1609, this was followed by **Keizersgracht** (after Holy Roman Emperor Maximilian I) in 1612 and **Prinsengracht** (commemorating William, Prince of Orange) in 1622. They were dug with picks and shovels by legions of labourers working waist-deep in water, many of them refugees from cities then occupied by the Spanish (*see p53* **War & Reformation**).

(*see p53* **War & Reformation**).

TECHNICAL TRIUMPH

For the time, the canals were an astonishing engineering feat. One particularly impressive aspect was the several dozen locks which could be closed at high tide to prevent floods and opened at low tide to flush the canals clean. Mains sewerage was a couple of hundred years away, and Amsterdam's canals served as the city's waste disposal system. Master carpenter Staets balanced drainage, rain water and the incoming tide so carefully that his lock system was perfectly adequate until 1876, when a dam was built across the harbour mouth in a vain attempt to stop it silting up. Writers of the period describe the consequences graphically: bacteria and algae multiplied so fast that the canal water turned vermilion.

The problem was solved by building sluice-gates into the dam, allowing a tidal flow to flush the city clean once more. But the system was scuppered again by the Afsluitdijk, the huge dike built across the Zuider Zee (turning it into the freshwater IJsselmeer) in 1932. Since then, tidal water has no longer reached the city and the canals have had their water flushed by mechanical means.

The organization responsible for the operation (*see below* **The sluices**) is the **Stadswaterkantoor**, Amsterdam's first water authority which was founded sometime in the seventeenth century. Its staff also keep an eye on the water level in the canals via a panel displaying water height at three spots in the city, as well as wind speed and direction. Should the water level become worryingly high after (not infrequent) periods of heavy rainfall, the pumping station on the artificial island of Zeeburg, to the east of the city, shifts into reverse gear and pumps the excess out into the IJsselmeer.

The sluices

Every night between about 7pm and 8.30pm some 15 sluice gates in the city centre are closed – still mainly by turning a pair of large wooden wheels by hand. Those on the River Amstel by the Koninklijk Theatre Carré (*see p118* **Dance** and *p126* **Theatre**)

There are about 1,280 bridges over Amsterdam's canals. Not surprisingly, most were originally built – of brick – at the same time as the canals in the seventeenth century. Many are lit up between April and November. The best place to view them, and the night-time illuminations, is at the junction of Keizersgracht and Reguliersgracht above: turn full circle and you'll see seven. A few of the old wooden drawbridges remain: the **Magere Brug** *or Skinny Bridge, see page 13* **Sightseeing***, is the most famous example, although the one leading to Prinseneiland is equally attractive. But the most sizeable bridges and expansive views of Amsterdam are on the Amstel: the* **Hogesluis**, **Toronto Brug** *and* **Amstelbrug** *are all more monumental than the canal variety.*

The boat service that combines sightseeing
with fun transportation!

HOP ON THE CANAL BUS!

Use it all day long with a day ticket

Moorings at the main attractions of
Amsterdam.

Canal Bus Nwe Keizersgracht 8 1018 DR Amsterdam tel. 020 - 623.98.86

offer the best city-centre view of the process. Once the sluices are shut, the pumping station swings into action, injecting some 700 million litres/154 million gallons of fresh IJsselmeer water into the canals every day between 10.15pm and 5.30am (till 9.30am on Saturdays and Sundays). Two or four sluices in the west of the city are left open – the choice varies so that every canal can get its turn – and the canal water flows out through these into the river IJ. The process replaces about a third of the water in Amsterdam's canals in a night.

IDLE TIMES

These days, Amsterdam's 160 canals (about 75.5 kilometres/47 miles in all) only have to cope with the sewage from some of the city's couple of thousand houseboats (see page 13 Sightseeing). Several of the canals were filled in – mainly in the nineteenth century – to make way for trams and city traffic: Elandsgracht, Vijzelgracht, Lindengracht and Rozengracht are a few examples. Spirited residents' campaigns saved others from the same fate, including Leidsegracht.

The canals' traditional role as dumping ground is not, alas, fully over. Old bicycles, cars with less than adequate handbrakes, pick-pocketed wallets and handbags, mattresses, empty safes, kitchen sinks, parking meters and, very occasionally, the odd corpse are all fished out by the council's fleet of nine boats: six for fishing out floating refuse, one for dragging out bikes (they haul up 5,000 to 10,000

every year) and three dredgers. Some one hundred million litres (22 million gallons) of sludge and rubbish are removed in a year; each canal is supposed to get a thorough dredging roughly once every ten years.

The canals serve less of a commercial purpose than in the Golden Age, when hardly any part of the city was further than 45 metres/50 yards from a canal bank or quay. The council uses them to transport rubbish in big barges from central dumps to the incinerator, and builders use flatboats to hold their Portakabins when they're working on a canalside building. Otherwise, the canals' main commercial use is in tourism, and one of the best ways to enjoy them is by boat (see page 3 Essential Information).

Apart from this, Amsterdam's canals are sadly idle. There may yet come a time in the not too distant future when the environment-conscious Netherlands will rediscover inner-city waterborne transport as a viable option to endless horn-tooting on the single-lane banks.

WATERSIDE STROLLS

Canalside walks remain one of the greatest pleasures Amsterdam can offer. Each canal has its own distinctive feel, which changes with the

hour of the day and the season. You need time to explore them properly and absorb their moods. But for glimpses, try the intimate, green-shaded calm of the Jordaan's narrow thoroughfares, Bloemgracht and Egelantiersgracht; see page 26 Amsterdam by Area. Compare those with the glaring, neon-lit upper reaches of Oude Zijds Achterburgwal and Voorburgwal, or the stately and relatively daunting middle stretches of Herengracht (known as the Gouden Bocht, or Golden Band).

There are some lesser-known beauties, too: the dark, almost walled-in peace of Rechtboomssloot, the tiny Blauwburgwal and Monet's favourite, Groenburgwal. The leafy, peaceful Brouwersgracht and its converted warehouses (see page 188 Business: picture and caption) is almost every visitor's favourite – though Leidsegracht is the most exclusive address in town.

But if there's one canal that fuses the different moods of all of these, it's Prinsengracht, the most interesting of the major waterways. A walk along it is easily punctuated by frequent stops in some of the city's best cafés, bars and galleries: Torch at No.218, Art & Project at No.758 and Printshop at No.845, see page 111 Galleries. A few diversions into some of the side streets reveal small, independent shops ranging from the trendy to the downright offbeat.

A WALK ALONG PRINSENGRACHT

Of the three canals that make up the grachtengordel (ring of canals), Prinsengracht is in many ways the most interesting: built on a smaller scale and with a more lived-in feel to it than the more grand-iose Keizersgracht and Herengracht, it is an attractive combination of elegance and tattiness. Prinsengracht has no museums or monuments – although many buildings are magnificent – and its only recognized attractions are the Anne Frank House and Westerkerk (see page 13 Sightseeing). But if you want to really capture the mood of the city, a day spent dawdling here is probably one of the best you'll have.

Starting quiet and stately by Brouwersgracht, with elegantly

restored old merchants' houses, converted warehouses and banks lined with houseboats (see page 13 Sightseeing), Prinsengracht becomes progressively more busy from Noordermarkt down to the Anne Frank House. A couple of notable squats (one with the categorical graffitti slogan 'US Out of Everywhere', see page 68 Post-war) mingle with bars, restaurants and dope cafés. Beyond the filled-in Rozengracht, the canal's character changes again as homes give way to offices, the houseboats disappear and the luxurious likes of the Pulitzer Hotel raise their wealthy heads. Between the central library (Prinsengracht 587) and Leidsestraat, Prinsengracht is simply

beautiful: open, tree-lined and calm with, on either side, the homes of some seriously rich people.

A brief stretch of sheer tackiness follows Leidsestraat – a couple of dubious Saturday-night bars and the perennially scruffy Easy Times coffee shop thudding to a hefty bass beat. The honourable exception is De Tap (see page 91 Cafés & Bars). Then Prinsengracht begins to get really grand, seeming to widen out as it passes Spiegelgracht and continuing with offices, hotels, consulates and some very desirable residences, on its way to the Amstel river. A cluster of houseboats at the understated little Amstelveld square are a final reminder of earlier, less moneyed moods.

Amsterdam by Season

Culture and carousing are the trademarks of Amsterdam's festivals. *Abi Daruvalla* takes you through the city's calendar.

Because of its puritan heritage, The Netherlands has few ancient traditions and the Royal Family tends to keep a low profile; your best chance of seeing Queen Beatrix is at the opening of parliament (*see under* **Autumn**) or on Remembrance Day (*listed under* **Spring**). But what Amsterdam lacks in pomp it makes up for with informal and colourful street celebrations such as Koninginnedag (Queen's Day) (*under* **Spring**) and New Year's Eve (*under* **Winter**).

More seasonal events in Amsterdam and the rest of the country are listed in most entertainment chapters, such as **Dance** (*page 118*), **Film** (*page 122*), and **Music** (Classical & Opera *page 130*; Rock, Folk & Jazz *page 135*). The VVV (*see page 3* **Essential Information**) has up-to-date information on all events going on in the city and publishes an events calendar in its *What's On* magazine (f2.50). For a list of public holidays *see page 3* **Essential Information**.

SPRING

The future of one of Amsterdam's best-known traditions, Vlaggetjesdag (Flag Day), is in doubt – owing to a shortage of herrings. The celebration usually marks the start of the new herring season at the end of May, but already it's clear that the 1991 yield (and probably 1992's) won't be anything worth making a song and dance about. Things are better in The Hague, however; the VVV there (*070 35 46 200*) can advise you of the date of its festival. Two of The Netherlands' signature sights, bicycles and windmills, are fêted every spring. On National Windmill Day, the second Saturday in March, about 650 of the country's 950 windmills turn their sails and are open to the public, including Amsterdam's four

working mills (*see page 13* **Sightseeing**). National Cycling Day takes place in May; roads are filled with cyclists following 220 routes worked out for the occasion (details from the ANBW auto club on *070 314 7147*). In March Amsterdam's RAI (*see page 188* **Business**) is the venue for the annual HISWA boat show and the Meervart (*see page 118* **Dance**) hosts a blues festival which is gradually growing in status. In April The Melkweg (*see page 135* **Music: Rock, Folk & Jazz**) hosts GRAP Day, when about 30 of Amsterdam's best local bands stage a day-long bonanza.

Stille Omgang (Silent Procession)

Dates 16/17 March 1991; 21/22 March 1992. **Contact** *Mr M Eisenburg, Grezelschap van die Stille Omgang, Zandvoorteweg 59, 2111 GS, Aerdenhout (023 245415). Phone after 7pm.*
Every year on the Sunday closest to 15 March, local Catholics commemorate the Miracle of Amsterdam with a silent night-time procession through the city. The Miracle took place in 1345; the story goes that a dying man vomited up the bread given in communion as part of the last rites. It was thrown on the fire and was found undamaged among the ashes the following morning. The sick man is said to have subsequently recovered (*see p52* **Early History**). The Procession follows the road that pilgrims have used for centuries, called, for that reason, Heiligeweg – Holy Way.

World Press Photo Exhibition

Nieuwekerk, Dam, C (Nieuwekerk foundation 626 8168). Tram 1, 2, 4, 5, 9, 13, 14, 16, 17, 24, 25. **Dates** 27 April-26 May 1991; 1992 to be decided. **Open** 11am-5pm daily. **Admission** f5; f3.50 students, over-65s. **No credit cards.**
The best of the preceding year's international newspaper and magazine photos go on show at Nieuwekerk from mid April to mid May. Along with the inevitable pictures of horrific news events, the photos also depict feats of individual courage and humorous moments.

Nationaal Museumweekend

Dates 20-21 April 1991; 25-26 April 1992. During National Museum Weekend many state-run museums offer reduced or free admission and mount special exhibitions and activities such as treasure hunts.

Opening hours are often extended, but even so most museums are predictably busy.

Koninginnedag (Queen's Day)

All over Amsterdam. **Date** 30 April 1991, 1992.
This is the party to end all parties. It's a national holiday and the Dutch really go to town, with thousands of people taking to the streets to eat, drink, and be generally very merry. The basic spirit of the festivities is to buy and sell anything and everything – children and grown-ups empty their junk onto home-made stalls outside their homes and in the city centre and indulge in the biggest shopping spree of the year (*see p37* **picture and caption**). Most of the action is in the centre with the result that Leidseplein, Rokin and the Dam get very crowded: claustrophobes should head for the quieter Jordaan instead. There are also all sorts of informal (and often free) performances, from singing to custard pie slinging, throughout the city centre (focal points are Leidseplein, Vondelpark, Spui and the Dam). Somewhat more sophisticated entertainment is provided by many bars, which erect outdoor stages for all sorts of bands from jazz (try along Egelantiersstraat) to pure pop (along Spui) and traditional Dutch folk (in the Jordaan).

Herdenkingsdag & Bevrijdingsdag (Remembrance Day & Liberation Day)

Remembrance Day *National Monument, Dam, C. Tram 1, 2, 4, 5, 9, 13, 14, 16, 17, 24, 25.* **Date** 4 May 1991, 1992.
Liberation Day *Vondelpark, OS. Tram 1, 2, 3, 5, 6, 12. Leidseplein, IS. Tram 1, 2, 5, 6, 7, 10.* **Date** 5 May, 1991, 1992.
On 4 May, those who died during World War II are remembered during a ceremony at the National Monument on the Dam. The service starts at 7.30pm; the Queen lays a wreath at 8pm; there follows a two-minute silence before the Chief of the Armed Forces and other dignitaries lay wreaths. Liberation is celebrated on the following day with various activities throughout the city. Vondelpark and Leidseplein are the best places to be, with music, speeches and information stands organized by political and ideological groups and (another) free market where you can sell all the unwanted things you bought on Queen's Day – if you've got over your hangover.

SUMMER

Outdoor events come out with the sun; ideal for a summer stroll, a book market springs up along the Amstel between 23 June and 8 August. In June there are usually rowing contests in Amsterdamse Bos (*see page 13* **Sightseeing**) and the motor racing season at Zaandvoort (*see page 183* **Sport & Fitness**) gets into full swing. A lesser-known and somewhat more ancient pursuit is ring tilting, whereby traditionally costumed horsemen try to catch rings on their spears. There are ring tilting events in July in Friesland and Zeeland; the best is at Middelburg (*see page 213* **The Provinces: Zeeland**).

Holland Festival

Dates 1-30 June 1991. **Admission** f10-f100.
The country's most prestigious arts festival, the month-long calendar of theatre, music, opera and dance attracts top-calibre performers from around the world. Performances are held at various venues throughout the country although the majority are in Amsterdam and The Hague. A new director has just taken over; he's famed for spectacle and extravagance, so this could be an event to watch. A fringe festival, The Off Holland Festival, runs concurrently. Advance programme information is available from **Holland Festival**, *Kleine Gartmanplantsoen 21, 1017 RP, Amsterdam (627 6566)*. The office is open 9am-6pm Mon-Fri. *See also p126* **Theatre**.

Kunst RAI (RAI Arts Fair)

RAI Congresgebouw, Europaplein, OS (549 1212;). Tram 4, 25/NS railway from Schiphol Airport to RAI Station. **Open** *office and enquiries* 9am-5pm Mon-Fri. **Dates** 29 May-2 June 1991, phone for dates in 1992.
Organized around a different guest country or theme every year, this annual exhibition of contemporary art includes everything from ceramics and jewellery to paintings and sculpture. About a hundred Dutch and international galleries take part. *See also p111* **Galleries**.

Echo Grachtenloop (Canal Run)

Information *Echo Newspaper, Basisweg 30, OW (585 9222).* **Dates** 9 June 1991; phone for exact date in 1992.
Around 5,000 people take part in this 5, 10 and 18 km (3, 6 and 11 mile) run along the city's canals (Prinsengracht and Vijzelgracht) on the second Sunday in June every year. You can register on the spot at the Stadsschouwburg on Leidseplein (*see p126* **Theatre**), where the run starts and finishes. Start times run from 11am. Leidseplein is a good place to watch but gets quite crowded; for a more sedate viewpoint stand on the banks of Prinsengracht.

World Roots Festival

Melkweg, Lijnbaansgracht 234, IW (624 8492). Tram 1, 2, 5, 6, 7, 10. **Dates** June 1991, 1992; phone for exact dates. **Tickets** f10-f20 plus membership. **Membership** f3.50 per month. **No credit cards**.
The Melkweg (*see p135* **Music: Rock, Folk & Jazz**) hosts nine days of music, dance and theatre from Africa and other non-Western countries. There are also workshops in, for example, dance and drumming.

Zomerfestijn (Summer Festival)

Dates July 1991, 1992; phone for exact dates. **Tickets** from first week in July *at the AUB Ticketshop and VVV tourist offices (see p3* **Essential Information**); during the Festival *ticket office/information centre, Grand Café Dulac, Haarlemmerstraat 118, C (627 4394).*
If progressive art appeals to you then Amsterdam's 10-day Summer Festival is not

The whole point of **Koninginnedag** *(Queen's Day, see under* **Spring***) is to buy and sell for fun, and there are plenty of bargains, although sadly the spectre of commercialism is looming and big businesses are muscling in on the act. Another recent development is that people's determination to stake out the best sales spot and the total dedication of the bargain hunters has meant that the whole jamboree is starting increasingly earlier – it's no longer a question of getting up at the crack of dawn but of going out the evening before. Perhaps all the festivity is more than one day can cope with and Queen's Day will expand into a two-day affair.*

to be missed. There is an impressive programme of mime, fringe theatre, dance, art and technology, video and multi-media performances. On the whole, artists shun the traditional venues in favour of strange locations (often open-air) such as disused warehouses, shipyards and waste ground. All the performances have a strong visual character, so language is no problem.

Prinsengracht Classical Concert

Information *Stichting Cristofori, Prinsengracht 579, IS (626 8485/8495).*
Date one evening in last week in Aug.
A stroll along Prinsengracht on this August evening (date not confirmed at time of writing) could hold an unexpected surprise – you could be confronted by musicians playing a classical concert from a boat. It takes place in front of the Pulitzer Hotel (Prinsengracht 315-331), which organizes the event with the piano manufacturers Cristofori. Get there early for a good view. It's free, but liable to be cancelled if it rains. *See also p130* **Music: Classical & Opera**.

Uitmarkt

Museumplein, OS. Tram 2, 3, 5, 12, 16. **Dates** 23-25 Aug 1991; 1992 to be decided.
A wonderful tradition, the Uitmarkt previews The Netherlands' coming cultural season with a huge fair giving information on amateur and professional theatre, opera, dance and music of all sorts. There is also a host of performances to whet your appetite, both on outdoor stages and in the city's various theatres. Everything is free and, not surprisingly, it's very crowded all day and into the evening. *See also p126* **Theatre**.

Dammen Op De Dam

Rabobank, Dam 16, C (626 8731). Tram 1,

2, 4, 9, 13, 14, 16, 17, 24, 25. **Dates** 10 Aug 1991; 8 Aug 1992.
Draughts (checkers) is extremely popular in The Netherlands and the opening of the season is celebrated with an open-air tournament on the Dam. Two concurrent events go on; one is for invited players only, the other allows 20 players to challenge a present or former world champion simultaneously. If you want to take part, pick up an entry form in advance from any branch of Rabobank (*see p188* **Business**).

AUTUMN

The Amsterdam marathon has recently been rescheduled to take place sometime in November in 1991 but might subsequently revert to its May date. It starts and finishes at the Dam. The more sedate sport of show-jumping is staged at the RAI (*see page 188* **Business**) at the end of October. Out of Amsterdam, the 1991 Holland Dance Festival is held in The Hague (6 Sept-1 Oct) and a respected annual antiques and art (nothing modern) fair takes place in Delft (*see page 208* **The Randstad**) in mid October. One of The Netherlands' few state occasions is the opening of parliament, at the beginning of September (3 Sept 1991) in The Hague. The queen drives to the Binnenhof, the parliament building, in a gilded coach, accompanied by soldiers in ceremonial uniform. If you're in The Hague, the best place to go is the Binnenhof; if you're not, you can watch it all on television.

Jordaan Festival

The Jordaan, IW. Tram 13, 14, 17. **Dates** second and third weeks of Sept. **Opening ceremony** in Westerkerk. **Admission** f5. **No credit cards.**

This is the most famous and the most typically Dutch of a series of neighbourhood street festivals held in September. A stage is usually erected for musical entertainment by local performers, including talented (or otherwise) children, and there are various stalls and barbecues. This is your opportunity to see the locals enjoying themselves in traditional style.

Bloemen Corso (Flower Parade)

Route *leaves from Aalsmeer at 9.30am; Olympic Stadium, Stadionplein, OS at 1pm (Tram 16); Overtoom, OS (Tram 1, 6); Leidseplein, IS (Tram 1, 2, 5, 6, 7, 10); Leidsestraat, IS (Tram 1, 2, 5); Spui, C (Tram 1, 2, 5); Spuistraat, C (Tram 1, 2, 5); Dam, C, at 4pm (Tram 1, 2, 4, 9, 13, 14, 16, 17, 24, 25); Rembrandtsplein, IS (Tram 4, 9, 14); Vijzelstraat, IS (Tram 16, 24, 25); Weteringschans, IS (Tram 6, 7, 10).* **Date** 7 Sept 1991, 5 Sept 1992.

For over 40 years a spectacular parade of floats bearing all kinds of flowers (except tulips, which are out of season) has made its way from Aalsmeer (the home of Holland's flower industry – *see p203* **Trips out of Town: Excursions in Holland**) to

Amsterdam on the first Saturday of September. Crowds line the pavements for a glimpse of the beautiful and fragrant displays. At 4pm the parade reaches the Dam, usually packed, where there is a civic reception, after which it sets off back for an illuminated cavalcade through Aalsmeer (9-10pm).

National Monument Day

Monumentenzorg, Keizersgracht 123, IW (626 3947). **Date** 14 Sept 1991, 12 Sept 1992. **Free.**

On the second Saturday in September the National Monument Society arranges for as many as possible of The Netherlands' listed buildings to be open to the public. In Amsterdam, this means you can see inside some of the city's finest canal houses, as well as windmills and pumping stations. Write or phone for details.

WINTER

The advent of winter is signalled by the conversion of Leidseplein into an ice rink, usually in mid October, depending on the weather. For the Dutch, St Nicholas' Day (5 December) is as important as Christmas. In the evening gifts are exchanged (sometimes seasonal sweets; *see page 150* **Special Occasion Food**), accompanied by poems hinting at the nature of the gift and the character of the recipi-

ent. The Dutch festivities are very family oriented and the city closes down early. New Year's Day is also celebrated in a big way, mainly in the streets (*see below*). Lots of tourists come over for it so all reasonably priced hotels are full. There are festive New Year's Day concerts at Nieuwekerk and Westerkerk (*see page 13* **Sightseeing**), usually accompanied by mulled wine. On Sheveningen beach (*see page 208* **The Randstad: The Hague**) there's a New Year's Day dive. On February 25 every year there's a ceremony at the Dokworker statue in Amsterdam to commemorate the protest strike of 1941; *see page 64* **World War II**.

Sinterklaas (St Nicholas' Arrival)

Route *Barbizon Palace Hotel, Prins Hendrikkade, C (Tram 1, 2, 4, 5, 9, 13, 16, 17, 24, 25); Damrak, C (Tram 4, 9, 16, 24, 25); Dam, C (Tram 1, 2, 4, 5, 9, 13, 14, 16, 17, 24, 25); Raadhuisstraat, IW (Tram 13, 14, 17); Rozengracht, IW (Tram 13, 14, 17); Marnixstraat, IW (Tram 7, 10); Leidseplein, IS (Tram 1, 2, 5, 6, 7, 10).* **Date** 16 Nov 1991; 15 Nov 1992.
See **picture and caption.**

Oudejaarsavond (New Year's Eve)

All over Amsterdam. **Date** 31 Dec, 1 Jan.
Along with Koninginnedag (*see above* **Spring**), New Year's Eve is the city's best celebration and, in true Amsterdam style, the excitement comes from being out on the streets – bring your own champagne and be prepared to share it with total strangers. Lots of fireworks are set off (the need for caution is obvious), including strings of firecrackers suspended across the streets. There's revelry throughout the city but the best spots are Nieuwmarkt and the Dam, both of which get seriously crowded. The Dutch celebrate by having a special meal with the family until midnight; many bars don't open until then.

Carnival

Information *Stichting Carnival Mokum (623 2568).* **Route** *Prins Hendrikkade, C (Tram 1, 2, 4, 9, 13, 16, 17, 24, 25); Damrak, C (Tram 4, 9, 16, 24, 25). Dam, C (Tram 1, 2, 4, 5, 9, 13, 14, 16, 17, 24, 25); Rembrandtsplein, IS (Tram 4, 9, 14); Vijzelstraat, IS (Tram 16, 24, 25); Weteringlaan, IS (Tram 6, 7, 10, 16, 24, 25); Stadhouderskade, OS (Tram 6, 7, 10); Leidseplein, IS (Tram 1, 2, 5, 6, 7, 10).* **Date** 9 February 1991; phone for date in 1992.
Carnival was originally a southern tradition celebrating the coming of spring, but not wanting to miss out on an opportunity to party, Amsterdammers have adopted in over the last decade. It must be said, however, that the festivities in the capital are nowhere near as much fun as the three-day jamborees in the provinces of Noord Brabant and Limburg (*see p213* **Trips out of Town: The Provinces**). The main activity is drinking, to the accompaniment of 'oompah-pah' Dutch songs. The event may be cancelled in 1991.

In mid November (see under **Winter**) *St Nicholas, the Dutch equivalent of Santa Claus, steps ashore from a steamboat at Amsterdam's Centraal Station before parading through the city on his traditional white horse while his helpers distribute sweets. He is given the keys to the city by the mayor on the Dam, but it's best to watch the early stages of the procession from Utrechtsestraat and Rembrandtsplein. The actual St Nicholas celebrations are held on the evening of 5 December. St Nicholas has not become as commercialized as Christmas Day yet, but the whole razzamatazz of Christmas (which used to be a very low-key affair in The Netherlands 10 years ago) is catching on, and children now want presents on 5 December and 25 December. Children also expect to be taken to the circus at the Koninklijk Theatre Carré (see page 118 Dance).*

Accommodation

Imagine being in bed with John and Yoko. *Julie Sinclair-Day* **calms your nightmares, rolls you into the Amstel's yacht and settles you in a canal house.**

Still a small city by European standards, Amsterdam has more than its fair share of accommodation problems, and long-term visitors in particular should be prepared for a struggle. As far as hotels go, however, a reasonable room can be found without too much effort so long as reservations are made well in advance, especially for peak periods (Christmas, New Year, and from March to September).

On the whole, Amsterdam's hoteliers are a dedicated bunch, doing their bit for the Dutch reputation for hospitality. This goes some way towards making up for the high **price** of hotel rooms: the cheapest you can expect to find will be about f50 for a single (f70 double), while at the top end of the market charges are around f400 for a single (f500 double). On average, a comfortable, no-frills room will cost about f100 for a single (f150 double). Bargains are hard to find here and basically you get what you pay for. Even dormitory beds cost from f20. The cheaper hotels generally offer clean, small rooms with little furniture other than a bed, and shared washing facilities. At the other extreme, your wish is the staff's command.

Canal houses, some of them of historic interest, generally make for pleasant hotels with typically Dutch atmosphere – few have lifts and their staircases are invariably very steep and narrow. Rooms will also vary in size in these houses. To avoid disappointment, leave little to chance. Obtain a full description of your room from the proprietor before making a reservation. There are no bed and breakfast establishments as such, but many small hotels are family-run and have an intimate atmosphere, and prices often include breakfast.

Amsterdam's growing prominence as a business centre is mirrored by its increasing number of **business hotels**, most of them at the top end of the market. These tend to target their clientele precisely, and seem to place brisk efficiency above convivi-

ality. All provide comprehensive business facilities, including fax, telex, telephones and meeting rooms, at extra cost.

The city's hotels are classified by the Benelux (Belgium, Netherlands, Luxembourg) hoteliers' association, by a **star system** ranging from one to five stars. But the usefulness of this system is debatable because each hotel is graded simply on the facilities it offers and classification does not take into account such factors as location, state of repair, quality of service or food. The listings below aim to give a rounded idea of what to expect from each establishment. Each has been visited by *Time Out* staff and judged according to its overall appeal.

For listings of some more hotels, and university halls of residence, *see page 169* **Gay**, *page 176* **Women** and *page 196* **Students**.

Unless otherwise stated, breakfast is included in the price. A typical **Dutch breakfast** consists of bread, Gouda cheese, a boiled egg, salami, jam, orange juice and tea or coffee. The Dutch generally serve tea without milk – ask if you require it.

RESERVATIONS

Advance bookings need to be made early as demand is generally high, and most hotels will require a deposit; if the establishment does not accept credit cards, this will have to be sent by post. Alternatively you can make use of the free Dutch hoteliers' reservation service (*see below*), which handles bookings for the whole of The Netherlands. For those already in the country, the VVV (*see page 3* **Essential Information**) also offers a national hotel booking service. In Amsterdam, this service costs f3.50 plus f4 room deposit; the deposit is later deducted from your hotel bill. Enquiries or instructions are not taken over the phone or by post. For those wanting to make their own reservations, the VVV produces a comprehensive guide to hotels in the city, available from their offices and costing f1.50.

National Reserverings Centrum

PO Box 404, 2260AK, Leidschendam (070 320 2500/fax 070 320 2611/telex 33755). **Open** 8am-8pm Mon-Fri; 8am-2pm Sat. Many of the hotels recommended by the VVV can be booked through this bureau. The booking service is free and the hotel bill is paid as normal. The VVV staff can provide a brochure of the hotels the centre deals with and, if you decide to book through them, they will send confirmation of your reservation by post.

DE LUXE

American Hotel

Leidsekade 97, 1017 PN; IS (624 5322/fax 625 3236/telex 12545 CBO NL). Tram 1, 2, 5, 6, 7, 10. **Rates** *single f295-f340; double f365-f410; extra bed f75.* **Credit** AmEx, CB, DC, JCB, MC, TC, V.

A listed building just off the Leidseplein and overlooking the Singel, the American Hotel is an impressive, multi-turreted structure dating from the early twentieth century. The stunning ground-floor art deco café is the hotel's centre-piece and is busy throughout the year, attracting a mainly young and arty crowd. The rest of the building has been renovated in a more modern style with constant echoes of art deco in colour, lighting, textile patterns and furniture design. The rooms are large, airy and luxuriously appointed, some with a picturesque canal view, others overlooking the bustle of Leidseplein. Extensive double glazing means all the rooms are quiet. The illuminated, red 'American Hotel' sign on the roof offers a good night-time landmark for the newly-arrived – and easily lost – visitor. If you can afford to stay here you probably won't mind breakfast costing an extra f27.

Hotel services *Café. Conference rooms. Dry cleaning. Fitness centre. Gift shop. Lifts. Limited parking. Room service (24-hour). Valet.* **Room services** *Clock radio. Double glazing. Hairdryer. Minibar. Telephone. TV and free in-house movies.*

Amstel Hotel Inter Continental

Professor Tulpplein 1, 1018 GX; IE (622 6060/fax 622 5808/telex 11004). Tram 6, 7, 10. **Rates** *single f415; double f525.* **Credit** AmEx, DC, JCB, MC, TC, V.

The five-star Amstel is perhaps the most luxurious – and expensive – hotel in Amsterdam. It's due to close between November 1990 and spring 1992 for renovation, after which it will be even more luxurious. How many other hotels offer Rolls Royces and a motor yacht for guests' use? The Amstel has been running since 1867 and part of its lasting appeal is the beautiful and quiet location on the River Amstel. The service is calm and discreet, ideal for those looking for star treatment – celebrity spotters take note. The communal areas are furnished in an exceptionally luxurious style.

Hotel services *Bar. Brasserie. Business centre. Conference rooms. Health centre. Library. Lifts. Motor yacht. Parking. Restaurant. Rolls Royce cars. Room service. Secretarial services. Shops. Swimming pool. Wheelchair access with assistance.* **Room services** *Minibar. Telephone. TV.*

Hotel Hegra

Hotel Hegra is situated on one of the most beautiful canals of Amsterdam, the Herengracht.

Herengracht 269, 1016 BJ Amsterdam
Holland
Telefoon 020-623 78 77 - 623 53 48

"King" HOTEL

Canal House Budget Hotel. Centrally located next to Leidseplein and museums. Rooms from f 50 to f 95.

Leidsekade 85 - 86
1017 PN
Amsterdam

Phone:
020 - 624 96 03
020 - 627 61 01

W HOTEL WILHELMINA

Superior Tourist Hotel. Centrally located near museums, RAI and WTC. Rooms with shower, wc and tv. Rates from f|80 to f 150.

Koninginneweg
167 - 169
1075 CN
Amsterdam

Phone:
020 - 662 54 67

FAX 020 - 620 72 77   TELEX 10873

TWENTY FOUR CANALHOUSES...

The location of the Hotel Pulitzer could hardly be more charming or convenient.

Its situation in the historic heart of Amsterdam means that attractions like the Royal Palace, the main shopping districts and museums, are just a pleasant stroll away...

HOTEL PULITZER
Amsterdam

Prinsengracht 315-331,
1016 GZ Amsterdam, Holland.
Phone 020 - 523 523 5, fax 020 - 276 753
Telex 16508.

Amsterdam Hilton

Apollolaan 138-140, 1077 BG; OS (678 0780/fax 662 6688/telex 11025). Tram 5, 24. **Rates** *single f360-f440; double f430-f510; no charge for children sleeping in same room as parents.* **Credit** AmEx, DC, MC, TC, V.

This enormous, rather anonymous building houses 263 rooms which overlook either the Amstel Kanaal or the Apollolaan. The décor throughout is muted and fairly unexciting, but the comprehensive hotel facilities and services give few other causes for complaint. Beatlemaniacs can book the room where John Lennon and Yoko Ono staged their 'Bed-In' – *see* **picture and caption**.

Hotel services *Banquet facilities for up to 600. Bar. Business facilities. Conference rooms. Dry cleaning. Hairdresser. KLM bus service. Laundry. Lifts. Parking. Restaurants. Shops. Water taxi service. Wheelchair access with help.* **Room services** *Double glazing. Hairdryer. Minibar. Telephone. TV.*

Holiday Inn Amsterdam

De Boelelaan 2, 1083 HJ; OS (646 2300/fax 646 4790/telex 13647). Tram 4. **Rates** *single f315-f330; double f375-f405.* **Credit** AmEx, DC, MC, TC, V.

An ideally placed business hotel, close to the Rai Congresgebouw and World Trade Centre. It's just ten minutes by car to the airport and the same by train for a night out in the city. Luxurious rooms and service as efficient as you'd expect for the price.

Hotel services *Bars. Business facilities. Conference rooms. Lifts. Parking. Restaurant. Room service (24-hour). Wheelchair access with help.* **Room services** *Coffee and tea making facilities. In-house video. Minibar. Telephone. Trouser press. TV.*

Grand Hotel Krasnapolsky

Dam 9, 1012 JS; C (554 9111/fax 622 8607/telex 12262 KRAS NL). Tram 1, 2, 5, 13, 14, 16, 17, 24, 25, 49. **Rates** *single f280-f335; double f340-f410; extra bed f75; under-12s in parents' room at half price, under-2s free.* **Credit** AmEx, DC, MC, TC, V.

An enormous building on Dam Square, facing the Royal Palace, this externally impressive four-star hotel has over 300 rooms of differing sizes. Inside, the impression is functional rather than grand. Some of the larger suites have particular themes to their décor, including a number decorated with typical Japanese restraint, and even the smaller rooms are designed with soothing colour schemes. With an eye to the nature of its clientele, the hotel offers particularly good business facilities, including a convention centre for up to 2,000 people.

Hotel services *Bar. Coffee shop. Convention centre for up to 2,000 people. KLM bus service. Shopping arcade. Restaurants. Wheelchair access.* **Room services** *Air conditioning. Coffee and tea making facilities. Minibar. Radio. Telephone. TV showing in-house movies.*

Hilton International Schiphol

Herbergierstraat, 1118 ZK; OSW (603 4567/fax 648 0917/telex 15186). Shuttle bus from Schiphol airport. **Rates** *single f350-f395; double f410-f455.* **Credit** AmEx, DC, JCB, MC, TC, V.

A luxury business hotel in the heart of the Schiphol complex. Should you hanker for a

little nightlife, Amsterdam is just 20 minutes away by train.

Hotel services *Bar. Business facilities. Conference rooms. Gift shop. Laundry. Lifts. Parking. Restaurant. Room service. Sauna. Swimming pool. Wheelchair access with help.* **Room services** *Minibar. Telephone. TV.*

Holiday Inn Crowne Plaza

Nieuwezijds Voorburgwal 5, PO Box 2216, 1000 CE; C (620 0500/fax 620 1173/telex 15183 HICPA NL). Tram 1, 2, 5, 13, 17. **Rates** *single f325-f350; double f450-f470.* **Credit** AmEx, DC, JCB, MC, TC, V.

Nothing to complain about here. This overtly luxurious five-star hotel is in a premium site within a stone's throw of the Dam, and its rooms are spacious, quiet and decorated in unobtrusive good taste. That said, once inside you could be in any Holiday Inn across the world. Breakfast will cost you an extra f25.

Hotel services *Bar. Business facilities. Coffee shop. Fitness centre. KLM bus service. Parking. Photo developing service. Restaurant. Room service. Sauna. Solarium. Swimming pool. Wheelchair access (limited).* **Room services** *Air-conditioning. Double glazing. Hairdryer. Minibar. Telephone. Trouser press.*

As a crass attempt to cash in on heavily-moneyed fans of the late Beatle, the **Hilton** (see under **De Luxe**) has made this luxurious suite – the very room where John and Yoko staged their 'Bed-In' in 1969 – available for a cool f1,500 a night. At a cost of around f100,000 the room has been renovated and done up with Beatle-related décor: white curtains and carpets, J & Y etchings and works of art, a painting on the ceiling depicting bars from All You Need Is Love and The Ballad of John and Yoko, some original lyrics from Imagine... get the idea? Bagism breaks new ground here – the suite's minibar is draped in a rough cotton bag, the TV, video and CD player are wrapped in another. It would be funny if it weren't so sad, but one suspects it will be a big hit.

Hotel de L'Europe

Nieuwe Doelenstraat 2-8, 1012 CP; C (623 4836/fax 624 2962/telex 12081). Tram 4, 9, 14, 16, 24, 25. **Rates** *single f330-f430; double f450-f550.* **Credit** AmEx, DC, MC, TC, V.

Built in 1895, this centrally located five-star hotel retains a period charm and elegance. The rooms are large and tastefully furnished and there's an attractive ground-floor terrace overlooking the River Amstel. The pick of the rooms are those with balconies overlooking the river.

Hotel services *Bar. Business facilities. Coffee shop. Fitness centre. Lifts. Limousine service. Restaurant. Sauna. Swimming pool.* **Room services** *Hairdryer. Minibar. Telephone. TV.*

Hotel Pulitzer

Prinsengracht 315-331, 1016 GZ; IW (523 5235/fax 627 6753/telex 16508). Tram 13, 14, 17. **Rates** *single f305; double f355; suite f810.* **Credit** Airplus, AmEx, Bank Americard, DC, JCB, MC, TC, V.

Arguably the best of Amsterdam's five-star hotels, the Pulitzer comprises 24 seventeenth-century canal houses between Prinsengracht – the hotel's entrance – and Keizersgracht. The architecture may be charming but it does mean that there's a labyrinth of angular corridors and steep

stairs. It's ideal, however, if you're seeking a characterful and intimate atmosphere. All the rooms are different; the most pleasant overlook the hotel gardens, where classical concerts have traditionally been held in the summer (a recent change in management may mean these no longer take place). Breakfast here costs an extra f27.50.
Hotel services *Airline reservations. Art gallery. Bar. Coffee shop. Conference rooms. Currency exchange. Dry cleaning. Gift shop. KLM bus service. Laundry. Lifts. Photo developing service. Restaurant. Room service (24-hour). Valet parking (f22.50).* **Room services** *Hairdryer. Minibar. Safe. Telephone. TV.*

Hotel Victoria
Damrak 1-6, 1012 LG; C (623 4255/fax 625 2997/telex 16625 VIC NL). Tram 4, 9, 14, 16, 24, 25. **Rates** *single* from f300; *double* from f375. **Credit** AmEx, DC, MC, TC, V.
The four-star Victoria has recently been refurbished in a conventional yet tasteful style and proves popular as an elegant business hotel close to Centraal Station. Its publicity boasts of its Victoria Gallery, which turns out to be little more than a glorified walkway. Nevertheless, the gallery is light, airy and has plants galore, characteristics common to all the communal areas.
Hotel services *Bar. Business facilities. Fitness centre. Parking. Residential apartments. Restaurant.* **Room services** *Hairdryer. Minibar. Telephone. TV.*

Marriott Hotel
Stadhouderskade 21, 1054 ES; OS (683 5151/fax 607 5555/telex 15087). Tram 1, 2, 5, 6, 7, 10. **Rates** *single* f425; *double* f500; discounts at weekends, under-18s free in parents' room.* **Credit** AmEx, DC, MC, TC, V.
A modern, large and efficient five-star hotel within easy access of Leidseplein and the museums, providing all you would expect for the price except breakfast, which costs between f23 and f28. There is a bright and pleasant café area overlooking the busy Stadhouderskade. One piece of advice – beware the ghastly piped music in the lobby.
Hotel services *Bar. Coffee shop. Dry cleaning. Laundry. Lifts. Parking. Restaurant. Room service (24-hour). Secretarial services. Shop. Valet. Wheelchair access.* **Room services** *Air-conditioning. Minibar. Telephone. TV.*

MODERATE

Agora
Singel 462, 1017 AW; C (627 2200/fax 627 2202/telex 12657). Tram 1, 2, 5. **Rates** *single* f132-f142; *twin/double* f158-f185. **No credit cards.**
See p43 picture and caption.
Room services *Telephone. TV.*

Ambassade Hotel
Herengracht 335-353, 1016 AZ; IS (626 2333/fax 624 5321/telex 10158). Tram 1, 2, 5. **Rates** *single* f170-f180; *double* f195-f210. **Credit** AmEx, DC, MC, V.
A good value three-star hotel on the Herengracht, home of embassies and consulates, comprising seventeenth- and eighteenth-century merchant houses. All the rooms are individually furnished in a variety of refined styles but, as is typical in

canal houses, the stairs are narrow and steep, and not all houses are connected. The ground-floor lounge and breakfast rooms have huge ceiling-to-floor windows, affording a fine canal view. Elsewhere in the building however, as in all canal houses, the light tends to vary. Antique furnishings help the building to retain much of its former graciousness. The location is central yet quiet.
Hotel services *Bar. Lifts. Room service.* **Room services** *Telephone. TV.*

Het Canal House
Keizersgracht 148, 1015 CX; IW (622 5182/fax 624 1317/telex 10412). Tram 13, 14, 17. **Rates** *single* f150-f165; *double* f165-f200. **Credit** AmEx, DC, MC, TC, V.
See p45 picture and caption.
Hotel services *Bar. Lift.* **Room services** *Bath or shower. Telephone.*

Cok First Class Hotel
Koninginneweg 34-36, 1075 CZ; OS (664 6111/fax 664 5304/telex 11679 COKNL). Tram 2. **Rates** *single* f220; *double* f250-f300; *junior suite* f450; *senior suite* f550; *extra bed* f50.* **Credit** AmEx, DC, MC, TC, V.
Of the three hotels in the Cok complex (*see below*), close to the Vondelpark and museums, this has the most character. Rooms are spacious and modern, decorated with bright paintings and lush plants. Apartments, suites and a number of rooms with kitchenettes are available.
Hotel services *Bar. Conference rooms. Dry-cleaning. Gift shop. Laundry. Lift. Parking. Restaurants. Room service. Secretarial service.* **Room services** *Coffee and tea making facilities. Hairdryer. Minibar. Safe. Telephone. TV. Trouser-press.*

Cok Superior Tourist Class
Koninginneweg 34-36, 1075 CZ; OS (664 6111/fax 664 5304/telex 11679 COKNL). Tram 2. **Rates** *single* f170-f190; *double* f210-f240; *extra bed* f50. **Credit** AmEx, DC, MC, TC, V.
The student-class Cok was closed in 1989 and renovated to reopen in March 1990 as this new-look building. Rooms are slightly less spacious than in the First Class above, but all are tastefully furnished in a modern style.
Hotel services *Bar. Conference rooms. Gift shop. Ironing facilities. Kitchen facilities. Lift. Parking. Restaurants.* **Room services** *Coffee and tea making facilities. Minibar. Safe. Telephone. TV. Trouser-press.*

Cok Tourist Class
Koninginneweg 34-36, 1075 CZ; OS (664 6111/fax 664 5304/telex 11679 COKNL). Tram 2. **Rates** *single* f130; *double* f175; *triple* f195; *quad* f220. **Credit** AmEx, DC, MC, TC, V.
The rooms have rather institutional furnishings and décor but this is more than compensated for by access to the excellent amenities in the other Coks (*see above*).
Hotel services *Bar-restaurant. Conference rooms. Gift shop. Ironing facilities. Kitchen facilities. Lifts. Parking.* **Room services** *Safe. Telephone. TV.*

Dikker & Thijs
Prinsengracht 444, 1017 KE; IW (626 7721/fax 625 8986/telex 13161). Tram 1, 2, 5. **Rates** *single* f225-245; *double* f285-

f320; *extra bed* f70. **Credit** AmEx, DC, MC, TC, V.
A small building, conveniently located near Leidseplein, furnished throughout in tasteful art deco style with grey, pink and black predominating. The English-speaking staff are helpful and pleasant. This four-star hotel has a first-class restaurant (*see p79* **Restaurants**), linked to a popular delicatessen, where you can get breakfast for an extra f20. A wise choice for visitors who seek luxury in intimate surroundings and enjoy their food.
Hotel services *Bar. Brasserie. Conference room. Lifts. Limited parking. Restaurant. Room service (7am-midnight).* **Room services** *Bath. Double glazing. Minibar. Radio. Shower. TV.*

Estherea
Singel 303-309, 1012 WJ; C (624 5146/fax 623 9001/telex 14019). Tram 1, 2, 5. **Rates** *single* f125-f170; *twin or double* f155-f200. **Credit** AmEx, DC, JCB, MC, TC, V.
See p47 picture and caption.
Hotel services *Bar. Lift. Lounge. Wheelchair access with assistance.* **Room services** *Double glazing. Hairdryer. Safe. Telephone. TV.*

Ibis Amsterdam Airport
Schipholweg 181, 1171 PK, Badhoevedorp (02968 91234/fax 02968 92367/telex 16491). NS train Schiphol station, then taxi or bus. **Rates** *single* f155; *double* f200. **Credit** AmEx, DC, MC, V.
A large and comfortable hotel with reasonable business facilities. The 68 bus will take you the short distance to the airport.
Hotel services *Bar. Conference rooms. Laundry. Restaurant. Secretarial services. Shops.* **Room services** *Telephone. TV.*

Jan Luyken Hotel
Jan Luykenstraat 58, 1071 CS; OS (676 4111/fax 676 3841/telex 16254). Tram 2, 3, 5, 12. **Rates** *single* f230; *twin* f250-f280; *triple* f345. **Credit** AmEx, DC, MC, V.
Close to the Concertgebouw, in a peaceful location. At time of writing, the hotel was undergoing refurbishment, although it hardly seemed to need it. It appears the management is striving for the crisp, efficient décor found across the road at the Jan Luijken building, which houses extensive business facilities. Hotel staff have a professional approach.
Hotel services *Exchange facilities. Lifts. Lounge. Wheelchair access.* **Room services** *Hairdryer. Minibar. Radio. Telephone. TV.*

Novotel Amsterdam
Europaboulevard 10, 1083 AD; OS (541 1123/fax 646 2823/telex 13375). Tram 4. **Rates** *single* f235; *double* f285. **Credit** AmEx, DC, MC, TC, V.
Another hotel within a stone's throw of the Rai Congresgebouw. This one has large, comfortable rooms and offers comprehensive business facilities.
Hotel services *Bar. Conference rooms. Gift shop. Laundry. Lifts. Restaurant. Wheelchair access with help.* **Room services** *Minibar. Telephone. TV.*

Park Hotel
Stadhouderskade 25, 1071 ZD; OS/PO Box 50600, 1007 DC (671 7474/fax 664 9455/telex 11412). Tram 1, 2, 5, 6. **Rates**

single f210; twin f270; extra bed f60. **Credit** AmEx, DC, MC, TC, V.

Recently taken over by the Principal hotel group, the enormous Park has been extensively refurbished in bland, business-like tones. Rooms at the top of the building have spectacular views across Amsterdam. The hotel is on a busy road near Leidseplein, but double glazing makes for relative quiet in all front-facing rooms. Staff are well-trained and multi-lingual. Breakfast (f20) is not included in the price.

Hotel services *Bar. Business facilities. Conference room. Hairdresser. KLM bus service. Parking. Restaurant. Secretarial services. Tax-free shopping.* **Room services** *Hairdryer. In-house video. Telephone. Trouser press. TV.*

Schiller Karena

Rembrandtsplein 26-36, 1017 CV; C (623 1660)/fax 624 0098/telex 14058). Tram 4, 9, 14. **Rates** *single* f190-f245; *double* f245-f335. **Credit** AmEx, DC, MC, V.

Recently refurbished, the building housing this four-star hotel dates from the late nineteenth century, when the painter Schiller turned his brush to architecture and designed it. To commemorate its creator, the hotel features his paintings throughout, and these give the building a personality rare to a chain hotel. There are attractive stained-glass sunlights, oak beams and panels in the restaurant. It's part of the Crest chain, and as you would expect, there are good business facilities and service is effi-

cient. The hotel is located in one of the main night-life areas.

Hotel services *Business facilities. Café. Lifts. Restaurant. Room service.* **Room services** *Hairdryer. Telephone. Trouser press. TV.*

BUDGET

Abina

Amsterdamseweg 193, 1182 GW, Amstelveen (641 2261). Bus 173. **Rates** *single* f60; *double* f90. **Credit** AmEx, DC, MC, TC, V.

These cheap rooms next to the Amsterdamse Bos (Amsterdam's main wooded area, on the southern outskirts of the city) have no facilities, but they are clean and comfortable. The bus journey to Centraal Station takes about 30 minutes.

Hotel services *Bar. Restaurant.*

Adam and Eva

Sarphatistraat 105, 1018 GA; IE (624 6206). Tram 6, 7, 10/Metro Weesperplein. **Rates** f18.50 per person; *sheets* f6. **No credit cards.**

A sensible option for those on a tight budget seeking no-frills accommodation. There are 90 beds in mixed and single-sex dorms accommodating between six and 20 each; there is no night-time curfew. The bar is open every day from 4pm to 2am. It's a ten-minute walk from Rembrandtsplein.

Hotel services *Bar-restaurant. Garden. TV room.*

De Admiraal

Herengracht 563, 1017 CD; OS (626 2150). Tram 4. **Rates** *single* f65-f115; *double* f85-f165. **Credit** MC.

De Admiraal is a friendly and homely hotel close to the Rembrandtsplein. Room number 6 has four beds and a stunning view of the Reguliersgracht and Herengracht. The hearty Dutch breakfasts are not to be missed.

Room services *Safe.*

Amsterdam Wiechmann

Prinsengracht 328-330, 1016 HX; IS (622 5410). Tram 1, 2, 5. **Rates** *single* f75-f135; *double* f150-f175. **No credit cards.**

The friendly hoteliers take great pains to ensure their establishment is scrupulously clean and comfortably furnished. Pleasantly situated and with a canal view, the hotel is close to Leidseplein. At time of writing, the breakfast room and lounge were undergoing complete refurbishment.

Hotel services *Lift. Lounge.* **Room services** *Double glazing. Telephone. TV.*

Bob's Youth Hostel

NZ Voorburgwal 92, 1012 SG; C (623 0063). Tram 1, 2, 5, 13, 17. **Rates** *dormitories for 4-18 people* f19. **No credit cards.**

Big (160 beds), brash and commercial, the hostel's low prices and central location means it is extremely popular with international back-packers all through the year. Those with a preference for quiet may not enjoy the noise and surrounding decadence. Most dorms are mixed, but there are four women-only dorms sleeping four to 16. The bar (snacks available) is open from 8am to 3am daily. There's a 3am curfew, and breakfast and sheets are included in the price.

Hotel services *Bar. Lockers. Showers in all rooms.*

Concert Inn

De Lairessestraat 11, 1071 NR; OS (675 0051). Tram 16. **Rates** *single* f105-f150; *double* f135-f175. **Credit** AmEx, DC, MC, V.

The rooms vary in size and though some are a little cramped for the price, all are spotlessly clean, have private bathrooms and are plainly furnished. There is a pleasant breakfast room with garden. The hotelier is friendly and welcoming.

Hotel services *Lift. Wheelchair access with assistance.* **Room services** *Telephone. TV.*

De Gouden Kettingh

Keizersgracht 268, 1016 EV; IW (624 8287). Tram 13, 14, 17. **Rates** *single* f110; *double* f150; *luxury* f180. **Credit** AmEx, DC, MC, V.

Inevitably, the best rooms are those with a view of Keizersgracht, at the front of the hotel. But all are decorated in shades of brown and cream, basically equipped and far more spacious than many found in canal houses. One of three luxury rooms is on the ground floor, and the hoteliers like to reserve this for people who have difficulty climbing more than a few steps.

Hotel services *Bar.* **Room services** *Alarm clock radio.*

Hans Brinker Budget

Kerkstraat 136-138, 1017 GR; IS (622 0687/fax 622 0687/telex 12127). Tram 1, 2, 5, 16, 24, 25. **Rates** *single* f54-f71; *double* f95-f119; *dormitory* from f27. **Credit** AmEx, DC, MC, V.

Built in 1735 and renovated in 1989 to create a modern, comfortable and clean environment, the **Agora** *(see under* **Moderate***) is situated on the Singel, close to the centre of the city. There are masses of plants in the pretty communal areas, and a large family room at the top of the house has angled ceilings and exposed beams. The staff are friendly and the hotelier is happy to give advice on eating out and excursions. All rooms have telephone and television.*

There's something special about

"De Stadhouder" Restaurant

at one of
Amsterdam's best loved hotels.

A friendly welcome from staff
who know and care about food and wine.
An international menu
carefully selected to cater for all palates.

Just ring **20 717474**
(from 1.3.1991 Tel: 20 6717474)
for a reservation and experience something special,
at one of Amsterdam's most central hotels, with it's
own private underground parking.

Ask for details
of our outstanding
conference and
business facilities

Parkhotel

A M S T E R D A M

Stadhouderskade 25, 1071 ZD Amsterdam, Netherlands.

✱✱✱HOTEL TERMINUS

**A stylish hotel in the heart of exciting Amsterdam.
5 minutes walk from the Central Station, with a train link to
Schiphol Airport. 100 metres from the main shopping area.**

* 75 rooms with bath-shower-wc-tel
* rooms with colour tv
* spacious apartments
* à la carte restaurant
* group restaurant
* intimate bar
* prices from NLG 115,- for a single room

* pleasant lounge with colour tv
* 24-hour service for drinks and snacks
* safety deposit facilities
* lift
* souvenir corner
* telex + fax facilities

**BEURSSTRAAT 11-19, 1012 JT AMSTERDAM
TEL: 020-62205 35.**

A very popular and lively hotel, awash with international backpackers in high season. Facilities are basic but the building is well-maintained and clean. Its location is a definite bonus, being just a short distance from the Leidseplein nightlife.
Hotel services *Café. Lifts. Wheelchair access with help.*

De Harmonie
Prinsengracht 816, 1017 JL; IS (625 0174). Tram 4. **Rates** *single* f60; *double* f90; *triple* f125; *quad* f150. **No credit cards.**
Nicely situated, close to the Rembrandtsplein and River Amstel. The hotel is not as pretty as its near neighbour the Prinsenhof (*see below*), but good value nevertheless. Rooms are small and none have any facilities.

Hotel de Filosoof
Anna van den Vondelstraat 6, 1054 GZ, OW (683 3013). Tram 1, 6. **Rates** *single* f65-f95; *double* f85-f140. **Credit** AmEx, V.
This small hotel is something of a centre of philosophy (*see p165* **Services**); even the décor has a philosophical theme, with each room in the style of a well-known thinker. The Plato room, for example, is decorated in black and white, with paintings mounted on trompe l'œil pedestals. You don't have to be a philosophy enthusiast to stay here, but it helps.
Bar.

Hotel Kabul
Warmoesstraat 38-42, 1012 JE; C (623 7158/telex 15443). Tram 4, 9, 16, 24, 25. **Rates** *ten-bed dormitory* f20; *six-bed dormitory* f23; *four-bed dormitory* f27.50; *double* f65-f85; *triple* f100. **No credit cards.**
Within easy walking distance of Centraal Station and on the edge of the red light district. Rooms and dormitories are basic and rather cramped; all have lockers and sheets are included in the price. The bar regularly plays host to live music through to the early hours.
Hotel services *Bar. Hotel open 24 hours. Lockers. Restaurant.*

Hotel Mikado
Amstel 107-111, 1018 EM; IE (623 7068/fax 623 7068). Tram 9, 14. **Rates** *single and double* **no credit cards.**
Situated on the Amstel, the quiet Mikado has spacious rooms furnished with deep armchairs and sofas – perfect for sinking into after a hard day's sightseeing. Amenities include an Italian restaurant and a sauna in the neighbouring buildings.
Hotel services *Bar.* **Room services** *Telephone.*

Hotel Prinsenhof
Prinsengracht 810, 1017 JL; IS (623 1772/627 6567). Tram 4. **Rates** *single* f60; *double* f88-f135; *twin* f93-f145; *triple* f140-f165; *quad* f185. **No credit cards.**
The Prinsenhof is simply and tastefully decorated throughout. Five of the ten rooms have private bathrooms. A charming, friendly and reasonably priced hotel, close to the River Amstel.
Room services *Clock radio. Telephone.*

Hotel Terdam
Tesselschadestraat 23, 1054 ET; OS (612 6876/fax 683 8313/telex 14275). Tram 1, 2,

The American owner of the **Canal House** *(see under* **Moderate***), a series of beautiful seventeenth-century canal houses close to the Jordaan, has restored it with exceptional good taste. Antiques adorn every nook and cranny, and features include exposed beams, patchwork quilts, a floodlit garden and a breakfast room with piano and crystal chandelier. Rooms do not have television, but that will give you more of a chance to enjoy the view of the garden from the back rooms and that of the canal from the front rooms. The hotel's appeal is reflected in a long waiting list; bookings should be made well in advance.*

3, 5, 6, 12. **Rates** *single* f110; *double* f152; *extra bed* f39. **Credit** AmEx, DC, MC, TC, V.
Very popular with package tour operators, this hotel is situated in a pretty and quiet street close to Leidseplein. The restaurant area, where a buffet breakfast is served, has a pleasant garden outlook. Communal areas are decorated in a low-budget, geometric style. Reception staff are well-informed and helpful.
Hotel services *Bar. Exchange facilities. Restaurant. Room service.* **Room services** *Telephone. TV.*

Hotel Verdi
Wanningstraat 9, 1071 LA; OS (671 1941). Tram 2, 3, 5, 12. **Rates** *single* f65-f95; *double* f85-f135. **Credit** AmEx.
See p49 **picture and caption.**
Hotel services *Telephone in reception. TV lounge.*

Parkzicht
Roemer Visscherstraat 33, 1054 EW; OS (618 1954/0897). Tram 1, 2, 3, 5, 6, 12. **Rates** *single* f55-f85; *double* f120-f140. **Credit** MC, V.
A simple, quiet hotel, close to the museums. Most of the rooms have *en suite* shower and toilet. The chunky wooden furniture is a little worn, but this and the dark wooden panelling make for an authentic Dutch feel. No lift or wheelchair access.

Room services *Telephone. TV in most rooms.*

PC Hooft
PC Hooftstraat 63, 1071 BN; OS (662 7107). Tram 3, 12. **Rates** *single* f60; *double* f85-f95. **Credit** V.
A small one-star hotel with 16 rooms, the PC Hooft is very basic but clean and cheerful. It's located close to the museums on a busy road which is home to some of Amsterdam's most elegant shops. Vondelpark is a short walk away.
Hotel services *Coffee shop.*

Seven Bridges
Reguliersgracht 31, 1017 LK; IS (623 1329). Tram 4. **Rates** *single* f60-f100; *double* f90-f130. **No credit cards.**
A lovely, cheap hotel. The 11 rooms are tastefully and simply furnished. As there is no dining area breakfast is served in the room.
Room services *TV.*

Sleep-In Mauritskade
's Gravesandestraat 51, 1092 AA; OE (694 7444). Tram 6, 10/Metro Weesperplein. **Open** *Easter-1 July* weekends only; *2 July-1 Sept* daily. **Closed** Sept-Easter. **Rates** f12.50 per person; *sheets* f3. **No credit cards.**
Situated close to the Oosterpark, three stops

Hotel Agora
* *

In the centre of Amsterdam near to the flower market.

Singel 462
1017 AW
Amsterdam
Phone
(0)20-627 22 00
Fax (0)20-627 22 02

HOTEL PETERS

**

Near to the Concert Hall, Van Gogh Museum and Rijksmuseum

Nic. Maesstraat 72
1071 RC Amsterdam
Phone (0)20 - 673 34 54

Hotel Belga **

Near to Dam Square, the centre of Amsterdam

Hartenstraat 8
1016 CB Amsterdam
Phone (0)20 - 624 90 80

Fax (for both hotels) (0)20 - 623 68 62

Grand Hotel Krasnapolsky (since 1866), Dam 9, 1012 JS Amsterdam, Telephone 020-5549111, Telex 12262, Telefax 020-228607. 330 Rooms and suites, 5 restaurants. World-famous Wintergarden. 14 Function rooms. Meeting and convention facilities for groups of up to 2000 persons.

When Amsterdam is your destination, you really should stay at the spot where the city originated.

GRAND —— HOTEL
KRASNAPOLSKY
A M S T E R D A M

THE CENTRE OF THE CENTRE IN AMSTERDAM

on the metro from Centraal Station. The mixed and single-sex dormitories are vast, accommodating up to 90 people. The hostel is closed between noon and 4pm each day for cleaning, but there is no night-time curfew, and the bar is open from 4pm to 2am during the summer. There's a luggage room but no individual lockers, and breakfast costs from f1.50 extra.
Hotel services *Bar. Garden. Lift.*

Slotania
Slotermeerlaan 133, 1063 JN; OW (613 4568/fax 613 4565/telex 17050). Tram 13. **Rates** *single* f70-f135. **Credit** AmEx, DC, MC, V.
A comfortable hotel in a western suburb, close to the Sloterpark with its lakes and recreational facilities. Handy for those interested in car travel outside Amsterdam. Although there are no hotel parking facilities there's plenty of space in the thoughtfully meterless street. The tram journey to Centraal Station takes 20 minutes.
Hotel services *Bar. Conference room. Lift. Restaurant. TV lounge.* **Room services** *Private bathroom.*

Toren
Keizersgracht 164, 1015 CZ; IW (622 6352/6033). Tram 13, 14, 17. **Rates** *single* f75-f145; *double* f125-f210. **Credit** AmEx, DC, MC, V.
A seventeenth-century canal house, very close to Amsterdam's beautiful Jordaan area. A gentle, quiet atmosphere is created by the tall ceilings, elegant décor and the antiques dotted around. All rooms have bathrooms. Have breakfast in the dining-room or have it delivered to your room.
Hotel services *Bar. Dining-room. Room service.* **Room services** *Telephone.*

Wijnnobel
Vossiusstraat 9, 1071 AB; OS (662 2298). Tram 1, 2, 3, 5, 6, 12. **Rates** *single* f55-f65; *double* f80-f95. **No credit cards.**
A small hotel with just 12 rooms on four storeys. The stairs are, as ever, narrow and steep, and there is no lift. The tone is basic, with shared washing facilities, but the rooms are clean and the hotel is well situated, close to Vondelpark and the museums. There is no dining area, so the continental breakfasts are served in the room.

YOUTH HOSTELS

The Dutch Youth Hostels Association (NJHC) has two hostels in Amsterdam (*listed below*). You have to be a member of the International Youth Hostel Federation (IYHF), but you can enrol in the Dutch Association at the hostel itself; membership costs f30 for non-natives (no concessions available), but Federation membership can be up to 50 per cent cheaper if you join in your own country. It is also possible to become a temporary member at a cost of f5 per night, but full members are given preference during

busy periods. For information on NJHC hostels throughout The Netherlands, contact the **NJHC**, *Professor Tulpplein 4, 1018GX Amsterdam (551 3155)*; the office is open for enquiries from 9am to 5pm, Monday to Friday.

NJHC Hostels
Vondelpark *Zandpad 5, 1054 GA; OW (683 1744/telex 110 31). Tram 1, 2, 5.* **Stadsdolen** *Kloveniersburgwal 97, 1011 KB; C (624 6832). Tram 4, 9, 14, 16, 24, 25.* **Both open** 8am-midnight daily. **No credit cards.**
Multinational staff provide a cheery welcome at both sites, of which the Vondelpark is larger and far more pleasantly situated; the Stadsdolen is in a seedy area on the edge of the Red Light district. Rates for both sites are f18.50 per night (including breakfast) for IYHF or NJHC members, 23.50 per night non-members, with sheet and pillowcase hire at f5.50; full board (breakfast, packed lunch, dinner) costs f35 for members, f40 non-members. There is a seasonal supplement of f2.50 per night from May to September for all guests. Facilities at both sites include communal rooms, non-smoking areas, kitchen, lockers and a bar. There are no lifts or wheelchair access at either building. All accommodation is in dormitories, generally mixed although there is one women-only dorm, for 16 to 40 people in bunk beds. There is also a limited amount of

two- and four-bed rooms, intended mainly for group leaders. Curfew at both sites is 2am. Groups are advised to book at least two months in advance.

Eben Haezer (Christian Youth Hostel)
Bloemstraat 179, 1016 LA; IW (624 4717). Tram 13, 14, 17. **Open** 8am-midnight Mon-Thur, Sun; 8am-1am Fri, Sat. **Rates** f13.50. **Credit** f:TC.
This is perhaps the better of the two Christian hostels because of its pleasant location on the edge of the Jordaan. The same excellent standards of cleanliness apply in both, but the single-sex dormitories here are smaller, with between 18 and 20 beds. The same house rules apply as at The Shelter (*see below*).
Hotel services *Exchange facilities. Snack bar (open 7.30-11.30pm daily).*

The Shelter (Christian Youth Hostel)
Barndesteeg 21, 1012 BV; C (625 3230). Tram 1, 2, 4, 5, 9, 13, 16, 17, 24, 25. **Open** 8am-midnight Mon-Thur, Sun; 8am-1am Fri, Sat. **Rates** *dormitory* f13.50. **Credit** TC.
No membership is required and religion is optional although you will receive a Christian leaflet on arrival and gentle Christian messages throughout your stay. These will seem a contrast to the 'temptations' of the red light district where the Shelter is located. There are separate male and female dormitories with bunk beds.

The **Estherea** *(see under* **Moderate**) *is made up of eight canal houses which have been recently refurbished. Some rooms are very small, but even those are uncluttered as furnishings are comfortable and neat; others look over the canal. The hotel's communal areas are lined with dark wooden panelling, which is due to be renovated to maintain a traditional Dutch atmosphere.*

HOTEL* ATLANTA

On the famous Rembrandt Square,in the middle of the business and shopping center. Within a few minutes walk of many shops, restaurants, bars, discos, galleries and the internationally renowned "red-light district". By tram 5 min. from Central Station.

Most rooms have bath or shower, private toilet and mini-bar. All rooms have color television and telephone.

Groups up to 30 persons. 24-hour guarded parking possible.

**Rembrandtplein 8 - 10, 1017 CV Amsterdam
Phone 020 - 6253585 Fax 020 - 6249141**

LOW BUDGET
Hotel Brian

In the centre of the city overlooking the Singel canal.

Singel 69 1012 VE Amsterdam

☎ 020-6244661

HOTEL IMPERIAL

✳ ✳

THORBECKEPLEIN 9
1017 CS AMSTERDAM
TEL. 020 - 622 00 51
FAX 020 - 624 58 36

Small, cosy and clean, on a picturesque square in the heart of the city, surrouded by fine restaurants, shops, entertainment, museums and parking. Private showers and toilets, cable TV (European/American stations), telephones and wall safes are standard with most rooms.

ROOM RATES:SINGLE NLG 90 - 125,
DOUBLE NLG 90 - 170.
LARGER ROOMS AVAILABLE

The larger ones can be rather cramped, with up to 40 beds squeezed in. The smaller dormitories sleep 16. The age limit is 35. Alcohol is absolutely forbidden on the premises, as is anyone under the influence. The building is spotlessly clean, and pleasant gardens and a fountained courtyard adjoin the building. Weary and hungry backpackers can leave their belongings in lockers, which cost 50c per day to hire, and have dinner for f6.50.
Hotel services *Café (open 7.30am-11pm). Exchange facilities. Lifts.*

BARGES

Amstel
Steiger 5 (pier number), De Ruijterkade, C (626 4247). Tram 1, 2, 4, 5, 9, 13, 16, 17, 24, 25. **Open** 24 hours daily. **Rates** *single* f47; *double* f36 per person; *twin* f31-f34 per person; *triple* f29-f31 per person; *4-6 bed rooms* f25 per person. **No credit cards.**
See p50 picture and caption.
Hotel services *Bar (open 10am-1am).*
Room services *TV in private rooms.*

CAMPSITES

There are a number of camping grounds in and around Amsterdam; we list below four recommended by the VVV. Two are just to the north of the city, a 15-minute bus-ride from the centre, two are further out and more rurally situated. If you're intent on staying under canvas, it's worth remembering the climate is very changeable, but you can always hire a cabin should you fall foul of a downpour. During the summer, the weather is reliably mild. Note that the Gaasper, Vliegenbos and Zeeburg sites are classified by the VVV as youth camp-sites; they welcome people of all ages but be prepared for noise and high spirits late into the night.

Gaasper Camping
Loosdrechtdreef 1108 AZ (696 7326). Metro Gaasperplas/Bus 59, 60, 158. **Reception open** *June-Aug* 8am-10pm daily; *Sept-May* 9am-9pm daily. **Rates** f4.50 per person per night; under-12s f2.25 per night; camper/caravan f6.25, tents f3.50-5.75, electrical connection f3.35, all per night; hot showers f1.25. **Credit** TC.
This campsite is in the south-east of Greater Amsterdam, easily accessible by either Metro or bus. It's on the edge of the Gaasperplas park, which has a lake with a watersports centre. Ground facilities include shop, café, bar and restaurant.

Het Amsterdamse Bos
Kleine Noorddijk 1, 1432 CC, Aalsmeer (641 6868). Bus 171, 172. **Reception open** *April-Oct only* 8am-10pm daily. **Rates** inclusive of car, tent, shower f7 per night per

The **Hotel Verdi** (see under **Budget**), *just behind Museumplein, is small and has steep staircases, but all rooms have good light, with white walls and occasional bold, primary-coloured prints. There are tables and chairs in the garden, where breakfast can be taken if desired. At time of writing, the multi-lingual Japanese owners were redecorating the rooms and public areas in bright, cheerful colours, contrasting with the previous, rather basic style.*

person; 4-12s f3.50 per night; under-4s free; electricity for caravans/campers f3.35 per night. **Credit** TC.
The site is several miles from Amsterdam, a long and dreary cycle ride. However, half-hourly bus services for the 30-minute trip into town stop 300m from the grounds, which are on the southern edge of the beautiful Amsterdamse Bos, a large park with facilities for horse-riding and watersports. Wooden cabins sleeping up to four people can be hired for f44 per night. These are equipped with stoves and mattresses, but you will have to provide your own cooking utensils and sleeping bags. Site facilities include phones, a shop, a bar and a restaurant, lockers, and bike hire in July and August.

Vliegenbos
Meeuwenlaan 138, 1022 AM (636 8855). Bus 32. **Reception open** *April-Sept only* 8am-11pm daily. **Rates** over-30s f6 per person per night; 14-30s f4.75 per night; 3-14s f3.50 per night; under-3s free; car f3, motorbike f2, electricity f3, all per night; hot showers f1.25. **No credit cards.**
The grounds are close to the River IJ to the north of Amsterdam, a 10-minute bus journey from Centraal Station. Facilities include bar, restaurant, a safe at reception, and a small shop with exchange service. Cabins sleeping up to four people cost f44 per night.

Zeeburg
Zuider IJ Dijk 44, 1095 KN (694 4430). Bus 37. **Reception open** *April-Sept only* 9am-11pm daily. **Rates** f4.50 per person per night; 5-12s f2.25 per night; under-5s free; tents f1.25, motorbikes f2, cars f2.50, campers f7.50 incl electricity, all per night; hot showers f1. **Credit** TC.
Facilities at these grounds just north of the River IJ include a bar, a small restaurant, lockers, a shop and bike hire. Caravans can be hired for f32 per night (including the f4.50 nightly charge), tents for f8.50 per night (not including nightly charge). Cabins sleeping up to four people are available from f55 per night.

APARTMENT RENTALS

Flat seekers in Amsterdam require two vital commodities: tenacity and luck. Competition for all apartments is fierce, and landlords have little trouble in quickly filling empty properties, whatever their size and location. There follows some basic advice and tips on finding a reasonable place to live as quickly and with as little bother as possible.

Don't count on a cheap flatshare, which is rare here in comparison to London or Paris. The Dutch seem rather shy of sharing their living space, and many of the available properties are simply too small to accommodate more than one person. However, it is common for the Dutch to let their flats during holidays or periods spent working abroad.

The property agencies listed below, and others found in the *Gouden Gids* (*Yellow Pages*) may be worth contacting, but be prepared for a hefty commission if they find you a flat. You can also try looking in the daily newspapers *De Telegraaf* and *De Volkskrant* under the *Te Huur* (To Let) sections, particularly on Wednesdays, Fridays and Saturdays, when there are more ads. If you spot something you will need to act very swiftly. Most desirable properties are usually snapped up within a few hours. Also, don't be surprised if the landlord instantly dismisses your enquiry if you can't speak Dutch.

The noticeboard in the main public library (*see page 221* **Survival**), plus many supermarkets and tobacconists, display cards advertising available lets. If you're having no luck it may even be worth placing a card saying you are looking for a place.

Many people eventually get lucky by trying the above methods, but many more simply find a place through word of mouth. Be sure to let your friends, workmates, associates, everybody, know that you are looking and something may turn up.

When you find a flat, the landlord will probably charge you a *borgsom*, a refundable deposit ranging from a week's to a month's rent. The previous occupants may also attempt to charge an *overname* (key money), to cover the costs of any furniture they leave. Though often unavoidable, such charges are often inflated and can only be recouped by similarly charging the next tenant when you leave. If you already have furniture you may be paying for a lot of unwanted junk, or for little more than light bulbs, paper blinds and toilet roll holders.

When you register with the Aliens' Police (Bureau Vreemdelingenpolitie) on arrival in Amsterdam (*see page 3* **Essential Information**) you will be directed to the *Bevolkings Register* (Housing Register). Following registration, after a minimum of two years' continuous residence in Amsterdam, you may be eligible for council accommodation at a controlled rent. To prove that you have been in continuous residence in Amsterdam, remember to keep getting your visa renewed every three months at the Bureau Vreemdelingenpolitie. When you become eligible for council accommodation you will be given at least two refusals on apartments somewhere within the city limits.

Bevolkings Register
Herengracht 531-537, IS (551 9911). Tram 4, 9, 14. **Open** 8.30am-3pm Mon-Fri.

Amsterdam Apartments
Nieuwezijds Voorburgwal 63, 1012 RE; C (626 5930). Tram 1, 2, 5, 13, 17. **Open** 9am-9pm Mon-Sat. **No credit cards.**
Privately owned furnished, self-contained flats in the centre of town. Rates start from f600 per week for a one-person studio or one-bedroom flat. The minimum let is one week, maximum two months.

GIS Apartments
Keizersgracht 33, 1015 CD; IW (625 0071). Tram 13, 14, 17/Bus 18, 22, 44. **Open** 10am-5pm Mon-Fri. **Credit** AmEx, MC, TC, V.
This agency deals with a wide variety of accommodation, from simple holiday flats whose owners are away, to luxurious canal-view apartments. Most of the flats are in the centre of town, but the agency also handles property in outlying villages and towns. Short-term flats (minimum stay four days) cost between f500 and f1,000 per week including commission. Longer-term rentals (over three months) average f1,000 per month, plus a commission of 10% (minimum f350), plus 18% tax on commission. For rentals of more than five months the commission is one month's rent. Bookings should be made one month in advance, but the agency may have something available at short notice.

Intercity Room Service
Van Ostadestraat 348, 1073 TZ; OS (675 0064). Tram 3, 4. **Open** 10am-5pm Mon-Fri. **Credit** DC, MC, TC, V.
The place to try if you're in Amsterdam and require something – anything! – very quickly. This agency specializes in flatshares, and occasionally offers entire apartments. Flatshares in the centre of town cost from f50 per day, self-contained flats from f1,200 per month. The minimum stay is one day, maximum is indefinite. The agency charges two weeks' rent as commission.

Riverside Apartments
Amstel 138, 1017 AD; C (627 9797). Tram 9, 14. **Open** 9am-5pm Mon-Sat; by appointment other times. **Credit** AmEx, DC, MC, V.
These privately owned, luxury furnished flats in central Amsterdam cost f4,5000 per month for two to three people. Services include telephone, fax, laundry, cleaner and linen. The apartments are available for a minimum of one week, a maximum of three months.

It used to be commonplace for back-packers to stumble out of Centraal Station to the city's piers, looking for cheap dormitory accommodation on one of many barges. However, battles with authorities over fire prevention regulations has meant all but one of these floating hotels – the **Amstel** *(see under* **Barges**)– *has closed. The* Amstel *is no longer forced to take nightly cruises to placate the authorities, so adding to a sense of permanence. Don't expect a quaint and cosy Dutch barge; this is a large, efficiently run hotel, which just happens to float. Rooms are neat, if rather small, and functional.*

History

Fire and redevelopment have left few relics of medieval Amsterdam, when it was a precarious settlement on a bog beside the Zuider Zee. But since the seventeenth-century Golden Age, when the city was elegantly rebuilt with profits from maritime trade, the architecture of each era has been preserved almost intact. The Begijnhof retains its cloistered calm; and gablestones illustrate ancient professions. Squatting communes and the red light district are not modern developments, but typical of the port's ribald past. In the following chapters, we've looked beyond the gabled façades to show you Amsterdam's turbulent history.

CONTENTS:

Early History

Emerging from a swamp when the River Amstel was dammed, Amsterdam swiftly became a thriving centre of trade. _Sophie Marshall_ traces its development.

North Holland was one of the few places the Romans preferred to ignore. The waterlogged swamp land that changed shape and location every time the tide turned was apparently not the stuff empires were built on, so the legions headed for firmer footholds elsewhere in northern Europe. Archaeologists have come up with no evidence of settlement at Amsterdam before AD 1000, although there are prehistoric remains further east in Drenthe (_see page 213_ **The Provinces**).

It looks as though Amsterdam's site was partially under water for most of history, forsaken by all but the birds. The River Amstel had no fixed course in this marshy region until enterprising farmers from around Utrecht began the laborious task of building dikes in the area during the early eleventh century. Once the peasants had done the work, the nobility took over.

During the thirteenth century, the most important place in the newly reclaimed area was Oudekerk aan de Amstel. In 1204, the Lord of Aemstel built his 'castle' near this tiny hamlet on what is now the outskirts of Amsterdam. Once the Amstel was dammed (in about 1240), a village grew up on the site of Dam Square, acquiring the name _Amestelledamme_. The Lord of Aemstel at this time was Gijsbrecht. A pugnacious man, Gijsbrecht was continually in trouble with his liege lord, the Bishop of Utrecht, and with his nearest neighbour, Count Floris V of Holland.

Tension in this power struggle increased when Floris bestowed toll rights – and thus some statutes and independence – on the young town in 1275. Events culminated in Floris' murder by Gijsbrecht at Muiden (Floris' castle can still be seen here _see page 203_ **Excursions in Holland: Castles**). Gijsbrecht's estates were confiscated by the Bishop of Utrecht and given to the Counts of Holland, and Amsterdam has remained part of the province of North Holland ever since.

The Count of Holland's overlordship was essentially nominal as Amsterdam, like many European cities with charters of rights, was effectively self-governing throughout this period.

ROLL OUT THE BARREL

The saying goes that Amsterdam's prosperity was launched in a beer barrel. This commercial boost came courtesy of a later Count of Holland, Floris VI, who in 1323 made the city one of only two toll points in the province for the import of brews. This was no small matter at a time when most people drank beer instead of water (drinking the local water was equivalent to attempting suicide). Hamburg had the largest brewing capacity in northern Europe and within 50 years a third of that city's production was flowing through Amsterdam. Because of its position between the Atlantic ports and the Hansa towns (such as Hamburg and Lübeck), Amsterdam increased its trade in a wide assortment of essential goods, including grain. The city's ships became a common sight all over Europe. (For Amsterdam's commercial history, _see page 188_ **Business**.)

Schreierstoren

Prins Hendrikkade, C. Tram 1, 2, 4, 5, 9, 13, 16, 17.

Dating from 1487, this is one of the few really old buildings in Amsterdam, and is a reminder of the city's maritime prominence. Translating roughly as the Weeping Tower, it's said to be the place where sailors' wives waved a tearful farewell to their men. On the other hand, _schreier_ also means saddle, and the tower does indeed straddle two canals. The tower was part of the city's medieval fortifications defending the approaches on the former Zuider Zee. Nothing else remains of the walls, except the former St Antoniespoort (St Anthony's Gatehouse), which dates from 1488, but became the Waag (Weigh House) in 1617. _See also p13_ Sightseeing: Heritage.

BUILDINGS & FIRES

Although a major trading force, Amsterdam remained little more than a village until well into the fifteenth century. In 1425, it consisted of a few blocks of houses with kitchen gardens and two churches, by this time neatly and compactly arranged along the final 1,000-metre/1,094-yard stretch of the River Amstel and bor-

dered by the present Zeedijk, Spui and Nieuwezijds Voorburgwal. The buildings, like the Houtenhuis (_see page 13_ Sightseeing: Begijnhof) were virtually all wooden, so fire was a constant threat. In the great fire of May 1452, three-quarters of Amsterdam was razed.

Not surprisingly, very few buildings predate 1452, and those built later had to be faced with stone and roofed with tiles or slates. Limited urban expansion first occurred around this time. Foreign commerce led to the development of shipbuilding. Numerous craftsmen in related trades set up shop outside the city walls (of which nothing remains) in what is now the Nieuwmarkt quarter.

CATHOLIC CONTROL

It is almost impossible to over-estimate the role of the Catholic Church in early medieval society. It permeated every aspect of life throughout Europe, and Amsterdam was no exception. Contemporary chronicles show that the city became an independent parish sometime before 1334. Documents from this date are the first to refer to the Oudekerk; the Nieuwekerk was built at the start of the fifteenth century (for both _see page 13_ Sightseeing).

Cloisters known as _Beguinages_ proliferated as the city became more prosperous; no fewer than 18 were dotted around the tiny urban enclave. The only remaining example, the Begijnhof (_see page 13_ Sightseeing), shows their original structure.

Historians haven't come up with any concrete reasons for such a concentration of cloisters, but one explanation could be the 'miracle' which occurred in 1345. From that date Amsterdam attracted large numbers of pilgrims (_see page 36_ **Amsterdam by Season: The Silent Procession**). The _Heiligeweg_ (Holy Way) was the road within the city leading to the chapel that was built on Rokin, close to where the miracle took place. Its length (roughly 70 metres/77 yards) is an indication of just how small Amsterdam was.

The cloisters in Amsterdam were also the main source of social welfare, providing hospital treatment, orphanages and poor relief for both inhabitants and travellers. Nothing remains of these complexes, as the Protestant élite which took over the city after the Reformation obliterated every trace of popery.

War & Reformation

The sixteenth-century Reformation united the Dutch and set them on a collision course with Spain. *Sophie Marshall* tells how Amsterdam profited from the 80 years of war that ensued.

None of the wealth and glory of Amsterdam's seventeenth-century Golden Age would have been possible without the turbulent events of the sixteenth century. During these hundred years, Amsterdam's population increased five-fold, from about 10,000 (a level low even by medieval standards) to 50,000 by 1600. Its first major urban expansion took place to accommodate the growth, yet people flocked to the booming city only to find poverty, disease and squalor in the hastily erected working-class quarters. But Amsterdam's merchants weren't complaining. During this century the city started to emerge as one of the major trading powers in the world.

Amsterdam may have been almost autonomous as a chartered city, but on paper it was still subject to absentee rulers. Through the intricate and exclusive marriage bureau known as the European aristocracy, the Low Countries (today's Netherlands and Belgium) had passed into the hands of the Catholic Austro-Spanish House of Hapsburg. The Hapsburgs were the mightiest monarchs in Europe, owning most of South America and claiming the English throne – Amsterdam was a comparative backwater among their European possessions. However, events in the sixteenth century soon gave the city a new prominence.

THE REFORMATION HITS HOLLAND

Amsterdam's burgeoning trade led to the import of all kinds of radical – in other words, religious – ideas which were flourishing throughout northern Europe at the time. It started with Martin Luther's audacious condemnation of the all-powerful Catholic Church in 1517. Luther's revolutionary notions about how God should be worshipped sparked off a domino effect as fast and all-encompassing as recent events in Eastern Europe. Religious wars, civil conflicts and insurrections swept through the Old World leaving no ruler or country unaffected.

The German princelings sided with Luther, but the Hapsburg kings of Spain gathered all the resources of their enormous empire and set about putting the upstart protesters in their place – back in the Catholic Church.

Although Luther's beliefs failed to catch on with Amsterdammers, many people were drawn to the austere and sober creeds of first the Anabaptists and later Calvin. Advocating a revolutionary Christian equality, the Anabaptists insisted on adult baptism. Calvinist doctrine was intertwined with principles of sober, upright citizenship.

When the Anabaptists first came to the city (from Germany) in about 1530, the Catholic city fathers tolerated the new movement. But when they seized the Town Hall in 1534 during an attempt to establish a 'New Jerusalem' on the River Amstel, the authorities clamped down. The leaders were arrested and subsequently executed, signalling a period of religious repression unparalleled in the city's history. Protesters of every persuasion had to keep a low profile – heretics were burned at the stake on the Dam (*see* **Witches' Weigh House**, *page 203* **Excursions in Holland** *under* **Oudewater**).

The Calvinist preachers came to the city from Geneva (where the movement started), or via France (as the Principality of Orange, in the south of France, had links with Holland and was one of the few safe pockets of Protestantism outside Switzerland and parts of Germany). Their arrival caused a sweeping transformation in Amsterdam. In 1566, religious discontent erupted into the **Iconoclastic Fury**, the most severe such outbreak in European history. In the space of two months, a popular, spontaneous uprising led to the sacking of all the churches and monasteries in the country. Statues, altar pieces and priceless religious art were dragged into the streets and burned or smashed. The iconoclasm had two major effects: one was that a church in Amsterdam was allocated to the Calvinists; the other was Philip II of Spain's decision to send an army to suppress the heresy.

Zuiderkerk

Zuiderkerkhof, Zandstraat 5, C (Zuiderkerk foundation 9am-5pm Mon-Fri 623 2334). Tram 9, 14/Metro Nieuwmarkt. **Open** *Church by prior arrangement only; tower 1 June-15 Oct 2-5pm Wed, Thur; 11am-2pm Fri; 11am-4pm Sat.* **Admission** fl. **No credit cards.** The South Church is Amsterdam's earliest post-Reformation church, and was the first to be built expressly for the Calvinists. The architect was the ubiquitous Hendrick de Keyser, who was able to introduce innovations in design because the religious requirements were no longer Catholic. All De Keyser spires are distinctive; this one is braced with columns and topped by an onion dome. Construction started in 1603 and the first service was held here in 1611.

UNITY AGAINST SPAIN

The **80 Years War** (1568-1648) between the Hapsburgs and the Dutch is often seen as primarily a struggle for religious freedom, but there was a lot more at stake than that. The Dutch were looking for political autonomy from an absentee king who meant little more to them than a continual drain on their coffers, through taxation for his interminable wars. By the last quarter of the sixteenth century, Philip II of Spain was fighting wars on almost every front in Europe – in Germany; against England (to whom he sent his Armada); in the East, against the infidel Ottoman Turks; and for control of his colonies in the New World. The last thing he needed was a revolt in the Low Countries.

Amsterdam at first stayed on the political fence, ostensibly supporting Philip II until it became clear that he was losing. Only in 1578 did the city patricians declare for the rebels, who were led by Willem of Orange. A year later the Protestant states of the Low Countries united in opposition to Philip when the first modern-day European Republic was born at the **Union of Utrecht**. The Republic of Seven United Provinces comprised the provinces of Friesland, Gelderland, Groningen, Overijssel, Utrecht, Zeeland and, most impor-

The **Oudemanhuis** *(see under* **Calvinist Clique***) was originally a home for elderly men. It was set up by the Regents, the Calvinist élite that took over social welfare after the Reformation. Its gateway, Oudemanhuispoort, survives, but the surrounding buildings of 1754 are now part of the University of Amsterdam and instead provide shelter for booksellers' stalls.*

tantly, Holland. Although lauded as the start of the modern Netherlands, it wasn't the unitary state that William of Orange had wanted, but a loose military federation with an impotent *States General* assembly (for more information on the political structure after the Union of Utrecht *see page 55* **The Golden Age**).

The provinces appointed a so-called *stadhouder*, a rank which in Hapsburg times had been held by the king's deputy. The *stadhouder* commanded the Republic's army and navy and had the right to appoint some of the individual cities' regents or governors. *Stadhouders* of each province sent delegates to the assembly, which was held at the Binnenhof in The Hague (*see page 208* **The Randstad**). The treaty also enshrined freedom of conscience and hence of religion – except for Catholics (until French rule in 1795). The Union of Utrecht was in part a response to the Union of Arras, whereby the southern provinces of the Low Countries declared for Spain and Catholicism.

CALVINIST CLIQUE

From its earliest beginnings, Amsterdam had been governed by four burgomasters and a **city council** representing the citizens' interests. This sounds pretty Utopian and it may have begun that way, but by 1500 city government had become an incestuous business. The city council's 36 members were supposed to be both rich and wise, but they were appointed for life and themselves 'elected' the burgomasters from among their own ranks. Selective intermarriage meant that the city was, in effect, governed by a handful of families. When Amsterdam joined the rebels in 1578, the only real change in civic administration was that the formerly Catholic élite was replaced by a Calvinist faction comprising equally wealthy families.

However, **social welfare** was transformed. Formerly the concern of the Catholic Church, it was now incorporated into city government. The Regents, as the Calvinist élite became known, took over the con-

vents and monasteries, establishing charitable organizations including orphanages and homes for the elderly. But if you had fallen on hard times through your own fault, there was little sympathy from the Regents, whose hard-work ethic and abstemious way of life would not tolerate any kind of excess. Crime, drunkenness, immorality, all were condemned and anyone who found themselves in front of a magistrate for this kind of offence was immediately sent to a house of correction (*see page 55* **The Golden Age: Social Welfare**).

Law and order in the city was the province of the civic guard or militia who, fortunately for artists like Rembrandt, had a penchant for having their portraits painted. Street names like *Voetboogstraat* (Bowman's Street) indicate the location of their barracks.

Municipal Orphanage

Kalverstraat 92, C. Tram 4, 9, 14, 16, 24, 25. The Municipal Orphanage (now the **Amsterdams Historisch Museum**, *see p100* **Museums**) was housed in an ex-convent. It was demolished in 1634 and rebuilt incorporating designs by De Keyser and Van Campen.

Oudemanhuis

Oudezijds Achterburgwal, C. Tram 9, 14/Metro Nieuwmarkt. See **picture and caption**.

PROFITING IN WAR

During the two centuries before the 80 Years War, Amsterdam had developed a powerful maritime force, expanding its fleet and broadening its trading horizons to include Russia, Scandinavia and the Baltic. Yet until Antwerp was taken by the Spanish in 1589, Amsterdam remained overshadowed by that Belgian port. The Hapsburg Spanish, rather than engaging in pitched battles against the rebellious Low Countries, adopted siege tactics, primarily in what is now Belgium. Thus Amsterdam was unaffected by the hostilities and benefited from the crippling blockades suffered by rival commercial ports. Thousands of refugees fled north, including Antwerp's most prosperous Protestant and Jewish merchants. They brought with them the gold and craft skills, and most famously the diamond industry, that would set Amsterdam on course to becoming the greatest maritime trading city in the world.

The Golden Age

Sophie Marshall **describes the Amsterdam of 1590 to 1660, when, through relentless trading, the city gained prosperity and power.**

History is cluttered with Golden Ages – any country with the least claim to fame seems to boast one. But in Amsterdam's case, the first six decades of the seventeenth century truly deserve the title. The small city on the River Amstel came to dominate world trade and establish important colonies, resulting in a population explosion at home and a frenzy of urban expansion. The still-elegant girdle of canals excavated around the city centre was one of the greatest engineering feats of that century. Extraordinarily, this all happened while the city was at war with one of the greatest powers in the world. And equally startling, this growth was presided over not by kings but by businessmen.

THE FIRST MULTINATIONAL

The East India Company doesn't have much of a ring to it – to modern ears it sounds rather like an enterprise specializing in cottons or joss sticks. Yet the name of the mighty *Verenigde Oost Indische Compagnie* (VOC) definitely loses something in translation, as this was the first ever transnational company. The VOC was created in 1602 by a group of respectable businessmen from all the main cities in the Republic of the Seven Provinces. Its initial purpose was to finance the wildly expensive and hellishly dangerous voyages to the East. Drawn by the potential fortunes to be made out of spices and silk, the shrewd Dutch saw the sense in sending out merchant fleets, but they also knew that one disaster could leave an individual investor penniless. As a result, the main cities set up trading 'chambers' which evaluated the feasibility (and profitability) of ventures, then equipped ships and sent them east. The VOC had enormous powers, including the capacity to found colonies, establish its own army, declare war and sign treaties.

Brouwersgracht warehouses
Brouwersgracht, IW. Tram 1, 2, 3, 5, 13, 17.
North of the Brouwersgracht canal is the former shipping quarter where goods from

VOC shipping were unloaded. Brouwersgracht is lined with warehouses; once storerooms for spices and East Indies produce, they've now mostly been converted into luxury apartments. The hauntingly severe architecture of the warehouses is in dramatic contrast to the heavily ornate merchants' houses of the period. *See also p188* **Business: picture and caption.**

VOC Headquarters
Oude Hoogstraat at Klovenierburgwal, C. Tram 4, 14, 16, 19, 24, 25/Metro Nieuwmarkt.
See p56 **picture and caption.**

THE STRAITS OF LEMAIRE

The story of Isaac Lemaire, whose name would be immortalized in atlases, is a good illustration of just how powerful the VOC became. Lemaire had fled to Amsterdam from Antwerp in 1589 and became a founder member of the VOC, initially investing f90,000 – about £30 ($50) million in today's terms. But, accused of embezzlement, he was forced to leave the company and, in businesslike fashion, cast around for ways to set up on his own. But the Republic had given the VOC a monopoly on trade with the East via the Cape of Good Hope and at that time there was no alternative route.

However, Portuguese seamen claimed the Cape route was not the only passage to the East. They believed the fabulous spice islands of Java, the Moluccas and Malaya could also be reached by sailing to the tip of South America where a strait would lead into the Pacific. In 1615, Lemaire financed a voyage, led by one of his sons, and discovered the strait that still bears his name. His son perished on the voyage home and Isaac died of a broken heart.

While the VOC concentrated on the spice trade, a new company received its charter from the Dutch Republic in 1621. The **Dutch West India Company** (*Verenigde West Indische Compagnie*, VWC) was not as successful as its Eastern sister, but it did dominate trade with the Spanish and Portuguese possessions in Africa and America. The VWC was also first to colonize a small island in the mouth of a river in North America in 1623.

The settlement on Manhattan Island was laid out on a grid system similar to Amsterdam's and subsequently it adopted the Dutch city's name. New Amsterdam flourished and more land was cleared on the banks of the River Hudson and named after other enterprising towns with a stake in the new colony: Haarlem (Harlem) and Breukelen (Brooklyn). Staten Island was so-called in honour of the States General, the 'national' council of the Republic.

But after an invasion by the Duke of York in 1664, the terms of the peace treaty between England and The Netherlands determined New Amsterdam would change its name to New York and come under British control. The Dutch were given Surinam as a consolation prize.

Lelystad
Battaver Oostvaardijk 19, Lelystad (032 0061409). Bus 150 from Lelystad station. **Open** 10am-5pm daily. **Admission** f10; under-16s f5; over-65s f6. **No credit cards.**
A visit to the shipyard in Lelystad will reveal exactly what kind of vessels the Dutch used to conquer the trading world. Master shipwrights and apprentices – on a new youth scheme for the unemployed – are now building a full-size replica of the *Batavia*, one of the VOC's biggest East-Indiamen, lost on its maiden voyage in 1628. When this is completed in 1991, the yard will begin work on a second project, the *Saerdam*. Lelystad is about 40 minutes by train from Centraal Station. *Café. Wheelchair access.*

NAP
Off Waterlooplein, C. Tram 9, 14/Metro Waterlooplein.
In the passage between the City Hall and the Muziektheater you can still see the height of the NAP (*Normaal Amsterdams Peil* or normal Amsterdam water level), set over 300 years ago in 1684. This became the basis for measurements of altitude for most of Western Europe. Three glass columns are filled with water; two indicate the water level at the coastal towns of Vlissingen and IJmuiden – at high tide the water rises well above knee level. In the third column, the water level is far over your head, indicating the height of the North Sea during the disastrous floods in Zeeland in 1953. The real NAP, which is a large bronze plate, can be seen by descending the staircase by the water columns.

Scheepvaart Museum
Kattenburgerplein 1, IE (523 2222). Bus 22, 28. **Open** 10am-5pm Tue-Sat; 1-5pm Sun, public holidays. **Closed** 1 Jan. **Admission** f5; CJP card holders f3.75; 6-17s f3; under-6s free; free with Museum Card. **No credit cards.**
Located in a restored, former VOC naval arsenal (*see p100* **Museums**), this well-organized museum charts the history of the Company using ship models, period sea charts (works of art in their own right), instruments and paintings. It has a rather nice waterside coffee shop overlooking the harbour.
Wheelchair access.

The **VOC Headquarters** (see under **The First Multinational**) *was the meeting place for the most influential chamber of the mighty East India Company. Many wealthy Protestant and Jewish refugees settled in the city after the fall of Antwerp and it was their money that helped to finance the lucrative voyages to the East Indies (now Indonesia). Ships berthed here before unloading; provisions for the ships were stored and the more precious booty (such as rare spices and silk) was laid up to await a rise in prices. The building dates from 1606, shortly after the founding of the VOC, and is now used as offices by the University.*

MONOPOLY MONEY

Extensive though commerce with the Indies became, it never surpassed Amsterdam's European business. The city became the major European centre for distribution and trade. Grain from Russia, Poland and Prussia, salt and wine from France, cloth from Leiden and tiles from Delft all flowed through the port. Whales were hunted by Amsterdam's fleets in the waters round Spitsbergen, generating a flourishing soap trade, and Surinam sugar and spices from Dutch colonies were distributed to ports throughout Scandinavia and the north of Europe. This manifold activity was financed by the Amsterdam Exchange, a bank set up in the cellars of the Town Hall by Amsterdam's municipal council as early as 1609. The Amsterdam bank was a unique initiative and was considered the money vault of Europe, its notes being freely exchangeable throughout the trading world – the seventeenth-century equivalent of an AmEx Gold Card.

ORANGE AID

The political structure of the young Dutch republic was complex. When the Treaty of Utrecht was signed in 1579, no suitable monarch or head of state was found, so the existing system was adapted to new needs. The seven provinces were represented in a 'national' council known as the States General. In addition, the provinces appointed a *stadhouder* (*see page 53* **War & Reformation**).

The most popular and obvious choice for *stadhouder* after the treaty was Willem of Orange, the minor aristocrat from Holland who had led the rebellion against Philip II of Spain. Willem was succeeded by his son, 'Prince' Maurits, who was as militarily successful against the Spanish as his father had been, securing the 12 Years Truce (1609-1621). Although each province could, in theory, elect a different *stadhouder*, in practice they usually chose the same person. It became something of a tradition to elect an Orange as *stadhouder*, and by 1641 this family had become sufficiently powerful for a later Willem to marry a princess of England. It was their son who, backed by Amsterdam money, set sail in 1688 to accept the throne of England in the so-called Glorious Revolution.

HOLLAND OUT-WITTS ORANGE

But the Oranges weren't popular with everyone. The provinces' representatives at the States General were known as *pensionaries*, and Holland's (read Amsterdam's) was so powerful he was in a position to challenge the authority and decisions of the *stadhouder*. In 1650 this power was used. The crisis was precipitated by Holland's decision to disband its militia after the end of the 80 Years War with Spain. The *stadhouder*, Willem II of Orange, wanted the militia maintained (and paid for) by Holland. In response to the disbandment, he got a kinsman, Willem Frederik, to launch a surprise attack on Amsterdam. The attack met with no resistance, but three months later Willem II died. The leaders of the States of Holland then called a Great Assembly of the provinces, which decided that (apart from in Friesland and Groningen, which remained loyal to Willem Frederik) there should be no *stadhouders*. Johan de Witt, Holland's powerful *pensionary*, swore no prince of Orange would ever become *stadhouder* again. This became law in the Act of Seclusion of 1653.

CIVIC PRIDE

Amid all these political machinations, you may wonder how anyone ever got any work done. But the powers that be in Amsterdam, the Lords (Heren) XLVIII (composed of a sheriff, four mayors, a 36-member council and seven jurists) kept a firm grip on all that went on both within and without the city walls. Although this system was self-perpetuating, these people were merchants rather than aristocrats, and anyone who made enough money could, in theory, become a member. The mayors and the council usually came from a handful of prominent families, the most powerful being the Witsen, Bicker, Six and Trip families. Their wives, nieces and daughters made up boards of governesses at the multitude of charitable institutions scattered throughout the city (*see below* **Social Welfare**).

Koninklijk Paleis (Royal Palace)

Dam, C (624 8698 ext 217). Tram 1, 2, 4, 5, 9, 13, 14, 16, 17, 24, 25. **Open** *mid June-1 Sept* 12.30-5pm daily. **Admission** f3.50; under-12s f1.50. **No credit cards.**
Although this building has been called the Royal Palace for the past 180 years, it was built in the seventeenth century to be the

City Hall. The impressive Palladian design reflects the civic pride of the period. This pride was also expressed when the city élite refused permission for a nearby church to have a tower – in case it detracted from their City Hall's dominance of the Amsterdam skyline. *See also p13* **Sightseeing**.
Guided tours throughout year 1.30pm Wed booking required. Guided tours by arrangement throughout year: Mon-Fri f25 for 15-30 people, f35 for 10-15 people, plus admission; Sat, Sun f35 for 15-30 people, f50 for 10-15 people, plus admission.

Trippenhuis
Kloveniersburgwal 29, C.
This palatial abode gives some idea of the opulence enjoyed by the Trip family, one of the powerful merchant clans that ran Amsterdam during the Golden Age. Built in 1662 by Justus Vingboons, it features Corinthian columns and a grandly friezed pediment. Although the interior isn't open to the public, it was big enough to house the entire Rijksmuseum collection for most of the nineteenth century.

GUILDS & PROTECTIONISM
The less elevated folk, the craftsmen, artisans, shopkeepers and the like, were equally active in maintaining their position. A system of guilds had developed in earlier centuries, linked to the Catholic Church, but under the new order, guilds were independent organizations run by their members. The original Amsterdammers were known as *poorters*, deriving from the Dutch for gate (they originally lived within the gated walls of the city). As the city was expanding fast, the *poorters* saw their livelihoods threatened by an influx of newcomers who were prepared to work for lower wages.

Things came to a head when the shipwrights' trade began to be lost to less expensive competitors in the nearby Zaan region. The shipwrights' lobby was so strong that the city regents decreed that Amsterdam ships had to be repaired in Amsterdam yards. This kind of protectionism extended to almost all industrial sectors in the city and effectively meant that most crafts became closed shops. Only *poorters* or those who had married *poorters'* daughters were allowed to join a guild, thereby protecting Amsterdammers' livelihoods.

Werf 't Kromhout
Hoogte Kadijk 147, IE (627 6777). Bus 22, 28. **Open** *10am-4pm Mon-Fri; also open noon-5pm Sat, Sun in summer; phone for exact dates.* **Admission** *f3; f1.50 under-12s.* **No credit cards.**
The Kromhout Shipyard Museum is sited in the eastern port area of the city where there were numerous shipyards in the seventeenth century. Old vessels undergo repair and restoration here and the work in

progress is open to view. *See also p100* **Museums**.
Guided tours. Wheelchair access with assistance.

URBAN EXPANSION
In 1600 Amsterdam's population was no more than 50,000 but in about 50 years the figure quadrupled. This increased opportunities for trade and industry, but brought inevitable headaches for the city fathers. The city was obliged to expand. The first and most elegant of the major canals girdling the city centre was *Herengracht* (gentlemen's canal); begun in 1613, it was where many of the Heren XLVIII had their homes. Just so there would be no misunderstanding about who was most

important, *Herengracht* was followed further out by *Keizersgracht* (emperor's canal) and *Prinsengracht* (prince's canal). In contrast, the tens of thousands of immigrants were housed along the mass of narrow transverse streets and waterways that linked the major canals.

The frenzy of building also included churches, as the wave of immigrants brought with them an amazing range of variations on the Protestant theme. Renaissance influences were already noticeable in Hendrick de Keyser's Calvinist Zuiderkerk (*see page 53* **War & Reformation**), but his classical Westerkerk (*see page 13* **Sightseeing**) marked a watershed in Amsterdam architecture. De Keyser's

Hidden in the attic of the **Amstelkring Museum** *(see under* **Urban Expansion***) is the only intact clandestine church left in Amsterdam. During the seventeenth century, Roman Catholic worship was banned in the city, and this chapel, '***Our Lord in the Attic***', was one of several used for secret Catholic ceremonies. The chapel has three tiers of balconies, a huge organ (which must have been anything but clandestine when played) and an altarpiece by Jacob de Wit. It's a fun place for children as there are numerous secret ways to reach the chapel and you can try to find these yourself. The rest of the house is preserved in its seventeenth-century state, giving an insight into the domestic life of the period.*

Noorderkerk followed in 1620-23 to a Greek Cross ground plan, and Dortsman's Nieuwe Luthersekerk (1668-71) (*see page 13* **Sightseeing**) acquired a baroque dome. But the most striking Palladian new building was the City Hall (now called the **Royal Palace**, *see above* **Civic Pride**).

For the first few decades of the century Catholics, Baptists, Lutherans and Jews were obliged to hold services in secret. But towards the end of this period the location of most of the clandestine churches was common knowledge and they were tolerated by the authorities.

Amstelkring Museum, 'Our Lord in the Attic'
Oudezijds Voorburgwal 40, C (624 6604). Tram 1, 2, 4, 5, 9, 13, 16, 17, 24, 25. **Open** 10am-5pm Mon-Sat; 1-5pm Sun, public holidays. **Admission** f3.50; f2 under-14s, CJP card holders; free with Museum Card; group discount. **No credit cards.** *See p57* **picture and caption.** *Guided tours by prior arrangement.*

Museum Van Loon
Keizersgracht 672, IS (624 5255). Tram 4, 9, 14. **Open** 10am-5pm Mon. **Admission** f5; free under-12s. **No credit cards.** *See* **picture and caption.** *Guided tours (min 10 people) by prior arrangement.*

SOCIAL WELFARE
Despite the city's wealth, and the reputation of its people as masters of transport, famine hit Amsterdam with dreary regularity in the seventeenth century. Guilds had benevolent funds set aside for their members in times of need, but social welfare was primarily in the hands of the ruling merchant class. Amsterdam's élite was noted for its philanthropy, but only *poorters* were eligible for assistance and they had to fall into a specific category, known as 'deserving poor'.

Those seen as undeserving poor were sent to a house of correction. At first these had been rather Utopian places, run on the premise that hard work would ultimately produce reformed, useful citizens. But this soon changed and the institutions became little more than prisons.

Rasphuis
Heiligeweg 19, C (620 4070). Tram 1, 2, 4, 5, 9, 14, 16, 24, 25. Justitia Hal: **Open** 10am-10pm daily. **Admission** f7.50; f4.75 under-14s; f5.50 with Museum Card, students, CJP card holders. **No credit cards.**
One of the charitable organizations that the Calvinist Regents set up. Built in a former monastery, it was a place of correction where criminals would rasp Brazil wood to produce dyes. The gateway survives and is adorned with De Keyser-esque sculptures dating from 1603. The building now houses **Justitia Hal**, a museum of torture instruments through the ages, *see p100* **Museums.** Lots of implements for use on witches are kept here.

Spinhuis
Oudezijds Achterburgwal 28, C. Tram 1, 2, 4, 5, 9, 13, 16, 17, 24, 25.
The Spinning House was a house of correction for women. In the seventeenth century the governors made a bit of cash on the side by allowing sightseers to watch the inmates at work. It is now used as offices by the city and is not open to the public.

ARTS & SCIENCES
Amsterdam's seventeenth-century Golden Age did not only affect its commercial life. Some of the world's greatest artists also happened to live there. Names like Rembrandt, Hals and Vermeer immediately spring to mind, but hundreds of long-forgotten artists also made a good living from their work. United in the Guild of St Luke, these artists are estimated to have produced no fewer than 20 million paintings. Art historians believe that almost every family had at least three or four paintings in the home. Rembrandt may have died in poverty, but when he managed to keep his temper and not offend his rich patrons, he had a remarkably comfortable life. The house where he lived still exists, now as a museum (*see below*), and it's no garret.

Unlike other European countries, The Netherlands wasn't liberally scattered with ancient universities. In fact, Amsterdam didn't have one at all. The first move towards establishing a centre of higher education came in 1632 when the Athenaeum Illustre (Illustrious School) was opened. It was attended by (male) members of the élite who studied Latin, Greek, law and the natural sciences. But two of the era's scientific pioneers, Anthonie van Leeuwenhoek, who pioneered microbiology, and the physicist Christiann Huygens, didn't go to a university at all. They did their work in improvised laboratories at home. Amsterdam's guild of surgeons, as Rembrandt records, held public demonstrations of anatomy, using the bodies of executed criminals for practice.

Rembrandthuis
Jodenbreestraat 4-6, C (624 9486). Tram 9, 14. **Open** 10am-5pm Mon-Sat; 1-5pm Sun, public holidays. **Admission** f4; f3.50 over-65s, 10-15s; free under-9s; free with Museum Card; group discount (min 15 people). **No credit cards.**
The great master lived here for around 20 years. The museum includes a good collection of his etchings and paintings by his pupils. *See also p100* **Museums.** *Guided tours by prior arrangement.*

The **Van Loon Museum** (see under **Urban Expansion**) *is housed in a beautifully restored and rather grand seventeenth-century home. The Van Loon family was one of the most powerful in Amsterdam at the time – Willem Van Loon helped to found the VOC (Dutch East India Company) in 1602. The house was built in 1672 by Adriaan Dortsman; the painter Ferdinand Bol was the first tenant. Among the collection of period pieces there is an enormous number of family portraits. Although there are none by a great master, all are excellent examples of contemporary portraiture.*

Decline & Fall

Sea wars with Britain, competition in trade and invasion by Napoleon reduced Amsterdam to poverty.
Sophie Marshall **charts the decline.**

After Amsterdam's intoxicating Golden Age came the hangover. The city remained one of the wealthiest in Europe until the early nineteenth century, but after 1660 its dominant trading position was lost to England and France. Wars at sea and invasions by land would gradually milk the small country dry.

DUTCH COURAGE

It's no accident that the English language is littered with 'Dutch' adjectives, all of them pretty derogatory. 'Double Dutch' (incomprehensible jargon), 'going Dutch' (each person paying only their share of the bill), 'Dutch courage' (bravery fuelled by alcohol) – all are indications of how the British viewed their major rivals in maritime trade. The United Provinces spent a couple of centuries bickering about trade and politics with Britain and the other main powers: France, Spain and the Austrian Hapsburg Empire. International relations were only straightforward when war broke out – which it did frequently. Major sea conflicts included battles against the Swedes and no fewer than four Anglo-Dutch wars (_see below_ **Monuments to Admirals**), from which the Dutch came off slightly the worse.

It wasn't that the Dutch didn't win many of the wars, it was more that the small country ran out of men and money. Amsterdam became the most vociferous opponent of the Orange family's attempts to acquire kingdoms – although it was one of Willem III's staunchest supporters when this Orange crossed the sea to become King of England in 1688. The city fathers believed a Dutchman on their rival's throne could only be advantageous to them. For a while that proved true, but Billy was soon knocking on the Amsterdammers' doors for more money to fight even more wars – this time against France.

Monuments to Admirals

Nieuwekerk, N Z Voorburgwal/Dam, C (626 8168). Tram 1, 2, 5, 13, 14, 17. **Open** 11am-4pm daily. **Admission** free.

The admirals who led the wars against Britain are Dutch heroes, and the Nieuwekerk (New Church) has monuments to Admirals Van Kinsbergen (1735-1819), Bentinck (1745-1831) and, most celebrated of all, Michiel de Ruyter (1607-76). The most famous incident, though not prominent in British history books, came during the Second English War (1664-67). In 1667, De Ruyter cheekily sailed up the River Thames to Chatham naval base, stormed the dockyards and burnt _Royal Charles_, the British flagship, as it lay at anchor. In Delft's Oudekerk are memorials to the equally illustrious Admirals Piet Heyn (1577-1629); and Maarten Tromp (1598-1653). Naval battles of this period are a frequent theme of Delftware tiles in Huis Lambert van Meerten Museum, also at Delft (_see p208_ **The Randstad**).

RICHES & RIOTS

Despite diminished maritime prowess, Amsterdammers of all classes still had the highest standard of living in Europe well into the eighteenth century. The prestigious Plantage district (_see page 26_ **Amsterdam by Area**) was the period's principal city development, of which the sole remaining patrician's villa is **Frankendael**, _see below_. Tradesmen and artisans flourished and their role in society can still be gauged by interpreting the shapes and carvings on gablestones (_see page 60_ **Gables & Gablestones**). The cause of improving society through the practice and development of the arts and sciences, and the encouragement of commerce, was promoted by the Felix Meritis brotherhood. The brotherhood included pioneers in anatomy and astronomy.

Unlike the general upheavals elsewhere, civil unrest was rare in Amsterdam. One exception was the Undertakers' Riot of 1696, which was provoked by city interference in their trade and the imposition of a tax on weddings and funerals. Fifty years later, in 1748, the entire province of Holland was shattered by a series of popular uprisings against the notorious tax farmers (collectors).

Felix Meritis Building

Keizersgracht 324, IW. Tram 1, 2, 5. **Open** _Café_ 5pm-midnight daily. **No credit cards.** Napoleon was once received at this magnificent edifice, designed in 1787 by Jacob Otten Husly. The building was initially constructed for the Felix Meritis brotherhood and has a somewhat chequered past. In the nineteenth century, the fine oval concert hall became the centre of Amsterdam's music scene, until financial problems forced the building's sale to a printing company. In 1932 it was burnt down, but was soon restored. The Dutch Communist Party took residence in 1946 (_see p68_ **Post-war**), and in 1956, the building was attacked as a protest against the Soviet invasion of Hungary. Since the late seventies, it has housed the Amsterdam Summer University (_see p196_ **Students**) and the Shaffy Theatre (_see p126_ **Theatre**).

Frankendael

Middenweg 72, OE. Tram 9. **Open** _Gardens only_ sunrise-sunset daily. **Admission** free.
This is the only surviving 'country house' in the Plantage area, which was the most significant land development in Amsterdam during the eighteenth century. The area south from Plantage Middenlaan was converted into a residential district where rich businessmen constructed such villas as Frankendael. The area had lots of green space which has now been parcelled as Artis Zoo (_see p13_ **Sightseeing**), Oosterpark and Frankendael's grounds (open to the public). You can't enter the villa, but the entrance is rich with Louis XVI ornamentation and there's a fountain with statues of river gods.

The Golden Curve

Herengracht between Leidsegracht and Vijzelstraat, IS. Tram 1, 2, 5, 16, 24, 25.
This stretch of Herengracht has some of Amsterdam's best examples of eighteenth-century architecture. The buildings are faced with expensive sandstone and are wider than most canal houses. Most notable are numbers **475** (architect Hans Jacob Husly, 1730); **485** (Jean Coulon, 1739), **493** and **527** (both of Louis XVI design, 1770). At **284** (Van Brienen House, 1728) there's another Louis XVI façade.

BANKING ON NO FUTURE

The Republic began to lag behind the major European powers in the eighteenth century. The Agricultural and Industrial Revolutions were taking off elsewhere, starting in Britain, but they didn't get off the ground in The Netherlands.

Amsterdam was nudged out of the shipbuilding market by England, and its lucrative textile industry was lost to other provinces, but the city exploited its position as the financial centre of the world – until the final and most devastating Anglo-Dutch War (1780-1784). The British hammered the Dutch fleets, both naval and merchant (which also carried heavy guns), crippling the Dutch's profitable trade with their far-eastern colonies. This was the beginning of the end of prosperity, but the death blow would come not from the English, but from the French.

OCCUPATION

The closest the Dutch had to the republican movements of France and the United States was the Patriot Party. The Patriots attempted to shake off the *stadhouders'* influence in the 1780s, but were foiled, partly by the intervention of the Prince of Orange's brother-in-law, Frederick William II, the king of Prussia, whose troops actually occupied Amsterdam in 1787. Hundreds of Patriots fled to exile in Paris, where their welcome convinced them of Napoleon's philanthropic intentions towards the wealthy Dutch Republic. The Patriots returned in triumph in 1795, backed by a French army of 'advisers'. With massive support from Amsterdam, they proclaimed the Batavian Republic (named after an early barbarian tribe from the mouth of the Rhine).

It sounded too good to be true, and it was. According to one contemporary: 'The French moved over the land like locusts.' Over f100 million (about a billion guilders in today's currency) was extracted from the Dutch people – Amsterdam paid a particu-larly high toll as it was one of the wealthiest cities. According to the French, this sum was appropriated in 'payment' for advice on the restructuring of the Dutch government along revolutionary, republican lines. The French also sent a standing army, all 25,000 of which had to be fed, equipped and billeted by its Dutch 'hosts'. The promised republican ideals seemed increasingly hollow when Napoleon installed one of his numerous brothers as King of The Netherlands. Piling insult on injury, the symbol of Amsterdam's mercantile ascendancy and civic pride, the City Hall on the Dam, was requisitioned as Louis Bonaparte's royal palace, Koninklijk Paleis (*see page 55* **The Golden Age**). Even Louis was disturbed by the increasing impoverishment of a nation that had been one of Europe's most prosperous. After Louis had allowed Dutch smugglers to break Napoleon's blockade of Britain in 1810 and the Low Countries were absorbed into the French Empire.

Government by the French wasn't an unmitigated disaster for the Dutch. The foundations of the modern Dutch state were laid in the Napoleonic period, a civil code was introduced and there were advances in education. However, trade with Britain ceased and the growing price of Napoleon's wars prompted the Dutch to do something about what was a problem of their own making.

London has its Waterloo Station, and Amsterdam has a Waterloo Square – Waterlooplein – for exactly the same reason. The Dutch joined the revolt against France and after Napoleon's defeat at Waterloo in 1815, Amsterdam became the capital of a constitutional monarchy, incorporating what is now Belgium. This was the unity dreamt of by Willem the Silent of Orange before the Treaty Of Utrecht in 1579, and once again an Orange claimed the throne – Willem VI of Orange was crowned King Willem I in 1815. Although the Oranges still reign in the northern provinces to this day, the United Kingdom of The Netherlands, as it then existed, was to last only until 1831.

GABLES & GABLESTONES

The façades of Amsterdam's houses tend to be tall and narrow, offering little scope for ornamentation. Only at the top is there an outburst of creativity in the shaped and often ornate gables at the apex of their roofs. This characteristic is peculiarly Dutch; similar gables exist elsewhere, but none are as elaborately decorated as those in areas of Dutch influence. In Amsterdam the number and variety of gables is impressive; even now almost 7,000 remain. The tradition dates largely from the seventeenth and eighteenth centuries, when a growing population within a finite area – the *grachtengordel* ring of canals – meant that houses were built more closely together. The fact that city taxes were based on the width of a building probably had its effect too. Because of the architectural constraints this gave rise to, builders channelled their creativity upwards into gables, which became at once their signature and an advertisement for their work. The shapes were subject to fashion; gables can be more recent than the house they cap if the occupants were concerned about having the latest design.

Another individual feature to look out for is the gablestone, usually positioned either halfway up the house or just over the door. Before Napoleon instituted a system of street numbers, householders used these plaques to identify their homes. Frequently beautifully crafted and brightly coloured, they bore illustrations giving clues to the identity of the householder; usually his profession, but sometimes his home town or religious persuasion. The variety of occupations depicted illustrates the diversity of trade in seventeenth- and eighteenth-century Amsterdam: they include druggists, fishermen, spinners, butchers, sailors, writers and fruit merchants. Sometimes the professions were represented allegorically or biblically; an apple dealer, for example, was identified by a scene of Adam and Eve in the Garden of Eden. The gablestones are now officially preserved even if the house bearing them is demolished.

Types of gable
The earliest gables are called step gables and, as you would expect from the name, have graded horizontals. An example can be seen at Herengracht 77 (IW). Spout gables, shaped like inverted funnels, are common on early warehouses. You can see bell gables at Reguliersgracht 37 and 39 (IS). These have decorated concave sides and sometimes a rounded top – hence the name. The neck gable, like that at Herengracht 168 (IW), can look similar; it's a protruding rectangle with decorative mouldings filling in the corners at the base. Flatter but even more elaborate is the cornice gable, often with a balustrade.

Gablestones
Because of its working class history, the Jordaan is a good hunting ground for gablestones. There's a large rectangular tableau of elks at Elandsgracht 125 (IW), denoting a tanner's (tanning was a principal industry here in the early seventeeth century), for example, and a stone featuring chairs at a former furniture maker's at Brouwersgracht 52 (IW). At Keizersgracht 104 (IW) a man's hat indicates that a hatmaker lived there; at Keizersgracht 320 (IW) an illustration of Bordeaux harbour reveals the origins of a former occupant; Singel 39 (C) has a Louis XIV-style gable and a stone showing a ship under full sail. Clusters of preserved gablestones can be found at Sint Luciensteeg (IW) and just inside the Spui entrance of the Begijnhof (C), where one shows Abraham sacrificing Isaac. The Begijnhof is also the site of one of only two remaining wooden gables in Amsterdam; that of number 34 dates from 1475.

Between the Occupations

Amsterdam struggled towards economic recovery in the nineteenth century, but was knocked reeling by the 1930s' slump and the German invasion. *Sophie Marshall* chronicles the period.

When the French were finally defeated and left Dutch soil in 1813, Amsterdam emerged with a fancy title – the capital of the new kingdom of The Netherlands – but very little else. The city wasn't even the seat of government. With its coffers almost totally depleted and its colonies abroad occupied by the British, Amsterdam would have to fight hard for recovery.

Recovery was made more difficult by two huge barriers. First, Dutch colonial assets had been reduced to present-day Indonesia (then known as Dutch East Indies), Surinam and the odd island in the Caribbean. The second problem was the Dutch failure to jump onto the Industrial Revolution bandwagon. The Netherlands has few natural resources to exploit, and Dutch business preferred to keep its hands clean by relying on the power of sail. Moreover, Amsterdam's opening to the sea, the Zuider Zee, was too shallow to accommodate the new, larger, steam-powered ships.

In an attempt to link the city to the North Sea port of Den Helder, the circuitous Great North Holland Canal was dug in 1824. But because it had too many bridges and locks, it was slow and thus expensive. Rotterdam gradually took over the capital's position as the most progressive industrial centre.

PROSPERITY RETURNS

Prosperity returned to Amsterdam after the 1860s. The city readjusted its economy to meet modern demands, and its trading position was greatly improved by the building of two canals. The opening of the Suez Canal in 1869 speeded up the passage to the Orient, producing a giant increase in commerce. But what the city needed most was easy access to the major shipping lanes of Northern Europe. Opened in 1876,

the North Sea Canal (from Amsterdam to IJmuiden) enabled Amsterdam to take advantage of German industrial trade and to become The Netherlands' greatest ship-building port again – at least temporarily.

Industrial machinery was introduced late to Amsterdam. However, by the late nineteenth century, the city had begun to modernize production of the luxury goods it would become famous for – chocolates, cigars, liquors, beers and cut diamonds.

Although there had been a local railway track between Haarlem and Amsterdam since 1839, the city finally got a major rail link and a new landmark in 1889. Centraal Station (*see page 3* **Essential Information**) was designed by PJH Cuypers, who was known mainly for neo-Gothic churches. The terminal was initially intended to be in the Pijp, but it was finally decided that the track should run along the Zuider Zee, shutting the city off from its seafront; much local objection ensued. There was also much controversy when the Rijksmuseum (*see page 100* **Museums**) was sited at what was then the fringe of the city, and about the selection of Cuypers as its architect. With Catholics demanding a neo-Gothic style and Protestants advocating neo-Renaissance, the result was, like Centraal Station, uniquely eclectic and led to the museum being ridiculed as a 'cathedral of the arts'; yet perhaps that is an appropriate label, given the contemporary boom in culture.

In 1877, the Carré Theatre opened (*see page 126* **Theatre**), to be followed a year later by the Concertgebouw (*see page 130* **Music: Classical & Opera**), then by the neo-Renaissance municipal theatre, the Stadsschouwburg

(1894; *see page 126* **Theatre**), the Stedelijk Museum (1895; *see page 111* **Galleries**) and, in 1926, by the Tropen Institute (now the Tropenmuseum, *see page 100* **Museums**). The city's international standing improved to the point that in 1928 it hosted the Olympic Games.

Beurs van Berlage (Berlage Stock Exchange)

Damrak 277, C (626 5257/fax 620 4701). Tram 4, 9, 16, 24, 25. **Open** *office and enquiries* 9am-5pm Mon-Fri.

This former stock exchange, designed by Hendrik Petrus Berlage (1856-1934), looks like a cross between an Italian *palazzo* and a railway station. It was intentionally experimental in its use of modern technology. Berlage advanced principles that would guide modernism: the building's function was fundamental to the design. Where Berlage departed from purists like *De Stijl* (*see below* **Openluchtschool** *under* **A New Metropolis**) was in his use of other arts, such as sculpture and decoration, to symbolize the building's place in society. The Beurs displays all these ideas and is now revered as one of modernism's embryonic masterpieces. However, it aroused outrage when it opened in 1903. It is now used for cultural events and trade fairs.

SOCIAL FACETS

Social welfare in Amsterdam, for so long dependent on the goodwill of the élite, was transformed in the nineteenth century. But until prosperity returned in the last third of the century, the living conditions of the working population were appalling. Amsterdam's solution before 1850 was to follow central government policy and round up the destitute, sending them off to do hard agricultural work. Yet, throughout this period, Amsterdam spent a relatively large amount of money on poor relief.

In the second half of the century, however, the notion that assistance only made the poor lazy gained more ground, and relief was cut back. But towards the end of the 1800s, the newly formed trade unions set up some forms of poor relief for their members. Socialist ideas began to permeate, and the way was paved for the development of one of the best social security systems in the world.

A SHORT CUT TO WEALTH?

The story of diamonds in Amsterdam is also the history of social change in the city (to visit working factories, *see page 13*

Sightseeing). Diamond-working in Amsterdam had first been recorded in 1586. Fabulous stones such as the Koh-i-Noor (Mountain of Light) and the giant Cullinan diamond, both among the British crown jewels, were cut by Amsterdammers. But as the industry depended on the discovery of rare stones, it was in a continual state of flux. In the early 1870s, diamond cutters could light cigars with f10 notes (the average weekly wage for the rest of the workforce was then f8) and travel to work in a hansom cab. Yet a decade later, the city would have to issue proclamations prohibiting diamond workers from begging naked in the streets. The working classes, meanwhile, had become more literate and politicized, so the ideas behind the old guild system (*see page 55* **The Golden Age**) took on a new resonance. Funds were established to protect diamond workers during

slumps, and this led to the formation of the first Dutch trade union; numerous other trades soon followed suit.

In the early days of the trade union movement, socialists and the upper classes got on well together, but by the 1880s the early activists had dispensed with their forelock-tugging ways. The movement needed an articulate leader and it found him in Ferdinand Domela Nieuwenhuis (*see below*), who also set up a political party, the Social Democratic Union. The SDU faded into obscurity after a split in 1894, but the splinter group, the Social Democratic Labour Party (SDAP), went on to win the first-ever socialist city-council seat for the diamond workers' union chief, Henri Polak in 1901. The SDAP went on to introduce the welfare state after World War II.

Educational reform was perhaps the greatest step forward made in

the late nineteenth century. A network of free primary schools was set up to teach the working classes the rudiments of reading, writing and arithmetic.

Ferdinand Domela Nieuwenhuis Museum
Herengracht 266, IW (622 5496). Tram 13, 14, 17. **Open** 10am-4pm Mon-Fri; phone first during school holidays as access is through a school. **Admission** free.
See picture and caption.

General Diamond Workers' Union building
Henri Polaklaan, IE.
This building was designed by Berlage to house the offices of The Netherlands' first trade union. Plans are afoot to convert it into a trade union museum, but no date has been set for its opening.

A NEW METROPOLIS
Amsterdam's population had stagnated at around a quarter of a million for two centuries after the Golden Age, but between 1850 and 1900 it more than doubled. This increased labour force was desperately needed to meet the demands of a revitalized economy, but the major problem facing the council was how to house the new workers. Today, the old inner city quarters are desirable addresses, but they used to be home to Amsterdam's poorest. The picturesque Jordaan (*see page 26* **Amsterdam by Area**), where riots broke out with increasing regularity, was occupied primarily by the lowest-paid workers. Canals were used as cesspits and the mortality rate was high. Oddly enough, the Jordaan was the first area in the city to have Tarmac streets. The decision wasn't philanthropic; it came after Queen Wilhelmina had been pelted by cobblestones as she was driven through the Jordaan's streets.

Around the old centre, entirely new neighbourhoods were constructed. The new housing developments – the Pijp (*see page 26* **Amsterdam by Area**), Dapper and Staatslieden quarters – weren't luxurious by any means, and most of them were cheaply built by speculators, but they had simple lavatory facilities (though no bathroom). Wealthier city-dwellers found elegance and space in homes built around Vondelpark and in the south of the city.

The expensive fashions for art nouveau and art deco largely bypassed

This statue of **Ferdinand Domela Nieuwenhuis** (see under **A Short Cut to Wealth**), *on Haarlemmerplein (OW), is a tribute to the man who became the father of Dutch socialism. Once a Protestant pastor, Nieuwenhuis (1846-1919) threw himself into the task of making the lower classes politically aware. His growing influence worried employers, and many of them co-operated in engineering social change. The* **Ferdinand Domela Nieuwenhuis Museum** *pays a touching homage to the great man in the form of personal effects, his library, letters, photos and some great posters. Documents focus on the labour movement of the period and on Nieuwenhuis's life.*

the city, although the Tuschinsky Cinema (*see page 122* **Film**) is a fine example of art deco, and the luxurious café of the otherwise 'Amsterdam School' **American Hotel** of 1900-1902 (*see p39* **Accommodation**) has both art nouveau and art deco features. Perhaps the paucity of these styles is due to the Dutch inclination towards elegant functionalism, rather than decadent decoration. The purist **De Stijl** movement (*see below* **Openluchtschool**) took modernism to an extreme.

Greenpeace building

Keizergracht 174, IW.
This former headquarters of the ELHB insurance company is one of the few decent examples of art nouveau in the city. Designed by G van Arkel in 1906, it's now the head office of environmental campaigners Greenpeace.

Openluchtschool (Open-air School)

Cliostraat 36-40, OS. Tram 5, 24. Bus 26.
This is Amsterdam's main example of the **De Stijl** movement, which started in 1917 in Rotterdam with Theo van Doesburg's journal *De Stijl* (The Style). The movement soon included the painter Piet Mondrian and the furniture-maker and architect, Gerrit Rietvelt. Its design group advocated severe functionalism in order to house large numbers of people. Influenced by Soviet constructivism, it was contemporary with the German *Bauhaus*. Characteristic features include rectangular planes and grids in white, black and primary colours, arranged in harmony. This school was a typically idealistic project. There are huge windows and classroom-sized balconies for *al fresco* teaching, which embraced the fitness ethic of the period. The best *De Stijl* buildings are JJP Oud's **Café de Unie** in Rotterdam and the **Rietvelt-Schröder House** in Utrecht, which looks like a Mondrian painting projected in 3-D (for both, *see page 208* **The Randstad**).

WAR & DEPRESSION

The city didn't fare badly in the first two decades of this century, but Dutch neutrality during World War I brought problems. While the élite lined their pockets selling arms to both sides, the poor were confronted with continual food shortages. In 1917, with food riots erupting, especially in the Jordaan, the city had to open soup kitchens and introduce rationing.

The army was called in to suppress another outbreak of civil unrest in the Jordaan in 1934. This time the cause was unemployment, endemic throughout the industrialized world after the Wall Street Crash of 1929. In the worst year of the Depression, 1936, historians estimate that 19 per cent of the workforce was unemployed.

Unfortunately, the humiliation of means testing for unemployment benefit meant that many families suffered in hungry silence. Many Dutch workers even moved to Germany where Hitler's National Socialism was creating a mass of new jobs. At home, Amsterdam initiated extensive public works, under the 1934 General Extension Plan, whereby the city's southern outskirts were developed for public housing (*see below* **The Amsterdam School**). The city was just emerging from the Depression by the time the Nazis invaded in May 1940.

THE AMSTERDAM SCHOOL

Mention council housing projects and most people think of cheaply constructed, darkly oppressive tower blocks. However, when the rest of Europe was smashing itself to pieces in World War I, the Dutch managed to create a model of successful urban planning. The *Amsterdaamse School* produced both superlative public buildings and housing on a human scale with an individualistic touch.

Prevailing socialist thinking elevated the status of the working class, and the council determined that workers' homes should be models and of high quality. HP Berlage was the city council's chief architect of the period (*see above* **Beurs van Berlage** *under* **Prosperity Returns**) and he implemented its *Plan Zuid* (plan for Amsterdam South). Michel de Klerk and Pieter Kramer, two leading Amsterdam School architects, were commissioned by the council. They came up with an innovative design: long, low housing blocks, culminating in landmark towers, and incorporating expressionist features such as curved and slanted walls, ruffles of brick and playful shapes for windows.

Through his architecture, Berlage hoped to encourage the working

classes to adopt a more bourgeois way of living. He designed kitchens to be tiny spaces so people would be obliged to eat in the dining room he provided. Also, he usually set window sills at eye- rather than waist-level, to prevent people from frittering away the day, gossiping with neighbours. One of the best preserved examples of this kind of architecture is at **Hembrugstraat**, OW, built by De Klerk in 1917. The end of the housing block has an extraordinary tower which serves no useful purpose (like most of De Klerk's elaborations). Other examples include the apartments at **Henriëtte Ronnerplein** (1921-23),

in Amsterdam South, and housing at **PL Takstraat**, OS (1921-22), which is dominated by the fanciful pleated walls of the Dageraad building (*see picture*). These projects have widely been judged successes by residents as well as architects.

Some of the most distinctive examples of Amsterdam School architecture are not houses, but public buildings. A VVV walking tour takes in many of the prominent buildings of the genre (for details, *see page 13* **Sightseeing**). The earliest example (1911-16) is the peculiar, turreted **Scheepvaarthuis** (Shipping Building), Prins Hendrikkade 8, C. Designed by Kramer and De Klerk, it's decorated with maritime reliefs and is sculptural both inside and out. The **Lydia House**, Roelof Hartplein, OS, is a witty variation by De Klerk on the typical Dutch *buurthuis* (neighbourhood house), a community centre. In the Zaanstraat neighbourhood (OW) is the extraordinary **Spaarndammerbuurt Post Office** (1917-20) Spaarndammerplantsoen, OW. This squat community centre has a ruffled, drum-like tower and eccentrically shaped window frames.

World War II

The Nazi occupation took The Netherlands by surprise. *Kees Neefjes* describes how Anne Frank and the Dutch Resistance became international symbols of courage.

Remarkably, Amsterdam endured World War II without being flattened by bombs, although a lot of its buildings, infrastructure and inhabitants were reduced to a terrible state by Nazi occupation. The Holocaust also left an indelible scar on a city whose population in 1940 was ten per cent Jewish. You can trace these experiences through the photographs and relics of the small World War II collection at the Amsterdams Historisch Museum (*see page 100* **Museums**).

INVASION

Early in the morning of 10 May 1940, German bombers mounted a surprise attack on Dutch airports and military barracks in order to destroy the Dutch air force. The government and people had hoped that The Netherlands could remain neutral, as they had in World War I. Thus the armed forces were unprepared for war. Yet the Dutch aimed to hold up the Germans until the British and French could come to their assistance. This hope was in vain. Queen Wilhelmina and the government fled to London to form a government in exile, leaving Supreme Commander Winkelman in charge of state authority. Many Dutch considered this cowardice, but later the Queen's broadcasts on *Radio Oranje* boosted the morale of the Dutch public and the Resistance. She and the government would not return to The Netherlands until the liberation in summer of 1945, *see below* **Liberation**.

The centre of Rotterdam was destroyed by bombing, and when the Germans threatened the same for cities like Utrecht and Amsterdam, Winkelman capitulated on 14 May 1940. French and Dutch troops continued to fight in Zeeland, but succumbed three days later.

The Dutch colonies of Indonesia and New Guinea were also invaded (by the Japanese), in January 1942. After their capitulation on 8 March, many Dutch colonials were imprisoned in Japanese concentration camps and the Indonesian nationalists Soekarno and Hatta proclaimed an independent republic.

NAZIFICATION

Hitler appointed Arthur Seyss-Inquart, an Austrian Nazi, as *Rijkskommissaris* (State Commissioner) of The Netherlands. His policy was to tie the Dutch economy to the German one and to *nazificeren* (Nazify) Dutch society. The National Socialist Movement (NSB) was the largest and most important Fascist political party in The Netherlands, although it was much smaller than those in Italy and Germany. In the 1939 elections the NSB won less than five per cent of the votes, but it was, of course, the only Dutch party not prohibited during the occupation. Its doctrine greatly resembled German Nazism, but the NSB wanted to maintain Dutch autonomy under the direction of Germany. In the beginning the Germans operated very carefully, hoping to reduce resistance to a minimum and win the population over to the National Socialist cause. Thus, not all important posts were delegated to NSB members, because most Dutch rejected them as racists and betrayers of their country.

During the first years of the war, the Nazis allowed most people to continue their normal daily life relatively undisturbed. But because of rationing, the Dutch became vulnerable to the black market and cinemas and theatres eventually closed because of curfews, censorship and disrupted transport, although there were no travel restrictions. This soft approach failed to Nazify the locals, so the Germans adopted more aggressive measures. Dutch men were forced to work in German industry and economic exploitation assumed appalling shapes. In April 1943 all Dutch soldiers – who'd been captured during the invasion, then released in summer 1940 – were ordered to give themselves up as prisoners of war. In an atmosphere of deep shock and outrage, strikes broke out during April and May throughout the country, only to be bloodily suppressed.

COLLABORATION

Ordinary people, as well as the political and economic élites, at first didn't have to choose between collaboration and resistance. They 'accommodated' their daily routines as much as possible to the new situation. In this cautious atmosphere the Germans took the first measures against the Jews (see below The Holocaust). As Nazi policies became more virulent, opposition swelled and a growing minority of people were confronted with the difficult choice of whether to obey German measures or to resist. But most of the population were neither collaborators nor Resistance workers.

There were many patterns of collaboration. Some people joined the NSB, others intimidated Jews, were involved in economic collaboration, or betrayed people in hiding or members of the Resistance; a few even signed up for German military service. In Amsterdam several social institutions gave information about Jews to the Germans, who had lied by saying that the Jews would be employed in the German camps. The most shocking institutional collaboration was by the police, who dragged Jews out of their houses for deportation. Sometimes on these *razzias* (raids) they even caught Jews who weren't on their lists. After the war between 120,000 and 150,000 people were arrested for collaborating. Mitigating circumstances – as in the case of NSB members who helped the Resistance – made judgements very complicated and eventually 60,000 people were brought to justice.

RESISTANCE

The Resistance comprised chiefly Calvinist Protestants and Communists. The latter gained much public support and many red flags were to be flown after liberation, although the Protestant élite ensured that there was no communist take-over. Anti-Nazi activities took several forms. Illegal newspapers, unlike the censored press, kept the population properly informed and urged resistance; copies can be seen in the **Verzetsmuseum Amsterdam** *below*.

There were many kinds of underground groups, which spied for the Allies, fought an armed struggle against the Germans through assassination and sabotage, or falsified identity cards. A national organization took care of people who wanted to hide because they refused to work in German industry. It also helped the railway strikers, Dutch soldiers and illegal workers who were being searched for by the Germans. Other groups helped Jews into hiding, which was a lot more difficult and risky. By the end of the war, more than 300,000 people had gone underground in The Netherlands.

Resistance Monuments

Apollolaan *at Beethovenstraat, OS. Tram 5, 24, 65, 67.*
H M van Randwijkplantsoen *Singelgracht at Weteringlaan, IS. Tram 6, 7, 10, 16, 24, 25.*
Weteringplantsoen, *IS. Tram 6, 7, 10, 16, 24, 25.*
The **Apollolaan** sculpture of three men waiting to be shot on 24 October 1944 as a reprisal against the killing of a member of the German Sicherheits Dienst, an espionage organization, by the Resistance. Sculpted by Jan W Havermans, it was unveiled in 1954. The **H M van Randwijk Pleasure Garden** was named after an important Resistance figure. The 1970 monument, designed by Gerda van der Laan, has the text: 'A people that gives in to tyrants will lose more than body and goods; then the light is extinguished.' Nearby on **Weteringplantsoen** 35 people were shot on 12 March 1945, as punishment for a Resistance attack on Rauter, head of the German police in The Netherlands. The sculpture of a man shot with a bugle in his hand is by G Bolhuis.

Verzetsmuseum Amsterdam (Museum of the Resistance)

Lekstraat 63, OS (644 9797). Tram 4, 25.
Open 10am-5pm Tue-Fri; 1-5pm Sat, Sun, public holidays. *Closed* 25, 31 Dec; 1 Jan.
Admission f3.50; f1.75 under-17s; f1.75 CJP card holders; f8.75 family ticket (2 adults and 2 children); free with Museum Card; group discount (min 15 people). **No credit cards.**
This collection is housed in a former synagogue in a part of town, the Rivierenbuurt, where Anne Frank lived between escaping Nazi Germany in 1933 and hiding in the Prinsengracht attic. In addition to the permanent collection (*see* **picture and caption**), exhibitions highlight contemporary developments such as extreme right wing Dutch political parties, about which there is general concern. There are other Resistance Museums in Leeuwarden in Friesland (*see p213* **The Provinces**) and Gouda (*see p208* **The Randstad**).
Wheelchair access and toilets for the disabled.

THE HOLOCAUST

'I see how the world is slowly becoming a desert, I hear more and more clearly the approaching thunder that will kill us,' wrote Anne Frank in her diary on 15 July 1944. As well as to Jews, Anne's words applied to the less publicly mourned gypsies, homosexuals, the mentally handicapped

and political opponents, who were all severely persecuted during the war (*see below* **Gypsies & Homosexuals**). The genocide of the Jews, especially, was carried out in an astonishingly accurate and systematic way by means of the latest industrial techniques. Anti-semitism had not been as virulent as in Germany, France or Austria. Yet most – but not all – of the Dutch closed their eyes to the persecution, because of which there's still a feeling of national guilt.

There were three stages to the Holocaust. First came measures to enforce the isolation of the Jews: the ritual slaughter of animals was prohibited, Jewish government employees were dismissed, Jews were banned from public places such as restaurants, cinemas and libraries and, eventually, all Jews were made to wear a yellow Star of David. Some non-Jewish Dutch courageously wore the badge as a demonstration of solidarity. Concentration was the second stage. From the beginning of 1942 all Dutch Jews were obliged to move to three areas in Amsterdam, which were isolated by signs, drawbridges and barbed wire.

The final stage was deportation.

Between July 1942 and September 1943, most of the 140,000 Dutch Jews were deported, via **Kamp Westerbork** (*see below* **Gypsies & Homosexuals**), to death camps, where over 100,000 were killed. Although some 27,000 went underground, about half of these were in the end captured and sent to the gas chambers. In 1941, public outrage at the first deportations from Amsterdam provoked the most dramatic protest against the anti-semitic terror, the impressive **February Strike** (*see below* **Dokworker statue**).

Anne Frankhuis

Prinsengracht 263, IW (626 4533). Tram 13, 14, 17. **Open** *Sept-May* 9am-5pm Mon-Sat; 10am-5pm Sun, public holidays; *June-Aug* 9am-7pm Mon-Sat; 10am-7pm Sun, public holidays. *Closed* 25 Dec, 1 Jan, Yom Kippur. **Admission** f5; f3 10-17s; free under-10s; group discount. **No credit cards.**
Along with thousands of other visitors to the Anne Frankhuis, you can see the tiny annexe at the rear of the building where Anne wrote her famous diary (*see p66* **picture and caption**), which gives a harrowing impression of the living conditions of people who went into hiding. The archive contains a photo album of Mr Dussel, one of the Jews in hiding with Anne, which was found in 1978 at Waterlooplein Flea Market. There's also an exhibition on the Jews, and their persecution in the war, and a display of different editions of the diary (known as *Het Achterhuis – The*

The imaginative ways in which the Dutch undermined the Nazi occupation can be seen in the **Verzetsmuseum** *(see under* **Resistance***). Artefacts, documents and interactive displays explain matters such as sabotage, espionage and the February Strike. You can hear radio broadcasts, look around a mock-up hiding place and see this bicycle-powered machine used to print illegal papers. Much of today's Dutch press started underground, namely: Het Parool (The Password), Vrij Nederland (Free Netherlands), Trouw (Loyalty) and De Waarheid (The Truth, now called Forum); see page 145* **Media***. Early editions of these are on display.*

The **Anne Frankhuis** (see under **The Holocaust**) *is one of Amsterdam's most visited sights, all because the diary of a Jewish girl who hid here from the Nazis became one of the most widely read books in history. Having already fled from persecution in Germany in 1933, Anne, her sister Margot, her parents and four other Jews went into hiding on 5 July 1942. Living in an annexe behind Prinsengracht 263, they were sustained by friends who risked everything to help them but were not themselves betrayed. Eventually, on 4 August 1944, they were all arrested and transported to concentration camps, where Anne died along with Margot and their mother. Her father, Otto Frank, survived and decided that Anne's moving and perceptive diary should be published.*

Annexe – in The Netherlands). Exhibitions chart current developments in racism, neo-Fascism and anti-semitism; there are explanatory texts in English. The museum is managed by the Anne Frank Foundation, whose aims are combating prejudice, discrimination and oppression. The Educational Service devises special programmes for schools and other groups. A **statue of Anne Frank** by Mari Andriessen (1977) stands where Westermarkt and Prinsengracht meet. *Documentation department: Keizersgracht 192, IW (626 4533). Tram 13, 14, 17. Open 1-5pm Mon-Fri for reference.*

Dokworker statue
Jonas Daniel Meijerplein, C. Tram 9, 14. See p67 **picture and caption.**

Hollandse Schouwburg (Dutch Theatre)
Plantage Middenlaan, IE. Tram 14.
For about 50,000 Jews the Hollandse Schouwburg was their last residence in Amsterdam and there's a monument here to all those deported between 1940 and 1945. The Germans had formed the Jewish Council, a so-called interest group for Dutch Jews, whose members were forced to prepare the deportations of their own people. One member was Etty Hillesum, whose published diary, *Etty: A Diary*, recounts her voluntary decision to go to Westerbork (she ended up at Auschwitz), explaining the fatalistic submissiveness of so many Dutch Jews as a refusal to play the role of victim in an unequal fight.

Jews who didn't show up voluntarily for 'work' in Germany were dragged out of their houses or hiding places and brought to this building, which had been a Jewish theatre since 1941. In the theatre there was a Resistance group led by Walter Süskind, who helped Jews – children above all – to escape deportation; there's a plaque here to his memory.

Holocaust Monuments
Ravensbrückmonument *Museumplein, OS. Tram 2, 3, 5, 12, 16.*
Jewish Resistance Monument
Zwanenburgwal at Amstel, C. Tram 9, 14.
The **Women of Ravensbrück** memorial by J van Santen, G Eckhardt and F Nix was unveiled in 1975. Light flickers from a central silver column to illuminate metal panels set in a semi-circle; the text runs, 'For women who to the utmost kept saying no to Fascism'. The memorial to the dead of the **Jewish Resistance**, designed by JJ Glatt and made by EM Glatt, is a column of black marble which bears the quote from The Bible: 'If my eyes were a well of tears I would cry day and night for the fallen fighters of my beloved people'.

Joods Historisch Museum
Jonas Daniel Meijerplein 24, C (626 9945). Tram 9, 14. **Open** 11am-5pm daily; *closed* Yom Kippur. **Admission** f7; f3.50 10-17s; free under-10s and with Museum Card. **No credit cards.**
The Jewish Historical Museum, located in the former Ashkenazic synagogue complex,

has a permanent exhibition on the Holocaust, but also much else. The displays, with explanations in English, are divided into three subjects: Jewish identity, Jewish religion and culture, and the history of the Dutch Jews. The Museum won the Museum Award of the Council of Europe in 1989, and also hosts exhibitions on different subjects. *See also p100* **Museums.**

GYPSIES & HOMOSEXUALS
The Nazis wanted to eliminate Dutch gypsies in as systematic a way as they had dealt with German gypsies much earlier. On 16 May 1944 the Dutch police were ordered to arrest all the gypsies in the country. They deported 578 to **Westerbork** transit camp (*see below*), but 279 of them were returned home because, according to Nazi race laws, they weren't gypsies. More than 200,000 European gypsies, about 200 of them Dutch, were exterminated in concentration camps. The Nazis exploited the prejudices of many Dutch against gypsies, whose slaughter was virtually ignored.

Homosexuals were also threatened with extermination, but because they were not easily recognizable their persecution had a less systematic character. Public morality acts prohibited homosexual behaviour and gay pressure groups ceased their activities. Gays were sometimes arrested in bars and sent to the German labour service, and men arrested for other activities were punished more severely if it was found out that they were gay. Amsterdam has the world's first memorial to persecuted gays, the **Homo-monument** (*see page 169* **Gay Amsterdam**), which appropriately incorporates pink triangles in its design, turning the Nazi badge of persecution into a symbol of pride.

Gypsy monument
Museumplein, OS. Tram 2, 3, 5, 12, 16.
The *hel van vuur* (hell of fire) sculpture by Heleen Levano, unveiled in 1978, was the world's first monument to gypsy persecution by the Nazis. The gypsies hold a commemoration ceremony here every 1 August.

Kamp Westerbork
Herinneringscentrum (Remembrance Centre) *Oosthalen 8, Hooghalen, Drenthe.* **Getting there** *Car Centre and site of Kamp are signed from A28 between Hoogeveen and Assen (05939 600). No public transport.* **Open** *Centre* 9.30am-5pm Mon-Fri; 1-5pm Sat, Sun; *Site of Kamp* 24 hours daily. **Admission** *Centre* f3.50; f1.50 8-18s, CJP card holders; free under-8s; group discount (min 10 people); *Site of Kamp* free. **No credit cards.**
Westerbork transit camp was originally built in 1939 to handle Jews who fled to The Netherlands from Nazi Germany. Between

1942 and 1945, Jews and gypsies passed through the camp and were treated relatively well, because the Germans wanted them to believe they were going to Germany to work, not to die. Today, the site is parkland. Informed by text panels, you can see the house of a camp commandant, a cellar, a small pill-box bunker, a reconstruction of a watch-tower and traces of canals, although the housing sheds have been demolished. A monument by Ralph Prins symbolizes the ascension of the prisoners' souls using railway track (from the line to the death camps) bent up towards the sky. The Remembrance Centre is a 2½km (1½ mile) car drive away (the centre has just three cycles and there are no buses). It has several exhibitions: on Westerbork Camp; on World War II in The Netherlands, stressing the Holocaust; on the history of Dutch Jewry; and a duplicate of the Netherlands display in Poland's Auschwitz Museum. You can also see some drawings by two young Westerbork prisoners.
Books for reference and sale. Toilet for the disabled. Tours by prior arrangement. Wheelchair access.

HUNGER WINTER

The 'Hunger Winter' of 1944 was the result of three developments. The supply of coal had ceased after the liberation of the south (*see below* **Liberation**), and a railway strike, called by the Dutch government in exile in London to hasten German defeat, was disastrous for the supply of food. In retaliation for the strike, the Germans damaged Schiphol Airport and the harbours of Rotterdam and Amsterdam, and resorted to stealing cars, bicycles, ships, machines, food, textiles, fuel and so on. In Amsterdam, walking became the only means of transport, domestic refuse was no longer collected, sewers overflowed and the population, suffering malnutrition and cold, was vulnerable to disease.

There were three survival strategies. The first was stealing food. More than 20,000 trees were cut down, four million brick-sized wooden sleepers were taken from tram rails and 4,600 buildings were demolished. Floors, staircases, joists and rafters were plundered, causing the collapse of many houses, particularly those left by deported Jews; Jodenbreestraat and Sint Antoniesbreestraat were ruined. The second scheme was black marketeering. At the end of the war the Dutch were given vouchers for food, clothes and fuel. But supplies were scarce and many people couldn't even afford to buy their allowance, let alone the expensive produce on the black market. The last resort was 'hunger expeditions', whereby citizens took pushcarts to the countryside and tried to buy food from farmers. By the end

The **Dokworker statue** *(see under* **The Holocaust***), sculpted by Mari Andriessen, commemorates an anti-Nazi protest unparalleled in occupied Europe. In February 1941, members of the Jewish Resistance got into a fight with Dutch Nazis, who had been intimidating and terrorizing Jews. When one of the Fascists was killed, the SS and the 'Grüne Polizei' (Dutch Police) rounded up 400 Jews here on J D Meijerplein and deported them to Mauthausen for execution. In protest, the local population started a general strike on 25 February, led by dockers and transport workers. After just two days, the strike was suppressed with brutal violence. As a warning against future anti-semitism, and recently to stress the plight of Soviet Jews, a ceremony is held at the statue every 25 February.*

of winter, 20,000 people had died of starvation and disease and much of the city was damaged.

LIBERATION

The Allies liberated the south of The Netherlands on 5 September 1944, *Dolle Dinsdag* (Mad Tuesday). But celebrations in the north were premature because the Allies' priority was to reach Germany. Complete liberation came after the Hunger Winter (*see above*) on 5 May 1945, when it became apparent that The Netherlands was the most badly hit country in Western Europe. In spite of the chaos, destruction, hunger and the loss of so many lives, there were effusive celebrations. But in Amsterdam tragedy struck on 7 May, when German soldiers opened fire on a crowd gathered to welcome their Canadian liberators, killing 22 people.

Nationaal Monument

Dam Square, C. Tram 1, 2, 4, 5, 9, 13, 14, 16, 17, 24, 25.
Unveiled on 4 May 1956, this national memorial was erected for all the Dutch who lost their lives in the war. The 22m (72 ft) obelisk decorated with sculpted figures was designed by De Stijl architect JJP Oud and sculptor John Raedecker. It's fronted by two lions (national symbols) and embedded in the wall behind it are urns containing soil from each province and from the colonies of Indonesia, Surinam and The Netherlands Antilles. Every year, on 4 May, all the Dutch war victims are commemorated here in a remembrance cere-

mony (liberation feasts take place on 5 May); *see p36* **Amsterdam by Season.**

National War & Resistance Museum

Museumpark 1, Overloon, Noord Brabant; 35 miles south of Nijmegen (04788 1820). **Open** 9.30am-6pm daily. **Closed** 1 Jan. **Admission** f6; f4 13-19s, CJP card holders; f3 4-12s; free under-4s, with Museum Card; group discount (min 20 people). **No credit cards.** Overloon was the site of intense fighting (27 Sept-14 Oct 1944) as the Allies pushed towards Germany; east of the town is the British war cemetery. Set in parkland, the Nationaal Oorlogs- en Verzetsmuseum displays relics of both Allied and German militaria. There are some fascinating documents and photographs, plus tanks, aircraft and a V-1 flying bomb.

Nieuwe Oosterbegraafplaats Cemetery

Kruislaan 126, OS (694 0074). Tram 4. **Open** 8am-4pm Mon-Sat; 10am-4pm Sun. This cemetery has several Allied war graves, many of soldiers only 'known unto God'. The three most notable memorials are in section 76. The **Buchenwald Monument** is a flat, white stone with two hands holding an urn, which the text says contains soil from every country whose citizens were among those killed at Buchenwald concentration camp. The famous Dutch writer-sculptor Jan Wolkers made the **Never Again Auschwitz** memorial with the words *nooit meer Auschwitz* standing in glass letters on a plate of glass. In a sunken urn containing the ashes of Jews from Auschwitz are three broken mirrors, so that heaven will never again be reflected perfectly. A statue of a woman waving a flag represents **Resistance** fighters whose deaths, says the text, teach us that tyrants cannot prevail where people refuse to be slaves.

Post-war

After the war, workaholic Amsterdam witnessed radical Provos, rioting squatters and hash-addled hippies. *Mark Fuller* tunes in and tells it how it was.

The Netherlands was deeply scarred by the German occupation, losing about ten per cent of all housing, 30 per cent of industry and 40 per cent of its total production capacity. The transport system had been immobilized and some of the country's dykes had been blown up, leaving large areas flooded. Amsterdam tried to put a brave face on its pains. Although it had escaped the bombing raids which devastated Rotterdam, it had borne the brunt of the deportations, and only 5,000 out of a pre-war total Jewish population of 80,000 remained.

NATIONAL REVIVAL

Despite intense poverty and drastic shortages of food, fuel and building materials, the Dutch tackled the massive task of post-war recovery and restoration with the spirit of the Resistance. There was a strong sense of optimism, excitement and unity, which was sustained until the end of the forties. In 1948, people threw street parties, firstly to celebrate the inauguration of Queen Julianna and then the achievements of Amsterdam athlete Fanny Blankers-Koen, who'd won four gold medals at the London Olympics.

For a time, the Dutch political tendency to *verzuilen* (divide up into small, competing interest groups) threatened to undermine this heady mood. Some Dutch flirted briefly with Communism directly after the war, but in 1948 a compromise was struck between the Catholic party KVP and the newly created Labour party PvdA. The two governed in successive coalitions until 1958. Led by Prime Minister Willem Drees, the government resuscitated pre-war social programmes and laid the basis for the country's lavish welfare state. Under the firm but benevolent hand of Drees, the Dutch reverted to the virtues of a conservative, provincial society: decency, hard work and thrift.

The country's first priority after the war was economic recovery. The Amsterdam city council concentrated on reviving the two motors of its economy: Schiphol Airport and the port of Amsterdam, which was boosted by the opening of the Amsterdam-Rhine Canal in 1952. Joining Belgium and Luxembourg in the Benelux bloc brought the country trade benefits and The Netherlands was the first to repay its Marshall Plan loans – $133 million out of a total $978 million received in aid. The authorities dusted off pre-war development plans and embarked on a period of rapid urban expansion. To the west, garden cities were created, such as Sloterplas, Geuzenveld and Osdorp. The architecture was sober, but the setting was airy and spacious. But as people moved out to the new suburbs, businesses moved into the centre (*see page 188* **Business**), worsening congestion on the already cramped roads, which had to deal with an explosive growth in car traffic on top of the trams, buses and push-bikes. Road casualties soared.

A quite unanticipated blow to the economy was the great flood disaster of 1953. An unusually high spring tide broke the sea defences in Zeeland, flooding large sections of south-west Netherlands, claiming almost 2,000 lives and causing billions of guilders of damage. The Delta Works (*see page 213* **The Provinces: Zeeland**) was built to prevent a repetition.

COLONIES & CULTURE

Directly after the war, the Dutch colonies of Indonesia and New Guinea (now West Irian), liberated from Japanese occupation, pushed for independence. With Indonesia accounting for 20 per cent of their pre-war economy, the Dutch were unwilling to hand over power and launched military invasions on 20 July 1947 and 18 December 1948. These could not prevent the transfer of sovereignty to Indonesia on 27 December 1949. The dispute with New Guinea dragged on until 1962, and did much to damage The Netherlands' international reputation. Colonial immigrants, including the later arrival of Surinamese, Turkish and Moroccan 'guest workers', now comprise 16 per cent of the population. Although they have tended to be landed with poorer jobs and housing, racial tension has been relatively low. Only those from The Moluccas, denied independence from Indonesia, have not integrated so well: the Dutch train hijacks in the seventies were carried out by Moluccan separatists.

By the end of the fifties the economy was reviving and the welfare state was in place, but memories of the war lingered and there was much civil unrest. Strikes flared at the port, and council workers defied a ban on industrial action. In 1951, protesters clashed violently with police outside the Concertgebouw (*see page 130* **Music: Classical & Opera**), angered by the appointment of the pro-Nazi Paul van Kempen as conductor of the Concertgebouw Orchestra. In 1956, demonstrators also besieged the Felix Meritis Building, the base of the Dutch communist party CPN from 1946 until the late seventies and now the Shaffy Theatre (*see page 59* **Decline & Fall**, *page 118* **Dance** and *page 126* **Theatre**), hurling stones in outrage at the Soviet invasion of Hungary.

As the fifties progressed, Amsterdammers began to turn back to pre-war pursuits: fashion and interviews with celebrities filled the newspapers and cultural events mushroomed. In 1947, the city had launched the prestigious **Holland Festival**, which is still held every June (*see page 36* **Amsterdam by Season**). The élite held events called 'Boekenbal', where writers met royalty and other dignitaries. New avant-garde artistic movements emerged, notably the COBRA art group (*see page 111* **Galleries**), whose 1949 exhibition at the Stedelijk Museum caused an uproar. The *vijftigers*, a group of experimental poets led by Lucebert, also sent shock waves through the literary establishment. Many of these writers, intellectuals and artists gathered in brown cafés around Leidseplein, particularly **Café Eijlders** (*see page 26* **Amsterdam by Area: Leidseplein**).

Bop Street

2e Leliedwarsstraat 10, IW (622 2845). Tram 13, 14, 17. **Open** 1-6pm Mon-Fri. **No credit cards.**
Memorabilia from the fifties and sixties is stocked here, including badges, leathers and reconditioned watches. The Dutch had a rock 'n' roll culture in the fifties, with rival gangs of *Dijkers* (Rockers from rural polders) and *Pleiners* (Mods who hung out in

trendy Leidseplein) dressing and fighting just like their British counterparts.

SIXTIES HEYDAY

The sixties must go down as one of the most colourful and intoxicating decades in Amsterdam's history. There were genuine official attempts to improve society and make it more prosperous. The IJ Tunnel eased communications to North Amsterdam and the national economy took off. There were high hopes for vast rehousing developments, such as the Bijlmermeer (*see below* **Housing Crisis**), and there was influential new architecture by Aldo van Eyck and Herman Herzberger; *see page 196* **Students** for the latter's University Arts Faculty and Weesperstraat Student Flats and Restaurant.

Yet the generous hand of the welfare state was being bitten: 'Welfare is not well-being', ran a common slogan of the day. Discontent began early in the decade on a variety of issues: the nuclear threat; rampant urban expansion and industrialization; the consumer society and authority in general. Amsterdam then experienced similar popular movements to other West European cities, but with a zaniness and creativity not found elsewhere. Because protest and dissent have always been a vital part of The Netherlands' democratic process, and the Dutch have a habit of keeping things in proportion, many popular demonstrations took a playful form.

Design for Netherlands Railway & ptt Post

Designers in Amsterdam and The Hague have set the world pace in graphics, drawing on the Dutch appetite for avant-garde, spartan design with a touch of fun. You'll encounter their work whether travelling, posting a letter or spending money. International attention was drawn by Gert Dumbar's sixties' redesign of **Netherlands Railways**, from their distinctive colour scheme and signs to their timetable, which is one of the best-selling books in The Netherlands. Dumbar's studio also created a new corporate identity for the **Rijksmuseum** in the eighties and in 1977, with Total Design (the first Dutch design consultancy, set up in 1963, famous for the Schiphol Airport sign system), for **ptt Post**, including many stamps. Since the sixties, the head of ptt Post's design branch, RDE Oxenaar, has modernized Dutch **bank-notes**, introducing vivid colours and the first use of relief points for the blind (*see p221* **Survival**).

Municipal Orphanage

IJsbaanpad 3, OS (676 9753).
Built in 1960-61 behind the Olympic Stadium, this is one of Van Eyck's most important works. Low-level and on a human scale, its modular units were inspired by African styles and in turn became an international model of school architecture. Unfortunately poor construction has threatened its existence, but it may become the College for Visual Arts. In 1981 Van Eyck designed a similarly sensitive building for the **Moederhuis**.

PROVO HAPPENINGS

The feeling of discontent gained focus in 1964, when *ludiek* (happenings) around **'t Lieverdje statue** (*see* **picture and caption**), at Spui, to highlight political or social problems, became the springboard for a new radical subculture, the Provos (from *provocatie* – provocation). Founded by Roel van Duyn, a philosophy student at Amsterdam University, the Provos only numbered about two dozen, but they appealed to a wide group of young people. When police cracked down heavy-handedly on a happening in 1965, clashes followed, culminating in two serious bouts of civil disorder which drew international attention.

On 10 March 1966, protests about the cost of Princess Beatrix's wedding to Claus von Amsberg at the Westerkerk, and about the fact that her groom was German, turned into a riot. Demonstrators threw smoke bombs at the wedding procession and fought police throughout the city. On 13 June, during a demonstration by building workers, the (false) assumption that a marcher's death was caused by police resulted in four days of violent clashes. After a month, Amsterdam's police chief was forced to resign, followed a year later by the city's mayor.

As opinion turned against the council's large-scale planning, the Provos gained increased public support, winning 2.5 per cent of the municipal vote and a seat on the council in 1966. However, their manifesto – the so-called **White Plans** (*see below* **Amsterdam Collection**) – tended towards the naïve and Utopian and by May 1967 the Provos had outgrown themselves and disbanded. Van Duyn's next move was to lead the Kabouters, named after a helpful gnome in Dutch folklore. They set up an alternative 'Orange Free State', with its own 'ministers' and policies, and had considerable success in the early seventies, adopt-

The Lovable Rascal, or **t' Lieverdje statue** (see under **Provo Happenings**), *became famous as the site of the first Provo happenings in 1964. Sculpted by Carel Kreulman, the little figure was donated to the city in 1960 by a cigarette manufacturer. It was proclaimed the emblem of 'tomorrow's addicted consumer' by window-cleaner turned self-proclaimed 'anti-smoke sorcerer and medicine man of the Western asphalt jungle', Jasper Gootveld. He was a founder of the Provo movement, whose happenings on Saturday evenings became a focal point for anti-establishment protest. No longer a hotbed of revolution, Spui, flanked by cafés, is still a meeting-place.*

Painted on one of the few surviving squats, the exuberant **Spuistraat Mural** (see under **Squat Thrust**) *illustrates the squatters' alternative lifestyle. The movement forged links with other anti-establishment groups at home and abroad, even organizing its own communications system, radio station and newspaper. The self-sufficient communities had their own crèches, shops, hairdressers, theatre groups and cafés. Given the lack of council housing, there was outrage at the huge cost of Queen Beatrix's investiture, so her inauguration day – 30 April 1980 – was declared the National Day of Squatting. When revellers joined in with the protest, the festivities degenerated into a full-scale riot.*

ing some of the more realistic White Plans and winning seats in six municipalities (five in Amsterdam). The movement described its form of socialism as not 'of the clenched fist, but of the intertwined fingers, the erect penis, the escaping butterfly...'. It disintegrated in 1981 amid quarrels about ideology.

The Provo actions somewhat concealed the beginnings of the Dutch feminist, gay rights and pacifist movements; for details of these, see page 169 **Gay Amsterdam**, page 176 **Women's Amsterdam** and page 196 **Students**. The changing mentality on the street also affected national politics. New parties emerged such as the pacifist party PSP and the eclectic Democrats 66 (D66), which today is enjoying a popular resurgence. However, they forced little change on the traditional, substantially conservative power base.

Amsterdam Collection

Centrale Bibliotheek, Prinsengracht 587, IW (623 5065). Tram 1, 2, 5, 7, 10. **Open** *1-9pm Mon; 10am-9pm Tue-Fri; 10am-6pm Sat.*
This department of the Central Library holds reams of documents and press clippings on the city's history. With the courteous assistance of the staff, you can refer to, but not borrow, items relating to the city's radical movements. The most significant and publicized radical initiative was the Provo's White Plans. These proposed that the council ban cars from the city centre and provide 20,000 white bicycles for citizens to pick up free of charge and then leave for someone else's use. This evolved into the White Car Plan, whereby small, economical cars would be available at suburban 'stations'. Given a trial run in 1974, it didn't catch on (although Georgetto Guigaro, designer of the VW Golf and Fiat Panda, is reviving the idea). They also hoped to stop reckless driving by placing a white plaster cast of every road victim where their accident occurred. For full library details, *see p221* **Survival**.

Fort van Sjakoo

Jodenbreestraat 24, C (625 8979). Tram 9, 14/Metro Waterlooplein. **Open** *11am-6pm Mon-Fri; 11am-5pm Sat.* **No credit cards.**
Radical politics of the kind championed in the sixties and seventies is the lifeblood of this shop. It stocks books, pamphlets, badges, iconography and other paraphernalia of interest to activists, squatters and right-on browsers.

HIPPY SLEEP-INS

Meanwhile, foreign hippies flocked to the city, attracted by its tolerant attitude to soft drugs. Although the possession of up to 30 grammes (1oz) of hash wasn't decriminalized until 1978, the authorities turned a blind eye to its use in the sixties, preferring to prosecute dealers, who increasingly pushed hard drugs. Amsterdam subsequently suffered a heroin (and AIDS) epidemic and has developed a well-defined drugs policy, *see page 221* **Survival**. The hundred or so smoker's bars selling soft drugs (*see page 91* **Cafés & Bars**) are very much left alone, so long as they don't become too conspicuous, foster civil disorder or sell hard drugs.

The focal points of hippy culture were the **Melkweg** (Milky Way) and **Paradiso** (*see page 135* **Music: Rock, Folk & Jazz** and *page 141* **Night-clubs**), from both of which the pungent aroma of marijuana could allegedly be smelled hundreds of metres away in Leidseplein. Set up in 1969 in a former church, Paradiso became famous for its psychedelic slide shows. In March 1969 John Lennon and Yoko Ono gave the sub-culture global publicity through their 'sleep-in' for peace in the Amsterdam Hilton; the room can now be booked (*see page 39* **Accommodation**).

Towards the end of the decade, with the Dam and Vondelpark becoming unruly camping sites, public tolerance of the hippies waned. After a group of off-duty marines evicted hippies from Centraal Station, the hippy population went into decline. In the seventies, along with most West European cities, Amsterdam's popular culture shifted towards a rougher, tougher expression of disaffected urban youth. Yet Vondelpark, the Melkweg and the Dam remained a Mecca for ageing hippies, even into the eighties.

HOUSING CRISIS

Perhaps the most significant catalyst for discontent in the seventies – which exploded into full-scale civil conflict by the eighties – was housing. Amsterdam's compact size and historic city centre had always been a nightmare for city planners. There was a dire housing shortage and many inner city homes were in need of drastic renovation. The population had swelled during the sixties, reaching its peak (nearly 870,000) by 1964 (later dipping to 673,000). The numbers were swelled by immigrants from The Netherlands' last major colony, Surinam, who came to settle in Amsterdam ahead of the country's independence in 1975. Many of the Surinamese immigrants were dumped in the forbidding **Bijlmermeer** high-rise housing project, which quickly degenerated into a ghetto.

The **Metro** link to the Bijlmermeer is itself a landmark to some of the most violent protests in Amsterdam's recent history. Passionate opposition erupted against the proposed clearance in February 1975 of a particularly sensitive site – the Jewish quarter of the **Nieuwmarkt**. Civil unrest culminated in 'Blue Monday', 24 March 1975, when heavy-handed police tactics once again sparked off violent clashes with residents and over 1,000 supporters. Police fired tear-gas into the homes of those who had refused to move out and battered down doors with armoured cars. Thirty people – over half of them police – were injured and 47 arrested. Despite further clashes a few weeks later, the plans went ahead and the Metro was opened in 1980, though only one of the four lines planned for the city was every completed.

Faced with inner city problems, the city planners were shocked by the fervent opposition to their schemes for large, airy suburbs and the wholesale demolition of old neighbourhoods. It was simply not what people wanted; they cherished the narrow streets, the small squares and cosy corner cafés. The shortage of residential space in the city centre made it a target for property speculators. The public felt very strongly that the council was selling out to big business and complained that the city centre was becoming unaffordable for ordinary people. Eventually, in 1978, the council decided to improve housing through small-scale development, renovating houses street by street. But with an estimated 90,000 people (13 per cent of the city's population) still on Amsterdam's housing list in 1980, there was growing public concern about the shortages.

Bijlmermeer
Amsterdam South-east, OE. Metro Bijlmer.
The city council intended this futuristic estate in the south-east of the city to solve its housing problems. But as so often happens with such ambitious schemes, it fast became a very undesirable address. Designed to the principles of Le Corbusier, the housing blocks had decent interiors and stood in parkland. People were separated from traffic, but they were also separated from each other: it wasn't a community and didn't even get a town centre until the mid-eighties. Rents ended up higher than planned and many people understandably refused to move here from the city centre – however dilapidated their houses were. The city council has since planned to improve some parts and demolish other sections of it – and if you take a Metro ride out there, you'll see why.

Nieuwmarkt Metro Station
Nieuwmarkt, C (GUB Information 627 2727). Tram 9, 14/Metro Nieuwmarkt.
Open 6am-midnight Mon-Fri; 6.30am-midnight Sat; 7.30am-midnight Sun.

The vast **NMB Postbank headquarters** (see under **Down to Business**) *is a monument to Amsterdam's current financial prowess, but is probably the city's oddest building. Unlike a conventional office 'block', it has no right angles; instead there are organic forms and running water in every room, making it the world's most energy-efficient building. Opened in 1987, it was designed by Ton Alberts and Max van Huut to the anthroposophical theories of George Steiner, and is more clearly described by the public as a cross between a sandcastle and a herd of galloping dromedaries. It seems a happier place to work in than the characterless glass towers that were also built in this southern suburb to relieve pressure on the cramped city centre. Group tours can be booked (563 9111), but there's a six-month waiting list.*

As a genuine gesture of tribute, the council dedicated this station to those who fought against its existence. It uses bricks from the demolished houses of what was the city's oldest quarter, and sculptures and photographs of the protests decorate the platform. The modern community buildings now surrounding the Nieuwmarkt have been widely judged a success and the area has a lively character.

SQUAT THRUST
Speculators who left property empty for many years caused acute resentment, which was soon mobilized into direct action – vacant buildings were occupied illegally by squatters. The squatting movement took off through two significant events in 1980. In March, police turned against the squatters for the first time and used tanks to evict squatters from a former office building in Vondelstraat; the ensuing battle attracted hundreds of demonstrators and flung the city into chaos. The building was quickly resquatted, and the movement was further strengthened by the riots on Coronation Day a month later (*see page 70* **picture and caption: Spuistraat squat**). Defeat and the expense of eviction forced the council to rethink its tactics.

In 1982, while the squatting movement reached its peak with an estimated 10,000 members in Amsterdam and a highly organized structure, clashes with police escalated. The eviction of Lucky Luyk, a lavish villa in the select museum area of the city, was the most violent and expensive. Riots went on for three days as demonstrators destroyed property and wrecked cars, forcing the mayor to declare a state of emergency. A year later, Amsterdam had a dynamic new mayor, Ed van Thijn, who took tough action to eradicate the squatters. One of the last of the city's important squats, Wyers, fell amid tear-gas in February 1984. It was pulled down to make way for a Holiday Inn hotel, despite the squatters' coherent plans for a community-oriented refurbishment. The squatters were no longer a force to be reckoned with, but their ideas of small-scale regeneration have become absorbed into official planning.

Café Huyschkaemer
Utrechtsestraat 137, IS (627 0575). Tram 4.
Open *bar* noon-1am Mon-Thur, Sun; noon-2am Fri, Sat; *kitchen* 6-10pm daily. **No credit cards.**

The polarization of Amsterdam society in the eighties is typified by this coffee house. Once a major haunt of squatters, it has since become a super-trendy café (*see p91* **Cafés & Bars**). More authentic is the bar **PH31** (*see p135* **Music: Rock, Folk & Jazz**), housed in an ex-squat, where class warriors are still consoled by political bands.

Spuistraat mural

Spuistraat, opposite Wijdesteeg, C. Tram 1, 2, 5, 13, 14, 17.
See p70 **picture and caption.**

Tetterode

Bilderdijkstraat 165, OW. Tram 3, 12.
One of Amsterdam's biggest squats, Tetterode was bought by the city council in the eighties and rented to the original squatters for a minimal sum, but it still retains its 'squatted' atmosphere. Like the squats of the movement's heyday, this large, rambling former Linotype factory has sprouted numerous small businesses, including hairdressers, a bicycle repair shop, Aschenbach art gallery (*see p111* **Galleries**), a café and Trut night-club (*see p169* **Gay Amsterdam**). A similar example of urban renewal is **Leeuwenberg**. Although some historic buildings suffered at the hands of squatters, this former 1930s milk factory on Zwanenburgwal was rescued from demolition as part of the Stopera construction, *see below* **Stopera!**. It's now refurbished, brightly painted and occupied mostly by its original squatters.

DOWN TO BUSINESS

Born and bred in Amsterdam, Ed Van Thijn embodied a new approach to Dutch politics, and launched a two-pronged plan to raise the city's international profile. Although a socialist, he took tough action against 'unsavoury elements' – hard drug traders, petty criminals, squatters – and upgraded facilities to attract new businesses and tourists. A new national political era also emerged, with the election in 1982 of Rotterdam millionaire Ruud Lubbers as leader of the centre-right coalition government of Christian Democrats and right-wing Liberals (VVD). He saw to it that the welfare system and government subsidies were trimmed to ease the country's large budget deficit, and aimed to revitalize the economy, which had been flagging since the 1973 oil crisis, with more business-like policies; *see page 188* **Business**.

The price of Amsterdam's new affluence (among most groups, except the poorest) seems to be a definite swing towards commercialism. Van Thyn has found it hard to live down a clumsy remark he made

about turning Amsterdam into a 'pleasure park'. Yet the evidence can be seen in the new casino, luxury apartments and shopping complex at the Leidseplein and the massive redevelopment of its docklands (for both, *see page 26* **Amsterdam by Area**.

NMB Postbank headquarters

Bijlmerplein 888, OS. Bus 59, 60, 61, 62, 137/Metro Bullewijk. **Open** 9am-4pm Mon-Fri.
See p71 **picture and caption.**

STOPERA!

The scruffy hordes of squatters have been largely supplanted by the well-groomed yuppie. Flashy cafés, galleries and *nouvelle cuisine* restaurants replaced the alternative scene and a mood of calm settled on the city – with just the occasional glimpse of Amsterdam's dissenting spirit. Apart from housing, the other great issue of the eighties was the Peace Movement, with its attendant anti-Americanism. Van Thijn also pushed through plans to build the **Stadhuis-Muziektheater** (City Hall-Opera House) complex, dubbed '*Stopera*' ('Stop the Opera') by the campaign waged against it. Another classic example of Dutch free expression was provoked by the city's campaign in the mid-eighties to host the 1992 Olympics. Amsterdam became the first city ever to send an (ultimately successful) official anti-Olympics delegation.

Peace Sculpture

Museumplein, OS. Tram 6, 7, 10/bus 26, 65, 66, 67, 170, 179.
Europe's largest anti-nuclear demonstrations were held in Amsterdam (November 1981) and The Hague (October 1983). This white sculpture commemorates the site where 400,000 people protested against the placing of NATO Cruise missiles on Dutch soil, supported by a petition of over four million people – 35 per cent of the population. It depicts two human figures embracing in such a way that they resemble a nuclear warhead. The Dutch insistence on neutrality was mocked by the Americans as 'Hollanditis' and the resultant anti-American sentiment is tatooed on Keizersgracht (between Leliegracht and Brouwersgracht) in graffiti demanding 'US out of everywhere!' A Cruise base was built at Woensdrecht, but USA-USSR arms negotiations aborted the missiles' deployment.

Stadhuis-Muziektheater

Waterlooplein, C (City Council 552 9111).
Tram 9, 14/Metro Waterlooplein.
See **picture and caption.**
See also p13 **Sightseeing**, *p118* **Dance** and *p130* **Music: Classical & Opera.**

The swish **Stadhuis-Muziektheater** (see under **Stopera!**), *designed in 1979 and opened in 1985, is now widely accepted. Yet plans for a new city hall had been in deadlock for most of the century, and the proposal to integrate an opera house was damned as élitist. Its location on a historic site and its f300 million price-tag mobilized the campaign against it, named Stopera – 'Stop the Opera'. Also controversial was the mongrel-like design, since it's the work of three architects – Cees Dam, Wilhelm Holzbauer and Berhnhard Bijvoet. The section pictured above is a bold landmark on the Amstel – particularly when lit at night – and the locals dub it the 'set of dentures'. Inside, the wedding rooms have been individually decorated by artists.*

Amsterdam Today

As the liberal approach of the seventies comes head to head with the hard-line policies of the nineties, *Sara and Jon Henley* examine the issues that will shape the future of Amsterdam.

Many issues Amsterdammers talk, worry and complain about – inside the town hall and out – are common to any major Western city in the nineties. But the legacy of the seventies has given Amsterdam some specific problems; and the city's progressive approach to solving them is being increasingly blunted as Europe's nations slide towards union.

There are two concerns outsiders would expect to be high on Amsterdam's guilt-list: drugs, which are an issue; and sleaze, which is not. Prostitution is contained through tolerant acceptance – residents need not suffer directly from it and it is not a problem that grows every year. But drugs do make people fear for their safety and for that of their children: there is bourgeois disgust at the squalor and petty crime they generate; and there is a strong human concern for addicts who are slowly and visibly destroying themselves.

SERIOUS DRUGS PROBLEM

No-one doubts that, like many Western cities, Amsterdam has a serious drugs problem. In 1989, 60 people were killed by drugs in the city; and 558 kilos (1,230 pounds) of marijuana, 600 kilos (1,323 pounds) of hash, 82.5 kilos (182 pounds) of cocaine and 196.5 kilos (433 pounds) of heroin were seized by the police. Some would say that Amsterdam's problems have been exacerbated by the police's toleration of dope trading. Many Amsterdammers disagree. There is no evidence that dope use automatically escalates into hard drug abuse, they point out. But this does not mean that others are not increasingly angry about the drug-driven degeneration of parts of the old city centre (like the Zeedijk, *see page 26* **Amsterdam by Area:**

Red Light District) or the crimes junkies perpetually and openly commit.

In characteristic style, Amsterdammers have blocked the streets to demonstrate their impatience with what they see as official incompetence in countering the problem. The official approach is still 'softly, softly': serious addicts have been helped by official programmes to provide substitutes and clean needles. There is a policy of acquitting addicts from petty criminal sentences if they agree to attend a treatment centre. But today's officials face a sharpening conflict between the prescriptions of the liberal seventies and a rigid hard-line approach. Mayor Ed van Thijn now has the power to approve police requests to ban problem individuals from the Zeedijk area for up to a fortnight. And as Brussels extends its influence in post-1992 Europe, Amsterdam's unique approach may come under closer scrutiny.

RESURGENT RACISM

The issues of drugs and race are never far apart in Amsterdam: the vast majority of people arrested for drug-related offences in 1989 were from Surinam and Morocco. Amsterdam is not isolated from the resurgent tide of extreme right-wing politics that first washed over Europe in the eighties: three right-wingers (of the inappropriately named *Centrum Partij* or CP and *Centrumdemocraten*) won seats on the city council in the 1989 elections. The Anne Frankhuis (*see page 100* **Museums**) was the epicentre of hefty rumblings in 1990 when it staged an exhibition on the far right, which included displays naming contemporary politicians in Holland and Belgium. The CP wanted the exhibition banned – instead, authorities throughout the country banned CP

press conferences intended to publicize their views. This deprivation of free speech underlines how high passions on the issue run: World War II memories of fascism are as sharp as is the racial tension in largely immigrant areas outside the centre.

The practice of dumping immigrants in places *burgers* don't want to live was not unique to Amsterdam, but attempts are now being made to integrate racial groups. The council's highest-profile responsibility is housing; and its efforts on this aspect of *stadsvernieuwing* (urban renewal) come in for a considerable (if not entirely fair) amount of abuse. The simple fact is that there are not enough homes (in 1989 the council estimated the city's tramps numbered 4,000 and rising).

But approaches to solving this problem are a debate in themselves. The philosophy of providing cheap, council-funded rental homes has spawned budgetary and moral problems: yesterday's impoverished student with a right to cheap rent is today's advertising executive with no intention of quitting that bargain canalside flat. The nineties answer is to build new homes for sale at subsidized prices, which are attracting the better off. But central government, dogged by deficits, is slowing down the rate at which the council can build the new cheap rental flats it needs, and so the problem goes on.

IDENTITY CRISIS

Amsterdammers are now less in control of housing matters than ever before. The squats that sprouted throughout the city in the seventies are being emptied with less and less ceremony. In some cases, the council buys a squatted building cheap from its disheartened owner and converts it into cheap housing in consultation with the squatters. But this option is not always open: owners aware of the post-1992 potential value of their investment won't play ball, and squatters are increasingly seen as cynically manipulating the council's conscience as a way of securing a cheap home. The ideologically motivated squatter protesting with reason is, the view seems to be, all but extinct.

Fears that *stadsvernieuwing* may mean nothing more than accentuating existing problems are perhaps most aptly illustrated by doubts about the showpiece development plans for the banks of the river IJ on either side of Centraal Station. An IJ boulevard – flanked by offices, hotels and, last and maybe least, homes – is to be the Manhattan of old Amsterdam, securing its place as a major metropolis in unified Europe. The NMB Postbank, which is putting the financing together, has already said it is not sure how profitable the multi-billion guilder plan will be. Socially, there are fears that this bid to drag little Amsterdam into the twenty-first-century limelight is too synthetic: opponents say that over-internationalizing the city will erase its social and cultural base. At the root of all this is a profound identity crisis, expressed by the local paper *Het Parool* as Amsterdam's 'never-ending dread of mediocrity'.

But like it or not (and many do not), the planners' bid to transform Amsterdam from provincial city to metropolis is changing the city's face. On Stadhouderskade (a much-trodden tourist route) two building sites greeted visitors in the summer of 1990. On one side of the road, Byzantium was to be a squeaky-clean shop, flat and office complex of the kind that litters modern Europe's cities and tends to look the same whether it's in Madrid or Manchester. On the other side, Amsterdam's first legal, purpose-built casino was under construction (*see* **picture and caption**).

Neither development has been as vociferously and violently opposed as the Stopera was (*see page 68* **Postwar**): it would be a sad thing if this were because Amsterdammers are indifferent to the schemes. Some aspects of the 'yuppification' of the city arouse strong resentment, but other new projects have been welcomed as cosmetic improvements. Council plans to clean up the shoddy Damrak and Rokin thoroughfares, and the Kalverstraat shopping street, for instance, have been greeted with warm words in the pages of *Het Parool*.

ON YER BIKE

Gagging the buskers has been another priority in the authorities' bid to smarten up Amsterdam. From Vondelpark to the Damrak, these representatives of all that was mellow about the seventies (the noise they make aside) are being deprived of their amplifiers and drums and at time of writing are not allowed to play 'loudly'. What difference this will make to the livelihood of most is not clear, although policing their decibel levels has helped provide work for a handful of the city's long-term unemployed. These are the *stadswacht* (city watch, as in Rembrandt's *Nightwatch*): a council 'Guardian Angels' initiative to beat unemployment and petty crime together. Patrolling in blue-uniformed pairs and distinguishable from policemen by their lack of weaponry and their red trim, they are one, small example of the official progressiveness that separates Amsterdam from other European cities.

Although it has dipped recently, Amsterdam's 10 per cent unemployment rate is still higher than the national average. One palliative the town hall has dreamed up, in co-operation with local businesses, is the *stadspas*, where the elderly and unemployed are given fat 'chequebooks' allowing them discounts on items ranging from a loaf of bread to a *rondvaart* canal tour. Another new – and successful – initiative has been to tackle the problems of young unemployed people individually, interviewing them to find out what they might be interested in *before* bombarding them with vacancies. An extra benefit is that the scheme will give a fuller insight into the problem which one prominent British politician thought could be solved by everyone getting on their bikes.

That this is, in fact, not always easy for the cycle-crazy Amsterdammers – 5,000 bikes were stolen in 1989 – is another problem entirely, and a prime source of the day-to-day grousing about their city that residents so relish. The dog mess is an other favourite topic. Some things will never change.

One of several building projects designed to transform the city into a modern metropolis, Amsterdam's first legal, purpose-built casino (see under **Identity Crisis**) is at the time of writing rising from the remains of the city prison. The project was so close to Mayor Ed van Thijn's heart that he threatened to resign if it did not go ahead. At the half-way stage, at least, the resemblance it bore to the architecturally controversial Muziektheater was ominous.

Green Issues

The Dutch are more keenly aware of environmental issues than many other Europeans. As *Sara Henley* explains, this concern reflects the scale of their own problems.

The fact that you can't swim in Amsterdam's canals – and that some streets are liberally smeared with dog dirt or strewn with litter – forms the tip of an environmental iceberg.

The Netherlands collects much of Continental Europe's muck (in the atmosphere and from the rivers Rhine, Maas and Schelde); its six million cars belch out noxious fumes; and the advanced Dutch chemical industry adds to the hazardous substances wafting out of waste incinerators (the heavy metal cadmium and the poison dioxin are household words). The country's five million cows and 13 million pigs account for around 100 million tonnes of dung per year. Contaminated by the chemicals in fodder, the dung is slowly poisoning ground water, and fears about the state of drinking water have led to a costly programme to clean up the soil. Belated concern for the Third World countries that The Netherlands formerly used as dumping grounds has prompted a decision to stop exporting waste, but finding the space for it in this tiny land is a tall order.

Half of The Netherlands lies below sea-level, so the Dutch have more to fear than most from global warming. Strategies to prevent flooding are being proposed (*see page 213* **The Provinces: Fighting the Sea**), but one cynical environmentalist commented: 'Global warming is no problem. We can just sit on our rubbish'.

It's hardly surprising that the Dutch are having to stretch their imaginations to find solutions. More unusual is that the government has taken a lead in the search for solutions, aiming for 'sustainable growth' and stimulating Dutch industry to introduce green products and methods. But its goals and proposed methods are, say Green movements, still not good enough.

MELTING THE ICEBERG

The environmental iceberg started to melt in 1989 when the Dutch adminis-

tration became the world's first government to topple on a green issue. A rift on how to pay for the comprehensive National Environment Policy Plan clean-up programme (NMP – an EC first) split open an already fissured coalition government. But by summer 1990, the new Dutch environment minister, Hans Alders, had come up with an even more stringent 'NMP-Plus'.

Estimated to cost about f17 billion by 1994, both the NMP and the NMP-Plus are hefty documents boiling down to a goal of cutting pollution in water, air and soil by between 70 and 90 per cent. Their principle that the polluter will foot the bill – through taxes on fuel – is already in practice. But, as Greens point out, the politicians are tending to shift the goalposts as the industrial lobby gains force and 'being Green' loses its political lustre. An example is the way Prime Minister Ruud Lubbers lowered his goals on cutting output of ozone-damaging CO2. In 1989, he wanted a ten per cent cut by the year 2000. In the NMP-Plus, he supported a three to five per cent cut. And in budget discussions in late 1990, a plan to raise fuel taxes to pay for public transport investment was being eased aside.

Nonetheless, the Dutch are widely acknowledged as being at the forefront of environmental policy. The NMP-Plus focuses on better insulation, energy conservation and a switch to renewable energy resources – wind and solar power (*see below* **Alternative Energy**). Through increased recycling, it is hoped to reduce the incineration and dumping of waste from 20 million to 12 million tonnes by the end of the century. Various sectors of industry are signing covenants with the government to invest in clean or emission-reducing systems (although even the Organization for Economic Co-operation and Development suspects these are too voluntary to be effective) and plans are afoot to set up manure processing plants to recycle dung into organic fertilizer.

LOCAL ACTION

The environment has become an everyday concern. Yellow bottle banks and grey paper and battery banks are scattered over Dutch towns (new models are lined to make them less noisy). Most soft drink and beer bottles – including plastic ones – are returnable for a deposit (*statiegeld*; there's no refund if it says *geen statiegeld*); offices use special blue refuse bags for paper; and Dutch supermarkets have been stacked with so-called 'environment-friendly' goods for years. Because there is always an element of uncertainty about such claims, advertisers have set up a voluntary 'green code' regulating 'environment-friendly' claims. **Vereniging Milieu Defensie**, the Dutch arm of Friends of the Earth, has a helpline to advise consumers on how green products really are.

Environmental pressure groups are well-supported in The Netherlands, the largest being **Greenpeace International**. The first major 'green' political party, **Groen Links**, was not formed until 1989, but already has seats in parliament. Another party, **De Groenen**, is represented on Amsterdam's city and district councils.

Vereniging Milieu Defensie
Damrak 26, 1012 LJ (622 1366/Helpline 9am-2pm Mon-Fri 626 2620).
The Dutch branch of Friends of the Earth can advise on environmentally sound products and on how to recycle various kinds of waste.

Stichting Greenpeace Nederland
Keizersgracht 174, 1016 DW (626 1877; fax 622 1272).
Greenpeace Nederland was founded in 1978, when its major campaign was against whaling. It has now grown into the country's largest environmental organization. Over the past decade, chemical land pollution and nuclear-waste dumping in the North Sea have been among the most pressing issues that Greenpeace has addressed. Many of Greenpeace's protest ships, including the replacement for *Rainbow Warrior*, are registered in Amsterdam.

De Groenen
Postbus 3244, 1001 AA Amsterdam (617 9543).
This party has two seats on the Amsterdam city council and six seats on the district council. It's mounting protests against the proposed building of a coal-fired power station near Amsterdam and the pollution of drinking water from the Rhine. It wants offending pesticide manufacturers to pay for filters, which cost Amsterdam householders an estimated f70 million a year.

Groen Links

Postbus 700, 1000 AS Amsterdam (624 5515/620 2212).
This coalition of four small left-wing parties was formed in 1989. In the September 1989 elections, it won six seats (out of a total of 150) in the Dutch national parliament. Its manifesto included a commitment to the clearance and cleansing of polluted soil, the promise of more money to build and maintain cycle paths, and a pledge to reduce speed limits.

ALTERNATIVE ENERGY

Serious money is being spent both by the government and by business on alternative energy, from solar energy (demonstrated at **Zonnehuis**) and wind power to biomass (vegetable matter used as a source of energy). The Netherlands has more windmills than any other country, about 900 in all, and although there's still some

scepticism about the viability of wind power, the current wind development programme aims to meet 30 per cent of Dutch energy needs by the middle of next century. *See below* **Wind Power**.

The Dutch also have an official commitment to build no new nuclear power stations before the year 2000 at the earliest. Fall-out from the Chernobyl disaster gave them a serious fright, although by mid 1990, doubts about the economics of alternative energy sources had the administration inching towards a shift of position.

The Netherlands is the world's fourth largest producer of natural gas, thanks to its sizeable inland gas field in Groningen. This fuel is reckoned to

be 'clean' because it emits less sulphur dioxide and nitrogen oxides than coal and oil, and vehicle engines which run on gas are being developed. Experimental buses in Groningen already run on gas and one company is developing a household pump to fill up cars with natural gas from the mains grid. Another Dutch company is even developing a commercial engine that runs on vegetable oil.

Zonnehuis (Sun House)

Het Lageland 1, off Laan van Alberthoeve, Castricum, near Alkmaar (information and appointments 023 143671). **Open** by appointment (usually Fri).
This housing estate home is identical to its neighbours to live in, but is unique in being powered by solar energy. Visitors get a guided tour in English of the house and its annex, where the sun's rays are converted.

WIND POWER

In 1987, as part of its environmental programme, the Dutch Government set the target of having 1,000 megawatts of electricity supplied by wind power by the year 2000. The Amsterdam region's generating board, the **Provinciaal Electriciteitsbedrijf van Noord-Holland (PEN)**, aims to supply 300 megawatts of this total. It has built wind farms along the Noordhollands Kanaal near Alkmaar and at Enkhuizen (for both *see page 203* **Excursions in Holland**). By the end of 1988, a total of 31 wind turbines had been built, costing nearly f40 million, of which f16 million was state subsidy. Together they produce enough energy for over 2,500 households every year – still a minute amount.

Dominating the flat, exposed landscape, these wind farms comprise sleek, statuesque turbines (technically called aerogenerators), built in series to reduce costs. However, wind energy remains expensive, so to reach its target and to become profitable after 1996 when subsidies stop, the industry will have to develop larger models. Presently, the country's biggest aerogenerator is at Wieringermeerpolder near Medemblik (*see page 203* **Excursions in Holland**). With a height of 60 metres (197 feet) and rotor blades measuring 45 metres (148 feet) in diameter, it can generate one megawatt on its own. For English-language details on how aerogenerators work, contact PEN (*see below*).

In a scheme copied from

Denmark, individuals have formed ten **windmill co-operatives** in Noord Holland. Members contribute money to finance local aerogenerators; three have already built turbines (*see below*). Since 1988, the co-operatives have been paid 12.5c for each kilowatt-hour supplied to the grid.

Amsterdam Energy Authority has one turbine at Oostzaan, called **Skoon**, meaning 'beautiful' in the local dialect. It's on the way to the museum village of Zaanse Schans (*see page 203* **Excursions in Holland**), where there's a windmill museum, so you can compare ancient and modern wind power.

PEN wind farms

Information: PEN, Postbus 150, 2060 AD, Bloemendaal (023 222514; fax 023 222173). **Burgervlotbrug** *along Noordhollands Kanaal.* 50km (31 miles) north-west. **Callantsoog** *along Noordhol Kanaal.* 50 km (31 miles) north-west. **Enkhuizen** *along a dike into the IJsselmeer lake.* 45km (28 miles) north-east/by train direct to Enkhuizen.

Skoon wind turbine

Oostzaan; visible 20m (66ft) from Kolkweg; or from A10 motorway. 5km (3 miles) north-east.

Windmill co-operatives

Camperduin *between Alkmaar and Burgervlotbrug wind farm* (above). *(information 072 155446).* One turbine. 55km (34 miles) north-west. **Venhuizen** *near Enkhuizen (information 02284 2540).* Three turbines. 45km (28 miles) north-east. **De Waal** *Texel Island (information 02223 673).* One large, 250kw turbine. 80km (50 miles) north.

Eating & Drinking

You won't find many traditional Dutch restaurants in Amsterdam, but almost every other national cuisine is well represented. Indeed, Indonesian cooking has been wholeheartedly adopted by the Dutch as their own. French cuisine has had the greatest influence, so there are plenty of places where the visiting gourmet can dine well for a reasonable price.

Amsterdam's cafés and bars do, however, possess a uniquely Dutch character. From yodelling locals in the Jordaan brown bars, to communal reading tables in the city's many style bars, each has its own atmosphere and appeal.

CONTENTS:

Café
De garage
Restaurant

the hottest
rendez-vous!

Ruysdaelstraat 54 - 56
1071 XE Amsterdam-Zuid
Phone: (0)20 - 679 71 76

Restaurants

The Netherlands may not have a gourmet tradition of its own, but in Amsterdam the quality and variety of imported cuisines, and the lovely settings, more than make up for it.

The dichotomy between capital and country is nowhere more pronounced than in The Netherlands. Amsterdam is a bustling and cosmopolitan melting pot which probably has more in common with New York or London than with the rest of the country. This difference is probably best appreciated when it comes to eating out, for unless you specifically seek out a Dutch restaurant you are likely to be making your choice between Filipino, Indonesian, Thai and Caribbean cuisines, to name but a few. Restaurants with no nationality tag are most likely to serve French food interpreted by Dutch chefs. French kitchens are still considered the best, as they have been ever since the days of the Napoleonic occupation, but even the most *haute* of cuisine is subject to international influences. Almost all the celebrated chefs listed below borrow from Japanese, Indian and Italian ingredients for their *nouvelle* dishes.

The Chinese and Indonesians from the Far East, 'guest workers' from the Mediterranean and hippies with their penchant for Indian and vegetarian cooking have also contributed to internationalizing the menus. As the capital of a post-colonial country with strong links to Indonesia, Amsterdam has an abundance of Indonesian restaurants – in fact, Indonesian food has been adopted to such an extent that it is almost considered a national speciality.

In the past few years, Thai, Japanese and Filipino food have been on the tip of everyone's tongue, while Surinam cuisine is on the verge of mass discovery. Surprisingly, despite the number of Surinamers in Amsterdam, very few restaurants feature Surinam cuisine, a spicy blend of mainly Chinese, Hindustani and African flavours refecting the country's mix of nationalities. The best places to look for it are cafés and takeaways in the Albert Cuypmarkt area. Restaurants serving Surinam food tend to offer *bami* (noodle) and *nasi* (rice) dishes and typical snacks such as *roti* (a stuffed, Indian-style pancake), *bojo* (a quiche-type

item of cassava and coconut) and *telo* (baked cassava with peanut sauce). *Pitjil*, baked vegetables with peanut sauce, is said to be a contribution from the Japanese. The largest eating place, and probably the one most recommended by members of the Surinam community, is the Marowijn (Albert Cuypstraat 68-70, tel 662 4845; open noon to 10pm daily), which has a Chinese/Surinam kitchen. It's not a top-of-the-line place, but it's pleasant, with linen table-cloths and Chinese lanterns.

GOING DUTCH

There is little in the way of a distinctive Dutch cuisine and no restaurants serve exclusively Dutch food. Such traditional dishes as there are are designed to stick to ribs in winter. Typical are potatoes, sausage and curly kale (*boerenkoo met rookworst*), meat and vegetable stew (*stamppot*) and thick split-pea soup (*erwtensoep*). Correctly made, the soup is thick enough to hold the spoon upright and is normally eaten with thick slabs of rye bread and raw bacon. Dutch breakfast is also hearty: several types of bread, cheese, cold meats, a boiled egg and coffee or tea.

Before World War II, meat was mainly for special occasions. Fish and dairy products, especially cheese, were the primary sources of protein. Herring and onions, both eaten raw, are still a national delicacy available on every street corner. Best is the new herring in May, the same month that asparagus from the province of Limburg is served with butter and nutmeg as a meal in itself.

Apple cake, cream cakes and pancakes are sweet treats. The Pancake Bakery, in a seventeenth-century warehouse (Prinsengracht 191, 625 1333), is the premier stop for plate-size pancakes with a choice of some 30 toppings.

FINDING YOUR WAY AROUND

Several streets are literally lined with restaurants from around the globe.

Those on Warmoesstraat (near Centraal Station) and Utrechtsestraat are among the more moderately priced, while those on Reguliersdwarsstraat, parallel to the flower market, and around Leidseplein tend to be pricier. Most recently, Van Baerlestraat (in the museum area) entered the gourmet sweepstakes with a number of former local shops now transformed into restaurants. The Jordaan is also liberally sprinkled with eating places, two of which (**De Kikker**, *listed under* **French**, and **Tout Court**, *under* **Celebrated Chefs**) were at time of writing all the rage.

Every restaurant is required by law to post menus and price lists outside. As well as à la carte selections, many restaurants have set-price menus; these are often posted on a blackboard after the chef has been to the market in the morning and decided what to serve. Particularly good value is the **Tourist Menu**, which offers three courses for about f20. The 500 or so restaurants throughout the country that participate in this programme are easily recognizable by the knife and fork logo in the window. For a round-up of basic terms found on a menu, *see page 80* **The Menu**.

Dining in Amsterdam is leisurely, and most meals are cooked to order. The Dutch eat early (about 6pm at home, 7pm to 9.30pm in restaurants), and many kitchens close at about 10pm, but customers are welcome to linger over coffee and dessert until about midnight. Restaurants open late into the night are listed in **Early Hours** *page 144*. It is always advisable to book (at least early in the day) for dinner at leading restaurants. If you do, turn up on time – the Dutch prize punctuality.

For a decent meal out consisting of a starter, main course and dessert you can expect to pay upwards of f30. In the haute cuisine establishments the sky really is the limit, although in eetcafés (literally cafés where you can eat) you can pay a lot less, *see page 91* **Cafés & Bars**. In the past decade, most restaurants have started to accept credit cards; many of the smaller ones still do not, however, so check before ordering. Bills always include 18.5 per cent tax and a 15 per cent service charge. It is customary to leave the small change as well, if the service merits it. We have indicated any special facilities, such as wheelchair access and high chairs for children, but if you intend to make use of them you should phone ahead to let the restaurant know your needs.

Prices listed below are based on the average cost of a starter, a main course and dessert, WITHOUT drink. You could spend less – or a lot more – depending on what you order and how much you drink.

CITY LANDMARKS

1e Klas
Platform 2B, Centraal Station, C (625 0131). Tram 1, 2, 4, 5, 9, 13, 16, 17, 24, 25. **Open** 9.30am-11pm Mon-Wed; 9.30am-midnight Thur-Sat; 10.30am-11pm Sun. **Lunch served** noon-2pm daily. **Dinner served** 5.30-10pm Mon-Wed, Sun; 5.30-10.30pm Thur-Sat. **Average** f40. **Set lunch** f35. **Credit** AmEx, DC, MC, V.
See p81 picture and caption.
Book 6-8pm. Children welcome; children's menu; high chair. Vegetarian dishes. Wheelchair access to restaurant; toilets for the disabled in the station.

De Blauwe Parade and Blauwe Poort
Hotel Port van Cleve, NZ Voorburgwal 178-180, C (624 4860). Tram 1, 2, 4, 9, 24, 25, **26. Meals served** *Parade* noon-2pm, 6-10pm, Mon-Fri; 6-10pm Sat, Sun; *Poort* noon-9.30pm daily. **Average** *Parade* f65; *Poort* f45. **Set menu** *Parade* f57.50; *Poort* f37.50. **Credit** AmEx, MC, V.
In the 1890s, Brietner, Witsen and Klos were among the renowned artists who gathered regularly at this beer house which later expanded into two restaurants and, in 1954, the Hotel Port van Cleve. The pricier Blauwe Parade (Blue Parade) is quintessentially Dutch, with walls of antique Delft tiles. The companion Blauwe Poort (Blue Door) across the hall has murals of old Amsterdam cityscapes and serves authentic Dutch dishes, including pea soup. Both are famous for their numbered steaks (at time of writing, almost 5½ million sold since the place opened in 1870).
Booking advisable. Children welcome; high chair.

Café Americain
Leidseplein 28, IS (623 4813). Tram 1, 2, 5, 6, 7, 10. **Open** 6am-1am daily. **Lunch served** 11am-2pm. **Dinner served** 6-11.30pm. **Average** f45. **Buffet** (served throughout the day) f30. **Credit** AmEx, DC, EC, MC, V.
See p83 picture and caption.
Booking advisable. Babies, children very welcome; reduced-price children's portions; high chairs. Vegetarian menu.

Dikker en Thijs
Prinsengracht 444 (625 8876). Tram 1, 2, 5. **Dinner served** 7-10pm Mon-Sat. **Average** f75. **Set menu** (four courses) f85. **Credit** AmEx, DC, MC, V.
This old and distinguished Dutch restaurant has received mixed reviews in recent years.

On a good night, the classically furnished second-floor dining-room overlooking Prinsengracht offers haute cuisine with heavy sauces. Other options here are a Franco-Dutch meal in the cellar restaurant, Prinsenkelder, where seasonal game is a speciality; a light à la carte meal in the ground-floor brasserie; or takeaway dishes from the adjoining delicatessen of the same name. All are under the same management and chef.
Children admitted but not welcome. Book always, Fri, Sat a week in advance. Vegetarian dishes by arrangement.

Keuken van 1870
Spuistraat 4, C (624 8965). Tram 1, 2. **Meals served** noon-8pm Mon-Fri; 4-9pm Sat, Sun. **Average** f10. **No credit cards.**
Probably the best value in town, this no-frills old-fashioned establishment was set up as a soup kitchen in 1870 (the name means 'Kitchen from 1870') and still serves copious, plain meals for less than f10. It closes at 8pm.
Bookings not accepted. Children welcome.

Keyser's Bodega
Van Baerlestraat 96, OS (671 1441). Tram 3, 5, 12, 16. **Open** 9am-midnight Mon-Sat. **Meals served** noon-11.30pm. **Average** f55. **Set menu** f49.75 three courses incl coffee. **Credit** AmEx, DC, MC, V.
Musicians from the Concertgebouw next door have made this café-restaurant their second home since 1903, and Amsterdam's literary set favours it as well. The décor and Oriental wool table coverings (an Amsterdam tradition) look the same as they did then – only central heating has been added. Some of the formally dressed waiters

---

THE MENU

Most restaurant staff speak English, and many menus are printed in several languages. A few Dutch words are helpful, however: *ober* (waiter); *kellnerin* (waitress); and *Mag ik de rekening, graag?* (May I have the bill, please?). This basic list picks out the terms that are hard to recognise with a combination of English and common sense.

Snacks
Boterham sandwich
Broodje roll
Eieren eggs
Erwentsoep pea soup (with bacon or sausage)
Kaas cheese
Suiker sugar
Stokbrood French bread
Uitsmijter ham or cheese with fried egg on bread

Drinks
Anijsmelk warm milk flavoured with aniseed
Huis wijn (wit/rood) house wine (white/red)
Jenever Dutch gin-tasting spirit; **bessenjen-ever** blackcurrant-flavoured *jenever*
Pils Dutch beer
Sinaasappelsap orange juice

Spa Rood (brand name) fizzy mineral water
Thee tea
Vrisdranken soft drinks

Main meals
Voorgerechten starters
Hoofdgerechten main courses
Visgerechten fish dishes
Vleesgerechten meat dishes
Nagerechten desserts

Terms
Gebakken fried or baked
Gebraden roast
Gekookt boiled
Gerookt smoked
Gestooft stewed
Vers fresh

Meat
Bitterballen small meatballs (eaten with apéritif)
Eend duck
Gehakt minced meat
Kalkoen turkey
Kalfsvlees veal
Kip chicken
Kroket meat croquette
Lamsvlees lamb
Spek bacon
Varkensvlees pork
Worst sausage

Fish
Garnalen prawns

Haring herring
Kabeljauw cod
Paling eel
Schol plaice
Zalm salmon

Vegetables
Groenten vegetables
Aardappelen potatoes
Bloemkool cauliflower
Bonen beans
Champignons mushrooms
Erwten peas
Knoflook garlic
Patates frites chips
Prei leek
Sla salad; **gemengde sla** mixed salad
Zuurkool sauerkraut
Uien onions

Desserts
Fruit: Aardbei strawberry; **druiven** grapes; **framboos** raspberry; **kers** cherry; **peer** pear; **perzik** peach; **pruim** plum/prune; **swarte bessen** blackberries

Gebak tart, pastry; **Appelgebak** Dutch apple tart
Ijs ice-cream
Pannekoeken pancakes
Poffertjes small doughnut-like pancakes
Slagroom whipped cream
Vlaai fruit tart
Vla custard

could have been here just as long. Sole meunière and smoked eel are specialities, in addition to classic French dishes. Many local business people lunch here, and shoppers tend to stop in for tea. Newspapers are available on the reading table. The place is really busy between 7pm and 8pm, before concerts next door.
Booking advisable. Children not admitted. Vegetarian dishes.

CELEBRATED CHEFS

Beddington's
Roelof Hartstraat 6-8, OS (676 5201). Tram 3, 5, 12, 24. **Lunch served** noon-2.30pm, **dinner served** 6-10.30pm, Mon-Sat. **Average** f70. **Set lunch** f55 three courses. **Set dinners** from f75. **Credit** AmEx, DC, JPL, MC, V.
Meals at Englishwoman Jean Beddington's establishment are a sumptuous feast. She has perfected the art of French cuisine, adding her own original touches gained during a long trip through the Far East. Reflecting the Japanese influence, the menu includes beautifully presented fish dishes (salmon sashimi as a starter); desserts betray Mrs Beddington's Derbyshire origins. Some diners find the starkly modern décor with almost no colour a bit sterile. *Babies, children admitted; children's portions on request. Private room for 16 with balcony view over gardens. Book dinner always. Vegetarian dishes.*

Le Ciel Bleu
Okura Hotel, Ferdinand Bolstraat 333 , OS (678 7111). Tram 12. **Dinner served** 6-11pm daily. **Average** f100-f125. **Credit** AmEx, DC, MC, V.
For the height of elegant dining, try the Okura Hotel's twenty-third floor restaurant. Great views of the city, French/Japanese creations by chef Dick Sinnema and soft music make this a place for special occasions. Drinking in the sights at the adjoining bar is less costly.
Booking advisable. Dress: jacket and tie.

Excelsior
Hotel l'Europe, Nieuwe Doelenstraat 2-8, C (623 4836). Tram 4, 9, 14, 16, 24, 25. **Breakfast served** 7-11am daily. **Lunch served** 12.30-2.30pm Mon-Fri, Sun. **Theatre dinner served** 6-7pm daily. **Dinner served** 7-10.30pm daily. **Average** f65. **Set breakfasts** f20-f50. **Theatre menu** f65. **Credit** AmEx, DC, MC, V.
Imko Binnerts took over the kitchen at this famous establishment in 1988 and his influence is already apparent. Although still classically based, the cuisine now includes Oriental starters as well as traditional dishes such as slices of roe deer with cabbage and mushrooms. Grand style, views of the Amstel and 40,000 bottles in the wine cellar are other reasons for the Michelin star. *Booking required. Children welcome; children's portions on request; high chairs. Dress: jacket and tie. Vegetarian dishes. Wheelchair access.*

De Graaf
Emmalaan 25, OS (662 4884). **Lunch served** noon-2pm, **dinner served** 6-10pm, Mon-Sat. **Average** f95. **Set lunch** (two

The lofty **1e Klas** *(see under* **City Landmarks**)*, restored in grand turn-of-the-century style, is in Centraal Station's former first-class waiting room. Its menu offers excellent à la carte nouvelle cuisine to Amsterdammers and travellers alike. Dutch specialities are featured in season. With the trains rolling by outside, it's a trip back to the heyday of rail travel.*

courses) f45, **set dinner** (four courses) f70. **Credit** AmEx, DC, MC, V.
Opened in 1988, this former town house in the chic Vondelpark area has won a steady following and a Michelin star for Harry de Graaf's cooking. A mirrored wall, cream-coloured décor and antique sculptures set the tone, but the centrepiece is the round table with a giant bouquet and lavish display of pastries – the house speciality. Stew of grilled shrimp and scallops in lobster sauce, and braised duck breast with ginger are typical main courses.
Booking advisable. Children welcome; reduced-price portions on request.

De Kersentuin
Garden Hotel (separate entrance), Dijsselhofplansoen 7, OS (664 2121). Tram 16. **Lunch served** noon-2.30pm Mon-Fri. **Dinner served** 6-10.15pm Mon-Sat. **Average** f125. **Set lunch** f65, **set dinner** (4 courses) f100. **Credit** AmEx, DC, MC, V.
Lekker Eten, the premier Dutch guide to cuisine, ranks Jon Sisterman among the top ten chefs in the country. His wizardry with nouvelle cuisine and the sophisticated Oriental cherry garden setting have been attracting Amsterdam's *beau monde* since the early eighties.
Booking required. Dress: jacket and tie.

De Molen 'de Dikkert'
Amsterdamseweg 104A, OS (641 1378). Bus 175. **Lunch served** noon-2pm, **dinner served** 6-10pm, Mon-Sat. **Average** f100. **Credit** AmEx, DC, MC, V.
An authentic windmill dating from 1672, 5km/3miles south of the city centre, is the setting for the classic French cuisine of chef

Didier Besnard. Scottish beef is among the dishes served in the spacious traditional dining-room. A good place for expense account dining.
Booking required. Dress: jacket and tie.

't Swarte Schaep
Korte Leidsedwarsstraat 24, IS (622 3021). Tram 1, 2, 5. **Meals served** noon-11pm daily. **Average** f60. **Credit** AmEx, DC, MC, V.
The name means 'black sheep', but this is a misnomer. The restaurant, set in this 300-year-old building since 1937, is noted for its excellent wines (especially reds), authentic antiques and chef Ton van der Boogaard's subtle blend of classic, nouvelle and post-modern cuisine. Even Prince Willem-Alexander dines here. The window tables have great views of Leidseplein below (the restaurant is on the second and third floors, up a long, steep staircase).
Bookings required. Children admitted.

Tout Court
Runstraat 13, IW (625 8637). Tram 7, 10. **Dinner served** 6-11.30pm Tue-Sat. **Average** f60. **Credit** AmEx, DC, MC, V.
Another stop on the circuit of beautiful people is the Jordaan restaurant of John Fagel, the eldest of six Dutch brothers who are all celebrated chefs. The nouvelle-based menu changes every four or five weeks, and a range of set menus offers good value. No alcohol other than wine is served, and some critics find the butcher-aproned waiters too slow, but people still come in droves to see and be seen.
Booking advisable Fri, Sat. Children admitted; children's portions on request. Vegetarian dishes. Wheelchair access with help.

Spuistraat 4
Amsterdam
Tel. 020 - 6248965

„De Keuken van 1870"

OPENING HOURS:

MON - FRI 11.30 - 20.00 HRS.
SAT - SUN 16.00 - 21.00 HRS.

OVER MORE THAN 100 YEARS
WELL-KNOWN FOR CHEAP AND
WELL-PREPARED DUTCH MEALS.

MAYUR
INDIAN RESTAURANT

Where you will enjoy original
Curry + Vegetarian food.

Kitchen open: 12:30 - 14:30 hrs.
and 17:00 - 23:00 hrs.
Lunch closed on Tuesdays,
5 minutes from Rijksmuseum.

AMSTERDAM
Korte Leidsedwarsstraat 203
Tel. (0)20 - 623 21 42

HAARLEM
Prinses Beatrixplein 43
Tel. (0)23 - 35 97 57
(Mondays closed)

QUICK TAKE-AWAY SERVICE

we don't fish for compliments
we serve fish for pleasure

Monday - Friday
12.00-24.00 hrs

VISRESTAURANT
LE PÊCHEUR

Saturday - Sunday
17.00-24.00 hrs

REGULIERSDWARSSTRAAT 32 - AMSTERDAM - PHONE: 020-24 31 21

Le pecheur, famous fish restaurant

MODERATE

Crignon Culinaire

Gravenstraat 28, C (624 6428). Tram 1, 2, 4, 9, 14, 16, 24, 25. **Dinner served** 6-10.30pm daily. **Average** f35. **Credit** AmEx, DC, MC, V.

'Intimate' best describes this cheese restaurant located in a sixteenth-century building in a narrow street by the Nieuwekerk. Previously the mezzanine annex of a local cheese shop (now closed), where customers sampled some of the 140 varieties on sale, the restaurant specializes in fondues. It also offers meat and fish selections, including a marinated salmon made according to an old (Scandinavian) family recipe. The staircase are impossibly narrow and winding, typically Dutch, but the owner has a dumbwaiter to help. *Booking advisable.*

De Impressionist

Keizersgracht 312, IW (627 6666). Tram 13, 14, 17. **Dinner served** 6-10.30pm Mon-Thur, Sun; 6-11pm Fri, Sat. **Set menus** f30-f50. **Credit** AmEx, DC, MC, V.

Roy Verwey named his small cellar restaurant so people of all nationalities would remember it, and the menu reflects this international approach. A team of British cooks produces English, American, Chinese, Japanese and Italian dishes, along with imaginative vegetarian selections. *Children admitted; children's portions on request. Book a day in advance. Vegetarian dishes.*

Jean Jean

1e Anjeliersdwarsstraat 12-14, IW (627 7153). Tram 3, 10/bus 18. **Dinner served** 5-11pm Tue-Sun. **Average** f20-f30. **No credit cards.**

Run by French brothers Jean-Olivier and Jean-Daniel Rous, this simply decorated and popular establishment serves excellent crêpes (from f8), soups, salads and main courses. The pastries are authentic and dreadfully tempting – try the lemon tartelettes. *Children welcome.*

Pier 10

De Ruijterkade, Steiger 10, C (624 8276). Tram 1, 2. **Dinner served** 6.30-11pm daily. **Average** f50. **Credit** AmEx, DC, MC, V.

A former shipping line office behind Centraal Station houses one of Amsterdam's newest and most unexpected restaurants. An unusual combination of functional décor, candlelight, shipside vistas, innovative food and casual atmosphere attracts a regular following. The three waterside tables are the most coveted. *Children admitted; children's portions on request. Booking advisable noon-2pm, 7-10pm. Terrace with 50 seats. Vegetarian dishes.*

Piet de Leeuw

Noorderstraat 11, IS (623 7181). Tram 16, 24, 25. **Meals served** noon-10.30pm Mon-Fri; 6-10.30pm Sat, Sun. **Average** f30. **Credit** DC, MC, V.

Most of the customers at this small, friendly steakhouse come for inexpensive steaks and french fries. People tend to mix and mingle (they may ask to sit at your table if there's

space), which makes it a good place to meet the Dutch. *Children welcome.*

Salad Garden

Weteringschans 75, IS (623 4017). Tram 6, 7, 10. **Meals served** 8am-11pm daily. **Average** f30. **Salad bar** f18.50. **Credit** AmEx, DC, MC, V.

On the Singel near Leidseplein, this indoor-outdoor restaurant has a covered garden popular with locals for lunch. French onion soup, salmon on toast and pâté can be accompanied by one of the excellent salads that give the place its name. Hard-to-find English, American and Continental breakfasts are also available, and robust evening dishes include steaks, lamb cutlets and trout. *Children welcome; children's portions on request. Book in summer 7-10pm. Covered terrace with 40 seats.*

De Smoeshaan

Leidsekade 90, IS (627 6966). Tram 1, 2, 5, 6, 7, 10. **Café open** 10am-1am Mon-Thur, Sun; 10am-2am Fri, Sat. **Restaurant open** 5pm-1am Mon-Thur, Sun; 5pm-2am Fri, Sat. **Last orders** 10pm. **Average** *restaurant* f35; *café* f20. **Credit** AmEx, DC, MC, V.

An old Dutch and usually busy café-bar downstairs and an only slightly more formal upstairs restaurant with a more varied menu (and higher prices) are the choices here. Both serve the same tasty Franco-Dutch food, lots of fresh vegetables and salads, and both attract a young, lively

crowd, including performers from the nearby theatres. An excellent casual venue for dinner. *Children admitted; children's portions on request. Booking advisable after 6pm. Vegetarian dishes.*

CAFÉS & BRASSERIES

Most cafés and bars serve snacks throughout the day and hot dishes at meal-times, *see page 91* **Cafés & Bars.** Here we list a few that specialize in serving food.

Bern

Nieuwmarkt 9, C (622 0034). Metro Nieuwmarkt. **Open** 4pm-1am Mon-Thur, Sun; 4pm-2am Fri, Sat. **Dinner served** 6-11pm daily. **Average** f32. **No credit cards.**

A brown café-restaurant with a reputation for its delicious cheese fondue made, of course, to a secret recipe. Peppered steak is also recommended. The kitchen closes at 11pm and it's advisable to book. *Children admitted. Booking advisable 7-10pm. Pavement tables for drinking only. Vegetarian dishes.*

Brasserie van Baerle

Van Baerlestraat 158, OS (679 1532). Tram 3, 5, 12, 16. **Open** 11am-11pm Mon-Fri;

One of a kind, the glorious Jugendstil *(art nouveau) interior of the* **Café Americain** *(see under* **City Landmarks***) is a listed monument decorated with murals and marbled amber lampshades. Theatrical personalities, the après-theatre crowd and tourists meet under the high vaulted roof. Some pop in for coffee and pastries; others relish meals from the buffet, where f30 entitles you to help yourself to as much as propriety allows.*

10am-11pm Sun. **Average** f55. **Credit** AmEx, DC, MC, V.
The media crowd has been hanging out at this turn-of-the-century town house brasserie since it opened about ten years ago. The food is strictly modern: Oriental salads and home-made soups. The table at the rear window gives the most privacy. On warm days, the garden is delightful. Sunday brunch is served here too.
Booking advisable.

Café Cox
Marnixstraat 427, IS (620 7222). Tram 1, 2, 5, 6, 7, 10. **Open** 10am-1am Mon-Thur, Sun; 10am-2am Fri, Sat. **Lunch served** 12.30-3pm, **dinner served** 5.30-11.30pm, daily. **Average** f30-f40. **Credit** MC.
This modern (white walls, functional furnishings) café-restaurant adjoins the Stadsschouwberg, one of the city's main theatres. Situated on the first floor, it serves reasonably priced but modest meals. Hungry diners are invited to ask for seconds of vegetables. Worth noting, the restaurant is busiest before 8pm. Post-theatre dining is more relaxed (less crowded).
Children welcome; meals adapted for them. Booking advisable before 8pm. Vegetarian menu.

Gerrit van Beeren
Koningsstraat 54, C (622 2329). Metro Nieuwmarkt. **Dinner served** 5-10pm daily. **Average** f24. **No credit cards.**
On a side-street off the Nieuwmarkt, this cheerful neighbourhood café-restaurant has been run by the same person since 1936, though only recently in its present form. It was a greengrocers first, then a bar, and was refurbished in 1989. The bouillabaisse for f12.50 has to be the best value dinner in town, and the steak and fish dishes are also very reasonably priced. The owner is very accommodating, but some of the staff can be a bit off-hand.
Children admitted; children's portions on request. No reservations. Terrace with 20 tables. Wheelchair access with help.

Grand Café Beurs van Berlage
Beursplein 3, C (638 4639). Tram 4, 9, 16, 24, 25. **Dinner served** 6pm-midnight daily. **Average** f65. **Credit** AmEx, MC, V.
Informality is the keynote of this modern café-bar-restaurant recently opened in the former stock exchange designed by noted Amsterdam architect HP Berlage (*see p61* **Between the Occupations**). Jan Toorop tile murals called 'Past', 'Present' and 'Future' depict the changing roles of workers and women at the turn of the century. The city's money-makers congregate in the restaurant; shoppers and tourists primarily in the café. Both offer an international menu (French, Dutch, Spanish and Italian dishes) cooked by Dutch and British chefs, in what has become one of the latest places to see and be seen.
Booking advisable. Children admitted; children's portions on request; high chairs with reservation. No-smoking areas. Terrace seating. Vegetarian dishes.

Witteveen
Ceintuurbaan 256-258, OS (662 4368). Tram 3. **Dinner served** 5-11pm daily. **Average** f55. **Credit** AmEx, DC, MC, V.
Deeply Dutch, this popular working class café-restaurant attracts all ages. Its lengthy

menu is supplemented by Cajun dishes from the Cajun Louisiana next door (*see below* **International**), which has the same owner.
Children welcome; children's portions on request; high chairs. Booking advisable around 7pm. Pavement tables for drinks only. Vegetarian dishes.

Amsterdam offers plenty of good cooking at prices ranging from reasonable to dirt cheap. Here are our favourites:

De Blauwe Hollander
Leidsekruisstraat 28, IS (623 3014). Tram 6, 7, 10. **Dinner served** 5-10pm daily. **Average** f22. **No credit cards.**
People come here for the slightly musty Dutch ambiance and the simple, inexpensive Dutch cooking; this is the only restaurant in Amsterdam that you could legitimately label Dutch. The four big tables – there's no separate seating – are always busy, but small parties seldom have to wait long.
Children admitted (if quiet). No reservations.

De Schutter
Voetboogstraat 13-15, C (622 4608). Tram 1, 2, 5, 14, 16, 24, 25. **Open** 11am-1am Mon-Thur, Sun; 11am-2am Fri, Sat. **Average** f20. **No credit cards.**
This upstairs bar has a marvellous atmosphere: students, musicians, yuppies and hippies mingle in the two bars and lean out of the enormous stained glass windows in summer. At lunch-time, there are French bread sandwiches (*stockbrood*), salads and pancakes for about f5. From 6pm to 9pm, the smaller bar has a selection of meals (listed on the board above the door) for f10-f20. Delicious steaks and other good bar food, and lots of Belgian beers – but go easy, they're strong.

Small Talk
Van Baerlestraat 52, OS (671 4864). Tram 2, 3, 5, 12. **Open** *coffee shop* 8am-7pm daily; *restaurant* 11am-9.30pm daily; *traiteur* 10.30am-8pm Mon-Sat. **Average** f30. **Credit** AmEx, DC, MC, V.
Two cafés side by side offer some of the most pleasant people-watching in town. Located halfway between the Concertgebouw and the PC Hoofstraat, Small Talk attracts a fairly well-heeled clientèle but the lunches and snacks remain reasonably priced. Dinners upstairs carry rather steeper tariffs. No-one will object if you linger, especially in the tiny corner café, which serves heavenly apple cake and hot chocolate.
Booking advisable for dinner.

Julia
Amstelveenseweg 169, OS (679 5394). Bus 146, 147, 170, 171, 172, 173. **Dinner served** 5-10pm daily. **Average** f35. **Set menu** f32.50. **Credit** AmEx, DC, MC, V.
For a real neighbourhood Dutch dinner, head out of town to Julia. It's a zany suburban place that encourages diners to let their

hair down – patrons may occasionally burst into song. It's probably the platter with ten kinds of fish, three vegetables, potatoes and salad for f32.50 that generates all this energy – and brings people from all over the region to these doors.
Children welcome; children's menu f19.50; high chairs.

Lucius
Spuistraat 247, C (624 1831). Tram 1, 2, 5, 13, 14, 17. **Dinner served** 5.30-11pm daily. **Average** f50. **Set menus** f30-f75. **Credit** AmEx, DC, MC, V.
Lucius is a fish-eater's paradise. The fish in the wall aquariums (not for eating) are a backdrop for a dinner of fresh ocean fish (as opposed to the normal North Sea variety), poached, grilled or fried, and shellfish in season. Lobster should be ordered in advance. Old-fashioned Dutch décor, right down to the tiles.
Children welcome; children's portions on request; high chairs. Booking advisable. Pavement seating. Vegetarian dishes on request. Meat dishes by arrangement. Wheelchair access.

Oesterbar
Leidseplein 10, IS (626 3463). Tram 1, 2, 5, 6, 7, 10. **Meals served** noon-midnight daily. **Average** f50. **Credit** AmEx, MC, V.
Some fish-lovers have come to this hundred-year-old restaurant every week for decades. Options are the enclosed (heated) pavement terrace with views on Leidseplein, the ground floor ringed by aquariums, or the upstairs dining-room with soft music. All three serve only fresh North Sea fish (no imports). Specialities are delicate Zeeland oysters in season, herring in May and mussels in June.
Children admitted. Book in summer. Covered terrace. Vegetarian dishes on request.

Sluizer
Utrechtsestraat 45, IS (626 3557). Tram 4. **Meals served** noon-midnight Mon-Fri; 5pm-midnight Sat, Sun. **Average** f50. **Credit** AmEx, DC, MC, V.
The old-fashioned flavour of this restaurant is hard to beat: marble-topped tables, fringed lampshades, good service, friendly atmosphere. The menu lists a dozen or more fish cooked in every conceivable way, but dishes of the day offer the best of the catch from the morning market. The meat restaurant of the same name next door is less impressive.
Children admitted; children's menu f13.50; one high chair. Book 7-10pm. Terrace with 40 seats. Vegetarian dishes.

CAJUN

Cajun Louisiana
Ceintuurbaan 260, OS (664 4729). Tram 3. **Dinner served** 5-11pm daily. **Average** f37.50. **Credit** AmEx, DC, MC, V.
A light and airy restaurant serving good southern American cuisine to a mainly trendy clientèle. Blackened catfish is a speciality.
Children welcome; children's portions on request; high chairs. Book for 7pm. Pavement tables for drinking only. Vegetarian dishes.

CARIBBEAN

Rum Runners
Prinsengracht 277, IW (627 4079). Tram 13, 14, 17. **Open** 4pm-1am Mon-Fri; noon-2am Sat; noon-1am Sun. **Dinner served** 6-11.30pm daily. **Average** f27.50. **Credit** AmEx, DC, MC, V.
A cocktail spot with a tropical feel to it, right down to the caged parrots. In keeping with the theme you can dine on Caribbean cuisine (spicy stews a speciality), but expect to be surrounded by much bustle and noise. *Children admitted; children's portions on request. No reservations. Two terraces. Vegetarian dishes. Wheelchair access.*

CHINESE

Sea Palace
Oosterdokskade 8, C (626 4777). Bus 22, 44, 47. **Open** noon-10.30pm daily. **Average** f60. **Credit** AmEx, DC, MC, V.
Oriental gourmets don't rush to this floating Chinese temple in Amsterdam's inner harbour, but lots of tourists, including those from the Dutch provinces, go for the Peking duck and rijsttafels. A dim sum buffet, served from noon to 3.30pm, includes many Chinese delicacies. Ask for a window table for views of old sailing ships.

FILIPINO

Filipino cuisine is rice-based and uses many exotic fruits (mango, coconut, banana). Fish is a favourite ingredient in the dishes, which range from the spicy to the very hot.

Adobo
Utrechtsestraat 42, OS (625 9251). Tram 4. **Dinner served** 5-10.30pm daily. **Average** f55. **Rijsttafel** f42.50. **Set dinner** f47.50. **Credit** AmEx, DC, MC, V.
The Adobo is a classy choice if you want to experience Filipino cuisine. The rijsttafel, a selection of various dishes, is a good way to experiment. The service is friendly and attentive, and the cooking is authentic. Every November the restaurant celebrates its anniversary with entertainment, gifts and a special menu. *Children welcome; children's menu. Book Fri, Sat, Sun. Pavement tables. Vegetarian menu.*

At Mango Bay
Westerstraat 91, IW (638 1039). Tram 3, 10. **Dinner served** 6-11pm Mon-Wed, Fri-Sun. **Average** f45. **No credit cards.**
This restaurant lives up to its somewhat exotic name with a variety of distinctive sweet and spicy dishes which use a lot of exotic fruits. It's both tiny and popular so reservations are necessary. Live music Wednesday and weekends. *Children welcome; children's portions on request. Book advisable Wed, Fri, Sat, Sun. Pavement tables. Vegetarian dishes by arrangement.*

FRENCH

Bartholdy
Van Baerlestraat 35-37, OS (662 2655). Tram 2, 3, 5, 12, 16. **Open** 11am-midnight daily. **Lunch served** noon-2.30pm daily,

Cirelli (see under **International: Italian**), *in the now very much cleaned up Zeedijk where formerly most feared to tread, is an elegantly but slightly outrageously furbished restaurant – look out for the leopard skin table legs and bizarre chandeliers that wouldn't look out of place in a modern art gallery. A tempting menu and home-made pasta make for a rather special night out.*

dinner served 6-9.30pm (11pm if concert) daily. **Average** f55. **Set lunch** f42.50 three courses. **Pre-theatre dinner** f49.50 three courses. **Credit** AmEx, MC, V.
Located in a recently converted fire station, and named after the composer Felix Mendelssohn Bartholdy, this restaurant continues the musical theme in its décor, with a grand piano and portraits of major composers. Upmarket, elegantly served French food is its forté. *Children admitted. Book one week in advance if there is a concert. Pavement tables with 40 seats. Vegetarian dishes on request. Wheelchair access.*

Bordewijk
Noordermarkt 7, IW (624 3899). Tram 3. **Dinner served** 6.30-10.30pm Tue-Sun. **Set menus** f55-f75. **Credit** AmEx, MC.
You probably need to be a yuppie at heart to fully appreciate the qualities of this restaurant. Dutch designer Rob Eckhardt conceived the flamingo walls and black furniture décor; Wil Demandt and Hans Mosterd are responsible for the 'French-oriented' menu. *Children welcome; children's portions on request. Book 8-9pm. Vegetarian dishes on request. Wheelchair access.*

Le Campagnard
Willemsparkweg 6, OS (662 6206). Tram 2. **Open** 9am-midnight daily. **Dinner served** 6-10pm. **Average** f40. **Set menu** f29.50. **Credit** AmEx, MC, V.
This small corner restaurant near the Stedelijk Museum offers decent portions of nicely presented French regional cooking with more fried food than most. The mezzanine has the best tables and overlooks a small patio.

Children admitted; children's portions on request. Booking advisable for dinner. Vegetarian dishes.

De Gouden Reael
De Zandhoek 14, Westerdok, IW (623 3883). Tram 3/bus 28. **Lunch served** noon-2pm Mon-Fri. **Dinner served** 6-10pm daily. **Average** f67. **Set menu** f50 three courses. **Credit** AmEx, DC, MC, V.
Slightly out of the centre of town on Reael Island in the western docks is a seventeenth-century gabled house. It now houses this 12-year-old portside split-level restaurant with a bar on the ground floor, wainscoting on the walls and boats at anchor at the door. The young chef Miek Blommestein is gaining renown for her regional French food. A new region is introduced every three months, along with new art displays. To make the trip to the island very special, take a water taxi (*see p3* **Essential Information**). *Children admitted; children's portions by arrangement. Book always. Waterside terrace with 25 seats. Vegetarian dishes by arrangement.*

Kikker
Egelantiersstraat 128-130, IW (627 9198). Tram 3, 10. **Dinner served** 6-10pm daily. **Average** f67.50. **Set meals** f75 four courses; f90 five courses. **Credit** AmEx, DC, MC, V.
This two-storey restaurant is tucked away in the Jordaan. The cooking is best described as 'almost French': French with strong Japanese and Italian influences. Chef Theo Koster changes the menu every day, depending on what the best produce at the market was that day. There's live music and Dutch cabaret at weekends.

VILLA MAX

RESTAURANT - CAFÉ

Adventurous French Food

GELDERSEKADE 109 (hoek Rechtboomssloot)
1011 EN AMSTERDAM – TEL 020-6205283
(5 minuten lopen van De Stopera)

RESTAURANT

ANNO
1520

- Old Dutch interior
- open for lunch and dinner
- DUTCH KITCHEN
- moderate prices
- restaurant open from 12:00 till 24:00 hrs on Sundays from 17:00 hrs
- 250 seats

SPUISTRAAT 275
AMSTERDAM

please reserve seat: phone (0)20 - 624 99 98

*Children admitted. Booking advisable.
Vegetarian dishes.*

Van Hale
*Saenredamstraat 39, OS (676 2495). Tram
16, 24, 25.* **Dinner served** *6-10pm Tue-Sat.*
Average *f40.* **No credit cards.**
Light colours, black marble tables, an interesting menu and an open kitchen identify
this pleasantly trendy restaurant as post-modern; but the home-made desserts,
especially, are old-fashioned goodness.
*Children admitted; children's portions on
request. No reservations. Vegetarian dish.
Wheelchair access with help.*

Vivaldi's
*Van Baerlestraat 49, OS (679 8888). Tram
2, 3, 5, 12, 16.* **Dinner served** *6-11pm Tue-Sun.*
Credit AmEx, DC, MC.
So called because of its position opposite
the Concertgebouw and because 'dis'
means table in Dutch, this is a suitably elegant venue for pre- and post-concert-goers.
The high point of the week is the surprise
menu on Sundays: clients choose between
meat or fish, nothing more, and are
rewarded with the chef's latest creation.
Recorded classics provide the background
music.
*Children welcome; children's menu. Booking
advisable. Vegetarian menu. Live classical
violin and guitar one Sat monthly.*

GREEK

Aphrodite
*Lange Leidsedwarsstraat 91, IS (622 7382).
Tram 1, 2, 5, 6, 7, 10.* **Dinner served** *5pm-midnight daily.* **Average** *f30.* **Credit** DC,
MC, V.
This Greek restaurant is the result of a
mixed marriage. Run by Costas Perandonis
and his Dutch wife, it offers a balanced mix
of Mediterranean hospitality and northern
European simplicity of style. The bill won't
break the bank.
*Children welcome; children's portions
available. Booking essential. Pavement tables.
Vegetarian dishes.*

INDIAN

Mayur
*Korte Leidsedwarsstraat 203, IS (623
2142/625 0776). Tram 1, 2, 5, 6, 7, 10.*
Lunch served *12.30-2.30pm Mon, Wed-Sun.* **Dinner served** *5-11pm daily.* **Average**
f30. **No credit cards.**
A friendly, casual atmosphere makes this a
good family restaurant, while the well-prepared and varied selection will satisfy the
most knowledgeable palate.
*Children welcome; high chairs; children's
menu f16. Vegetarian thali. Wheelchair
access.*

Tandoor
*Leidseplein 19, IS (623 4415). Tram 1, 2, 5,
6, 7, 10.* **Dinner served** *5-11pm daily.*
Average *f20.* **Credit** AmEx, DC, MC, V.
When it opened in 1970, the Tandoor was
Amsterdam's first commercial Indian
restaurant (as opposed to some sixties'
hippy co-operatives). The excellent quality
of the food, the varied menu and reasonable prices go a long way towards making
this one of the most popular Indian restau-

rants in the city. It is famous for tandoori,
but many other regional dishes are
offered as well. The Tandoor looks out on
Leidseplein – it's well worth booking a
window seat, as the passing crowds and
street performers are great entertainment.
Children welcome; children's menu f13.

INDONESIAN

Lonny's
*Rozengracht 48, IW (623 8950). Tram 13,
17, 24.* **Dinner served** *6-10.45pm daily; Oct-Easter 5-9.45pm daily.*
Average *f35.* **Credit** AmEx, MC, V.
A relatively new restaurant, Lonny's has a
good kitchen which has quickly earned it a
loyal clientèle. Small and personal, with a
cheerfully elegant décor, it offers reasonably
priced, authentic meals in a peaceful, pleasantly unhurried environment.
*Children admitted; children's portions on
request. Vegetarian dishes.*

Orient
*Van Baerlestraat 21, OS (673 4928). Tram
10.* **Dinner served** *5-9.15pm daily.* **Rijsttafel**
f36. **Credit** AmEx, DC, MC, V.
See **picture and caption.**
*Booking advisable. Children welcome.
Vegetarian dishes.*

Sama Sebo
*PC Hooftstraat 27, OS (662 8146). Tram 2,
3, 5, 12.* **Lunch served** *noon-1.45pm,*
dinner served *6-9.45pm, Mon-Sat.* **Average**
f30. **Rijsttafel** *f42.50.* **Credit** AmEx, DC,
MC, V.
One of the earliest rijsttafel restaurants,
Sama Sebo is now suffering from a surfeit of
visitors from abroad; booking is essential.
Good Indonesian nibbles can be ordered at
the bar. There are two evening sittings, one
at 6pm and one at 8pm, so be sure to ask for
the second if you like a leisurely meal.
*Children welcome; children's portions on
request. Book always. Terrace area for drinks
only.*

Speciaal
*Nieuwe Leliestraat 142, IW (624 9706).
Tram 10, 13, 14, 17.* **Dinner served** *5.30-11pm daily.* **Average** *f40.* **Rijsttafel** *f39.50.*
Credit AmEx, DC, MC, V.
When Indonesian food comes up in conversation in Amsterdam, so does the Speciaal.
Be sure to book because the food is appreciated by Amsterdammers and tourists alike,
and if you are feeling brave order the
rijsttafel. Recent reports indicate that standards may have fallen
*Children admitted; one high chair. Booking
advisable Fri, Sat. Pavement tables.
Vegetarian dishes and rijsttafel on request.*

The **Orient** (see under **International: Indonesian**) *is small but authentic,
with antique shadow puppets on the walls and cuisine from the former Dutch
East Indies on the menu. Top of the list is rijsttafel, the traditional Indonesian
feast of about 20 dishes served simultaneously, accompanied by a bowl of rice. The
idea is to build a meal around the rice by adding each of the items: chicken, pork,
beef, eggs, vegetables, fruits and nuts all prepared in various ways (spicy, mild,
sweet and sour). Connoisseurs also add sambal – red-hot pepper sauce. The
Wednesday night all-you-can-eat buffet (about f30) is another treat. An English-language menu explains the history of Indonesian customs and the dishes.*

Tempo Doelo
Utrechtsestraat 75, IS (625 6718). Tram 4.
Dinner served 6-11.30pm daily. **Average**
£39.50. **Rijsttafel** (vegetarian, meat, fish)
£47.50. **Credit** AmEx, DC, MC, V.
Another Indonesian institution – here you
can test your tongue on the hottest food in
town. The waiters, however, can be relied on
to warn you in advance about the dangerous
dishes. Unusually for an Indonesian restaurant, fish is a speciality.
Children admitted; children's portions by
arrangement. Book always. Vegetarian dishes.
Wheelchair access with help.

ITALIAN

Casa di David
Singel 426, C (624 5093). Tram 1, 2, 5.
Dinner served 5-11pm daily. **Average** £15.
Credit AmEx, DC, MC, V.
This romantic, dark-wooded and beamed
restaurant is popular with visitors and locals
alike. The pasta is made on the premises
and is first-rate (try the fettucine with
salmon sauce) and the crusty pizzas are
made in a wood-fired oven (illegal in the UK,
so British visitors may enjoy the slightly
charcoaled flavour). Tables by the window
give a good view of the canal.
Children welcome; children's portions on
request. Book at weekends. Vegetarian dishes.

Cirelli
Oude Zijskolk, C (624 3512). Bus 100, 104,
105, 106, 110, 111, 112, 114, 115. **Dinner**
served 5-10pm Mon-Thur, Sun; 5-11pm Fri,
Sat. **Average** £50. **Credit** AmEx, MC, V.
See p85 picture and caption.
Children admitted; half portions available
(also for adults). Booking appreciated.
Vegetarian dishes. Live music occasionally.

Da Damiano
Jan Pieter Heijestraat 139, OW (685 0795).
Tram 1, 6, 7, 17. **Dinner served** 5-10.30pm
daily. **Average** £10. **No credit cards.**
Though out of the city centre (just north of
Vondelpark), this popular neighbourhood
Italian is a find – a true piece of Italy with
excellent pizzas (plus pasta and more substantial main dishes) and a house red to
match. For those staying in the area it's one
to return to again and again.
Children admitted; children's portions on
request. Book after 7pm. Vegetarian dishes.

Mirafiori
Hobbemastraat 2, OS (662 3013). Tram 1,
2, 5, 6, 7, 10. **Lunch served** noon-3pm,
dinner served 5-9.30pm Mon, Wed-Sun.
Average £45. **Credit** AmEx, MC, V
Located in a grandiose building at the
Leidseplein corner of Vondelpark, this is
reputed to be the classiest Italian in town.
For all its elegance and the excellence of its
cuisine, it isn't outrageously expensive, and
two can dine very well on three courses with
house wine for not much more than £100.
Veal dishes are melt-in-your-mouth tender
and the service is attentive for a middle-
range establishment.
Children welcome. Vegetarian dishes.

Piccolino
Lange Leidsedwarsstraat 63, IS (623 1495).
Tram 1, 2, 5, 6, 7, 10. **Meals served** noon-
11pm daily. **Average** £20. **No credit cards.**
One of the several cheap but very cheerful

Italian restaurants in this street near
Leidseplein, Piccolino is a good pre-cinema
dining spot. House wine is served by the
glass.
Children admitted. Vegetarian dishes.

Pizzaria Capri
Lindengracht 63, IW (624 4940). Tram 3,
10/bus 18. **Open** 10am-9pm Mon, Tue,
Thur-Sun. **Average** £25. **No credit cards.**
Angela and Nicola Tritatepe give the impression of having been magically transported
from central Italy, pizza ovens and all. They
make their own ice-cream, and their version
of Dutch apple cake is just the thing to complement an espresso or cappuccino. Simple
home-style pastas and pizzas, well-chosen
robust Tuscan wines and an unpretentious
setting are other attractions.

JAPANESE

In 1970, the **Yoichi** was the only
Japanese restaurant in Amsterdam.
Since then, they've been sprouting
like shitake mushrooms. All of them
are good, and everyone has their
favourites. We list a selection below.

Aska
Handweg 1-5, Amstelveen (647 1740). Bus
68. **Lunch served** noon-2pm, **dinner**
served 6-10pm, Mon-Sat. **Average** £50.
Credit AmEx, DC, JCB, MC, V.
Well worth the short trip south to
Amstelveen, as is evidenced by the many
Japanese, mostly business executives, who
eat here. The purpose-built octagonal building of woods and natural materials offers
customers a choice of teppan-yakki tables,
where customers can watch as chefs prepare the food, lakeview tables or tatami
seating (upstairs). Tempura, sashimi and
sushi are superbly presented.
Children welcome; children's menu for over-
4s. Book always. Vegetarian dishes.

Oshima
Prinsengracht 411, IW (625 0996). Tram 7,
10. **Open** 6-10pm Tue-Sun. **Average** £50.
Credit AmEx, DC, MC, V.
Reservations are essential for this compara-
tively cheap but good restaurant located on
one of Amsterdam's major canals. The owners have put all their investment into
maintaining the freshest sushi bar around,
rather than into luxurious décor. Customers
can opt for chairs or tatami mats, and neither
the simple (spotlessly clean) surroundings
nor the relatively peaceful crowd distract
from the well-prepared and presented meals.

Teppan-Yaki & Yamazato
Okura Hotel, Ferdinand Bolstraat 333, OS
(678 7111). Tram 12, 25. **Lunch served**
noon-2.30pm Mon-Fri. **Dinner served** 6.30-
10.30pm daily. **Average** £75. **Set menus**
from £86. **Credit** AmEx, DC, JCB, MC, V.
These sister restaurants are among the
finest purveyors of Japanese fare.
Customers at the Teppan-Yaki are treated to
amazing showmanship by master Japanese
chefs, while at the Yamazato, chefs sliver
fish with the same dexterity. The artfully
presented sushimi-sushi can be a meal in
itself; sukiyaki is downright ceremonial.
Tatami rooms are available.
Children welcome; children's portions on

request; high chairs. Book always. Vegetarian
dishes. Wheelchair access.

Yoichi
Weteringschans 128, IS (625 0996). Tram
13, 14, 17. **Dinner served** 6-10pm daily.
Average £60. **Credit** AmEx, DC, MC, V.
A big favourite with Japanese businessmen
and Nipponophiles, Yoichi changed management a few years ago – thank heavens,
because for a long time it was the only
Japanese restaurant in town, and the freshness of the sushi could not be guaranteed.
These days, the service is quick and special
orders can be accommodated. The manager
will explain what everything is, and answer
questions about Japan in general. The
Japanese waitresses are polite and unobtrusive, but attentive.

MEXICAN

El Mareton
Johannes Verhulststraat 104, OS (662 7218).
Tram 16. **Open** 5-10.30pm daily. **Average**
£40. **No credit cards.**
A Spanish-run neighbourhood bar that has
grown into a relatively low-key Mexican
restaurant. Start with margaritas in the
postage stamp-size bar before heading up
the circular stairs to the relaxed dining-room
full of Mexican memorabilia. The action
spreads to the pavement in summer.
Children welcome; children's menu £14.50.

Pancho Villa
Spuistraat 30, C (620 0140). Tram 1, 2, 5.
Dinner served 5-11pm Tue-Sun. **Average**
£30. **Credit** AmEx, DC, MC, V.
Some loyal customers will swear that this is
the home of the best tequila cocktails in
Amsterdam (others vote for Rose's Cantina
below). In any case, the teetotaller will also
find plenty to enjoy. Chocolate fiends take
note of the mole rojo enchilada – a savoury-
filled enchilada covered with dark chocolate.
Children admitted; children's menu.
Vegetarian dishes.

Rose's Cantina
Reguliersdwarsstraat 38, IS (625 9797).
Tram 16, 24, 25. **Dinner served** 5.30-11pm
Mon-Thur, Sun; 5-11.30pm Fri, Sat. **Average**
£23. **Credit** AmEx, MC, V.
So crowded you have to keep an eye on
whose tacos you are dipping into whose
sauce. It's definitely not the place for a quiet
night out, and not particularly authentic
either; but the ingredients are top-quality
and the portions are more than generous.
Rose's gets our vote for the best margaritas
in town.
Children welcome; children's portions on
request. No reservations. Vegetarian dishes.

NORTH AFRICAN

Hamilcar
Overtoom 306, OW (683 7981). Tram 1, 6.
Dinner served 5-10.30pm Wed-Sun.
Average £30. **Cous-cous** £17-£34. **Credit**
AmEx, DC, MC, V.
Just outside the centre of town, Hamilcar is
definitely worth the walk up Overtoom.
Delicious dishes, including cous-cous of
course, are prepared by owner-chef
Kamoun and served by his Dutch wife in a
relaxed and spacious setting.
Children welcome; children's portions on

request; one high chair. Book Fri, Sat, Sun. Vegetarian dishes.

Marakech
Nieuwezijds Voorburgwal 134, C (623 5003). Tram 1, 2, 5, 13, 17. **Meals served** 3-11pm daily. **Average** cous-cous f14. **Credit** MC, V.
Genuine cous-cous at reasonable prices. Mint tea with honey and luscious pastries brought on a tiered silver stand make the menu even more enticing. The obligatory cat is enormous, orange, and very cuddly.

PORTUGUESE

Portugalia
Kerkstraat 35, IS (625 6490). Tram 1, 2, 5. **Meals served** noon-midnight daily. **Average** f30. **Credit** AmEx, DC, MC, V.
Piri-piri sauce, cataplana, stuffed squid and – rare in Amsterdam – grilled swordfish are some of the delicacies served here. Portuguese crafts and frescoes contribute to the authentic feel in this excellent restaurant.

SPANISH

Centra
Lange Niezel 29, C (622 3050). Tram 4, 9, 16, 24, 25. **Open** 11am-11pm daily. **Average** f20. **No credit cards.**
Known for good, wholesome, home-style cooking, this restaurant doesn't look very inviting at first glance. Cafeteria tables and fluorescent lighting aren't very atmospheric, but you know you're in the right place because of the large and satisfied Spanish clientèle. House wines are very good value. It's in the heart of the red light district, so read your map well if you go after dark.

Iberia
Hoogte Kadijksplein 16, IE (623 6313). Tram 1. **Open** 5-11pm daily. **Average** f45. **Credit** AmEx, DC, MC.
See picture and caption.

El Naranjo
Boomstraat 41A, IW (622 2402). Tram 3, 10/bus 18. **Open** 4pm-1am Tue-Sun. **Average** f40 **Credit** MC.
This is the only Spanish restaurant in Amsterdam to offer a reasonable selection of tapas. The Spanish owner is friendly and helpful, as are the staff. Friday nights feature live Spanish music and the crowd is the real sing-and-clap-along type. There are probably better places for the food, but not for sheer enjoyment and fun.

Rias Altas
Westermarkt 25, IW (624 2510). Tram 13, 14, 17/bus 21, 67, 170, 171, 172. **Open** 3-11pm daily. **Credit** AmEx, DC, MC.
Despite its rather touristy appearance, Rias Altas is a favourite among the Spanish community, and it certainly has a first-rate paella. It is also very easy to find, being right across from Westerkerk and a stone's throw from Anne Frankhuis.

VEGETARIAN

Baldur
Weteringschans 76, IS (624 4672). Tram 6, 7, 10, 16, 24, 25. **Open** 5-9pm Mon-Sat.

Flamenco music sets the scene at **Iberia** *(see under* **International: Spanish**), *the first authentic Spanish restaurant in Amsterdam when it opened 25 years ago. The paella, zarzuela (fish stew) and tapas are still popular with the new breed of residents moving into the old dock area conversions.*

Average f25. **Unlicensed. No credit cards.**
Peaceful, soothing simplicity of décor and soft new-age or classical background music combine to make this restaurant a wonderful refresher for frazzled nerves. The meals (vegan, lacto-ovo and 'biological') are basically nouvelle cuisine; the menu changes frequently to include many seasonal offerings, and offers some of the best deals for vegetarians in the city. In the summer there are tables on the back balcony, overlooking the herb garden.

Bolhoed
Prinsengracht 60, IW (626 1803). Tram 13, 14, 17. **Open** noon-10pm Mon-Fri; 10am-10pm Sat, Sun. **Average** f20. **No credit cards.**
Choose hearty vegan dishes à la carte or on the daily-changing set-price menu (f19.50). The restaurant is licensed, and there's a sumptuous selection of pastries; the banana cream pie is a *tour de force*, properly tackled by two. It's a pleasingly eccentric mix of folklore, new age and modern.

The Egg Cream
St Jacobsstraat 19, C (623 0575). Tram 1, 2, 5, 13, 17. **Meals served** 11am-8pm daily. **Unlicensed. Average** f14. **Credit** EC.
Good, imaginative vegetarian food has been served in these simple surroundings for over 20 years. Several cooks of different nationalities work a rota, and the menu changes every day.
Children admitted. Booking advisable 6-8pm. Vegan dishes sometimes available.

Hemelse Modder
Oude Waal 9, C (624 3203). Metro Nieuwmarkt. **Dinner served** 6-10pm Mon, Wed-Sun. **Average** f35. **No credit cards.**

Booking is the only way of getting a table here. The creative mixed meat/vegetarian menu is based on French and Italian-inspired dishes, and the friendly service makes for a cheerfully upbeat atmosphere. The *pièce de resistance* is a rich chocolate mousse, which goes by the name of Heavenly Mud (*Hemelse Modder*), and is well worth the f6.50 tag. The restaurant is licensed.
Children welcome; children's portions on request.

Klaverkoning
Koningsstraat 29, C (626 1085). Metro Nieuwmarkt. **Dinner served** 5.30-9.30pm Tue-Sat. **Average** f30. **Credit** DC, MC, V.
A light, airy atmosphere and friendly service set this vegetarian and fish restaurant apart from others. All vegetables are organically grown. Desserts are always a highlight – the ice-cream is made from fresh cream: fattening but delicious. The restaurant is licensed.
Children welcome; children's portions on request; high chairs. Smoking not encouraged. Terrace seating. Vegan dish available.

De Waaghals
Frans Halsstraat 29, OS (679 9609). Tram 16, 24, 25. **Dinner served** 5.30-9pm Tue-Sat. **Average** f20. **No credit cards.**
Popular and inexpensive, this dedicated vegetarian establishment serves organically grown food that you can wash down with organic wine. Like The Egg Cream (*see above*) they don't believe in eating late here and the place empties by around 9pm. A few vegan dishes are usually on the menu, but phone to check and for other special dietary requirements.
Children welcome. Nö-smoking area.

DE BRAKKE GROND

Theatercafé & Restaurant

Nes 43, Amsterdam
International kitchen with a Flemish touch.

opened: daily
reservations: (0) 20-626 00 44

Enjoy a special Dutch dinner in a classic Dutch ambiance

The "Port van Cleve" has been a meetingpoint in the heart of the Capital city for over 100 years. You too should enjoy a typical Dutch dinner or one of those famous numbered steaks from around the world. Get to know Dutch Cuisine and meet up at the Port van Cleve.

die Port van Cleve

N.Z. Voorburgwal 178-180, 020-240047

Cafés & Bars

Barflys will get a real buzz out of Amsterdam, whether they're after a genial atmosphere, designer décor or the local liquor. *Jon Henley* **does the honours.**

Amsterdam has 1,402 cafés and bars (approximately one per 700 residents), according to the statistic-obsessed VVV. But what is really worth knowing is that they are one of the city's major assets. A gentle tipple, a quiet read on a rainy afternoon or a sustained drinking bout – most bars offer congenial surroundings for all three.

Except for the most glaringly tourist-oriented joints around Damrak, Rembrandtsplein and Leidseplein, they're relaxed places with a regular and characteristic clientele – gilded youth, tarnished hippies, beautiful 'meedja' people, solid burghers or solitary *pils* drinkers who have occupied the same stool since Liberation Day 1945. It's worth seeking out the good ones: they have an atmosphere that's difficult to quantify but will draw you back – probably against your better judgement – time and again.

DESIGNER vs BROWN

Roughly speaking, there are two types of bar in Amsterdam: the 'brown café' and the 'designer bar'. The first, as the name suggests, are the small, dark, smoke-stained, invariably friendly watering-holes where the prevailing activity – except on Friday and Saturday nights – will be quiet and more or less considered conversation, accompanied by equally quiet and considered drinking. The second are the bright, chrome-and-glass alternatives: call them what you will, in Amsterdam it's hi-tech, post-modernist, new realist or functionalist. Here one tends to be seen and hopes to be talked about.

Almost all bars cater for more intellectual tastes with a selection of newspapers and magazines – although not often, unfortunately, in English. Several also provide large, central reading tables at which you can spread out luxuriously – and usually over a single coffee or beer – for a whole afternoon. **Het Molenpad**, the **Luxembourg** (listed *under* **Brown Cafés**) and the

Waterloo (*under* **Designer Bars**) are among the best for this.

GOING DUTCH

Drinking in Dutch is a straightforward matter. Lager beer (Heineken, Amstel, Oranjeboom, Grolsch, Ridder) is called *pils* and is usually served in a small, thin glass with a two-finger head skimmed flat with a plastic knife. (Complaints about the foam/liquor ratio are generally met with blank incomprehension.) It should cost around f2.25-f2.50, although in some places – particularly those with waiter service – this can reach f2.75, and bars featuring live music might charge even more.

More exciting alternatives are *witbier*, a light, lemon-flavoured beer recommended for summer;

Dentergem, Raaf, Hoengaarden are some examples. Darker beers, either draught or bottled, tend to be Belgian. Perhaps most popular is De Koninck, widely available and a welcome respite for determined English bitter drinkers; Duvel is a lighter-tasting but considerably stronger alternative. The remaining Belgian bottled beers (Trappist, Kriek – cherry flavoured – and several dozen others) should be treated with extreme caution . Most are brewed by monks with a seemingly perverse sense of humour: one bears the accurate name of Mort Subite (Sudden Death).

Except with their meals, the Dutch are not big wine drinkers. While you shouldn't expect to find many wine bars, or a particularly wide range of wines, most bars will have a tolerable dry white or red, often of indeterminate origin. Ask for *wijn*, either *rood* or *wit*.

Almost all bars stock a considerable variety of foreign spirits (starting at f3.50-f4) along with the cheaper locally produced hooch: *jenever* (or *genever*) and *vieux*. The former is known as Dutch gin, although it's actually made from

One of the pleasures of Prinsengracht, **Het Molenpad** *(see under* **Brown Cafés***) is long, dark and narrow with a large reading table at the back, good tapes, changing art exhibitions and exceptionally good food from f18. Worth a detour, despite the occasionally surly barstaff.*

One of the Jordaan's classic bars, **De Tuin** *(see under* **Brown Cafés***) is stone-floored, dark and always lively. Generally frequented by slightly alternative locals, it has excellent apple tarts in the afternoons, and there's always someone to challenge to a game of chess or backgammon.*

remarkably imaginative food at more than reasonable prices (starting with *dagschotel*, or dish of the day, from about f15-f19).

It's difficult to be categorical about opening hours; most bars open between 10am and noon, although several don't open until 4pm. Unless they have a special licence (*nachtvergunning*), most close at 1am Sunday to Thursday and 2am on Friday and Saturday. For the seriously dedicated, a minority open at 9pm or 10pm and close at 4am or later. These include **De Doffer** and **Koophandel** (*under* **Brown Cafés**).

BROWN CAFES

The following is a selection of convivial cafés: places for an afternoon read or an evening drink. Where indicated, the *eetcafés* among them serve lunch-time snacks and/or an evening meal of varying degrees of sophistication – but be warned, most brown café kitchens close at around 9pm.

Aas van Bokalen
Keizersgracht 335, IW (623 0917). Tram 1, 2, 5. **Open** *bar* noon-1am Mon-Thur; noon-2am Fri; *kitchen* 5.30-10pm daily. **No credit cards**.
A stunningly unpretentious little bar serving some of the best-value food in town (from f16). It has a fine collection of seventies' tapes and a varied, largely young clientele. Usually full by mid-evening.

Bern
Nieuwmarkt 9, C (622 0034). Metro Nieuwmarkt. **Open** 4pm-1am Mon-Thur, Sun; 4pm-2am Fri, Sat. **No credit cards**.
Small and very brown, this is the genuine article in a seedy area where you really wouldn't expect to find it. Friendly service, very good food – particularly the fondue – from f17. *See also p79* **Restaurants: Cafés & Brasseries**.

Café Nol
Westerstraat 109, IW (624 5380). Tram 10. **Open** 9am-3am Mon-Thur, Sun; 9am-4am Fri, Sat. **No credit cards**.
This way over-the-top Jordaan bar is always crowded with lustily singing locals and the occasional stray tourist. Something of an institution and not to be attempted unless you're happy to lose almost every inhibition you ever had.

De Doffer
Runstraat 12, IW (622 6686). Tram 1, 2, 5. **Open** *bar* 11am-2.30am Mon-Thur; 11am-3.30am Fri, Sat. **No credit cards**.
A scruffy, friendly, down-to-earth brown bar with billiards at the back and cheap, filling food from f16. Much patronized by students, possibly because of its opening hours (rising before lunch not being a general requisite of Amsterdam student life).

molasses and only flavoured with juniper berries. It comes in a variety of ages (*jong*, *oud* and *zeer oud*: young, old and very old), its flavour mellowing progressively up the scale. It also comes in more exotic flavours: *citroenjenever* (lemon), *bessenjenever* (blackcurrant) and in the form of an old North Holland fisherman's drink, a *schelvispekel*. This herb-flavoured *jenever* has its equivalent in all the regions of The Netherlands; the Limburg version, for example, is *els*. If you want to sound truly *Amsterdams*, ask for a *jonge* or *oude borrel* (young or old *jenever*). Those prepared to wake up with amnesia should ask for a *kopstoot* (pils with a *jenever* chaser).

Vieux is a rather weak and insipid Dutch brandy. Drink it only if you can't afford the French version, or if you don't want to get drunk in a hurry. *Advocaat* needs no description.

The Dutch find cocktails a bit too flamboyant, and you won't find them on offer at many places; your best bet is to go to the bars of the more 'international' hotels such as the Café Americain (*under* **Designer Bars**) or the Pulitzer (*see page 39* Accomm-

odation). Rum Runners (*see page 79* **Restaurants**) is the only place to make a point of serving cocktails, and you can get margaritas at Tex Mex and South American restaurants.

BAR FOOD
Solid refreshment is also available at many bars. Apart from meals, there is a traditional range of nibbles with which the Dutch assuage pre-dinner hunger. Particularly worth trying in winter are *bitterballen*: deep-fried cases of breadcrumbs around a tongue-singeing gunge of puréed meat, served with mustard and much more delicious than they sound. Common alternatives include chunks of cheese with mustard, unshelled peanuts, chorizo sausage, *osseworst* (raw minced beef in sausage form) and, lately, insipid tortilla chips with throat-clearing sauce.

More serious sustenance is often available: a roll at lunch-time, a cheap and cheerful meal in the evening, or a full three-course menu. Generally speaking, *eetcafés*, a sort of brasserie (which can be either 'brown' or 'designer'), are an excellent alternative to restaurants; some serve

De Druif

_Rapenburgerplein 83, C (624 4530). Tram
1/Metro Waterlooplein/bus 22, 31._ **Open**
11am-1am Mon-Thur, Sun; 11am-2am Fri,
Sat. **No credit cards.**
A little-known bar of immense charm, situated on the water's edge behind the
harbour. If you make it out there you'll be
the only non-local – but they're a very
friendly bunch.

Engelbewaarder

Kloveniersburgwal 59, C (625 3772). **Metro**
Nieuwmarkt. **Open** noon-1am Mon-Thur;
noon-2am Fri, Sat; 2pm-1am Sun. **No credit
cards.**
A 'literary café' featuring occasional Sunday
live jazz, this is a scruffy but attractive dive
whose clientele (including students, retired
American hippies and perspiring writers)
will welcome you providing you have something intelligent to say. There is additional
outdoor seating on a barge moored outside.

Frascati

_Nes 59, C (624 1324). Tram 4, 9, 14, 16, 24,
25._ **Open** _bar_ 4pm-1am Mon-Thur, Sun;
4pm-2am Fri; noon-2am Sat; _kitchen_ 5.30-
10pm daily. **No credit cards.**
The Frascati is more Victorian purple than
brown, with a disconcertingly large mirror
behind the bar and excellent, cheap food
from f15. Popular with students and theatrical
types from the numerous fringe venues in the
street. It was undergoing renovation at time
of writing – pray the atmosphere is retained.

Gollem

Raamsteeg 4, C (626 6645). Tram 1, 2, 5.
Open 4pm-1am Mon-Thur, Sun; 4pm-2am
Fri, Sat. **No credit cards.**
An unbelievably wide range of often lethal
bottled beers explains this small, crowded
bar's popularity. There's even a 'menu' to
help you choose. For obvious reasons, early
evening is the best time to go if you want
anything resembling conversation.

Het Hok

_Lange Leidsedwarsstraat 134, IS (624 3133).
Tram 1, 2, 5._ **Open** 9am-1am Mon-Thur;
9am-2am Fri, Sat; noon-1am Sun. **Credit**
AmEx, DC, MC, V.
A friendly chess and board games café with
a dedicated local clientele. On the edge of
the neon-lit Leidseplein night-life scene, this
place couldn't be further removed in mood.

Heuvel

_Prinsengracht 568, IS (622 6354). Tram 1,
2, 5, 16, 24, 25._ **Open** 10am-1am Mon-Thur;
10am-2am Fri, Sat; noon-1am Sun. **No
credit cards.**
A dark but cheerful and unpretentious bar
in a lovely location at the edge of two canals.
It's generally full of locals who tend to get
rather raucous late at night. The 'terrace'
(pavement) catches the sun till late into the
afternoon.

Hoppe

_Spui 18-20, C (623 7849). Tram 1, 2, 4, 5,
9, 14, 16, 24, 25._ **Open** 11am-1am Mon-
Thur, Sun; 11am-2am Fri, Sat. **No credit
cards.**
An Amsterdam institution, Hoppe allegedly
dates from 1670. Popular at the best of
times, it becomes impossibly crowded from
5pm to 6pm, when it's filled with stripy

shirts and braces on their way home from
the office. In any event, you're likely to have
to sup your _pils_ standing up.

De IJsbreker

_Weesperzijde 23, OE (665 3014). Tram 3, 6,
7, 10._ **Open** _bar and snacks_ 10am-1am Mon-
Thur, Sun; 10am-2am Fri, Sat. **No credit
cards.**
The bar at this contemporary music centre
(_see p130_ **Music: Classical & Opera** and
_p135_ **Music: Rock, Folk & Jazz**) isn't
strictly speaking a brown bar but it's very
pleasant nonetheless. Well worth the bike or
tram ride for its terrace on the Amstel, off-
beat clientele and high-class modern
classical music. One of the few places open
for breakfast on Sunday, it has food available
all day.

De Kalkhoven

_Prinsengracht 283, IW (624 8649). Tram
13, 14, 17._ **Open** 11am-1am Mon-Thur;
11am-2am Fri, Sat; noon-1am Sun. **No
credit cards.**
An unremarkable but very pleasant brown
bar, generally less crowded with jolly
Jordaaners than other Prinsengracht alternatives. The clientele is relaxed and friendly,
as is the service.

Koophandel

_Bloemgracht 49, IW (623 9843). Tram 10,
13, 14, 17._ **Open** 4pm-very late daily. **No
credit cards.**
A late-night bar for the very dedicated.
Situated in a former warehouse beside the

Jordaan's prettiest canal, the Koophandel
looks abandoned and remains virtually
empty until midnight, when things get
steadily livelier. Closing time is flexible but
isn't usually much before dawn.

Luxembourg

_Spuistraat 22, C (620 6264). Tram 1, 2, 5,
13, 17._ **Open** _bar_ 10am-1am Mon-Thur, Sun;
10am-2am Fri, Sat; _kitchen_ noon-11pm daily.
No credit cards.
Still going strong as _the_ place to be seen for
the trend-conscious and generally monied
Amsterdammer, the Luxembourg is a fine
bar: elegant, high-ceilinged and serving an
excellent range of high-quality snacks (from
f12) culled from the kitchens of various
restaurants (_dim sum_ is delicious, club sandwiches colossal).

Het Molenpad

_Prinsengracht 653, IW (625 9680). Tram 1,
2, 5, 7, 10._ **Open** _bar_ noon-1am Mon-Thur,
Sun; noon-2am Fri, Sat; _kitchen_ noon-
3.30pm, 6-10.30pm, daily. **No credit cards.**
See p91 **picture and caption.**

Nieuwe Lelie

_Nieuwe Leliestraat 83, IW (622 5493).
Tram 10, 13, 14, 17._ **Open** 2pm-1am Mon-
Thur; 2pm-2am Fri, Sat. **No credit cards.**
A charming split-level Jordaan brown bar,
one of the few where you can be sure of a
table until quite late in the evening. It's very
quiet and relaxed, and chess boards are
often unoccupied; there's an exceptionally
friendly cat.

Perched on a second floor, **De Kroon** (see under **Designer Bars**) _is high-
ceilinged and spacious, has a covered balcony overlooking Rembrandtsplein and
serves evening meals (f14-f30) as well as bar snacks and light lunches. The
Regency-style furniture and apron-clad waiters are clearly aimed at office staff from
the surrounding banks; somehow, it just fails to avoid feeling ever-so-slightly tacky._

**amsterdam
tourist
office**

The best way
to find your way
in AMSTERD⟨⟩M

The VVV AMSTERDAM TOURIST OFFICE: an expert multilingual couter staff to answer all your questions ● Hotel reservations ● Reservations for excursions, concerts, theaters ● City maps ● Walking tours ● Shopping guides ● Souvenirs ● T - shirts ● What's on in Amsterdam ● Video films ● Posters ● Linen bags ● Picture postcards ● Recreational guides to all Dutch tourist centres ● Road maps ● Etc.

Stationsplein 10
Opposite Central Station
Leidsestraat 106

Phone (0)20 - 626 64 44

Oosterling
Utrechtsestraat 140, IS (623 4140). Tram 4.
Open noon-1am daily. **No credit cards.**
A stone-floored, unpretentious local that also, unusually, doubles as an off-licence. Good for a drink before or after a meal in one of the street's many restaurants; popular at office closing time with BP and Nederlandsche Bank slaves.

Orangerie
Binnen Oranjestraat 15, IW (623 4611). Tram 3/bus 18, 22, 44. **Open** 3pm-1am Mon-Thur, Sun; 3pm-2am Fri, Sat. **No credit cards.**
A delightful, relaxed and very brown bar a stone's throw from Brouwersgracht and its converted warehouses; good for quiet evenings and private conversations. The clientele includes a couple of notable north Jordaan eccentrics and squatters.

De Pieter
St Pieterspoortsteeg 29, C (623 6007). Tram 4, 9, 14, 16, 24, 25. **Open** 11pm-3am Mon-Thur, Sun; 11pm-4am Fri, Sat. **No credit cards.**
A very small, very dark, night café close to the Dam. Popular with students, it can get very rowdy when the owner squeezes in a live band. An experience, undoubtedly.

De Prins
Prinsengracht 124, IW (624 9382). Tram 13, 14, 17. **Open** *bar* 10am-1am Mon-Thur, Sun; 10am-2am Fri, Sat; *kitchen* 6-10pm daily. **No credit cards.**
Not to be confused with De Prinses, a little way down the canal, De Prins is usually full of students and a good bet if you're young and feeling in need of company. Very pretty setting, excellent food from around f17.

Van Puffelen
Prinsengracht 377, IW (624 6270). Tram 1, 2, 5, 7, 10. **Open** *bar* 2pm-1am Mon-Thur, Sun; 2pm-2am Fri, Sat; *kitchen* 6-10pm daily. **No credit cards.**
Two in one: a very popular, sawdust-strewn brown bar at the front; a high-ceilinged and up-market restaurant (from f20) at the back – beware the low-flying Cupids that adorn the ceiling. It's one of the haunts of the beautiful people, particularly on summer evenings when you can sit on the barge moored outside.

De Reiger
Nieuwe Leliestraat 34, IW (624 7426). Tram 10, 13, 14, 17. **Open** *bar* 11am-1am Mon-Thur, Sun; 11am-2am Fri, Sat; *kitchen* 6-10.30pm daily. **No credit cards.**
The style-conscious alternative to the Nieuwe Lelie (*see above*) down the street, this is a light and airy brown bar and one of the most popular in the Jordaan. Get there early, particularly if you want to eat (very good food including, in season, mussels, from f17).

Reijnders
Leidseplein 6, IS (623 4419). Tram 1, 2, 5, 6, 7, 10. **Open** 9am-1am Mon-Thur, Sun; 9am-2am Fri, Sat. **No credit cards.**
With its neighbour Eylders (*see p26 Amsterdam by Area: Leidseplein*), Reynders is probably the only bar worth considering on Leidseplein. Both are sur-

The **Waterloo** (see under **Designer Bars**) *is one of the new breed of 'grand cafés': light and airy, with abundant chrome, textured concrete and greenery. It has a television screen (permanently tuned to MTV) embedded in the floor and one of the best views of any café in Amsterdam, overlooking the Amstel. The lunch-time snacks are good (if pricey and often slow to arrive) and there is an up-market restaurant.*

vivors of a bygone era, with white-aproned waiters and high-ceilinged, antique interiors.

Scheltema
NZ Voorburgwal 242, C (623 2323). Tram 1, 2, 5, 13, 17. **Open** 8am-11pm Mon-Sat. **No credit cards.**
The Scheltema was once thronged with journalists from the national dailies based down the road. Now that they've all moved out to the concrete wilderness, the bar has become quieter, though it retains an attractive, slightly highbrow atmosphere. Note the early closing time.

't Smackzeyl
Brouwersgracht 101, IW (622 6520). Tram 1, 2, 5, 13, 17. **Open** 11.30am-1am Mon-Thur, Sun; 11.30am-2am Fri, Sat. **No credit cards.**
About as brown as you could wish for, this idyllically situated bar on the corner of two canals is one of the few to serve draught Guinness. As a result, getting served generally involves social intercourse with Irishmen in various stages of inebriation.

't Smalle
Egelantiersgracht 12, IW (623 9617). Tram 10, 13, 14, 17. **Open** *bar and kitchen* 11am-1am Mon-Thur, Sun; 11am-2am Fri, Sat. **No credit cards.**
Small, cosy and almost impossible to get a seat. In summer the terrace is wonderful; in

winter it's all candles and calm; the cat is friendly all year round. Very good lunch-time rolls and pre-dinner snacks.

Smoeshaan
Leidsekade 90, IS (625 0368). Tram 1, 2, 5, 6, 7, 10. **Open** *bar* 4pm-1am Mon-Thur, Sun; 4pm-2am Fri, Sat; *kitchen* 6-10pm daily. **No credit cards.**
If 'new brown' were a style, this would be one of its exponents. The Smoeshaan is a low-ceilinged, noisy joint serving food from around f18, and is mainly frequented by theatrical types. *See also p79* **Restaurants: Moderate.**

De Tap
Prinsengracht 478, IS (622 9915). Tram 1, 2, 5, 6, 7, 10. **Open** 4pm-1am Mon-Thur, Sun; 4pm-2am Fri, Sat. **No credit cards.**
A long, narrow, wood-panelled bar not far from the frantic Leidseplein, serving abundant pre-dinner snacks – mainly of unshelled peanuts. It's popular for student reunions and office parties; should you ever walk in on a medical student gathering, stay at your peril.

De Tuin
2E Tuindwarsstraat 13, IW (624 4559). Tram 3, 10, 13, 14, 17. **Open** 10am-1am Mon-Thur; 10am-2am Fri, Sat; 11am-1am Sun. **No credit cards.**
See p92 **picture and caption**

Twee Prinsen

Prinsenstraat 27, IW (624 9722). Tram 3, 10. Open 11am-1am Mon-Thur, Sun; 11am-2am Fri, Sat. No credit cards.
Opposite the Vergulde Gaper (*see below*), this is an exceptionally friendly bar full of young and vaguely off-beat local residents. Situated in the middle of the Jordaan, it forms an integral part of the Great Prinsengracht Pub Crawl (*see p33* Canals). The outdoor terrace is heated in chillier evenings.

Twee Zwaantjes

Prinsengracht 114, IW (625 2729). Tram 13, 14, 17. Open 3pm-1am daily. No credit cards.
A slightly (but only just) less rowdy version of the Café Nol (*see above*): a tiny bar usually crammed to bursting point with accordion playing, yodelling Jordaaners.

Vergulde Gaper

Prinsenstraat 30, IW (624 8975). Tram 3, 10. Open 11am-1am Mon-Thur, Sun; 11am-2am Fri, Sat. No credit cards.
An up-market and larger version of the Twee Prinsen (*see above*), the Vergulde Gaper is much reviled by the locals of the former as the 'yuppie pub across the road'. All that can truthfully be said is that the skirts are shorter and the braces more colourful. It also has a heated terrace.

De Wetering

Weteringstraat 37, IS (622 9676). Tram 6, 7, 10, 16, 24, 25. Open 3.30pm-1am Mon-Thur; 4.30pm-2am Fri, Sat; 4.30pm-1am Sun. No credit cards.

A split-level, very brown studenty bar tucked away in a side-street off Prinsengracht. Friendly locals, a huge roaring fire in winter and an antiquated television only turned on for vital football matches. Light snacks (rolls, toasted sandwiches, and so on) are available on demand.

Wildschut

Roelof Hartplein 1, OS (676 8220). Tram 3, 5, 12, 24, 25. Open *bar* 9am-2am daily; *kitchen* noon-5pm, 6-10pm, daily. No credit cards.
The Wildschut tries hard to be a brasserie rather than a bar, serving snacks from around f10. It's very popular with well-dressed office folk and crowded to overflowing when the terrace is open in summer.

DESIGNER BARS

The alternative: generally larger, shinier and populated with an altogether fancier kind of individual. Designer bars tend to serve good but often quite expensive food, and though you won't be thrown out for being underdressed, it's worth bearing in mind that designer bars attract would-be designer people. They're also among the few places in Amsterdam where you can get away with carrying a black leather Filofax.

De Balie

Kleine Gartmanplantsoen 10, IS (624 3821). Tram 1, 2, 5, 6, 7, 10. Open *July, Aug* 5pm-1am Mon-Thur, Sun; 5pm-2am Fri, Sat; *Sept-June* 11am-1am Mon-Thur, Sun; 11am-2am Fri, Sat. No credit cards.
Part of the cultural/political centre of the same name, the Balie is a slightly sterile, marbled place full of more-or-less active activists watching the riff-raff of Leidseplein from large windows. Reasonably good food is served upstairs (from f17).

De Beiaard

Herengracht 90, IW (625 0422). Tram 1, 2, 5, 13, 14, 17. Open noon-1am Mon-Thur, Sun; noon-2am Fri, Sat. No credit cards.
A beer drinkers' paradise: a high-ceilinged bar with a fifties' atmosphere to it, stocking a huge assortment of draught and bottled beers, served by a beer connoisseur.

Café Americain

American Hotel, Leidseplein 28-30, IS (624 5322). Tram 1, 2, 5, 6, 7, 10. Open 6am-1am daily. Credit AmEx, DC, MC, V.
Still the haunt of the rich and would-be famous, though beginning to lose out to some aggressive rivals, the Americain is worth visiting if only for the amazing art deco interior. The price of the drinks and food (from f25) reflects the surroundings. *See also p79* Restaurants: City Landmarks.

Huyschkaemer

Utrechtsestraat 137, IS (627 0575). Tram 4. Open *bar* noon-1am Mon-Thur, Sun; noon-2am Fri, Sat; *kitchen* 6-10pm daily. No credit cards.
Transformed from a former existence as an old-style brown bar, the Huyschkaemer is now all rag-rolled pastels and intricate mosaics. Popular with the gilded youth of the up-and-coming Utrechtsestraat, it serves excellent food (from f20).

De Jaren

Nieuwe Doelenstraat 20, C (625 5771). Tram 4, 9, 14, 16, 24, 25. Open *bar* 10am-1am Mon-Thur, Sun; 10am-2am Fri, Sat; *kitchen* 5.30-8.30pm daily. No credit cards.
A beautifully restored old building overlooking the Amstel, with exposed brickwork, a tiled mosaic floor and high cream walls, De Jaren serves snacks downstairs and a full restaurant menu upstairs (main courses from f20). With sunny balconies on both floors, down-to-earth service and an impressive range of beers and spirits, it's the most elegant and unpretentious of Amsterdam's new 'grand cafés'.

Kapitein Zeppos

Gebed Zonder End 5, C (624 2057). Tram 4, 9, 14, 16, 24, 25. Open *bar* 4pm-1am Mon-Thur, Sun; 4pm-2am Fri, Sat; *kitchen* 6-10pm daily. No credit cards.
Tucked away at the end of a cul-de-sac, this bar has a cobbled courtyard for summer evenings and loud music, live on Sunday afternoons. The tortilla chips have flavour; the menu is interesting and wide-ranging (from f20).

De Kroon

Rembrandtsplein 17, IS (625 2011). Tram 4, 9, 14. Open 11am-1am Mon-Thur, Sun; 11am-2am Fri, Sat. Credit MC.
See p93 picture and caption.

Metz (see under **Coffee Shops**) *is a post-modern café on the sixth floor of the famous department store, offering one of the best views of Amsterdam. Prices for the more gourmet than gourmand snacks reflect its location. Food includes smoked salmon on toast and pastrami on rye plus soups and, for larger appetites (and wallets) entrecôte, Metzburgers and so on. Metz claims to serve English afternoon tea: we've yet to be convinced.*

Land van Walem

*Keizersgracht 449, IW (625 3544). Tram 1,
2, 5.* **Open** *bar* 9am-1am Mon-Thur; 9am-
2am Fri, Sat; 9.30am-1am Sun; *kitchen*
9.30am-10.30pm daily. **No credit cards.**
Land van Walem is one of the earlier
designer bars: long, narrow and bright. The
seriously self-important clientele is worth
braving for the food; although it can be
pricey (from f17) it is good and comes in
large portions. Excellent vegetarian quiches
and big, cheap salads.

Malvesijn

*Prinsengracht 598, IW (638 0899). Tram 1,
2, 5, 6, 7, 10.* **Open** *bar and snacks* 10am-
1am daily; *kitchen* 5.30-10pm daily. **No
credit cards.**
Not very designer, but certainly not brown,
this friendly, recently opened bar looks like
a Habitat ad and serves good value food at
lunch-time and in the evenings (from f17).
Rarely full.

Morlang

*Keizersgracht 451, IW (625 2681). Tram 1,
2, 5.* **Open** *bar* 10am-1am Mon-Thur, Sun;
10am-2am Fri, Sat; *main kitchen* 5.30-10pm
daily; *snack kitchen* 10am-11pm daily. **No
credit cards.**
Next door to Land van Walem (*see above*)
and a competitor in the style stakes,
although the greenish psychedelic cloth
ceiling is not very appetising. There's an
awesome selection of foreign spirits, and
good food downstairs (from f18).

L'Opera

*Rembrandtsplein 27, IS (620 4754). Tram 4,
9, 14.* **Open** 10am-1am Mon-Thur, Sun;
10am-2am Fri, Sat; *kitchen* 11am-10pm daily.
Credit MC, V.
Another 'grand café', with an imposing
Parisian-style interior full of mirrors and gilt.
Unfortunately the overall sense of style is
not matched by the service, which is
appallingly slow. There's a good range of hot
snacks until late into the evening (from f10).

Paris Brest

*Prinsengracht 375, IW (627 0507). Tram 1,
2, 5, 7, 10.* **Open** *bar* 10am-1am Mon-Fri;
4pm-1am Sat, Sun; *kitchen* 10am-midnight
Mon-Fri; 4pm-midnight Sat, Sun. **No credit
cards.**
A hi-tech stainless steel and glass *eetcafé* that
is now an established haunt of those who
consider themselves too cool for (or can't
get into) the Van Puffelen next door (*see
above* **Brown Cafés**). Excellent food from
f30 for two courses.

Schiller

*Rembrandtsplein 26, IS (624 9846). Tram 4,
9, 14.* **Open** *bar* 4pm-1am Mon-Thur, Sun;
4pm-2am Fri, Sat; *kitchen* 9.30-11pm daily.
Credit AmEx, DC, MC, V.
This beautiful bar is a reminder of how
things were on Rembrandtsplein before
neon was invented. A legendary art deco
Amsterdam bar, it belongs to the hotel of the
same name.

Tisfris

*St Antoniesbreestraat 142, C (622 0472).
Metro Nieuwmarkt.* **Open** *bar* 10am-1am
daily; *kitchen* 6.30-10.30pm daily. **No credit
cards.**
A hi-tech but undaunting split-level bar with

Recently expanded, the slick and sanitized **Fancy Free** (see under **Smoking
Bars**) *is part of a chain and features lurid pink furniture, chrome trimmings
and a scattered selection of fifties' memorabilia. Masters of self-promotion, Fancy
Free sells its own brand of T-shirts, lighters and cigarette papers as well as juices,
coffee, toasties and rolls.*

good and wholesome food (from f16) and a
young and largely arty clientele. Tisfris is a
good bet if you're in the Jewish
quarter/Waterlooplein area.

Waterloo

*Zwanenburgwal 15, C (620 9039). Tram 9,
14.* **Open** *June-Sept: bar* 10am-1am daily;
kitchen 11am-10pm daily, to 11.30pm if
there's an opera; *Oct-May: bar* 10am-
midnight Mon-Fri; 11am-midnight Sat, Sun;
kitchen 11am-10pm daily. **Credit** AmEx, DC,
MC, V.
See p95 **picture & caption.**

PROEFLOKALEN

Generally little larger than a
wardrobe, *proeflokalen* or tasting
houses were originally tap-house
annexes where the distiller or
importer would serve potential
clients a selection of his flavoured
jenevers and liqueurs before persuad-
ing them, several hours later, to buy
a bottle. The free sample element
disappeared long ago, but *proeflokalen* remain a feature of
early-hours drinking. Most close at
around 8pm: probably a good thing
given the potency of their wares.

De Admiraal

*Herengracht 319, IW (625 4334). Tram 1, 2,
5.* **Open** noon-midnight Mon-Fri; 5pm-
midnight Sat. **No credit cards.**
A large *proeflokaal* offering – uniquely –
sofas and armchairs so you can get sozzled
in comfort. Bizarre-sounding liqueurs from
Amsterdam's only remaining independent
distillery, De Ooievaar, line the bar.
Unusually, it stays open till midnight. Be
warned!

De Drie Fleschjes

*Gravenstraat 16, C (624 8443). Tram 1, 2,
4, 5, 9, 13, 16, 24, 25.* **Open** noon-8.15pm
Mon-Sat. **No credit cards.**
There's virtually nowhere to sit here: just
knock back your liqueur (ask for the bar-
man's recommendation) and come back for
more in the company of large numbers of
locals, the odd student and office workers –
some of whom have their own reserved
cask on the wall.

Het Hooghoudt

*Reguliersgracht 11, IS (625 5030). Tram 4,
9, 14, 16, 24, 25.* **Open** noon-8pm Mon-Fri;
for groups at other times by arrangement.
No credit cards.
The Hooghoudt is more of a brown bar than
a *proeflokaal*, really, although it still calls
itself one. Casks are stacked high around
the walls, but this dark, appealing hole also
has a reading table – not the idea of a *proeflokaal* at all....

COFFEE SHOPS

The word 'coffeeshop' is open to misinterpretation in Amsterdam: as well as being a place for genteel afternoon tea or coffee and cakes, it can also denote the kind of place gran would sniff at: the hash bar or 'smoking' coffee shop (*see below* **Smoking Bars**). The two are in fact pretty easy to tell apart; one look at the customers should be enough, but if in doubt, ask the staff. We list below a selection of Amsterdam's best places for cakes and snacks.

While not succumbing to the orgies of gâteaux and whipped cream common in Germany and Austria, the Dutch are no mean cake eaters. Coffee is by far the best option to accompany your *taart* (cake): no one would claim that the Dutch make good English-style tea (and if you must have tea, don't expect to get milk without specifically asking for it). The best place to go for afternoon tea is PC Hooftstraat, Amsterdam's most elegant street, which is littered with up-market tearooms catering to shoppers trying not to look concerned about the f400 they've just spent on a shirt. Two of the best are **Patricia's** and **PC** (*see below*). There are few sandwich bars as such, but a number of the chic eateries provide light lunches or afternoon snacks.

Berkhoff
Leidsestraat 46, IS (624 0233). Tram 1, 2, 5. **Open** 9am-6pm Mon-Fri; 9am-5pm Sat. **No credit cards.**
Still one of the best for chocolate- and calorie-laden pastries and cakes, the Berkhoff has a small salon attached. It's usually full of little old ladies who seem to manage, astonishingly, to remain so.

Caffé Esprit
Spui 10A, C (622 1967). Tram 1, 2, 4, 5, 9, 14, 16, 24, 25. **Open** 10am-10pm Mon-Wed, Fri; 10am-midnight Thur; 10am-7pm Sat; *kitchen* 10am-9pm Mon-Wed, Fri; 10pm-10pm Thur; 10am-5pm Sat. **Credit** AmEx, MC, V.
Owned by the next-door fashion store of the same name, this ultra-modern café serves a full menu of Californian-style food as well as classy rolls and salads. It's at its best in summer, when the large terrace catches the sun and provides a welcome break from traipsing up Kalverstraat looking for bargains.

Lanskroon
Singel 305, C (623 7743). Tram 1, 2, 5. **Open** 8.30am-5.30pm Tue-Sat. **Credit** DC, MC, V.
For many people's money the most refined *banketbakkerij* (patisserie) in town, Lanskroon makes mouth-watering fruit pies and chocolate cakes. Devour them on the premises in a rather cramped tearoom.

Metz
Keizersgracht 455, IS (624 8810). Tram 1, 2, 5. **Open** 9.30am-5.30pm Mon-Wed, Fri, Sat; 9.30am-8.30pm Thur. **Credit** AmEx, DC, MC, V.
See p96 **picture and caption.**

Noord Zuid Hollands Koffiehuis
Stationsplein 10, C (623 3777). Tram 1, 2, 4, 5, 9, 13, 16, 17, 24, 25. **Open** *café* 9am-9pm Mon-Sat; 10am-9pm Sun; *kitchen* 9am-8.30pm Mon-Sat; 10am-8.30pm Sun. **Credit** AmEx, DC, MC, V.
Most people shoot straight past this on their way out of Centraal station, which is a shame because, while not worth a special journey, it is pleasantly relaxed, has a fine waterside terrace and serves reasonably-priced, light food.

PC
PC Hooftstraat 83, OS (671 7455). Tram 2, 3, 5, 12. **Open** 10am-7pm Mon-Fri; 10am-5.30pm Sat, Sun. **No credit cards.**
A pleasant and relaxed coffee shop, low-ceilinged and with wicker furniture, serving a good-value range of rolls, cakes and toasted sandwiches. Less imposing than some of its competitors.

Patricia's
PC Hooftstraat 128, OS (673 5595). Tram 2, 3, 5, 12. **Open** *café* 10am-6pm Mon-Sat; *kitchen* 10am-5pm Mon-Sat. **No credit cards.**
Doyen of the PC Hooftstraat coffee houses, Patricia's features matt grey furniture and large, sliding windows for maximum client exposure. Make sure you're clutching the right brand of carrier bag. Cold lunches from f15, meals from f17.50 and up-market rolls from f5.

Pompadour
Huidenstraat 12, IW (623 9554). Tram 1, 2, 5. **Open** 8.30am-6pm Tue-Sat. **No credit cards.**
Chocolatiers of distinction in a remarkable gilt and mirrored interior: your chance to follow Marie Antoinette's instructions in appropriate period surroundings.

SMOKING BARS

There are still plenty around, but dope bars are not the rage they once were. Strictly speaking, possession is illegal but the Amsterdam police turn a half-blind eye to soft drugs for personal use, working on the principle that semi-controlled outlets such as smoking coffee shops at least narrow down potential sources of harder stuff. However, official policy could change at any time. The authorities don't like large-scale trading, and have clamped down on over-commercial bars: the green cannabis leaf sticker that used to distinguish many bars has now disappeared, or been replaced by a question mark or just a blank space; some names have been altered to eliminate obvious references to intoxication and the hash menu is kept behind the bar. The range and the quality of the goods on offer are pretty standard across town.

It's difficult to generalize about the bars that remain. Some are slick, clean and hygienic, serving juices, coffee and tea as well as hash, and provide video games for customers lively enough to use them; others are little more than glorified holes in the wall, filled with pale, glazed teenagers.

The Bulldog
Leidseplein 13-17, IS (627 1908). Tram 1, 2, 5, 6, 7, 10. **Open** 9am-1am daily. **No credit cards.**
The grandaddy of them all, this also has branches at OZ Voorburgwal 90 and 132 and at Hekelveld 7, and recently opened an outlet in The Hague. First-time visitors take note: the smoker's bar is in the basement of The Palace, which features cocktail and juice bars, a souvenir shop, and even bike hire (*see p3* **Essential Information**).

Fancy Free
Martelaarsgracht 4, C (620 0457). Tram 1, *2, 4, 5, 9, 13, 16, 17, 24, 25.* **Open** 10am-midnight daily. **No credit cards.**
See p97 **picture and caption.**
Branch: Haarlemmerstraat 64, IW (627 8596).

Prix d'Ami
Haringpakkerssteeg 5, C (627 1019). Tram 1, 2, 4, 5, 9, 13, 16, 17, 24, 25. **Open** 9am-midnight daily. **No credit cards.**
Virtually indistinguishable from Fancy Free (*see above*). So respectable you could almost find a Filofax here.

Rusland
Rusland 16, C (627 9468). Tram 4, 9, 14, 16, 24, 25. **Open** 11am-9pm Mon-Sat; noon-9pm Sun. **No credit cards.**
Small, full and far more intimate than the chains.

So Fine
Prinsengracht 30, IW (622 6795). Tram 13, 14, 17. **Open** noon-midnight daily. **No credit cards.**
A scruffy but long-established dive, a favourite with local squatters. Food of a reasonable standard costs from f14.

Museums & Galleries

Some of the world's greatest art and museum collections are in Amsterdam. But if museum-going gives you a cultural overdose, try some of the more unusual specialist museums. These vary from the sacred – a clandestine church, the Bible Museum or Anne Frank's House – to the profane: take your pick from displays on sex, cannabis or torture instruments.

Masterpieces by Rembrandt, Van Gogh and others pull in millions of visitors each year. Contemporary Dutch artists may be less well known, but the city's commercial galleries display vibrant, exciting works for you to view or buy.

CONTENTS:

Museums

The Golden Age lives on in many of Amsterdam's museums. Others reflect the atmosphere of tolerance that has given the city its particular flavour. *Judi Seebus* steers you from fine art to wind machines.

With an average of one per 40 square kilometres (about 15 square miles), The Netherlands has the highest concentration of museums in the world. In Amsterdam the collections are diverse. Some are world-class; others are small gems and a few are unique.

The past few years have been characterized by dramatic cuts in the already ungenerous government funding of the arts. The present funding system of the Amsterdam museums is confusing, even for insiders. Three of the Amsterdam museums (the **Rijksmuseum** and the **Van Gogh Museum**, *listed under* **The Big Three**; and the **Nederlands Sheepvaart Museum**, *under* **Maritime**) are financed by the state but, in order to minimize bureaucracy, the government plans to give them a more independent structure. Another four (the **Stedelijk Museum**, *under* **The Big Three**; the **Fodor**, *under* **Art**; the **Amsterdams Historisch Museum**, *under* **Historical**; and the **Willet-Holthuysen Museum**, *under* **Golden Age**) are financed by the city of Amsterdam, while the rest are private. The majority of the museums are private collections that were donated to the city or to a specific foundation. Many are also classified as monuments (the Rijksmuseum, the **Theatermuseum**, *under* **Theatre**, and the **Bijbels Museum**, *under* **Religion**, for instance) and their upkeep is supported by Monumentenzorg, an administrative organization set up to preserve Amsterdam's architectural heritage.

FUNDING SCHEMES

Commercial sponsorship of museums and exhibitions has become a hot item recently; some observers are predicting that a new Golden Age will descend upon The Netherlands, with generous patrons subsidizing the arts. Cuts brought some talk of museums having to close down (the **Hortus Botanicus**, *under* **Botanical**, for example), but special activities were organized to save them and focus public attention on their problems. This coincided with the appearance of groups such as Friends of the Hortus Botanicus.

In the past, Dutch companies favoured sponsoring sports events rather than the arts, but times are changing and it is now becoming more prestigious for companies to have their name linked to that of an important museum, through the financing of special exhibitions or restoration of specific paintings. And foundations such as the Rembrandt Vereniging (Rembrandt Association), which provides funds for purchases, or the Prins Bernhard Fonds, which subsidizes restoration projects, assist several museums including the Rijksmuseum.

Temporary exhibitions, such as the 1990 special exhibition on Van Gogh to commemorate the centenary of his death, have been all the rage recently; organizers have found such events to be a quick and relatively easy way of increasing attendance figures to make the museum eligible for subsidies.

Charging for admission is not a recent thing – the Rijksmuseum introduced entrance fees in the thirties. While increases in admission prices provoke no real outcry, there were grumbles about the recent jump in the cost of the Annual Museum Card (*see below* **Tickets & Discounts**), which rose from £25 to £40.

While government funds are drying up for existing museums, the tap has been turned on for a new multi-million-guilder project planned for a location near Centraal Station. Some time in early 1993, the present **Technologie Museum NINT** (*under* **Technology**) will be reborn there in the form of a world-class Science Centre. Designed by the architect of the Centre Pompidou in Paris, the 'supermuseum' will be the first technological museum in the world to give chemistry a prominent position.

FURTHER AFIELD

With museums spread throughout the country devoted to the likes of clogs, clocks, salt, skates, wine and cheese, there will be something to tickle the fancy of even the staunchest museum hater. We list below a few of the major art collections (*under* **Further Afield**), but for more museums outside Amsterdam, *see page 203* **Excursions in Holland**, *page 208* **The Randstad** and *page 213* **The Provinces**. A guide brought out by the Museum Card foundation containing listings (in Dutch) of some 830 museums can be bought from various bookshops. The VVV tourist offices (*see page 3* **Essential Information**) are also helpful.

MUSEUM BOAT

Amsterdam is among the few major Dutch cities that offers the possibility of reaching a museum by water (another is Giethoorn; *see page 213* **The Provinces: Overijssel**). The Museum Boat is remarkably good value, even for tourists on a tight budget. Tickets entitle holders to get on and off at any of the five stops serving 16 of the capital's 40-odd museums located on or near one of the concentric canals or by the River IJ near Centraal Station. Tickets also give up to 50 per cent discount on admission prices; *see also below* **Tickets & Discounts**.

Museum Boat
Office and main boarding point: Stationplein 8, C (622 2181). Tram 1, 2, 4, 5, 9, 13, 16, 17, 24, 25. **Departs** every 45 mins, 10am-3.15pm daily. **Stops at** *Prinsengracht/Egelantiersgracht* (for Anne Frankhuis); *Singelgracht in front of Rijksmuseum* (for Museumplein); *Herengracht/Leidsegracht* (for Bijbels, Fodor, Amsterdam Historisch, Allard Pierson); *Amstel/Zwanenburgwal* (for Rembrandthuis, Jewish Historical); *Oosterdok/ Kattenburgergracht* (for Tropenmuseum, Werf 't Kromhout). **Tickets** f12 per day; f10 under-13s, CJP card holders; *combination tickets* (boat plus free admission to 3 museums) f20 per day; f18 under-13s, CJP card holders. **No credit cards.**

TICKETS & DISCOUNTS

Most museums are reasonably priced, between around f3 and f7. If you're thinking of taking in more than a few – in Amsterdam or elsewhere in the country – the **Annual**

Museum Card (*Museumjaarkaart*) is a good buy. Costing f40 (f15 for under-18s, f25 for pensioners), the ticket offers free or reduced-price admission to almost 400 museums throughout The Netherlands. Special exhibitions are normally not covered by the ticket, but you may be entitled to a reduction. The ticket can be purchased at one of the participating museums (indicated in the listings below) or at the VVV tourist offices. Reductions can often also be obtained with a valid student identity card, or a CJP under-26 card, available at the AUB Uitburo (*see page 3 Essential Information*).

Top of the list for good value is the **national museum weekend** (20-21 April 1991; 25-26 April 1992) – two days on which some 350 museums throughout the country are open free of charge (*see page 36 Amsterdam by Season*). But it's only really worthwhile if you're on a shoestring budget, since you'll have to vie with the large number of locals taking advantage of this popular freebie.

Temporary exhibitions at the major museums are often popular at weekends for family outings. It's also wise to avoid Wednesday afternoons if you're going to a museum that may be popular with children, as most primary schools have the afternoon off. Many museums are closed on Monday, with the notable exception of the **Museum Van Loon** (*under* **Golden Age**), which is only open on this day. Some museums do not always have captions and explanations in English, but many sell reasonably-priced English-language guidebooks. Enquire about this when you buy your ticket. Several museums also offer guided tours in English for groups; always phone to enquire or to make a booking.

Many museums are closed on public holidays (*see p3* **Essential Information**). Always phone to check.

THE BIG THREE

Rijksmuseum
Stadhouderskade 42, OS (673 2121). Tram 6, 7, 10. **Open** 10am-5pm Tue-Sat; 1-5pm Sun, public holidays. **Admission** f6.50; f3.50 under-17s; free with Museum Card; group discounts (min 20 people). **No credit cards.**
If you've been to Amsterdam's Centraal Station, you might think you're seeing double when you glimpse The Netherlands' largest national museum, the Rijksmuseum.

The **Van Gogh Museum** (see under **The Big Three**) *is the only museum in The Netherlands devoted to a single artist. The exterior may be bland, but the collection is remarkably colourful. Apart from the bright colours of his palette, Van Gogh is also known for his productivity, and both are clearly reflected in the 200 paintings and 500 drawings that form part of the permanent exhibition. An exceptionally good selection of works by Van Gogh's contemporaries, such as Toulouse-Lautrec, Bernard and Gauguin, is also on view. Van Gogh was influenced by Japanese prints and a selection of these is housed on the second floor. His development as an artist is further illustrated by changing exhibitions. From March to May 1991 a special exhibition will present the works of a number of Van Gogh's Dutch contemporaries including the Maris brothers, Isaac Israels, Breitner and Toorop.*

Both of these splendid neo-Renaissance buildings were designed by the architect PJH Cuypers (*see p61* **Between the Occupations**). Opened in 1885, the Rijksmuseum is backed by a small garden with sculptures, a pleasant end to what will probably be a tiring visit. The Museum gets some one million visitors per year – almost twice as many as its closest rivals, the Van Gogh Museum and the Stedelijk (*see below*), which respectively have 600,000 and 500,000 annually. The collection has expanded tremendously since eighteenth-century *stadhouder* Willem V started bringing pieces together for his private amusement. A single day won't be enough to view all the treasures, which include a fabulous collection of paintings from the fifteenth century until around 1850 and decorative and oriental arts; *see p103* **The Rijksmuseum**. Temporary exhibitions are often held in the National Print Room. A major exhibition on Rembrandt will be held from late 1991 until early 1992, featuring 50 paintings by the Dutch master as well as drawings and prints.
Café. Educational department. Films and slide shows. Guided tours. Shop. Wheelchair access with assistance.

Stedelijk Museum
Paulus Potterstraat 13, OS (573 2911/Dutch recorded information 573 2737). Tram 2, 3, 12, 15, 16. **Open** 11am-5pm daily; 11am-4pm public holidays. **Admission** f7; f3.50 under-17s, CJP card holders; under-7s free; free with Museum Card; group discounts (min 50 people). **No credit cards.**
Picking up where the Rijksmuseum (*above*) leaves off, the Stedelijk (Municipal Museum) has the best collection of modern art in Amsterdam. After occupying various locations around the city, the Stedelijk finally settled down in its present neo-Renaissance abode, designed by AW Weissmann, in 1895. The building soon became too small for the ambitions of its directors and an ugly new wing was tacked on in 1954. The Museum focuses on particular trends or the works of specific artists which are exhibited in spacious, well-lit rooms. Highlights include paintings by Monet, Cézanne, Picasso, Matisse, Kirchner and Chagall. In addition, the Museum has a prize collection of paintings and drawings by the Russian artist, Kasimir Malevich. Also well-represented is the Dutch De Stijl group, of which Piet

Rembrandt *may not have painted everything he signed, but the controversial Dutch master must have had his hands full just working on the large legacy of etchings that he left behind. About 250 of these are on display at the charming three-storey house (1606) in which he lived for over 20 years of his life (see under Art: Rembrandthuis). The museum has an intimate atmosphere, enhanced by the low-level lighting used to preserve the etchings. The etchings themselves are well-illuminated, however, allowing visitors to trace Rembrandt's development as an etcher and his interest in biblical scenes and human emotions. The only paintings here are by Rembrandt's teacher, Pieter Lastman, and his pupils. Don't miss the drawings (by Rembrandt) indicating the men's and women's toilets in the basement – they're good for a giggle.*

Mondrian is probably the most famous, as well as other post-1945 artists including De Kooning, Newman, Ryman, Judd, Stella, Lichtenstein, Warhol, Nauman, Middleton, Long, Dibbets, Van Elk, Kiefer, Polke, Merz and Lounellis. Interior design buffs will enjoy the extensive collection of furniture by Gerrit Rietveld. Don't forget to pop into the Appelbar or the restaurant – both are decorated by the designs of another Dutch artist, Karel Appel. The restaurant has a terrace overlooking the sculpture garden, and is a lovely place to sit on a sunny day. Outstanding temporary exhibitions are replaced in the summer by a selection of the permanent collection.
Café and restaurant. Guided tours f65 (book at least two weeks ahead). Occasional lectures with special exhibitions (f5-f10). Library (open to library card holders only, phone for details), closed July, Aug. Art History courses, f75 for 8 sessions, advance booking essential. Shop. Wheelchair access and toilets for the disabled.

Van Gogh Museum
Paulus Potterstraat 7, OS (570 5200). Tram 2, 3, 5, 12, 16. **Open** 10am-5pm Tue-Sat; 1-5pm Sun, public holidays. **Admission** f10; f5 under-18s, CJP card holders; f3.50 with Museum Card; group discounts (min 20 people).* **No credit cards**.
See p101 picture and caption. Library (10am-4pm Tue-Fri). Restaurant. Shop. Cassette tours f7.50. Wheelchair access and toilets for the disabled.

Allard Pierson Museum
Oude Turfmarkt 127, C (525 2556). Tram 4, 9, 16, 24, 25. **Open** 10am-5pm Tue-Fri; 1-5pm Sat, Sun, public holidays. **Admission** f3.50; f1 11-15s; free under-11s; f1.75 CJP card holders. **No credit cards**.
A rather uninspiring collection of archaeological exhibits – albeit the world's richest university collection of its type – from Egypt, Greece, Rome and other ancient civilizations. The displays are unimaginative, sometimes even amateurish, and the exhibits look static and dull. Established in 1934, the Museum moved to this building, originally built in 1934 to house the Netherlands Central Bank, in 1976. It's normally fairly quiet, but the temporary exhibitions tend to draw larger crowds.

Texts are sporadically in English, but often in obscure places or in such small print that they are difficult to read. The renovation of several sections of the permanent exhibition in 1991 is supposed to bring about some improvement – but we're not holding our breath.
Cassette tours f1. Wheelchair access with assistance.

ART

Fodor Museum
Keizersgracht 609, IS (624 9919). Tram 16, 24, 25. **Open** 11am-5pm daily. **Admission** f1; 50c under-12s; free with Museum Card. **No credit cards**.
The Fodor has close connections with the Stedelijk Museum (*see above* **The Big Three**), but it tends to be even more avant-garde. There is no permanent collection; temporary exhibitions focus on the works of contemporary local artists and recent acquisitions of the city of Amsterdam. These are accommodated in the starkly modern interior of an old canal house. Check the garden as well – modern sculptures are sometimes on view. Major reconstruction work is due to start in autumn 1991, during which opening times may vary; phone to check.

Rembrandthuis
Jodenbreestraat 4-6, C (624 9486). Tram 9, 14. **Open** 10am-5pm Mon-Sat; 1-5pm Sun, public holidays. **Admission** f4; f2.50 10-15s; free under-9s; free with Museum Card; group discount (min 15 people). **No credit cards**.
See picture and caption. Guided tours by prior arrangement.

BOTANICAL

Bosmuseum
Koenenkade 56, Amsterdamse Bos, OS (643 1414). Bus 146, 147, 170, 171, 172. **Open** 10am-5pm daily. **Admission** free.
This exhibition recounts the history, use and management of the extensive forest – the Amsterdamse Bos – located on the outskirts of the city (see p13 **Sightseeing**). Don't interrupt a picnic to see it, but keep it in mind if it starts to rain.
Café. Shop. Wheelchair access.

Hortus Botanicus
Plantage Middenlaan 2, IE (525 5403). Tram 7, 9, 14. **Open** Oct-March 9am-4pm Sat, Sun, public holidays; April-Sept 9am-5pm Mon-Fri; 11am-5pm Sat, Sun, public holidays. **Admission** f5; f3 under-14s.
If Amsterdam's other museums have left you exhausted, head to a living museum: the Hortus Botanicus. You don't need to be a keen gardener to enjoy the greenery of more than 6,000 herbs, shrubs and plants. Established in 1682, when ships from the East Indies Company brought back tropical plants and seeds from faraway locations, to create a medicinal garden for doctors and pharmacists, the Hortus is a haven for those wanting respite from the concrete jungle.
Wheelchair access.

Hortus Botanicus of the Vrije University

Van der Boechorststraat 8, OS (548 4142). Bus 23, 65, 173. **Open** 8am-4.30pm Mon-Fri. **Admission** free.

As it was only created in 1967, the Hortus of the Vrije University doesn't have the historical charm of its older counterpart in the city centre (above), but it's a very pleasant place for a stroll if you happen to be in the neighbourhood – on the outskirts of town near Amstelveen. The fern collection is one of the largest in the world, while the Dutch garden shows the great variety of flora originally found in this country. *Wheelchair access.*

Nederlands Filmmuseum

Vondelpark 3, OS (589 1400). Tram 1, 2, 3, 5, 6, 12. **Open** box office 8.30am-¼ hour before last film ends Mon-Fri; 1pm-¼ hour before last film ends Sat; 11am-¼ hour before last film ends Sun; library 10am-5pm Tue-Fri. **Tickets** cinema f6-f8.50; reduced (matinées only) f2.50; ten-visit cards f50; 25-visit cards f100; 60-visit cards f200; library and exhibition f2.50; members, students, over-65s free. **Membership** f25-f100. **No credit cards.**

An extensive renovation project will keep the doors of the late nineteenth-century pavilion closed until September 1991, but after that date film buffs can obtain an insight into the history and development of the cinema, and play with the magic lanterns and other early animation techniques that form part of the permanent exhibition. During the renovations films from the extensive national and international collections will be shown at the Kriterion cinema (see p122 **Film** for details of both the Kriterion and the Filmmuseum's

collection). The museum's trendy café Vertigo will also be undergoing a facelift in early 1991, but should be open in time for Amsterdam's sun lovers to catch the first rays of spring sunshine on the café terrace overlooking Vondelpark.

Tropenmuseum (Tropical Museum)

Linnaeusstraat 2, OE (568 8200/8295). Tram 9, 10, 14. **Open** 10am-5pm Mon-Fri; noon-5pm Sat, Sun, public holidays. **Admission** f6; f3 under-18s, CJP card holders; free with Museum Card. **No credit cards.**

When it was built in the twenties, the Tropenmuseum was designed to justify and glorify the activities of the Dutch in their colonies. However, the permanent exhibitions have changed course dramatically since World War II. Instead of focusing on the noble deeds of the Dutch in their overseas territories, the Museum now takes an honest look at daily life and problems in all tropical and subtropical regions. The well-integrated displays vividly depict the present situation in the Third World, new developments and the responsibility of industrialized countries. The 'bazaars' and other displays (reproductions of an Indian village with taped sounds, an African compound, a nomad tent and so on) are so lifelike that they suspend reality for a moment. Compared to these, the collection of cultural/historical exhibits such as textiles, musical instruments and Oceanic art tends to become a bit dull. A highlight during the winter season is the gamelan concert series (3pm first Sunday of each month, from September to June, free). Excellent temporary exhibitions are mounted in the large, airy hall on the

ground floor. Until September 1991 a special exhibition focuses on the development of the Tropenmuseum from a colonial museum. The shop has a good selection of souvenirs and books from or dealing with Third World countries. Attached to the main museum is the Tropenmuseum Junior, for children aged between 6 and 12, see p180 **Children & Parents.**

Amstelkring Museum, 'Our Lord in the Attic'

Oudezijds Voorburgwal 40, C (624 6604). Tram 1, 2, 4, 5, 9, 13, 16, 17, 24, 25. **Open** 10am-5pm Mon-Sat; 1-5pm Sun, public holidays. **Admission** f3.50; f2 under-14s, CJP card holders; free with Museum Card; group discount. **No credit cards.**

One of the most surprising of the smaller museums in Amsterdam, the Amstelkring is undeservedly neglected by most visitors. Located in the heart of the red light district, this unique building, housing the only remaining attic church in Amsterdam (see p55 **The Golden Age**), was happily saved from demolition in the late nineteenth century by a group of historians who called themselves the Amstelkring (Amstel 'circle') and were mainly concerned with preserving the city's Catholic past. The lower floors of the house feature furnished living rooms that could have served as the setting for some of the seventeenth-century Dutch masters. Upstairs, the chaplain's room features a cupboard bed. The pilgrimage upwards leads visitors to the highlight of the Museum: the beautifully preserved attic church, the altarpiece of which features a painting by eighteenth-century artist Jacob de Wit. Built in 1663, the church is still used for services and a variety of other meetings. *Guided tours by prior arrangement.*

Unless you want to get lost, don't start a tour of the Rijksmuseum (The Netherlands' largest national museum, see under **The Big Three**) without a map or a guidebook. The shop on the first floor stocks an English-language guidebook (f7.50) and also has a choice of 24 Viewfinders (25c), fold-out floor plans each devoted to a particular theme. These include 'The Dutch Abroad', 'Tapestries with Plants and Animals' and 'Dramatic Moments in History'.

If you only have a limited amount of time, head first for the exhibition on the first floor, which features Holland's claim to artistic fame: the seventeenth-century Dutch masters. Top of the list of the best works in this section would have to be Rembrandt's *Nightwatch*. If you can't understand why, visit the exhibition

in the room next door which explains why the painting was so innovative. Rembrandt was indisputably the most prolific of the Dutch masters, but also impressive are the works by his contemporaries.

The Kitchen Maid and *The Young Woman Reading a Letter* by Johannes Vermeer capture a moment in the lives of two women from totally different backgrounds. Pieter de Hooch was another seventeenth-century painter to excel in scenes of domestic interiors, while Jan Steen focused on life in the lower social classes. Together with the landscapes of Jacob van Ruisdael and Paulus Potter, the winter scenes of Hendrik Avercamp and Jan van de Capelle, and the maritime scenes of Willem van de Velde the Younger, this section of fifteenth- to seven-

teenth-century Dutch art offers an excellent insight into life in The Netherlands during the Golden Age.

If this has served to whet your appetite for Dutch art, return to the ground floor to view representatives from The Hague and Amsterdam Schools such as Mauve and Breitner. Other attractions elsewhere include superb examples of Delftware, porcelain, pottery, silverware, costumes and oriental art. Dutch history is interesting but the section devoted to this subject on the ground floor isn't – the presentation is badly thought out and there are no English explanations. Worth a visit, however, are the early eighteenth-century doll's houses on the ground floor, which give a good impression of the sort of houses works by Rembrandt and Vermeer were hung in.

Allard Pierson Museum

Egyptian, Greek, Etruscan and Roman antiquities and objects from the near East.

Opposite 't Rokin

AMSTERDAM

Nederlands Filmmuseum
Vondelpark 3, 1071 AA Amsterdam.
Telephone 020 - 589 14 00

FILM PERFORMANCES - PERMANENT AND CHANGING EXHIBITIONS - LYBRARY
Due to extensive renovation, films will be temporarily shown in Kriterion, Roetersstraat 170, Amsterdam (daily at 17:30 and 19:30 hrs). From 1st September 1991 all exhibitions and film performances will return to the renovated Vondelpark pavilion. During this renovation the library will be open as usual at Vondelstraat 69 - 71, Amsterdam.

Stedelijk Museum ∎

A Museum of Modern Art

painting   sculpture   video   prints   drawings
photography   applied art   industrial design   posters

The collection contains among others works by:

Monet   Cézanne   Van Gogh   Matisse   Picasso   Chagall   Kirchner
Kandinsky   Mondrian   Malevich   Appel   Lucebert   Fontana
Klein   Schoonhoven   Johns   Warhol   Oldenburg   Lichtenstein
Ryman   Andre   Dibbets   Van Elk   Nauman   De Maria   Kounellis
Merz   Fabro   Kiefer   Polke   Daniels   Scholte   Koons

Open daily from 11 a.m. to 5 p.m.

Paulus Potterstraat 13 telephone 020-5732911 infoline 020-5732737

∎ **Amsterdam**

Museum Willet-Holthuysen

*Herengracht 605, IS (523 1870). Tram 4, 9,
14.* **Open** 11am-5pm daily. **Admission** f2.50;
under-12s f1.25; group discount (min 15 people). **No credit cards.**
See **picture and caption.**

Museum Van Loon

*Keizersgracht 672, IS (624 5255). Tram 4, 9,
14.* **Open** 10am-5pm Mon. **Admission** f5;
free under-12s. **No credit cards.**
Behind the classical seventeenth-century
façade of this canal house lies a furnished
interior, showing how wonderful it was to be
a wealthy resident of Amsterdam in
Holland's Golden Age. Apart from the Louis
XV décor, the Museum has an unusually
large collection of family portraits from the
seventeenth and eighteenth centuries,
added after the purchase of the house in
1884 by Hendrik van Loon. The eighteenth-
century garden, laid out in the French style,
contains a coach house from the same
period (now a private home).
*Guided tours (min 10 people) by prior
arrangement.*

HISTORICAL

Amsterdams Historisch Museum

*Kalverstraat 92, C (523 1822). Tram 1, 2, 4,
5, 9, 14, 16, 24, 25.* **Open** 11am-5pm daily.
Admission f5; under-16s f2.50; f12.50 family
ticket (2 adults, 2 children); free with
Museum Card; group discount (min 20
people). **No credit cards.**
The courtyard of the Amsterdam Historical
Museum is an oasis of peace in the midst of
the busy Kalverstraat, one of Amsterdam's
main shopping thoroughfares. The main
entrance is hard to find, though – look out for
a tiny alley and a lopsided arch bearing the
three crosses of the city's coat of arms. The
Museum is housed in a former convent and
orphanage dating from the sixteenth century.
The development of the city from the
thirteenth century to the present day is illustrated in a masterful way by various *objets
d'art*, archaeological finds and interactive displays. The best view of the Civic Guard
Gallery – a covered street gallery with several massive group portraits commissioned
by wealthy burghers in the sixteenth and seventeenth centuries – is from the second floor
of the Museum. Another attraction is the
adjacent Begijnhof (beguines' courtyard, *see
p13* **Sightseeing**). The 'life-size' model of
Goliath in the Museum's adjoining restaurant
is a favourite with kids, as are the pancakes.
It's a good place to take a well-earned rest –
this is definitely a museum for sensible walking shoes.
Restaurant.

Anne Frankhuis

*Prinsengracht 263, IW (626 4533). Tram
13, 14, 17.* **Open** *Sept-May* 9am-5pm Mon-
Sat; 10am-5pm Sun, public holidays;
June-Aug 9am-7pm Mon-Sat; 10am-7pm Sun,
public holidays. **Admission** f5; f3 10-17s;
free under-10s; group discount. **No credit
cards.**
The Anne Frank House was opened to the
public in 1960 and now attracts more than
half a million visitors a year. The building, on
the border of the Jordaan, dates from 1635,

Originally built in 1689, the interior of this pleasant patrician's mansion, now
the **Museum Willet-Holthuysen** (see under **Golden Age**), on one of
Amsterdam's most elegant canals is more reminiscent of a French château than
a Dutch canal house. Both the Louis XV and neo-Louis XVI styles are very much
visible. The latter was mainly introduced by the Willet-Holthuysen couple who
acquired the house in 1860 and who gave the Museum its name. Their passion
for overembellishment is also apparent in their legacy of rare objets d'art: glassware, silver, fine china and paintings. There are no English texts to accompany
the exhibits, but an English-language video on the ground floor gives a comprehensive review of what visitors can expect. The charming eighteenth-century
garden is unfortunately overshadowed by several twentieth-century buildings.

but the upstairs annex where Anne's family
and four other Jews hid before being
deported to concentration camps toward the
end of World War II was added a century
later. A bookcase marks the entrance to the
sober, unfurnished rooms which sheltered
the eight inhabitants for two long years.
Unfortunately, it's hardly ever quiet enough
to imagine what their lives must have been
like during that time. To avoid the crowds,
go early or take advantage of the longer
opening hours in summer. The permanent
and temporary exhibitions on the fight
against anti-semitism and other forms of discrimination are sobering, but enlightening.
Translations of Anne's diary can be bought
in the bookshop downstairs. *See also p64*
World War II.
*Bookshop. Documentation department
(Keizersgracht 192, tel 626 4533).
Educational department. Guided tours by
prior arrangement. Videos.*

Verzetsmuseum Amsterdam (Museum of the Resistance)

Lekstraat 63, OS (644 9797). Tram 4, 25.
Open 10am-5pm Tue-Fri; 1-5pm Sat, Sun,
public holidays. **Admission** f3.50; f1.75
under-17s, CJP card holders; f8.75 family
ticket (2 adults and 2 children); free with
Museum Card; group discount (min 15
people). **No credit cards.**
Out of the way, but worth the extra effort,
the Verzetsmuseum is located in a former
synagogue in the southern part of the city,
an area renowned for its early twentieth-century architecture typical of the Amsterdam

School (*see p61* **Between the
Occupations**). The hardships of World War
II and the heroic deeds of the Dutch
Resistance fighters are depicted by photos,
tape recordings, newspaper clippings and
other objects from the war. *See also p64*
World War II.
*Computer games. Guided tours by prior
arrangement, f1. Library and video access by
prior arrangement. Wheelchair access and
toilets for the disabled.*

MARITIME

Nederlands Scheepvaart Museum (Maritime Museum)

*Kattenburgerplein 1, IE (523 2222). Bus 22,
28.* **Open** 10am-5pm Tue-Sat; 1-5pm Sun,
public holidays. **Admission** f5; f3 6-17s; free
under-6s and with Museum Card; f3.75 CJP
card holders. **No credit cards.**
The national maritime museum takes visitors on a voyage back to Roman times. It is
housed, appropriately, in what was the Sea
Arsenal of the United Provinces of The
Netherlands, in the heart of Amsterdam's
nautical district (*see p26* **Amsterdam by
Area**). Dating from 1656, this monumental
edifice was used as a warehouse for the
upkeep of the city's fleet of warships.
Exhibitions trace the importance of water to
The Netherlands' development as a major
trading nation. *See also p106* **picture and
caption.**
Café.

Werf 't Kromhout

Hoogte Kadijk 147, IE (627 6777). Bus 22, 28. **Open** *10am-4pm Mon-Fri; also open noon-5pm Sat, Sun in summer, phone for exact dates.* **Admission** *f3; f1.50 under-12s.* **No credit cards.**

Located diagonally opposite the Netherlands Maritime Museum (*above*) the Kromhout is one of the few survivors of the once-numerous shipyards in the eastern port area of Amsterdam during the seventeenth and eighteenth centuries. Antique vessels being repaired under the cast-iron roof are photogenic (completed ships are not on show), but the steam engines, tools and instruments on display in the adjoining museum are only interesting for real connoisseurs. *See also p55* **The Golden Age.**

Guided tours. Wheelchair access with assistance.

RELIGION

Bijbels Museum (Biblical Museum)

Herengracht 366, IW (624 7949). Tram 1, 2, 5. **Open** *10am-5pm Tue-Sat; 1-5pm Sun, public holidays.* **Admission** *f3; f2*

under-16s; free with Museum Card and for CJP card holders. **No credit cards.**
See p107 **picture and caption.**
Café. Library (10am-5pm Tue-Fri). Shop. Slide shows every half hour. Walks: July, Aug only: Tue 11am and 2pm, f5 (1½ hours); Thur 11am and 2pm, f7.50 (2½ hours).

Joods Historisch Museum (Jewish Historical Museum)

Jonas Daniel Meijerplein 24, C (626 9945). Tram 9, 14. **Open** *11am-5pm daily; closed Yom Kippur.* **Admission** *f7; 3.50 10-17s; free under-10s and with Museum Card.* **No credit cards.**

Located in a former High German Synagogue in the heart of what used to be a prominent Jewish neighbourhood (*see p26* **Amsterdam by Area**), the Museum is a short walk from Waterlooplein and the nearby Muziektheater (*see p130* **Music: Classical & Opera**). Until 1987, the Museum was housed in the Waag (Weigh House, *see p13* **Sightseeing**), near the red light district. The new premises are both a suitable and interesting backdrop for an exhibition on the Jewish religion and the history of this minority group in The Netherlands. The permanent display contains some beautiful *objets d'art*, but these

are somewhat overshadowed by a gripping exhibition on the persecution of Jews during World War II (*see p64* **World War II**). The Museum organizes walks around the Jewish neighbourhood and group visits to the nearby Portuguese Synagogue. The Jewish character of the coffee shop on the premises is not particularly prominent, but bookings can be made in advance for kosher lunches. The Museum gets particularly crowded on Jewish religious holidays.

Guided tours by prior arrangement.

TECHNOLOGY

Technologie Museum NINT

Tolstraat 129, OS (664 6021). Tram 4. **Open** *10am-5pm Mon-Fri; noon-5pm Sat, Sun.* **Admission** *f7; f5 5-12s; free under-5s.* **No credit cards.**

Until its grand transformation into a super Science Centre at the end of 1992 or the beginning of 1993 (*see above* **Introduction**), NINT will continue to be housed in the former workshop of Asscher, one of Amsterdam's best-known gem companies. Even those who loathe science get a buzz out of the place – it takes the principles of physics out of stuffy textbooks and into the real world. Some of the more popular exhibits deal with automation in shops, car repair, holography and micro-computers. Eight multi-media machines help explain such things as CAD/CAM and fractals. The Museum is popular with kids and teenagers, who love getting their hands on the displays to discover the basic principles of nature; *see also p180* **Children & Parents.**

Café (closes at 4pm). Shop (closes at 4pm).

THEATRE

Theatermuseum

Herengracht 168, IW (623 5104). Tram 13, 14, 17. **Open** *11am-5pm Tue-Sun.* **Admission** *f2.50; f1.50 under-14s, CJP card holders; free with Museum Card.* **No credit cards.**
See p108 **picture and caption.**
See also p126 **Theatre.**
Café. Guided tours (f3.50; 1pm and 3pm Wed, noon and 2pm Sun). Library closed Sun.

TOWN PLANNING

Informatiecentrum Ruimtelijk Ordening

Zuiderkerkhof, C (596 1357). Metro Nieuwmarkt. **Open** *12.30-4.30pm Tue, Wed, Fri; 12.30-4.30pm, 6-9pm, Thur.* **Admission** *free.*

Unless you're really interested in town planning and housing, the setting of this museum – a beautifully restored seventeenth-century church located near the red light district, run by the Urban Planning Information Centre – is possibly more interesting than the temporary exhibitions. These focus on current housing projects, through photographical and textual displays (English texts are planned for 1991). There

Some of the old maps at the **Nederlands Scheepvaart Museum** *(maritime museum, see under* **Maritime***) are quite spectacular – their size alone is astonishing – and the antique sailing ships and models on display in the spacious rooms transport you back into the past. The paintings of famous sea battles and voyages are also evocative. If you feel overwhelmed by it all, take a break in the restaurant, which offers good views of barges and other vessels passing by. Don't forget to visit the replica of the VOC ship* De Amsterdam *(above) on the dockside (see also page 55* **The Golden Age***). There are no English explanations in the Museum, but a reasonably-priced guidebook can be bought in the shop downstairs.*

are also model reproductions and slide shows. The Amsterdams Historich Museum (*see above* **Historical**) is a better place to trace the development of the city through the ages.
Wheelchair access with assistance.

TRANSPORT

Aviodome

Schiphol Centre (604 1521). Train to Schiphol Airport. **Open** *Oct-May* 10am-5pm Tue-Fri; noon-5pm Sat, Sun; *May-Sept* 10am-5pm daily. **Admission** f6; f4.50 4-12s; free under-4s. **No credit cards.**
It helps to be mad about aviation to enjoy this place. There are over 30 historic aircraft on display (some suspended from the ceiling), including the first motorized plane – the Wright Flyer from 1903 – and the Spider, designed by Dutch aviation pioneer Anthony Fokker. Kids enjoy clambering into a cockpit and pretending to be Biggles in an exhibit especially reserved for that purpose. Also popular is the Space Department, which contains the American Mercury capsule. The hangar-like aluminium dome also shows films and has a large collection of models, photos and airplane parts. The Dutch-language guidebook has a summary in English. There are special weekend aviation markets and fairs, as well as theme weekends focusing on subjects such as restoration – information available from VVV tourist offices (*see p3* **Essential Information**), the local press or from the Museum. An information centre, opened in 1990, houses a permanent exhibition detailing the future and the role of Schiphol Airport, and related environmental issues.
Films and slide shows. Shop. Wheelchair access except to 1st-floor Space Department.

Electrische Museumtralijn (Electric Tram Museum)

Amstelveenseweg 264, OW (673 7538). Tram 6, 16. **Open** *April-Oct* 10.30am-5.30pm Sun. **Trams depart** every 20 minutes 10.30am-5.30pm Sun; *July, Aug* also at 1pm, 2.15pm, 3.30pm Tue-Thur, Sat. **Admission** f4; f2 4-11s, CJP card holders; free under-4s. **No credit cards.**
When open, the Electric Tram Museum is almost always on the move. Some of the antique trolleys, collected from cities throughout Europe, are still in use. Kids in particular love going for a 30-minute ride in one of the Museum's colourful conveyances through the nearby – and surprisingly rural – Amsterdamse Bos (forest); *see p180* **Children & Parents.**
Café at Haarlemmermeer station.

UNIVERSITY HISTORY

Universiteitsmuseum De Agnietenkapel

Oudezijds Voorburgwal 231, C (525 3341) Tram 4, 9, 14, 16, 24, 25. **Open** usually 9am-1pm, 2-5pm, Mon-Fri; may open at weekends, phone to check. **Admission** usually free; small charge (max f2.50) for special exhibitions.

The Agnietenkapel (chapel), built in 1470 and part of the University since its foundation in 1632, is one of the few Gothic chapels to have escaped the demolisher's hammer. It has a sober, Calvinistic beauty, with lovely stained glass windows and old wooden beams and benches. The chapel is more stimulating than the collection, which focuses on the history of education, research and student life at the University of Amsterdam. One of the most interesting things in the University Museum is the *Grote Gehoorzaal* (Large Auditorium) where respected seventeenth-century academics Vossius and Barlaeus gave their first lectures. It has a beautiful wooden ceiling, decorated with soberly painted ornamental Renaissance motifs such as angels, masks, flowers and a portrait of Minerva, the Roman goddess of Science and Arts. The Auditorium is now used for symposia, the presentation of certificates and occasional lectures.

ZOOLOGICAL

Artis Zoologisch Museum

Plantage Kerklaan 40, IE (623 1836). Tram

7, 9, 14. **Open** 9am-5pm daily; last Planetarium show 4pm. **Admission** zoo, *Planetarium and Zoological Museum* f16; f9 under-10s; group discount (min 20 people). **No credit cards.**
This zoo, planetarium and zoological museum makes a great outing for kids – although it's a bit pricey at f9 for children and f16 for adults. Apart from the usual range of animals, including a section for nocturnal creatures and a fascinating aquarium, the beautiful gardens of the 150-year old Artis Zoo (*see p13* **Sightseeing**) contain a small but interesting zoological museum featuring thematic exhibitions and a collection of stuffed animals. A slide show presents scenes of wildlife in the Dutch coastal dunes. Also on the premises is a planetarium; although the narration is in Dutch, the spectacular visuals make it well worthwhile. The feeding ground for humans is ideally situated between a pond with pink flamingoes and a popular children's playground; *see also p180* **Children & Parents.**
Café and restaurant. Guided tours by prior arrangement (free). Schools educational programme. Shop. Wheelchair access and toilets for the disabled.

Many tourists visit the **Bijbels Museum** (*biblical museum, see under* **Religion**) *for the two adjoining patrician's houses in which it is accommodated. Built in 1660-1662 by the renowned Dutch architect Philip Vingboons, the houses feature stunning early-eighteenth century ceiling paintings by Jacob de Wit and a splendid spiral staircase which connects them. The Museum itself is also remarkable. Life in Biblical times is vividly illustrated by archaeological finds from Egypt and the Middle East, a reconstruction of a Palestinian house, models of Solomon's temple and various audio-visual displays. In conjunction with the Amstelkring Museum (see under* **Golden Age**), *the Biblical Museum organizes walks around historical monuments of religious significance in July and August; unfortunately, the commentary is in Dutch only.*

Featuring the first neck gable in Amsterdam (built in 1638 by the architect Philip Vingboons), the **Theatermuseum** *(see under Theatre) is an architectural gem worth visiting simply for its interior. The eighteenth-century plasterwork, the ceiling paintings by Jacob de Wit and the spiral staircases are simply magnificent. This delightful décor distracts somewhat from the permanent and temporary exhibitions which relate the story of Dutch theatre. Important chapters include stage costumes, models of stage scenery and a selection of related drawings and prints. Children enjoy creating wind and rain with the special machines on display. Tea and cake in the lovely old garden behind the house is a treat in summer. The Museum also boasts an extensive library.*

over the world by an eccentric former bank director. Silver savings banks and other antique curiosities are juxtaposed with the more numerous ceramic and plastic versions in all sorts of shapes and sizes. The presentation is rather unimaginative, but some of the individual pieces are quite extraordinary. The collection is housed in neon-lit toyshop-like premises near the Dam. It tends to be busy during school holidays.
Wheelchair access.

Sex Museum
Damrak 18, C (622 8376). Tram 4, 9, 16, 24, 25. **Open** 10am-11.30pm daily. **Admission** f3.75. No credit cards. *See p109 picture and caption.*

Boymans-Van-Beuningen, Rotterdam
Mathenesserlaan 18-20 (010 441 9400). **Open** 10am-5pm Tue-Sat; 11am-5pm Sun, public holidays. **Admission** f3.50; f1.75 CJP card holders; free under-16s, and with Museum Card; group discount (min 15 people). No credit cards.
The Boymans rivals the Rijksmuseum (*see above* **The Big Three**) in the quality of its canvases and outstrips it in organization. Much of the best Dutch art isn't in Holland, but the Boymans has gems by Van Eijck, Rembrandt, Bosch and the other masters. A lot of the best French and surrealist art is here too, along with modernist paintings and sculpture, industrial design and major exhibitions.
Guided tours by prior arrangement. Wheelchair access.

De Lakenhal, Leiden
Oude Singel 28-32 (071 254620). **Open** 10am-5pm Tue-Sat; 1-5pm Sun, public holidays. **Admission** f2.50; f1.25 6-16s; free with Museum Card. No credit cards.
An awe-inspiring collection of decorative arts and paintings. There's almost too much to see here, but don't overlook the extraordinary *Last Judgement* by Lucas van Leyden, Pieter Xavery's charming terracotta court scene *De Leidsche Vierschaar* or the reconstructed guild room upstairs.
Guided tours by prior arrangement. Library (10am-12.30pm Tue, Thur, Fri; 2-5pm Wed).

Frans Hals Museum, Haarlem
Oudmannhuis, Groot Heiligland 62 (023 319180). **Open** 10am-5pm Tue-Sat; 1-5pm Sun, public holidays. **Admission** f4; f2 10-18s; free under-10s and with Museum Card; group discount (min 20 people). No credit cards.
Some of Hals' finest canvases are here, plus paintings by his illustrious contemporaries. There are reconstructed rooms illustrating the building's original use as an almshouse or *hofje*, the Oudmannhuis (for elderly men). Hals is famous for his group portraits of civic guards and almshouse regents; two of the eight displayed here depict the regents of the Oudmannhuis itself.
Guided tours 1.30pm Sun. Wheelchair access to most of the museum and toilets for the disabled.

Cannabis Info Museum
Oudezijds Achterburgwal 150, C (624 0386). Tram 4, 9, 16, 24, 25/Metro Nieuwmarkt. **Open** usually 11am or noon-9pm Fri, Sat, Sun; occasionally open during the week, phone to check. **Admission** f4. No credit cards.
The only one of its kind throughout Europe, the Museum explains the use of marijuana throughout the ages. Various paraphernalia more recently associated with cannabis, such as comics and T-shirts, would be more at home in the shop next door, which sells all the accoutrements for growing the stuff at home. The opening hours of the Museum are not reliable; always phone to check. Moreover, the authorities would like to see both the Museum and the shop shut down.
Wheelchair access with assistance.

Justitia Hal (Torture Instruments through the Ages)
Heiligeweg 19, C (620 4070). Tram 1, 2, 4, 5, 9, 14, 16, 24, 25. **Open** 10am-10pm daily. **Admission** f7.50; f4.75 under-14s; f5.50 students, CJP card holders, with Museum Card. No credit cards.

Definitely not a museum for the queasy, Torture Instruments through the Ages – otherwise known as Justitia Hal – is accommodated (some hope temporarily) in a former swimming pool in a busy shopping street just off Kalverstraat. The dark and dingy rooms contain over 60 torture instruments showing the depths that man can sink to. The instruments, which come from all over Europe, are antique (from the Middle Ages to the nineteenth century). Some of the more gruesome items include a guillotine and the chair of nails from the Inquisition. Each device is accompanied by a historical poster showing how it was used, plus an explanation in ungrammatical English. Nothing in the exhibition prepares you for the deplorable state of the toilets.

National Spaarpottenmuseum (Piggy Bank Museum)
Raadhuisstraat 12, C (556 7425). Tram 13, 14, 17. **Open** 1-4pm Mon-Fri. **Admission** f1; 50c under-13s, CJP card holders; free with Museum Card. No credit cards.
A good place to take kids, the permanent exhibition consists of over 2,000 examples from a vast collection of 12,000 money boxes and piggy banks, brought together from all

Mauritshaus, The Hague

Korte Vijverberg 8 (070 346 9244). **Open**
10am-5pm Tue-Sat; 11am-5pm Sun, public
holidays. **Admission** f6.50; f3.50 under-18s.
No credit cards.
This, in one of the country's finest Golden
Age houses (recently restored), has master-
pieces by Rubens, Van Dyke, the Flemish
School and rooms devoted to Rembrandt,
Van Steen, Holbein and Vermeer.

UNIVERSITY & OTHER COLLECTIONS

The collections listed can only be visited by appointment; telephone or
write in advance.

LITERARY

Frederik van Eedenmuseum

*University Library, Singel 425, 1012 WP; C
(525 2476). Tram 1, 25.*
The collection includes objects, manuscripts
and letters relating to the Dutch poet, physi-
cian and writer Frederik van Eeden
(1860-1932).

Multatuli-Museum

*Korsjespoortsteeg 20, 1015 AR; C (638
1938). Tram 1, 2, 5, 13, 17.*
The life of the nineteenth-century writer E
Douwes-Dekker (who wrote under the
pseudonym Multatuli) is illustrated by photographs and other objects. There is also a
library.

Schriftmuseum JA Dortmund

*University Library, Singel 425, 1012 WP; C
(525 2284). Tram 1, 25.*
The focus is on the art of writing from
approximately 3000BC to the present.

RELIGIOUS

Historisch Documentatiecentrum Van de Vrije Universiteit

*De Boelelaan 1105, 1082 SB; OS (548
3637). Bus 8, 23, 26, 49, 64, 65, 67, 68, 158,
173, 197.*
The history of the Dutch Protestant
University and its founder Abraham Kuyper
is explained with the help of documents,
photos, and artefacts.

'Museum' is a pretentious title for the **Sex Museum** *(see under*
Miscellaneous)*, a commercial enterprise behind a fairly respectable-looking
façade on a busy shopping street. The scientific basis of the Museum is dubious.
The endless display of erotica, including historic objects and images such as
lithographs, etchings, oil paintings, photos, movies and statues surprises and
shocks at first, but becomes somewhat monotonous after a while. Not for those
wanting a healthy family outing.*

Rothaan Museum

*Krijtbergkerk, Singel 448, C (623 1933).
Tram 1, 2, 5.*
The collection concentrates on the life of J P
Rothaan (1785-1853) who became General
of the Jesuits.

SOCIAL HISTORY

Ferdinand Domela Nieuwenhuis Museum

*Herengracht 266, IW (622 5496). Tram 13,
14, 17.*
Documents focusing on the life of
Ferdinand Domela Nieuwenhuis
(1846-1919, *see p61* **Between the
Occupations**) and the labour
movement.

Instituut voor Sociale Geschiedenis

*Cruquiusweg 31, OE (668 5866). Tram 6,
10/bus 22.*
An international library specializing in the
social history of the Western world, run by
the Institute for Social History. The library
also contains original writings by Karl Marx
and Friedrich Engels.

ZOOLOGY

Instituut voor Taxonomicsch Zoologie

*Entomology Department, Plantage
Middenlaan 64, IE (525 6258). Tram 7, 14.*
Insects from all over the world for scientific
research.

NOT TO BE MISSED...

Amsterdam's museums contain
some of the world's best and most
famous paintings. Here's our (admit-
tedly subjective) top ten:
Rijksmuseum (*listed under* **The Big
Three**) *The Nightwatch*, Rembrandt;
The Milkmaid, Johannes Vermeer;
The Singel Bridge by the Paleisstraat

in Amsterdam, George Hendrik
Britner
Stedelijk Museum (*under* **The Big
Three**) *Composition with Red, Black,
Yellow and Grey*, Piet Mondrian; *The
Fiddler*, Marc Chagall; *An
Englishman in Moscow*, Kasimir
Malevich; *Nude Behind a Curtain*,

Ernst Ludwig Kirchner
Van Gogh Museum (*under* **The
Big Three**) *Wheatfield with Crows*,
Van Gogh; *Among the Mangoes at
Martinique*, Paul Gauguin
Theatermuseum (*under* **Theatre**)
The Story of Jeptha, Jacob de Wit and
Isaac de Moucheron

AMSTERDAMS MOST BEAUTIFUL
18TH CENTURY MONUMENT
ON SINGEL CAN BE VISITED
BY APPOINTMENT BETWEEN
11.00 A.M. AND 21.00 P.M.
SHOWING AN IMPORTANT
COLLECTION OF RUSSIAN
PAINTINGS
"NEW RUSSIAN REALISM".

Telefoon (0) 20 - 38 56 55
Telefoon (0) 20 - 38 27 36
Telefax   (0) 20 - 38 29 01

THE INNA KAUFMAN GALLERIE
monument
"Huis met de neuzen"
Singel 116
Amsterdam

HOGENDOORN & KAUFMAN
EUROPEAN CRYSTAL AND PORCELAIN, RUSSIAN ART,
OLD AND NEW DELFTWARE, RARE MATRYOSHKA'S
PALEKH AND FEDOSKINO LACQUER MINIATURES

Rokin 124
Amsterdam

Telefoon (0) 20 - 38 27 36
Telefax   (0) 20 - 38 29 01

From: Fieldings - U.S.A. 1991:
"If you have a discerning eye don't
miss this spectacular house."

All Travel Guides and Literature ... Allert de Lange
Bookshop at Damrak 62 & 60 (near Dam Square)
020 - 624 67 44/624 67 46

All Art and Literature ... Robert Premsela
Bookshop at Van Baerlestraat 178 (near Museum Square)
020 - 662 42 66

Even more Guides and Maps... 'A la Carte
Bookshop at Utrechtsestraat 110 (near Rembrandt Square)
020 - 625 06 79

Galleries

Amsterdam's eclectic art scene is one of the most fascinating in Europe – there's no better place in which to buy, browse or even borrow. Sculptor *Mari Shields* guides you around the galleries.

The variety of Amsterdam's art life is astounding, given the city's size and its neighbourhood atmosphere. Tourists may teem around the Van Goghs and Rembrandts in the city's museums (*see page 100* **Museums**), but there is also a wealth of more contemporary art, with over 1,500 artists working in the city. Much of their work can be seen in the privately owned galleries which now total more than 250 throughout Amsterdam.

A country of painters, The Netherlands is very strong in graphics, printmaking, meticulously executed small paintings and clean, approachable sculpture. This applies to both figurative and abstract art. Amsterdam's galleries always have a broad variety of this work on show.

Modern Dutch art, and gallery tastes, follow two major directions. One is orderly, continuing the traditions of De Stijl (*see page 61* **Between the Occupations: The Amsterdam School**) and Piet Mondrian; the other is anarchic, exemplified by Cobra, the abstract movement of the fifties. The style of Cobra is quite unlike the clean lines of Mondrian. Carel Appel is its hero in The Netherlands, though Corneille, Lucebert, Lucassen, Constant and others may be better respected elsewhere. Cobra has become a respected, virtually institutionalized tradition. Amsterdam remains the focal point for Cobra art; and some of the artists are still doing excellent work.

Space is a major consideration for Amsterdam's art world. The genius of the artists, galleries and buyers in getting the maximum use out of the minimum of space is taken for granted. There is an enormous selection of unobtrusive but concentrated art in a small place – and in small spaces. This makes Amsterdam's galleries ideal for collectors outdone by ten-yard paintings and six-figure prices.

DOUBLE DEALERS

Some confusion is caused over the difference between a gallery and a kunsthandel. A *kunsthandel* (which means art dealer) is more likely to buy and resell art; to carry multiples of paintings as prints; and to go for established names. A gallery, strictly speaking, acts as a sort of agent to the artist, exhibiting and selling art and taking a commission, though not buying the art outright. But to complicate matters, many *kunsthandels* decided to call themselves galleries when 'gallery' became fashionable in the sixties. In short, there is considerable overlap between the two terms.

ART AND THE ESTABLISHMENT

Since World War II, art has been heavily supported, notably in subsidies to individual artists. Artists were thus guaranteed a market – the government, which bought large quantities of work. This was more a social programme – to keep the artists off the street – than a subsidy to the arts. In the mid-1980s there were over 3,500 artists on this programme, about half of them in Amsterdam. Because artists could sell to the government, commercial galleries weren't a necessity and the gallery scene was not particularly strong.

Those days are now over and enormous reshuffling is taking place. The massive artists' support programme was discontinued. At the end of the eighties, caution and consolidation prevailed. Artists no longer had a secure market. Initially there were inevitable hiccups and flickers of panic, but these quickly righted themselves and a keener sense of the world outside the studio has developed. Dutch artists are reconsidering their public and putting maximum energy into the presentation of their work; they are forced to write grant proposals and CVs, go after funds and find their own markets. Whatever artists think of the changing situation, even the controversy it has provoked is enlivening the gallery scene: how will commercial sponsors and a capitalist market-structure affect creative freedom?

That official subsidies provided so many artists with the opportunity to 'discover themselves' for so long is unique, and has lent a special quality to the art now in Amsterdam's galleries. Moreover, today, the wide range of art that it has produced is available to galleries, which are now overwhelmed by artists. Business and industry are slowly warming to the idea of sponsoring and buying art, and changes in attitude are producing an ever more exciting climate.

A BUYER'S MARKET

At the beginning of the nineties, new movements, new stars and new names are lurking in the wings. The last important changes occurred nearly a decade ago (when a dozen or so new Dutch artists came to prominence), so artists and galleries are awaiting the next outburst. It is difficult to predict what form this will take; and which galleries will sense it first and reap the rewards, but there is no shortage of galleries showing new and unknown artists.

In fact, an extraordinary number of internationally-known artists were – and are – shown here first. They are often picked up by big-name galleries from New York and elsewhere, with the consequence of fame and skyrocketing prices. Artists often stay loyal to the Amsterdam gallery which believed in them in their pre-fame days, but prices here stay at reasonable levels (measured in hundreds, rather than thousands of guilders). Despite these bargain prices, artists – thus far – show in Amsterdam and sell elsewhere, as The Netherlands has few private collectors. The main market here is the government and the museums. As an incentive for individual buyers, the government has introduced new subsidies and loans to facilitate the buying of art. Foreigners may be eligible: information on this is available at the galleries.

ART IN MUSEUMS

Relationships between museums and galleries are always convoluted. In The Netherlands, the art world is dominated by five of the world's best museums. The Haags Gemeentemuseum (The Hague, *see page 208* **The Randstad**), Amsterdam's Stedelijk Museum (*see page 100* **Museums**), the Rijksmuseum Kröller-Müller (Otterlo, *see page 213* **The Provinces: Gelderland**), the Groningen Museum (Groningen, *see*

The two young publishers at **Picaron Editions** (see under **Galleries**) *invaded the gallery scene in 1989, earning immediate respect. Picaron Editions is in a beautiful space near Centraal Station and is one of the hot, up-and-coming galleries. Young, promising Dutch and foreign artists are shown alongside established names. Gadella and Happel are out to get an international market with individualistic work that survives the years. Two-dimensional work is a speciality, but they also show installations and produce multiples (including sculptures) and books by artists.*

page 213 **The Provinces)** and the Van Abbe Museum (Eindhoven, *see* page 213 **The Provinces: Nord Braband).** All 'discover' relatively new artists and are known for their 'eye' for art which will be in demand. They provide a standard and sometimes a market for privately-owned art galleries, but they are a very hard act for the galleries to follow, without access to public funding.

The Amsterdam gallery guide, *Alert* (available at all galleries) is in Dutch, but it has maps of all districts, with the gallery locations clearly marked, and is very helpful when finding your way around. Custom-made guided tours of the galleries are run by Amsterdam Gallery Guide, *see* page 13 **Sightseeing.** Many of the galleries listed below close for a month, either in July or August, so it's best to phone before setting out to visit one in these months.

Apunto
Damrak 30, C (620 4384). Tram 4, 9, 16, 24, 25. Open 1-5pm Tue-Sat. No credit cards.
A young gallery with young artists, Apunto is

a place to watch. You won't find abstract expressionists, rather a space-age propensity for clean-cut, hard-edged irony and humour. The gallery was Amsterdam's first to show baroque fantastic artists. It also shows installations. Apunto is in a spacious building and the location couldn't be more central, but it's above a store and easy to miss.

Art Affairs
Wittenburgergracht 313, OE (620 6433). Bus 22, 28. Open 1-6pm Wed-Sat; also by appointment. No credit cards.
Art Affairs is this writer's favourite gallery, showing 'concrete' art (with solid, strong forms) in all materials. It inclines towards elementary forms concerning nature and the elements. Art Affairs emphasizes and excels in sculpture, but also shows painters with related strong concepts. *Wheelchair access.*

Art & Project
Nieuwesluizerweg 42, Slootdorp (02277 375/fax 02277 385). Open 11am-5pm Thur-Sun. No credit cards.
Although this is technically no longer an Amsterdam gallery (it's based in a western suburb), there are rumours that it might return to the city. Art & Project is the oldest conceptual gallery in the Amsterdam area and is also the best. Struycken, Schuil, Van Elk and Geurts are a few of the top names. *Wheelchair access with assistance.*

Aschenbach
Bilderdijkstraat 165C, OW (685 3580).

Tram 3, 12, 13, 14. Open 1-6pm Wed-Sun. No credit cards.
Aschenbach was the first Amsterdam gallery to show Russian artists, but it also concentrates on new German expressionist painters and shows a mixture of famous and new names, including AR Penck and J Jonkers. Its lack of concern about being 'established' gives the gallery added charm. *Wheelchair access with assistance.*

Asselijn
Lange Leidsedwarsstraat 198-200, IS (624 9030). Tram 1, 2, 5, 6, 7, 10. Open noon-5pm Tue-Sat. No credit cards.
A typically Dutch gallery which has been around for over 20 years. It is consistent and representative of the prevailing atmosphere. Asselijn won't knock your socks off: it prefers the soft approach to the shocking and adventurous. *Wheelchair access.*

Barbara Farber
Keizersgracht 265, IW (627 6343/fax 627 8091). Tram 13, 14, 17. Open 1-6pm Tue-Sat. No credit cards.
A top gallery and an absolute phenomenon in Amsterdam. Barbara Farber has put the lid on myths, such as the need to survive for a decade before being taken seriously. She shows new avant-garde work and has an eagle eye for unlaunched artists, particularly young Americans. The gallery has been responsible for an entire list of discoveries who've shot to the top, and also carries established artists like Merz, Paolini, Qucka and Lewitt.

Brinkman
Rozenstraat 59, OW (622 7493/fax 638 4558). Tram 13, 14, 17/Bus 21, 47, 67, 170, 171, 172. Open noon-6pm Tue-Sat. No credit cards.
Brinkman is considered important in the Amsterdam art world: old-guard to some, not to others. The gallery is a frequent exhibitor at art fairs, and shows Dutch and foreign artists – art you can live with. Quality is a little variable, but Brinkman has done some good things.

Collection d'Art
Keizersgracht 516, IS (622 1511). Tram 1, 2, 5. Open 1-5pm Tue-Sat. No credit cards.
An old gallery (founded 1969) which corners the market for good, established Dutch artists: Armando, Constant, De Kooning and a stable of big names.

D'Eendt
Spuistraat 272, C (626 5777). Tram 1, 2, 5. Open noon-6pm Tue-Sat; 2-6pm Sun. No credit cards.
Once a real trendsetter, d'Eendt is now living on an old reputation gone stale. New management is trying to find an exciting new image, but there are some doubts about the direction it's taking. Classic-moderns and good naïve figuratives are the strongest work. D'Eendt is another Dutch miracle of space utilization.

Espace
Keizersgracht 548, IS (624 0802). Tram 1, 2, 5, 16, 24, 25. Open noon-5.30pm Tue-Sat. No credit cards.
Based in Amsterdam since 1960, Eva Bendien is one of Amsterdam's *grande dames* of art. Her gallery shows Cobra artists: Lucassen, Lucebert and Pierre

Alechinsky. Co Westerik's popular, odd, Dutch realism is another highlight.

Galerie A

Johannes Verhulststraat 53, OS (671 4087/fax 675 2602). Tram 2, 16. **Open** *2-5pm Tue-Sat; also by appointment.* **No credit cards.**
Situated behind the Concertgebouw, this highly specialized gallery shows Fluxus art (an international movement of the sixties) and international conceptualists. The accent is on editions, so sales are often negotiated through catalogues, over the telephone or by fax. However, Galerie A also shows artists such as Wim T Schippers who are still producing new work. Prices are relatively low. *Wheelchair access.*

Galerie Rob Jurka

Singel 28, C (626 6733). Tram 1, 2, 4, 5, 9, 13, 16, 17, 24, 25. **Open** *12.30-5.30pm Wed-Sat.* **No credit cards.**
Established in 1970, Jurka is one of the oldies which once had a big name and superb exhibitions. This is a laid-back, non-aggressive gallery with very specific, perhaps decorative art. Jurka was the first to show photographer Robert Mapplethorpe before anyone seemed able to digest his work.

Geert Schriever

Prinsengracht 258A, IW (625 9757/fax 622 5973). Tram 13, 14, 17. **Open** *2-6pm Thur-Sat.* **Credit** *AmEx.*
Geert Schriever is a graphic designer who owns a publishing house and lives in his gallery. He takes younger artists who've proved their staying power. The accent is on painting.

Van Gelder

Planciusstraat 9A, OW (627 7419). Tram 3/Bus 22, 44. **Open** *1-5.30pm Tue-Sat.* **No credit cards.**
Kees van Gelder has a young gallery showing young up-and-coming artists. He has a good, appreciative eye that reacts quickly to new talent, although he's been accused of ignoring young Dutch artists. A lot of sculpture and several Scandinavian artists are shown.

Van Krimpen

Prinsengracht 629, IW (622 9375). Tram 1, 2, 5. **Open** *2-6pm Tue-Sat.* **No credit cards.**
Thought by some to be among the best galleries around, Van Krimpen was established in 1971. The owner's personal taste is paramount in deciding which artists are shown, but the accent is on new developments. Works reflect the current scene and can be anything from big sculpture to tiny paintings. *Wheelchair access.*

Kunsthandel Leeman

Keizersgracht 556, IS (627 4142). Tram 1, 2, 5, 16, 24, 25. **Open** *11am-5pm Thur-Sat; also by appointment.* **No credit cards.**
An enthusiastic, proud example of the traditional *kunsthandel* (art dealer), Leeman buys and resells works by Cobra artists, associated abstract expressionists of the fifties and sixties, and 'informal' art.

Laurens A Daane

Kerkstraat 127, IS (622 9963). Tram 1, 2, 5. **Open** *noon-5pm Tue-Sat.* **No credit cards.**
Laurens Daane was a collector before opening this gallery full of 'nice' paintings. The

Galerie Binnen (see under Specialized Galleries: Interior & Industrial Design) *is Amsterdam's foremost gallery for industrial and interior design and the applied arts (binnen means 'inside' or 'indoors'). The owners have a great roomy space to show new work by Dutch designers, including installations and spatial projects, plus glass, ceramics, jewellery and Czechoslovakian design. Surprisingly, Binnen is the only gallery of its kind and calibre in Amsterdam.*

work has an easy-going Dutch flavour, comparable to Asselijn *(see above).* According to Ms Daane, her shows feature 'current, contemporary tendencies in art', but concentrate on the expressive, not the geometric. Mostly young Dutch, French, Italian and Spanish artists are exhibited. *Wheelchair access.*

The Living Room

Laurierstraat 70, IW (625 8449). Tram 13, 14, 17. **Open** *2-6pm Tue-Sat.* **No credit cards.**
A top spot, often thought to carry only Dutch artists, but which also has international work that Bart van de Ven feels challenges Dutch artists. The gallery actively promotes artists such as Ton van Sumeren and Peer Veneman abroad and specializes in installations. *Wheelchair access.*

Lumen Travo

Nieuwezijds Voorburgwal 352, C (627 8049). Tram 1, 2, 5. **Open** *2-6pm Wed-Sat.* **No credit cards.**
Marianne van Tilborg is extremely ambitious and on the look-out for up-and-coming artists (both Dutch and foreign) who 'break new ground'. The gallery began with design (functional or applied art) but has moved to more spatial work and installations. It is trendy, and Guillaume Bijl and Thom Puckey are two hot names. Having established her reputation from a living-room, from April 1991 Marianne will be in a beautiful gallery space at Paulus Potterstraat 38; the phone number will remain the same.

Maghi Bettini

Warmoesstraat 16A, C (622 4301). Tram 4, 9, 16, 24, 25.. **Open** *1-5.30pm Wed-Sat.* **No credit cards.**

Swiss-born Maghi had an uphill struggle for a decade because her central location is on a picturesque but hardly classy street. However, the gallery is doing very well now. Maghi prefers artists who've 'found themselves' to youngsters starting out, and presents them abroad. Not one to shock, she has targeted a growing, young middle-class market.

Mokum

Nieuwezijds Voorburgwal 334, C (624 3958). Tram 1, 2, 5. **Open** *noon-6pm Tue-Sat; 2-4pm Sun.* **No credit cards.**
Mokum specializes in Dutch realism, an extremely well-developed school of its own here. Magic (or fantastic) realists are also represented. 'Mokum' is the popular Jewish nickname for Amsterdam.

Nanky de Vreese

Singel 37, IW (627 3808). Tram 1, 2, 4, 5, 9, 13, 16, 17, 24, 25. **Open** *11am-5.30pm Tue-Sat; also by appointment.* **No credit cards.**
Nanky de Vreese shows lyrical abstract work by generally older artists, inclining towards decorative, milder art you can live with. She has had good shows and a fair amount of sculpture as well as drawings, prints and paintings, but is not always consistent. *Wheelchair access to ground floor.*

Onrust

Prinsengracht 627, IW (638 0474). Tram 1, 2, 5. **Open** *2-6pm Tue-Sat.* **No credit cards.**
This little gallery is run by Milco Onrust, an inscrutable, respected fellow who says he likes boring art. Artists represented are young, poetic, sensual and conceptual. Prints and drawings are particular strengths, but paintings are also featured. An important gallery, at least locally.

Paul Andriesse
Prinsengracht 116, IW (623 6237). Tram 13, 14, 17. **Open** 10am-1pm, 2-6pm, Tue-Fri; 2-6pm Sat. **No credit cards.**
The Paul Andriesse gallery has been around since 1977 and is one of the best to promote both Dutch and foreign artists of repute. It is one of the few Amsterdam galleries doing well overseas. Marlene Dumas' big and disconcerting faces, Guido Geelen's outrageous ceramics and Henk Visch's sculptures are all noteworthy.

Picaron Editions/Gadella & Happel
Binnenkant 29, C (620 1484). Bus 22, 32, 33, 34, 35, 56, 91, 92, 94, 100, 104, 105, 106, 110, 111, 112, 114, 115. **Open** 1-6pm Wed-Sun. **No credit cards.**
See p112 **picture and caption.**

Van Rooy
Kerkstraat 216, IS (622 9621). Tram 16, 24, 25. **Open** 1-6pm Tue-Sat. **No credit cards.**
Luce van Rooy shows contemporary architectural work and what she describes as 'related forms of visual art' in this upstairs gallery. The definition is broad, and not exclusive, but there is a consistent thread and identity. This is the Mondrian side of Dutch art, resisting anarchy. Van Rooy has good shows and her own following.

De Selby
Nieuwe Teertuinen 16, IW (625 0990). Tram 3. **Open** 1-5pm Tue-Sat. **No credit cards.**
The Selby is an important place for young Amsterdam artists, serving as a forum for discussions. A low-budget space, it is installation-oriented and has a New York atmosphere. The Selby isn't easy to find – it's in the western harbour area – but has a pleasantly shabby and laid-back feel.

Suzanne Biederberg
Oudezijds Voorburgwal 223, C (624 5455). Tram 4, 9, 16, 24, 25. **Open** 2-6pm Wed-Sat; also by appointment. **No credit cards.**
Suzanne Biederberg, an Australian, has had a gallery here since 1985. Its competent, appealing Dutch and foreign artists, if no resounding names. Take a look at Nan Hoover's work, when she is showing.

Swart
Van Breestraat 23, OS (676 4736). Tram 2, 3, 5, 12, 16. **Open** 2-6pm Wed-Sat; 3-5pm Sun. **No credit cards.**
Riejke Swart is the undisputed *grande dame* and godmother of the Amsterdam art scene. She began in 1964 with constructivism and didn't show women because they weren't aggressive enough for her (she does show them now, occasionally). Nowadays nobody's sure how to classify her style, but it's always good. She is critical, opinionated and is looking for young people because 'no one buys expensive artists here'. Artists love her and galleries admire her. She showed Donald Judd first (nobody came) and couldn't sell Lucio Fontana's work, so she bought it herself. *Wheelchair access.*

Torch
Prinsengracht 218, IW (626 0284). Tram 13, 14, 17. **Open** 1-6pm Thur-Sat. **No credit cards.**
Adriaan van der Have says he has the most international gallery in Amsterdam. Torch specializes in current developments in photography and includes video, installations and sculpture. It is classy by local standards, with artists like Joel Peter Witkin and Cindy Sherman. This is a trendy gallery trying to make it big from a small space up a flight of narrow Amsterdam stairs.

Wetering Galerie
Lijnbaansgracht 288, IW (623 6189). Tram 3, 10. **Open** noon-5pm Tue-Sat. **No credit cards.**
The Wetering Galerie has a reputation for showing sculpture. Michiel Hennus searches for individuals, not 'school' trends, and believes there is a serenity and neatness to Dutch art in the De Stijl (Peter Struycken) tradition – flashiness is equated with foreign influence and insincerity.

Witzenhausen Meyerink
Laurierstraat 41, IW (638 2305). Tram 13, 14, 17. **Open** 2-6pm Thur-Sat. **No credit cards.**
A recent addition to Amsterdam's galleries that stands out for its self-assurance and professional approach. The effect is heady, serious and refreshing. There's a German/Austrian emphasis with five Viennese artists represented and exchange exhibitions held with Austria. The art is super-realism with a twist, achieved by narrative strategy using old, apparently traditional techniques that are almost bourgeois. You are tricked into asking: 'Is it art?'. Together with Apunto *(see above)*, Witzenhausen Meyerink commands this genre.

SPECIALIZED GALLERIES

CERAMICS

De Witte Voet
Kerkstraat 149, IS (625 8412). Tram 1, 2, 5. **Open** noon-5pm Tue-Sat. **No credit cards.**
Annemie Boissevain hesitates to use the term ceramics to describe her exhibits – people still seem to think in terms of pots, not sculpture. But this is *the* ceramics gallery, mounting solo shows of predominantly Dutch artists. Boissevain says the market is growing, and that traditional ceramics galleries (selling pots) are 'popping up everywhere'.

INTERIOR & INDUSTRIAL DESIGN

Galerie Binnen
Keizersgracht 82, IW (625 9603/fax 627 2654). Tram 1, 2, 5, 13, 17. **Open** noon-6pm Tue-Sat. **No credit cards.**
See p113 **picture and caption.**
Wheelchair access.

Although **Ra** (see under Specialized Galleries: Jewellery) *isn't the only place for jewellery, it's the one everyone will send you to. There is a thin line between sculpture and jewellery these days, as a look around this gallery will show – you may prefer putting these works on your mantlepiece to wearing them. Opened in 1976, the gallery is now well established. The artists/designers are both Dutch and foreign and a wide variety of materials are used.*

JEWELLERY

RA
Vijzelstraat 80, C (626 5100). Tram 4, 9, 14, 16, 24, 25. **Open** noon-6pm Tue-Fri; 11am-5pm Sat. **Credit** AmEx, V.
See p114 **picture and caption.**
Wheelchair access to ground floor.

MEDIA ART

Montevideo/Rene Coelho
Singel 137, C (623 7101). Tram 1, 2, 5, 13, 17. **Open** *Montevideo* 9am-5pm Mon-Fri; *gallery* 1-6pm Tue-Sat. **No credit cards.**
Montevideo is a media artists' organization; its gallery puts on solo shows of work related to electronic media, photography, sculpture and installations.

Time Based Arts
Bloemgracht 121, IW (627 2620/622 9764). Tram 13, 14, 17. **Open** *exhibitions* 1-5pm Wed-Sat; *archives and library* 9am-5pm Fri. **No credit cards.**
This is the place for information on video arts and for good shows. Time Based Arts is an organization of media artists.

PHOTOGRAPHY

22 x 42 Fotogalerie
Prinsengracht 356, IW (626 0757). Tram 13, 14, 17. **Open** 2-6pm Thur, Fri; noon-5pm Sat. **No credit cards.**
Together with Canon *(see below)*, this is the survivor among a number of photography galleries which have come and gone. There is a broad range of solo shows.

Canon Image Centre
Leidsestraat 79, IS (625 4494). Tram 1, 2, 5. **Open** noon-5.45pm Tue-Fri; 11am-4.45pm Sat. **Credit** AmEx, MC, V.
See **picture and caption.**

PRINT-MAKING

De Expeditie
Leliegracht 47, IW (620 4758). Tram 13, 14, 17. **Open** 2-6pm Wed-Sat. **No credit cards.**
The one-man shows at De Expeditie take months of preparation. Siguidur Gudmunsson, Tony Cragg, Barry Flanagan and a number of Dutch artists have all worked and exhibited here. The gallery's aim is to get artists started in printmaking and help them, technically, to realize it.

Printshop
Prinsengracht 845, IS (625 1656). Tram 16, 24, 25. **Open** 10am-1pm, 2-5.30pm, Mon-Sat. **No credit cards.**
Printshop is the grand-daddy of the print-maker's studio-galleries – it has been an atelier since 1958, a gallery since 1968. Artists do their own prints and the gallery also exhibits their drawings and paintings. Standards are somewhat limited and mixed.

Steendrukkerij Amsterdam
Lauriergracht 80, IW (624 1491). Tram 13, 14, 17. **Open** 1-5.30pm Wed-Sat. **No credit cards.**
Steen is stone; *drukker* is printer, and the *drukkerij* is the place where printers print. The gallery, not surprisingly, shows lithos,

woodcuts, and experimental prints. It has a straightforward approach.

SCULPTURE

Fons Welters
Bloemstraat 140, OW (622 7193). Tram 13, 14, 17. **Open** 2-6pm Tue-Sat. **No credit cards.**
Fons Welters is a solid, red-headed country fellow who is impossible to dislike. This is the only gallery exclusively for sculpture and is one of the top ten galleries in the city. It shows everything from multiples to spatial projects and installations. Sculpture is extremely strong in The Netherlands, if not breathtakingly exciting. However, Welters considers Dutch sculptors to be the most international (eclectic) in the world, and he has the pick of 'em.

SUBSIDIZED SPACES & COLLECTIVES

Amsterdam has about half a dozen subsidized exhibition spaces apart from its museums, but funding has been reduced in the past decade, with predictable results. Recent sub-sidies for open studios and weekend art events will result in artists preferring annual events to maintaining co-operative spaces year-round. Several non-profit-making private and co-operative initiatives throughout The Nether-lands organize outstanding exhibitions. Oddly, not many of these are in Amsterdam, but that may change.

SCULPTORS' COLLECTIVE

ABK/Amsterdams Beeldhouwers Kollektief
Zeilmakerstraat 15, IW (625 6332). Tram 3. **Open** 10am-5pm Wed-Fri; 1-5pm Sat, Sun. **No credit cards.**
Amsterdam's sculptors' collective was not big, flashy or exceptionally professional, but it has now greatly expanded its space and taken on new artists. It has a spectrum of figurative sculptors, in particular.
Wheelchair access.

SUBSIDIZED ART SPACES

De Appel
Prinseneiland 7, OW (625 5651). Tram 3. **Open** 1-5pm Tue-Sat. **No credit cards.**

The **Canon Image Centre** (see under **Specialized Galleries: Photography**) *is based in a multi-storey building, with exhibition space – large by Amsterdam standards – on the ground and first floors. It's run by a team of well-informed staff, led by manager Adrian Monshouwer. The exhibitions, which change every three weeks, are good, sometimes great. Two photographers, one Dutch, one foreign, are usually shown at the same time, and shows range from exhibitions of portraits of Dutch personalities and news photography to experimental, abstract works. Above the gallery is an excellent bookshop.*

An Amsterdam institution, dating from 1975, De Appel presents films, lectures and exhibitions, with the accent on theoretical approaches to contemporary art.

Arti et Amicitiae
Rokin 112, C (623 3367). Tram 4, 9, 14, 16, 24, 25. **Open** noon-5pm Tue-Sun. **No credit cards.**
This beautiful building houses Amsterdam's oldest and most elegant club for artists and the patrons who support them. It has a beautiful, large upstairs exhibition space. Occasionally, this is rented out, but primarily it hosts excellent theme shows and projects by members.

Nieuwe Vleugel Stedelijk Museum (New Wing Stedelijk Museum)
Paulus Potterstraat 13, OS (573 2911/Dutch recorded information 573 2737). Tram 2, 3, 12, 15, 16. **Open** 11am-5pm daily; 11am-4pm public holidays. **Admission** f7; f3.50 under-17s, CJP card holders; under-7s free; free with Museum Card; group discounts (min 50 people). **No credit cards.**
A monument to Amsterdam idealism, the new wing of the Stedelijk Museum (*see p100* **Museums: The Big Three**) was built and funded to be used exclusively as exhibition space for Amsterdam's artists' guilds and clubs. Sculptors, watercolourists, illustrators, photographers, graphic designers and several mixed-discipline organizations exhibit works of wildly varying content and calibre. This confuses anyone associating it with the museum – which is everyone. Together with the Fodor Museum (*see p100* **Museums: Art**), the New Wing is Amsterdam artists' official alternative to a gallery. Get there soon, there is controversy over the New Wing's future: its days could be numbered.

Oudekerk
Oudekerksplein 23, C (625 8284). Tram 4, 9, 16, 24, 25. **Open** 15 Apr-15 Sept 11am-5pm Mon-Sat; 16 Sept-14 Apr 1-5pm Mon-Sat. **No credit cards.**
Artists are able to rent space for exhibitions

in Amsterdam's oldest church. The shows vary enormously.
Wheelchair access with assistance.

De Ruimte
2nd floor, Rozengracht 207, IW (625 0235). Tram 13, 14, 17. **Open** 1-5pm Wed-Sat. **No credit cards.**
Ruimte means space. And this is an expensive one for artists to rent. Exhibitors are strictly screened, hence the Ruimte maintains a reputation for high standards. Once approved, artists use the space as they wish.

W 139
Warmoesstraat 139, C (622 9434). Tram 4, 9, 16, 24, 25. **Open** noon-6pm Tue-Sun. **No credit cards.**
This ground-floor space is gigantic by Amsterdam standards. W139 has close links with the art schools and offers young artists excellent opportunities to produce space-related works and theme shows.
Wheelchair access.

ARTISTS' BOOKS

Few people are aware of the talents put into books made by and for artists – not Rembrandt, Van Gogh or Mondrian, but the folk currently sweating over the work in the galleries, designing, drawing and publishing their own books. There are several small publishers and book designers in Amsterdam producing books by and for artists. Some, like **Picaron Editions** (*see above* **Galleries**), support their gallery this way, others support their own non-applied arts by making books for their colleagues.

Boekie Woekie
Gasthuismolensteeg 16, C (625 9360). Tram 1, 2, 5, 13, 14, 17. **Open** noon-6pm Tue-Fri; noon-5pm Sat. **No credit cards.**

Boekie Woekie exhibits and sells graphics and books by artists. Graphics is a broader term in Dutch than in English – it includes all forms of printmaking – so if Dutch artists say they make graphics (as a huge number will) don't assume they're layout people at an advertising firm.

EVENTS

ART FAIRS
Amsterdam's annual art fair is called the **KunstRai** (the Rai is Amsterdam's congress centre) and it takes place in late May or early June. So much art in one place at one time can be overwhelming, but everything is there – at least as far as the 'accepted' gallery circuit is concerned. You may buy art at the KunstRai or simply go to admire it. *See also page 36* **Amsterdam by Season**.

OPEN ATELIERS
Neighbourhoods with large artist populations and artists' studio complexes hold open days, often in the spring or autumn. Recent open days have been held at Prinseneiland, Jordaan, and at WG Terrein. Dozens of studios are open to the public for a weekend or more; most present a group show. The events have become popular and have succeeded in reaching a broader spectrum of the public than would normally go to a gallery. If you see 'Open Atelier' banners or posters during your visit, try and go – it may provide a memorable insight into artists' lives and studios, and behind-the-scenes art.

ARTOTEEKS

In Amsterdam you can borrow works of art as you do books from a library – for a week, a month or a year. The *artoteek* (a play on words with *bibliotheek* – the Dutch word for library) and the *kunstuitleen* (*kunst* means 'art', *uit means* 'out', and *leen* means 'lend') work on the same principle as libraries. The main difference between the two is that the *kunstuitleen* is subsidized, rather than run by the city. At both, borrowers can take a work of art home on loan, with the option to buy. Because of the astounding over-supply of artists and the cautious (to put it

mildly) market, *artoteeks* and *kunstuitleens* carry huge numbers of artists. They provide a good cross-section of art, within the restrictions of size, and durability to withstand frequent transport. Artists sometimes sell to these lending libraries, but work is usually rented for a percentage of its value.
The *artoteeks* have proved to be a success, and they provide an excellent means of getting art across to the public. There are five neighbourhood *artoteeks* run by the city. All have exhibition spaces for solo shows and have hundreds of works

in stock, but none are in the centre of Amsterdam. As for *kunstuitleens*, only the **SBK** has maintained a semi-independent structure and fairly high standards. It is easily reached, has the large space it requires (there are about 10,000 works by 900 artists), and also represents artists from outside Amsterdam.

SBK Kunstuitleen (Stichting Beeldende Kunst/Fine Arts Foundation)
Nieuwezijds Voorburgwal 325, C (623 9215). Tram 1, 2, 5. **Open** 11am-9pm Tue; 11am-5pm Wed-Fri; 9am-5pm Sat. **Hire cost** *basic* £25 per month; *deposit* f75. **No credit cards.**

Entertainment

Amsterdam's entertainment scene is very accessible to the foreign visitor, mainly because you don't have to speak Dutch to enjoy it. Most films are shown in their original language with Dutch sub-titles, as are British and American programmes on Dutch television. There are even English-language theatre companies. And of course, the city's impressive dance companies need no translation.

Music is highly international in Amsterdam, whether it's pumped out live or on the radio. We give a DJ's mix of night-clubs, a tour of the rock and jazz venues and an expert look at Amsterdam's famous classical music makers. After a night on the town, whether you need a late-night chemist, a kebab at 3am or a drink at dawn, we tell you where you to go. And how to get home.

CONTENTS:

Dance

Amsterdam's dance scene is burgeoning, with performances from international stars and homegrown talent, says dance critic _Ariejan Korteweg_.

The Netherlands has been exposed to a diverse collection of cultures through its pre-eminence as a trading nation. In recent years this contact has given Dutch dance a refreshing vitality. Practitioners are constantly looking for new challenges, causing the scene to change rapidly – artistic liaisons are often made for one production only. The trend is marked by elaborate interplay with other disciplines and a tendency to play at unusual locations.

But this explosion of variety is a novel phenomenon. The country lacks a strong indigenous tradition of dance, partly because of the influence of Calvinism. Apart from clog-dancing – which at the moment is only practised when there are foreigners around – dance is an imported art form and until the eighties the choice was quite limited. Two companies dominated the scene in the seventies: the **Nationale Ballet** and the **Nederlands Dans Theater** (for both _see under_ **Companies**). But modern dance companies were few at that time.

Over the past decade, the situation has changed dramatically. Amsterdam has attracted many artistes from abroad who have settled in the city, causing dance to prosper and diversify. The two main companies are still top of the heap, but a flowering of modern dance has resulted in many new groups. Now you can find post-modern dance influenced by New York, expressionistic dance following the example of the Germans, and dance with its roots in the Orient or in jazz. Amsterdam is where most companies are located and most premières take place.

Dance in The Netherlands tends to emphasize the ideas of the choreographer rather than being a gallery for dancers to show off their virtuosity. Indeed, the ideas are sometimes better than the performance itself. Recently, however, the quality of the dance academies has improved, and Dutch dance has benefitted considerably as a result. If you are looking

for something special, look out for Truus Bronkhorst, a solo dancer who stands out as an intense and very personal performer, dancing on the edge of a shiver and a moan. Her Amsterdam performances usually take place in the **Shaffy Theater** (_under_ **Venues**). Roxane Huilmand and Angelika Oei are two young Dutch choreographers whose work is also worth watching. They are not attached to any particular group, but tend to work with dancers or musicians for one-off productions.

SUBSIDY SQUABBLES

Although it took a long time for the government to open its eyes to the new developments in Dutch dance, subsidies are now more in tune with current trends. A number of the more established modern companies now receive an annual grant. However, counter-forces are raising their voices, insisting that it's unfair that taxpayers who would never go to an 'élitist' dance performance should have to pay a share of the ticket. If subsidies are to become closely related to public attendance, it will mean the end of avant-garde dance in The Netherlands.

So how can you get to see the exciting dance groups while the scene is still effervescing? Below we have listed all the main companies and venues in Amsterdam and the surrounding area. Tickets can be purchased from **AUB Uitburo** or the **VVV** (for both _see page 3_ **Essential Information**). To find out which companies are currently performing in the city, pick up the latest edition of _Uitkrant_ magazine, free at every venue. The **Nederlands Dans Instituut** (_see below_ **Festivals & Events**) also provides information on festivals and performances.

FESTIVALS & EVENTS

One way of sampling new trends in dance, without being overloaded by interminable performances, is by attending a concourse, where prizes are awarded to the best acts. Groningen, for instance (_see page_

213 **The Provinces**), had an International Concourse for Choreographers in 1988 and 1990 and will probably stage another in 1992. Information on these competition events, courses, workshops, festivals and performances is provided by the **Nederlands Dans Instituut**; _see also below_ **Events** and **Courses & Workshops**.

Nederlands Dans Instituut
Herengracht 174, IW (623 7541). Tram 13, 14, 17. Open 9am-5pm Mon-Fri.

VENUES

Bellevue
Leidsekade 90, IS (624 7248). Tram 1, 2, 5, 6, 7, 10. Open _information and bookings_ 10am-4pm Mon-Fri; 11am-4pm Sat, Sun; _ticket office_ 7.30-8.30pm before performances. Tickets f17.50; CJP card holders f12.50. Performances 8.30pm. No credit cards. Modern dance companies such as Dansgroep Krisztina de Chatel (_see below_ **Companies**) and Reflex (_see below_ **Companies: Out of Town**) often perform at this handsome, small theatre. _Café._ Wheelchair access by arrangement.

De Brakke Grond (The Salty Ground)
Nes 45, C (626 6866). Tram 4, 9, 14, 16, 24, 25. Open _box office_ 10am-4pm, 7-9pm, Mon-Sat. Tickets f15; CJP card holders f10. Performances 8.30pm. No credit cards. You'll find this place in a small street near the Dam which boasts the unofficial title of 'Amsterdam's theatre boulevard'. De Brakke Grond is a Flemish centre for the arts, and is where to see the best of Belgian dance. _Café (open 11am-1am Mon-Thur; 11am-2am Fri, Sat). Wheelchair access to Expozaal and Rodezaal only._

Captain Fiddle
Kloveniersburgwal 86, C (626 0363). Tram 9, 14, 16, 24, 25/Metro Nieuwmarkt. Open _information and bookings_ 9am-5pm Mon-Fri; _box office_ 8-8.30pm Wed-Sat. Tickets f10. Performances 8.30pm. No credit cards. A fringe theatre, permanently suffering from a lack of money, where young dance and theatre companies stage productions. Performances are staged every week from October to June. _Bar. Wheelchair access with assistance._

Danslab
Overamstelstraat 39, OE (694 9466). Tram 8, 15/Metro Wibautstraat. Open _box office_ one hour before performance. Tickets f10; f7.50 CJP card holders. Performances usually 8pm. No credit cards. _See p119 picture and caption._

Engelenbak
Nes 73 (above Nes 45), C (626 6866). Tram 4, 9, 14, 16, 24, 25. Open _box office_ 10am-4pm, 7-9pm, Mon-Sat. Tickets f15; CJP card holders f10. Performances 8.30pm. No credit cards. The programming at the Engelenbak

emphasizes semi-professional and non-Western performances. It sometimes surprises with African or South American dance that you won't find elsewhere.

Folkloristisch Danstheater
Kloveniersburgwal 87, C (623 9112). Tram 9, 14/Metro Nieuwmarkt. **Open** *box office* 11am-3pm Mon-Fri; one hour before performance; *information* 9am-5pm Mon-Fri. **Tickets** f7.50-f20. **No credit cards.**
This is the permanent residence of the company that performs folk dances both from The Netherlands and abroad. In summer, special events are staged for tourists, combined with a boat trip through the canals. The company regularly tours, both in The Netherlands and abroad, so you may not be able to catch it in Amsterdam. During the winter it gives one-hour Sunday 'coffee concerts'.

Frascati
Nes 63 (box office Nes 45), C (626 6866). Tram 4, 9, 14, 16, 24, 25. **Open** *box office* 10am-4pm, 7-9pm, Mon-Sat. **Tickets** f15; CJP card holders f10. *Frascati 1* 8.30pm; *Frascati 2* 9pm. **No credit cards.**
Two halls that house modern dance companies such as Dansproduktie (*see below* **Companies**).
Café (open 4pm-1am Mon-Thur; 4pm-2am Fri, Sat). Wheelchair access. Toilets for the disabled.

Koninklijk Theater Carré
Amstel 115-125, OS (622 5225). Tram 6, 7, 10. **Open** *box office* 10am-7pm Mon-Sat; 1-7pm Sun. **Tickets** f25-f75; reductions for CJP card holders, over-65s. **Performance** 8.15pm. **Credit** DC.
This former circus theatre on the quay of the Amstel provides a stylish venue for occasional dance performances. *See also* p126 **Theatre.**

Muziektheater
Waterlooplein 22, C (625 5455). Tram 9, 14/Metro Waterlooplein. **Open** *box office* 10am-6pm Mon-Sat; noon-6pm Sun. **Tickets** f20-f45; reductions for CJP card holders, over-65s. **Performances** 8.15pm. **No credit cards.**
The new Muziektheater is Amsterdam at its most ambitious. The plush crescent-shaped building with the Stadhuis (town hall) at the back, opened in 1985, seats 1,500 and is the home of both the Nationale Ballet (*see below* **Companies** and the Nederlands Opera. The big stage is also used by visiting companies such as the Royal Ballet, the Frankfurt Ballet and the Merce Cunningham Company. *See also* p68 **Post-war** and p130 **Music: Classical & Opera.**
Wheelchair access and toilets for the disabled.

Shaffy Theater
Felix Meritis Building, Keizersgracht 324, IW (bookings 623 1311/information 9am-5pm Mon-Fri 620 0225). Tram 1, 2, 5. **Open** *box office* 3pm-start of performance Tue-Sat; *telephone bookings* 3-7.30pm daily. **Tickets** f10. **Performances** 9pm. **No credit cards.**
Many of today's outstanding companies gave their first performances at the Shaffy and the programmers still have a taste for talent, mainly from abroad. *See also* p126 **Theatre.**

De Stadsschouwburg
Leidseplein 26, IS (624 2311). Tram 1, 2, 5, 7, 10. **Open** *box office* 10am-6pm Mon-Sat; 75 mins before performance. **Tickets** f15-

Although dance productions can be seen all over Amsterdam, the **Danslab** *(see under* **Venues**) *is the only venue permanently dedicated to the art. It's a small, informal theatre, situated a little outside the city centre near Wibautstraat, the city's Fleet Street. Four or five nights a week it hosts shows by mostly new companies and artists. You might have the good fortune to see young and gifted dancers giving their first performances, but there's a chance you'll encounter a few duds.*

f45; reductions for CJP card holders, over-65s. **Performances** 7.30pm, 8.15pm. **No credit cards.**
Together with the Hotel Americain, this nineteenth-century building dominates Leidseplein. Performances range from musicals to experimental theatre and modern dance. The small *bovenzaal* (upper room) often gives space to small dance companies. *See also* p126 **Theatre.**

Tropen Instituut
Mauritskade 63, IE (568 8490). Tram 9, 10, 14. **Open** *telephone bookings* 2-4pm Mon-Fri; *box office* one hour before performance. **Tickets** f12.50-f22.50. **Performances** usually 8pm. **No credit cards.**
From September to June, performances of Indian music and dance are held once or twice per month as part of the Classical India Series, in the main Institute hall. The Soeterijn Theater includes dance in its regular programmes of Third World music and theatre. Balinese dance has been among the highlights.

Het Veemtheater (The Warehouse Theatre)
Van Diemenstraat 410, IW (626 0112). Tram 3/bus 28. **Open** *box office and information* 10am-9pm Mon-Sat. **Tickets** f12.50; CJP card holders f10. **Performances** 9pm. **No credit cards.**
A former warehouse next to the port which specializes in mime and movement theatre.
Café (open 8pm-1 hour after performance ends).

OUT OF TOWN

AT&T Danstheater
Schedeldoekshaven 60, 2511 EN, Den Haag (070 360 9931). **Open** *box office* 10am-3pm Mon-Sat; one hour before performance. **Tickets** f35; occasional reductions for CJP card holders. **Performances** 8.15pm; *matinées* 2.30pm. **No credit cards.**

Since 1987 this venue in The Hague has been the home of the Nederlands Dans Theater (*see above* **Companies**). The building's design, by leading Dutch architect Rem Koolhaas, is both daring and handsome. Many dance companies perform here throughout the year and it's considered to be a much better venue than Amsterdam's Muziektheater (*see above* **Venues**).
Wheelchair access by arrangement.

Rotterdamse Schouwburg
Schouwburgplein 25, 3012 CL, Rotterdam (010 411 8110). **Open** *box office* 11am-7pm daily; one hour before performance. **Tickets** f25-f45; reductions for CJP card holders, over-65s. **Performances** 8.15pm, 8.30pm. **Credit** Schouwburg credit card.
Designed by Dutch architect Wim Quist, this large theatre first opened its doors in 1988. It plays host to the bigger national companies as well as dance troupes from abroad.
Bar. Café. Shop. Wheelchair access. Toilets for the disabled.

Toneelschuur (Theatre Barn)
Smeedestraat 23, 2011 RE, Haarlem (023 312 439). **Open** *box office* 3-6pm Mon-Sat; also from 7.30pm. **Tickets** f15; CJP card holders f10. **Performances** 8.30pm. **No credit cards.**
Many dance and theatre lovers from Amsterdam go to Haarlem (15 minutes by train, *see* p208 **The Ranstad**) to congregate at the Toneelschuur. This theatre has two halls and is nationally renowned for its programmes of theatre and modern dance.

Nationale Ballet
Information from Muziektheater (*see above* **Venues**).
When the Dutch National Ballet left the Stadsschouwburg in 1986 to move to the

Amsterdam, NDT stages regular performances in the Muziektheater, and NDT2 usually performs in the Stadsschouwburg (*see above* **Venues**). *See also* **picture and caption**.

Dansgroep Krisztina de Châtel
Plantage Muidergracht 155, 1018 TT; IE (627 3970). Tram 7, 14. **Open** *office* 9am-5pm Mon-Fri.
An outstanding modern dance company. Hungarian-born de Châtel formerly based her choreography on repeated movements, but in recent years she has taken to a more theatrical approach. Performances in Amsterdam usually take place in the Bellevue, *see above* **Venues**.

Dansproduktie
Plantage Kerklaan 61, IE (624 2166). **Information and programmes** from Frascati (*see above* **Venues**).
Dansproduktie has been the pioneer of Dutch modern dance. Led by Bianca van Dillen, this group clings to sophisticated, Cunningham-oriented dance with scores by modern Dutch composers. Video and film clips are often used in the performances. Frascati (*see above* **Venues**) is the company's home base in Amsterdam.

De Nieuwe Dansgroep
Lootsstraat 39, 1053 NV, (616 2153). Tram 7, 17. **Open** 9am-5pm Mon-Fri.
De Nieuwe Dansgroep is as close as a Dutch company can get to 'abstract' modern dancing. Jacqueline Knoops, its main choreographer, is strongly influenced by post-modern dancing from the USA. She usually manages to gather fine young dancers in her company. Daily courses are run for professional dancers.

OUT OF TOWN

Djazzex
In 1983 Djazzex started in The Hague as a middle-of-the-road, jazz-cum-showdance company, but it soon developed its own style – a mixture of jazz and modern dance. The company has been a pioneer of jazz dance in The Netherlands.

Introdans
Introdans is a touring company, based in Arnhem, that tries not to be too highbrow. Productions vary from easy-going dramatic ballet to some fine work by young Dutch choreographer Ed Wubbe.

Reflex
Reflex, based in Groningen in the far north, has in a few years built up a repertoire that is both varied and tasteful. Most of the choreographers are European. Don't miss this company when it performs works by Hans Tuerlings, its finest native choreographer.

Rotterdamse Dansgroep
Information from Schouwburg (*see above* **Venues Out of Town: Rotterdam**).
This company is one of the most vigorous exponents of New York dance in The Netherlands. Imported dance routines are mixed with work by young Dutch choreographers. The nervous and precise ballets of Ton Simons are outstanding.

The **Nederlands Dans Theater** (see under **Companies**) *has a Czech (Jiri Kylian) for artistic director, and nine out of ten of its dancers hold a foreign passport. In 15 years Kylian has given the company a solid reputation for quality, both in The Netherlands and abroad. He was famous for his lyrical ballets based on music from middle-European composers, but recently he has taken a promising, sharper-edged direction. In 1986 the company appointed Hans van Manen, a choreographer who specializes in almost mathematical neo-classicism. The NDT's international repertoire includes this production of* Visions Fugitives *with music by Prokofiev and choreography by van Manen.*

Muziektheater, its repertoire changed markedly. The innovative choreographer Hans van Manen did not feel at ease in the prestigious surroundings of the Muziektheater and left to join the Nederlands Dans Theater *below*. Now that 1,500 seats have to be filled every night, the company tends to lean heavily on classical ballets such as *Swan Lake* and *Sleeping Beauty*, which are performed with consummate skill. This is the largest company (over 80 dancers, many non-Dutch) in The Netherlands and it has over 20 Balanchine ballets in its repertoire, the largest collection outside New York. Rudi van Dantzig and Toer van Schayk are the main choreographers, both dwelling on expressionistic classical dance. After having been in charge for over 20 years Rudi

van Dantzig retires as artistic director in 1991.

Nederlands Dans Theater
Information from AT&T Danstheater (*see above* **Venues: Out of Town**).
In 1987 the Nederlands Dans Theater left its shabby housing near Centraal Station in The Hague to settle in its own theatre. This clever building suits the repertoire of the company, the black stage walls directing all the attention towards the quality of the movements. Ballets from the Czech artistic director Jiri Kylian form the core of the programming. The company also has a group of younger dancers (under the age of 20) named NDT2. Its repertoire is similar to that of the NDT and the technical skills of the dancers are surprisingly good. In

Scapino Ballet
Information from Schouwburg (*see above* **Venues Out of Town: Rotterdam**).
Scapino is the oldest company in the country and until recently put emphasis on youth dance and 'family' programmes. But under the artistic leadership of Nils Christe this is now changing to a more up-to-date style. Ed Wubbe, one of the country's most promising choreographers, has been appointed.

THEATRE & DANCE

Theatre and dance in The Netherlands are closely related. At the beginning of the eighties, the Nationale Ballet surprised audiences with *Bacchanten*, a dance performance directed by a stage director. Ever since, companies and artists have balanced on the boundary between the two disciplines. These performances are easily accessible to non-Dutch speakers, because movement and image are usually more important than speech. And often when text is involved, it is spoken in English. The following are worth looking out for (further information from the Nederlands Dans Instituut, *see above* **Festivals & Events**).

Barbara Duyfjes & Lisa Marcus: A Dutch-American duo who combine dance with whatever happens to cross their minds. The blend often produces performances with a hallucinatory quality.

Cloud Chamber: Cloud Chamber provides the truest representation of the so-called post-modern multi-media spectacle, which is often convincing while you are watching, but leaves you with many questions afterwards.

Het Concern: Het concern can mean either 'the company' or 'caring'. This group of dancers in their late thirties often collaborates with stage directors to fuse the best of theatre and dance.

Onafhankelijk Toneel: Onafhankelijk Toneel was a pioneer in mixing dance and theatre. Its trademark is a very precise style, combining movement and speech. You will find the results either highly sophisticated or utterly boring.

EVENTS

Spring Dance
Information and bookings (*030 332032*).
Spring Dance, until now held in both Utrecht and Rotterdam in late April-early May, is one of the oldest annual festivals for modern dance in Europe, dating from the end of the seventies. It attempts to give an overview of recent developments in modern

dance all over the world, including work from Dutch artists. The festival played a leading role in acquainting Dutch audiences with the many aspects of modern dance. From 1992, the festival will take place either in Utrecht or Rotterdam; no decision had been taken at time of writing.

Holland Festival
Bookings (from February) *Nationaal Reserverings Centrum, Postbus 404, 2260 AK Leidschendam (070 320 2500).* **Credit card bookings** *freephone 06 321 2101.*
Direct sales (from May) from AUB Uitburo and VVV tourist offices (*see above* **Subsidy Squabbles**) and individual theatres.
Premières by both large and small Dutch dance companies are held at this annual festival of performing arts (June). Major companies from abroad also appear. *See also p36* **Amsterdam by Season**.

Off Holland
For some years the Holland Festival has had its own fringe – Off Holland. Under this banner, a random gathering of small groups perform mostly dance and music routines in both Amsterdam and The Hague. *See also p126* **Theatre**. At the time of writing, the future of the festival is in doubt as one of the major sponsors has pulled out. However it is likely that the event will continue in one form or another.

Zomerfestijn
Tickets from first week in July *at the AUB Ticketshop and VVV tourist offices* (see above **Subsidy Squabbles**).
'Language no problem' is the motto of the Zomerfestijn. This mix of theatre, dance, music and multi-media performances takes place every summer (July) in unusual venues such as factories and boats. *See also p36* **Amsterdam by Season**.

Uitmarkt
Museumplein, OS. Tram 2, 3, 5, 12, 16.
Dance, music, theatre and cabaret are performed *al fresco* in the last weekend of August every year. *See also p36* **Amsterdam by Season**.

Holland Dance Festival
Information and bookings *AT&T Danstheater (070 360 9931).*
Every other September (1991, 1993), the Holland Dance Festival takes place in The Hague's Danstheater. Many of the world's larger companies are attracted to the event, and the Nederlands Dans Theater usually performs.

COURSES & WORKSHOPS

Artemis Kunstcentrum
Keizersgracht 676, IS (623 2655). Tram 4, 16, 24, 25. **Open** 10am-3.30pm Mon-Sat.
Classes 11am-12.30pm, 1-2.30pm, Mon-Fri; 11am-12.30pm Sat. **Cost** f10. **No credit cards.**
See **picture and caption**.
Coffee shop (open 10.30am-when they feel like closing).

Perron 2
Arie Biemondstraat 107, OW (612 4324).
Tram 1, 6, 7, 17. **Classes** 10.15am-noon Mon-Sat. **Cost** f12.50 per class; weekly workshops approx f350. **No credit cards.**
Perron 2 has daily classes in t'ai chi, yoga, improvisation and the Alexander technique. Modern dance classes are run for experienced dancers. Workshops are run during summer and at weekends. You can walk in for classes, but must book for workshops.

The **Artemis Kunstcentrum** (see under **Courses & Workshops**) *is a former church which has been turned into a handsome centre for the arts. Courses and workshops in both modern and classical dance are run, often by dancers from the Nationale Ballet or other modern dance companies. Because of this activity, Artemis is turning into a meeting place for those involved in dance. There are daily training possibilities and an international mix of students and teachers.*

Film

European premières; student screenings; art-house revivals; Amsterdam has it all – and most of it's in English. *Chris Fuller* puts you in the picture.

Amsterdam's internationalism is perfectly reflected by its cinema. There may not be as many screens as there are in London or Paris, but they offer as much variety as anywhere in Europe – in fact Amsterdam's multi-screens are often a step ahead of the rest of Europe with new, mainstream movies. Central Cannon complexes such as **City**, **Bellevue Cinerama** and especially the **Tuschinski** (*listed under* **First Run & Mainstream**) regularly offer European premières, sometimes a month ahead of London. And almost all films are shown in the original language with Dutch subtitles (the few that are dubbed into Dutch are indicated in the publicity with the words *Nederlands Gesproken* by the title).

Because of their international nature Amsterdam audiences are regarded as a good cinematic testing ground. *Batman*, for example, received some re-editing for the rest of the continent, based on the reaction it got here. The pick of the 30 or so commercial picture houses are either in or near the city centre and offer a wholly cosmopolitan mix of Hollywood blockbusters, European art movies, Third World documentaries, re-runs and retrospectives. Venues range from tiny canal house theatres such as **De Uitkijk** (*under* **Revival & Art Houses**) through the conventional multi-screen to the spectacularly grandiose **Tuschinski** (*under* **First Run & Mainstream**).

The wide variety of film available enables Amsterdam to retain its status as The Netherlands' film capital, despite competition in recent years from Rotterdam, where a growing world film festival runs in January, and Utrecht, where the 'Dutch Film Days' event takes place in September (*see below* **Film Festivals**). Amsterdam has no all-embracing film celebration of its own but throughout the year there are many mini-festivals, saluting particular directors, countries, genres, actors or actresses, at art houses (*filmhuizen*) such as **The Movies, Desmet, Rialto** and **Kriterion** (*under* **Revival & Art Houses**).

HOME-GROWN TALENT

It may seem ironic to visitors that, in view of Amsterdam's international embrace, Dutch movies generally get a low billing, with cinema owners blaming the public's lack of enthusiasm for the home-grown. This is particularly surprising since Amsterdammers are keen filmgoers. This negative attitude to Dutch films sadly extends abroad, with only one or two of the dozen-odd new Dutch productions each year making it onto the world circuit, and these confined to art houses. Such prejudice appears unfair, especially considering the international reputation for excellence of Dutch cameramen such as Robby Muller, who's the regular choice of German director Wim Wenders and the man responsible for the cinemascapes of *Paris, Texas*, and Jan de Bont (*The Jewel of the Nile, Ruthless People*); plus a small army of editors and technicians in regular demand in Hollywood.

As in the UK, in the Dutch film industry budgets are small, with a total annual government subsidy of around f13 million available through two funds, the Netherlands Film Fund (aimed more at documentaries and art house movies) and the Production Fund (for feature films). In recent years the most successful Dutch movies at home and abroad have been carefully paced, intelligent thrillers, usually heavy with eroticism and black humour. The best of these come from directors Dick Maas (*The Lift, Flodder, Amsterdamned*), Fons Rademaker (*The Assault*), George Sluizer (*The Vanishing*) and Paul Verhoeven (*Soldier of Orange, The Fourth Man, Robocop, Total Recall*). Verhoeven in particular is one of the Dutch industry's biggest and most charismatic talents, whose previous achievements include a 1973 Oscar nomination for *Turkish Delight* and the 1979 Golden Globe award for *Soldier of Orange*. His 1987 English-language *Robocop*, a foreign-backed, hi-tech romp featuring a metallic law enforcer, was a major US box-office hit. This was followed in 1990 by *Total Recall*, an even higher-tech

romp, complete with Arnold Schwarzenegger and a $65 million budget.

In front of the camera, Rutger Hauer (star of *Blade Runner, The Hitcher* and Guinness advertisements) is still the most visible Dutch actor worldwide, although Jeroen Krabbe (*The Living Daylights, Crossing Delancy, Melancholia*) and Derek de Lint (*The Unbearable Lightness of Being, Stealing Heaven*) are fast gaining ground. Actresses are less in demand, though Renee Soutendijk, a star in the Netherlands for *Het Meisje Met Het Rode Haar (The Girl With The Red Hair)* and Monique van de Ven (*Turkish Delight*) have successfully moved into American TV drama. For those actors who stay at home there is a living to be made in film combined with stage and TV work. But, as with anywhere else, there are many unemployed Dutch actors and actresses.

STUDENT WORK

Like Verhoeven and cameraman Jan de Bont, many Dutch film-makers begin their careers at the Nederlandse Film en Televisie Academie (*De Lairessestraat 142, telephone 673 8811*), a faculty of the city's school of arts, the Amsterdam Hogeschool Voor De Kunsten. Here around 250 students attend four-year courses in all aspects of feature film and documentary production. Most of the teaching is in Dutch and the Academie only admits a handful of foreign students each year. Those that are admitted have to be very determined and demonstrate a talent for film (videos, references, and so on). Knowledge of Dutch is essential. For those students who do get onto courses, future prospects are good since the Academie's high international reputation means that 75 per cent of graduates find work in the film industry. Unfortunately, the Academie does not run workshops for the public. If you want to get your hands on a steadicam the only chance would be at the film festivals (*see below* **Film Festivals**).

In the final year, students' films are given public showings at the school and occasionally on Dutch TV or in the city's art houses. One recent triumph was in 1990, when Academie student Mike van Diem won a student Oscar from the US Academy of Motion Picture Arts and Sciences for *Alaska*. The Academie is a member of the international CILECT body (Centre Internationale De Liaison Des Ecoles De Cinéma et Télévision), which operates as an information exchange on films and filming for its 36 member countries. It promotes international meetings and exchange screenings for students' work. Foreign students' films are generally shown at the Academie. On rare occasions **The Movies** or the **Kriterion** (*under* **Revival & Art Houses**) may be used.

THE CINEMAS

There's really no excuse for being ignorant of Amsterdam's film programme. In virtually every café, bar and cinema box office weekly listings of the main venues are prominently displayed. Other reliable sources include *Uitkrant's* 'Filamagenda' section and the Wednesday edition of *Het Parool*. The VVV tourist offices (*see page 3* **Essential Information**) stock the English-language *What's On In Amsterdam*. There is also an excellent monthly Dutch film mag, *De Filmkrant*, which has comprehensive information and is free. Although most of these listings are in Dutch they can be easily understood by the non-native.

Programmes change each Thursday. In the multi-screens prices range between fl1-fl2.50 (there are usually discounts for children), while in the Cannon theatres on Wednesdays most evening shows are reduced to f9. First shows are generally around 2pm, the evening programmes begin around 7pm and 9.30pm, with the film itself starting some 15 minutes later. Late shows are generally confined to Friday and Saturday nights and start about midnight. In the art houses (*filmhuizen*) times vary greatly and prices tend to be a little lower. At most venues a ticket can be reserved in advance for a nominal charge of 50c.

A few negative points. Be prepared for an obligatory 15-minute *pauze* (interval), slapped into every main picture of whatever length, and usually at a crucial moment. From fringe to mainstream, nearly all cinemas operate this dreaded *pauze*. Also (a common European problem) some of Amsterdam's out-of-centre multi-screens are hastily designed, have bad acoustics and, particularly for

non-smokers in the smaller screens, can prove uncomfortably airless. For those who enjoy the sight of smoke drifting through the projector's beam, smoking is allowed in the multi-screens; policy varies elsewhere.

FIRST RUN & MAINSTREAM

Alhambra
Weteringschans, IS (623 3192). Tram 6, 7, 10. **Open** *box office* 1-3pm, 6-10pm, Mon-Fri; 12.30-10pm Sat, Sun. **Tickets** f12.50, f12; Wed f9. **No credit cards.**
A small and rather drab Cannon house on a busy road, though its bold metallic exterior suggests more glorious days long past. The films are usually transfers from the City or Tuschinski *below* and tend to run and run until well and truly exhausted. Little wonder the staff look bored.
Wheelchair access with assistance to screen 2 downstairs.

Calypso/Bellevue Cinerama
Marnixstraat 400, IW (623 4876). Tram 7, 10. **Open** *box office* 1-11pm Mon-Fri; noon-

11pm Sat, Sun. **Tickets** f12.50, f12; Wed f9. **No credit cards.**
Two separate and glitzy cinema complexes, next to each other and sharing a common box office. The titles tend to lack the weight of those at the Tuschinski and City *below*, though the more highbrow Bellevue is always worth a visit. Also home to the occasional first-run or European première.
Wheelchair access to all screens with assistance.

City
Leidseplein, IS (623 4579). Tram 1, 2, 5, 6, 7, 10. **Open** *box office* 12.15-10pm daily. **Late** shows midnight Fri, Sat. **Tickets** f12.50, f10.75; Wed f9. **No credit cards.**
Where the Tuschinski *below* has charm, its Cannon cousin the City has hard sell. The large frontage and huge electronic advertisement hoarding dominate the Kleine Gartman Plantsoen, a small feed road to the Leidseplein, and a bank of TV sets in the foyer runs a constant diet of trailers. Much frequented by tourists, the City is Amsterdam's largest cinema with a total seven-screen audience capacity of some 2,094. The fare is family-oriented mainstream, and non-English-language are films pretty rare; trade is heavy all week, with long queues at weekends. There are occasional premières. For special screenings the City 1 and City 7 theatres are combined into

The **Tuschinski** *(see under* **First-Run & Mainstream**)*was built in 1922 by Polish tailor-turned-architect Aram Tuschinski, originally as a variety theatre for rich merchant families. The interior décor owes much to the tailor's eye for colour, material and design and has been well preserved, including a large, domed lobby, intricate wood carving on the staircases, richly patterned carpets, silk hangings and tapestries, stained glass and lamps. As well as the seven-screen programme, the building's stunning art deco design attracts many visitors, so much so that tours of the cinema are organized each July and August. Tours are at 10.30am and 11.45am on Mondays and Sundays; tickets (f5) are available from the box office.*

one enormous whole, and City 1 is also available for hire for conferences and parties. *Wheelchair access with assistance to screens 1-4.*

Tuschinski
Reguliersbreestraat 26, IS (626 2633). Tram 9, 14. **Open** *box office* 12.15-10pm daily. **Tickets** f12.50, f11; Wed f9; deluxe and selected balcony seats f15-f20; eight person box (with glass of champagne) f25. **No credit cards.**
One of Europe's most beautiful and unusual cinemas, the Tuschinski is Amsterdam's most prestigious cinema, which inevitably means long box office queues spilling out into the street at evenings and weekends. Blockbusters go straight to the magnificent Screen 1 and then switch from screen to screen, usually finishing their run at Screen 7, housed in a separate building called the Cineac, immediately opposite. The Tuschinski is Amsterdam's showcase cinema, home to regular premières and occasional Royal screenings, but, for a mainstream venue, the film choice is lively and occasionally inspired. *See also p123* **picture and caption.**
Wheelchair access with assistance to all screens apart from Screen 5.

REVIVAL & ART HOUSES

Alfa
Hirschgebouw, Leidseplein, IS (627 8806). Tram 1, 2, 5, 6, 7, 10. **Open** *box office* 1-3pm, 6-11pm, Mon-Thur; noon-midnight Fri-Sun. **Late shows** midnight Fri, Sat. **Tickets** f12.50, f11.50; Wed, matinées, f9. **No credit cards.**
A Cannon art house, no less, the Alfa is a former dance-hall whose entrance is tucked down a little sidestreet. The décor is austere but the film choice reliably intelligent, if a little too predominantly English-language. There are also kids' matinées most afternoons and a documentary festival each summer. Packed houses at the City (*see above* **First-Run & Mainstream**), which is just across the road, usually means the overspill will find its way here, so expect a crush at weekends.
Wheelchair access to all screens with assistance.

Cinecenter
Lijnbaansgracht 236, IS (623 6615). Tram 1, 2, 5, 6, 7, 10. **Open** *box office* 2.15-10.30pm daily. **Tickets** f12.75; Wed, matinées f9.75; no charge for ticket reservations. **No credit cards.**
The Cinecenter, on a Leidseplein sidestreet cluttered with Indian and Indonesian restaurants, requires some seeking out, but it's worth the effort. It's a novel and welcoming venue, with Commedia prints adorning the walls and stairways; the four screens each have their own name and décor – Coraline, Peppe Nappa, Pierrot and the tiny 52-seat Jean Vigo. The movie fare is around 60% French to 40% English-language, with Spanish and Russian screenings also common. A pleasant café adjoining the theatres sells toasties and apple pie.

Wheelchair access to all screens with assistance.

Desmet
Plantage Middenlaan 4A, IE (627 3434). Tram 7, 9, 14/Metro Waterlooplein. **Open** *box office* 6.30pm-½ hour before last film ends daily. **Late shows** 11pm daily. **Tickets** f10; reduced f8; ten-visit cards f70. **No credit cards.**
The art house answer to the Tuschinski (*see above* **First-Run & Mainstream**), the Desmet is far smaller but of similarly striking art deco design. Its ornate downstairs café area is usually adorned with an exhibition of paintings or photographs. The film choice is steadily imaginative and wholly international, with regular festivals and Dutch or even European premières common, and documentaries shown every Sunday at 2pm. The weekend gay screenings are well attended, while the lates are far more Hollywood than normal Desmet fare.
Wheelchair access with assistance by prior arrangement.

Kriterion
Roetersstraat 170, IE (623 1708). Tram 6, 7, 10/Metro Weesperplein. **Open** *box office* 1-10.30pm Mon-Thur, Sun; 1pm-midnight Fri, Sat. **Late shows** 12.15am Fri, Sat. **Tickets** f10. **No credit cards.**
An exuberant and slickly designed venue run entirely by volunteer students, with a broad film choice which includes children's matinées on Wednesday, Saturday and Sunday. Festivals are a speciality but the late-night screenings centre on cult American or erotic French movies. At time of writing the downstairs bar, lively in the evenings and at weekends, was due for a face-lift, and on completion will be open all day to non-filmgoers. Until September 1991 the upstairs theatre will feature the daily programme of the Nederlands Filmmuseum (*see below* **Film Museum**) while its Vondelpark premises undergoes renovation.
Wheelchair access to Screen 1.

The Movies
Haarlemmerdijk 161, IW (624 5790). Tram 3. **Open** *box office* 2pm-½ hour before last film ends Mon-Sat; noon-½ hour before last film ends Sun. **Late shows** midnight Sat, Sun. **Tickets** f12.50, f11; under-14s f7.75. **No credit cards.**
The most aesthetically pleasing of the city's art houses, The Movies dates from 1928, when it was a prominent feature of what was then a bustling main street. The Haarlemmerdijk may have faded because of tram rerouting after World War II, but the cinema, complete with a beautiful café, recaptures its former glory thanks to renovations which began in the early seventies. The small theatres have an intimacy which is enhanced by a busy collection of posters on the interior walls. The café, which is worth a visit regardless of the generally fine film programme, has been restored to its full thirties' charm. There's regular live jazz and folk music to while away the time before a late screening, plus a jukebox crammed with sixties' hits. The films themselves are international, from obscure to near-mainstream, but almost always feature something worthwhile. Children's films are shown at 2.30pm on Wednesday

Amsterdam's oldest cinema, 'he staunchly independent **De Uitkijk** *(see under* Revival & Art Houses*) dates from 1913 and is a charming, 158-seat converted canal house. Films that prove popular tend to stay put – Paul Bogart's* Torch Song Trilogy *appeared immovable for almost a year in 1989/90. In co-operation with the Nederlands Filmmuseum (see under* **Film Museum***) there are occasional afternoon screenings of historic and silent movies, sometimes with live piano accompaniment. The grand on the left was installed shortly after the cinema was built and, though long since unplayable, is too big to be removed. The owner's 'movies over ice-cream' policy means there are no refreshments, though we suspect lack of space may have something to do with this. Best of all, De Uitkijk refuses to use the dreaded* pauze.

and Saturday, and 12.30pm on Sunday.
Wheelchair access with assistance.

Rialto
*Ceintuurbaan 338, OS (662 3488). Tram 3,
12, 25.* Open *box office* 5.30-10pm daily.
Tickets f10; under-14s f6.50; members f7.50;
five-visit cards f37.50. Membership f20, f50.
No credit cards.
A stylish alternative cinema just a short journey from the centre of town. Recently
refurbished, and run mostly by volunteers,
it offers a mixed diet of new and old international flicks, children's matinées on
Wednesday and Sunday plus regular tributes to directors. In more playful vein, the
daily 'Six O'Clock Cinema' in Rialto 2 centres on cult science fiction movies while the
twice-weekly children's matinées (Wed, Sat)
often feature excellent little-seen animation
from around the world. The membership
packages entail ticket discounts and permanent seat reservations.
Wheelchair access to Rialto 2 downstairs.

De Uitkijk
*Prinsengracht 452, IS (623 7460). Tram 1,
2, 5.* Open *box office* ½ hour before film
starts. Tickets f12.50; no charge for ticket
reservations. No credit cards.
See p124 picture and caption.
Wheelchair access with assistance.

MULTI-MEDIA CENTRES

De Melkweg
*Lijnbaansgracht 234A, IW (624 1777).
Tram 3.* Open *box office* noon-1am daily.
Late shows 12.30am Fri, Sat. Tickets
f10.50. Membership f3.50 (included in
admission price). No credit cards.
Though better known as a rock venue and
theatre, De Melkweg runs a consistently
imaginative film programme in its cosy first-
floor cinema, running from mainstream
action/adventure through cult films to art
house movies. *See also p135* Music: Rock,
Folk & Jazz.

Soeterijn
*Linnaeusstraat 2, OE (568 8500). Tram 9,
10, 14.* Open *box office* 10am-4pm Mon-Fri;
10am-8pm Sat, Sun. Tickets f10. No credit
cards.
Situated right next to the Tropenmuseum
(*see p100* Museums), the Soeterijn stages
regular ethnic music, theatre and, occasionally, documentaries and feature films from
the developing countries. Film night is
Monday, with one show at 8.30pm. During
occasional festivals celebrating the Third
World, films are shown throughout the
week.

FILM MUSEUM

Nederlands Filmmuseum
*Vondelpark 3, OS (683 1646). Tram 1, 2, 3,
5, 6, 12.* Open *box office* 8.30am-¼ hour
before last film ends Mon-Fri; 1pm-¼ hour
before last film ends Sat; 11am-¼ hour
before last film ends Sun; *library* 10am-5pm
Tue-Fri. Tickets *cinema* f6-f8.50; ten-visit

The Nederlands Filmmuseum *(see under* Film Museum*) concentrates most of its energies on film programming, but also worth seeing is its
well-constructed exhibition on the development of European cinema, with video
displays, magic lanterns, 'What the butler saw' machines, cameras and projectors,
plus an original 1900 cinema box office. Because of renovation work, the main
museum building, though not the adjoining library, will be closed to the public for
one year from September 1990. The library (Vondelstraat 69-71) houses the
country's largest collection of film books and periodicals, but sadly, because of theft,
books can no longer be borrowed. The museum also holds an excellent 30,000-
plus hoard of posters and stills.*

cards f50; 25-visit cards f100; 60-visit cards
f200; *library and exhibition* f2.50; members,
students, elderly free. Membership f25-
f100. No credit cards.
Idyllically housed in the former nineteenth-
century tea-room in the Vondelpark, the
Government-subsidized Filmmuseum was
established in the forties and boasts a
strong three-films-a-day programme aimed
at pleasing all tastes. Most of the titles at
the 5pm screenings are drawn from the
museum's own 60,000-plus collection of
Dutch and European movies dating back a
century, while the later shows pursue a varied diet of themes, from Egyptian
documentaries to Ealing comedies. Silent
movies get live piano accompaniment. In
the ground-floor Café Vertigo there are
Sunday afternoon film seminars and discussions, of which about half are in
English, and in the summer occasional
screenings are held outdoors on the first-
floor terrace. Due to renovation, the main
building, including the film theatre, exhibition space and café, will be closed for a
year from September 1990, during which
time the film programme will continue at
the Kriterion cinema (*see above* Revival &
Art Houses). The adjoining Filmmuseum
library (*Vondelstraat 69-71*) will remain
open during renovations. *See also* picture
and caption.

FILM FESTIVALS

Dutch Film Days
*Festival office, Hoogt 4, 3512 GW, Utrecht
(030 322 684).* Open 10am-6pm Mon-Fri.

Tickets *pass for all films* f90; *pass for three
films* f21; *one film* f8.50. No credit cards.
An all-Dutch affair aimed at the Dutch public and film industry, running for a week in
the third week of September, and celebrating its tenth anniversary in 1991. The
festival features around 100 feature films in
a variety of venues, plus shorts and a selection of TV programmes. All new Dutch
productions are shown here, along with a
selection of students' efforts from the
Amsterdam Film Academie. As in
Rotterdam (*see below*), there are also lectures from guest speakers and workshops
on technique aimed at students. The festival presents its own awards to those films
judged the year's best.

Rotterdam Film Festival
Tickets f10 per film.
Now going for over 20 years, the
Rotterdam Film Festival is the biggest film
festival in The Netherlands and is international in scope, with around 70 films in its
main programme, and up to a hundred
others compiled in retrospectives. There's
also an accompanying series of lectures
and seminars by guest directors, actors,
producers and others involved in the
industry. Each afternoon there are workshops, aimed at film students, on film
technique. The festival is non-competitive
(no awards), with an accent on 'art'
movies. For information and exact dates –
end of January to the beginning of
February – contact any VVV office; *see p3*
Essential Information for Amsterdam
offices, or *p208* The Randstad for
Rotterdam's.

Theatre

For a country renowned for its sobriety, The Netherlands has a surprisingly rich theatrical tradition, with strong links to Britain, writes *Bert Verheij*.

Theatre in The Netherlands is characterized by its wide variety. Musicals, revues and cabaret are surprisingly popular in a country that has a reputation for sobriety.

The Dutch theatrical tradition dates back to medieval times. Seventeenth-century Dutch theatre companies used to perform all over Europe, as far afield as the Baltic. In the Golden Age, Dutch was the international language of trade. The Dutch playwrights of that period – Hooft, Bredero and Vondel – are still performed; traditionally, Vondel's *Gijsbrecht van Aemstel* (*Gijsbrecht of Amstel; see page 128* **picture and caption**) is staged nearly every year at the Stadsschouwburg (*see below* **Venues**) for a fortnight from 1 January.

'They don't think the profession of an actor the only trade a man ought to have, so they won't allow anybody to grow rich on a profession that so little conduces to the good of the commonwealth', wrote Joseph Addison after seeing a play in Amsterdam in 1703, performed by 'tradesmen that after their day's work is over earn about a guilder a night by personating kings and generals'. Throughout the eighteenth and nineteenth centuries, theatre was still by and for the people. It was not until the end of the nineteenth century that it became an élitist affair, something for those with an 'education' – actors and public alike. This attitude is still fairly entrenched.

FROM REVOLT TO RESPECTABILITY

In 1968 a group of young actors and drama students started the 'Tomato Action' by literally throwing tomatoes during performances by their older, established colleagues. At the time, theatre was controlled by a small, exclusive group of actors and directors. The aim of the tomato-throwing was to provoke discussion between those on the stage and those who wanted to be there, with a view to livening up the scene with new ideas and forms. The rebels were so successful that they now form the 'establishment' in the theatre world –

and ironically are now themselves discovering classic works and method acting. Consequently Dutch theatre is experiencing a lull; it is striking how few Dutch-language plays are staged and how little avant-garde work is going on. The most innovative fringe groups are Orkater and De Mexicaanse Hond (Mexican Dog); both are occasionally featured at the Nes theatres (*listed under* **Festivals & Events: International Theatre School Festival**). Otherwise the emphasis is on form at the expense of freshness; a pro-

duction may major on clever costumes and staging, but the impact is diffused because the acting is self-conscious, alienating the audience. However, there are signs that things are changing for the better; modified training methods are producing actors with a more natural technique.

There is no national theatre company; the best of the mainstream Dutch groups are Toneelgroep Amsterdam, resident at the Stadsschouwburg (*under* **Venues**), whose interpretations are solid if not inspiring; and Theater van het Oosten, Art & Pro, De Appel, Ro-Theater and Maatschappij Discordia, all based outside Amsterdam but frequent visitors to the Nes theatres.

CUT-BACKS AND MERGERS

The view of the present Dutch government is not so different from

The first **Stadsschouwburg** (see under **Venues**) *was built in 1638 on Keizersgracht; it was destroyed by fire in 1772 – to get more light on stage the number of candles used for illumination was doubled, resulting in the curtain catching fire. The second Schouwburg was built soon afterwards in the present location, Leidseplein, which in those days was on the outskirts of the city: the proper place for actors and other disreputable people. A replica of that building can be seen at the Nederlands Theater Museum (see under* **Museums**). *The present theatre was opened in 1894, after the second Schouwburg was also destroyed by fire. The beautiful and impressive baroque theatre was built in the traditional horseshoe shape and seats about 950. During the summer, backstage tours of the building are run, lasting – depending on the guide's enthusiasm – an hour or more. English is spoken. Tours start at noon (or by arrangement) every day and cost f5.*

that of the early eighteenth-century described by Addison. Dutch theatre only enjoyed the luxury of subsidies from the end of World War II, and in the mid-eighties the government started a programme of drastic cutbacks in arts support. Like some of the major orchestras (*see page 130* **Music: Classical & Opera**), several companies have been forced to merge, and a few have disappeared altogether. And, as so often happens in these situations, 'serious' theatre loses out to more popular forms of entertainment, such as cabaret and musicals, which can attract more sponsors and investors and bigger audiences.

Very few actors are able to make a decent living from the theatre alone. The absurdity of putting actors on welfare rather than supporting a theatre company is beyond the comprehension of the average person, but is probably quite logical to the average politician. The recent production of *Going to the Dogs* by Wim T Schippers, using only German shepherds, satirized the notion that actors are obsolete.

Based at **De Stalhouderij** (see under **Venues**), *American actor Joe Weston (above, with Mary Donovan) and friends are a safe bet for interesting and relatively high-standard performances of contemporary English-language plays. The success of these expatriates is an example of what can be achieved without subsidies through ingenuity and sheer hard work. Their diligence has finally been rewarded with some corporate sponsorship and a growing list of individual patrons. In addition, the company runs a workshop studio, where teachers from English-speaking countries and The Netherlands offer a broad variety of courses, ranging from scene study to technical movement. Workshops run from September to June and last for seven days or evenings.*

LOCATION THEATRE & FESTIVALS

Festivals and location theatre are the latest trends. During the summer festivals are held not only in Amsterdam (*see below* **Festivals & Events**), but also in most of the major cities in the Randstad. For those prepared to travel further out, try the Oerol Festival in June, on the northern island of Terschelling (*see page 213* **The Provinces: Friesland**). Location theatre is another new development: venues such as warehouses, factories, stables and fortresses form an integral part of the performance. One of the highlights of the Oerol Festival is a bicycle tour with theatrical interruptions, encouragement and rest-stops.

ENGLISH-LANGUAGE THEATRE

Because virtually everyone in Amsterdam speaks English there is a (potentially) large audience for English-language theatre in the capital. Some of the major English-language companies have disappeared over the last few years, unable to survive the subsidy cut-backs. The present Amsterdam-based companies are the Stalhouderij Theatre Company (*see below* **Venues:** De Stalhouderij) and Panache (*see below* **Venues: De Stadsschouwburg**). LEST (Leiden English Speaking Theatre) can be seen regularly at various venues in Amsterdam. Impresarios such as Ritsaert ten Kate, Jaap van Baasbank and Wim Visser are doing a great job getting top-quality productions from Britain (sometimes with backing from the British Council), the United States and South Africa. The roots of English-language theatre in The Netherlands go back as far as the Golden Age: *see page 129* **English-language Theatre**.

INFORMATION & BOOKINGS

Uitkrant is a monthly freesheet, published by the AUB Uitburo cultural office (*see page 3* **Essential Information**), with listings for almost every venue in Amsterdam. It's available in most theatres, bookshops and tourist information centres. For information (not reservations) on performances and concerts, phone *621 1211*, 10am to 6pm Monday to Saturday (English is usually spoken). The *Amsterdam Times* (free from most Amsterdam hotels) and *What's On In Amsterdam* (f2.50 from VVV tourist offices, *see page 3* **Essential Information**) give a run-through of selected events in English.

Tickets can be bought or reserved direct from theatre box offices, or from the Uitburo, from 10am to 6pm Monday to Saturday (till 9pm Thursday). There is a f2 booking charge. You can also book or purchase tickets from the VVV tourist offices, or through their telephone reservation service (*620 4111*); there is a f3 surcharge.

't Fijnhout Theater

Jacob van Lennepkade 334, OW (618 4768). Tram 3, 7, 12, 17. **Open** 9am-5pm Tue-Fri. **Tickets** f10; reductions for CJP card holders, over-65s. **Performances** 9pm Fri, Sat. **No credit cards.**
This small theatre, housed in a converted factory, puts on two English-language shows a week by various international companies.

Koninklijk Theater Carré

Amstel 115-125, OS (622 5225). Tram 6, 7, 10. **Open** *box office* 10am-7pm Mon-Sat; 1-7pm Sun. **Tickets** f25-f75; reductions for CJP card holders, over-65s. **Performance** 8.15pm. **Credit** DC.
This former circus is home for some of the best Dutch comedians and solo performers. This is one of the places where you may catch Jango Edwards, an Amsterdam-based

American whose shows are a wild mixture of stand-up comedy and rock 'n' roll, and not to be missed. Rudi van Dantzig's dance-music-theatre spectacle 'Live Life' was staged here to international acclaim. The Carré is the traditional venue for musicals in Amsterdam; recent productions include *Cats* and *Sweet Charity*, and in 1991 you can expect a Dutch staging of *Les Misérables*. Circus can still be seen here around Christmas. Other offerings include folk dance, cabaret and revues. A word of warning to those who don't like heights: the cheap seats are right up in the rafters. A backstage tour (3pm Wednesday and Saturday, Sept-June, f2.50) leads you through the stables and memories of the good old days – this is still the only theatre in Amsterdam that has ever hosted a true water ballet. *See also p118* **Dance.**

De Melkweg

Lijnbaansgracht 234A, IS (624 1777/624 8492). Tram 1, 2, 5, 7, 10. **Open** *box office* 10am-5pm Mon-Fri; 7.30pm-start of performance Wed-Fri; 4pm-start of performance Sat, Sun.* **Tickets** *theatre tickets* f10 plus membership.* **Membership** monthly f3.50; 3 months f5; yearly f15. **No credit cards.**

This multi-media centre behind the Stadsschouwburg (*see below*) opened its doors in 1970 in a former milk factory. The symbol of Amsterdam liberalism and tolerance in the seventies, the Melkweg has managed to survive its own legend and still has a worldwide reputation as a cultural meeting place. In 1983 it became a founding member of Transeuropehalles, an international network of multi-media cultural platforms. The theatre provides an important stage for new international groups and solo performers, and offers space to young directors and groups to develop new ideas. The Melkweg's director, Cornelius Schlösser, and theatre programmer Suzanne Dechert keep coming up with interesting and often refreshing new acts – ethnic, gay, lesbian, stand-up comedy, improvisation and gestural theatre, you name it. In some cases, the Melkweg has been a stepping-stone to stardom; Whoopi Goldberg, for example, performed here in 1982. *See also p122* **Film,** *p135* **Music: Rock, Folk & Jazz,** and *p141* **Night-clubs.**

Shaffy Theater

Felix Meritis Building, Keizersgracht 324, IW (bookings 623 1311/information 9am-5pm

Mon-Fri 620 0225). Tram 1, 2, 5. **Open** *box office* 3pm-start of performance Tue-Sat; *telephone bookings* 3-7.30pm daily. **Tickets** f10; reductions for CJP holders, over-65s. **Performances** 9pm. **No credit cards.**

The centre of fringe theatre in the early seventies, the Shaffy is struggling to survive after serious financial and subsidy problems. Occasionally you can catch the odd English-language theatre group in this beautiful, early nineteenth-century building. During July and August the Amsterdam Summer University (*see p196* **Students**) runs an extensive daytime programme of courses, workshops and seminars in the arts and sciences (all in English) to an international group of participants. In the evenings a multi-cultural programme covers theatrical performances, dance, music, video and seminars.

De Stadsschouwburg

Leidseplein 26, IS (624 2311). Tram 1, 2, 5, 6,7, 10. **Open** *box office* 10am-6pm Mon-Sat; 75 mins before performance. **Tickets** f15-f45; reductions for CJP card holders, over-65s. **Performances** 7.30pm, 8.15pm. **No credit cards.**

The present Stadsschouwburg (municipal theatre) is in fact the third building with this name: *see p126* **picture and caption.** Director Cox Habbema is responsible for a new policy which offers opportunities not only for traditional Dutch theatre, but also for a wide variety of national and international productions. The **Bovenzaal**, originally the prop room and situated right underneath the roof, is now a space for small-scale productions. One of the residents of the Bovenzaal is Panache, the theatre group that rose from the ashes of ESTA (English Speaking Theatre Amsterdam). It specializes in new plays, often featuring no more than two performers.

De Stalhouderij

1e Bloemdwarsstraat 4, IW (bookings noon-5pm Mon-Sat 626 2282). Tram 13, 14, 17. **Open** *box office* 8pm-start of performance; reserved tickets to be collected before 8.15pm. **Tickets** f15; CJP card holders, over-65s, students f12.50. **Performances** 8.30pm. **No credit cards.**

For a number of years this former stable (*stalhouderij* is Dutch for livery-stable) has been the home of the Stalhouderij Theatre Company, an international collective of artists (*see p127* **picture and caption**). It's the smallest theatre in Amsterdam – the size of an average living-room (40 seats) – and is unusually intimate. 'My kingdom for a horse!' will never be heard in these small quarters, but *Equus* could be staged with devastating effect. The friendly little bar upstairs is often manned by actors and actresses not involved in the current production. Booking in advance is imperative, as productions tend to be popular.
Wheelchair access with help.

Perhaps the best-known of the Dutch classics, **Gijsbrecht van Aemstel**, *written in 1638 by Joost van den Vondel, is performed every January at the Stadsschouwburg* (see under **Venues**). *The story is loosely based on history and the doings of Gijsbrecht van Aemstel, a feudal lord of Amsterdam, during the siege of Amsterdam in the fourteenth century. Enemy soldiers trick their way into the city and proceed to slash and burn their way to the centre of town. Lord Gijsbrecht tries to hold them off at the Dam, fails and flees to his castle across the Amstel. He plans to make a stand there, but the angel Raphael appears in a dream saying: "Go to Prussia and found a city and call it Holland and don't feel guilty because Amsterdam will prosper anyway." Being a good Christian, he does as he was told and splits. The play was written to celebrate both the opening of the first Stadsschouwburg and the prophesied Golden Age of Amsterdam* (see page 55 **The Golden Age**).

Holland Festival

Bookings (from February) *Nationaal Reserverings Centrum, Postbus 404, 2260 AK Leidschendam (070 320 2500).* **Tickets** f10-f100. **Credit card bookings** *freephone*

06 321 2101. **Direct sales** (from May) from AUB Uitburo and VVV tourist offices (*see above* **Information & Bookings**) and individual theatres.

Amsterdam's most prestigious entertainments festival takes place throughout June every year, and presents not only theatre, but also music and dance in the major venues. It will be interesting to see how the Festival will develop under its new director Jan van Vlijmen, who has a reputation for spectacle and extravagance – good for the Festival's publicity, but not so good for fiscal continuity. Advance programme information is available from Holland Festival, *Kleine Gartmanplantsoen 21, 1017 RP, Amsterdam (627 6566)*, open 9am-6pm Mon-Fri.

Off Holland Festival

The official 'fringe' of the Holland Festival *above*, and certainly no less interesting than the real thing: one-man shows, mime, music, dance and combinations by Dutch and international performers. The Off Holland schedule is available in the *Holland Festival Daily* (from participating theatres and the usual ticket outlets; *see p3* **Essential Information**). At time of writing, the future of the festival is in the balance, as one of the major sponsors has pulled out, but it will probably continue in one form or another.

International Theatre School Festival

Tickets *De Brakke Grond, Nes 45, C (day 626 6866/evening 624 0394). Tram 4, 9, 14, 16, 24, 25.* **Open** box office 10am-4pm Mon-Sat. Tickets f7.50. **No credit cards.**
An interesting festival of theatre school productions from all over the world takes place

throughout June at the so-called Nes theatres: De Brakke Grond (Nes 45), De Engelenbak (Nes 71) and Theatre Frascati (Nes 63). English-speaking touring groups make occasional visits here year-round.

Zomerfestijn (Summer Festival)

Tickets from first week in July at the AUB Ticketshop and VVV tourist offices (see above **Information & Bookings**).
This multi-media theatre arts festival (10 days in July) uses unusual and unique locations in Amsterdam. A shipyard, a grain-elevator and a freezer warehouse have in the past served as background for spectacular performances and visual 'happenings'. A chance to witness the splendour of location theatre and see sides of Amsterdam you would normally not encounter.

Uitmarkt

Museumplein, OS. Tram 2, 3, 5, 12, 16. **Dates** 23-25 Aug 1991.
This is a cultural market rather than a festival. In the last weekend of August every year, theatres, performing artists and companies preview and sell their programmes for the coming season. From Friday to Sunday Museumplein turns into a lively marketplace, with free music, dance, theatre and cabaret performances on several outdoor stages.

THEATRE MUSEUM

Nederlands Theater Museum

Herengracht 168-170, IW (623 5104). Tram

13, 14, 17. **Open** 11am-5pm Tue-Sun. **Admission** f2.50; CJP card holders, over-65s, students, under-14s f1.50. **No credit cards.**
The museum forms part of the Netherlands Theatre Institute, which also houses an excellent library and a theatre bookshop. The building itself is an example of seventeenth-century splendour, with beautifully decorated walls and ceilings (all in perfect symmetry). The collection includes a fine eighteenth-century miniature theatre, modelled after the second Stadsschouwburg (*see above* **Venues**), working rain, thunder and wind machines and several other old-fashioned stage machinery. In various, regularly-changing exhibitions you can admire a wonderful collection of costumes, masks, posters and anything relating to Dutch theatre. *See also p100* **Museums**.
Guided tours: f3.50; 1pm, 3pm, Wed; noon, 2pm, Sun.

BOOKSHOP

International Theatre & Film Books

Leidseplein 26 (in the Stadsschouwburg building, to the right of the main entrance), IS (622 6489). Tram 1, 2, 5, 6, 7, 10. **Open** 10am-6pm Mon-Fri; 10am-5pm Sat. **Credit** AmEx, MC.
This bookshop offers a wide variety of international magazines and books on the stage and screen. There are hard-to-find books on everything from history to theatre management, often in English, as well as texts of current productions.

ENGLISH-LANGUAGE THEATRE

English theatre companies visited The Netherlands as early as 1590, playing the theatres of The Hague, Leiden, Utrecht and Amsterdam, and – if they could get the permission of the city authorities – at fairs outside the towns. In the middle of the seventeenth century, Utrecht could even boast a resident company of 'comedians'. Their Dutch colleagues were thus familiar with the English repertoire, and this enabled them to write Dutch adaptations of works by Shakespeare, Kyd and Marlowe. Sometimes, with the Dutch playwrights stealing a little here and borrowing a little there, the original English material is difficult to spot. Other plays are clearly Dutch versions of popular English works: *The Taming of the Shrew, The Spanish Tragedy* and *Doctor Faustus* were reworked and staged in Amsterdam and elsewhere in Holland.

Seventeeth- and eighteenth-century Holland had a considerable

English-speaking community. Audiences would include English politicians and soldiers in The Hague, medical students in Leiden, merchants and bankers in Amsterdam and Scottish law students in Utrecht. There were plenty of theatre-loving tourists: Holland was the starting or finishing point for many a well-heeled young gentleman on his Grand Tour. There were English churches, English taverns and English booksellers in Amsterdam and The Hague. In 1710 one bookseller, Thomas Johnson, whose shop was right next to The Hague's theatre, started publishing a collection of English plays – 70 in all – which included works by Shakespeare, Dryden and Vanbrugh.

By the end of the eighteenth century, however, Holland had fallen under the spell of French language and culture. A contest in Paris even established that the best actress in the French Empire (which Holland

was a part of at that time) was Dutch. It was not until the end of the nineteenth century that there was a resurgence of interest in English plays. Works by Oscar Wilde and later Bernard Shaw were staged in Dutch translations. But it was quite a long time – the 1960s in fact – before English theatre companies were treading the boards again in The Netherlands. The occasional production by the Royal Shakespeare Company paved the way for other, less established groups. Amsterdam, a hotbed of creative activity, proved fertile ground for English-language theatre, both mainstream and fringe. It is not surprising that this resurgence coincided with a growing population of English and American expatriates. But the audience at English-language productions is still largely made up of natives, some of them seeing Shakespeare for the first time and finding out they can get the gist without recourse to subtitles.

Music: Classical & Opera

Government cuts, poor facilities, cautious managements – Amsterdam's classical performers have really had to face the music. But, writes flautist *Rose Anne Hamilton*, they've caught on to the new rhythm.

Until 1988, Amsterdam was not usually a touring stop for top-rank classical performers. The only exceptions were specialists in baroque, which is extremely popular in The Netherlands, and most of those were Dutch. It was a received wisdom in the concert management business that nobody would ever be prepared to fork out more than f50 for a ticket, and the resulting scene was unexciting, average in quality, and not very international. In fact provincialism had become deeply rooted in public and players alike.

Then in 1988 came Vladimir Horowitz and the subsequent renovation of the **Concertgebouw** (*listed under* **Venues**). The concert pianist easily sold out the hall at an unheard of f200 per seat. Encouraged by this success, the Concertgebouw arranged a series of benefit concerts by major international orchestras to help raise money to rebuild the foundations of the 100-year-old monument. Since then, Amsterdammers have discovered that there is a whole world of musicians out there – and managements are waking up to the smell of money in their own back yard.

CUTTING EDGE

The eighties was a very controversial decade for The Netherlands, as the government decided to no longer support the arts from cradle to grave. Many of the cuts were dramatic and ill-considered, and they have often encouraged provincial attitudes, enforced poor standards and wiped out entire sectors of the musical establishment. At the top, the number of major orchestras has been reduced from 13 to eight; at grass roots level, the organization that arranged about 80 per cent of concerts by young musicians in The Netherlands has been guillotined. On the other hand, there is suddenly a lot of room for the really enterprising artist to seek unusual venues and

business sponsorship, and experience the freedom (and often heartache) of the marketplace.

Competition is keener and the atmosphere has a liveliness in it that would have been unimaginable a few years ago. Amsterdam now enjoys something of the best of both worlds: enough international stars to spark a high level of interest and quality; and a stronger, tighter local scene that still has plenty of Dutch flavour and idiosyncrasy. It's the breath of fresh air that The Netherlands was gasping for, although it has been achieved at a terrible price in lost jobs and wrecked careers.

WHAT'S ON

To find out what's on where, get a copy of the free Dutch listings paper *Uitkrant*. For details of where to get both magazines *see page 145* **Media**. The VVV (*see page 3* **Essential Information**) can give details of forthcoming concerts. Small recitals are often advertized on lamp-post posters.

The best seats are booked up quickly, especially for opera. If you haven't booked, try and get to the theatre at least half an hour before the show starts to avoid long queues. Although ticket prices are still relatively low, you won't find any bargains: there are no cheap returns, stand-bys or unreserved standing tickets. The only discounts are for students, over-65s (and some venues only accept Dutch ID) and CJP card-holders (*see page 3* **Essential Information**). For ticket outlets *see page 3* **Essential Information: Tourist Information.**

VENUES

AGA Zaal and Wang Zaal

Damrak 213, 1012 ZH, C (627 0466). Tram 4, 9, 16, 24, 25. **Open** *box office mid Aug-June* 12.30-6pm Tue-Sat; 75 mins before performance for ticket sales and collection.

Tickets f12.50-f35; reductions for CJP card holders. **No credit cards.**
Nobody was ever very happy in the old stock exchange, whose tenants included various branches of the city government until the merging of the Amsterdam Philharmonic with the Netherlands Chamber Orchestra and Netherlands Opera Orchestra made a home for the new conglomerate an urgent matter. The new ensemble (the Netherlands Philharmonic) was offered the building, designed by the Amsterdam School architect Berlage, but not the money for the necessary alterations. Thus began one of the most innovative funding partnerships in the history of corporate arts sponsorship. The agreement finally arrived at was that the major sponsor of each hall or foyer (Wang Computers for the large hall, AGA Gas for the recital hall and Arke Travel for the foyer) would have its name used for a renewable 10-year period, in return for a grant. The necessary architectural changes were carried out sensitively (*see p132* **picture and caption**) and the overall result has been pleasing to all concerned, financially and artistically. The Wang Zaal is now the home of the Netherlands Philharmonic Orchestra; the Netherlands Chamber Orchestra rehearses and performs in the AGA Zaal (for both *see below* **Ensembles**). In addition, these two halls are busy filling the desperate need for more medium-size and small recital spaces in this concert-hall-poor city and play host to themed chamber music series. The box office has a recorded message giving programme and ticket details; an English translation follows the Dutch version. For details of tours of the building, *see p13* **Sightseeing: Tours**. *See also p61* **Between the Occupations.**
Wheelchair access and toilets for the disabled.

Concertgebouw

Concertgebouwplein 2-6, Van Baerlestraat, OS (ticket reservations 10am-5pm daily 671 8345/recorded information in Dutch 675 4411). Tram 3, 5, 12, 16. **Open** *box office* 10am-5pm Mon-Sat; 40 mins before performance for ticket sales and collection.
Tickets f25-f50; CJP card holders, students f15-f30. **Performances** 8.15pm. **Credit** AmEx, DC, MC.
Both the hall and its world-renowned orchestra (*see below* **Ensembles**) celebrated their hundredth birthdays in 1988 with films, concerts and a renovation of the building (*see p131* **picture and caption**). The controversy surrounding the aesthetics of the new glass wing has died down; as the coffee is hot and the views inside and out provide plenty of entertainment, there seems to be less criticism and more enjoyment of the 'improvements' (coffee in the interval is a sacred Dutch tradition, and it is a poor performance indeed that cannot provide it). The Grote Zaal (Large Hall) hosts orchestral performances and recitals by major artists who can generate the necessary ticket sales. The world-famous acoustics are among the planet's most divine for both players and listeners throughout the hall. The Kleine Zaal (Small Hall) is a home from home for dozens of recitalists and chamber ensembles throughout the season. Acoustically and visually it is a small replica of the Grote Zaal. Here is where young Dutch and visiting soloists make their débuts, and there are also a number of lunch-time and chamber music series.
Wheelchair access by arrangement.

Engelsekerk

Begijnhof 48, C (624 9665). Tram 1, 2, 4, 5, 9, 14, 16, 24, 25.
This lovely English Reformed Church (Presbyterian), nestled in the courtyard of the most beautiful 'hof' in Amsterdam (*see p13 Sightseeing*), schedules up to four concerts a week; monthly programmes are available from the church. The series of free lunch-time concerts in July and August (phone for details) generally feature young players and new ensembles. Evening concerts may include well-known Dutch musicians, visiting artists and groups, choirs and chamber music. The acoustics are very live, the audiences informal and tickets are generally quite reasonably priced.
Wheelchair access.

IJsbreker

Weesperzijde 23, C (668 1805/recorded information in Dutch 693 9093/fax 694 6607). Tram 3, 6, 7, 10/Metro Weesperplein. **Open** box office 9am-5.30pm Mon-Fri; *café* 10am-1am Mon-Thur, Sun; 10am-2am Fri, Sat. **Tickets** f15-f20; CJP card holders f12.50-f15. **Performances** 9pm. **No credit cards.**
This is the famous Dutch centre for contemporary music, run by director Jan Wolff (*see p133 picture and caption*). Because of his years of determined subsidy-hunting and publicity, the vast majority of the artists get paid for their performances – something of a record in the twentieth-century music business. Many of the concerts feature Dutch works and musicians. One of the most interesting features of the IJsbreker are the 'Weeks' dedicated to specific instruments or composers. The foundation also hosts weekly concerts broadcast live by the Concertzender cable radio station (*see p145 Media*). There is a pleasant café in the front of the building, open all day and after the concerts (*see p91 Cafés & Bars*).
Wheelchair access with assistance.

Muziektheater (Stopera)

Waterlooplein 22, C (625 5455). Tram 9, 14/Metro Waterlooplein. **Open** box office 10am-6pm Mon-Sat; noon-6pm Sun. **Tickets** *opera* f20-f80; *ballet* f20-f45; reductions for CJP card holders, over-65s. **Performances** *opera* 8pm; *ballet* 8.15pm. **No credit cards.**
The result of a building project that has provoked controversy for the best part of the twentieth century (*see p68 Post-war*), this is internationally known as the lemon to top (bottom?) them all. One of the architects defended it by claiming that there were so many zoning and building restrictions on the site that it couldn't have been designed a centimetre differently. Acousticians were called in from all over, at an ever-mounting cost, to come up with solutions. At last the top expert arrived. He opened the door, glanced around the theatre, shrugged his shoulders expressively, said mournfully, 'I'm sorry, it's hopeless,' and flew home with a suitable five-figure fee in hand. Every musician in Amsterdam could have offered the same advice for nothing, and did. Acoustics are not the only problem. The ballet rehearsal rooms have low ceilings, making it impossible to practise lifts. Although the orchestra was provided with a spacious pit and sumptuous dressing rooms, there is no purpose-built rehearsal room. Now they have a heated basement storage area. The ground and stage level loading entrances are at opposite ends of the building from the scenery lifts,

The **Concertgebouw** *(see under* **Venues***) has recently undergone extensive renovations. In the early eighties it was discovered that the wooden piles supporting it were disintegrating because of dry rot, causing shifts and cracks in the walls and threatening the structure with eventual collapse. A monumental project was undertaken to replace the old piles with new concrete supports, installed with sophisticated hydraulic engineering, while a full concert and rehearsal schedule proceeded unabated in the halls above. The resulting new basement area has been made into a long-desired dressing and extra rehearsal space, and a new entrance, box office and café area has been added on to the east side of the building.*

which are too small to accommodate harps in cases or tall props. The list goes on. In fact the only success of the structure is the public area, which is strongly reminiscent of New York's Lincoln Center and commands a breathtaking view of the Amstel River. This is the only venue in Amsterdam where you can see grand opera performed, and if you can get a seat in the centre of the first row of the first balcony it may be possible to hear the orchestra and singers in reasonable balance. Otherwise, you may be disappointed. Several conductors and visiting companies have taken to using microphones and the management is also experimenting with 'over-titling' – translations of the libretti projected on a screen above the stage (in Dutch, of course). The Muziektheater is home to the National Ballet and the Netherlands Ballet Orchestra (*see p118 Dance*) as well as the Netherlands Opera Foundation and Opera Orchestra (which draws its members from the Netherlands Philharmonic Orchestra conglomerate). Musicians from the Opera and Ballet Orchestras give free lunch-time concerts in the Boekman Zaal (Sept-June). Tours of the building are given on Wednesdays and Saturdays at 4pm, costing f8.50. If you book in advance, the guide will be prepared with English translations.
Wheelchair access and toilets for the disabled.

Nieuwekerk

Dam, C (Nieuwekerk foundation 626 8168). Tram 1, 2, 4, 5, 9, 13, 14, 16, 17, 24, 25. **Open** 11am-5pm daily. **Tickets** f7.50; CJP card holders, students f5. **Performances** 8pm Thur, Sun. **No credit cards.**
Hosts primarily organ concerts of the top Dutch and visiting international players. Gustav Leonhardt (*see below* **Ensembles**) is the resident organist, and frequently plays on the magnificent sixteenth-century organ. There's no regular programme, but it's a popular venue for organ series. *See also p13 Sightseeing.*
Wheelchair access with assistance.

Oudekerk

Oudekerksplein 23, C (625 8284). Tram 4, 9, 16, 24, 25. **Open** 15 Apr-15 Sept 11am-5pm Mon-Sat; 16 Sept-14 Apr 1-5pm Mon-Sat. **Tickets** f6.50-f15; CJP card holders, over-65s f5-f12.50. **Performances** *July, Aug* 8.15pm Wed, Sat. **No credit cards.**
Jan Sweelinck, The Netherlands' most famous seventeenth-century composer, was organist here, and a host of other important musicians have been associated with the Oudekerk over the centuries. Concerts include organ and carillon recitals (*see p134 Carillons*) and chamber music concerts. *See also p13 Sightseeing.*
Wheelchair access with assistance.

Sweelinck Conservatorium

Van Baerlestraat 27, OS (664 7641). Tram 2, 3, 5, 12. **Performances** *Oct-June* 12.30pm Thur.
Students at this conservatory give free lunch-time recitals.

Waalsekerk

Oudezijds Achterburgwal 157 (623 2074). C, Tram 4, 9, 16, 24, 25.
Small, elegant, and intimate, the Waalse church was the French Huguenot church for Amsterdam. It is now a very popular location for chamber music, early music and choral concerts. Musica Antiqua Köln from Germany, The Netherlands Chamber Choir and Gustav Leonhardt are frequent performers here. The church is scheduled to reopen in spring 1991 after restoration work.

The redecoration of the **AGA** *and* **Wang** *concert halls (see under* Venues) *has been a fascinating story. Apart from two fire doors, no damage has been done to the existing structures – everything is 'added on'. Amsterdam School architect Berlage's intention when designing his stock exchange was to preserve the old building crafts in the fabric of the edifice itself. Wrought iron girders, colourful tilework, intricate patterns of bricks; none of these lovely details have been destroyed or hidden. In the case of the AGA Zaal, above, the solution to the street noise coming through the glass roof was to build a glass recital hall within the larger room. An acoustical nightmare to design, it was a year late in opening, but the results have silenced the doubters.*

OUT OF TOWN

Anton Philipszaal
Houtmarkt 17, 2511 DM, Den Haag (box office 070 360 9810/information 070 360 7927). **Open** *box office* 10am-3pm; 75 mins before performance. **Tickets** f20-f80; reductions for CJP card holders; over-65s. **Performances** usually 8.15pm. **No credit cards.**
The home of The Hague's Residentie Orchestra since 1987. The old concert hall burned down in 1964 and the Orchestra was buried in a conference hall at the great Congressgebouw (congress building) for over two decades. The horrendous non-acoustics nearly destroyed morale and did nothing for the sound either. You couldn't find a happier bunch now as the Orchestra grows into its new quarters. It's an odd-looking structure from the outside, resembling a crashed UFO, but inside it's a soundly designed rectangular hall with excellent acoustics.
Wheelchair access and toilets for the disabled.

Doelen
Schouwburgplein 50, 3012 CL, Rotterdam (010 413 2490). **Open** *box office* 10am-6pm Mon-Thur, Sat, Sun; 10am-9pm Fri. **Tickets** f16-f150; reductions for CJP card holders,

students. **Performances** 8.15pm. **No credit cards.**
The Doelen is a large, modern, black edifice housing large and small concert halls and the Rotterdam Philharmonic Orchestra. The sound in the large hall is one of the reasons why the Rotterdam Phil sounds so wonderful on tour: it has to really work for a warm, expressive sound at home. The Doelen hosts about two dozen series a year, ranging from orchestral contemporary to jazz and just about everything in between, in addition to the RPO's schedule, which runs from September to June. The ticket office is one of the most efficient in the country and the audience is chic. Standing ovations are the rule at every concert regardless of quality, but if the audience really likes it, there will be plenty of stamping, cheering and vocal appreciation as well. Another eccentricity: the management lengthened the interval rather than making the coffee service more efficient.
Wheelchair access and toilets for the disabled.

ENSEMBLES

Academy of the Begijnhof
Named for its original rehearsal and performance space in the Begijnhof, this chamber

orchestra now gives concerts throughout The Netherlands. It offers interesting programmes, often with choral ensemble, and is one of the few groups not either on holiday or doing the *Messiah* at Christmas-time. Repertoire from the fourteenth to the nineteenth centuries; performances of a reasonable standard.

Concertgebouworkest
Postal and telephone enquiries to Jacob Obrechtstraat 51, 1071 KY (679 2211).
The one and only, resident in the Concertgebouw (*see above* **Venues**), and just turned 100 in 1988. Newly appointed conductor Riccardo Chailly is changing a lot of things – including getting the players to look up from the music now and again. It's not every conductor's favourite orchestra; it became rather sluggish and set in its ways under Bernard Haitink's somewhat lopsided programming: Brahms, Mahler, Brückner, and some more of the same. They've still got that lush sound, particularly in the Concertgebouw, but the relatively average quality of individual players (notably in the brass section) does show, and often appallingly. A sacred cow, harder to renovate than the building, the Concertgebouw is definitely a prima donna among orchestras and suffers from many of the faults and perfections of an arrogant old eccentric, though recent concerts have shown signs of greater flexibility. If Chailly can replace retiring members with top-ranking players he might have himself a truly great orchestra.

Gustav Leonhardt
The grandfather of modern baroque keyboard practice still gives plenty of concerts in Amsterdam. He is the resident organist at Nieuwekerk (*see above* **Venues**), and also gives harpsichord recitals and continuo contributions in other venues.

Nederlands Kamerkoor (Chamber Choir)
Postal and telephone enquiries to Paulus Potterstraat 16, 1071 CZ (662 5199).
World-renowned and for good reason. That this group manages to stay in voice with such an exhausting schedule is a miracle in itself. Its concerts are varied and highly polished. This is without doubt one of the world's finest vocal ensembles. It has no base of its own: catch it at venues across the city.

Nederlands Kamerorkest (Chamber Orchestra)
Postal and telephone enquiries to Beurs van Berlage, Damrak 213 , 1012 ZH (627 1161).
Now under the wing of the Netherlands Philharmonic (*below*), the Kamerorkest draws its players from the larger orchestra, and is struggling to maintain its identity and quality. In spite of the complaints, it remains one of the world's finest chamber orchestras, and gets top-rate soloists and conductors reasonably often as well. Based at the AGA Zaal (*see above* **Venues**).

Nederlandse Opera
Postal and telephone enquiries to Waterlooplein 22 , 1011 NV (551 8922).
Since this Muziektheater-based company (*see above* **Venues**) began co-productions with the English National Opera, standards

have risen in both staging and singing. It's still nothing like the major international opera companies, but at least the performances are now adequate, and sometimes quite good in the case of new works.

Nederlands Philharmonisch Orkest

Postal and telephone enquiries to Beurs van Berlage, Damrak 213, 1012 ZH (627 1161).
Still suffering from all the upheavals caused by the cutbacks and mergers, this orchestra used to be three different ensembles, and must still form and reform constantly to meet the schedules of a chamber orchestra, symphony orchestra and opera orchestra. The quality of all three have definitely suffered, and difficulties with conductors don't improve matters. They are now resident in the Beurs van Berlage (Wang and AGA halls, *see above* **Venues**) which has helped improve morale – the old Amsterdam Philharmonic used to rehearse in an old skating rink. A good bet if you're interested in the up-and-coming young soloists from The Netherlands and the rest of Europe.

Orchestra of the 18th Century

Postal and telephone enquiries to Oudezijds Voorburgwal 225-227, 1012 EX (626 8236).
Flautist and recorder player Frans Brüggen wanted an orchestra, and what Frans wants he gets. You could do a lot worse than a band made up of the *crème de la crème* of baroque and classical players from around the globe. They play in Amsterdam on their thrice-yearly whirlwind tours. Daring tempos, brilliant string passages, and wild exploits from natural horns (with no valves) make for some of the most exciting performances available anywhere. Not for the faint of heart or the closed of mind.

Residentie Orchestra

Postal enquiries to Stichting het Residentie Orkest, PO Box 11543, 2502 AM, Den Haag.
The Hague's resident orchestra suffered for years in a wretched hall, which was finally replaced with palatial new quarters in 1989 (*see above* **Venues: Out of Town**). Conductor Hans Vonk is not noted for charisma or daring interpretations, and this very good band frequently gives better results under guest batons. The company does more contemporary work than many orchestras, but its Dvorak tells its story best. The Residentie plays occasionally in Amsterdam – most often as an opera orchestra.

Rotterdam Philharmonic Orchestra

Postal and telephone enquiries to De Doelen, Kruisstraat 2, 3012 CT, Rotterdam (010 414 2911).
The Netherlands' best-kept orchestral secret. Youthful, energetic, and full of the cream of Dutch players, the ensemble is also very liberally salted with top-quality foreigners. This organization has vigorously bucked the political system at every possible turn in order to get the best players available, and the results have been well worth the trouble. Under James Conlon, Rotterdam developed into the kind of orchestra that young conductors like to challenge and old conductors like to make music with. They work hard to sound good in the Doelen (*see above* **Venues: Out of Town**), and given a kinder hall sound full

and lush. Unfortunately they rank third behind Concertgebouw and Residentie for funding and don't often get the first-rank conductors they deserve.

Schoenberg Ensemble

Postal and telephone enquiries to Weesperzijde 24, 1091 EC (663 1415/fax 668 4935).
Reinbert de Leeuw's band of intrepid performers of contemporary chamber music is often on tour so it's hard to catch in Amsterdam. Well-presented programmes, although sometimes on the conservative side, have a depth and subtlety that can be missing from American and British performances. De Leeuw's tempos, gruellingly slow at times, may not be to your taste but the standard is high. The Ensemble plays all over town, most frequently at the Concertgebouw and the IJsbreker.

EVENTS

As well as the annual events listed below, look out for the occasional 'Grand Piano Festival', a series of grand piano recitals sponsored by piano shop Cristofori, which also arranges the Prinsengracht classical concert (*see page 36* **Amsterdam by**

Season). The heats of the Gaudeamus Concours, an international competition for contemporary music held every spring in Rotterdam, are not open to the public, but for details of tickets for the final, contact the venue, the Doelen (*listed under* **Venues: Out of Town**). The Vredenburg Music Centre in Utrecht (*see page 208* **The Randstad**) is the venue for 1992's Liszt Piano Competition (9-23 May), an international event growing in importance. Free Sunday lunch-time concerts are held at the Nieuwe Lutheran Church (*see page 13* **Sightseeing**). The AUB Uitburo and the VVV (*see page 3* **Essential Information**) can give further details on all the events listed below.

Holland Festival

Dates 1-30 June 1991. **Admission** fl0-fl00.
Highlights of this internationally famous annual festival are plenty of Dutch contemporary music, performances by the best of Dutch theatre, musical and dance ensembles, and reasonable ticket prices. *See also p36* **Amsterdam by Season.**

The **IJsbreker** (see under **Venues**) *is the famous Dutch foundation for contemporary music, where about half of the new music going on in The Netherlands can be heard. The other half doesn't get along with director Jan Wolff (above), a man of enormous energy and talent – and the self-will necessary to found, develop and run such an enterprise. Wolff is the absolute dictator of everything that goes on within the walls of the IJsbreker, and many an innocent has run afoul of the unwritten law: Thou shalt clear every idea with Jan first, middle, and last. Plenty of good music stays on his benevolent side, however, and Wolff produces varied and stimulating programmes, series, and master classes (open to public view) nearly every night of the week.*

Uitmarkt

Dates 23-25 Aug 1991. **Admission** free. Held in August on and around Museumplein, this annual event is a hugely popular open-air 'music-market'. Musicians and ensembles play on temporary stages, previewing concerts scheduled for the coming season. The public can buy series tickets and other music-related bargains. See also *p36* Amsterdam by Season.

Utrecht Festival for Early Music

Dates 30 Aug-8 Sept 1991. **Admission** f10-f40. Held in Utrecht (see *p208* **The Randstad**) late in the summer. All your favourite baroque and classical artists and ensembles from around the world. There are also a book, recordings and sheet music market, midnight concerts and very nicely priced tickets. Visiting musicians can go to classes and join in workshops.

Vokalise

Between October and May, Dutch Radio (Hilversum 4) sponsors a Sunday morning programme broadcast live from the Grote Zaal at the Concertgebouw (see *above* **Venues**). The public can attend; all tickets are f6 and must be bought in advance. The show starts at 11am and previews musical events scheduled in and around Amsterdam for the next week or two with mini-recitals and short interviews with both famous and unknown musicians. It's

pretty lively in the hall as everybody brings the kids.

MUSICAL ASIDES

There's a lot more to music than just concerts. Here is a selection of shops and cafés which have a strong connection with the world of music.

SHOPS

Donemus

Paulus Potterstraat 14, OS (676 4436). *Tram 2, 3, 5, 12.* Open 9am-5pm Mon-Fri. No credit cards.
The Dutch contemporary music publisher. This office is here to promote contemporary Dutch music and is not a shop as such, but the friendly staff will bring out reasonably priced music by Dutch and Netherlands-resident composers. There's also a large library of compositions from decades back.

G N Landré b.v. Muziekantiquariaat

1e Anjeliersdwarsstraat 36, IW (624 7056). *Tram 3.* Open 11am-5pm Wed-Sat. No credit cards.
Georges Landré comes from a long line of musical families who have had their fingers in every sort of melodious pie, from composing to criticizing. His musicological and

performing background and his wife Angela's energy and organizing ability come together in a collection of about 20,000 books and pieces of sheet music, plus musical postcards, fine music boxes, posters, etchings and book plates.

Muziekmagazijn Opus 391

Rustenburgerstraat 391, OS (676 6415). *Tram 12, 25.* Open 10am-6pm Tue-Sat. No credit cards.
If it was popular in the sidewalk cafés of Europe in the twenties and thirties, then here's your shop: sheet music for tea dance, early jazz and salon ensembles; there's even a service to locate a fox-trot trio for parties. Owner Anke Kuiper is herself a member of the Max Tak Film Orchestra, and really knows her stuff.

CAFE

Lindsay's Tea Shop

Basement of the American Discount Book Center, Kalverstraat 185, C (625 9441). *Tram 4, 9, 16, 24, 25.* Open 11am-6pm Tue-Sat; noon-6pm Sun. No credit cards.
Lindsay Shackleton serves cream teas that have sustained many a musician between rehearsals (the café is close to both the Muziektheater and the Begijnhof). Her friendly chat and informal networking keep the atmosphere lively and personal. If you arrive on a holiday – such as St Andrew's Day – you might find the staff in fancy dress, and there will be traditional cakes to celebrate.

CARILLONS

To British ears accustomed to an altogether more majestic clang, Amsterdam's seemingly perpetual jingle of pint-sized bells clattering out intricate tunes can be irritating: why don't they just get on with it and tell the time? This, of course, is what the carillons (in Dutch, *beiaard*) are doing – and have been, on the quarter-hour, for about four centuries. Amsterdam has five regular carillons: **Oudekerk** (see *under* **Venues**), **Zuiderkerk** (see *page 53* **War & Reformation**), **Westerkerk**, **Koninklijk Paleis** (Royal Palace) and **Munttoren** (for all three see *page 13* **Sightseeing**) all have carillons which chime every 15 minutes. And from time to time the **Rijksmuseum** (see *page 100* **Museums**) spills forth a few notes. If you're a light sleeper it is worth avoiding accommodation that may prove too close for comfort (and insomniacs should bear in mind that Dutch clocks strike half-to rather than half-past the hour – 5.30am is signalled by the chime plus six 'bongs' – so it seems later than it is). The time-telling chimes are pre-

programmed along music box lines, but the carillon is also a musical instrument which can be played by a *carillonneur*. It has a keyboard of large wooden keys (one for each bell) and a pedal board like an organ's. Unlike an organ, however, they are not usually on public view. The *carillonneur* thumps the keys with the fist, rather than fingering them gently; they are connected via a complicated system of rods and wires to the bells in the tower. Like pianists, *carillonneurs* can vary the volume depending on how hard they hit the keys. Played as an instrument since 1510, the carillon can (and does) render anything from Bach to the Beatles. Carillon concerts are a feature of many churches' calendars: in Amsterdam these are held at the Westerkerk most Wednesdays at noon, and at the Oudekerk most Saturdays at 4pm. You'll hear them best from the street.

For enthusiasts, the **Carillon School** in Amersfoort, 40 kilometres (25 miles) east of Amsterdam, has a splendid specimen in the civic tower. This is played at 10am on Fridays

and 10am, noon and 5pm on Saturdays. The School has a small collection of campanological exhibits, including a model chiming cylinder and a model keyboard. It has no formal opening hours; phone in advance or try ringing the doorbell. The **National Beiaardmuseum** in Asten in the south of The Netherlands has a collection of clocks and bells from around the world, including a carillon that chimes every half-hour. Museum guides will play a tune on the one-octave keyboard if you ask nicely.

The Carillon School

Grote Spui 11, Amersfoort (033 752638). **Admission** free. *Wheelchair access.*

National Beiaardmuseum (Bell Museum)

Ostaderstraat 23, Asten (04936 1865). Open 10am-5pm Tue-Fri; 1-5pm Sat, Sun. **Admission** f4.50; f2.50 under-15s; group rates. No credit cards. *Wheelchair access and toilets for the disabled. Coffee bar.*

Robert Perry

Music: Rock, Folk & Jazz

Got the blues? *Maz Weston* **takes you from Edenhal to Paradiso via the Milky Way.**

The Dutch love anything that 'rocks', especially if it's done live. They thrive on it. Any excuse – a festival, birthday or wedding, you name it – and a band is sure to be playing. The magic word 'band' can open doors that otherwise would remain firmly closed: the authorities permit live performances to take place almost any time, any place, anywhere. Unlike the house and dance-music scene, with live music there is no interference from the police and no complaints from neighbours.

The Amsterdam scene reflects the multi-cultural, multi-racial nature of the city in the wide range of musical styles on offer. On any night of the week, you can travel the world, musically speaking, from South America to Africa, Eastern Europe to the States. This is partly due to a unique management system that has its roots in the radical movements of the sixties and seventies: many of the larger venues were forced to become legal as *stichtings*: non-profit-making foundations. The result is that one busy night can support a whole month of experimental and minority-appeal music. This allows a venue to programme chart toppers, a reggae legend, a Brazilian combo or an unknown local band all in the same week.

There are very few internationally famous Dutch artists, although those who have made it to the top, however briefly, are never forgotten by their fans. Ancient one-hit-wonders Golden Earring still sell out concerts wherever they play. But the new generation of bands, such as Fatal Flowers, Urban Dance Squad and Claw Boys Claw are beginning to receive the international recognition that Dutch rock has long been denied. You don't always have to pay to see well-known artists perform – it's often possible to catch guitar hero Jan Akkerman or saxophonist Candy Dulfer playing for free in Vondelpark.

International superstars such as Prince and Madonna usually skip Amsterdam on their European tours, as there are no venues big enough to accommodate them. Instead they play at the Feyenoord football stadium in Rotterdam, or the Vredenburg in Utrecht; both are easily accessible by train from Amsterdam.

To find out what's going on, look out for posters and leaflets in bars and record shops or pick up a free copy of *Luna*, which lists most of the live events in Amsterdam. For a wider view, *Oor* magazine (the Dutch equivalent to *NME*) covers events throughout The Netherlands and gives information (in Dutch) on local talent and visiting international names.

VENUES

The venues listed below range from large multi-media centres such as Melkweg to small squat venues and back-street bars where you can hear live music every night of the week.

Akhnaton
Nieuwezijds Kolk 25, C (624 3396). Tram 1, 2, 5, 13, 17.
The policy of this venue is to provide a forum for the city's ethnic bands to meet and perform. At time of writing it was being refurbished and was temporarily closed (phone for details of opening times), but in the past Akhnaton was renowned for its non-profit-making hip hop and rap nights, and these look set to continue into the nineties with the new building, partly funded by the city council, also providing recording studios and rehearsal facilities.

Cruise Inn
Zeeburgerdijk 272, OE (692 7188). Tram 6, 10. Open 8pm-2am Fri, Sat. **Admission** usually free. **No credit cards.**
See p137 picture and caption.

Jaap Edenhal
Radioweg 64, OE (694 9894). Tram 9. Open *for information* 9am-5pm Mon-Fri; *music* about 8pm various nights. **Tickets** f25-f35. **No credit cards.**
This large sports hall is not regularly used as a venue, but occasionally plays host to international performers, most recently Bunny Wailer and the Cramps. It seats 3,000 and an event needs to be well attended for any atmosphere to survive the coldness of the steel and concrete. It's easily reached by tram, even though it is situated on the edge of town near the Ajax football stadium. Events are always well-publicized by fly-posting in the city centre and listings in various papers.

Korsakoff
Lijnbaansgracht 161 (625 7854). Open 11pm-1am Mon-Thur, Sun; 11pm-2am Fri, Sat. **Admission** usually free. **No credit cards.**
A hang-out for a very young post-punk and goth crowd. Plenty of local bands of varying quality play here and usually go down well with the home supporters. It's especially busy after a big name has played in town. The admission fee is either very low or non-existent.

Maloe Melo
Lijnbaansgracht 160, IW (625 3300). Tram 10, 13, 14, 17. Open 10pm-3am Mon-Fri. **Admission** free. **No credit cards.**
They like to call this place 'The Home of the Blues' although it's unclear how long the venue has actually been in operation – some of the acts that appear here have certainly been around a very long time. It's a dark, smoky bar with a small stage area, and is always very cramped. Having said that, there's an earthy and friendly atmosphere. Cheap drinks and free admission make this worth investigating.

Mazzo
Rozengracht 114, IW (626 7500). Tram 13, 14, 17. Open *Sept-June* 11pm-5am Tue-Sun; *July, Aug* 11pm-5am daily. **Admission** f7.50 Mon-Thur, Sun; f10 Fri, Sat. **No credit cards.**
This club puts on a wide range of music throughout the week, from live house and PAs at weekends to a regular live band night on Tuesdays. Most performers featured are new or well-established local bands. Many international acts hold after-gig parties here, which are open to the public although they get very crowded so admission can be restricted. It's a small, compact place to see a live performance – most notable in recent years was a surprise appearance by Public Enemy who played to a packed house of only 400 people. Great atmosphere. *See also* p141 **Night-clubs**.

Melkweg (Milky Way)
Lijnbaansgracht 234, IW (624 1777). Tram 1, 2, 5, 6, 7, 10. Open 7.30pm-late Tue-Sun; *disco* 1am-4 or 5am Fri, Sat. **Admission** f10-f20; includes admission to disco, theatre and cinema. **Membership** f3.50 per month. **No credit cards.**
See p139 picture and caption.
See also p122 **Film** and p141 **Night-clubs**.

Paradiso
Weteringschans 6-8, IS (626 4521). Tram 6, 7, 10. Open 8pm-1am (approx) various days, phone for details. **Admission** f7.50-f17.50. **Membership** f3 per month. **No credit cards.**
From the outside, the Paradiso is dark and foreboding – it's a blackened old church that looks like a goth's paradise. But the interior is light and airy and this is an excellent place to see bands. The weekly programme caters for a wide range of musical tastes, from local band nights to bigger names on tour. There's also a strong emphasis on reggae, African and Latin music. It's a great place to

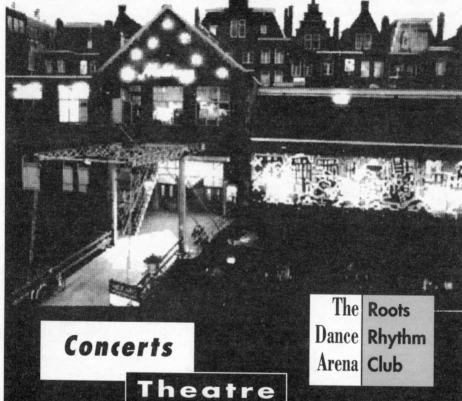

multi media

Melkweg

Concerts

Theatre

The Dance Arena | Roots Rhythm Club

Expositions

Video

CINEMA

Café-Restaurant

Anti-apartheids bookshop

Workshops

Open from 7.30 pm until 1 am on weekdays
and 3 am on Fridays and Saturdays
Lijnbaansgracht 234a,
telefoon 241 777; fax 201 209

see someone who would usually fill several nights at Wembley Arena; some acts take a while to catch on in The Netherlands and can be surprisingly badly attended, as were De La Soul and Happy Mondays when they appeared. Tickets can be bought at the door, but are also available from the AUB ticket office, VVV tourist offices (for both *see p3* **Essential Information**) and major record shops.

PH 31
Prins Hendriklaan 31, OS (673 6850). Tram 2. **Open** 8pm-2am daily; closed July, Aug. **Music** Thur. **Admission** free. **No credit cards.**
This ex-squat bar, now a one-room venue with a small stage and a separate theatre room, is situated in an unlikely residential area of town, beyond Vondelpark. Local residents seem to tolerate noisy comings and goings, which is lucky as the sound system is powerful. Politically motivated local bands are regular performers.

Roxy
Singel 465, C (620 0354). Tram 1, 2, 4, 5, 9, 14, 16, 24, 25. **Open** 11pm-4am Wed, Thur, Sun; 11pm-5am Fri, Sat. **Admission** f10. **No credit cards.**
As well as featuring PA spots during weekend dance nights, the Roxy is sometimes hired out on Mondays for various events and bands on European tours. These nights are always well publicized by posters all over town and the strict membership rules are waived. *See also p141* **Night-clubs.**

Sleep-In
's-Gravesandestraat 51, OE (694 7444). Tram 6, 10. **Open** 10pm-3am Wed, Thur; 10.30pm-3am Fri. **Admission** free (Wed)-f5. **No credit cards.**
This venue is part of one of the main youth hostels in Amsterdam (*see p39* **Accommodation**). The agenda consists of local bands, student discos and reggae nights. A little way out of the centre, it's handy if you're staying in the area or actually in the hostel.

Vondelpark
OS. Tram 1, 2, 3, 5, 6, 12. **Open** dawn-dusk daily.
During the summer months the open-air theatre is the focal point of activities in the park. On Sunday afternoons it seems that the whole town turns up to wander around and watch buskers, jugglers and African drummers in a scenario that hasn't changed much since the sixties. The main podium has a programme of live performances from local musicians and singers. Look out for some of the more famous Dutch names such as Mathilde Santing and The Nits, who always get an enthusiastic reception for their brand of folk-influenced indie pop. The future of the live shows is in doubt; check with the VVV (*see p3* **Essential Information**) before going.

FOLK & WORLD MUSIC

Amsterdam has always been a meeting place for travellers from all over

Take a tram out to the eastern edge of town and travel back in time a couple of decades. **Cruise Inn** *(see under* **Venues***) is the stronghold of the few rock 'n' roll enthusiasts, complete with motor bikes, quiffs and brothel-creepers, left in Amsterdam, who hang out in this wooden club house. Live rockabilly bands and visiting DJs often appear on Saturday nights, and there is a 'Rock 'n' Roll Jamboree' open-air event every summer in the middle of June (phone for details).*

Europe and the rest of the world. Some are just passing through, while others stop off and make the city their home. As a result of The Netherlands' colonial history, there is a large population of Surinam and Indonesian descent in Amsterdam, each with their own music styles. Major venues such as the **Paradiso** and **Melkweg** (*see above* **Venues**) regularly feature world music nights. For free outdoor performances, Amsterdam has a never-ending supply of street musicians who can usually be found on Leidseplein or outside Centraal Station. Look out for the Peruvian buskers who are an especially colourful troupe.

The Dutch have their own brand of folk, of the oom-pah-pah sing-along variety. The Jordaan (*see page 26* **Amsterdam by Area**) is the best place to find it.

Canecao
Lange Leidsedwarsstraat 68 (638 0611). **Open** 8pm-1am Mon-Thur, Sun; 8pm-2am Fri, Sat. **Admission** free. **No credit cards.** *See p140* **picture and caption.**

Iboya
Korte Leidsedwarsstraat 29, IS (623 7859). **No credit cards.**
A small theatre, restaurant and live music venue catering for South American music lovers. There are live bands at weekends unless a theatre production is taking place; phone for details. Regular customers are a friendly and enthusiastic mixed Dutch and Surinam crowd. The admission charge varies according to the programme.

MART
106.8FM. **On air** 10pm-3am daily.
Not a venue, but a local radio station, MART is proud to be able to boast the world's longest salsa show, every Friday from 10pm to 3am. Presented by the extremely laid-back (English-speaking) Dr Salsa, it's a great show to tune in to before going out, or even when you get home. It's often possible to go along and dance in the studio itself – listen in for details. Other nights feature country-and-western, African and reggae shows.

Mulligans
Amstel 100, IS (622 1330). Tram 4, 6, 7, 10. **Open** 4pm-1am Mon-Thur; 4pm-2am Fri; 2pm-2am Sat; 2pm-1am Sun. **Music** Fri, Sat. **Admission** free. **No credit cards.**
Home-from-home Irish bar with great atmosphere and live music provided on Friday and Saturday evenings by the resident crew and visiting folk musicians. Weekends are always busy and the Guinness may take a long time to pour, but it tastes twice as good once you get it. Centrally situated on the Amstel in an otherwise mainly gay area.

Nieuwe Kroeg
Lijnbaansgracht 163, IW (626 8910). Tram 10. **Open** 10pm-3am Tue-Thur; 10pm-4am Fri, Sat. **Music** Tue, Wed, Fri. **Admission** f3.50-f5. **No credit cards.**
A visit to the old Kroeg was quite an experience – it used to be a seedy dive complete with pimps, dealers and cockroaches, but since its refurbishment its image has been cleaned up and, sadly, it has lost some of the original atmosphere. In the back room, reggae sound systems and salsa groups are the main focus, along with the occasional local rock band.

R

WE KNOW WHO YOU AM

ROXY

CLUB-THEATRE-SALON

SINGEL 465 AMSTERDAM PHONE (31) 20200354, FAX (31) 20269454

Rembrandt Bar

Rembrandtsplein 3, IS (623 0688). Tram 4, 9, 14. **Open** 4pm-1am Mon-Thur, Sun; 4pm-2am Fri, Sat. **Admission** free. **No credit cards.**
One of the best of the several brown bars (*see p91* **Cafés & Bars**) around Rembrandtplein which have live Dutch folk music. The beer flows and the music gets louder as the night wears on.

Rodos Bar

St Jacobsstraat 40, C (622 0168). Tram 1, 2, 5, 13, 17. **Open** noon-1am Mon-Thur, Sun; noon-2am Fri, Sat. **Admission** free. **No credit cards.**
A dingy hang-out for street musicians and old hippies who occasionally get up and pay off their drink tabs with a performance. It can get rowdy as the night goes on and the *jenever* takes effect.

Roothaanhuis

Rozengracht 133, IW (623 5969). Tram 13, 14, 17. **Open** varies with performance; phone for details. **Admission** f5-f10. **No credit cards.**
This basement dive popular with a Turkish and Surinam crowd can get rather heavy at times. Reggae sound systems and live Surinam bands make regular appearances at weekends.

Royal Star

Paardenstraat 9 (opposite Café Vive La Vie), C (620 9472. Tram 4, 9, 14. **Open** 11pm-4am Mon-Thur, Sun; 11pm-5am Fri, Sat. **Admission** f15-f25. **No credit cards.**
This glitzy disco venue stages live Brazilian, reggae and salsa acts at weekends. Popular with a mixed Surinam/Dutch crowd, the entertainment often covers the more commercial end of the market, with cabaret evenings alongside serious dance nights. Prices are relatively high for Amsterdam.

Soeterijn Theatre

Linnaeusstraat 2, OE (568 8500). Tram 9, 10, 14. **Open** *information and reservations* noon-4pm Mon-Fri; *box office* one hour before performance. **Admission** f12.50-f22.50. **No credit cards.**
The Soeterijn is a small theatre attached to the Tropenmuseum. The Museum itself exhibits artefacts from all over the world (*see p100* **Museums**) and the Soeterijn follows the same policy in its music programming, featuring international folk musicians. It's not necessarily the best context for some performances, as the presentation is very formal (all-seated audience). Listings of events can be found in *Uitkrant, see p145* Media.

Spinoza

De Wittenstraat 100, OW (688 0127). Tram 10. **Open** irregularly, phone for details (2-6pm Wed). **Admission** f2.50-f5. **No credit cards.**
Sound systems occasionally play in this one-room venue to a laid-back reggae crowd. Spots Roadshow is well recommended – tune in to AFM radio (106.8FM) on Sunday afternoons (1-2pm) for a sample of its style.

String

Nes 98, C (625 9015). Tram 4, 9, 14, 16, 24, 25. **Open** 8pm-2am Mon-Thur, Sun; 8pm-

3am Fri, Sat. **Admission** free. **No credit cards.**
This back-street bar is home to the city's buskers when the sun goes down. There's barely enough room to swing a guitar, so solo/duo folk and blues musicians are the most frequent performers.

JAZZ

In summer, Holland comes alive to the sound of jazz, with outdoor festivals in the centre of Amsterdam, as well as the North Sea Jazz Festival in The Hague (*see below* **Festivals**). But throughout the year, venues play host to the big names in jazz and many small, relaxed bars have live sessions every night of the week.

Alto Jazz Café

Korte Leidsedwarsstraat 115, IS (626 3249). Tram 1, 2, 5, 6, 7, 10. **Open** 9pm-3am Mon-Thur, Sun; 9pm-4am Fri, Sat. **Admission** free. **No credit cards.**
This cosy and relaxed traditional brown bar is in an otherwise commercialized tourist

area just off Leidseplein. Live jazz is played every night of the week by the in-house quartet and guests.

Bimhuis

Oudeschans 73, C (623 3373). Tram 9, 14/Metro Nieuwmarkt. **Open** *box office* 8-9pm Thur-Sat. **Tickets** f9.50-f20. **No credit cards.**
The city's major regular jazz venue stages a mixture of well-known international artists as well as local talent in a subdued and reverent atmosphere. It's often hard to get a seat, so arrive early. There are free sessions on Monday and Wednesday evenings when regulars like saxophonist Hans Dulfer and friends provide the entertainment. Tickets cannot be booked but can be bought on the day from the AUB or VVV tourist offices (*see p3* **Essential Information**), or on the door before performances.

Gambrinus

Ferdinand Bolstraat 180, OS (671 7389). Tram 3, 12, 24, 25. **Open** 11am-1am Mon-Thur, Sun; 11am-2am Fri, Sat. **Admission** free. **No credit cards.**
A small bar in the *Oude Zuid* (Old South) area of Amsterdam, beyond the Heineken brewery. A good place for an early evening meal (kitchen open 6pm-10pm daily), with

Housed in a wonderful old wooden building that was once a dairy (hence the name), the **Melkweg** *(see under* **Venues***) opened in the sixties, and is still run on a co-operative basis. The multi-media centre is open from Tuesday to Sunday for bands, theatre, dance and film. If the main hall gets too crowded, there's a separate bar where you can relax and get something to eat. The Melkweg is one of the few remaining places where you can 'legally' buy dope and space cake. Friday night is the Roots Rhythm Club, with live African or South American musicians; live bands, usually of the British or American indie rock variety, play on Saturdays. Look out for posters or pick up one of the monthly information sheets from the foyer.*

local jazz musicians providing the background music on Sunday afternoons from 4pm onwards.

IJsbreker
Weesperzijde 23, IS (668 1805). Tram 3, 6, 7, 10/Metro Weesperplein. **Open** *box office* 9am-5.30pm Mon-Fri; *café* 10am-1am Mon-Thur, Sun; 10am-2am Fri, Sat. **Admission** to shows f15-f20. **No credit cards.**
This venue is situated on the picturesque banks of the Amstel river. The programming concentrates on classical and experimental jazz, and performance and art films. Even when there's no live performance, it's worth a visit for the bar alone, especially on summer evenings. *See also p130* **Music: Classical & Opera.**

Joseph Lam Jazz Club
Van Diemenstraat 8, IW (622 8086). Tram 3. **Open** 9pm-3am Sat; 9pm-2am Sun. **Admission** f6 Sat; free Sun. **No credit cards.**
This venue is a little off the beaten track, in an old harbour area to the west of Centraal Station. The crowd is an older group of jazz enthusiasts who go there to hear traditional and Dixieland jazz.

Odeon Jazz Kelder
Singel 460, C (620 9722). Tram 1, 2, 4, 5, 9, 14, 16, 24, 25. **Open** 10pm-3.30am Mon-Thur, Sun; 10pm-4.30am Fri, Sat. **Admission** f5-f10. **No credit cards.**
Housed in a cellar that was formerly a gay club, this recent extension to the Odeon

disco survived the fire that gutted the club. Live jazz every night of the week. A wide range of Dutch artists provide traditional jazz entertainment for a mature audience of jazz fans in an intimate café/restaurant.

Rum Runners
Prinsengracht 277, IW (627 4079). Tram 13, 14, 17. **Open** 4pm-1am Mon-Thur; 4pm-2am Fri; noon-2am Sat; noon-1am Sun. **Admission** free. **Credit** (bar and restaurant) AmEx, DC, MC, V.
A cool and relaxing Caribbean bar/restaurant most of the week, at weekends it gets very crowded. Live jazz combos and Latin bands provide the entertainment once a week, from 4pm to 9pm on Sunday. The place is easy to find, being sandwiched between the Westerkerk and Anne Frankhuis. *See also p79* **Restaurants.**

FESTIVALS

Koninginnedag
Date April 30.
This Dutch national holiday is the best day of the year to be in Amsterdam. In honour of the former Queen's birthday, all laws concerning sales taxes and licensing are suspended and a massive jumble sale engulfs the city. The trading is accompanied by music, which blasts out from every street corner. Stages are erected in every available space and bands of all kinds play from midday to midnight, by which time everybody is too drunk to go on. In recent years more

sound systems with DJs have sprung up to challenge the traditional domain of the bands, and outdoor 'raves' are much more frequent. *See also p36* **Amsterdam by Season.**

Pink Pop & Park Pop Festivals
Dates *Pink Pop* 1 day in mid to late May (20 May 1991); *Park Pop* 1 day in late June (30 June 1991). **Information and tickets** available in Amsterdam from VVV tourist offices (*see p3* **Essential Information**), from December; tickets for Pink Pop approx f15; admission to Park Pop free.
Taking place around Whitsuntide in The Hague (Park Pop), and in a small village outside Rotterdam (Pink Pop) these major outdoor pop festivals have impressive line-ups of famous Dutch and international stars. Expect to find a diverse mixture of artists such as Van Morrison, Nick Cave, De La Soul, Urban Dance Squad and the Red Hot Chili Peppers on the bill. But be warned, it always seems to rain on the day.

Drum International Jazz Festival
Date about one week, usually in early July (4-9 July 1991). **Information and tickets** Jazz Inn record shop, *see p153* **Shopping Around**; tickets cost from f15 to f85 for the opening concert (average price f45).
Artists in 1990 included Michael Brecker, Celia Cruz, Astrud Gilberto and Nina Simone. Venues range from the Carré (*see p126* **Theatre**) and the Paradiso (*see above* **Venues**) to open-air performances in Amsterdamse Bos (free, bring a picnic), *see p13* **Sightseeing.**

North Sea Jazz Festival
Dates 3 days in mid-July. **Information** *Festival organizers* PO Box 87840, 2508 DE Den Haag. **Tickets** from f30 per day, available in Amsterdam from Uitburo and VVV tourist offices (*see p3* **Essential Information**).
Founded in the early seventies, the North Sea Jazz Festival (in The Hague's Congresgebouw) plays host to an astonishing list of international performers, from traditional jazzmen such as Miles Davis and Dizzy Gillespie to the soulful George Benson and crazy funkateer George Clinton. At time of writing, dates for the 1991 and 1992 festivals had not yet been set.

Amsterdam Jazz Festivals
Several jazz events take place in Amsterdam throughout the summer; from July to the end of September there can be as many as five or six festivals catering for every taste in jazz. The main events, such as the **Drum International Jazz Festival** (*see above*) and **Amsterdam and All That Jazz**, coincide with the **Holland Festival** in July (*see p36* **Amsterdam by Season**) and consequently attract a large, international crowd of traditional jazz fans. These events take place in venues throughout the city, with the main focus being the stages and marquees erected on the Dam. There are also performances in the Amsterdamse Bos, a large park to the south of the city (*see p13* **Sightseeing**). Information for all the festivals can be obtained from the VVV or AUB offices, *see p3* **Essential Information.**

The **Canecao** (see under **Folk & World Music**) *is a centrally-located bar that throbs to the sound of live samba every weekend. It's one of the few places in Amsterdam that serves cocktails (reliably potent), and the tropical décor adds to the atmosphere. The club gets extremely busy, so arrive early to claim a seat.*

Night-clubs

Local DJ *Paul Jay* puts you in step with Amsterdam's relaxed night life.

Amsterdam nightlife has a relaxed and carefree mood that overrides the lack of an individual style. In recent years the post-house music crowd has started something of a club-culture scene in music and fashion, but it's the laid-back attitude of the locals that gives special appeal to a night out.

A great advantage is that nearly all clubs are situated within the relatively small city centre. Distances between venues are walkable, and for many people an evening out a trek around a few different clubs. Another advantage is that admission prices are extremely low, although they can rise a little at weekends. Bar prices are also very reasonable. However, tipping the doorman when you leave is an established custom – expect to donate at least five guilders.

Most clubs open at 11pm but rarely get going until 1am or 2am. Although there has been a crackdown on late licences, most places stay open until 4am and an hour later at weekends. Watch out for rogue taxi drivers who sometimes wait outside busy clubs (official taxis never do this). They have been known to threaten to drop you off in the middle of nowhere unless you give them all your cash.

The Roxy is the only club with a strict membership policy.

GOING UNDERGROUND

It was once possible to attend what locals would call a 'new-wave' club and hear a mixture of music ranging from punk through to hip hop. These have now been replaced by specialist clubs and one-nighters. Often top guest DJs from the UK or USA are the attraction, although local DJs are reaching very high standards themselves.

In the Leidseplein and Rembrandtsplein areas you will find a selection of commercial discos playing chart music. Some are quite tacky, attracting an out-of-town crowd known locally as the 'Leidseplein Public', and the Saturday night drunken punch-up may be hard to avoid. One of the better venues is **De Bunnies**.

For something altogether different, check out one of the many South American nights – a legacy of Dutch colonial interest in Surinam – when sharply dressed couples execute finely rehearsed dance steps to salsa and Latin music at venues like **Star-Sky**. It's an experience not to be missed.

But the most exciting events of the last few years have not taken place in the clubs. Many spectacular underground dance parties have been held in large, empty warehouses on the edge of town. Unfortunately, here, as in other countries, the authorities have tried to stamp out all illegal events. There are still many smaller all-night parties going on, although it can be difficult for visitors to find out where to go.

With this in mind, a recommended stop-off point before embarking on a night out is the WILD! clubwear shop (*see page 153* **Shopping Around**). There you can pick up a copy of a local fashion/club scene quarterly magazine written in English, also called *WILD!* (f2.75), which is full of club listings and gossip. This is also a good place to pick up club and party leaflets, as are dance record shops such as Black Beat (*see page153* **Shopping Around**). Another source of up-to-date nightlife information is the excellent Amsterdam FM dance-music radio station (106.8FM), which is on air between 1am and 6pm daily. Many of the shows are presented in English.

THE CLUBS

Boston Club
Kattengat 1, C (624 5561). Tram 1, 2, 4, 5, 9, 13, 16, 17, 24, 25. **Open** 10pm-4am Mon-Thur, Sun; 10pm-5am Fri, Sat. **Admission** free. **Credit** AmEx, MC, V.
This is adjacent to the up-market Sonesta Hotel and you'll need to put on your best suit and tie or evening dress to gain entry. Admission is free but take a credit card along to pay for the drinks. The fabulous cocktails just about compensate for the mediocre selection of chart music and the small dancefloor.

De Bunnies
Korte Leidsedwarsstraat 26, IS (622 6622). Tram 1, 2, 5, 6, 7, 10. **Open** 10pm-4am

Mon-Thur, Sun; 10pm-5am Fri, Sat. **Admission** f2.50. **No credit cards.**
One of the better Leidseplein-area discos, with a cosy bar area next to the dancefloor.

Cash
Leidseplein 12, IS (627 6544). Tram 1, 2, 5, 6, 7, 10. **Open** café 10pm-4am daily; *disco* 10pm-4am Thur-Sun. **Admission** f10. **Credit** £STC.
An appropriately named pick-up joint in the heart of the Leidseplein nightlife area playing commercial dance music. The décor comes complete with plastic palm trees and thick pile carpets. It gets very busy at the weekend, attracting a conservatively dressed working crowd, although in summer Italian tourists seem to outnumber the locals.

Chic
Rozengracht 133, IW (622 1031). Tram 13, 14, 17. **Open** 11pm-4am Thur-Sat. **Admission** f5. **No credit cards.**
A small Caribbean-flavoured club playing African, reggae and salsa music to a local Turkish and Surinam crowd. You'll have to dress formally and look smart to gain entry.

Dansen Bij Jansen
Handboogstraat 11, C (620 1779). Tram 1, 2, 5. **Open** 11pm-4.30am Mon-Thur, Sun; 11pm-5.30am Fri, Sat. **Admission** f3.50 Mon-Thur, Sun; f4 Fri, Sat. **No credit cards.**
This is officially a student-only club but just saying you attend a college, even a non-Dutch one, should be enough to get you in. A very safe music selection played on a poor sound system nevertheless packs in a young crowd, especially in term time. Sundays are enlivened by different theme parties, such as fancy dress, salsa and jazz-dance.

Escape
Rembrandtsplein 11-15, IS (622 3542). Tram 4, 9, 14. **Open** 10pm-4am Thur (students only); 10pm-5am Fri, Sat. **Admission** free Thur; f10 Fri, Sat. **No credit cards.**
The dancefloor at this cavernous disco can accommodate 1,000 people. The impressive computerized lighting show complete with giant video screen and lasers have failed to attract the vast numbers needed to give the place atmosphere; even on a Saturday night it's often half empty. The bland music selection coupled with indifferent staff hasn't helped. There are occasional live performances by hip hop and soul acts, including some big names (recently Alexander O'Neal, Ten City and De La Soul).
No trainers.

Havana
Reguliersdwarsstraat 17, IS (620 6788). Tram 1, 2, 5, 16, 24, 25. **Open** *bar* 4pm-1am Mon-Thur, Sun; 4pm-2am Fri; 2pm-2am Sat; 2pm-1am Sun; *disco* 10pm-3am Mon-Thur, Sun; 10pm-4am Fri, Sat. **Admission** free. **No credit cards.**
An early-closing free-entry bar with a separate dance area upstairs. It's popular with a yuppy-ish pre-club crowd, largely gay, who stand around watching each other, occasionally venturing onto the small floor to dance to commercial, soul-based music. Jazz-dance on Sundays.

Julianas
Apollolaan 138, OS (673 7313). Tram 16. **Open** 10pm-4am Mon-Thur, Sun; 10pm-5am

You are more than welcome to:
AMSTERDAM'S MOST CIVILISED DISCOTHEQUE

HOMOLULU

An unusual experience, where happy people and friendly service all go together.

❖ Amsterdam's only dinner dance club

❖ Amsterdam's only discotheque which is open every night.

❖ Amsterdam's only discotheque, where regardless of your sexual persuasion you can enjoy a free and friendly atmosphere.

HOMOLULU is open every night 10 pm - 4 am
weekends 10 pm - 5 am

International food is served in a candlelit bistro until closing time.
Excellent food for very reasonable prices.

Kerkstraat 23 - 1017 GA Amsterdam
Tel: 624 63 87

Fri, Sat. **Admission** f5. **Credit** AmEx, DC, MC, V.
Situated a little way out of the city centre underneath the Hilton Hotel, this is Amsterdam's premier up-market club. Not surprisingly, it attracts an older, conservative crowd. Bar food, cocktails, a tasteful décor and chart music are the attractions.
No trainers.

The iT
Amstelstraat 24, IS (625 0111). Tram 4, 9, 14. **Open** 11pm-4am Thur; 11pm-5am Fri, Sat. **Admission** free Thur; f10 Fri, Sat. **No credit cards.**
What started as an exclusively male gay club is now attracting an increasingly mixed young crowd. The nude transvestites and outrageous cabaret acts have now given way to dated non-stop house music, strobes and smoke. The club can be difficult to get into as it fills up quickly.

Mazzo
Rozengracht 114, IW (626 7500). Tram 13, 14, 17. **Open** *July, Aug* 11pm-5am daily; *Sept-June* 11pm-5am Tue-Sun. **Admission** f7.50 Mon-Thur, Sun; f10 Fri, Sat. **No credit cards.**
Plenty of space to sit and talk as well as great visuals and a neat compact dance area make this one of the best clubs in town. The music policy changes throughout the week as different DJs, playing anything from jazz dance to hard acid, are featured. At time of writing Friday is the best night, with guest acts and DJs from London adding to a great atmosphere. Often very busy, this club tends to have a selective door policy.
Wheelchair access with help.

Melkweg
Lijnbaansgracht 234, IW (624 8492). Tram 9, 10, 14. **Open** 1-5am Fri, Sat. **Admission** f5. **Membership** f3.50. **No credit cards.**
This multi-media centre (*see also p122* **Film** and *p135* **Rock, Folk & Jazz**) turns into a dance club after the bands have finished. It's one of the few places where you'll get alternative rock music on the turntables, although Saturday is a hardcore house and hip hop night. You have to buy a temporary membership to gain entry.
Wheelchair access with assistance.

(36 Op de schaal van) Richter
Reguliersdwarsstraat 36, IS (626 1573). Tram 1, 2, 4, 5, 9, 14, 16, 24, 25. **Open** midnight-3.30am Mon-Thur, Sun; midnight-4.30am Fri, Sat. **Admission** f5 Mon, Tue; f7.50 Wed-Sun. **No credit cards.**
The name refers to the earthquake-style décor (shattered mirrors, cracks in the wall) inside this small two-tiered club. It used to attract the city's rich and beautiful as well as famous pop stars, but most have now moved across the canal to the Roxy (*see below*). Consequently a less desirable bunch – mainly groups of men on the pick-up – fills the empty spaces.

Roxy
Singel 465-467, C (620 0354). Tram 1, 2, 4, 5, 9, 14, 16, 24, 25. **Open** 11pm-4am Wed, Thur, Sun; 11pm-5am Fri, Sat. **Admission** f5 Wed, Thur, Sun; f10 Fri, Sat. **No credit cards.**
See **picture and caption.**

To enter the **Roxy** *(listed under* **The Clubs***), an old canal-side converted cinema, you go through the basement and then climb a grand stairway into a high-ceilinged dance area. A further staircase leads to an upstairs bar overlooking the DJ and the activities below. The Roxy was one of the first places in The Netherlands to play house music. It consequently became quite notorious and hugely influential in the creation of a new dance subculture. Although these days it seems to have lost a little of its vitality, it still gets very busy – you may not be able to get a seat – and many of the city's 'in-crowd' will turn up. Look out for some spectacular décor that changes every month. Food is available and there's a small shop selling T-shirts and jewellery. The Roxy has a strict membership policy. It is extremely difficult to join, so the best way to gain entry is to dress up, go early, look confident and try to impress the doorman.*

Star-Sky
Warmoesstraat 151, C (627 1545). Tram 4, 9, 16, 24, 25. **Open** 10pm-4am Wed, Thur, Sun; 10pm-5am Fri, Sat. **Admission** f5 Wed, Thur, Sun; f10-f25 Fri, Sat. **No credit cards.**
Aimed at the local South American population, Star-Sky plays salsa, swing-beat and soul. It's housed in an old roller-skating hall in the heart of the red light area. Smart, traditional clothes are essential.

OUT OF TOWN

Distances from Amsterdam are so small that many people regularly make the effort to travel out to these three clubs. All three frequently charter a free coach service to and from the centre of Amsterdam for special events.

The Metropool
Korte Hogendijk 2, Zaandam (075 70 0811). **Open** 9pm-4am Thur-Sun. **Admission** f5 Thur, Fri, Sun; f10 Sat. **Credit** AmEx, MC, V.
A huge, purpose-built, glittering discotheque with expensive lighting effects and a large and loud sound system. Hip hop and swing-beat are very popular. Many local and a few big-name American acts perform live.

Stalker
Kromme Elleboogsteeg 20, Haarlem (023 31 4652). **Open** 11pm-3am Thur; 11pm-5.30am Fri, Sat; 10pm-3am Sun. **Admission** free Thur, Sun; f5 Fri, Sat. **No credit cards.**
Hidden down a dark alley in this picturesque town (*see p208* **The Randstad**) is this small but ambitious club. Lots of guest DJs and acts from Amsterdam perform here. A lively crowd and an excellent sound system.

De Waakzaamheid
Hoogstraat 4, Koog A/D Zaan (075 28 5829). **Open** *café* 7pm-2am daily; *disco* 7pm-5am Fri, Sat. **Admission** f7.50. **No credit cards.**
In the middle of a sleepy village just outside Zaandam, this adventurous venue attracts a mixed crowd from the surrounding towns. Housed in a beautiful old wooden venue, it claims to have staged one of the last concerts by Billie Holiday in the fifties. Nowadays you get a surprisingly upfront dance mix from a variety of local DJs and the occasional guest from the UK. A good range of different beers, excellent bar food and a separate salsa/jazz room are also big attractions.

Early Hours

If you're on the streets after a night on the town, hungry and tired, we show you where to find some food and how to get home.

To the outsider it may seem that Amsterdam closes down at 1am, but if you know where to look, there are still places open to assuage hunger and slake thirst before setting off home as the sun rises.

But first, if something disastrous should happen, ring *0611* for **police**, **fire** or **ambulance** and then ask for the relevant emergency service. For less major **medical emergencies** *see page 221* **Survival** for a list of 24-hour casualty departments.

If you need a **chemist** or **pharmacist** late at night phone the **Central Medical Service** (*Centraal Dokters Dienst*) on *664 2111* or *679 1821* (24 hours daily) or consult the daily newspaper *Het Parool* which publishes details of which *apotheek* are open late that week. Details are also posted in the local *apotheek*.

If you need to change some money, the GWK **bureau de change** in Centraal Station stays open 24 hours daily, as does the branch in Schiphol airport.

The tram and Metro systems stop running after midnight and don't start again until 6am. **Night buses** are numbered from 71 to 77, with numbers 73 to 76 running through the city centre. A night bus stop is shown by a black square with the bus number printed on it. However, even the night buses stop running between 2am and 4am Monday to Friday and 2.30am to 3.30am on Saturday and Sunday, so between those hours the only alternatives are walking or taking a taxi. Since Amsterdam is a small city walking may well be the best choice, but for those whose feet refuse to carry them any further **taxis** can usually be found at the ranks at Centraal Station, Rembrandtsplein, Leidseplein and the junction of Kinkerstraat and Marnixstraat. Taxis can't be hailed in the street, but one can be ordered by phoning the 24-hour central taxi control on *677 7777*. For car drivers, the following are the main 24-hour **petrol stations** (*benzinestation*) within Amsterdam: Gooiseweg 10-11, OE; Sarphatistraat 225, IE; Marnixstraat 250, IW; Spaarndammerdijk 218, OW.

SHOPS

Throughout the city are 'nightshops' (*avondwinkel*), usually open until 1am. Although the goods are overpriced, they are the only places open for those late-night necessities: coffee, tea, milk and cigarettes.

Avondmarkt
De Wittenkade 90-96, OW (686 4919).
Tram 10. **Open** 6pm-1am Mon-Fri; 5.30pm-1am Sat, Sun. **No credit cards.**

Baltus Sterk
Vijzelstraat 127, IS (626 9069). Tram 16, 24, 25. **Open** 4pm-1am Mon-Fri; 1pm-1am Sat; 6pm-1am Sun. **No credit cards.**

Dolf's Avondverkoop
Willemsstraat 79, OW (625 9503). Tram 3.
Open noon-1am daily. **No credit cards.**

Doorneveld
De Clercqstraat 3-7, OW (618 1727). Tram 12, 13, 14. **Open** 6pm-1am daily. **No credit cards.**

Heuft's First Class Night Shop
Rijnstraat 62, OS (642 4048). Tram 4, 25.
Open 4pm-1am daily, telephone orders for lunch accepted earlier. **Credit** AmEx, DC.
Go in person, or phone and ask for a delivery of anything from champagne and oysters to fully-catered meals.

BARS

Bars in Amsterdam are usually open until 1am from Monday to Thursday and Sunday, and 2am on Fridays and Saturdays. For the dedicated barfly, we list below three very late night bars.

Café Nol
Westerstraat 109, IW (624 5380). Tram 10.
Open 9am-3am Mon-Thur, Sun; 9am-4am Fri, Sat. **No credit cards.**
You don't need to be drunk to venture into this Jordaan institution featuring pink neon lights and inebriated locals bawling sentimental Dutch songs, but it probably helps.

Koophandel
Bloemgracht 49, IW (623 9843). Tram 10, 13, 14, 17. **Open** 4pm-very late daily. **No credit cards.**
A bar for the dedicated drinker. Don't bother turning up before midnight, when the bar is virtually empty, and be prepared not to leave before dawn.

De Pieter
St Pietersteeg 29, C (623 6007). Tram 4, 9, 14, 16, 24, 25. **Open** 11pm-3am Mon-Thur, Sun; 11pm-4am Fri, Sat. **No credit cards.**
Something of a student hang-out, this is a small, dark and noisy bar that gets even smaller and noisier when the owner squeezes in a live band.

RESTAURANTS

Most of the so-called night restaurants are located around Leidseplein and vary from okay to awful. They can get crowded after 1am. An alternative for hungry homeward-bound clubbers is the **Febo** chain (*see picture*), which does a virtually

round-the-clock service of food from slot machines. Heated dishes, plus good chips and sauces from mayonnaise to piccalilli, are available. There are branches throughout the city, but there are particularly popular ones in Leidsestraat and Kalverstraat.

Bojo
Lange Leidsedwarsstraat 51, IS (622 7434). Tram 1, 2, 5, 6, 7, 10. **Open** 5pm-2am Mon-Thur, Sun; 5pm-5.30am Fri, Sat. **No credit cards.**
An Indonesian restaurant of variable quality in the middle of Amsterdam's late-night district. It's often crowded and noisy, with a long wait to be served. You'll see all kinds of crazy types here, and at an average price of f14 it makes for good entertainment.

Mama's Shoarma
Between Sedap and Christine LeDuc Sex Shop, Korte Leidsedwarsstraat, IS (no phone). Tram 1, 2, 5, 6, 7, 10. **Open** 5pm-5am daily. **No credit cards.**
Mama's serves the best (and one of the cheapest) shoarma (or kebab) in Amsterdam – f6 for a single shoarma. This Middle Eastern speciality is perfect for late-night appetites, and the Egyptian staff are friendly and not into the drug dealing that goes on in some of the other grill-bars.

Sedap
Korte Leidsedwarsstraat 60, IS (627 4743). Tram 1, 2, 5, 6, 7, 10. **Open** 4pm-3am daily. **Credit** AmEx.
A relatively quiet place with Indonesian food of acceptable quality. Most dishes range from f10 to f15. Open until 5am on weekends if it's busy.

Media

From soaps to soft porn, gossip to highbrow analysis, this cabled city has it all, in nearly every language. *Sara Henley mediates.*

THE PRESS

For those who can handle the language (and if you know a bit of German you should be able to read some) the Dutch press is extensive – in shades of opinion as well as bulk. One of the most striking aspects of the Dutch press is that several leading papers started life as underground news-sheets during the Nazi occupation. Although today this does not mean these journals fly in the face of injunctions to print investigative truths, it does occasionally give them a mildly anarchic flavour, and a loyal readership.

FOREIGN PRESS

Beyond a couple of superficial listings magazines such as *What's On In Amsterdam* (*listed under* **Listings Magazines**) and in-depth financial journals such as *Het Financieele Dagblad* (*under* **Newspapers**), little Dutch-printed English is available. But foreign papers from *El País* to *Sporting Life* and major magazines are easily available at branches of the Bruna and AKO newsagent chains (Leidsestraat, Beethoven-straat and Centraal Station are the most accessible outlets; for addresses *see page 221* **Survival**), and most major European and US newspapers are available on the day of publication.

NEWSPAPERS

De Telegraaf

Politically similar to its British namesake, the conservative *Daily Telegraph*, *De Telegraaf* (f1.10, Saturday edition f1.75) was the only Dutch paper allowed to publish during the Nazi occupation – not because the people who worked on it were collaborators or even convinced Nazis, but because unlike other papers, it never overtly criticized the occupying government. But any resemblance to the *Telegraph* stops on the front page; it's the closest the Dutch get to a morning tabloid, dressed up as a broadsheet. And like the most notorious of the British tabloids, *The Sun*, it has far and away the biggest circulation, although the titillation is less of the sexual than the pop star/TV personality scandal variety. Worth buying for the accommodation ads on a Wednesday (get it early to stand a chance).

Algemeen Dagblad

Milder than *De Telegraaf* (although with headlines still out-screaming the stories), and with a more progressive outlook than most British tabloids, this populist sheet (f1.10, Saturday edition f1.75) takes the shock-horror approach to more off-beat issues. Its financial pages, like those of *De Telegraaf*, are quite highly regarded.

De Volkskrant

Set up as Catholic paper in 1922, it shed the religious tag to attract a broadly left-wing audience after the war (when it had been censored out of print). Now the Dutch equivalent of the British *Guardian* or the American *Washington Post*, with occasional eccentric quirks, it's widely read and respected by the professional classes – and very much a paper with which to be seen in cafés. Published by the same company as *Trouw* and *Het Parool* (*see below*), and carrying the same small ads, it's another useful source for local services and accommodation. Price f1.35, Saturday edition f1.95.

NRC Handelsblad

Although sometimes mocked for its intellectual pretensions (some say it thinks it's *Le Monde*) the *NRC* is probably the most respected national, with a well-educated, business-oriented readership. The Thursday *Donderdag Agenda* supplement is an encyclopaedic guide to cultural events nationwide.

Trouw

Protestant in origin, this national daily (f1.25) went underground during the war but has been less successful in expanding circulation and moving away from religious identification than *De Volkskrant*: it still publishes a regular church page.

Het Parool

See p146 picture and caption.

Het Financieele Dagblad

Strictly for those who need Dutch business/financial news, this paper's international business coverage is thinner that the *Financial Times*, which is easily obtainable on the day of publication. But it is the only Dutch daily with a summary in English, and this gives much more coverage of Dutch affairs that the FT. Price f1.95.

PERIODICALS

Avenue, Elegance

A monthly upmarket style-bible for glossy living, the large-format *Avenue* (f7.95) appeals to yuppies of both sexes as well as to would-be yups who dream of affording some of its exotic travel recommendations. A similar publication, *Elegance* (f9.75), is directed at wealthy, mature women. Both have beautifully produced photos.

Elsevier, De Tijd, Haagse Post, De Groene Amsterdammer, Forum

Weekly current affairs magazines, these fit into a category known in The Netherlands as *opiniebladen* and as such offer readers a weekly dose of their favourite political medicine.

Nieuwe Revu, Panorama, Privé

Few serious opinions are offered by these high-colour titillators. *Nieuwe Revu* (f2.85) has youth appeal; *Privé* (f2.35) is famous for its dirt-mongering salaciousness.

Vrij Nederland

Another Resistance baby, this Friday weekly (f4.75) has a strong emphasis on long, mildly investigative stories and culture, particularly literature. Its colour supplement boasts many an arty photo.

LISTINGS MAGAZINES

Agenda

A monthly listings magazine available free in bars, with an English section badly in need of a mother-tongue editor. Only sporadically useful as a guide, but still worth picking up.

Uitkrant

Although written in Dutch, this monthly listings freesheet is relatively straightforward, easily decipherable, and is the most comprehensive guide to what's on in town. Available from the Uitburo (*see p3* **Essential Information**), central library (*see p221* **Survival**) and several bookshops.

What's On In Amsterdam

Amsterdam's weekly English-language listings magazine (f2.50). Since it's published by the VVV tourist information office (*see p3* **Essential Information**), criticism does not rate as an editorial priority, but it's probably still the best you can do in English.

RADIO & TV

Anyone with access to a television in Amsterdam should engage in a bout of channel-hopping – an endless stream of music videos, recycled soap operas and serials, old-fashioned movies, soft porn, sports footage and round-the-clock news is churned out in various languages by the 15 or so satellite television channels cabled through the city. These supplement the three national channels, which are as a rule either unexcitingly worthy or in very dubious taste. The vast majority of British or American programmes have Dutch subtitles rather than being dubbed.

The Netherlands remains one of the few countries in Western Europe not to have national commercial radio and television: the broadcast media's role as a public service is

Het Parool *('The Password') was first published in 1941 and rapidly became the main organ of the Resistance* (see page 64 **World War II**). *Now trying to inch away from strong socialist associations, it has successfully emphasized its role as Amsterdam's local paper – although it is also distributed nationally and covers national and international news (often translating articles from the British* Independent). *At one time seen as the pinnacle of well-written journalism, with novelists such as Simon Carmiggelt providing regular columns, it lost ground during the eighties and is trying to claw back its market share – partly through the 'local' tag. Written in fairly straightforward Dutch, it's a good paper for foreigners to practise on.*

still jealously guarded. Legislation is tabled to introduce commercial stations in the early nineties, but they will operate under very strict conditions.

Holland is one of the most densely cabled countries in Europe. Over 80 per cent of Dutch homes get perfect reception of up to 20 television channels and dozens of radio stations, including many foreign broadcasts.

The home-grown Dutch broadcasting system is ludicrously complicated. Based on the highly democratic principle that even the tiniest minority group should be able to air its views, the resulting system involves a clear distinction between channels and 'stations'. In radio as well as TV, each 'station' or broadcasting organization is allocated airtime according to its popularity. Which 'stations' the three national TV and five national radio channels broadcast on depends on their identity and the kind of programming they produce. So, for instance, you will find at least four different 'stations' on the Nederland I TV channel.

Each broadcaster's popularity is measured, for some obscure reason, by subscription sales of the individual radio and TV guides they publish (they're also on sale at newsagents and supermarkets). So when the Dutch buy their *TV Times* they are effectively making a political statement, although each prints programme details of the other broadcasters.

Commercials are allowed to take up around five per cent of airtime and are scheduled in blocks at regular times: for instance, before and after the news. No programme may be interrupted by an advertisement, and each individual commercial begins and ends with recognizable (and excruciating) jingles to distinguish it from the programme.

TV

Nederland 1
Carries programmes of the 'stations' with a clearly identifiable 'message': the Catholic KRO, the orthodox Dutch reformed NCRV, socialist Vara and evangelical EO, for example. Programming is largely documentary.

Nederland 2
The home of the 'big three' broadcasters, none of which have an ideological base: Avro, Tros and Veronica. Programming consists mainly of glittering quiz shows, films, imported soaps such as *Neighbours* and other mainstream viewing. Highly successful and very rich, these broadcasters make few pretensions to providing anything other than mass-market entertainment: Veronica has a late-night soft porn slot, and Tros gave rise to a new Dutch word, *vertrossing*, meaning a general lowering of standards. An isolated exception is the VPRO, seen as the intellectual's entertainer and with quality documentaries, talk shows and comedy. But it only gets airtime on Sunday evenings.

Nederland 3
Major sporting and cultural/entertainment events are broadcast by the NOS, the broadcasters' umbrella organization which also provides the news on all three channels. Nederland 3 is also the home of the smaller, minority-interest broadcasters and of the Dutch Open University, *Teleac*.

RTL 4
This Luxembourg-based commercial channel won a court battle with the state in 1989 (because it is beamed via satellite from outside the country, the government was powerless to ban it). It is now well established and spews forth a largely uneventful diet of soaps, quiz shows, comedy and (sometimes watchable) films. Its news coverage is excellent, and the – Holy Reruns! – at time of writing it was repeating early *Batman* shows.

Cable Stations
The Amsterdam cable network also carries the following foreign stations: **BRT1** and **2** (Belgium), **BBC1** and **2**, three German channels, **TV5** (France), **Rai Uno** (Italy), **Super Channel** (youth-oriented pan-Europap), **MTV**, **Eurosport** (usually oldish sport footage), **CNN** (24-hour US news channel, often devoid of European content), **FilmNet** (pay-TV film channel) and the Amsterdam local station **Salto** offers an eccentric mix of straight and weird programming. Those unable to decide which channel to watch can gaze at the Infokanaal, which has two alternating screens showing what's on all the channels simultaneously.

RADIO

Roughly speaking, **Radio 1** (747kHz AM for non-cabled listeners) consists of news, documentaries and regional broadcasters, interrupted by the occasional record. **Radio 2** (92.6mHz) is similar but with more easy-listening music. **Radio 3** (96.8mHz) is pop, **Radio 4** (98.9mHz) classical and **Radio 5** (1008kHz AM) information for and about ethnic minorities and minority-interest groups. **BBC Radio 4** is rather crackly on 198kHz AM but much better on cable, as is the **BBC World Service** (1296, 3955 and 6045kHz AM).

Other cabled radio includes British Forces Broadcasting Service, Voice of America, Deutschlandfunk, three Belgian and two German stations. And there are a couple of foreign all-music commercial stations: Sky Radio (DJ-free) and Radio 10. You can even get a direct feed from the Dutch Lower House of Parliament on cable.

Shops & Services

Amsterdam has plenty of major stores, but one consequence of its trading role, past and present, is the great diversity of markets and specialist shops. Outlets for tobacco, tea and Delftware are direct links to the past; more eccentric are the shops devoted to items such as teeth, condoms, fifties' memorabilia and Christmas.

Dutch food isn't limited to cheese and pickled herrings – there seems to be a delicacy for every occasion. And should you need to hire a cocktail dress, repair a pipe or a suitcase, or consult a philosopher, we show you where to go.

CONTENTS:

HOGENDOORN & KAUFMAN

EUROPEAN CRYSTAL AND PORCELAIN, RUSSIAN ART,
OLD AND NEW DELFTWARE, RARE MATRYOSHKA'S
PALEKH AND FEDOSKINO LACQUER MINIATURES

Rokin 124
Amsterdam

Telefoon (0) 20 - 38 27 36
Telefax   (0) 20 - 38 29 01

From: Fieldings - U.S.A. 1991:
"If you have a discerning eye don't
miss this spectacular house."

BV

*A beautiful selection of Dutch flowers
available right by Central Station Amsterdam*

OPEN EVERY DAY 7:00 AM - 21:00 PM
PHONE (0)20 - 627 11 33

WH SMITH
English Bookshop

WHERE can you find

JD   Salinger
Dorothy Sayers
Simon Schama
Sir Walter Scott
Clifford D Simak
Delia Smith
Spot
and William Shakespeare

under one roof?

*At WH Smith you can choose
from a comprehensive range of
English and American
fiction and non-fiction,
children's books, greeting cards,
newspapers and
magazines.
Moreover, WH Smith
offers a prompt order service.*

WH SMITH
More to discover

Kalverstraat 152
1012 XE Amsterdam
tel. 020 - 38 38 21

Food & Drink

Made-to-measure marzipan to savour in private, exotic snacks to eat on your feet... *Jonette Stabbert* **gets her teeth into Amsterdam's food shops.**

You will never go hungry in Amsterdam. The Dutch are extremely partial to snacks, and in addition to an abundance of shops selling every kind of food and drink your palate could ever crave, fast-food counters and stalls offering native and exotic nibbles flourish in practically every street-corner. The favourite national snack is Belgian-style chips (*patates-frites*), eaten with mayonnaise. Don't knock it until you've tried it. The best stall is Vlaamsfrites at Voetboogstraat 33, off Spui. Fresh raw herring is almost as popular – the first day of the new season is quite an event (*see page 36* **Amsterdam by Season**). It's served with raw onions and purists eat it head first in one gulp, dangling it by the tail. Amsterdam's best herring stall is **Bloemburg Vis Specialiteiten** (*listed under* **Fish**).

Laws regarding the import of foods and alcoholic beverages vary from country to country. In general, most foods, except for dairy produce and unprepared meat products, can be freely imported within the EC, and you can almost always ship non-perishable items anywhere without problems. The best way to find out your allowances is to ask customs officials as you leave your home country. Your embassy (*see page 221* **Survival**) should also be able to help.

For late-closing shops, *see page 144* **Early Hours**.

BAKERIES

There are two kinds of bakeries. For bread, rolls and packaged biscuits, go to a *warme bakker*, for pastries and wickedly delicious cream-cakes, you need a *banketbakker*. See also *below* **Chocolate**.

Harrison's
Kinkerstraat 339, OW (612 2380). Tram 7, 17. **Open** 10am-6pm Tue-Fri; 10am-5pm Sat. **No credit cards.**
This is the place to go should you ever require a huge, multi-tiered and elaborately decorated wedding cake that will feed 3,000. You can custom-order a cake in any shape, colour or flavour – and even have it sent abroad. There is also a mouthwatering selection of French pastries and American cheesecakes, available in individual servings, and a wide choice of marzipan flowers and other edible cake decorations.

Hendrikse
Overtoom 472, OW (618 0472). Tram 1, 6. **Open** 8.30am-5.30pm Mon-Fri; 8.30am-4.30pm Sat. **Credit** AmEx, V.
Cake suppliers to the Dutch royal family, Hendrikse is unequalled for quality. More than 20 types of tart are sold, including advocaat, plus cream cakes and a wide choice of traditional Dutch pastries and biscuits from all over the country. No chemical additives are used.

Multi-Vlaai
Vijzelstraat 137, IS (688 0106). Tram 16, 24, 25. **Open** noon-6pm Mon; 8.30am-5pm Tue-Fri; 8.30am-5pm Sat. **Credit** AmEx, DC, MC, V.
A *vlaai* is a traditional pie from Limburg, in the south of The Netherlands. This shop has 22 varieties brought in fresh daily from Limburg. Buy a whole pie, or enjoy a slice with tea or coffee in the shop. The most traditional flavour is a rice-custard (*rijstevlaai*), but apple-lemon (*appel-citroen*) is currently very popular. Branches throughout Amsterdam.

Oldenburg
PC Hooftstraat 97, OS (662 8363). Tram 2, 3, 5, 12. **Open** 9am-6pm Mon-Wed, Fri; 9am-9pm Thur; 8.30am-5.30pm Sat. **No credit cards.**
This is one of two Oldenburg *banketbakker* in Amsterdam, specializing in fancy dessert cakes, bavarois and chocolate mousse tarts. You can also buy home-made chocolates and marvellous marzipan confections in winter and chocolate eggs and bunnies at Easter. Every month, a different theme is featured in the window, and the displays are admired by all.
Branch: Maasstraat 84, OS (662 2840).

Paul Anneé
Runstraat 25, IW (623 5322). Tram 1, 2, 5, 7, 10. **Open** 8am-5pm Mon-Fri; 9am-3pm Sat. **No credit cards.**
Everything at this *warme bakker* is freshly baked daily from organically grown grains. Try the popular sour-dough bread and the cakes. There is a display of the (non-edible) bread decorations for which the shop is famous. Unfortunately, these must be ordered at least one week in advance. There are also health food products for sale.

Pool
Ceintuurbaan 278, OS (662 1409). Tram 3, 12, 24, 25. **Open** 8am-5.30pm Mon-Fri; 8am-3pm Sat. **No credit cards.**
One of the best bread bakeries in Amsterdam; on Saturday mornings there is often a queue right around the block.

Choose from white or wholemeal loaves baked from a variety of grains. Particularly recommended is *roggevloer* (rye bread). You can also buy sandwiches.

CHEESE

Every Dutch adult consumes about 13 kilogrammes (six pounds) of cheese per year. There are plenty of varieties to choose from. In general, the younger (*jong*) the cheese, the creamier and milder it will be. Riper cheeses (*belegen* or even *extra belegen*) will be drier and sharper-tasting. The most popular cheeses are called *Goudse* (from Gouda), followed by *Leidse*, which is flavoured with cumin seeds, and *Edammer*, with its red crust. Four interesting cheeses to get you started are: *Friese nagelkaas*, a ripe cheese whose sharp flavour is enhanced by cumin seeds and cloves; *Kernhem*, a good dessert cheese; *Leerdammer* and *Maaslander*. These last two differ slightly from each other, but both are mild, with holes. If you are interested in visiting a cheese-producing town, *see page 203* **Excursions in Holland**.

Kef, French Cheesemakers
Marnixstraat 192, IW (626 2210). Tram 3, 10. **Open** 10am-6pm Tue-Thur; 9am-6pm Fri; 9am-4pm Sat. **No credit cards.**
French cheesemaker Abraham Kef set up shop over 35 years ago and his shop still imports the finest selection of French cheeses – more than 70 – in Amsterdam. The range of goats' cheeses is particularly good. The shop looks its age in the nicest possible way; it's tiny, dark and wood-furnished, with tastings from oak tables until an hour before closing time. You'll receive expert advice. There is also an assortment of good French wines, pâtés, sausages and baguettes.

Wegewijs Kaas
Rozengracht 32, IW (624 4093). Tram 13, 14, 17. **Open** 8.30am-6pm Mon-Fri; 8.30am-5pm Sat. **No credit cards.**
This authentic Dutch cheese shop has been run by the Wegewijs family at the same address for the past 100 years. The Rozengracht, now an avenue, was then still a canal and cheese was delivered by boat. On offer are 50 foreign cheeses and over 100 domestic varieties, including *gras kaas*, a grassy-tasting cheese only available in summer. You can taste the Dutch cheeses before making your selection. They also sell sandwich fillings, bread and wine, and will send cheeses abroad.

CHOCOLATE

Dutch cocoa is famous all over the world, and when made into chocolate, the taste defies description. Try some and you'll want to stay forever.

Hendrikse Le Confiseur
Overtoom 448-450, OW (618 0260). Tram 1, 6. **Open** 8.30am-noon, 1-5.30pm, Tue-Fri; 8.30am-4.30pm Sat. **No credit cards.**
Hendrikse specializes in the finest handmade chocolates. Try *gianduja*, a fudge-like chocolate log made with ground hazelnuts and almonds. Marzipan figures are also a speciality (can be designed to order), and you can get delicious fruit preserves.

Macrander
Vijzelstraat 125, IS (623 3102). Tram 16, 24, 25. **Open** 9am-6pm Mon-Fri; 8.30am-5pm Sat. **No credit cards.**
See p151 picture and caption.

DELICATESSENS

Dikker & Thijs
Prinsengracht 444, IW (626 7721). Tram 1, 2, 5. **Open** 11am-6pm Tue-Sat. **Credit** AmEx, DC, MC, V.
Frequented by foodies in search of gourmet ingredients, Dikker & Thijs is the last word in food shops. Expensive and exotic goodies such as truffles can be bought here, as well as complete take-away meals made to recipes served at their three top restaurants (*see p79* **Restaurants**).

Eicholtz
Leidsestraat 48, IS (622 0305). Tram 1, 2, 5. **Open** 10am-6pm Mon; 9am-6pm Tue, Wed, Fri; 9am-9pm Thur; 9am-5pm Sat. **Credit** (minimum f32) AmEx, V.

Lots of imported foods, notably from the USA and Britain, are available here, plus Dutch souvenirs (chocolate tiles and so on).

ETHNIC

Most general markets have stalls offering authentic foreign snacks such as Vietnamese or Indonesian egg rolls (*loempia*), filled Indian pancakes (*roti*) and Surinam chicken pasties (*kippepasteitje*). Favourite takeaway foods available at snack bars are Chinese-Indonesian rice (*nasi*) and noodle (*bami*) dishes, Indonesian skewered meat with spicy peanut butter sauce (*sateh*) and the ubiquitous pizza.

Florence Exotic Catering
Noordermarkt, IW (699 0868 after 6pm; home phone number, so please ring at reasonable times). **No credit cards.**
Once you've sampled the spicy, authentic Surinam take-away snacks from Florence's food stall at the Noorderkerk end of the Noordermarkt, you will probably come back for more. She also caters wonderfully exotic dinners and buffets for any number. Prices are reasonable and the food is delicious. The delivery charge is f30, and a week's notice is preferred. Tip: for those who like it hot, ask for the red sauce. For a

description of Surinam cuisine, *see p79* **Restaurants.**

Hellas
Hobbemastraat 26A, OS (662 7238). Tram 6, 7, 10. **Open** 9am-6pm Mon-Fri; 9am-5pm Sat. **No credit cards.**
Greek delicacies and wines, freshly-made snacks and salads, cheeses, filo pastry and vine leaves fill the shelves here.

Meidi-Ya
Beethovenstraat 18-20, OS (673 7410). Tram 5. **Open** 10am-6pm Mon-Wed, Fri; 10am-9pm Thur; 9am-5pm Sat. **No credit cards.**
A Japanese supermarket with every food and condiment necessary to the Japanese kitchen including fresh greens, flown in specially, and saké. Snacks can be eaten at the sushi bar and there are hot dishes and snacks for take-away.

Mouwes Kosher Delicatessen
Utrechtsestraat 73, IS (623 5053). Tram 4. **Open** 1-6pm Mon; 8.30am-6pm Tue-Thur; 8.30am-dusk Fri; 10am-7pm Sun. **No credit cards.**
Come here for a good range of kosher Jewish specialities such as bagels, gefilte fish, blintzes and American-style kosher pickles. Take-away or enjoy in their small dining area.

Smeraglia
Kinkerstraat 21, OW (616 6895). Tram 7,

Certain foods have long been associated with special celebrations in The Netherlands, but many of these traditions are now falling by the wayside. This has the dubious advantage that the more popular delicacies are becoming available year-round as they gradually metamorphose into tourist novelties.

December is a big month for sweet-giving. The excesses of the Christmas season have in the past centred around St Nicholas' Day (5 December), with Christmas Day itself reserved for more reverent celebrations, but recently the commercial jamboree has extended into Christmas proper (*see page 36* **Amsterdam by Season**). Exchanged as St Nicholas gifts are chocolate letters (you would give someone their initial), while artistically executed marzipan (*marsepein*) models are given throughout December. These are imaginative, detailed and varied; you can get pigs complete with a litter of piglets, money, cartoon characters and joints of meat.

It's customary for adults to play tricks on each other at St Nicholas

and they often buy (or commission) joke *marsepein* figures such as anatomically correct human figures (with or without fig leaf). Macrander, *listed under* **Chocolate**, keeps a selection all year round and has brought the tradition up to date by offering a marzipan computer. Another seasonal sweetmeat is *banket staf*, marzipan covered in butter pastry, either shaped into large letters or small rods meant to represent St Nicholas's staff. Models of St Nick himself are made out of *taai-taai*, a heavy gingerbread decorated with candied fruit and nuts. This tradition is dying: the figures used to be moulded on special wooden biscuit boards (still sold as souvenirs), but now they are mass-produced.

There's no respite from tooth-rot in the New Year, which is celebrated with *oliebollen* – large, deep-fried balls of dough coated in sugar. The story goes that doughnuts originate from a mis-shapen *oliebol*.

Birthdays are important occasions in The Netherlands: celebrants are expected to treat their friends, family and co-workers to cream cakes.

Marzipan-filled cakes in the shape of Abraham and Sarah are given as gifts. Tiny pancake puffs called *poffertjes* are associated with the celebrations for the Queen's birthday, when there used to be lots of stalls and competitions for the best *poffertje*. Now they are available all year round; there's an old-fashioned stand on Weteringcircuit at the top of Vijzelstraat.

When a baby is born, *muisjes op biscuit* (candied aniseeds on rusks) or *kandeel* (a heavenly mixture of warm wine with milk, sugar, egg yolks and cinnamon) is distributed to close friends of the family. *Kandeel*, originally given to the pregnant mother to keep evil spirits away, is a dying tradition, but there's still at least one shop in Amsterdam where you can buy it:

Van Gelder Fruitgeschenken
Parnassusweg 3, OS (662 8322). **Open** 8.30am-5.30pm Mon-Fri; 8.30am-3pm Sat. **No credit cards.**
VG's principal business is in fruit hampers, but it also sells *kandeel*, made and bottled specially. It comes in 50cl bottles (f14.50) lying in miniature ruffled pink or blue bassinets. A great gift for expectant parents.

17. **Open** 11am-6pm Mon-Fri; 10am-5pm Sat. **No credit cards.**
The friendly staff here can provide you with northern and southern Italian foods, wines and spirits.

Toko Ramee
Ferdinand Bolstraat 74, OS (662 2025).
Tram 16, 24, 25. **Open** 9am-6pm Tue-Fri; 9am-5pm Sat. **No credit cards.**
All the spices and ingredients used in Indonesian cooking are sold here, plus Chinese and Thai ingredients and take-away dishes. Fresh tropical greens on Fridays only.

FISH

Bloemberg Vis Specialiteiten
Van Baerlestraat, across from Concertgebouw and between Stedelijk Museum and the corner. *Tram 2, 3, 5, 12, 16.* **Open** 9am-5pm Tue-Sat. **No credit cards.**
This famous herring stall is a must for anyone wishing to sample Dutch herring or mackerel. The owner is a recipient of the coveted 'Golden Herring of Amsterdam' award for his delicious cured fish and fish sandwiches. Take-away, or snack at one of the outdoor tables.

Viscenter Volendam
Kinkerstraat 181, OW (618 7062). *Tram 7, 17.* **Open** 8am-6pm Mon-Sat. **Credit** AmEx, MC, V.
The family that runs this popular shop commutes from Volendam, a major fishing village. It offers a large selection of freshwater and sea fish, shellfish, cured fish (try the smoked eels – *gerookte paling*), take-away snacks and seafood salads.

HEALTH FOOD

Manna
Spui 1, C (625 3743). *Tram 1, 2, 5.* **Open** 1-6pm Mon; 9am-6pm Tue, Wed, Fri; 9am-9pm Thur; 9am-5pm Sat. **No credit cards.**
Amsterdam's most popular organic food store. Fresh, bottled and frozen foods, wine, beer, cosmetics and aromatherapy oils are all guaranteed free of artificial additives. Bread and pastry are baked daily on the premises. Take-away meals; café.

MINERAL WATER

Waterwinkel
Roelof Hartstraat 10, OS (675 5932). *Tram 3, 12, 24.* **Open** 9am-6pm Mon-Fri; 9am-5pm Sat. **No credit cards.**
Owner Jan Willem Bakker boasts of stocking 100 bottled mineral waters from around the world. Customers are encouraged to sample before buying, and bottles can be gift-wrapped and shipped. There is even mud from the Dead Sea; you don't drink it, you apply it as a balm for acne and arthritis.

OFF-LICENCES

The legal age for buying or being served beer is 16, and for wine and spirits it's 18. Beer (*pils*) and Dutch gin (*jenever*) are the most popular alcoholic drinks, although many people enjoy a good glass of wine.

Despair of dieting, all ye who enter **Macrander** *(see under* **Chocolate***). Sumptuous chocolate confections, rich chocolate cream cakes and truly wonderful marzipan figures (available all year round, see* **Special Occasion Food***) are on display, all made on the premises. Purchases can be gift-wrapped, and even shipped abroad. The shop is also a combination pastry bakery* (banketbakkerij) *and tea room, where you can enjoy a quiet cuppa while indulging your gluttony. Lunches are also served and include such specialities as Dutch pea soup* (erwtensoep). *The owners treat customers like honoured guests in the intimate Dutch décor.*

Wines often cost less at an off-licence than at the airport tax-free shopping centre. This is also true of spirits if they are on special offer.

De Bierkoning
Paleisstraat 125, C (625 2336). *Tram 1, 2, 5, 13, 14, 17.* **Open** 1-6pm Mon; 11am-6pm Tue, Wed, Fri; 11am-9pm Thur; 11am-5pm Sat. **No credit cards.**
'The Beer King', named for its location opposite the Royal Palace, stocks approximately 750 different brands of beer from around the world, as well as beer glasses.

De Cuyp
Albert Cuypstraat 146, OS (662 6676). *Tram 4, 16, 24, 25.* **Open** 9am-6pm Mon-Sat. **No credit cards.**
Specializing in miniature and giant bottles, De Cuyp stocks more than 3,000 miniatures. Huge bottles include an eight-litre bottle of *jenever* and a 21-litre bottle of champagne. There is a large international assortment of wines and spirits, including unusual Surinam drinks such as tropical fruit spirits.

Wijnkoperij Woorts
Utrechtsestraat 51, IS (623 7426). *Tram 4.*

Open 1-6pm Mon; 9am-6pm Tue-Fri; 9am-5pm Sat. **No credit cards.**
A wine lover's paradise, offering over 600 varieties, with the emphasis on those from Italy. Tasting sessions are held all day on Saturday and qualified advice is available. Some of the bottles have unique labels depicting the work of contemporary Dutch artists, and are becoming collectors' items.

TEA & COFFEE

Keizer
Prinsengracht 180, IW (624 0823). *Tram 13, 14, 17.* **Open** 9am-5.30pm Mon-Fri; 9am-5pm Sat. **No credit cards.**
This is *the* tea and coffee specialist. In business at the same address since 1839 and with much of the original tiled décor, Keizer carries everything and anything to do with brewing and serving. A vast selection of coffees and teas (some organically grown), spices, traditional Dutch sweets from all over the country and unusual utensils make shopping for gifts easy. For f20 you can buy a decorative tile made of pressed tea. In ancient China, these were used as currency when buying horses from Mongolia. No home should be without one.

metz&co ®

BY APPOINTMENT TO THE COURT OF THE NETHERLANDS

A world without boundaries
A world of romance and elegance
A personal adventure and a way of life.

metz&co
Since 1740

LEIDSESTRAAT   AMSTERDAM

Shopping Around

Small is not only beautiful, it borders on the ubiquitous when applied to the shops in this compact city. But, finds *Jonette Stabbert*, variety means vitality.

Amsterdammers love to shop. They especially love the intimacy of small shops, and that's just as well because their city has a significant lack of department stores and an abundance of tiny, quirky shops.

The best shopping street for fashion in Amsterdam is PC Hooftstraat (IS). Unfortunately, it is also the priciest. Beautiful window displays and smartly turned-out customers grace this ultra-chic street. Nearly every store carries top-name designer labels for men, women and children. Quality footwear is another strength. Most shops on the street offer tax-free shopping to tourists and it is worth taking advantage of this – Dutch VAT (called BTW) is a hefty 18.5 per cent on most goods. The tax is included in the price tag.

Van Baerlestraat (IS) has a junction with PC Hooftstraat and is beginning to rival it for smart shopping. The most interesting stretch of this long street is within the four-block area between Jan Willem Brouwersstraat and Vossiusstraat.

If you're on the look-out for unusual or handcrafted gifts or clothing, wander through the Jordaan (IW, *see page 26* **Amsterdam by Area**). The small side streets running parallel to Rozengracht, such as 1e and 2e Bloemdwarsstraat and their extensions, and Elandsgracht, will divulge a wealth of tiny, interesting businesses. Antiques can be found around Looiersgracht and also in the area around the Rijksmuseum, notably Spiegelgrach, IS.

If you're aiming to go on a spending spree, plan your visit to coincide with the sales. These are mostly in January and February, then again in July and August. And don't neglect the markets if you're looking for bargains. The Dutch claim that a guilder at a market will buy 2½ guilders' worth of merchandise, and this tends to be true.

Most tourists who want to do all their shopping in one area flock to Kalverstraat (IW), but it can be very crowded and merchandise is generally very run of the mill. Leidsestraat (IW) is full of bogus souvenirs – some are even made in Taiwan. Damstraat

(C) also has many souvenir shops, but also many pickpockets. Beethovenstraat (OS) is clean, uncrowded and has an attractive array of better, more diverse shops.

General opening hours are 9am to 6pm on weekdays. Many stores are closed on Mondays or are only open in the afternoon (1-6pm). On Saturdays, most businesses close by 5pm and some as early as 3pm. Late-night shopping is on Thursday evenings, when many stores are open until 9pm, but phone first to be certain. Credit cards were slow to catch on in Dutch shops, but these days most large stores and many small shops accept them.

AUCTION

All auctions held in The Netherlands are carried out in Dutch. However, the management will arrange for someone to bid for you. A premium of between 16 and 30 per cent is payable on all purchases; BTW (Dutch VAT, usually 18.5 per cent) must be paid on the premium. Sotheby's (*627 5656*) and Christie's (*575 5255*) each have a branch in Amsterdam, but their Dutch counterpart is Gijselman's.

L Gijselman
Overtoom 197, OW (616 8586). Tram 1, 6. **Open** 9am-5pm Mon-Fri. **Auctions** usually 10am, 2pm, Tue, Wed. **No credit cards.**
The only thing we don't auction are human beings', we were told by Gijselman's. The firm was established in 1813, making it one of the oldest auctioneers in The Netherlands; it is still owned by the Gijselman family. Recent specialized auctions have included sales of paintings by a student of Van Gogh, and unique toy collections. When an international public is expected, the catalogue is printed in English. Once a month, household goods are auctioned. This is a particularly good source of art deco furnishings.

BOOKS

GENERAL BOOKSHOPS

American Discount Book Center
Kalverstraat 185, C (625 5537). Tram 1, 2, 4, 5, 9, 14, 16, 24, 25. **Open** 10am-10pm

Mon-Sat; 11am-7pm Sun. **Credit** AmEx, DC, MC, V.
A huge stock of American and English titles is sold, both fiction and non-fiction, mostly in paperback. There is also a very large selection of magazines and some second-hand paperbacks. The shop has a good line in children's books.

Athenaeum Nieuwscentrum
Spui 14-16, C (624 2972). Tram 1, 2, 5. **Open** 8am-10pm Mon-Sat; 10am-6pm Sun. **Credit** (minimum f50) AmEx, MC, V.
A favourite hang-out of highbrow browsers, Athenaeum stocks newspapers from all over the world, as well as magazines and quality books in many languages. There is a section for fiction, but the shop's strength lies in its non-fiction collection.

The Book Exchange
Kloveniersburgwal 58, C (626 6266). Tram 9, 14/Metro Nieuwmarkt. **Open** 10am-6pm Mon-Fri; 10am-5pm Sat. **No credit cards.**
Second-hand English and American books, mostly paperbacks, both fiction and factual, are bought and sold. There is also a selection of books in Dutch, German and French.

The English Bookshop
Lauriergracht 71, IW (626 4230). Tram 7, 10/bus 25, 65, 66, 67, 170, 171, 172. **Open** 11am-6pm Mon-Sat. **No credit cards.**
English books (both fiction and non-fiction) share shelf space with a selection of British magazines, including *Time Out*.

Oudemanhuis Book Market
Oudemanhuispoort (off Oudezijds Achterburgwal), C. Tram 4, 9, 14, 16, 24, 25. **Open** 10am-4pm Mon-Sat.
A fabulous collection of printed matter finds its way onto the stalls of this market. Old magazines and postcards, second-hand books, sheet music, antique tomes – all in a hodgepodge of conditions, a mélange of subjects and in multifarious languages. *See also p53* **War & Reformation**.

De Slegte
Kalverstraat 48-52, C (622 5933). Tram 4, 9, 14, 16, 24, 25. **Open** 11am-6pm Mon; 9.30am-6pm Mon-Sat; 10am-6pm Thur; 9.30am-5pm Sat. **No credit cards.**
One of the city's largest bookshops, De Slegte carries a vast number of volumes in English, Dutch and other languages (including textbooks and children's books, fiction and non-fiction). It is mainly an antiquarian shop, but there are always some new titles on special offer. Prices are usually low.

W H Smith
Kalverstraat 152, C (638 3821). Tram 4, 9, 14, 16, 24, 25. **Open** 9am-6pm Mon-Wed, Fri; 9am-9pm Thur; 10am-5pm Sat; 11am-4pm Sun. **Credit** AmEx, MC, V.
A large, attractive establishment where you can take your pick from a great many titles (fiction and non-fiction) all in English. It also carries all the major English-language magazines.

SPECIALIST BOOKSHOPS

For other specialist bookshops, *see page 126* **Theatre**, *page 130* **Music: Classical & Opera**, *page 169* **Gay**

There's a nostalgic atmosphere at **De Speelmuis** (see under **Children: Toys**) *that emanates from the wide collection of wooden toy furniture, vehicles and garages. You can also buy handmade doll's house miniatures and teddy bears, musical instruments, Victorian-style gifts for adults, unusual wrapping paper, cards and child-size cooking utensils that really work. Children are allowed to play with many of the toys in the shop.*

Amsterdam, *page 176* **Women's Amsterdam**, and *page 196* **Students**.

Architectura & Natura
Leliegracht 44, IW (623 6186). Tram 13, 14, 17. **Open** 9am-6pm Tue-Fri; 9am-5pm Sat. **No credit cards.**
The name says it all: architecture and nature. The stock includes photographic books of buildings, field guides and animal studies. Many of the books are in English.

Canon Bookstore
Leidsestraat 79 (upstairs from Canon Gallery), IS (625 4494). Tram 1, 2, 5, 6, 7, 10. **Open** *summer* noon-5.45pm Tue-Fri; 11am-4.45pm Sat; *rest of year* noon-5.45pm Tue-Fri; 11am-4.45pm Sat, Sun. **Credit** AmEx, MC, V.
Every aspect of photography is covered at Canon, including technique, in beautiful volumes covering diverse subjects. Many are in English. The shop is above the Canon Photography Gallery, *see p111* **Galleries**.

Intertaal
Van Baerlestraat 76, OS (671 5353). Tram 3, 5, 12, 16. **Open** 9.15am-6pm Mon-Fri; 9.15am-5pm Sat. **Credit** AmEx, MC.
Grapplers with Dutch grammar might gain some succour from the language books, records and teaching aids kept at Intertaal. Students of English and other languages are also provided for.

Jacob van Wijngaarden (Geographische Boekhandel)
Overtoom 136, OW (612 1901). Tram 1, 6. **Open** 1-6pm Mon; 10am-6pm Tue-Fri; 10am-5pm Sat. **No credit cards.**
Every part of our planet comes up for inspection in the geography books, maps and travel guides sold at Wijngaarden. A great deal of the stock is in English.

Lambiek
Kerkstraat 78, IS (626 7543). Tram 1, 2, 5. **Open** 11am-6pm Mon-Fri; 11am-5pm Sat. **Credit** AmEx, MC, V.
Lambiek claims to be the oldest comic shop in the world (established in 1968) and has thousands of comic books from all over the world: some are collector's items. There's a cartoonists' gallery with a new exhibition of comic art for sale every two months. A brochure is given free to customers.

CAMERA SUPPLIES

Foto Professional
Nieuwendijk 113, C (624 6024). Tram 4, 9, 14, 16, 24, 25. **Open** 10am-6pm Mon-Wed, Fri; 10am-9pm Thur; 10am-5pm Sat. **Credit** AmEx, DC, MC, f£$DMTC, V.
This is an official dealer for Hasselblad, Leica, Nikon, Minolta, Canon, Pentax, Sony and Olympus. Cameras, camcorders and audio-visual equipment are sold new and second-hand.

CHILDREN

BABIES' NEEDS

Disposable nappies and bottled food can be purchased at groceries and supermarkets. Drugstores also carry dummies and powders.

Prénatal
Kalverstraat 42, C (626 6392). Tram 4, 9, 14, 16, 24, 25. **Open** 1-6pm Mon; 9.30am-6pm Tue, Wed, Fri; 9am-5.30pm, 6.30-9pm, Thur; 9.30am-5pm Sat. **Credit** AmEx.
Four floors of goods for expectant mothers and small children (new-borns to five-year-olds). There are stacks of clothing, toys and furniture, plus cotton nappies for babies.

BOOKS

De Kinderboekwinkel
Nieuwezijds Voorburgwal 344, C (622 7741). Tram 1, 2, 5. **Open** 10am-6pm Tue-Fri; 10am-5pm Sat. **No credit cards.**
The large selection of books in English and other languages is attractively displayed and arranged according to age.
Branch 1e Bloemdwarsstraat 21 (622 4761).

Lankamp & Brinkman
Spiegelgracht 19, IW (623 4656/4512). Tram 6, 7, 10. **Open** 1-6pm Mon; 9am-6pm Tue-Fri; 10am-5pm Sat. **Credit** AmEx, DC, MC, V.
The first floor of this bookshop has a special children's section containing quality books from all over the world, including *Little Golden Books*. The staff claim to have Amsterdam's largest collection of children's books in English.

CHILDREN'S CLOTHES

't Schooltje
Overtoom 87, OW (683 0444). Tram 1, 2, 5, 6. **Open** 1-6pm Mon; 9am-6pm Tue-Fri; 9.30am-5pm Sat. **Credit** AmEx, DC, MC, V.
The well-heeled, well-dressed child is fitted out here. The clothing and shoes for babies and children aged up to 16 are attractive but expensive.

Second Time
Frans Halslaan 31, Amstelveen, OS (647 3036). Bus 66. **Open** 10am-4pm Mon; 10am-5pm Tue-Sat. **No credit cards.**
Wonderful bargains in second-hand clothes for babies and children can be unearthed at this shop. Outfits are top brands and in good condition.

Wampie
2e Anjeliersdwarsstraat 19, IW (627 1675). Tram 3, 10. **Open** 11am-2pm Mon; 11am-6pm Tue-Fri; 11am-5pm Sat. **Credit** AmEx, MC, V.
Original fashions at affordable prices. Partners Henny and Lillian create casual clothing in brightly coloured fabrics (mostly cotton) for children aged up to seven. There are toys to amuse the kids while you browse.

TOYS

The Bell Tree
Spiegelgracht 10, IS (625 8830). Tram 6, 7, 10. **Open** 1-6pm Mon; 9am-6pm Tue-Fri; 9am-5pm Sat. **Credit** AmEx, MC, V.
Old-fashioned dolls and toys in natural materials are stocked here, along with children's books in various languages. The shop is run by a devotee of Rudolf Steiner.

De Speelmuis
Elandsgracht 58, IW (638 5342). Tram 7, 10. **Open** 10am-6pm Tue-Fri; 10am-5pm Sat. **No credit cards.**
See **picture and caption.**

FASHION

ACCESSORIES

Body Sox
Leidsestraat 35, IS (627 6553). Tram 1, 2, 5.
Open noon-6pm Mon; 9.30am-6pm Tue,
Wed, Fri; 9.30am-9pm Thur; 9.30am-5pm
Sat. **Credit** AmEx, MC, V.
Step out in the latest designer tights from
Mary Quant, Pierre Cardin and others.
There's a large assortment of socks, tights,
body stockings and lingerie.

The English Hatter
Heiligeweg 40, C (623 4781). Tram 1, 2, 5.
Open 1-5.30pm Mon; 9am-5.30pm Tue-Fri;
9am-5pm Sat. **Credit** AmEx, DC, JCB,
MC, V.
Hats, caps and other headwear at a variety of
prices find shelf space here, as do jumpers,
shirts and ties. Goods are directed at men,
but are popular with women.

BESPOKE TAILORING

Paul Neve
*Bilderdijkkade 70, OW (618 1129). Tram 7,
12, 13, 14, 17.* **Open** 10am-6pm Mon-Fri;
10am-5pm Sat. **Credit** AmEx, fTC.
Paul Neve has been making trousers here
for 21 years and he believes he's the last tailor in Amsterdam to specialize in them.
Denim trousers cost around f175 and wool
mohair between f250 and f300. Everything
is made to the client's specifications.

CLUBWEAR

WILD!
Kerkstraat 104, IS (626 0749). Tram 1, 2, 5.
Open 1-6pm Tue, Wed, Fri, Sat; 1-9pm Thur.
Credit AmEx, MC, V.
WILD! sells the latest clubwear and house
clothing, much of it designed and made in
Amsterdam. Look out for the exciting T-
shirts. *WILD!* magazine is on sale, giving
information on music and club events, par-
ties and fashions.

DESIGNER FASHION

Antonia
*Gasthuismolensteeg 12, IW (627 2433).
Tram 1, 2, 5, 13, 14, 17.* **Open** 11am-6pm
Tue-Sat. **Credit** AmEx, DC, MC, V.
The top young Dutch designers find a showcase at Antonia, including Gletcher, Imps,
Orson and Bodil. There are also underwear
and swimwear from True Falsies and fantastic footwear from Lola Pagola (suede and
crocodile). Men's garments include shirts,
suits and underwear.

Modegalerie Summat
*Zeedijk 39, C (638 2821). Tram 4, 9, 16, 24,
25/Metro Nieuwmarkt.* **Open** 10am-noon, 1-
6pm, Tue-Fri; 10am-noon, 1-5pm, Sat. **Credit**
AmEx, DC, MC.
Tina Withagen takes on four young designers every two months to show their work in
this gallery-cum-shop. Two of these are
clothes designers, the other two make
accessories such as bags, belts, hats, and
even lingerie. Most of the designers are
Dutch. Every November Ms Withagen features a collection for men.

HAUTE COUTURE

Edgar Vos
*PC Hooftstraat 134, OS (662 6336). Tram 2,
3, 5, 12.* **Open** 9am-6pm Mon-Wed, Fri;
9am-9pm Thur; 9am-5pm Sat. **Credit** AmEx,
DC, MC, TC, V.
Many of Mr Vos's customers are internationally fashionable businesswomen. His
good-looking suits are often severely tai-
lored, in gorgeous natural fabrics.

Frank Govers
*Keizersgracht 500, IS (622 8670). Tram 1, 2,
5.* **Open** 10am-6pm Mon-Sat. **Credit** AmEx,
fTC, V.
Given the prices of the clothes here, Frank
Govers attracts a surprisingly wide variety of
clients, ranging from a priestess wanting
vestments to a diamond heiress after a mil-
lion-guilder, diamond-embroidered wedding
dress. Ready-to-wear starts from f1,000 and
haute couture from f3,000.

HIGH-STREET FASHION

Kamikaze Broads
*St Luciensteeg 21, C (627 9702). Tram 1, 2,
5.* **Open** 11.50am-6pm Mon; 9.50am-6pm
Tue, Wed, Fri, Sat; 9.50am-9pm Thur. **Credit**
AmEx, MC, fTC, V.
Slightly off-beat high-street fashion for
young women brings in the cash at
Kamikaze. Casual clothing predominates.

Khymo
*Kalverstraat 66, IS (622 2137). Tram 1, 2,
5.* **Open** 10am-6pm Mon-Wed, Fri; 10am-
9pm Thur; 10am-5.30pm Sat. **Credit** AmEx,
DC, MC, V.
Trendy fashions for trendy twenty- and
thirty-somethings, both male and female.
Labels include Katharine Hamnett and Jean
Paul Gaultier.

Onadur
*Spiegelgracht 6, IS (626 3735). Tram 1, 2, 5,
6, 7, 10.* **Open** 10.30am-6pm Tue-Fri;
10.30am-5pm Sat. **Credit** AmEx, MC, V.
This boutique carries beautiful, timeless,
women's fashions in colours that compensate for the lack of sunlight in northern
climates and look good on every type of figure. Only natural fabrics are used. There's a
full range of clothing, including knitwear
and large sizes.

Need a pair of red stilettoes a foot long? The imaginatively named **Big Shoe**
(see under **Fashion: Shoes***) specializes in fashionable footwear for large sizes
only. Every shoe on display is available in size 46 to 50 for men (American size 12
to 16; British size 11 to 15) and size 41 to 46 for women (American size 10 to 15;
British size 8½ to 13½). Designs include modern, sporty, classical and chic styles
in the latest colours; high heels, sandals, boots and gym shoes are all available.*

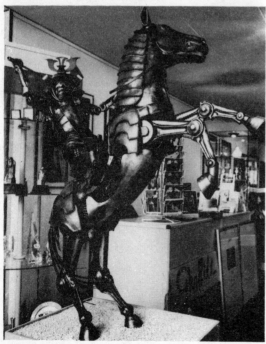

YIN & YANG

The International

THE INTERNATIONAL
ART & DESIGN GALLERY

OPENING HOURS
MO. 11.00 - 18.00
THUE/SAT 09.00 - 18.00
SUN 14.00 - 17.00
THU 9.00 - 21.00

PAINTINGS
SCULPTURES
LIMITED EDITIONS OF
LITHOGRAPS &
SILK - SCREEN PRINTS

REGULIERS-
DWARSSTRAAT 84
TEL: 020 - 620 49 77
FAX: 020 - 620 49 69

LARGE SIZES

Duco
Overtoom 167A, OW (683 0184). Tram 1,
6. **Open** 1-5.30pm Mon; 10am-5.30pm Tue-
Fri; 10am-5pm Sat. **Credit** AmEx.
Attractive women's clothing in bright
colours comes in size 46 up to 60 (American
size 16 to 30; British size 18 to 26).

G & G Special Sizes
Prinsengracht 514, IW (622 6339). Tram 1,
2, 5. **Open** 9am-5.30pm Tue, Wed, Fri; 9am-
5.30pm, 7-9pm, Thur; 9am-5pm Sat. **Credit**
AmEx, DC, MC, V.
This store stocks a full range of men's clothing from size 58 up to 75 (American and
British size 48 to 65). Staff also tailor garments to fit.

LINGERIE

Tony Tolo
Kinkerstraat 161, OW (612 0940). Tram 7,
17. **Open** noon-6pm Mon; 9am-6pm Tue,
Wed, Fri; 9am-9pm Thur; 9am-5pm Sat.
Credit AmEx, DC, MC, V.
The last word in lingerie shops. You'll find
garments from every designer imagin-
able, ranging in price from f16 to f500.
Cocktail dresses cost between f1,000 and
f1,500.

Victoria's Secrets
Leidsestraat 32, IW (638 4163). Tram 1, 2,
5. **Open** noon-6pm Mon; 9am-6pm Tue,
Wed, Fri; 9am-9pm Thur; 9am-5.30pm Sat.
Credit AmEx, DC, MC, V.
Victoria's Secrets is more expensive than
the average lingerie shop, since its attractive goods are all made of high-quality
materials, including silk. Bras cost from f89
to f250. Sleepwear and swimwear is also
stocked.

SHOES

In addition to the shops below, try
the numerous posh boutiques in PC
Hooftstraat for exclusive, expensive
footwear.

Big Shoe
Leliegracht 12, IW (622 6645). Tram 13, 14,
17. **Open** 10am-6pm Tue, Wed, Fri; 10am-
9pm Thur; 10am-5pm Sat. **Credit** AmEx,
DC, MC, V.
See p155 **picture and caption.**

Jan Jansen
Rokin 42, C (625 1350). Tram 4, 9, 14, 16,
24, 25. **Open** 11am-6pm Tue-Sat. **Credit**
AmEx, DC, MC, V.
Jan Jansen brings out two collections a year,
and has fashionable footwear produced for
him in Italy. Comfortable walking shoes
have been a best-seller for years, but many
styles are available.

Van Haren
Kalverstraat 153, C (623 3466). Tram 4, 9,
14, 16, 24, 25. **Open** 11am-6pm Mon;
9.30am-6pm Tue, Wed, Fri; 9.30-9pm Thur;
9.30am-5pm Sat. **Credit** AmEx, MC, V.
Van Haren carries affordable shoes for men,
women and children in the latest styles. This
is one of many branches around town.

VINTAGE & SECOND-HAND

Daffodil
Jacob Obrechtstraat 41, OS (679 5634).
Tram 2, 16. **Open** noon-6pm Tue-Fri; noon-
5pm Sat. **No credit cards.**
Second-hand haute couture for women –
including clothing, shoes, hats, shawls,
and jewellery – finds its way to Daffodil.
Names such as Hermès, Cardin and
Kenzo sell for one quarter to half the origi-
nal price.

Rose Rood
Kinkerstraat 159, OW (618 2334). Tram 7,
17. **Open** 11.30am-6pm Mon; 9.30am-6pm
Tue, Wed, Fri; 9.30am-9pm Thur; 9.30am-
5pm Sat. **No credit cards.**
Period women's clothing, from 1700 to the
sixties, is given real space in Red Rood. Take
a look at the Victorian undergarments, or
the long, luscious evening dresses.
Accessories and some new fashions are also
sold. Prices are on the low side.

GREETINGS CARDS

Cards for Days
Huidenstraat 26, IW (624 8775). Tram 1, 2,
5. **Open** noon-6pm Mon; 11am-6pm Tue-Fri;
11am-5pm Sat. **No credit cards.**
Greetings cards (most in English) to fit any
occasion are displayed here, alongside
unusual gifts such as walking balloons.

HANDICRAFTS

Annabelle
Elandsgracht 116, IW (625 9780). Tram 7,
10. **Open** 1-5pm Tue-Sat. **Credit** AmEx, DC,
MC, V.
Unusual handcrafted gifts and toys; specialities include miniature bears and mice for
collectors. Goods are made by craftswork-
ers throughout The Netherlands.

Cedille
Lijnbaansgracht 275, near Spiegelgracht, IS
(624 7178). Tram 6, 7, 10. **Open** *Mar-Sept*
1-6pm Mon; 11am-6pm Tue-Sun; *Oct-Dec* 1-
6pm Mon; 11am-6pm Tue-Sat; *Jan-Feb*
11am-6pm Tue-Sat. **Credit** AmEx, DC, JCB,
MC, TC, V.
On one side Cedille sells fashion jewellery,
mostly handmade in The Netherlands. The
other half has handmade wooden toys, including handsome and unique puppets. There's
also a large collection of music boxes.

Purple Heron Gallerie Atelier
1e Leliedwarsstraat 8, IW (626 9497). Tram
13, 14, 17. **Open** 1.30-6pm Mon, Wed-Sat.
Credit MC.
British potter Karen Masters models clay in
her workshop. Besides porcelain dolls, she
makes one-of-a-kind Amsterdam house
façades that resemble Anton Piek drawings.
You can order decorative clay pieces.

Tesselschade – Arbeid Adelt
Leidseplein 33, IS (623 6665). Tram 1, 2, 5,

The handcrafted gifts at **Tesselschade – Arbeid Adelt** *(see under*
Handicrafts) *are all made in The Netherlands. Toys, decorations and more util-*
itarian items (including tea cosies and decorated clothes hangers) are made and
sold on a non-profit basis by an association of Dutch women. This association (its
name is that of the shop; a rough translation is 'work ennobles') was founded in
1871 to give women the chance to work from home and make some money, and
it's still going strong.

6, 7, 10. **Open** 10am-6pm Tue-Fri; 10am-5pm Sat. **No credit cards.**
See p157 **picture and caption.**

HEALTH & BEAUTY

The Body Shop
Kalverstraat 157-159, C (623 9789). Tram 4, 9, 14, 16, 24, 25. **Open** 11am-6pm Mon; 9.30am-6pm Tue, Wed, Fri; 9.30am-9pm Thur; 9.30am-5pm Sat. **Credit** AmEx, MC, £STC, V.
Great aromas, attractive displays and knowledgeable staff make it hard to resist entering this British export. Natural ingredients are used for the assortment of shampoos, soaps and lotions.

Jacob Hooy & Co
Kloveniersburgwal 12, C (624 3041). Tram 4, 9, 14, 16, 24, 25/Metro Nieuwmarkt. **Open** noon-6pm Mon; 8.30am-6pm Tue-Fri; 8.30-5pm Sat. **No credit cards.**
Established in 1743, this old-fashioned chemist's sells kitchen and medicinal herbs, spices, natural cosmetics, organically-grown grains and other health foods and homoeopathic remedies.

Palais des Parfums
Van Baerlestraat 74, OS (662 5781). Tram 2, 3, 5, 12. **Open** 1-6pm Mon; 9am-6pm Tue, Wed, Fri; 9am-9pm Thur; 9am-5pm Sat. **Credit** AmEx, DC, MC, £STC, V.
A good place for both men and women to go and spend a lot of money on being pampered. Top brands of cosmetics and all the major perfumes are sold. Upstairs there are five salons, which offer one-hour facials for £50, a manicure for £22 and massage for £50.

LEATHER & LUGGAGE

Carina Lederwaren
Nieuwendijk 95, C (623 3305). Tram 1, 2, 4, 5, 9, 13, 16, 17, 24, 25. **Open** noon-6pm Mon; 10am-6pm Tue, Wed, Fri; 10am-9pm Thur; 10am-5pm Sat. **Credit** AmEx, DC, MC, V.
Leather bags, cases and luggage for a variety of budgets are kept here. Additional lines include umbrellas, aluminium cases, rucksacks and school briefcases. Samsonite, Delsey, Jolly Bag and Knirps are among the brands.

Façade
PC Hooftstraat 79, OS (676 4440). Tram 2, 3, 5, 12. **Open** 1-6pm Mon; 9am-5.30pm Tue-Fri; 9am-5pm Sat. **Credit** AmEx, DC, MC, V.
Top labels such as Cardin and Gucci appear here. You'll find travel articles, gloves, diaries and wallets along with umbrellas, men's ties, key rings, cuff-links and br:efcases.

Hester van Eeghen
Hartenstraat 1, IW (626 9212). Tram 1, 2, 5, 13, 14, 17. **Open** 11am-5.30pm Tue-Fri; 11am-5pm Sat. **Credit** AmEx, DC, MC, V.
Ms van Eeghen designs all her own goods and they are made in The Netherlands. Only leather is used, even for linings. Beautiful briefcases for women come in luscious

The chic **Zumpolle** *(see under* **Leather & Luggage***) supplies the opulent with the top names in suitcases – Rimowa (hi-tech aluminium), Rodelle (lightweight, dent-resistant), Modler (leather-trimmed canvas), Marco Tabini (crocodile) and Lark (carry-on hold-alls). There is a wide choice of briefcases and small leather goods, jewellery kits, British picnic hampers and leather writing folders.*

shades including peach and light blue, and there are also items for men – knapsacks and wallets. Be prepared to join a long waiting list if you insist on a custom-made article.

Pyramid Belts
St Antoniesbreestraat 3, C (620 6442). Tram 9, 14/Metro Nieuwmarkt. **Open** 10am-6pm Mon-Fri; 11am-5pm Sat. **Credit** AmEx, DC, MC, V.
Original designs in belts and bags are handcrafted from top-quality leather in Pyramid's workshop. Custom orders are accepted.

Zumpolle
PC Hooftstraat 103, OS (664 8334). Tram 2, 3, 5, 12. **Open** 1-6pm Mon; 9.30am-6pm Tue, Wed, Fri; 9.30am-6pm, 7-9pm, Thur; 9.30am-5pm Sat. **Credit** AmEx, DC, MC, V.
See **picture and caption.**

ONE-STOP

De Amsterdamse Poort
Bijlmerplein, OSE. Metro Bijlmer/bus 59, 60, 62, 137. **Open** 1-6pm Mon; 9am-6pm Tue, Wed, Fri; 9am-9pm Thur; 9am-5pm Sat.
Easily accessible by car or public transport, this huge shopping centre has stacks of chainstores; both inexpensive household goods and exclusive designer fashion can be found. There are numerous supermarkets, banks, hair salons, restaurants, outdoor terraces and boutiques, a post office and even a branch of C&A. The outdoor general market held on Mondays and Thursdays is well known for foreign delicacies and tropical fruits and vegetables.

De Bijenkorf
Dam 1, C (621 8080). Tram 1, 2, 4, 5, 9, 13, 14, 16, 17, 24, 25. **Open** 11am-6pm Mon; 9.30am-6pm Tue, Wed, Fri; 9.30am-9pm Thur; 9am-5pm Sat. **Credit** AmEx, DC, MC, V.

De Bijenkorf (The Beehive) is the best-known department store in The Netherlands. It has good clothing for all ages, jewellery, shoes and accessories, a fine book department, household furnishings and linens. The restaurant La Ruche is a good place to lunch.

Gelderlandplein
Gelderlandplein, OS. Bus 148, 149.

Osdorpplein
Osdorpplein, OW. Tram 1/bus 19, 23, 68.
Although not as large as the Amsterdam Poort *above*, both these shopping centres have a large selection of chain-stores for one-stop shopping.

Hema
Reguliersbreestraat 10, C (624 6506). Tram 4, 9, 14, 16, 24, 25. **Open** 9am-5pm Mon-Sat. **No credit cards.**
Hema is the Dutch answer to an American five-and-dime store. The prices are very low and the quality is surprisingly high. Goods include casual clothing and underwear, accessories, household wares, tools, stationery and assorted foods. Decent wines are sold cheaply. Hema has many branches around town.

Metz & Co
Keizersgracht 455, IS (624 8810). Tram 1, 2, 5. **Open** 9.30am-6pm Mon-Fri; 9.30am-5pm Sat. **Credit** AmEx, MC, V.
A great place to shop for gifts. You'll find trendy, modern, attractive furniture alongside small gift items such as ornaments and scented soaps. The top-floor restaurant is popular for business lunches and has a terrific view of the city (*see also p91* **Cafés & Bars**).

Vroom and Dreesman
Kalverstraat 201, C (622 0171). Tram 4, 9, 14, 16, 24, 25. **Open** 11am-6pm Mon; 9.30am-6pm Tue, Wed, Fri; 9.30am-9pm Thur; 9am-5pm Sat. **Credit** AmEx, MC, V.

Prices are a step up from Hema (*above*) but the range of goods is more extensive in this large branch of the V&D chain. Furniture, appliances, gardening supplies, sporting goods, records, inexpensive fashions, cosmetics and tableware can all be found.

MARKETS

GENERAL MARKETS

There are many pickpockets among the market throngs, so keep your money in a safe place.

Albert Cuyp Markt
Albert Cuypstraat, OS. Tram 2, 16, 24, 25. **Open** 9am-4.30pm Mon-Sat.
The international atmosphere of this market makes it the most popular in Amsterdam. There are many exotic foodstuffs for sale, a variety of fish, shellfish, fresh herbs, clothing, fabrics and houseplants. Many interesting shops line the street.

Lapjesmarkt
Westerstraat, IW. Tram 3, 10. **Open** 9.30am-1pm Mon.
As well as the colourful fabrics displayed at this superior market, you can also pick up fantastic bargains in clothing and accessories. There's a small but fascinating flea market near Prinsengracht, plus some exotic take-away foods, and a large stall with houseplants.

Organic Farmers' Market
Westerstraat/Noorderkerkstraat, IW. Tram 3, 10. **Open** 10am-3pm Sat.
All the fresh fruits, vegetables and herbs sold here are organically grown. There are also health foods and ethnic craft goods.

Ten Kate Markt
Ten Katestraat, OW. Tram 7, 17. **Open** 9am-6pm Mon-Fri; 9am-5pm Sat.
A very good market for fresh fruits and vegetables, clothing, cut flowers and houseplants.

FLEA MARKETS

Haggling over the price at a flea market is half the fun. Don't pay a lot for 'antiques' unless you are an expert.

Waterlooplein
Waterlooplein, C. Tram 9, 14/Metro Waterlooplein. **Open** 10am-5pm Mon-Sat.
The contents of other people's attics will be revealed to you at Waterlooplein market. A few genuine antiques nestle next to hopeless rubbish. Beware of rip-offs.

Zwarte Markt (Black Market) & Oosterse Markt (Eastern Market)
Industriegebied aan de Buitenlandenden, Beverwijk-Oost. Train to Beverwijk; N202 to A9, then Beverwijk junction. **Open** *Zwarte Markt* 7am-5pm Sat; *Oosterse Markt* 8am-6pm Sat, Sun.
See **picture and caption**.

'The largest indoor flea market in Europe' is how the **Zwarte Markt** (see under **Markets: Flea Markets**) announces itself. New goods, old goods, foreign goods – you name it, you'll find it. Bargains abound and your guilder will go far. The adjoining Oosterse Markt *is exactly that – Oriental merchandise from pottery and carpets to Vietnamese spring rolls and fresh produce pile the stalls: it's hard to believe you're in The Netherlands.*

RECORDS

Boudisque/Boudisque Black Beat
Haringpakkerssteeg 10-18, C (623 2603). Tram 1, 2, 4, 9, 13, 16, 17, 24, 25. **Open** 1-6pm Mon; 10am-6pm Tue, Wed, Fri; 10am-9pm Thur; 10am-5pm Sat. **Credit** AmEx, MC, V.
A wide selection of pop, rock, heavy metal and world music goes on sale at Boudisque. The Black Beat section features funk, disco, soul, jazz, hip hop and dance music.

Concerto
Utrechtsestraat 54-60, IS (626 6577/624 5467/623 5228). Tram 4. **Open** 10am-6pm Mon-Fri; 10am-5pm Sat. **Credit** AmEx, MC, V.
Albums and CDs, both new and secondhand, for music-lovers of every persuasion. This is the shop to look in for old Bach releases, odd Beatles items, that favourite Diana Ross album that got lost in the move. There are also new releases for slightly less than the usual prices. You can test your find before buying it.

Forever Changes
Bilderdijkstraat 148, OW (612 6378). Tram 3, 12, 13, 14. **Open** 1-6pm Mon; 10am-6pm Tue-Fri; 10am-5pm Sat. **No credit cards.**
Named after a hippy album by the band Love, this shop stocks mostly pop music imported from the USA and England. There

are many second-hand records and CDs, plus collector's items from the sixties, seventies and eighties.

Jazz Inn
Vijzelgracht 9, IS (623 5662/620 4313). Tram 6, 7, 10, 16, 24, 25. **Open** 10am-6pm Mon-Fri; 10am-5pm Sat. **Credit** AmEx, MC.
Jazz is the speciality here. You'll find the full spectrum, from thirties' stompers through to modern and Afro jazz.

Sound of the Fifties
Prinsengracht 669, IS (623 9745). Tram 1, 2, 5, 6, 7, 10. **Open** 10am-6pm Mon-Wed, Fri; 10am-9pm Thur; 10am-5pm Sat. **Credit** AmEx, MC, V.
The owners of this record store stretch a point and include sixties' as well as fifties' recordings in their stock. A place is also found for new releases of recordings from that era. Rock 'n' roll, soul, blues and jazz make up the bulk of the music.

SPORTS

Perry Sport
Kalverstraat 93-99, C (624 7131). Tram 4, 9, 14, 16, 24, 25. **Open** 11am-6pm Mon; 9.30am-6pm Tue, Wed, Fri; 9.30am-9pm Thur; 9.30am-5pm Sat. **Credit** AmEx, DC, MC, TC, V.
An all-purpose sports shop supplying tents, sport shoes, tennis racquets, exercise aids and winter and summer jackets.

You haven't been in Amsterdam, if you didn't visit 'de Bijenkorf'.

For that special gift or souvenir, for the latest fashion or for
the latest trends in home decoration,
you can't do better than shop in Amsterdam's leading
department store 'de Bijenkorf'.
Our opening times: Monday from 11.00 till 18.00,
Tuesday, Wednesday and Friday from 9.30 till 18.00,
Thursday from 9.30 till 21.00 and Saturday from 9.00 till 17.00.

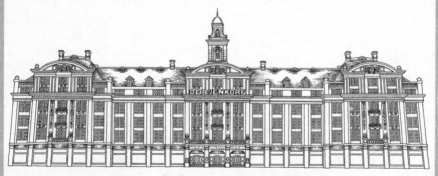

Every visit you'll discover something new in the Bijenkorf.

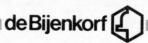

Specialist Shops

Many small shops and a small city centre make Amsterdam a great place for hunting out both traditional and quirky speciality buys, writes *Lyn Ritchie*.

Certain industries and goods are inextricably linked with The Netherlands, and their stories are an intrinsic part of the country's history. They include flowers, cut diamonds, pottery and glassware, and although they are sold in cities across the world, nowhere offers the variety found here. A lesser-known speciality is pewter, made by several Dutch companies. It comes both in traditional forms, similar to utensils seen in seventeenth-century paintings, and in sleek modern shapes. Goods range in size from spoons to tankards, trays, tea sets and samovars. There's a range of pewter at **Focke & Meltzer** (*listed under* **Pottery**); gift shops and some department stores (*see page 153* **Shopping Around**) also carry selections.

DIAMONDS

Amsterdam has had a lively relationship with these gems since the sixteenth century when refugee diamond workers from Antwerp settled here. By the 1920s, some 10,000 people, many of them Jewish, were employed in the city's jewellery business. The workforce was severly depleted during World War II (*see page 64* **World War II**); but the subsequent rebirth of the trade has been remarkable. If you are interested in a carat or two, do some careful comparative shopping and only buy from long-established, reputable firms such as those listed in **Sightseeing** (*see page 13*), where you can also see how a rough stone is transformed into a precious jewel.

FLOWERS

Tulip time is any time in The Netherlands – you will find them at numerous flower stands even in the dead of winter. Out-of-season blooms are grown in hothouses under carefully controlled conditions. Roses are another year-round speciality.

Each year countless packets of flower bulbs are bought by foreign travellers. Unfortunately, many are confiscated by customs officers because import regulations either prohibit the entry of bulbs entirely or require them to have a phytosanitary (health) certificate.

The following information was valid at time of writing; however, regulations often change. No certificate is needed to take less than 2 kilograms (4½ pounds) of bulbs into the UK. Bulbs with a phytosanitary certificate can be carried into the USA, Canada and the Irish Republic. Australia will not allow them in even with a certificate; and New Zealand's regulations are too fuzzy to give firm advice. You are allowed to bring one bunch of cut flowers into Britain (not gladioli or chrysanthemums); regulations on cut flowers vary from state to state in the USA. The best way to find out your entitlements is to ask as you leave your home country.

To avoid disappointment, get Dutch wholesale dealers to ship the bulbs to your home. This can be done at the annual Keukenhof flower show (late March to late May), or by mail order from the Frans Roozen Nurseries (minimum order varies depending on where you live). For both, and for details of visiting nurseries and gardens, *see page 203* **Excursions in Holland.**

Bloemenmarkt (Flower Market)
Singel, between Muntplein and Koningsplein, C. Tram 1, 2, 5, 16, 24, 25. **Open** 9am-6pm Mon-Sat.
Amsterdam boasts the world's only floating flower market. This fascinating collage of colour stretches four blocks along the southern side of the Singel canal. Some 15 florists and garden shops are permanently ensconced there on large barges. They offer a wide assortment of fresh and dried blooms, plants for the house or garden, flower bulbs, packets of seeds, novelty plants and souvenirs – including plastic tulips. Rufina van Zoomeren, Singel 526, and A Smit, Singel 502, can provide packets of bulbs with phytosanitary certificates.

GLASS & CRYSTAL

Royal Leerdam, one of the oldest glassworks in The Netherlands, is world-famous for its contemporary – and remarkably inexpensive – collections of glassware. Its 'Guild' wine goblet, created in co-operation with the Association of Dutch Wine Merchants in 1930, is still one of the company's most popular products. Amsterdam's better gift shops, such as **Focke & Meltzer** (*listed under* **Pottery**) carry Leerdam's lead crystal 'Unica' one-of-a-kind pieces. Cheaper glassware can be found at household furnishing stores throughout the city.

Glasgalerie Kuhler
Prinsengracht 134, IS (638 0230). Tram 13, 14, 17. **Open** 12.30-6pm Mon-Wed, Fri; 12.30-9pm Thur; noon-5pm Sat. **Credit** AmEx, MC, V.
A large, lustrous collection of contemporary European glass and crystal is kept at Kuhler. All pieces are unique, dated and signed by well-known artists, including two from The Netherlands. Glass-blowing is well represented, along with *pâte de verre* (a method of pouring molten glass into moulds) and cold laminated sculptures. Prices go from f85 to f17,000.

POTTERY

Early in the seventeenth century, merchant ships of the Dutch East India Company (VOC, *see p55* **The Golden Age**) sailed home with beautifully decorated porcelain from China. Seeing their livelihood threatened, Dutch potters began imitating those popular imports. That was the origin of today's **Delftware**, with its distinctive blue designs on an off-white background. By the middle of the century, there were over 30 small potteries in Delft alone. One of them, **De Porceleyn Fles** (The Porcelain Jar), is still in business. Traditionally, Delftware is made from white baking clay imported from Cornwall, and the pieces are formed on a potter's wheel or in plaster moulds. After one firing, each piece is dusted with a charcoal outline of its decoration and artists paint every detail, including their initials and the article's code number next to the company's trademark. The future heirloom is then given a transparent glaze coating and fired once more. Cheaper, machine-made imitations are only partially hand-painted. The decorations are usually applied by transfer or printed on the surface: look closely and you'll see the tiny dots.

Another type of entirely hand-painted pottery produced in The Netherlands is **Royal Makkum**. Named after its home town in

The collectable pottery at **Galleria d'Arte 'Rinascimento'** (see under Classic Dutch: Pottery) *ranges from a f40 thimble to an antique tile mural for f30,000. Both old and new Delftware, Porceleyne Fles and Makkum are featured and there's an amazing variety of ceramic clock cases (complete with timepieces). Also on sale are authentic copies of early seventeenth-century vases specifically designed to display precious tulips during Holland's 'tulipmania' – an orgy of speculation that took place in the 1630's, when the price of a tulip bulb rocketed to over f1,500. The replica of a blue and white tulip vase, pictured above (the original is in Hampton Court Palace, London), consists of seven sections and stands 1.5 metres/5 feet high.*

Friesland (*see page 213* **The Provinces**), the most notable is made by **Tichelaar**, which has been going for over 300 years. The company still uses local clay and seventeenth-century processes. The clay, which turns yellow after firing, must be coated with an opaque tin glaze to provide a background for the application of enamel paints. During the final firing, the colours blend with this glaze to create a special warmth and brilliance.

For non-specialist pottery and crafts shops, *see below* **Gifts**.

Focke & Meltzer
PC Hooftstraat 65-67, OS (664 2311). Tram 2, 3, 5, 12. **Open** 9.30am-6pm Mon-Wed, Fri; 9.30am-9pm Thur; 9.30am-5pm Sat. **Credit** AmEx, DC, MC, V.
Established in 1823, Focke & Meltzer specializes in elegant European china, crystal, silver and figurines. Its Dutch range includes the four Royals: Holland pewter, Leerdam crystal, Makkum pottery and Porceleyne Fles Delftware. Prices start at f20 for cups and saucers and rise to f15,000 for one-off vases.
Branch Tax-free Shopping Centre, Schiphol Airport (601 5205).

Galleria d'Arte 'Rinascimento'
Prinsengracht 170, IS (622 7509/fax 623 3431). Tram 13, 14, 17. **Open** 9am-6pm daily. **Credit** AmEx, DC, MC, V.
See **picture and caption**.
Export scheme. Packing and shipping, including insurance.

Kleikollektief (Clay Collective)
Hartenstraat 11, C (622 5727). Tram 13, 14, 17. **Open** 1-5pm Wed-Sat. **No credit cards.**
This showroom is shared by a group of Dutch ceramicists whose studios are scattered throughout the city. View examples of their work here and pick up an English-language folder that tells you where to find the individual artists.

De Porceleyne Fles
Rotterdamseweg 196, Delft (015 569214). **Open** 9am-5pm Mon-Sat. **Credit** AmEx, JCB, MC, V.
The Porceleyne Fles pottery dates from the seventeenth century and uses traditional methods to produce vases, bowls, tiles, candlesticks, display plates and many other pieces with modern as well as traditional motifs. Prices range from f65 to f3,000 for large vases. Except for some slightly flawed pieces (sold only at the factory) you'll pay the same as in shops in Amsterdam. A certificate of authenticity is supplied with every item that bears the Porceleyne Fles symbol.

Tichelaar's Royal Makkum Faience
Turfmarkt 61, Makkum (05158 1341/Telex 46424TKM). **Open** 9am-4pm Mon-Sat. **Guided tours** 10-11.30am, 1-4pm, Mon-Thur; 10-11.30am, 1-3pm, Fri. **Cost** f3; group discount (min 20 people) f2.50. **Credit** AmEx, DC, MC, V.
As well as traditional Royal Makkum ware, Tichelaar makes intricately patterned blue and white pottery, attractive ceramic brooches and striking art deco vases. A few pieces of Royal Makkum are found in Amsterdam's best gift shops, but dedicated collectors should visit the factory for the best range. Prices are similar wherever you shop: tiles from f25 to f100, plates from f100 to f3,000.

GIFTS

Holland Gallery De Munt
Muntplein 12, C (623 2271/fax 638 4215). Tram 4, 9, 14, 16, 24, 25. **Open** 9am-6pm Mon-Fri; 9am-5pm Sat. **Credit** AmEx, MC, V.
Stockists of Royal pottery (Makkum and Porceleyn Fles) plus other hand-painted objects such as traditional tiles and beautifully decorated wooden trays and boxes. Other highlights include miniature ceramic canal houses and dolls in traditional Dutch costumes. You'll find De Munt in the Munttoren (*see p13* **Sightseeing**).

Poppette Doll Studio
V. Speykstraat 30, OW (683 8862). Tram 1, 3, 6, 12. **Open** by appointment. **Credit** AmEx, V.
Jonette Stabbert is an American artist with a flair for caricature. Her unique handmade gifts include miniature teddy bears, ethnic dolls and life-size soft sculpture car companions – popular in the USA with women drivers travelling alone, as the dummies are sufficiently life-like to fool potential trouble-makers.

Silverplate
Nes 89, C (624 8339). Tram 4, 9, 14, 16, 24, 25. **Open** 11am-6pm Mon-Fri; 11am-5pm Sat. **Credit** AmEx, DC, MC, V.
Try this place for a stack of ideas for gifts: wine coolers, cocktail shakers, trays, serving dishes, candlesticks, photo frames and much more, all in silver; also damask napkins and table-cloths made to measure.

SPECIALITY SHOPS

Amsterdam has hundreds of specialist shops – usually small, fascinating places where the owners can indulge an obsession. Below we have listed a selection of the more interesting stores, but there are plenty more all over town: try, for example, wandering around the Jordaan (*see page 26 Amsterdam by Area*) and the area around Utrechtsestraat.

ANTIQUES

Most antique dealers can be found in the Spiegel quarter around the Spiegelgracht and the Nieuwe Spiegelstraat near the Rijksmuseum. Shops tend to specialize in one era or type of antique, including clocks, coins, paintings and maps; we list one gallery where you can see a wider range.

Amsterdam Antiques Gallery
Nieuwe Spiegelstraat 34, OS (625 3371). Tram 1, 2, 5, 16, 24, 25. **Open** 11am-6pm Mon-Sat. **Credit** AmEx, DC, MC, V.
Ten antique dealers under one roof. Among their hoard of booty are icons, nineteenth- and twentieth-century paintings, lamps, vases, bronze figurines, silverware and Dutch tiles.

De Haas
Kerkstraat 155, IS (626 5952). Tram 16, 24, 25. **Open** 11am-5.30pm Tue-Sat. **Credit** AmEx, DC, MC, V.
A repository for glass (including famous Dutch designs), pottery, silver articles and bronze figurines created between 1890 and 1940. Art nouveau and art deco vases, figurines and china are a speciality.

ARTISTS' SUPPLIES

J Vlieger
Two entrances: Halvemaansteeg 4-6 (near Rembrandtsplein) and Amstel 52, IS (623 5834/624 5741). Tram 4, 9, 14. **Open** noon-5.30pm Mon; 9am-5.30pm Tue-Fri; 9am-5pm Sat. **Credit** AmEx, MC, V.
An inspiring collection of brushes, pigments, pens and paper, plus artists' portfolios and book-binding materials is sold here.
Branch: Van Woustraat 102, OS (671 3733).

BEADS, BUTTONS & TRIMMINGS

André Coppenhagen
Bloemgracht 38, OW (624 3681). Tram 13, 14, 17. **Open** 9am-5.30pm Tue-Fri; 9am-5pm Sat. **Credit** AmEx, DC, MC, V.
Besides beads (*kralen*), spangles and bangles, this shop has chains, cords and clasps for necklaces, belts and handbags, and do-it-yourself gift boxes.
Branch: 1e Bloemdwarsstraat 10, OW (624 0679).

HJ van de Kerkhof
Wolvenstraat 9, IW (623 4084). Tram 1, 2, 5. **Open** 9am-6pm Mon-Fri. **No credit cards.**
Trimmings (*passementerie* in Dutch) of every type are Kerkhof's speciality – stock includes lace collars, feather boas, fringes, sequins, and satin rosettes.

CANDLES

Kramer
Reestraat 20, IW (626 5274). Tram 13, 14, 17. **Open** 10am-6pm Tue-Fri; 10am-5pm Sat. **No credit cards.**
Candles in a multitude of shapes and sizes find space at Kramer. Naïve forms from Swaziland, sleek art deco designs and ornamental showpieces (up to f285) are among the more interesting goods.

FABRICS

Capsicum
Oude Hoogstraat 1, C (623 1016). Tram 4, 9, 16, 24, 25/Metro Nieuwmarkt. **Open** 10am-6pm Tue, Wed, Fri; 10am-9pm Thur; 10am-5pm Sat. **Credit** AmEx, MC, V.
Capsicum is dedicated to natural fibres and splendid textures: cotton woven in India and Thai silk in glowing shades are highlights.

Het Kantenhuis (The Lace House)
Kalverstraat 124, C (624 8618). Tram 1, 2, 4, 5, 9, 14, 16, 24, 25. **Open** 11.45am-6pm Mon; 9.15am-6pm Tue, Wed, Fri; 9.15am-9pm Thur; 9.15am-5pm Sat. **Credit** AmEx, DC, MC, V.
In business for 90 years, 'Holland's only linen shop' sells reasonably priced tablecloths, place-mats, doilies and napkins that are embroidered, appliquéd or printed with Delft blue designs. There are also lace curtain material and kits to make cross-stitch pictures of Amsterdam canal houses.

McLennan's
Hartenstraat 22, IW (622 7693). Tram 1, 2, 5. **Open** 1-6pm Mon; 11am-6pm Tue, Wed, Fri; 11am-9pm Thur; 11am-5pm Sat. **No credit cards.**
Imperial Chinese silks are sold by the metre. They also come ready-made as kimonos, scarfs, lingerie or ever-blooming tulips and rose buds (f15 each).

TIKAL Native Expression
Hartenstraat 2A, IW (623 2147). Tram 1, 2, 5. **Open** 11am-5.30pm Mon-Fri; 11am-5pm Sat. **Credit** AmEx, MC, V.
Folk fabric from Guatemala is the speciality here. The hand-dyed, hand-woven, hand-washable cotton comes in pleasing patterns and harmonious hues. It's available by the metre (90cm-1m/about 1yd wide) from f23 to f45 per metre, or made up in clothing and accessories (shirts from f125 to f189).

GAMES & MODELS

Compendium
Hartenstraat 14, IW (638 1579). Tram 13,

With a do-it-yourself kit from the **Scale Train House** *(see under* **Speciality Shops: Games & Models***), you can build yourself a replica of Moscow's onion-topped St Basil's Cathedral or the Leaning Tower of Pisa (height 44 centimetres/about 17 inches). Further scaled-down construction work could leave you with wind-jammers (a three-masted ship kit costs f350), Dutch houses and windmills, or working models of miniature musical instruments (from about f70). The ready-made parade includes electric trains (with steam or diesel engines and all kinds of rolling stock) plus tracks, European railway stations, houses and scenery, and modern and vintage vehicles in various sizes.*

Every available inch of space in **Fifties-Sixties** (see under **Speciality Shops: Miscellaneous**) *is choc-full of authentic period pieces – toasters, blenders, lamps and even vacuum cleaners – all in good working condition (220 volts). Non-electrical goods include fifties' lighting fixtures and floor-standing chrome ashtrays.*

14, 17. Open 1-6pm Mon; 10am-6pm Tue, Wed, Fri; 10am-8pm Thur; 10am-5pm Sat. Credit AmEx, DC, MC, V.
Come here for games galore, including fantasy role-playing from the USA and Britain (Dungeons and Dragons, War Hammer Citadel). Tin soldiers, chess sets, computer games and the Japanese board game Go are also available.

Miniature Furniture
Prinsengracht 293, IW (626 7863/622 1113 private number; please ring at reasonable time). Tram 13, 14, 17. Open noon-4.30pm Saturday and by appointment. No credit cards.
The remarkable assortment of diminutive furnishings is made on a one-twelfth scale by Dutch craftspeople. Ring Mrs Louise Meertens for an appointment to see them.

Scale Train House
Bilderdijkstraat 94, OW (612 2670/fax 612 2817). Tram 3, 12, 13, 14. Open 9.30am-6pm Mon-Fri; 9.30am-5pm Sat. No credit cards.
See p163 picture and caption.

PARTIES

Center Stage
Nieuwezijds Voorburgwal 150, C (622 4903). Tram 1, 2, 5, 13, 17. Open 1-5pm Mon; 10am-6pm Tue, Wed, Fri; 10am-9pm Thur; 10am-5pm Sat. Credit AmEx, MC, V.
Three Californians offer a jolly variety of 2,500 items for every kind of party. They stock decorations, disposable eating utensils, balloons and a huge variety of chocolate figures including horses and carousels.

Christmas World
Nieuwezijds Voorburgwal 137-139, C (622 7047). Tram 1, 2, 5, 13, 17. Open Sept-Easter 8.30am-6.30pm Mon-Wed, Fri, Sat; 8.30am-9pm Thur; Easter-Aug 9am-6pm Mon-Sat. Credit MC, TC, V.
Cheery Yuletide decorations, made in the

USA and Britain, are sold here all year round. The selection includes personalized stockings for Santa to fill, table linens and old-fashioned tree ornaments.

Party House
Utrechtsestraat 90, IS (620 8304). Tram 4. Open 10am-6pm Tue-Fri; 10am-5pm Sat. No credit cards.
A multitude of masks – weird, funny, fantastic – hangs from the ceiling in this shop. There are also costumes and accessories for sale or hire and a plethora of practical jokes.

POSTERS & PRINTS

Art Unlimited
Keizersgracht 510, IS (624 8419/fax 623 6524). Tram 1, 2, 5. Open 11am-6pm Mon; 10am-6pm Tue-Fri; 10am-5pm Sat. Credit AmEx, DC, MC, V.
Among the large collection of posters you'll find reproductions of modern paintings, 400 black and whites (no film subjects), thousands of postcards and photos of famous and obscure poets, actors and other international personalities.

Cine-Qua-Non
Staalstraat 14, C (625 5588). Tram 4, 9, 14, 16, 24, 25. Open 1-6pm Tue-Sat. Credit MC.
Film fanatics flock here for posters (mostly Italian and French), photos and second-hand books concerning their hobby, plus videos of cult films such as Warhol's *Chelsea Girls*. Note that different signal formats prohibit the use of European videos in North America.

STAMPS & COINS

Outdoor Market
Pedestrian island in front of Nova Hotel, Nieuwezijds Voorburgwal 276, C. Tram 1, 2, 5, 13, 17. Open 11am-4pm Wed, Sat. No credit cards.
You don't have to be a philatelist to enjoy

this gathering of some 20 local dealers selling currency, stamps, old postcards and commemorative medals.

MISCELLANEOUS

Condomerie Het Gulden Vlies
Warmoesstraat 141, C (627 4174). Tram 1, 2, 4, 5, 9, 13, 16, 17, 24, 25. Open 1-6pm Mon-Fri; noon-5pm Sat. No credit cards.
Opened in 1987 by two Dutch women, The Golden Fleece was the first shop of its kind in the world. It's still the only one in The Netherlands to specialize in condoms. They come in all shapes, colours, textures, flavours and sizes, with different kinds of lubrication. Besides laboratory-tested, officially approved types, there are novelty sheaths (fluorescent or edible) and others packaged as chewing gum, sweets, or tucked into walnut shells. The illustrated English-Dutch catalogue costs f5.

Fifties-Sixties
Huidenstraat 13, IW (623 2653). Tram 1, 2, 5. Open 1-6pm Tue-Fri; 1-5pm Sat. No credit cards.
See picture and caption.

P G C Hajenius
Rokin 92-96, C (625 9985). Tram 4, 9, 14, 16, 24, 25. Open 10am-6pm Mon; 9am-6pm Tue-Fri; 9am-5pm Sat. Credit AmEx, DC, MC, V.
Hajenius was established as a tobacconist's in 1826, but has recently been bought by British tobacco giants Gallagher. The interior has been refurnished to resemble a photo of the shop taken in 1915. Famed for its own brand of cigars, Hajenius also stocks a splendid variety of pipes including the traditional Dutch clay pipe with either a 14-in or 20-in (35cm or 50cm) stem. The staff will organize the shipping of gifts.

Joe's De Vliegerwinkel
Nieuwe Hoogstraat 19, C (625 0139). Metro Nieuwmarkt. Open 11am-6pm Tue-Fri; 11am-5pm Sat; also open 1-6pm Mon in summer. Credit AmEx, EC, V.
Boomerangs handmade by Aborigines in Australia and hammocks from Columbia, Brazil and Mexico are sold at Joe's, as are Frisbees and kites (ready-made or in do-it-yourself kits). You can also order a custom-built kite. Prices? – the sky's the limit.

De Witte Tanden Winkel
Runstraat 5, IW (623 3443). Tram 1, 2, 5. Open 1-6pm Mon; 10am-6pm Tue-Fri; 10am-5pm Sat. Credit AmEx, DC, MC, V.
The White Teeth Shop has all you need for a sparkling smile, from junior-size toothbrushes with a Mickey Mouse or banana handle to champagne or whisky-flavoured toothpaste and electric brushing/rinsing equipment.

Wooden Shoe Factory
Nieuwezijds Voorburgwal 20, C (623 0632). Tram 1, 2, 5. Open 1 Apr-15 Sept: 10am-10pm daily; 16 Sept-31 Mar 10am-6pm daily. Credit AmEx, DC, MC, V.
Wooden shoes (*klompen* – the Dutch don't call them clogs) may not be the highest fashion in footwear, but are very useful for gardeners. Buy them large enough to wear over heavy socks and tell children the Dutch only wear *klompen* outside the house.

Services

If your backpack has disintegrated or your Rolex needs repairing, don't panic. *Jonette Stabbert* **puts Amsterdam at your service.**

Amsterdam is not the most service-oriented of cities. Employment law makes it difficult to get fired, so staff have no personal stake in pleasing their customers. The Dutch penchant for taking things literally can also lead to problems. You often have to be persistent and make sure you ask exactly the right question: enquire if your hotel does dry-cleaning and you may be told no. Only after you have trekked around the city with your grubby shirt crumpled in your bag will you find out that there was a great express dry-cleaners just around the corner that staff hadn't thought to mention.

HOTEL & SHOP SERVICES

These differ greatly, but the more expensive the hotel or shop, the more services it will offer. However, you'll find that even at budget hotels the staff will be able to recommend baby-sitters and other services if asked. Every department store (*see page 153* **Shopping Around**) has a customer service division (*klantenser-vice*), which will advise on packaging and shipping arrangements.

Business-related services are listed in our **Business** chapter (*see page 188*). For police, fire, ambulance and other emergency services, veterinary services and car hire companies, *see page 221* **Survival**. Bicycle hire shops can be found in **Essential Information** (*page 3*).

ALTERNATIVE HEALTH

Natuurlijk Gezondheidscentrum
Shackletonstraat 2, OW (616 4942). Tram 13. Open 9am-5pm Mon-Fri. **Consultations** f75 an hour. **No credit cards.**
This respected training centre offers consultations in tarot, astrology, acupuncture, foot reflexology, physiotherapy, iriscopy (the analysis of illness through examination of the irises), fasting, hypnosis and psychotherapy.

Roxy
Singel 465, C (620 0354). Tram 1, 2, 5, 16, 24, 25.
The Roxy is principally a discotheque (*see p141* **Night-clubs**), but one evening a month (8pm-midnight) the premises are

taken over by the Dolphin Club, an underground new-wave movement. 'Happenings' involve group participation in aromatherapy, brain-wave machines and other phenomena. Against a background of ambient music, soft lighting and bubble machines, and attended by some eccentric-looking visitors, it is an experience not to be missed. English is usually spoken. Phone for details of dates and themes.

CAMERA, TV & VIDEO HIRE

Ruad Foto
Overtoom 371, OW (618 1500). Tram 1, 5. Open 10am-6pm Mon; 9am-6pm Tue-Fri; 9am-5pm Sat. **Credit** AmEx, MC, V.
Cameras, computers, camcorders and video recorders are hired out on a short or long-term basis. A steep security deposit is required (f1,000 for a video recorder, for example), payable by credit card or cheque as well as in cash.

BEAUTY

Beauty and Shine
Leidsekade 100, C (624 7017). Open 10am-5pm Mon-Fri; evenings and weekends by appointment. **No credit cards.**
A wide range of services provided by therapist Henny Vledder includes facials, body massage, reflexology, aromatherapy, waxing, manicure, pedicure and colour analysis. Professional French cosmetics are used, suitable for black and Asian skins.

Beauty Form
1E Oosterparkstraat 101, OE (694 4957). Tram 3. Open 9.30am-5.30pm except evenings by appointment. **No credit cards.**
A full range of services for both sexes at reasonable prices. The 1½-hour 'traveller's special' (f55) is aimed at replenishing dehydrated skin and includes epilation, peeling, massage, a mask and compresses. All skin problems, including acne and ingrown beard hairs, are handled by multi-lingual Shirley Bueno-Bibaz.

PIPE & LIGHTER REPAIR

Han Schellings
Reguliersdwarsstraat 47, IS (627 8286). Tram 1, 2, 4, 5, 9, 14, 16, 24, 25. Open 9am-4.30pm Mon-Fri. **No credit cards.**
Mr Schellings is regarded as one of the best in the business and deals with customers worldwide by post. He offers a same-day service.

CLOTHING CARE

Clean Brothers
Jacob van Lennepkade 179, OW (618 3637). Tram 3, 12, 17. Open 8am-8pm Mon, Tue, Thur, Fri; 8am-6pm Wed; 9am-5pm Sat. **No credit cards.**
You can have a same-day service-wash done

at this launderette run by the white-suited British 'Clean Brothers'. If you prefer to DIY, the branches listed below are self-service only: the centrally-located Kerkstraat branch is open every day from 7am to 9pm.
Branches: Rozengracht 59, OW (623 7718). Kerkstraat 56, IS (no phone).

Cleaning Shop Express
Huidenstraat 22, IW (623 1219). Tram 1, 2, 5. Open 8.30am-6pm Mon-Fri; 8.30am-1pm Sat. **No credit cards.**
This establishment offers a full range of services, including dry-cleaning, laundering, leather and carpet cleaning, repairs, alterations and invisible mending. Staff will also hand-launder, and press shirts and sheets. Same-day service on request. You can trust them with your designer originals.

FLORIST

Ivy
Leidseplein 35, IS (623 6561). Tram 1, 2, 5, 6, 7, 10. Open 9am-6pm Mon-Fri; 9am-5pm Sat. **Credit** AmEx, MC, V.
This expensive shop puts together wonderful flower arrangements. Currently in vogue is the natural look, achieved with garden flowers and grasses. Ivy can arrange to send flowers by Interflora.

FOOD DELIVERY

Heuft's First Class Night Shop
Rijnstraat 62, OS (642 4048). Tram 4, 25. Open 4pm-1am daily, telephone orders for lunch accepted earlier. **Credit** AmEx, DC.
This is the place to call when you've got the midnight munchies. It has a huge selection of delicacies and ready meals for take-away or delivery: everything from champagne and oysters to fully-catered meals or the ingredients to create an authentic Mexican feast. Heuft's is expensive, but quality and service are excellent. Staff will vacuum-pack Dutch cheeses for you to take home.

Pizzalijn La Botte
Lijnbaansgracht 120, IW (623 5539). Tram 3, 10. Open 4-11pm daily. **No credit cards.**
Phone Pizza Line for super-quick delivery of pizza and other fast-food meals. There's no delivery charge on orders above f25.

FORMAL DRESS HIRE

Joh. Huijer
Weteringschans 153, IS (623 5439) Tram 6, 7, 10. Open 9am-5pm Tue, Wed, Fri; 9am-9pm Thur. **No credit cards.**
Men's formal dress hire. All clothing is from the German label Lacerna in Dutch sizes 46 to 60 (British and American sizes 34 to 50). A complete outfit, including cuff-links and bow tie, can be rented for f125. Pick up your outfit in the afternoon, return it the following morning.

Maison Van Den Hoogen
Sarphatipark 88-90, OS (679 8828). Tram 3. Open 9am-5pm Mon-Wed, Fri; 9am-9pm Thur; 9am-4pm Sat. **No credit cards.**
Women's formal dress hire – there is a choice of cocktail and evening dresses in Dutch sizes 36 to 40 (British 8 to 12; American 5 to 9). The deposit is f100 and the price range f85-f125.

Ida Jongsma is co-founder of the **Association of Practical Philosophy** (*see under* **Philosophy**)*. The aim of this unique and innovative organization, set up as recently as 1988, is to bring philosophy out of its ivory tower and into the world by arranging lectures and providing a forum for discussion. In addition, its members offer private consultations. Ms Jongsma rarely gives these herself, but the Association can put anyone interested in touch with one of its 16 practising members. Some clients have specific problems, often regarding their careers; some have more existential concerns and some just want a natter about philosophy. There's no reason why visitors shouldn't have a one-off consultation.*

HAIR SALONS

De Don's
Weteringschans 167, IS (626 3430). Tram 6, 7, 10. **Open** 9am-5pm Mon-Fri. **No credit cards.**
You can get an inexpensive, good hairstyle at this hairdressers' training institute. Cuts are done by advanced students and cost f23.50. Ten other locations in Amsterdam are staffed by graduates and so prices are higher, but still reasonable. No appointment necessary.

The Freaks
Leidsestraat 63, IS (627 8667). Tram 1, 2, 5. **Open** 9.30am-6pm Tue, Wed, Fri, Sat; 9.30am-9pm Thur. **Credit** AmEx, DC, MC, V.
Young and trendy styles on offer for men and women include hair extensions and stylized punk. Seriously rich types cross the Atlantic for the unique dyes used here. You'll need to make an appointment and be prepared to pay between f100 and f600.

H B Hairstylers
Hilton Hotel, Apollolaan 138-140, OS (679 0599). Tram 5, 24. **Open** 9am-7pm daily. **No credit cards.**
Styling for men and women. Expensive but excellent, and open to non-guests. Four other locations in town, phone for details.

JEWELLERY REPAIR

Elke Watch Cy
Kalverstraat 206, C (624 7100/623 6386). Tram 1, 2, 4, 5, 9, 14, 16, 24, 25. **Open** 9am-5.30pm Mon-Fri; 9am-4.30pm Sat. **Credit** AmEx, DC, MC, V.
Elke carry out quick repairs to jewellery and watches, and offer a 24-hour service for simple jobs.

LUGGAGE REPAIR

Wentholt Exclusive Luggage Repair Shop
Nieuwezijds Kolk 4, C (624 3252). Tram 1, 2, 4, 5, 9, 14, 16, 24, 25. **Open** 9.30am-5.30pm Thur, Fri. **No credit cards.**
Staff here are used to dealing with people on the hop; Wentholt is frequently used by hotels and airlines. It specializes in leather repair and will repair or replace locks, on luggage and handbags.

PACKING & REMOVALS

De Gruijter
Industrieweg 11-13, 2382 NR Zoeterwoude (071 89 9313). **Open** 8.30am-5pm Mon-Fri. **No credit cards.**
Accustomed to dealing with fragile and expensive items, De Gruijter will package and send your purchases or household belongings anywhere in the world by sea or air and also offers storage facilities. Service is friendly.

PASSPORT PHOTOS

Foto Coleur
Leidsestraat 87, IS (623 5687). Tram 1, 2, 5. **Open** 9am-6pm Mon-Fri. **No credit cards.**
If your passport is stolen or goes missing, you may need a new photo in a hurry. Foto Coleur can supply the requisite size and angle for US nationals. This service costs f27.50 and takes three hours. You can also get ordinary ID photos while you wait.

PHILOSOPHY

Amsterdam is home to the world's first Association of Practical Philosophy (*see* **picture and caption**), whose members offer the public private con-

sultations with a philosopher. Its headquarters are at the Hotel de Filosoof (*see page 39* **Accommodation**), where staff can put you in touch with any of the 16 practising philosophers in The Netherlands. It also hosts regular lectures, courses and intellectual gatherings, unfortunately in Dutch, but you could always try to turn the discussion into a multi-lingual event.

Dries Boele
Spaarndammerplantsoen 108, OW (686 7330 – private number, please ring at reasonable times). Bus 22, 28. **No credit cards.**
Mr Boele can advise on the philosophical aspects of important life decisions, such as career changes and make-or-break relationship dilemmas. Many of his clients have tried psychiatry and are now looking for a wider perspective. He is multi-lingual and charges about f100 for a 75-minute session (those on low incomes can negotiate a lower fee).

PHOTOCOPYING

Grand Prix Copyrette
Weteringschans 84A, IS (627 2703). Tram 6, 7, 10. **Open** 9.30am-5.30pm Mon-Fri; 11am-4pm Sat. **No credit cards.**
Come here for all your photocopying needs. Quick, friendly service – while you wait or DIY. Prices are low and the quality high. Colour copies, enlargements, spiral-binding, and a fax service are available. For more copy shops *see* p188 **Business.**

PHOTO PROCESSING

Capi
Leidsestraat 77, IS (623 3019). Tram 1, 2, 5. **Open** 9am-5.30pm Mon-Fri; 10am-5pm Sat. **Credit** AmEx, DC, MC, V.
Capi offers a one-hour service for colour film, three or four days for black and white; two days for slides.

"S" Color
Singel 356, IW (624 9102). Tram 1, 2, 5. **Open** 8am-10pm Mon-Fri; 2-5pm Sat; 4-8pm Sun. **No credit cards.**
This is the film laboratory used by top professional photographers, producing quality work quickly done (black and white ready in two hours). "S" Color is more expensive than other places, but it's the fastest and the best.

SHOE REPAIR

Luk's Schoenservice
Leidsekruisstraat 2, IS (623 1937). Tram 1, 2, 5. **Open** 8.30am-5.30pm Mon-Fri; 9am-1pm Sat. **No credit cards.**
A complete repair and cleaning service, Luk's is professional and quick. Trust him with your satin evening shoes. Top-quality work which can usually be completed in a day.

Mr Minit
Leidsestraat 71, IS (624 8368). Tram 1, 2, 5. **Open** 11am-6pm Mon; 9.30am-6pm Tue, Wed, Fri; 9.30am-9pm Thur; 9am-5pm Sat. **No credit cards.**
The service here is fast; usually while you wait. Repairs to shoes, handbags and other small leather goods by machine.

In Focus

This city has a huge diversity of general facilities. However, many visitors have specific interests, which can be particularly acute in a foreign environment. We've focused on the needs of women; children and their parents; gays and lesbians; and those whose stay isn't complete without watching or doing a little sport.

CONTENTS:

I N T E R M A L E
A M S T E R D A M

■ WIDE SELECTION OF ENGLISH, FRENCH, GERMAN AND DUTCH LITERATURE
■ OTHER SPECIALITIES: BIOGRAPHY, HISTORY, PHOTOGRAPHY AND SEXUALITY ■ EXTENSIVE RANGE OF CARDS, NEWSPAPERS AND MAGAZINES ■ COMPLETE SERIES OF AMERICAN TOM OF FINLAND PICTURE BOOKS AND GREETING CARDS ■ HOT PORN FROM THE STATES: BOOKS AND PHOTOMAGS ■ INTERMALE IS THE EUROPEAN DISTRIBUTOR FOR MAJOR GAY PUBLISHING COMPANIES THROUGHOUT THE WORLD ■ RETAIL MAIL ORDER TO ALL COUNTRIES ■ SEND FOR FREE CATALOGUE ■ INTERMALE IS OPEN MON.-SAT.10.00 A.M. - 6.00 P.M (THURS. UNTIL 9.00 P.M.) ADDRESS: SPUISTRAAT 251, 1012 VR AMSTERDAM TELEPHONE: (020) 625.0009

HOTEL NEW YORK
AMSTERDAM

HERENGRACHT 13
1015 BA AMSTERDAM
TEL (3120)|6243066
TELEFAX (3120) 6203230

IN THE HEART OF THE CITY
3 MIN FROM CENTRAL STATION
(DIRECT AIRPORT-TRAIN)
DIRECT DIAL TELEPHONES AND
CTV IN ROOMS
INSIDE PARKING

ONE MORE
REASON TO COME
TO AMSTERDAM

MAN around

GAY AMSTERDAM

Man Around, World leaders in Gay Travel, offer exclusively gay, or gay friendly hotels in Amsterdam! From a quick weekend break from every major UK airport, to accommodation only – we do it best.

All clients are supplied with up to date gay information listings, featuring Bars, Discos, Saunas, Cinemas, Cafes and Book Shops!

For a full colour brochure featuring this and many other gay holiday ideas worldwide, contact us on 071-376 5361.

Man Around – 270 Fulham Road, Chelsea, London SW10 9EW. Tel: 071-376 5361. Fax: 071-376 5534. Telex: 24740 Males G.

Gay Amsterdam

**Amsterdam is often called the gay capital of Europe.
Kees Neefjes assesses the scene, from protest
movements to leather bars.**

Amsterdam's gay scene rivals those
of Berlin, Paris and London, and for
many tourists is the main reason for
visiting the city. The gay organization, COC (*listed under* **Help &
Information**), has branches
throughout The Netherlands.
However, openly gay life is found
mainly in the big cities, to which
many young homosexuals migrate
from the less tolerant countryside.

ARTICLE 248 TO SECTION 28

The Netherlands originally decriminalized homosexuality in 1811. But
in 1911, pressure from moralizing
Catholics and Calvinists led to
Article 248-bis, which made the age
of consent 16 for heterosexuals, but
21 for homosexuals. The first wave
of protest, led by the newly-founded
NWHK (Dutch Scientific Humanity
Committee), furthered public understanding and increased gay
self-confidence. After World War II,
the Shakespeare Club was established; it was the forerunner of the
NVIH-COC, now known as COC.
COC gained status as a pressure
group, but was not recognized in law
until it was granted Royal Assent in
1973.

The high-profile gay rights movement of the sixties and seventies
outraged moralists, but generally won
tolerance. Traditional sexual roles
were being undermined by the new
welfare state and the student and feminist movements (*see page 196*
Students and *page 176* **Women's
Amsterdam**). These social movements fortified each other and
benefited from overlapping member-
ships and unity between gays and
lesbians, who, unlike in other countries, were covered by the same law.

Gay and lesbian groups were
formed in political parties, labour
unions, educational institutions and
churches – understanding for the
'homophile fellow-man' was even
advocated in ecclesiastical circles,
both Protestant and Catholic. The
Dutch Reformed Church is allowed
to bless gay relationships (*see below*
Remonstantse Broederschap).

Proud of their sexuality, influential
groups of radical homosexuals –
mostly students – adopted the old
nicknames *flikker* and *poot* (gay) and
pot (lesbian), criticizing COC for con-
centrating on integration with
heterosexual lifestyles. Article 248-
bis was finally abolished in 1971.
Groups such as *Roze Front* (Pink
Front; *see below* **Roze Zaterdag**),
which raised public awareness by
organizing publicity stunts and
demonstrations, redirected their
energies towards other issues such
as gay marriage and Section 28,
Britain's anti-gay law. The Dutch
branch of the AIDS activist group
Act-Up (*668 5488*) was founded in
1990 and has already secured the
availability of the AIDS medicine
DDI in The Netherlands.

Homo-monument

Westermarkt, IW. Tram 13, 14, 17.
This monument to people persecuted for
their sexual preference, unveiled in 1987,
was first proposed by a gay and lesbian section of the Pacifist Socialist Party, but from
1979 was supported by homosexuals from
all political parties. They united in a foundation, which raised finance from fund-raising
events, public subsidy and international private donations. You can read about its
history in a book by Pieter Koenders, *The
Monument*. Designed by Karin Daan, its
three triangles of pink granite form a larger
triangle that juts out into Keizersgracht. It
bears an inscription by gay writer Jacob
Israël de Haan, 'such an infinite desire for
friendship,' and is the focus for many events.
See also p171 **picture and caption**.

Remonstantse Broederschap

*Nieuwegracht 27, 3512 LC, Utrecht (030
316 970).*
If you want your relationship blessed,
whether or not you are Dutch or belong to
the Dutch Reformed Church, write to this
church giving your name, address and
phone number. You'll receive English-language information and then, if you wish to
continue, the address of the minister to contact. The process takes from three to six
months. At time of writing, such blessings
do not carry legal status in The
Netherlands.

Roze Zaterdag (Pink Saturday)

*Information on location and events from Gay
& Lesbian Switchboard (623 6565).* **Dates**
29 June 1991; 27 June 1992.
The *Roze Front* (Pink Front) is a co-operative organization embracing a number of
gay and lesbian groups. It organizes the

national gay pride demonstration, *Roze
Zaterdag* (Pink Saturday), which is held in a
different town every year. The day begins
with the *roze kerkdienst* (pink divine service); there are a lot of gay church groups.
Then between 5,000 and 10,000 people take
part in a march followed by a festival. In
recent years there's been a 'Festival of
Seduction' at Amsterdam's Melkweg (*see*
p141 **Night-clubs**) during the previous
week, but at time of writing this looked
unlikely to continue (phone the Switchboard
for news and details).

POLITICS OF CRUISING

The term 'cruising' is derived from
kruysen, the old Dutch word for seeking sexual contacts. In the seventies,
there were protests against municipal laws that enabled police to arrest
cruising gays as prostitutes and out-
lawed the 'alternative use' of public
urinals as gay meeting places. With
general support among councillors,
gay activists opposed the replacement of old two-man urinals with
one-man urinals and demanded that
the police should catch *potenram-
mers* (gay-bashers) instead of
harassing those being victimized.
After Amsterdam's Court of Justice
adjudged in 1985 that cruising was
not prostitution, the by-laws were
abolished.

Council policy is now more tolerant than ever before. Public
expressions of affection, cruising,
and even discreet sex in open spaces
(*see below* **Nudist areas**), are all
allowed, within reasonable limits in
places where offence is unlikely to
be taken. The liberal prostitution
laws also apply to gays, and the bor-
dellos and 'rent boy bars' in the gay
areas (*see below* **Clubs & Bars**) are
legal, if not all reputable. Bars and
discos that refuse admission to gays
or lesbians can lose their night
licence, and institutions that discrimi-
nate against homosexuals risk losing
municipal co-operation and subsidy,
although this doesn't always happen
in practice.

As cruising areas (*kruisenbaan*),
urinals have lost popularity and
cruisers now head for Vondelpark
(*see page 13* **Sightseeing**);
Julianapark, OE; Oosterpark, OE;
the Weteringscircuit (1e and 2e
Weteringsplantsoen), IS; and for
local nudist areas.

Nudist areas

Gaasperplas *south bank of Gaasperpark
lake, OE. Bus 174/Metro Gaasperplas.*
Nieuwemeer *on north bank, OW. Bus 43,
then along Jaagpad, then 10 mins past
Oeverland sign turn right down a short path.*
Spaarnwoude *north of Haarlem, near*

National Agency for Homosexuality

** Counselling

** Education & Prevention

** Schorer Publishing House

P.C. Hoofdstraat 5
1071 BL AMSTERDAM
Phone: (0)20 - 6624206
Fax: (0)20 - 6646069

Double/twin rooms with shower & toilet from 125 guilders singles from 70 guilders triples/luxury suite available breakfast till noon – your own key – bar central location – english owned – gay

Call Grant or John
31 - 20 - 62 30 230
or write to
ITC Prinsengracht 1051
1017 JE Amsterdam
Holland

AERO HOTEL
KERKSTRAAT 49
TEL. 6227728
NEWLY RENOVATED
YOUR OWN KEY
MOST ROOMS PRIVATE SHOWER

DE PUL TAVEERNE
KERKSTRAAT 45
TEL. 6221506
OPEN FROM 12.00 TILL 01.00

THE BRONX CINEMA BOOKSHOP
KERKSTRAAT 53 - 55
TEL. 6231548
OPEN FROM 12.00 TILL 24.00

THE BRONX VIDEOTHEEK
KERKSTRAAT 53 - 55
TEL. 6231548
SALE AND RENTAL ALL SYSTEMS

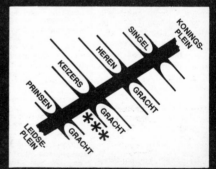

When in Amsterdam ...come see us!

Spaarndam; nudist area is Westhofbos. Bus 82 from Marnixstraat bus station/car via N5 (A5), then A9.
Het Twiske between Oostzaan and Landsmeer, N; nudist areas are Wezenlanden and Geldeveen. Bus 19, 68.
Zandvoort gay beach Train direct to Zandvoort/car via A5 to Haarlem, then follow signs.
These legal nudist areas are particularly visited by gays and don't get raided by police. They are cruisy, some with people having sex. Spaarnwoude open area has an official nudist section, Westhofbos, free for anyone, straight or gay. At the resort of Zandvoort, head south to the gay restaurant Zeezicht at the end of the promenade; the Zuidstrand (south beach) is nudist thereafter, but the gay area is a long walk further south (30 mins walk from station in total). The nudist area on the small islands at Sloterparkbad (see p183 Sport & Fitness: Water Sports) is popular with gay men.

GAY CULTURE

The Dutch have come to recognize the cultural and historical significance of homosexuality through both gay and lesbian studies and homosexual literature, whose readership extends beyond the the gay community. Early this century there were notable books published by Jacob Israël de Haan and Wilma Vermaat. The principal modern gay writers are Gerrit Komrij and Gerard Reve (see under Vrolijk). Reve has, like the lesbian writer Andreas Burnier (see page 176 Women's Amsterdam), been active in the gay movement. Translated Dutch literature and other gay books and publications in English can be found at American Discount Book Centre and W H Smith (see page 153 Shopping Around) and the shops listed below.

Gay & lesbian publications

Top Guide is a regularly updated English-language manual covering Amsterdam's gay scene in great detail. The annual Best Guide reviews (in English) gay places in Benelux (Belgium, Netherlands, Luxembourg), in which Amsterdam is prominent. Britain's monthly magazine Gay Times carries listings in English on Amsterdam for gays and lesbians. The following are in Dutch: Gay Krant, the country's most important gay newspaper; Homologie, a cultural and intellectual bi-monthly magazine; Man-to-Man, carrying listings of gay places throughout the country; Sekstant, magazine of the Netherlands Society for Sexual Reform, which has a list of organizations and information for special interest groups; and Sek, the COC's monthly.

Intermale

Spuistraat 251, C (625 0009). Tram 1, 2, 5, 13, 14, 17. Open 10am-6pm Mon-Wed, Fri, Sat; 10am-9pm Thur. Credit AmEx, MC, V.
This gay and lesbian bookshop has a large supply of titles (many in English) on litera-

The **Homo-monument** (see under **Article 248 to Section 28**) is the world's first memorial to persecuted gays and lesbians. Those victimized in World War II are commemorated here every 4 May, but flowers are frequently laid in more private grief. It's also a positive symbol for the homosexual community and a focus for demonstrations. The date of the monument's unveiling in 1987, 5 September, is celebrated as 'Coming Out Day' and parties are held here on occasions such as Queen's Day (see page 36 **Amsterdam by Season**).

ture, social science and art, plus a range of magazines and 'what's on' information.

Vrolijk

Paleisstraat 135, C (623 5142). Tram 1, 2, 5, 13, 17. Open 11am-6pm Mon; 10am-6pm Tue, Wed, Fri; 10am-9pm Thur; 10am-5pm Sat. No credit cards.
Vrolijk has an exhaustive range of new and second-hand gay and lesbian books, many in English, plus a huge stock of international magazines and details of events. It specializes in literature, so look out for works by Gerard Reve, one of the most popular and controversial Dutch authors. In the sixties, he was prosecuted and only partially acquitted of blasphemy for describing God as an incarnated donkey. Supported by the Attorney General, Reve appealed and was fully acquitted. A year later (1968) he received the PC Hooftprijs, the most important state award for literature.

Gay & lesbian studies

University of Amsterdam Oude Hoogstraat 24, C (525 2227). Tram 4, 9, 14, 16, 24, 25/Metro Nieuwmarkt.
University of Utrecht Haedelbarglaan 8, Utrecht (030 39 9111).
Courses on gay and lesbian topics can be taken by students on most degree courses. Courses at Amsterdam University concentrate on gay lifestyles and on homosexuality in society and history. Research at Utrecht University deals with gay emancipation (they advise the government on this) and the impact of AIDS.

HELP & INFORMATION

For sexual health matters, including AIDS, see page 221 **Survival**.

COC (National)

Rozenstraat 8, IW (623 1192). Tram 13, 14, 17. Open 9am-5pm Mon-Fri.
Thankfully, COC doesn't use its snappy full title: Nederlandse Vereniging tot Integratie van Homoseksualiteit – Cultuur en Ontspannigs Centrum (Dutch Union for Integration of Homosexuality – Centre for Culture and Relaxation). With about 6,000 members, and branches throughout the country, it's one of the world's biggest homosexual organizations.

COC (Amsterdam)

Rozenstraat 14, IW (information 1-5pm Wed-Sat 623 4079/office 626 3087). Tram 13, 14, 17. Open 9am-5pm Mon-Thur; coffee shop 1-5pm Wed-Sat; café 8pm-midnight Wed; 8pm-2am Fri. No credit cards.
COC can help with all matters relating to gays and lesbians, particularly if they're just coming out, but many come here to read magazines or to meet like-minded people in the coffee shop. COC discos are attended by people from all scenes and age groups, attracted by the friendly atmosphere, cheap drinks and varied music, from rock 'n' roll to acid. Discos are mixed on Fridays (10pm-2am) and lesbians-only on Saturday (10pm-3am), with admission f3.50 and a token system for buying drinks (a strippenkart costs either f4 or f12).

Gay & Lesbian Switchboard

(623 6565). Open 10am-10pm daily.
The English-speaking male and female employees of this phoneline are specially trained in giving information and advice on all gay and lesbian matters, from scene news to safe sex, and in talking about personal problems.

Mannen Hulplijn

(625 2225). Open 8-11pm Mon, Fri; 3-6pm Tue.

This is a listening and information phoneline for men.

Schorer Stichting
Nieuwendijk 17, C (624 6318). Tram 4, 9, 14, 16, 24, 25. **Open** *9am-5.30pm Mon-Fri.*
This state-funded social agency offers information, support and counselling for gay men and lesbians. Most calls are from people who can't handle their sexuality, but staff can advise on coming out, gay lifestyles and help for older homosexuals, but not legal matters. One department is solely concerned with AIDS and related matters. Phone for an appointment; they speak English.

Sjalhomo
PO Box 2536, 1000 CM Amsterdam (023 312318)
This national organization (the office is in Haarlem) for Jewish gays and lesbians organizes cultural, social and political activities on Jewish feast days. It has contacts with other Jewish organizations and with gay Jewish groups abroad, and welcomes visitors.

CLUBS & BARS

Amsterdam's gay men have a great choice of bars and discos, but there are far fewer for lesbians (*see page 176* **Women's Amsterdam**). The different gay scenes – **nichten, macho** and **trendy** – have distinct locations and types of bar, but, of course, the boundaries between them aren't rigid. We've selected some of the best, but the scene does change rapidly as venues open or close; comprehensive listings can be found in *Top Guide.* The following have a general, mixed appeal to gays of all ages and persuasions, as do the café and disco at COC (*see above* **Help & Information**)

The C'ring (Cockring)
Warmoesstraat 96, C (623 9604). Tram 4, 9, 16, 24, 25. **Open** *10pm-4am Mon-Thur, Sun; 10pm-5am Fri, Sat.* **Admission** free.
See p173 **picture and caption.**

IT
Amstelstraat 24, C (625 0111). Tram 4, 9, 14. **Open** *11pm-4am Thur, Sun; 11pm-5am Fri, Sat.* **Admission** free.
IT is a big disco with a *nichten* atmosphere (*see below* **Nichtenbars**) that's also popular with all kinds of young gays, lesbians and straights between 20 and 35, particularly students. The disco throbs to acid and house music and sometimes has drag or strip shows. The VIP room is a low-lit bar with quieter music.

John's Place
Beulingstraat 19, IS (624 1603). Tram 1, 2, 5. **Hotel rates** single from f85; double from f135. **Open** *bar* 7pm-1am Mon-Thur, Sun; 7pm-2am Fri, Sat. **Admission** free. **Credit** AmEx, MC, V.

John's is English-run and attracts many British ex-pats and tourists, as well as a mixed local crowd. The bar is modern, with Karel Appel posters on the walls and varied music quiet enough for proper conversation. There are four well-appointed hotel rooms upstairs and a restaurant with a traditional Dutch menu was due to open at time of writing.

NICHTENBARS

Nichten is a broad term identified with camp, effeminate gays, who heavily influenced the public image of homosexuals in the sixties, when most gay places were *nichtenbars.* Now concentrated in the Amstel-Rembrandtsplein area, *nichtenbars* are cosy and women-friendly, with an animated clientèle always willing to sing along with the music. Some of these venues are home to the drag scene.

Amstel Taveerne
Amstel 54, C (623 4254). Tram 4, 9, 14. **Open** *4pm-1am Mon-Thur, Sun; 3pm-2am Fri, Sat.* **Admission** free.
See p175 **picture and caption.**

Anthony Theater
Oudezijds Voorburgwal 30, C (622 4793). Tram 4, 9, 16, 24, 25. **Open** *drag shows* 6-7 weeks in spring and autumn at about 8pm Thur-Sat, lunch-time Sun.* **Admission** f25.
This tiny, old-fashioned theatre, as intimate as someone's front room, presents drag shows in spring and autumn. At other times it presents Yiddish theatre, so check the programme in *Uitkrant* or the VVV's *What's On.* Presided over by Dolly Bellefleur, the drag shows are very professional and aimed at an international audience, so are mostly in English. Relax in the bar after the show.

Chez Manfred
Halvemaansteeg 10, C (626 4510). Tram 4, 9, 14. **Open** *3pm-1am Mon-Thur, Sun; 3pm-2am Fri, Sat.* **Admission** free.
This cosy neighbourhood bar attracts the exuberant local *nichten* who sing along to the Dutch songs. As the name suggests, the camp bar is owned by singer-entertainer Manfred. Generally packed, it gets particularly busy at happy hour (5.30-7pm; two drinks for the price of one) and on public holidays the crowd overflows into the alley. There are frequent shows and people also get up to sing.

Le Montmartre
Halvemaansteeg 17, C (620 7622). Tram 4, 9, 14. **Open** *4pm-1am Mon-Thur, Sun; 4pm-2am Fri, Sat.* **Admission** free.
This cosy bar has original turn-of-the-century murals by Epoe Doeve and recent restoration makes the best of the old features. As at Amstel Taveerne (*see above*), the fun-loving regulars can't resist partying on public holidays and other occasions. There's frequent cabaret, sometimes drag.

Le Shako
's Gravelandseveer 2, C (624 0209). Tram 4, 9, 14, 16, 24, 25. **Open** *9pm-2am Mon-Thur, Sun; 9pm-3am Fri-Sat.* **Admission** free.
This is a tiny, gay brown café and its cosy

character attracts students and young, conversational types. It's less overtly *nichten* than the Amstel Taveerne opposite (*see above*).

MACHO SCENE

The cruisy, denim-and-leather scene is concentrated mainly around Warmoesstraat.

Argos
Warmoesstraat 95, C (622 6595). Tram 4, 9, 14, 16, 24, 25. **Open** *9pm-3am Mon-Thur; 9pm-4am Fri, Sat; 8pm-3am Sun.* **Admission** free.
This is one of the oldest, most famous leather-and-denim bars in town, and certainly the cruisiest. Although a dress code isn't enforced, the macho atmosphere in the very dark front and back bars is uncompromising – the wall decorations are chains. There's a back room with cabins and videos in the basement.

Club Jaques
Warmoesstraat 93, C (622 0323). Tram 4, 9, 16, 24, 25. **Open** *8pm-3am Mon-Thur, Sun; 8pm-4am Fri, Sat.* **Admission** free.
A lot of tourists favour this leather-and-jeans bar. It has a back room, but is perhaps more sociable than cruisy.

The Eagle
Warmoesstraat 90, C (627 8634). Tram 4, 9, 16, 24, 25. **Open** *9pm-3am Mon-Thur, Sun; 9pm-4am Fri, Sat.* **Admission** free.
Gays of all ages into leather and jeans make this bar with a dancefloor very busy after midnight, but it's not too crowded before then and the whole place is air conditioned. There are two back rooms, but it's not heavily cruisy.

De Spijker
Kerkstraat 4, IS (620 5919). Tram 1, 2, 5. **Open** *9pm-3am Mon-Thur, Sun; 9pm-4am Fri, Sat.* **Admission** free.
Spijker means 'nail' or 'tack', and there's a huge nail impaled into the counter of this American-style bar. It has recently become less leather-oriented, but is still very cruisy, with porno videos and regular 'jack-off parties', the f10 entry fees to which are donated to AIDS charities.

TRENDY SCENE

Gay students, artists, intellectuals and those who follow fashion rather than dress codes, frequent venues such as Havana (*see page 141* **Nightclubs**), which mostly have modern interiors and higher drink prices than other bars.

April
Café April Reguliersdwarsstraat 37, IS (625 9572). April's Exit (bar/disco) *Reguliersdwarsstraat 42, IS (625 8788). Tram 1, 2, 4, 5, 9, 14, 16, 24, 25.* **Open** *Café April* 2pm-1am Mon-Thur, Sun; 2pm-2am Fri, Sat; *April's Exit* 11pm-4am Thur, Sun; 11pm-5am Fri, Sat. **Admission** free. **No credit cards.**
April café-bar is large and relaxed, with friendly staff serving good light meals. The

décor is modern, with photos on display; there's also a notice-board. Quiet by day, it fills up with men after work for the happy hour (times vary); drinks are also cheaper in late evening. April's Exit is a smart new disco for trendy young gays. Reached via a quieter, comfortable bar, the disco room was once a hay loft, and there's much hay-making on the cruisy dancefloor, overlooked by a balcony. State-of-the-art equipment pumps out the lights and latest music.

Traffic
Reguliersdwarsstraat 11, IS (623 3298).
Tram 1, 2, 5. **Open** 10pm-3am Mon-Thur, Sun; 10pm-4am Fri, Sat. **Admission** free.
This modern bar, with car-inspired decorations, is favoured by the beautiful people and those who like to look at them, and is welcoming to like-minded, like-dressed foreigners. A rival of Havana (*see p141* **Night-clubs**), it has quieter music and is more conducive to conversation. It's busiest after other bars have closed.

De Trut
Bilderdijkstraat 165, OW (no phone). Tram 3, 7, 12, 17. **Open** 10pm-4am Sun.
Admission free.
The Trut disco is in the cellar of the Tetterode squat (*see p68* **Post-war**), and attracts young, trendy gays and lesbians, as well as squatters and students. Drinks are very cheap and the music's right up-to-date.

EATING

For the gay disco-restaurant Homolulu and women's eating places welcoming to gay men, *see page 176* **Women's Amsterdam**. Mandate Coffeebar (*see under* **Fitness Centre**) and the café at COC (*listed under* **Help & Information**) have wide gay appeal.

Adrian
Reguliersdwarsstraat 21, IS (623 9582).
Tram 4, 9, 14, 16, 24, 25. **Open** 6pm-midnight daily. **Credit** AmEx, MC, TC, V.
This high-quality gay restaurant has excellent French specialities; the daily-changing set menu costs f45. Dimly lit, it's perfect for a romantic treat.

Down Town
Reguliersdwarsstraat 31, IS (622 9958).
Tram 1, 2, 4, 5, 9, 14, 16, 24, 25. **Open** 10am-8pm daily. **No credit cards.**
Evidently successful with gays who know they look good, this modern, white café is still hospitable to individuals, since it's so small you have to share tables. You can people-watch through the large windows or from pavement tables in summer. Good-value light snacks, salads and cakes are served by pleasant, efficient staff. To a background of unintrusive music, you can peruse the art exhibitions and selection of magazines and newspapers (many in English).

The Eighties
Brouwersgracht 139, IW (626 9874). Tram 1, 2, 4, 5, 9, 13, 16, 17, 24, 25. **Open** April-

Sept 10am-8pm daily; *Oct-Mar* 10am-6pm daily. **Credit** MC.
The hi-tech design of this new café couldn't contrast more with the surrounding old warehouses (now up-market apartments). There are photographic exhibitions and plenty of magazines to read, plus an outside terrace.

Leto
Haarlemmerdijk 114-116, IW (625 5695).
Tram 3/bus 18, 22, 44. **Open** 5-11pm daily.
No credit cards.
This cheap, intimate restaurant is famous for its camp, impertinent waiters, whose jokes are hilarious on occasional visits, but could prove tiresome if you go often.

Le Monde
Rembrandtsplein 6, IS (626 9922). Tram 4, 9, 14. **Open** 8am-midnight daily. **No credit cards.**
The reasonably priced snacks and hot meals served here are popular with both local and visiting gays. A terrace faces the street entertainers on Rembrandtsplein and the staff are happy to give information on the gay scene.

HOTELS

It's illegal for 'straight' hotels (*see page 39* **Accommodation**) to refuse accommodation to gays, and it's rare to encounter excuses such as 'All rooms are engaged'. At the following gay hotels, no questions are asked if you take a guest to your room, but you'd be expected to pay for an extra breakfast. The same applies to John's Place (*listed under* **Clubs & Bars**), and Granada Hotel and Quentin Hotel (*see page 176* **Women's Amsterdam**). For a comprehensive list, consult *Top Guide*.

Greenwich Village Hotel
Kerkstraat 25, 1017 GA; IS (626 9746).
Tram 1, 2, 5. **Rates** *dormitory* f35; *double* f95. **No credit cards.**
Hotel services Bar. **Room services** TV.

International Travel Club (ITC)
Prinsengracht 1051, 1017 JE; IS (623 0230).
Tram 4. **Rates** *single* f63-f82; *double* f105-f145; *twin* f145; *triple* f190; *luxury suite* f175-f300. **Credit** AmEx, MC, V.
Hotel services Bar.

Hotel New York
Herengracht 13, 1015 BA; IW (624 3066/fax 620 3230). Tram 1, 2, 5, 13.
Rates *single* f80-f140; *double* f130-f145;

The C'ring *night-club* (see under **Clubs & Bars**) *has been such a success that it's one of the few gay venues for which you need to queue to get in at weekends. It attracts all types of gays under about 40, although it's located in the leather-and-denim district. The dancefloor sounds are house, hi-NRG and pop, with quieter music in the upstairs video bar. Despite the air-conditioning the pulsating mass of people raises the temperature. It's a lot quieter early in the week. The C'ring's a cruisy place, with a back room reached through the (clean) toilets.*

GIS
APARTMENTS

During the last few years a growing interest in renting apartments in the city of Amsterdam has developed. Fully furnished apartments are an attractive alternative to more impersonel hotel rooms. Not only attractive to the tourist in general but also to the temporary 'detached' business woman or man. GIS can offer you such an apartment for a period ranging between one week and one month or even longer. Rental prices for one week are from $600 and for one month from $1.000 to $3.000 or more, excluding the fee to GIS. You might be looking for an apartment for a holiday or other reasons. In that case we hope that you too will use the unique service GIS can offer.

If you want information you can always contact GIS by letter to: Keizersgracht 33, 1015 CD Amsterdam, or by fax: -31.20.6380475, or by telephone: -31.20.6250071.

General Manager,
Alain Stom.

**YOU CAN DANCE
ON THE FIRST FLOOR**

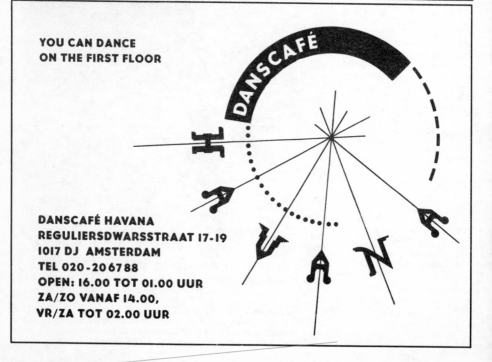

**DANSCAFÉ HAVANA
REGULIERSDWARSSTRAAT 17-19
1017 DJ AMSTERDAM
TEL 020-206788
OPEN: 16.00 TOT 01.00 UUR
ZA/ZO VANAF 14.00,
VR/ZA TOT 02.00 UUR**

luxury double f235; *triple* f275. **Credit**
AmEx, DC, MC, V.
Hotel services *Bar. Coffee shop. Laundry.*
Room service.

Orfeo Hotel
Leidsekruisstraat 14, 1017 RH; IS (623
1347/fax 620 2348). Tram 1, 2, 5, 6, 7, 10.
Rates *single* f65-f75; *double* f97.50; *twin*
f102.50; *studio apartment* f130-f140. **Credit**
AmEx, MC, V.
Hotel services *Bar. Laundry. Parking (f20*
per day). Sauna.

Unique Hotel
Kerkstraat 37, 1017 GB; IS (624 4785).
Tram 1, 2, 5. **Rates** *single* f70; *double* f95;
twin f125. **No credit cards.**
Hotel services *TV lounge bar.*

APARTMENTS

Gay Interhome Services
Keizersgracht 33, 1015 CD; IW (625
0071/638 0955/fax 638 0475). Tram 1, 2,
5, 13, 14, 17. **Cost** *one-bedroom apartment*
from f500 per week; *two-bedroom apartment*
from f800 per week. **Deposit** one month's
rent. **Credit** AmEx, MC, V.
Gay Interhome Services lets out furnished
flats for between three days and three
months. The flats, mostly one-bed and central, are owned by people away for an
extended period. This agency has a good
reputation and a big deposit is required.
Lesbians are welcomed.

AROUND TOWN

CINEMA

Gay & Lesbian Switchboard (*see*
above **Help & Information**) has a
list of cinemas and theatres with
shows on homosexual themes, such
as the movies at Desmet (*see page*
122 **Film**) every Saturday at midnight and Sunday at 4pm.

SHOPS

The Condomerie (*see page 161*
Specialist Shops) stocks a great
variety of condoms. For bookshops,
see above **Gay Culture**.

The Bronx
Kerkstraat 53-55, IS (623 1548). Tram 1, 2,
5, 16, 24, 25. **Open** noon-midnight daily.
Credit AmEx, MC, V.
A large selection of magazines, books and
cards, toys (not Monopoly). There's a wide
range of videos for hire or sale, and viewing cabins. A cinema is attached to the
shop.

Expectations...
Warmoesstraat 32, C (624 5573). Tram 1, 2,
4, 5, 9, 13, 16, 17, 24, 25. **Open** noon-6pm
Mon-Fri; noon-5pm Sat. **Credit** AmEx, DC,
MC, V.
If the off-the-peg leather and rubber gear
doesn't fit, you can have the item you want

The long-established **Amstel Taveerne** *(see under* **Clubs & Bars:**
Nichtenbars) *is about the best example of a Dutch neighbourhood bar you could*
find. As with other 'nichtenbars', it's gay in both senses of the word. The regulars
are very exuberant and liable to join in with the Dutch songs spun by the DJ, gen-
erating a fun, party-like atmosphere that's very welcoming to foreigners and
women. In fine weather, the crowd – and it does get busy, particularly during the
6-7pm happy hour – spills out onto the pavement; on occasions such as Queen's
Day, a bar is set up outside to cope with the demand for Amstel beer.

made to measure. Whatever your taste in
adult toys and bondage equipment they've
probably got it in stock.

RoB Gallery
Weteringschans 253, IS (625 4686). Tram 6,
7, 10. **Open** 9am-6pm Mon-Fri; 11am-5pm
Sat. **Credit** AmEx, MC, V.
Leather and rubber clothing and accoutrements can be bought direct or by mail
order, either from stock or made to measure. The shop has a two-floor gallery with
monthly exhibitions, on which RoB's series
of 'Amsterdam Cards' are based. Posters,
cards, videos and magazines are on sale and
there's also an S&M cellar.

FITNESS CENTRE

Mandate
Prinsengracht 715, IS (625 4100). Tram 1,
2, 5. **Open** 11am-10pm Mon-Fri; noon-
6pm Sat; 2-6pm Sun. **Membership** daily
f20; weekly f60; monthly f85. **No credit**
cards.
Mandate is a men-only fitness centre for
gays. The well-equipped gym has a trained
instructor. Sauna (no hanky-panky allowed),
shower and towels are included in the membership fee; sunbed and massage are extra.
Mandate Coffeebar is a good meeting
place for anyone, whether or not you're a

member or have just used the gym, and has
become fashionable for Sunday brunch
(from 2pm). Many well-priced videos are for
hire or sale.

SAUNAS

Egelantier
Egelantiersstraat 246, IW (625 3736). Tram
10, 13, 14, 17. **Open** 6-11pm Mon-Thur;
6pm-8am Fri; 10pm-8am Sat; 1-6pm Sun.
Admission f17.50. **No credit cards.**
Less hectic than rival saunas and welcoming
all age groups, Egelantier has a snack-bar, a
sunbed, a video and a safe sex area, with
condoms on sale.

Thermos
Thermos Day *Raamstraat 35, IW (623*
9158). Tram 1, 2, 5. **Open** noon-11pm Mon-
Fri; noon-6pm Sat, Sun. **Admission** f21. **No**
credit cards.
Thermos Night *Kerkstraat 60, IS (623*
4936). Tram 1, 2, 5. **Open** 11pm-8am daily.
Admission f22.50. **No credit cards.**
Both of these claret saunas have a steam
room, a dry-heat room, a bar, videos, private
cubicles and a snack bar. Both are very popular with an uninhibited clientèle. Thermos
Night is an alternative to spending money
on a hotel room – although you wouldn't get
much sleep.

Women's Amsterdam

The campaigners of the sixties and seventies won important victories in the battle of the sexes. Even during the current ceasefire, Amsterdam has plenty to offer women, writes Marieke Sjerps.

Amsterdam women are internationally famous for their campaigns to gain equal treatment for women and men. Their protests, Dutch tolerance and progressive legislation have all combined to make the city's feminist credentials impressive by the standards of most countries.

SUFFRAGETTE CITY

Like the suffragettes in other western countries, Dutch women struggled for the right to vote over several decades around the turn of the century. Besides this they claimed better healthcare and education for women. In 1871 a Dutch university admitted a woman student for the first time. This pioneer, Aletta Jacobs, became the first Dutch woman doctor and fought throughout her lifetime for the improvement of conditions for women.

When the right to vote was finally granted to women in 1919, the movement lost its strength and did not fully recover until the sixties. Feminist pioneers remained little known until the introduction of women's history onto the curriculum in Dutch schools. But in Amsterdam, several streets were named in tribute to the early campaigners, including Aletta Jacobslaan and Wilhelmina Druckerstraat.

THE FEMINIST WAVE

The origins of the second wave of the women's movement lie in the changing cultural climate of the fifties and sixties. The first wave had struggled for equal *rights* for men and women; now women campaigned for equal *treatment* of both sexes.

In 1967 Joke Smit articulated feminist grievances in her book *Het Onbeha gen de Vrouw* (roughly, 'the discontent of women'), which became the definitive reference on the subject. Smit was a founder member in 1968 of the radical group

MVM, *Man-Vrouw-Maatschappij* (man-woman-society), which aimed at fundamentally changing the roles of the sexes. One of its proposals was a five-hour working day for both men and women. In later years MVM started consciousness-raising groups. Another of MVM's founders, Hedy d'Ancona, became Minister for Welfare, Public Health and Culture in 1989, and has since campaigned on such issues as provision of childcare facilities for working women.

The feminist protest organizations became models for other social movements. One of the most remarkable was **Dolle Mina**, named after Wilhelmina Drucker, a feminist leader during the first wave. It was formed in 1968 by women (and some men) from all parts of the country and of society, ironically as an outraged reaction to student protests (*see page 196* **Students**). Students had occupied the administrative centre of the University of Amsterdam, but while the male students held meetings, their female colleagues were supposed to prepare sandwiches and clean the toilets. When prosecuted, the women students were sentenced less severely than the men, showing that the judge didn't take their protests as seriously. Dolle Mina activists later sang in front of City Hall, greeting newly-weds with the refrain: 'Faith forever, but who will clean the sink?'.

On the crucial demand that abortion should be decriminalized and made freely accessible, all feminist groups worked together, but the most notable action was by Dolle Mina (*see page 177* **picture and caption**). In 1970, a clinic that carried out abortions was threatened with closure by the Justice Minister, but an (ultimately successful) occupation of the clinic prompted an outcry that almost caused the fall of the government. An abortion law was finally passed in 1981, but to many women it

was a disappointing outcome after such a long political battle. After 50 days and before 22 weeks of pregnancy, a woman wanting an abortion has to wait five days after discussing the matter with a doctor, to give her time to reconsider.

IIAV (International Archives of the Women's & Lesbian Movement)
Keizersgracht 10, IW (624 2143/4268). *Tram 1, 2, 5, 13, 17.* **Open** 10am-4pm Mon, Wed-Fri; 10am-8.45pm Tue.
See p177 **picture and caption**.
Further archives: **Lesbian Archives**, *see below* **Lesbian Liberation; Centraal Bibliotheek**, *see page 221* **Survival**.

A CITY FOR WOMEN?

The women's movement as it was in the seventies no longer exists. During the eighties, the public diverted its protesting energies into anti-nuclear and environmental campaigns. Since then, as individuals, women have seemed more concerned with making an independent career than demonstrating. Moreover, feminism has become institutionalized: women are represented in all sorts of organizations. A Minister of State for Emancipation, J G Kraaijeveld-Wouters, was appointed in 1977, but the post was deemed unnecessary a decade later, as by then there was a commission for equal treatment at work and a Council for Emancipation (*Emancipatieraad*) advising the government. Many university departments have their own women's courses and you can graduate in Women's Studies from the University of Amsterdam (UVA); *see page 196* **Students**.

But in business, the equal wages act (1975) and equal treatment act (1980) have been undermined by more subtle sexism. On starting a family, women find that the lack of childminders forces them back into their traditional role at home. Because men still occupy most – and the most important – positions in business and society, the equality laws were combined in 1989 and a more effective law of equal treatment for all groups was proposed in 1990. But in the provinces, religious tradition still dictates that women keep to their child-rearing, home-making roles.

If you want to relax in female-only company, get sympathetic help or find out more about the women's movement, we've listed where to go. For advice, information or details on where to go out and find hotels, courses and women's festivals – there are often events on International Women's Day, 8 March – phone one of the following or contact **Café Saarein** (*see below* **Going Out: Cafés & Bars**).

Het Vrouwenhuis (The Women's House)
Nieuwe Herengracht 95, IE (625 2066). *Tram 7, 9, 14.* **Open** *information* 2-5pm Mon-Fri; *bar* 8pm-1am after classes. **Closed** June-early Sept.
There's a network of Women's Houses throughout The Netherlands. They organize events, such as festivities on International Women's Day (8 March), and activities, including workshops, courses and classes on things like massage, dance, contact and improvization. Non-lesbian women will appreciate the fact that the bar, which opens after evening classes have finished, is not part of the 'scene'. Vrouwenhuis also runs a women-only disco every second Friday of the month (10pm-2am, f5).

Vrouwen Bellen Vrouwen (Women Call Women)
(625 0150). **Open** 9am-noon, 10-11pm, Mon, Tue, Thur; 9am-noon, 1.30-4pm, Wed; 9am-noon Fri.
Women can get advice and support by ringing this phoneline.

Zwarte Vrouwentelefoon (Black Women's Telephone)
(085-42 4713). **Open** 9am-noon Mon; 1-4pm Tue; 7-10pm Wed.
This helpline for black women offers both support and information.

LESBIAN LIBERATION
The lesbian movement has had a significant role in changing views on sexuality. For a history of the movement for homosexual rights, *see page 169* **Gay Amsterdam**. These days, unlike the more coherent gay community, Amsterdam lesbians have a low profile and don't present themselves as a group anymore; there are very few purely lesbian establishments. But they do campaign with gay men for the freedom to adopt children and with feminist activists for the right to artificial insemination for single women and lesbians.

The lesbian scene of course overlaps with the gay scene and women (not just lesbians) are accepted at many gay clubs, bars and cafés. The lesbian and gay centre **COC** has a notice-board, a 'non-scene' café and a women-only disco on Sunday nights. The staff of the *COC vrouwensecretariat* (Lesbian Women's Secretariat) offer information and advice. You can also try the English-speaking help and information line **Gay & Lesbian**

*The **IIAV Archives** (see under* **The Feminist Wave***) relate the history of the women's and lesbian movements through international books, documents, press clippings and photographs. Among the many memorable images are some of Dolle Mina activists entering a meeting of gynaecologists displaying their bellies, labelled: 'Baas in eigen buik' – 'Control over our own bellies'. Around 1970 the group claimed back the streets in other creative ways, wolf-whistling at men and pinching their buttocks. And, in protest at the lack of women's public toilets, they tied up urinals with pink ribbons bearing the motto: 'Women too have the right to piss.'*

Switchboard on 623 6565. For all the above, *see page 169* **Gay Amsterdam**. A continuously updated printout of the *Top Guide's* comprehensive lesbian chapter is available for the price of postage (f6/£2/US$3) from: *Postbox 22643, NL-1100 DC Amsterdam*. Two monthly Dutch-language magazines listing what's on for lesbians are *Ma'dam* (Madame Amsterdam, f2.95) and *Sek* (f4), available from newsagents and bookshops (*listed under* **Shops & Business**).

Groep 7152
West Indie Café, De Ruijterkade 110, C (624 7769). *Tram 1, 2, 4, 5, 9, 13, 16, 17, 24, 25.* **Meetings** (phone to check) *Sept-June* 4-9pm 3rd Sun of month.
Group 7152 provides a social support group for lesbians and bi-sexual women, and meets for talking and dancing at West Indie Café. For information on this countrywide organization phone 662 0866, although little English is spoken there.

Lesbian Archives
1e Helmersstraat 17, OW (618 5879). *Tram 1, 6.* **Open** 1-5pm Mon, Fri; 6.30-10.30pm Tue; 9.30am-1.30pm Thur.
These archives are mainly audio-visual, including home-made videos of festivals and events, recordings of speeches and television and radio programmes, including ones in English, French and German. For IIAV general women's archives, *see above* **The Second Wave**.

The women's 'scene' is far smaller than it was in the seventies. Amsterdam women now seem to feel less of a need for female-only venues, many of which are run by volunteers and are struggling financially. The Melkweg (*see page 135* **Music: Rock, Folk & Jazz**) has occasional exhibitions for and about women. For child and baby minders, *see page 180* **Children & Parents**.

CAFES & BARS

There's a general women's bar at **Het Vrouwenhuis** (*see above* **A City for Women?**) and a café popular with lesbians at **COC** (*see page 169* **Gay Amsterdam**).

Café Sonja
Nassaukade 122, OW (684 3325). *Tram 10.* **Open** 8pm-2am Mon-Thur; 8pm-3am Fri, Sat. **No credit cards.**
The atmosphere in Sonja's can be compared to a *volkscafé* – a typical neighbourhood coffee shop. Many of the people here (mostly lesbians) know each other, but they welcome foreigners.

Café Vive-la-Vie
Amstelstraat 5, C (624 0114). *Tram 4, 9, 14.* **Open** noon-1am Mon-Thur, Sun; noon-2am Fri, Sat. **No credit cards.**

Mainly lesbian women go to this café for a drink and to meet others. The art deco-style interior is perfect for conversation, although the music can get a little too loud in the evening. Every first Friday of the month locals cross the road to the café's sister disco **Super-vie-night** (10am-5pm; f5) at the Royal Star, Paardenstraat 32, C (622 9418); *see p135* **Music: Rock, Folk & Jazz.**

Françoise
Kerkstraat 176, IS (624 0145). Tram 16, 24, 25. **Open** 9am-6pm Mon-Sat. **No credit cards.**
At this mixed, lesbian-owned café and gallery you can get tea, coffee, home-made pastries and full meals (including vegetarian) and see exhibitions of work by female artists, which change every month. The décor is old-Dutch style and the music is classical.

Homolulu
Kerkstraat 13, IS (624 6387). Tram 16, 24, 25. **Open** *restaurant & disco* 10pm-4am Mon-Thur, Sun; 10pm-5am Fri, Sat; *women-only evening* 1st Sun of month 6pm-midnight; then mixed lesbians and gay men midnight-4am. **Admission** free Mon-Thur, Sun; f5 Fri, Sat; *women-only evening* free. **Average meal** f40. **No credit cards.**
Owned and run by lesbians, this smart private restaurant/disco is frequented by lesbians, gays and a sprinkling of straights. There's a women-only night on the first Sunday of the month (except July and August). You can have a reasonably priced, candle-lit meal in the superb restaurant overlooking the mirrored dance-floor, where the music is mainly from the pop charts. The door policy can be selective, so dress up!

Café Saarein
Elandsstraat 119, IW (623 4901). Tram 7, 10. **Open** 8pm-1am Mon; 3pm-1am Tue-Thur, Sun; 3pm-2am Fri, Sat. **No credit cards.**
See picture and caption.

La Strada
Nieuwezijds Voorburgwal 93, C (625 0276). Tram 1, 2, 5, 13, 17. **Open** *bar* 3pm-1am Mon-Thur, Sun; 3pm-2am Fri, Sat; *kitchen* 5.30-10pm daily. **No credit cards.**
This spacious café is bang in the centre of Amsterdam, with a sprinkling of gay men, can have dinner here from 5.30pm to 10pm; main courses cost between f15 and f25 and vegetarian meals are available. Each month La Strada shows the work of a different artist.

Van den Berg
Lindengracht 95, IW (622 2716). Tram 3. **Open** 4pm-1am Mon-Thur, Sun; 4pm-2am Fri, Sat. **No credit cards.**
Have your dinner or simply a coffee outside on the terrace of this café-restaurant in the Jordaan. Van den Berg is a cosy place to have a good dinner – vegetarian meals are available – for between f10 and f20. It's mainly frequented by women, but men are welcome too.

CULTURAL CENTRE

Amazone
Singel 72, C (627 9000). Tram 1, 2, 5, 13, 17. **Open** 10am-4pm Tue-Fri; 1-4pm Sat. **Admission** free. **No credit cards.**
This foundation promotes artistic and cultural work by women, mostly Dutch. It holds exhibitions in its gallery; recent shows include photographic studies of women in sport and studies of the portrayal of women in children's literature. The bar is only open during the occasional lectures and poetry evenings, both in Dutch (normally last Thursday of the month, phone to check).

DISCOS

Amsterdam does not have many women-only clubs, but there are regular women's 'one-nighter' discos organized at the following clubs and by **Het Vrouwenhuis** (*see above* **A City for Women?**), **Vive La Vie** (*see above* **Cafés & Bars**) and **COC** (for this and **gay clubs** that accept women, *see page 169* **Gay Amsterdam**). Phone before setting out.

De Brug
Kuipersstraat 151 (postal enquiries to PO Box 6189, 1005 ED, Amsterdam), OS. Tram 3, 4. **Open** 8.30pm-2am 1st Sat of month. **Admission** f4. **No credit cards.**
On the first Saturday of every month there's a disco evening here for lesbians over 35.

De Club
Amstel 178, IS (623 4480). Tram 4, 9, 14. **Open** 10pm-4am Mon-Thur, Sun; 10pm-5am Fri, Sat. **Admission** free. **No credit cards.**
This club is owned and run by lesbians and lesbians form most of the crowd, although straight women and gay men come along to this busy venue. There are shows over public holidays and every Sunday evening, when volunteers are invited on stage to sing a favourite song. You ring the bell to gain admission and pay for drinks at the end of the night, having marked your orders on a card.

La Louve
Singel 447, C (623 3984). Tram 1, 2, 4, 5, 9, 12, 14, 24, 25. **Open** midnight-4am Tue-Sun. **Admission** free Tue, Wed, Sun; f5 Fri, Sat. **Meals** *average* f35; *snacks* f5. **No credit cards.**
La Louve is a straight club, but it attracts a lot of lesbians and gay men. There's a ground-floor bar, a first-floor disco and a decent restaurant on the second floor. Pop and chart music predominate.

Mae West
2e Constantijn Huygenstraat 31, OW. Tram 1, 2, 5, 6. **Open** 8.30pm-2.30am 3rd Sat of month. **Admission** f3.50. **No credit cards.**
The music is from the fifties and sixties, and there's a card system for drinks (pay when you leave).

BATHS & SAUNA

Almost every sports centre, swimming pool and sauna in Amsterdam has women-only sessions; *see page 183* **Sport & Fitness.** We list two women's saunas.

Sauna Kylpy
Mercatorplein 23-27, OW (612 3496). Tram 7, 13. **Open** 10am-11pm Mon-Fri. **Admission** f17.50. **Sunbeds** f15 for 20 mins. **No credit cards.**

Café Saarein (see under Going Out: Cafés & Bars) *is the hub of the women's scene in Amsterdam. It's a snug brown bar that women have to themselves in the centre of the Jordaan. The staff have a list in English of women's activities in the city and are happy to give help and information over the phone. It's often said that the Dutch women's scene has become insular. Many bars are frequented by women who all know each other, so foreigners often end up talking more with other visitors than locals. But at Saarein you can always find female company to chat to or play darts or billiards with in the interestingly furnished 'cellar'.*

You can take all kinds of baths, including Turkish, in this rustic building.

Sauna Aquafit

Van 't Hofflaan 4, OE (694 5211). Tram 9. Open 7-11pm Tue-Fri. Closed during the summer school holidays, Christmas holidays and for a couple of weeks around Easter so it's wise to ring and check first. Admission f16. No credit cards. The women-only sauna at this swimming school is open to the public.

SHOPS & BUSINESSES

The number of Dutch women owning businesses continues to grow. According to a recent survey, almost 30 per cent of businesses in The Netherlands – even more in Amsterdam – have a female managing director, although these are predominantly small firms. It's striking that only a few of the concerns are aimed just at female customers. For outsize and petite clothing shops, *see page 153* Shopping Around.

STEW

Weesperzijde 4, OE (665 5016). Tram 3, 6, 7, 10. Open 9am-5pm Mon-Thur. The association has information on women-run businesses and companies throughout The Netherlands.

Women's International Network

PO Box 15692, 1001 ND, Amsterdam (679 8088/co-founder Agnes Benjamin 679 9951). Membership Sept-June f150. No credit cards. The professional women members of this network are supportive of each other and have a wealth of contacts and advice for like-minded career women, particularly useful to those who have just moved to Amsterdam. To join you should be of managerial status, be over 25 and have been employed for a minimum of five years. Associate members are women with these qualifications who are temporarily out of work (due to children, a recent move, and so on). There's an international mix of women, but given that all communications and meetings are in English, Americans and Britons predominate. The Network holds monthly meetings, invites guest speakers and organizes lectures, workshops and visits, usually with a career theme.

BOOKSHOPS

For Vrolijk bookshop, *see page 169* Gay Amsterdam.

Antiquariaat Lorelei

Prinsengracht 495, IW (623 4308). Tram 1, 2, 5, 7, 10. Open noon-6pm Tue-Fri; noon-5pm Sat. No credit cards. *See picture and caption.*

Vrouwen in Druk

Westermarkt 5, IW (624 5003). Tram 13,

Antiquariaat Lorelei (see under Shops & Businesses: Bookshops) *stocks a huge selection of second-hand books by and about women. Titles in English cover all subjects from biography and feminist theory to travel and sociology. Among the fiction by women, you can find titles by the lesbian writers Wilma Vermaat, Andreas Burnier, Anna Blaman and Astrid Roemer. The latter was elected to The Hague city council, where she champions minority interests. Lorelei also has a notice-board with information on events and activities of interest to women.*

14, 17. Open 11am-6pm Mon-Sat. No credit cards.
Vrouwen in Druk stocks second-hand books (with dozens of shelves of English titles) by female authors of interest to women, covering feminist theory, history and literature.

Xantippe

Prinsengracht 290, IW (623 5854). Tram 1, 2, 5. Open 1-6pm Mon; 10am-6pm Tue-Sat. Credit MC, V.
This is the main women's bookstore, stocking new titles, with many in English. Staff are up to date with information on what's on for women in Amsterdam.

HOTELS

There are no women-only hotels, but the following are 'friendly'. Among the gay hotels, ITC Hotel is the most popular with women (*see page 169* Gay Amsterdam).

Granada Hotel

Leidsekruisstraat 13, IS (623 6711). Tram 1, 2, 5, 6, 7, 10. Rates dormitory f40; single f75-f85; double f85-f100; triple f130-f145; quad f160. Credit (minimum f120) AmEx, DC, MC, V.
This relaxed, mixed hotel is much frequented by women and gays on a tight budget. Many of the rooms have shared facilities and the dormitory rooms are popular with younger guests. There's a returnable deposit for keys and you won't be surcharged for overnight company.
Hotel services *Bar. Car park (enclosed) nearby. Laundry. Sitting room.*

Quentin Hotel

Leidsekade 89, IS (626 2187). Tram 1, 2, 5,

6, 7, 10. Rates single f55-f60; double f85-f100. Credit AmEx, DC, MC, V.
This is a 15-room straight hotel, but is particularly welcoming to lesbians, although not to small kids. The reasonably-priced rooms are decently sized. The staff are aware of what's on culturally and speak English. The hotel is closed in December and January but you can still make bookings for later.
Hotel services *Car park (guarded) nearby. Snacks and drinks available 24 hours daily.*

HEALTH & SAFETY

Amsterdam is a relatively unthreatening city for women, although it has places to avoid, particularly after dark. If you've been raped or sexually abused, you can contact Tegen Haar Wil (Against Her Will) phoneline on 625 3473 or Blijf-van-m'n-lijf-huis ('don't touch my body' refuge) on 694 2758. For other health establishments and counselling services, and for some safety tips, *see page 221* Survival.

Women's Health Centre

Obiplein 4, OE (693 4358). Tram 3, 6, 14. Open 9am-noon Tue; 7-10pm Thur; 1-4pm Fri. Women working at the *Vrouwen-gezondheidscentrum* give information and advice on all health matters. They refer patients to *vrouwvriendlijke arts* (doctors, clinics and therapists sympathetic to women's specific needs) and run self-help groups on such issues as pregnancy, over-eating and the menopause.

Children & Parents

Canaltown can be fun for families. *Marieke Sjerps* shows you where Amsterdam's youngest visitors can be entertained, exercised and fed.

Amsterdam wasn't built for kids – which city was? – but its narrow streets and beautiful canals with houseboats make it a rewarding place for children to explore. Moreover, there are always things to do: hiring a pedalo, watching a puppet show, or making huge soap bubbles in the NINT museum (*listed under* **Attractions**). The best source of information about events for children is the VVV (*see page 3* **Essential Information**). The free monthly events paper *Uitkrant* has listings on kids' entertainment under the heading *jeugd* (youth). This is in Dutch, but it does give telephone numbers, so you can investigate. If you want to buy books, clothing or toys for children, *see page 153* **Shopping Around**.

THE DUTCH FAMILY

Dutch families were traditionally quite large until the 1960s. By the early seventies, the norm was two kids per family, although three-child families are now more common. Women born after World War II have been inclined to start and complete their families at an older age.

The structure of Dutch households changed strikingly during the eighties, with one third of children having divorced parents. There are now many one-parent families; that parent is usually the mother, who in some cases has made a conscious decision to bring up a child by herself.

The Dutch don't make a great distinction between the worlds of children and adults. Therefore, little is organized especially for youngsters. Parents and guardians often take them along to restaurants, parties and other occasions. Usually nobody minds their presence and often things are improvised on the spot, such as child-sized portions of food.

SCHOOL DAYS

Most children spend between a few months and a couple of years at a pre-school crèche before going to a *basisschool* at five. At the age of 12, pupils make a complex choice between different kinds of secondary school, depending on their academic or practical ability and whether they want to start work as soon as possible, or take professional training or higher education. Each child is schooled for a minimum of ten years (normally by age 16): if they start work early, they must complete their studies part-time.

RIGHTS & WRONGS

About a third of the Dutch population – 5.5 million people – is under 25. Under the law, children become adults at 18, when they can vote, but parents are responsible for supporting them up to the age of 21, if required. It's forbidden to sell alcoholic drinks to children under 16.

Kinderrechtswinkel (Children's Rights Shop)
Brouwersgracht 44, IW (626 0067). Tram 1, 2, 4, 5, 9, 13, 16, 17, 24, 25. **Open** by appointment (*consultations* 2-5pm Wed, Sat). This office can be visited and phoned by children under 18, as well as by adults, for information about children's legal rights and the responsibilities of teachers and employers.

Kindertelefoon (Childline)
(622 4455). **Open** 2-8pm daily.
Young people from eight to 18 are welcome to phone this line to get an answer to questions on both the trivial, like cake recipes, and the important, such as matters concerning parents and teachers (victimization, incest, running away from home and so on). Staff do not give information on children's entertainment.

TRANSPORT

The centre of Amsterdam is small and well laid out, so almost all the interesting places for youngsters are easy to reach by foot. The fastest and most convenient way to get around is by tram, bus or Metro (*see page 3* **Essential Information**). But if you

have time, it's much more exciting to go by water taxi or rent a pedalo (*see page 13* **Sightseeing**). From about ten years old, children can steer and handle a pedalo by themselves, but remind them to navigate on the right hand side of the waterway. A pleasant, free excursion is to take the River IJ ferry to Amsterdam North; boats leave from behind Centraal Station every ten minutes.

Electrische Museumtramlijn
Haarlemmermeerstation, Amstelveenseweg 264 (673 7538). Tram 6, 16. **Departs** *Apr-Jun, Sept-Oct* every 30 mins, 10.30am-5.30pm Sun; *July, Aug* 10am, 2.15pm, 3.30pm Tue, Thur, Sat; every 30 mins, 10.30am-5.30pm Sun. **Admission** f4 adult; f2 4-12s; free under-4s. **No credit cards.**
This is not so much a museum as a pleasure ride. The antique electric tram carriages come from cities throughout Europe and children especially enjoy the 30-minute tram ride in one of the colourful old trolleys south through Amsterdamse Bos (*see p13* **Sightseeing** and *p183* **Sport & Fitness**) to Amstelveen.

ATTRACTIONS

CHILDREN'S FARMS

Artis Zoo Children's Farm
Artis Zoo Plantage Kerklaan 40, IE (523 3400). Tram 7, 9, 14. **Open** *Zoo* 9am-5pm daily; *Children's farm* 10am-1pm, 2-4.30pm, daily. **Admission** *Zoo & farm* f16 adults; f9 under-10s; group discount (min 20 people). **No credit cards.**
See p181 **picture and caption.**

De Dierenpijp
Lizzy Ansinghstraat 82, OS (664 8303). Tram 12, 25. **Open** 1-5pm Mon, Wed-Sun. **Admission** free.
Centrally located in the Pijp district (*see p26* **Amsterdam by Area**), this farm is also a short walk from NINT (*see below* **Museums**). You can meet all the usual farm beasts at Dierenpijp, but without the crowds at Artis Zoo (*above*), so the staff have more time to be helpful.

Het Ruige Riet
President Allendelaan 2, OW (611 8851). Bus 19, 68. **Open** 8.30am-5pm daily. **Admission** free.
This children's farm is situated in Sloterpark on the west side of town. There are animal feeding times at 8.30am and 4pm, and children can help. Between May and August, you can watch the staff make goat's cheese.

De Uylenburg
Staalmeesterslaan 420, OW (618 5235). Bus 18, 19, 48, 64. **Open** *Sept-Apr* 10am-4pm daily; *May-Aug* 10am-5pm daily. **Admission** free.
This city farm is part of Rembrandtpark, which also has a playground and a place where children can build simple huts under supervision. Free horse rides are also offered in the park.

MUSEUMS

See page 100 Museums for details of: the **Netherlands Maritime Museum**, where children can handle exhibits on the ships docked outside; the **Aviodome**, an aviation museum with an exciting flight simulator; and the **National Spaarpottenmuseum** (Piggy Bank Museum), which is filled with unusual money boxes. For **Artis Planetarium** and **Madame Tussaud's** wax museum, see page 13 **Sightseeing**.

TM Junior

Linnaeusstraat 2, OE (568 8300 Mon-Thur). Tram 9, 10, 14. **Open** school holidays 11am-4pm Mon-Fri; noon-4pm Sun; term time noon-4pm Sun. **Admission** f6 adults (must be accompanied by a child); 6-12s f3; under-6s free. **No credit cards.** See p182 picture and caption. Shop. Wheelchair access.

NINT Museum of Science & Technology

Tolstraat 129, OS (664 6021). Tram 4. **Open** 10am-5pm Mon-Fri; noon-5pm Sat, Sun. **Closed** 25 Dec, 1 Jan. **Admission** adults f7; under-13s f5; under-6s free. **No credit cards.** Everybody is busy doing something. That's what will strike you most when you enter NINT, one of the few museums in which visitors are allowed to touch and handle exhibits, and where children's needs are considered in the design; even the holograms are at kids' height. See, feel, hear and do! Test your reaction times, or see your shadow frozen on the fluorescent wall. In the main hall upstairs the computers ask you to play with them; they have menus in English and all display texts are in four languages, including English. NINT is particularly stimulating for children over the age of six, but younger kids will have a nice time there too. Staff are very helpful. Baby changing facilities. Café (10am-4pm Mon-Fri; noon-4pm Sat, Sun). Shop. Wheelchair access; toilets for disabled.

OUT OF TOWN

Children greatly enjoy trips to the windmills, castles, bulb fields and traditional towns near Amsterdam (see page 203 **Excursions in Holland**). The following are especially suitable for kids.

De Efteling, Kaatsheuvel

Europaweg 1, Kaatsheuvel, Noord Brabant (04167 088111). **Getting there** Car 110km (68 miles) from Amsterdam, off A267 just north of Tilburg; rail NS Day Excursion ticket (includes train, bus and admission). **Open** Easter-Oct 10am-6pm daily. **Admission** f21; group discount (min 20 people) f18. **No credit cards.** The brainchild of illustrator Anton Pieck, this is the most original theme park in The Netherlands. Pieck designed an enormous fairytale forest where Sleeping Beauty's bosom rises and falls with each breath, rubbish bins talk and fakirs fly on magic

The farm animals at **Artis Zoo Children's Farm** (see under Attractions: Children's Farms) are very used to visitors, so you can get up close and stroke some of them. But beware, they're inquisitive and will nibble your valuables if you don't keep them hidden. The farm's part of Artis Zoo, which also houses Artis Planetarium (for both, see page 13 Sightseeing) and Zoological Museum (see page 100 Museums), so you can have a full day out for one admission price. Its popularity is a problem, though; it gets very busy and the staff can't give as much attention as you will get at the free local kinderboerderijen (children's farms) we list.

carpets. Inevitably, there are also the usual roller-coasters and fairground rides. Café and restaurant. Shops. Wheelchair access; toilets for the disabled.

Land van Ooit, Drunen

Parklaan 40 (04163 77775). **Getting there** car A2, then before 'S Hertogenbosch, take A59 to Drunen; train to 'S Hertogenbosch then bus 137, or NS Day Excursion ticket (includes train, bus and admission). **Open** Easter-mid Oct 10am-6pm daily; closed selected Mon, Tue in Sept, Oct. **Admission** f14 adult; 4-11s f12; under-4s free. **No credit cards.** This fantasy park is particularly good for under-12s and is unusual in that there are no machine-powered rides. Children themselves operate pedal cars shaped like a shoe or a pie, or a swan-like pedalo on water, so they don't mind that the rides are slower – and safer – than those in other fun parks. Kids can climb into the tree-house café or over statues of giants and test their strength against them. Actors dress up as princesses, lords and such like, giving performances around the park (in Dutch, although if crowds are small they may explain in English). More easily understood are the shows in the puppet theatre. There's a brochure in English. Restaurants. Wheelchair access; wheelchairs available free; toilets for the disabled.

Linnaeushof, Bennebroek

Rijksstraatweg 4, Bennebroek (02502 7624). **Getting there** Car 20km (13 miles) on A5 to Haarlem, then on N208 south; rail NS Day Excursion ticket (includes train, bus and admission). **Open** Apr-Oct 10am-6pm daily. **Admission** f8.50; group discount (min 20 people) f7.50. **No credit cards.** Between Haarlem and the Lisse bulbfields is this huge leisure park, formerly the estate of the Swedish Botanist Carl von Linné. The attractive grounds of woods, gardens and pic-

nic areas contain some 300 attractions designed for children, such as a Wild West train, 'moonwalkers', pedalos, mini-golf, trampolines and (for an extra charge) go-karts. Café and restaurant. Shops. Wheelchair access; toilets for the disabled.

Madurodam, The Hague

Haringkade 175, The Hague (070 355 3900). **Getting there** Car 57km (35 miles) on A4; rail direct to The Hague or NS Day Excursion ticket (includes train, bus and admission). **Open** Mar-May 9am-10.30pm daily; June-Aug 9am-11pm daily; Sept 9am-9.30pm daily; Oct-Jan 9am-6pm daily. **Admission** f11 adult; f6 2-12s; under-2s free; group discounts. **Credit** AmEx, S£TC. This miniature village is popular with younger children, but somewhat uncomfortable for taller tourists prone to back-ache when wading through the knee-high buildings. An odd jumble of the country's most famous features, it incorporates working models of Rotterdam's port, Schiphol airport and the inevitable windmills. Less predictably, it prides itself on keeping up with the latest architecture. The best time to go is on summer evenings, when the models are lit up from inside. There's another miniature town at Middelburg, Zeeland (see p213 **The Provinces**), called **Walcheren**, Koepoortlaan 1 (01180 12525; open daily Apr-Oct). Café and restaurant. Cassette tour. Shop. Wheelchair access; toilets for the disabled.

ENTERTAINMENT

PARKS & PLAYGROUNDS

Parks (see page 13 **Sightseeing** and page 183 **Sport & Fitness**) are the best places for children's entertainment, whether it's a puppet show or boating lakes and playgrounds. **Vondelpark** is famous for its summer programme of free afternoon entertainment, such as musicians, mime artists and acrobats; Amstelpark on Europalaan has train and pony rides. But Amsterdam's larger green areas are on the edge of town: **Amstelandse Bos**, to the New South, has boating lakes, an open-air theatre, large playgrounds and wild deer; **Gaasperpark**, in south-east Amsterdam, has superb sport and playground facilities, including a paddling pool; and **Twiske**, north of the IJ River, is a pleasant area of countryside. Also, during school holidays, there are supervised activity sessions in sports halls, where activities include trampolining and organized games; phone the local government's Sport & Recreation Department on **596 9111** for details. For other sporty places to let off steam, such as **Mirandabad** swimming pool with its water-slides, *see page 183* **Sport & Fitness**.

All of the parks have **playgrounds**. In addition, many street corners in residential districts have a sand-pit and a climbing frame, where kids can have a great time playing – but beware of dog dirt. For further information on playgrounds, phone the

VVV on *626 6444 (see also page 3* **Essential Information**).

THEATRE & CIRCUS

The **children's theatre phoneline**, *622 2999*, has recorded information in Dutch.

Kindertheater Elleboog
Passeerdersgracht 32, IW (626 9370). Tram 7, 10. **Circus sessions** *non-members* alternate weekends 1.30-5pm Sat; 10.30am-4pm Sun; *club* 3.30-5.30pm Mon, Thur; 6.30-8.30pm Tue; 1.15-3pm, 3.30-5.15pm Wed; 10.30am-12.30pm Sat. **Admission** *non-member sessions* f5 Sat; f7.50 Sun; *club membership* f40 per year, plus f1.50 per visit. **No credit cards.**
At the Elleboog circus, kids aged from six to 16 can try out circus skills, including tricks, make-up, unicycles, juggling and tight-rope walking. The non-member sessions are always busy, mostly with Dutch kids, but the eight to ten volunteer staff do speak English and also welcome disabled children. The club has about 400 members, who attend once a week for drama sessions and to experiment with theatre and circus equipment. *Book in advance (Thur, by phone). Drinks provided. Wheelchair access.*

De Krakeling
Nieuwe Passeerdersstraat 1, IW (625 3284/624 5123). Tram 7, 10. **Shows** *suitable for 4-12s* 2pm Wed, Sat, Sun; *suitable for over-12s* 8pm Fri. **Admission** f7.50 adults; f5 4-16s. **No credit cards.**
De Krakeling has separate productions suitable for over-12s and under-12s. Happily for non-Dutch speakers, there are many puppet

and mime shows. Shows are listed in a programme available from the theatre and in *Uitkrant*. Wheelchair access.

Poppentheater Diridas
Hobbemakade 68, OS (662 1588). Tram 16. **Shows** *for under-5s* 11am Sun; *for over-5s* 3pm Sat, Sun. *Closed Aug.* **Admission** *under-5s show* f3; *over-5s show* f4. **No credit cards.**
Shows at Diridas Puppet Theatre use either marionettes or glove puppets. Every Sunday, there's a new play for the under-5s. The show for older kids is in Dutch, but if you're foreign, tell the puppeteer in advance and you'll be given a short summary of the plot before the play starts. Children celebrating a birthday will get special attention. *Book in advance (from 10am Fri-Sun).*

CHILDREN'S FILMS

There are a few special children's film shows at **Kriterion**, **Rialto** and **Filmmuseum**; *see page 122* **Film**. Films are usually in Dutch or without dialogue, but occasionally in English.

If there's somewhere you're unable to take your child to – or if you need a rest from your *enfant terrible* – contact the following supervising services. Unfortunately, babysitters are the only option, since Amsterdam lacks crèches where children can be left with others their own age (although **Oppascentrale** runs one for students at University of Amsterdam). Babysitting in a hotel is usually less comfortable than at a home, so you'll be charged a higher rate, although a number of hotels offer their own babysitting service. It's good manners to supply babysitters with drinks and – if it's for a long period – some food. After midnight only night-buses operate, so if you're staying in a suburb, you'll be asked to take the babysitter home or pay for a taxi.

Babyzitcentrale Babyhome
Chassestraat 97, OW (616 1119). Tram 12, 13, 14. **Open** *booking* 3-5pm Mon, Thur. **Rates** f5 per hour. **No credit cards.**
This babysitting agency employs women over the age of 17. It's advisable to book in advance.

Oppascentrale Kriterion
2E Rozendwarsstraat 24, OW (624 5848). Tram 13, 14, 17. **Open** *booking* 24 hours daily. **Rates** *Basic charge* f4, then: *7pm-midnight* f5 per hour; *midnight-3am* f7 per hour; *3am-8am* f10 per hour; *8am-7pm* f6 per hour; f2.50 supplement on total bill for Fri, Sat evenings. **No credit cards.**
This babysitting service employs male and female students, all of whom are vetted before employment. They're particularly busy at weekends, so it's best to book in advance.

TM Junior (see under **Attractions: Museums**) *is a branch of the* **Tropenmuseum** *(Tropical Museum) designed especially for children. Only one parent is allowed in with a child, so parents can also have time to themselves, maybe visiting the main Tropenmuseum (see page 100* **Museums***). TM Junior's long-running exhibitions – a recent one was on Senegalese families – introduce young people to the cultures of the Third World in a very personal way. The staff play with their young visitors, telling stories and answering questions. Children can participate in all sorts of workshop activities, from exploring tribal huts and cooking rice to playing drums and learning a dance that they've just seen in a film. The groups are quite small, and staff can speak English. Booking is advisable and it's essential on Saturdays. Note that TM Junior will be closed for renovation from summer 1991 to May 1992.*

Sport & Fitness

Do you fancy a sporting break from culture and canals? *Jeroen van den Berg* shows where to have a bash at basketball, a crack at korfball or a splash in a swimming pool.

Although Amsterdam's status as the cultural capital of The Netherlands is rarely disputed, few people are aware that the city is also a major centre for sports. The health craze has hit the city hard, with health and fitness clubs rapidly increasing in number, and more and more joggers pounding the parks and streets. Most parks have recreational facilities, but the best are Vondelpark, with its tennis courts and amateur footballers, and Amsterdamse Bos, which has a training circuit marked out and facilities for rowing, canoeing, fishing (carp, pike and perch) and even swimming, although the water's rather dirty. For both, *see page 13* **Sightseeing**.

The most popular sports in The Netherlands are soccer, skating, cycling and tennis. In winter skating comes to the fore – even when it doesn't freeze. The world and European skating championships become the main topic of conversation in bars, and the events are broadcast live on television. When it freezes, almost all the Dutch put their skates on.

For therapy centres, *see page 165* **Services**. For further information on sports and leisure facilities and events in Amsterdam, phone the city's Sport & Recreation Department on **596 9111**.

SPECTATOR SPORTS

BASEBALL

Pirates
Jan van Galenstraat Sportpark, Jan van Galenstraat, OW (616 2151). Tram 13/bus 19, 47. **Season** Apr-Oct. **Admission** f5. **No credit cards.**
The team to see if you want to catch a competition match in Amsterdam, the Pirates are the city's best club, attracting up to 2,500 spectators.

BASKETBALL

Canadians Amsterdam
Apollohal, Stadionweg, OS (671 3910). Tram 5, 24/bus 15. **Matches** end Sept-mid May 9pm Fri. **Admission** f5. **No credit cards.**

This is the best team in Amsterdam and one of the top five in The Netherlands. Both the men's and women's teams play in the first division.

CRICKET

KNCB (Dutch Cricket Board)
Nieuwe Kalfjeslaan 21B, PO Box 898, 1182 AA, Amstelveen (645 1756/fax 645 1715). Bus 125, 170, 171, 172, 173, 194. **Open** 10am-5pm Mon-Thur.
Cricket is still a minority sport in The Netherlands – the Dutch Cricket Federation has 4,500 members and 70 clubs. In comparison, The Dutch Skate Federation has almost 200,000 members. However the national cricket team is improving: in 1990, The Netherlands came second in the world championship of B-countries (the nations not yet eligible for the Test Match circuit). The Dutch also beat an England B team recently. Phone the KNCB for information and dates of fixtures. This ground is also home to several local sides: games are at 1pm on Saturdays and 11am on Sundays from May to August. Admission is free.

CYCLING

Cycling is a Dutch passion. The country has two great cycling advantages: it's flat (although also windy) and it has the best facilities in the world. Despite the flat terrain, The Netherlands has reared professional cyclists who have excelled in the French Alps during the Tour De France, in which the legendary Joop Zoetemelk came second six times before winning in 1980; in 1985, at the age of 38, he also became world champion in Italy. Most Dutch avidly follow the Tour de France on TV and afterwards watch the spate of criteriums (road races) around The Netherlands, in which Tour de France heroes ride round a village about 70 times and receive a lot of money for it. Although on the decrease, these criteriums sometimes attract crowds of over 50,000. For further information, contact the **Koninklijke Nederlandsche Wielren Unie** (Dutch Cycle Federation), *PO Box 136, Polanerbaan 15, 3447 GN, Worden (03480 11544).*

If you want to cycle in The Netherlands, contact the **Nederlandse Rijwiel Toer Unie** (Netherlands Cycletouring Union),

Ambachtsherenlaan 1162A, 2722 VJ, Zoetermeer (08385 21421). For cycle hire, *see page 3* **Essential Information**; for cycle touring, *see page 200*.

8 van Chaam
Chaam, Noord Brabant (Mr Coenraadf 01619 1503; private number, please ring at reasonable times). **Date** first Wed after Tour de France. **Admission** f10-f12.50. **No credit cards.**
This is the biggest and oldest criterium in The Netherlands (first run in 1933), attracting thousands of spectators. A hundred professional riders and twice as many amateurs cycle 12 times around the 8km circuit of this village in the south of the country.

FOOTBALL

Soccer has long been the number one sport in The Netherlands and there are now almost a million registered members of the KNVB, the national football federation. The Dutch national team has had mixed fortunes recently – winning the European Championships in 1988, but failing to play up to expectations in the 1990 World Cup. Amsterdam's major club is the world-famous Ajax.

If you want to play soccer yourself, the best place to go is a park. On a sunny day there will always be people playing and they are often happy for others to join in. We recommend Vondelpark (*see page 13* **Sightseeing: Parks**).

Ajax
Middenweg 401, OE (694 6515). Tram 9/bus 138, 150, 152, 154, 158. **Admission** standing f10; seated f16, f19, f25. **Matches** Sept-June 2.30pm Sun. **No credit cards.**
Under coach Leo Beenhakker, Ajax became Dutch champions in the 1989/1990 season, drawing an average crowd of over 16,000; only PSV Eindhoven had more, averaging 24,000. But Ajax has suffered recent setbacks. It was banned from European competitions for a year after an iron bar was thrown on to the pitch, hitting the visiting goalkeeper. The Club has also been stricken with financial problems since it was fined f2 million after the former board of managers made unauthorized transfer payments. *See also p184* **picture and caption**.

Feyenoord
Olympiaweg 50, Rotterdam (010 419 0457). **Admission** matches against Ajax and PSV f15, f20, f35; all other teams f12.50, f15, f30. **Matches** Sept-June 2.30pm Sun. **No credit cards.**
Although Feyenoord is no longer as strong as it was in the seventies it remains in the first division and still has the biggest stadium in the country. Almost all The Netherlands' internationals are played here.

PSV
Fredericklaan 10/A, Eindhoven (040 51 1917). **Admission** f17, f25, f35. **Matches** Sept-

Amsterdam is proud of its only professional football club, **Ajax** *(see under* **Spectator Sports: Football**). *It won three European Cups in the early seventies when Johann Cruyff was in the team. Now, the go-ahead for a new stadium just outside the city has been given. According to chairman Michael van Praag, this should be 'the most beautiful stadium in Europe'. Going to an Ajax match is reasonably safe, although there are some dodgy matches, which are heavily policed. These are usually against Feyenoord, FC Den Haag, FC Utrecht and PSV Eindhoven. We advise you to buy seat tickets.*

June 7.30pm Sat; 2.30pm Sun. **Credit** AmEx, DC, MC, V.
England's ex-manager Bobby Robson became manager of PSV in July 1990. It is owned by the Philips company and is the wealthiest club in The Netherlands, with a blissfully comfortable stadium.

HOCKEY

Although The Netherlands is the world champion of both men's and women's hockey, the sport is not as popular as football.

Amsterdam
Wagener Stadium, Nieuwe Kalfjeslaan, OS (640 1141). Bus 125, 170, 171, 172, 173, 194. **Admission** *league games* free; *internationals* f20. **Matches** *Sept-Pentecost women* 12.45pm Sun; *men* 2.30pm Sun. **No credit cards.**
This is the strongest club in the region. The team's ground also hosts most of the home matches of the national teams. To see The Netherlands play costs about f20, while all league matches are free. The stadium has a capacity of 7,000.

ICE HOCKEY

S IJ S Amsterdam '89
Jaap Edenhal, Radioweg 64, OW (694 9652). Bus 8, 120, 126, 136. **Admission** f12; under-16s, over-65s f6. **Matches** *Oct-Feb* usually 8pm Fri or 8pm Sun. **No credit cards.**
This is the only ice-hockey team in Amsterdam. It plays in the top league, but the best teams tend to come from the north of The Netherlands. Having won the second division in the 1989/1990 season, S IJ S Amsterdam (which stands for Stichting IJshockey Sport) hope to be challenging for the first division championships. Their current team has a blend of youth and experience, with three Czechs and one Canadian playing alongside the natives.

MOTOR SPORTS

TT Races
De Haar Circuit, Assen (05920 55000/ fax 05920 56911/race day information 05920 13800). Exit Assen South off motorway A28, then follow signs. **Dates** Tue-Sat 25-29 June 1991; Tue-Sat 23-27 June 1992. **Admission** *grandstand* f65; *other stands* f45; *circuit* f35. **No credit cards.**
More than 100,000 people come to see this spectacular event, lasting for a week, and culminating in the Grand Prix races for sidecars and 125, 250 and 500cc bikes on the final Saturday. On Tuesday the European championships are run for all classes of bike, and Thursday sees the TT Formula 1 and historic TT races. Real fanatics go along on the intervening days to watch the practice laps. Tickets can be booked in advance from *TT Assen, PO Box 150, 9400 AD, Assen.*

Zandvoort
Stichting Exploitatie Circuit Park, Burgemeester Van Alphenstraat (02507 18284). **Train** to Zandvoort from Centraal Station. **Admission** *paddock* f30; *grandstand* f15. **No credit cards.**
The car-racing track at the resort of Zandvoort, about 30km from Amsterdam (see *p208* **The Randstad**), was once a venue for Formula One racing and the new director hopes to bring it back for 1992. Meanwhile a programme of international races, including some nostalgic events, is in operation roughly every other weekend between March and October. Tickets are available from ESSO garages.

ACTIVITIES

BASKETBALL

Basketball fiends can play for free on Museumplein, near the Rijksmuseum. There are several courts where you can usually join the other players, but you have to be good.

FISHING

Dutch Fishing Federation
Nicolaas Witsenstraat 10, IS (626 4988). Tram 6, 7, 10. **Open** 10am-3pm Tue-Fri. **No credit cards.**
For a f35 annual fee and a five-minute wait, you can get the permit you need to fish legally in The Netherlands, plus a book telling you where to do it (in Dutch). Staff will need to see your passport. Het Amsterdamse Bos is a convenient place to fish (see *p13* **Sightseeing: Parks**); a local fishing permit can be obtained from any post office. *see also p213* **The Provinces: Overijssel**.

GOLF

Because major events are shown on BBC and Eurosport television, golf has become quite popular, but is still considered to be élitist by most Dutch people. If you're a member of a British club, you are allowed to play on any Dutch course. Otherwise, you can only play on public courses.
Further information can be obtained from **De Nederlandse Golf Federatie** (Dutch Golf Federation), *Soestdijkerstraatweg 172, 1213 XJ, Hilversum (035 830 565).*

Sloten
Sloterweg 1045, OSW (614 2402). Bus 179. **Open** *golf course* 8.30am-dusk Mon-Fri; *driving range* 8.30am-5.30pm Mon-Fri. **Cost** *golf course* f12.50 per day; *driving range including hire of 60 balls* f6. **No credit cards.**
A public course with nine holes and friendly staff. A half-set of golf clubs can be hired for f10.

Spaarnwoude
Het Hogalane 8, Spaarnwoude (023 385599). **Open** 8.30am-7pm daily. **Cost** *18-hole course* f22 per round; *12-hole course* f6 per round; *9-hole course* f10 per round. **No credit cards.**
A par 70 18-hole public course with water and wind hazards to trap the unwary or unskilled. There are also 12- and nine-hole courses for the less skilled or more hurried. No advance reservations are taken but you can book by phone for the same day from 8.30am.

HEALTH & FITNESS

For women-only saunas *see page 176* **Women's Amsterdam**; for saunas for gay men *see page 169* **Gay Amsterdam**.

Splash
Looiersgracht 26, IW (624 8404). Tram 7, 10. **Open** 10am-10pm Mon-Fri; 11am-6pm Sat, Sun. **Admission** *1-day pass* f25; *1-week pass* f50; *2-week pass* f75; *1-month pass* f97.50. **Credit** AmEx, V.

Facilities here include a weights room with room for up to 50 people, a Turkish bath, a massage service and a sauna. There are eight aerobics classes daily. Everything is free once you have paid to get in.

Sporting Club Leidseplein

Korte Leidsedwarsstraat 18, IS (620 6631). *Tram 1, 2, 5, 6, 7, 10.* **Open** 9am-midnight Mon-Fri; 10am-6pm Sat, Sun. **Admission** *1-day pass* f25. **No credit cards.**
This central health club has a weights room and a sauna. Aerobics classes (f7.50, f15 without day pass) are held at 7pm on Mondays, Wednesdays and Fridays. The interior is luxurious.

SKATING

When temperatures drop to freezing, many Dutch put on a Walkman and go skating over the iced-over polders, keeping warm by drinking hot chocolate and alcoholic drinks bought from stalls on the banks. When the ice gets very thick, Dutch people start talking about the *elfstedentocht*, an 11-city marathon in the province of Friesland (*see page 213* **The Provinces**) last held in 1986. If your visit coincides with the event, go to Friesland immediately; you'll never forget it. Amsterdammers skating on their canals also make a great spectacle. However, it's inadvisable to try this yourself as the canal water is dirty and the waterways hardly ever freeze completely in winter.

During the winter you can skate for free at Leidseplein (*see page 26* **Amsterdam by Area**), but the rink is very small. There are also many places close to Amsterdam (such as Loosdrecht, Vinkeveen, Muiden, Edam, Volendam or Broek-in-Waterland) where you can also go skating if the weather is cold enough. If the winter is mild, visit an indoor ice rink, but don't expect to be able to skate in the summer – all the rinks close and even the professionals are reduced to practising on roller skates.

Jaap Edenhal

Radioweg 64, OW (694 9652). *Bus 8, 120, 126, 136.* **Open** *Oct-Mar* for skating 10am-noon, 2-4pm, daily; ice disco 8-10pm Wed. **Admission** f5.50; under-13s f3.15. **Skate hire** f8. **No credit cards.**
You can hire skates here for a mere f8, but the staff will ask for a deposit of a passport, a driver's licence or f100. The rink is open from the middle of October until the end of March.

SNOOKER & CARAMBOLE

Potting the black is becoming popular, thanks to the BBC's snooker

coverage (which the Dutch can pick up), and there are several halls where you can play fairly cheaply, although there are no tables in bars. When it comes to *biljart* (billiards), carambole, played on a table without pockets, is still the major variation. A carambole is made when you cannon your white ball off both the red and the other white ball. Listed below are some snooker and carambole centres where drinks are also sold.

Biljartcentrum Bavaria

Van Ostadestraat 97, OS (676 4059). *Tram 3, 4, 12, 24, 25.* **Open** 11am-1am daily. **Cost** *snooker* f13.50 per hour; *carambole* f7.50 per hour. **No credit cards.**
See picture and caption.

Snookercentrum de Keizer

Keizersgracht 256, IW (623 1586). *Tram 13, 14, 17.* **Open** noon-1am Mon-Thur, Sun; noon-2am Fri, Sat. **Cost** f10 per hour before 3pm; f15 per hour after 3pm; half price if playing alone. **No credit cards.**
This place has eight snooker tables and is unique in Amsterdam in that each of these tables is in its own room. There are telephones in all the rooms so players can phone orders down to the bar and have drinks sent up. Members pay a reduced rate but anyone is welcome to play here.

Snookerclub Overtoom

Overtoom 209, OW (618 8019). *Tram 1, 6/bus 171, 172.* **Open** 10am-1am Mon-Thur,

Sun; 10am-2am Fri, Sat. **Cost** f10 per hour before 2pm; f15 per hour after 2pm. **Membership** f25 per year. **No credit cards.**
The atmosphere in this ex-church is quiet, making this a club for the serious snooker player. While anyone can play here, members pay f2.50 less per hour.

SPORTS CENTRE

Borchland

Borchlandweg 8-12, OSE (696 1441/1444). *Bus 169.* **Open** 10am daily. **Credit** AmEx, DC, MC, V.
This is the only big *omni-sportcentrum* (sports centre) in Amsterdam, offering squash, outdoor and indoor tennis, ten-pin bowling and badminton. Rates are higher in the evening and at weekends.

SQUASH

Dickysquash

Karel Lotsylaan 16, OS (646 2266). *Bus 26, 48, 65, 148, 158, 197.* **Open** 9am-midnight Mon-Fri; 9am-10pm Sat; 9am-11pm Sun. **Cost** *½ hour* f17.50; *1 hour* f32.50. **No credit cards.**
Dickysquash caters for the more experienced player.

Squash City

Ketelmakerstraat 6, IW (626 7883). *Bus 18, 22, 44.* **Open** 8.45am-11.15pm Mon-Fri; 8.45am-9pm Sat, Sun. **Cost** *during the day and Sat* f25; *evenings and Sun* f30. **Credit** AmEx, MC, V.
This is the place to head for if you see squash as more of a hobby than a battle. It

Biljartcentrum Bavaria (see under **Activities: Snooker & Carambole**) *is famous in Amsterdam for its billiards team, which plays in the first division of the league. There are four floors here, the third and fourth devoted to carambole and billiards, the second floor to snooker and the first to pool. The use of cues is included in the table hire. Phone before turning up, as some evenings are for members only.*

also has a sauna and weights room, which you can use for no extra charge.

SWIMMING POOLS

Watch out for thieves in public pools. Always make use of the key lockers and never leave your coat or jacket unattended. For **Sloterparkbad** open-air pool, *see under* **Watersports: Duikelaar.**

Marnixbad
Marnixplein 9, OW (625 4843). Tram 3, 7, 10. **Open** 7-9am, noon-1.30pm, 3-5pm, Mon; 7am-5.30pm Tue, Wed; 7-10am, 11am-5pm, Thur; 7-10am, 11am-5.30pm, Fri; 10am-noon Sat; 10am-noon, 3.30-5.30pm, Sun. **Admission** f3.80; under-18s f3.30; over-65s f2.50. **No credit cards.**
This is a 25m indoor pool, with water slides and a whirlpool. There's also a sauna.

Mirandabad
De Mirandalaan, OSE (644 6637). Tram 25/bus 8, 48, 60, 158. **Open** *indoor pool* 7am-10.15pm Mon, Fri; 3.30-10.15pm Tue; 12.15-10.15pm Wed; 7am-5.30pm, 7-10.15pm, Thur; 10am-5.30pm Sat, Sun; *outdoor pool May-Aug* 10am-5.30pm daily, depending on the weather. **Admission** f5.25; 4-17s f4.25; over-65s f3.25. **No credit cards.**
The only sub-tropical pool in Amsterdam, Mirandabad is very clean, with a stone beach and a wave machine that's switched on every half hour. There is also a water slide, a whirlpool and an outdoor pool in good weather.

Zuiderbad
Hobbemastraat 26, OS (679 2217). Tram 1, 2, 5/bus 26, 66, 67, 170, 179. **Open** 7am-6pm, 7-10.30pm, Mon; 7-9am, noon-6pm, 6-9.30pm, Tue; 7-10am, noon-10.30pm, Wed; 7-9.30am, noon-6pm, Thur; 7am-9pm Fri; 8am-5pm Sat; 10am-3.30pm Sun. **Admission** f3.80; under-18s f3.30; over-65s f2.50. **No credit cards.**
The Zuiderbad was built in 1912, making it one of the country's oldest pools. Though some renovations have been undertaken, it retains its original, picturesque detail. In

1982, an impromptu committee successfully fought against plans for its closure.

TENNIS

There are four busy open-air courts at Vondelpark (*see page 13* **Sightseeing**).

Amstelpark
Karel Lotsylaan 8, OS (644 5436). Bus 26, 48, 65, 148, 158, 197. **Open** 8am-midnight daily. **Hire costs** *indoor courts* f30 per hour; *outdoor courts* f25 per hour. **Racket hire** free. **No credit cards.**
The Amstelpark has 36 courts in all. During the summer there are ten indoor courts, and in the winter six of the outdoor courts are covered over, giving a total of sixteen indoor courts. You can make a reservation over the phone.

Buitenveldert
Van der Boechorststraat 38, OS (642 9641). Bus 23, 65, 173. **Open** 8am-midnight daily. **Hire costs** *outdoor courts* f25 per hour; *indoor courts* f27.50-f42.50 per hour depending on date and time. **Racket hire** free. **No credit cards.**
There are four indoor courts and 20 outdoor courts. The outdoor courts are often booked in the evenings by clubs, so phone first to check.

Kadoelen
Kadoelenweg, N (631 3194). Bus 91, 92. **Open** 9am-midnight daily. **Hire costs** *indoor courts mid Apr-mid Sept* f18 per hour; *mid Sept-mid Apr* f36 per hour; *outdoor courts Apr-Sept* f15.65 per hour. **Racket hire** f5. **No credit cards.**
Kadoelen is subsidized by the local council, so the 20 outdoor and six indoor courts cost a bit less to hire than in other places. Tennis lessons can be arranged in advance.

WATER SPORTS

As The Netherlands is a land of water, water sports are very popular. Sailboards are normal holiday lug-

gage for the Dutch, despite the wet climate. If you want to go sailing, visit Loosdrecht (25 kilometres/15 miles south-east of Amsterdam) or go to the IJsselmeer; in Muiden (20 kilometres/12 miles east of Amsterdam) catamarans can be rented. For information about canoeing phone the **Dutch Canoe-Federation** on *033 62 2341*, and *see page 213* **The Provinces: Overijssel**. Most watersports schools ask for a deposit when you rent a boat; in most cases a passport will suffice. The Dutch often take their sailboards out to the North Sea resorts (such as Zandvoort, *see page 208* **The Randstad**), where boards can also be hired.

Duikelaar, Sloterpark
Noordzijde 41, OW (613 8855). Bus 19, 47. **Open** 9am-6pm Mon-Fri; 11am-5pm Sat, Sun. **Hire costs** *sailing boat* f15 per hour; *one and two person canoes* f5 per hour; *three person canoe* f10 per hour; *sailboard and wetsuit* f15 per hour. **Deposits** *sailing boat and sailboards* f100 plus passport; **canoes** f25 plus passport. **No credit cards.**
At this water-sports centre on the banks of the Sloterplas lake (in the western suburbs), you can rent small sailing boats, canoes and sailboards. The season runs from May to October; from November to April only canoes are available for hire. Also here are the **Sloterparkbad** indoor and open-air (summer) swimming pools (*611 4565*).

Park Gaasperplas
OSE. Metro Gaasperplas/bus 59, 60, 158, 174. **Open** 24 hours daily.
Tucked away behind the Bijlmemeer in Amsterdam South-East, this park was laid out for 'Floriade 1982' (*see p203* **Excursions in Holland: Flowers**). Its large lake has become a centre for watersports and windsurfing. Equipment hire should be available from 1991. There's also a campsite.

KORFBALL

A hybrid of netball and volleyball, korfball was invented by a Dutch schoolteacher at the turn of the century. It's a genuinely mixed-team sport, which could explain its popularity in a country renowned for its egalitarianism. It caught on swiftly and now the national federation has 90,000 members. Korfball can be played indoors and out; the rules are the same but the size of the teams varies. Teams for indoor games comprise four men and four women; for the outdoor version the complement is six and six. The sexes compete on equal terms as players are only

allowed to mark opponents of the same sex. The aim is to shoot the ball into the net – similar to a netball hoop but considerably higher at 3.5 metres/11.5 feet. You are not allowed to run with the ball, which means that quick and accurate passing is essential for victory. Matches last for 60 minutes. The korfball season has three stages. From September until the middle of November and then from April to June matches are played outdoors; from the middle of November to mid-April the game goes indoors. There are about 20 teams in

Amsterdam; the two best are **Blauw Wit**, which has its own hall and fields, and **Rohda**, the national outdoor champions in 1989-90.

Blauw Wit
Joos Banckersweg, OW (Barbara Geeredzen 075 17 2784; private number, please ring at reasonable times). Tram 12, 14/bus 15, 85. **Admission** free. **Matches** 2pm Sun. **No credit cards.**

Rohda
Sportpark Ookmeer, Ookmeerweg, Osdorp, OW (611 0416). Bus 19, 68. **Admission** usually free; *finals* f5; f2.50 under-16s, over-65s. **Matches** 2pm Sun; occasionally 2pm Sat. **No credit cards.**

Business & Study

Many visitors to the Dutch capital have come on business. To make their trip go smoothly, we've provided details of sources of information and services such as couriers, translators, office equipment hire and photocopying.

The radical, permissive character of Amsterdam has made it a favourite destination for students on holiday. There's a lively student scene, which serves two universities, several colleges, summer schools, Dutch language classes – and visitors. We give the low-down on the study facilities, cheap eating places and student haunts.

CONTENTS:

Business

Financial journalist *Jon Henley* explains how Amsterdam has become a commercial hot-house, while *Julie Sinclair-Day* gives the low-down on services and information for business travellers.

Trade is inextricably bound up in the history of Amsterdam. Beginning life as a small fishing settlement that helped to supply herring to northern Europe in the Middle Ages, the town gradually developed into a transit point for grain and timber from the Baltic countries. Further expansion occurred when the wool trade with England took off: wool was imported, made into cloth in Leiden or Haarlem, and re-exported through Amsterdam. Dam Square became a major marketplace. In the fourteenth century, the city also benefited from the trade in beer (*see page 52* **Early History**).

After the Spaniards' initial defeat at the hands of Willem of Orange in the sixteenth century (*see page 53* **War & Reformation**), the merchant fleet expanded rapidly, fuelled by investment money from the thriving Baltic trade. Skilled workers and traders were drawn to Amsterdam: merchants armed with new book-keeping and banking techniques came from Italy and France; more than a thousand shipbuilders arrived between 1580 and 1664; and migrant Jewish diamond merchants and polishers set up workshops in the city after the fall of Antwerp to the Spanish in 1585.

VOC EMPIRE-BUILDING

Antwerp's collapse as a trading rival was the Amsterdam merchants' biggest opportunity to date, and they seized it with both hands. The first successful voyage to Indonesia returned, laden with spices, in July 1599. Three years later, the notorious *Verenigde Oost-Indische Compagie* (VOC), the Dutch East India Company, was founded in Amsterdam.

The VOC developed into possibly the most powerful trading organization the world has known (*see page 55* **The Golden Age**). It was one of the first companies to issue shares, and over the 200 years of its existence paid an average annual dividend of just over 18 per cent. But the VOC wasn't the main force driving Amsterdam's commercial life: the Baltic trade, mainly tin, grain and timber, still accounted for two-thirds of the city's collective capital as late as 1666.

Now used by the University, the original HQ of the Dutch East India Company is on Oude Hoogstraat at the corner of Klovenierburgwal. Ships berthed here before unloading; provisions for the voyages were stored in the building and the more precious cargoes were laid up to await a rise in prices. Cows were kept downstairs to slaughter before the next expedition left.

Brouwersgracht warehouses
Brouwersgracht, IW. Tram 3/bus 18.
See p189 **picture and caption.**

BANKS AND SHARES

To cope with the amount of money changing hands in what had, by the early seventeenth century, become the central marketplace of the western world, the city began to experiment with financial services. In 1609 – a full century before London – it opened a *wisselbank* (exchange bank), allowing merchants to complete their transactions in paper money and deposit certificates rather than gold and silver coins. Eminently respectable and solid, the Amsterdam bank did an enormous amount to promote trade through instilling confidence. Two years later its antithesis – the **Effectenbeurs** (Stock Exchange, *listed under* **Exchanges**) – opened its doors. It became the home of speculative money, trading in paper, and gambling largely on short-term price fluctuations on the exchange.

Amsterdam's giddy rise was halted abruptly in the late seventeenth century. British and French politicians and bankers broke the city's trading monopoly by forcing their merchants to use domestic-flagged ships, and British naval power grew. The adventure, the voyages and the plundering ground to a halt; wars with the British and the French punctuated the following century and the Dutch economy gradually became agrarian-based.

The country had to wait until the late nineteenth century – some would say until after World War II – for its small-scale industrial revolution. But throughout this period, and to a certain extent to the present day, the merchants of Amsterdam were not overly upset: they were sitting on a mountain of money. For a country one-tenth the size of California, The Netherlands today generates a surprisingly large amount of wealth.

THE MODERN ECONOMY

Given its history, it's not surprising that the Dutch economy today is dominated by international trade. Some 65 per cent of gross domestic product (GDP) is exported, and it was the ever-increasing sales abroad that paid for the country's rapid industrialization after 1945. Dutch agriculture, now highly mechanized and with one of the world's highest yields per hectare, accounts for around a quarter of total exports. The Netherlands is the world's largest exporter of dairy products, poultry and seed potatoes, and its outright earnings from agricultural exports rank second only to the USA. Horticulture makes up 20 per cent of total agrarian exports – the famous tulip bulbs (*see page 203* **Excursions in Holland**) account for only a fraction of this. Recent figures indicate that over half the world's cut flowers and pot plants originate in Dutch soil.

Dutch industry was developed largely during this century and is based around mostly small and medium-sized companies. However there are three notable exceptions to this trend – Royal Dutch/Shell, Unilever and Philips are Dutch-based companies and are among the 25 largest industrial concerns in the world.

The most important industrial sector is food, drink and tobacco manufacturing, which accounts for 18 per cent of industrial turnover. The chemicals and petroleum sector contributes 17 per cent and electrical engineering 14 per cent; printing and mechanical engineering follow. Then come vehicle manufacture, shipbuilding materials and rubber products.

SERVICE ECONOMY

The service sector – banking, insurance, transport, communications and tourism – is where the Dutch make much of their money. It now generates 50 per cent of net national income and employs half of the workforce. The two largest banks, Amro and ABN, merged at the end of 1990; both were previously among the world's top 50. The country is a net exporter of capital, and investment abroad by companies based in The Netherlands is still on the rise. The largest Dutch insurance company, Nationale-Nederlanden, ranks fifteenth in the world.

Transport and distribution account for eight per cent of The Netherlands' GDP. The Dutch play a vital role in the European Community (EC) in these sectors. Rotterdam is now easily the world's biggest port in terms of volume handled. With 292 million tonnes/287 million tons passing through in 1989, it's twice as big as its nearest rival, New York. The Netherlands today generates six per cent of total EC gross national product, but it handles 37 per cent of EC transport. Schiphol, Amsterdam's airport, carries much EC freight. It also handled 15.7 million passengers in 1989. The country's system of bonded warehouses and customs depots is designed to encourage the free movement of commodities. Goods in transit can be sorted, assembled and repacked or stored indefinitely without incurring duties or value added tax (BTW in Dutch).

FREE TRADE

The liberal and non-discriminatory attitude the Dutch developed over their centuries of trade has prompted some 3,500 foreign firms to set up Dutch offices. Companies such as Fuji, ITT, Nissan, IBM, EMI, Polaroid, Rank Xerox, Sony and Canon have established their European distribution centres in the country. There are very few restrictions on the repatriation or transfer abroad of profits, capital repayments, dividends or earnings. Free trade is enshrined in trading law, with no licence required for either importing or exporting in the majority of cases. Major corporations benefit from the free-enterprise economy – any company physically or statutorily based in The Netherlands is exempt from tax on the earnings of foreign subsidiaries in which they have at least a five per cent stake. Foreign international corporations, in other words, can set up a Dutch BV (private limited company) or NV (public

The **Brouwersgracht Warehouses** (see under **VOC Empire-Building**) *were originally owned by the merchants of the Golden Age – both family firms and larger enterprises such as the VOC. During this period they held spices, tobacco, silks, porcelain and other colonial gains. The buildings fell into disuse during the nineteenth and most of the twentieth centuries, but during the past 20 years, the majority have been converted into desirable private flats.*

company) and save on tax bills. This device has helped Dutch-registered companies become leading foreign investors in the USA.

But while the Dutch economy remains one of the most open and well-managed in Europe – and the Dutch guilder, linked to the Deutschmark, is traditionally strong – business predictions are not entirely optimistic. Export growth is projected to fall over the next few years and the country's exceptionally low inflation is set to rise. Wage costs are likely to climb, and the national debt ratio – 82 per cent of GNP in 1990 – is worryingly high. Against a background of declining world trade, the task of reducing this will not be eased by the combined facts that the Dutch run the most expensive welfare state in the EC; long-term unemployment persists; and income on exports of natural gas can be expected to wane during the next century (The Netherlands is the fourth largest gas producer in the world). The massive costs of cleaning up the environment (*see*

page 75 **Green Issues**) could brake economic growth further.

AMSTERDAM TODAY

So where does Amsterdam fit into today's Dutch business scene? The city's port is fighting back, but has a long way to go: throughput in 1989 was about one-tenth of Rotterdam's and it is currently the fourteenth largest in Europe. Around the port are petrochemical and petroleum-blending installations, distribution centres (Japanese car manufacturer Nissan is to be the latest) and ship repair yards. Hi-tech and light manufacturing – for example, the fashion industry – are in good health. The traditional diamond industry, now recovered from the destruction of its workforce during World War II (it was, and still is, largely run by Jewish people), numbers some 20 diamond workshops; the majority of production is geared to industrial use. Tours are run around several of these workshops (*see page 13* **Sightseeing**).

The city is home to the headquarters of the Nederlandsche Bank (the Dutch National Bank), the NMB Postbank and ABN AMRO banks, the European head offices of companies including IBM, and to countless trading houses and brokers. Tourism is a substantial earner, with nearly eight million people visiting Amsterdam in 1989.

Financial services are the city's biggest invisible money-spinner: Amsterdam contains over 400 stock-broking firms and 500 domestic and foreign bank branches. The Effectenbeurs lists some 250 Dutch companies and 315 foreign firms. It also trades around 1,500 bond issues. A system known as ASAS allows players to trade shares in a number of US stock issues directly from Amsterdam in dollars rather than guilders. Along with the Effectenbeurs, the **Optiebeurs** (the European Options Exchange, or EOE, *see below* **Exchanges** and *page 193* **picture and caption**) the major banks are part of a drive to make Amsterdam a European financial centre in the post-1992 single European market.

The Dutch capital may not be the commercial hub it was in the Golden Age, but behind the doors of the old merchants' canal houses and in the gleaming new office blocks of Amsterdam's *Zuid-Oost* business park, a lot of money is still changing hands.

INFORMATION

Many of the agencies listed below are in The Hague (Den Haag). For details of embassies and consulates, and libraries in Amsterdam, *see page 221* **Survival**.

American Chamber of Commerce
Carnegieplein 5, 2517 KJ, Den Haag (070 347 8292). Open 9am-4pm Mon-Fri.

British Embassy, Commercial Department
Lange Voorhout 10, 2514 ED, Den Haag (070 364 5800). Open 9am-1pm, 2.15-5.30pm, Mon-Fri.
Based in The Hague, this office co-operates with the British Department of Trade and Industry to assist British companies operating in The Netherlands.

British-Netherlands Chamber of Commerce
Bezuidenhoutseweg 181, 2594 AH, Den Haag (070 347 8881). Open 9am-4pm (trade enquiries 10am-noon, 2-4pm) Mon-Fri.

Centraal Bureau voor Statistiek (CBS)
Prinses Beatrixlaan 428, 2273 XZ, Voorburg (070 369 4341). Open 9am-noon, 2-5pm, Mon-Fri.
The Central Bureau for Statistics provides statistics on every aspect of Dutch business, society and the economy.

Commissariaat voor Buitenlandse Investeringen Nederland (Netherlands Foreign Investment Agency)
Bezuidenhoutseweg 91, 2500 EC, Den Haag (070 379 72333/fax 070 379 6322). Open 8am-6pm Mon-Fri.
Probably the most useful first port of call for business people wishing to relocate to The Netherlands.

Douane Amsterdam (Customs)
Leeuwendalersweg 21, OW (586 7511). Tram 12, 14/bus 21, 68, 80. Open 7.30am-5.30pm Mon-Fri.

Douane Rotterdam (Customs)
West Zeedijk 387, Rotterdam (010 478 7922). Open 8am-5pm Mon-Fri.

Economische Voorlichtingdienst, EVD (The Netherlands Foreign Trade Agency)
Bezuidenhoutseweg 151, 2594 AG, Den Haag (070 379 7883). Open 9am-4pm Mon-Fri.
A very useful library and information centre for business people. It incorporates the Netherlands Council for Trade Promotion (NCH), another handy source of information.

Kamer van Koophandel (Chamber of Commerce)
De Ruijterkade 5, C (523 6600). Tram 1, 2, 4, 5, 9, 13, 16, 17, 24, 25. Open 9am-4pm Mon-Fri.
See p191 picture and caption.

Ministerie voor Economische Zaaken (Ministry of Economic Affairs)
Bezuidenhoutseweg 30, 2594 AV, Den Haag (070 379 8911). Open 9am-4pm Mon-Fri.
The information department of this ministry will provide answers to general queries concerning the Dutch economy. Detailed enquiries will probably be referred to the EVD (Netherlands Foreign Investment Agency, *see above*).

Ministerie voor Buitenlandse Zaaken (Ministry of Foreign Affairs)
Bezuidenhoutseweg 67, 2594 AC, Den Haag (070 348 6486). Open 9am-4pm Mon-Fri.
Staff at the Ministry's information department will answer general queries only. Detailed enquiries will probably be referred to the EVD (Netherlands Foreign Investment Agency, *see above*).

BANKING

The branches listed below are head offices. Most do not have general banking facilities, but staff will be able to provide a list of branches that do. For information about foreign exchange, *see page 3* **Essential Information**.

ABN AMRO
Vijzelgracht 32, IS (629 9111). Tram 6, 7, 10, 16, 24, 25. Open 9am-5pm Mon-Fri.
ABN and AMRO were The Netherlands' two biggest banks. They merged at the end of 1990 and this is their main office. Before the merger, there were about 80 branches of both banks in Amsterdam.

Barclays Bank
Weteringschans 109, IS (626 2209). Tram 6, 7, 10. Open 9am-5pm Mon-Fri.
Deals with business transactions only.

Citibank NA
Herengracht 545-549, IS (551 5911). Tram 16, 24, 25. Open 9.30am-3pm Mon-Fri.
This company is affiliated to the US Citibank.

Credit Lyonnais Bank Nederland NV
Keizersgracht 515, IS (556 9111). Tram 1, 2, 5. Open 9am-4pm Mon-Fri.

Lloyds Bank
Leidseplein 29, IS (626 3535). Tram 1, 2, 5, 6, 7, 10. Open 9am-5pm Mon-Fri.
Only business transactions can be carried out here.

London Amsterdam Merchant Bank NV
Paleisstraat 1, C (550 2602). Tram 1, 2, 5, 14. Open 8.30am-5pm Mon-Fri.

NMB Postbank Group
Bijlmerplein 888, OE (563 9111). Bus 59, 60, 62, 137/Metro Bijlmer. Open 9am-4pm Mon-Fri.
This recently merged group now incorporates the 50 Amsterdam branches of the post office bank offering full banking and exchange services. *See also p68* **Post-war:** picture and caption.

Rabobank
Wilhelminaplantsoen 124, OS (569 0569). Bus 136. Open 9am-4pm Mon-Fri.
Rabobank has 29 Amsterdam branches, some of which are closed on Monday mornings.

Société Générale
Museumplein 17, OS (676 8321). Tram 3, 5, 12, 16. Open 9am-5pm Mon-Fri.
Only commercial transactions are undertaken by this bank.

Swiss Bank Corporation
Amstel 344, IS (626 4100). Tram 6, 7, 10. Open 8.30am-5.30pm Mon-Fri.
Commercial transactions only are offered by this investment bank.

Verenigde Spaarbank
Singel 548, C (520 5911). Tram 4, 9, 14, 16, 24, 25. Open 9am-5pm Mon-Wed, Fri; 9am-5pm, 6.30-8pm, Thur.
Full banking facilities are offered. There are 41 branches in Amsterdam.

EXCHANGES

Effectenbeurs (Stock Exchange)
Damrak 62A, C (523 4567). Tram 4, 9, 16, 24, 25. **Open** *10am-4.30pm Mon-Fri.*
Stock for officially-listed Dutch companies is traded here. Phone for an appointment to view proceedings from the visitors' gallery.

Nederlandse Termijnhandel (Dutch Association of Futures and Options Traders)
Damrak 261, C (638 2239). Tram 4, 9, 16, 24, 25. **Open** *10.45am-4pm Mon-Fri.*
This commodity exchange is where futures contracts are traded in potatoes and pigs.

Optiebeurs (European Options Exchange)
Rokin 65, IW (550 4550). Tram 4, 9, 14. **Open** *10am-4.30pm Mon-Fri.*
See p193 **picture and caption.**

CONFERENCES

Amsterdam has established itself as an important congress and conference venue. Most major hotels offer full conference facilities and the city's main congress centre, the **RAI** (*see below*) hosts some 65 international events a year. A number of specialist conference organizers have sprung up to arrange these events.

Grand Hotel Krasnapolsky
Dam 9, C (554 9111/fax 622 8607/telex 12262 KRAS NL). Tram 1, 2, 5, 13, 14, 16, 17, 24, 25, 49.
Bang in the centre of the city, the recently refurbished Krasnapolsky (*see p39* **Accommodation**) now has the most comprehensive in-hotel meeting facilities, including a convention centre for up to 2,000 people. The largest meeting room is suitable for conferences of up to 700.

RAI Congresgebouw
Europaplein, OS (549 1212; exhibition centre and restaurant: fax 646 4469/telex 1601). Tram 4, 25/NS railway from Schiphol Airport to RAI Station. **Open** *office and enquiries 9am-5pm Mon-Fri.*
A self-contained congress and trade fair centre in the south of the city. The building contains nine halls totalling 63,000sq m/56,000sq yds of covered exhibition space and 19 conference rooms which can seat between 40 and 1,750 people. Full translation and business services are available.

Stichting de Beurs van Berlage (Berlage Exchange Foundation)
Damrak 277, C (626 5257/fax 620 4701). Tram 4, 9, 16, 24, 25. **Open** *office and enquiries 9am-5pm Mon-Fri.*
This stunning building was completed in 1903, to be used as a commodity exchange, *see p61* **Between the Occupations.** Later (1978-1987) it was the venue for the European Options Exchange. It is now used

for cultural events and smaller trade fairs (up to 2,500 visitors can be provided with buffet dinners). Berlage Hall, within the building, provides a stylish conference venue for between 50 and 200 people.

World Trade Center
Strawinskylaan 1, OS (575 9111/fax 662 7255/telex 12808). Tram 5/NS railway from Schiphol Airport to RAI Station. **Open** *office and enquiries 9am-5pm Mon-Fri.*
Just about anything you might need to run a conference can be provided here. Facilities include an international press centre, small studios for top-level meetings and 14 business-class rooms seating from 4 to 40 people. A conference room seating up to 250 costs f1,740 per full day of 8am-11pm (excluding VAT and services). Worldwide conference facilities and secretarial, translating and legal services can be supplied. *See also below* **Office Services: Office Hire.**

CONFERENCE ORGANIZERS

NOVEP (Netherlands Organization Bureau for Events and Projects)
Paulus Potterstraat 40, OS (662 1922/fax 662 8136). Tram 2, 3, 5, 12. **Open** *9am-5pm Mon-Fri.* **Credit** *AmEx, DC, MC, V.*
NOVEP will organize congresses or conferences to your specifications.

QTL Convention Services
Keizersgracht 782, IS (626 1372/fax 625 9574/telex 14527). Tram 4. **Open** *9am-5pm Mon-Fri.* **Credit** *AmEx, MC, V.*
These specialists in teleconferencing will organize and supply the equipment for congresses and seminars.

BUSINESS SERVICES

You can send faxes from Telehouse 24 hours daily and some district post offices, but some commercial locations, such as Teletalk Centre, are less expensive. For details, *see page 221* **Survival.** Major hotels have fax services for guests (and sometimes non-guests, if the hotel is not too busy), but prices are high. The World Trade Center (*listed under* **Office Hire**) also has full reception and transmission facilities.

COURIERS & SHIPPERS

Intercontinental Couriers
Vrachtegebouw 1, Kamer 211, Schiphol (648 1636). Train to Schiphol Airport from

Amsterdam's **Kamer van Koophandel** (*Chamber of Commerce, see under* **Information**) *is a spanking new building on the harbour front. A sign of renewed confidence in Amsterdam, or just bluff? Staff have lists of import/export agencies, companies by sector and government trade representatives. They will also advise on legal procedure, finding an office and hiring local staff. The bureaucracy can be baffling, but persevere: once you've found the right person, you can get all the information you need.*

Thomas Cook
Foreign Exchange

Thomas Cook
Travel Management

MORE THAN 1600 OFFICES MAKES THOMAS COOK THE
LARGEST TRAVEL-DRIVEN BUSINESS IN THE WORLD.

Our foreign exchange bureaux offer the following services:
- Foreign currency exchange.
- Purchase and sale of travellers cheques.
- Money transfers throughout the world.
- Cash on major credit cards.
- Hertz car rental.
- Excursions.

Travel Management:

- Business and Leisure Travel.
- Hotel Reservations.
- Passport and visa service.
- Worldwide Network services.

TRAVELLERS HAVE TRUSTED US FOR 150 YEARS

In Amsterdam:
Travel Agency
Van Baerlestraat 40
Tel. 237273 / 267000
Foreign Exchange Bureaux:
Dam 23-25,
1012 JS Amsterdam
Tel. 250922

Leidseplein 31A,
1017 PS Amsterdam
Tel. 267000

Scandic Crown Hotel
Damrak 1-5,
1012 LG Amsterdam
Tel. 203236

Munt Tower
Muntplein 12A
1012 WR Amsterdam
Tel. 204016

Centraal Station. Open 24 hours daily. **No credit cards.**
Next-day delivery is guaranteed for many destinations, including London and Paris at a cost of f35 for the first 0.5kg/1.1lb and then f5 for each additional 0.5kg plus f35 if the package is subject to duty. All packages received before 4pm are delivered before noon the next day.

International Couriers
Amsterdam
Coenhavenweg Loods 10, Pier Europa, N (686 7808/7805). Bus 40. Open 24 hours daily. **No credit cards.**
This worldwide courier service will transport packages across Amsterdam within an hour for f17.50. Rates for London (up to 0.5kg/1.1lb, arriving before noon the following day) start at f65.

Randstad Koeriers
Andreas Schelfhoutstraat 48, OW (617 3622/617 8615). Tram 1, 6, 17. Open 24 hours daily. **No credit cards.**
Randstad transports documents across the world. Rates to London start at f60 for a 0.5kg/1.1lb delivery in 24 hours. Motorcycle delivery in Amsterdam within an hour costs from f20.50.

XP Express Systems
Hessenbergweg 8-10, OSE (06 099 1234/fax 020 912 050). Bus 48, 62, 158/Metro Bullewijk. Open 7am-7pm Mon-Fri. **No credit cards.**
Documents of up to 250g/9oz can be delivered to London within 24 hours for f100 (f130 for parcels up to 1kg/2.2lb). Overnight delivery to destinations throughout The Netherlands costs f40 plus f1 per kilogram.

FORWARDING AGENT

Geytenbeek BV
Kernweg 1, 3542 AE, Utrecht (030 469 212/fax 030 46 9316/telex 76438). Open 9am-5pm Mon-Fri. **No credit cards.**
A business removals, and exhibition delivery service, Geytenbeek deals with all customs formalities.
Branch RAI Congresgebouw, Europaplein 8, OS (644 8551/fax 644 0603).

PRINTING & DUPLICATING

Grand Prix Copyrette
Weteringschans 84A, IS (627 3705). Tram 16, 24, 25. Open 9.30am-5.30pm Mon-Fri; 11am-4pm Sat. **No credit cards.**
There are a number of branches of this firm around the city. Each offers both monochrome and colour copying, ring binding, fax services and laser printing.

Multicopy
Weesperstraat 65, IE (624 6208/620 4922). Bus 31. Open 9am-5.30pm Mon-Fri. **No credit cards.**
See p195 picture and caption.
Branch Zeilstraat 30, OS (662 0154/675 1650).

Prontaprint
Utrechtsestraat 138, IS (626 0033/fax 620 4163). Tram 4. Open 9am-5pm Mon-Fri. **Credit** AmEx, MC, V.
Both colour and black and white photocopy-

The new **Optiebeurs** *(the European Options Exchange or EOE, see under* **Exchanges***) opened in 1987 and is now the largest options exchange in Europe. Trading share, gold and silver options as well as bond and currency options, it books about 55,000 transactions daily: way ahead of the City of London. Tours around this impressive building are run every weekday morning at 10.30am and 11.30am. You can watch trading on the floor from a visitors' balcony. Phone to reserve a place.*

ing is undertaken, plus laser printing, offset printing and binding.

TRANSLATIONS (VERTALENG)

Anglo-Dutch Language Services
Pretoriusstraat 53, OE (693 6332/fax 694 4704). Tram 9, 14. Open 9am-5pm Mon-Fri. **No credit cards.**
Dutch/English or English/Dutch translations cost 30c per word. Copywriting, correction, layout and word-processing services are provided and language courses are run.

Berlitz Language Center
Rokin 87, C (622 1375/fax 620 3959). Tram 4, 9, 14, 16, 24, 25. Open 8.15am-9pm Mon-Fri. **No credit cards.**
Specialists in commercial, technical, legal and scientific documents. All European languages are translated, plus Japanese and Arabic. English/Dutch translation costs from f30 per 100 words.

Mac Bay Consultants
PC Hooftstraat 15, OS (662 0501/fax 662 6299). Tram 2, 3, 5, 12. Open 9am-5pm Mon-Fri. **No credit cards.**
This firm specializes in translating financial documents. Dutch/English translations cost f172.50 an hour. Other languages are also

translated and there is a copywriting service.

INTERPRETERS (TOLKEN)

Congrestolken – Secretariaat
Prinsengracht 993, IS (625 2535/fax 626 5642). Tram 4, 16, 24, 25. Open 9am-5.30pm Mon-Fri. **No credit cards.**
Highly specialized staff are supplied for conference interpreting. Languages offered include Arabic, Japanese, Cantonese and all European languages. Members of the Association Internationale D'Interprètes de Conference (AIIC).

Randstad Uitzenburo
Strawinskylaan 501, World Trade Center, OS (662 8011). Tram 5. Open 8.30am-5.30pm Mon-Fri. **No credit cards.**
This branch of the employment agency (*see below* **Office Services: Staff**) has a number of freelance interpreters and translators on its books. Costs for services vary widely.

EQUIPMENT HIRE

Apple Center
Hogehilweg 10, OSE (697 6166/fax 697 9766). Bus 48, 158/Metro Bullewijk. Open 9am-5pm daily. **No credit cards.**

SPECIAL
ISSUE

The
Best-Selling
Weekly
Guide To

LONDON

The Best
& Worst Of

FILM
MUSIC
THEATRE
ART
NIGHTLIFE
DANCE
TELEVISION
RADIO
BOOKS
SPORT
GAY
CABARET
KIDS EVENTS
POETRY
POLITICS
FASHION
EATING OUT
FITNESS
SHOPPING
TRAVEL

Plus
NEWS, SCANDAL,
GOSSIP . . .

EVERY
WEDNESDAY

Time Out

LONDON'S WEEKLY GUIDE

CIRQUE DU SOLEIL PHOTO: AL SEIB

Apple Mac computers are for hire from f285 per week, excluding BTW (the Dutch name for VAT: 18.5%). Desktop publishing services and training are also offered.

Avisco
Stadhouderskade 156, OS (671 9909). Tram 6, 7, 10. **Open** 7am-6pm Mon-Fri. **No credit cards.**
Slide projectors, video equipment, screens, cameras, overhead projectors, microphones and tape decks are hired out or sold.

Capi-lux
Basisweg 42, OW (586 6333). Bus 42, 44, 82. **Open** 8.30am-5.30pm Mon-Fri. **Credit** AmEx, DC, MC, V.
These audio-visual equipment suppliers specialize in photographic goods: Hasselblad cameras, lights and projectors.

Decorum Verhuut
Jarmuiden 21, OW (611 7905). Bus 44, 82. **Open** 8am-5pm Mon-Fri. **No credit cards.**
Office furniture can be hired from this firm.

Particuliere Telefoon Dienst (Personal Telephone Service)
Nassaukade 129, OW (686 6660). Tram 10. **Open** 9am-5pm Mon-Fri; 10am-4pm Sat. **Credit** AmEx, DC, MC, V.
Hiring a car phone costs from f350 per month plus f1,000 deposit. Fax machines are for hire from f100 per month plus f500 deposit.

Ruad Computer Hire
Kuiperbergweg 33, OSE (697 8191). Bus 62/Metro Bullewijk. **Open** 8am-5pm Mon-Fri. **Credit** AmEx, DC, MC, V.
IBM compatibles can be hired for f350 per month plus f1,500 deposit (invoice to be paid in cash). Hiring an IBM computer costs from f720 per month plus f2,000 deposit (invoice can be paid by cheque). Fax machines cost from f250 per month plus f1,500 deposit.

COMPUTER REPAIRS

De Vakman
Nieuwe Hemweg 6N, NW (684 2425/697 2511). Bus 41. **Open** 24-hour emergency repair service. **No credit cards.**
This firm will attempt to repair all models of computers. The call-out charge is from f41.50.

OFFICE HIRE

Euro Business Center
Keizersgracht 62, IW (626 5749/623 1433/fax 623 1506/telex 16183 EUROCNL). Tram 13, 14, 17. **Open** 8.30am-5.30pm Mon-Fri. **Credit** AmEx, DC, MC, V.
The fully-equipped offices for hire (long or short term) include the use of telex, fax, photocopier, phone and mailbox services and multilingual secretaries. Switchboard operators are also provided. For a minimum of three months, fully-equipped offices cost between f2,000 and f4,775 per month. Private offices cost between f125 and f200 per working day. Personal cheques not accepted.

Jan Luyken Residence
Jan Luijkenstraat 58, OS (676 4111/fax 676 3841/telex 16254 HTLIJNL). Tram 2, 3, 5,

12. **Open** *office* 9am-5pm Mon-Fri. **Credit** AmEx, MC, V.
Three fully-equipped offices are for hire, long or short term. Projectors, videos, phones, telex, fax and mailbox are among the many services that can be provided. Small temporary offices cost f250 per day. Conference rooms with capacities of up to 55 people cost f400 to f500 per day.

World Trade Center
Strawinskylaan 1, OS (575 9111/fax 662 7255/telex 12808). Tram 5/NS railway from Schiphol Airport to RAI Station. **Open** *office and enquiries* 9am-5pm Mon-Fri.
Over 200 companies work in the rather soulless, air-conditioned luxury of the trade centre. Offices can be hired long or short term from f125 to f305 for a day lasting 8am-5pm (from f160-f400 for a day of 8am-11pm). Audio and projection equipment is also for hire. Secretarial services cost f75 per hour, and telex, fax and photocopying facilities are offered. *See also above* **Conferences.**

RELOCATION

Formula 2
Stadionweg 190, OS (664 2759/fax 675 2820). Tram 24. **Open** 9am-4pm Mon-Fri. **No credit cards.**
Two British women set up this company six years ago and now have a team of employees settling non-Dutch managerial and executive staff in the Randstad area. Assistance is given on all aspects of relocation, from house-hunting to finding doctors and schools.

EMPLOYMENT AGENCIES (UITZENDBUREAU)

Content Uitzendbureau
Nieuwezijds Voorburgwal 156, C (625 1061). Tram 1, 2, 5, 13, 17. **Open** 8.30am-5.30pm Mon-Fri. **No credit cards.**
Office, secretarial, medical and technical staff are on this firm's books. There are six branches in Amsterdam; this is the head office.

Manpower
Van Baerlestraat 16, OS (664 4180). Tram 3, 5, 12. **Open** 8.30am-5.30pm Mon-Thur; 8.30am-6.30pm Fri. **No credit cards.**
A large employment agency with five branches in Amsterdam. Staff can be provided for general office, secretarial, computer and other work.

Randstad
AJ Ernststraat 593, OS (644 9135). Bus 8, 48, 49, 67. **Open** 8.30am-5.30pm Mon-Fri. **No credit cards.**
There are 13 branches of Randstad in Amsterdam supplying office and secretarial staff, translators and data-entry staff.

Tempo Team
Rokin 118, C (622 9393). Tram 4, 9, 14, 16, 24, 25. **Open** 8.30am-5.15pm Mon-Fri. **No credit cards.**
Secretarial, hotel and catering, medical, technical and academic staff are on Tempo's books.

Multicopy *(see under* **Printing & Duplicating***) is typical of Amsterdam's slickly run photocopy shops. The machines are metered, so rather than annoying staff by asking for change, you pay a total on your way out. You can make colour and black and white copies in A4, A3 and A2 sizes, on white or coloured paper.*

Students

Amsterdam is the hub of Dutch higher education and is famed for its student movement. Kees Neefjes studies the academic facilities and student social scene.

Amsterdam's 60,000 students constitute almost ten per cent of the city's population. Most are highly integrated with the rest of Amsterdam's inhabitants, as few join the student societies and clubs. Instead, they meet up in favoured bars and discos in the city centre – at least when they're not protesting. Amsterdam's student movement has made headlines ever since the radical heyday of the sixties (*see below* **Union Protest**).

Students in The Netherlands join student unions individually, and foreign students can also use the clubs' and unions' facilities if they become members. The **Foreign Student Service** and the **Student Information** phoneline (*both listed under* **Study**) can help with any queries.

DUTCH DEGREES

There are two sectors of Dutch higher education: **Universities** and **Institutes of Higher Vocational Education (HBO)**. The differences between them are similar to those between British universities and polytechnics, but are becoming less defined. Universities prepare undergraduates for independent research and work in an academic or professional setting. The minimum duration of study is four years, and the maximum six; students may continue their studies for longer, but will have to pay their own way.

HBOs provide the knowledge and skills necessary for specific professions, such as teaching, social work, drama, accounting and journalism, with work experience being an integral part. No academic research is conducted at HBOs.

There are 13 universities in The Netherlands; the oldest was founded in 1575 in Leiden (*see page 208* **The Randstad**); the youngest, University of Limburg in Maastricht, opened its first department in 1976. With two universities and three large and 17 small HBOs, Amsterdam is the educational and scientific centre of the country.

UVA (University of Amsterdam)

Maagdenhuis (administration), Spui, C (525 9111). Tram 1, 2, 5.
The *Universiteit van Amsterdam* was founded in 1877, but its roots go back to 1632 with the founding of the *Atheneum Illustre*, which prepared students for one of the existing universities. The University is a public building, and the public are free to visit. In St Agatha's chapel (Agnietenkapel), which now houses the University Museum (*see p100* **Museums**), the first two professors, Gerardus Vossius and Caspar Barlaeus, lectured in history and philosophy respectively. Within 33 years the curriculum was expanded to include mathematics, law, medicine and theology. The UVA is now the largest university in the country. Its 28,000 students are educated in a number of buildings in the city centre. The Lutheran Church, Singel 411, is now used as the university's auditorium.

Vrije Universiteit (VU, Free University)

De Boelelaan 1105, OS (548 9222/hospital 548 9111). Bus 8, 23, 26, 48, 49, 64, 65, 67, 173.
In 1878 a group of orthodox Protestants, led by the theologian and politician Abraham Kuyper, formed a society to establish a 'free' Christian university – free of church and state, committed only to the Word of God – which they founded two years later. The VU is no longer orthodox Protestant but Christian generally and, like all Dutch universities, almost fully financed by the state. It is mostly housed in a modern complex in Amsterdam-Buitenveldert, which includes a *mensa* (student restaurant) and an academic bookshop (*see below* **City Life**). The Historical Documentation Centre for Dutch Protestantism (1800-the present) organizes temporary exhibitions on the first floor of the main building. The original Vrije Universiteit site in *Keizersgracht 162-164*, but the buildings are no longer VU property.

UNION PROTEST

The student movement campaigned vigorously during the sixties and seventies, particularly for the democratization of the universities and for peace in Vietnam. The most dramatic action was the occupation of the Maagdenhuis, the administrative centre of the University of Amsterdam. As a result of the struggle, students gained a lot more input into University matters, for example, being represented on the University Board by student unions such as **ASVA** (left wing) and **OBAS** (liberal). The current system of funding for

students consists of a basic grant, and additional top-up loans that have to be paid back with interest after graduation. Students from low-income families get an additional payment on top of their grant. A new wave of protests erupted in the eighties against government proposals to economize in the education sector. These plans included shortening the duration of funded study; reorganizing the system of student grants and loans; and increasing tuition fees. Massive student protests, co-ordinated by LSVB, a federal organization of local university and HBO student unions, resulted in a somewhat less rigorous realization and delay of these plans.

ASVA

Spinhuissteeg 1, C (union 622 5771/accommodation agency 623 8052). Tram 4, 9, 14, 16, 24, 25. **Open** *Union* noon-5pm Mon-Fri. *Accommodation agency:* July, Aug 10.30am-4.30pm Mon-Fri; Sept-June 12.30-4.30pm Mon-Fri. **No credit cards**.
As the University of Amsterdam's main student union, ASVA can provide assistance for foreign students on all kinds of matters. The union bar and building are occasionally open during the evening, and evening meals are sometimes available. The *ASVA Kamerbureau* (accommodation agency) can find you a room from f250 to f350 per month, charging a fee of f10. Arrive early and wait for rooms to become available. Be prepared for numerous visits before something turns up.

OBAS

Voetboogstraat 2, C (525 2833). Tram 4, 9, 14, 16, 24, 25. **Open** 11am-12.30pm, 2.30-4.30pm, Tue-Fri.
This UVA union is most concerned with law students, but has general members, too. There are no facilities here, but foreign students can contact OBAS for help and information.

SRVU

De Boelelaan 1115B, OS (548 3600). Bus 8, 13, 26, 48, 49, 64, 65, 67, 173. **Open** July-mid Aug irregular hours, message in English on answerphone; mid Aug-June 12.30-3.30pm Mon-Fri; closed Christmas and Easter holidays.
The union for students at the Free University. SRVU's accommodation service also helps foreign students find a place to stay, as well as providing them with general advice and help.

CITY LIFE

It's not easy to find a house or a room in Amsterdam. Foreign students can apply to the **Foreign Student Service** (*listed under* **Study**) or to the *kamerbureau* of **ASVA** (*under* **Union Protest**). Another possibility for those seeking

emporary accommodation is to
advertise in the university papers *Ad
Valvas* (548 4330) and *Folia Civitates*
(525 3981). *See also page 39*
Accommodation.

Students are often entitled to discounts on admission at museums,
attractions and places of entertainment; details are given in the
relevant chapters of this guide.
Presenting an ISIC card is often sufficient, but you can also buy a *CJP
card* (discounts for under-26s) from
Uitburo (*see page 3* **Essential
Information**). Theatres popular with
students include the Shaffy and the
Stalhouderij, which often stage performances in English (*see page 126*
Theatre). Nightclubs frequented by
students include Dansen bij Jansen,
Roxy, Escape (*see page 141* **Night-
clubs**) and IT (*see page 169* **Gay
Amsterdam**). For discount travel
agencies, and advice on hitch-hiking,
see page 221 **Survival**.

CAFES & BARS

You're likely to find students congre-
gating at the following: Aas van
Bokalen, De Balie, Frascati, De
Huyschkaemer, Hoppe and De
Reiger; for details, *see page 91* **Cafés
& Bars**.

De Blincker
*St Barberenstraat 7-9, C (627 1938). Tram
4, 9, 14, 16, 24, 25.* **Open** 4pm-1am Mon-
Thur; 4pm-2am Fri, Sat. **No credit cards.**
The bar of the Frascati Theatre (*see p126*
Theatre). Many students visit this pub
with its modern interior of granite and
iron.

The Schutter Café
*Voetboogstraat 13-15, C (622 4608). Tram 1,
2, 5.* **Open** *bar* 11am-1am Mon-Thur, Sun;
11am-2am Fri, Sat; *kitchen* 5.45-10pm daily.
No credit cards.
This café is frequented by students and
tourists. There are 35 types of beer, including English varieties, and snacks; drinks
prices are average, snacks are cheap. Meals
are also available; there are two *dagschotels*
(dishes of the day) for fl3, as well as vegetarian dishes. Lunch is served between
noon and 2.45pm.

MENSAE (STUDENT RESTAURANTS)

There are several large *mensae* (student restaurants) in Amsterdam
where the food is good and the
prices rather low. The mensae are
subsidized, and are open to the public, but generally only students and a
few budget-conscious people use
them. *Trefcentrum* means meeting
place.

Het Trefcentrum Atrium (see under **City Life: Mensae**) *is a buffet/self-
service restaurant where fl7.50 buys a meal of soup and a daily choice of meat, fish
and vegetarian dishes. The restaurant's architecture is an interesting blend of old
and new: this former inner court of the building of political science now has a
pyramid of white glass for a roof. The building once housed the university hospital,
and the original separate entrances for men and women can still be seen.*

Het Trefcentrum Atrium
*Oudezijds Achterburgwal 237, C (525 3999).
Tram 4, 9, 14, 16, 24, 25/Metro
Nieuwmarkt.* **Open** 9am-7pm Mon-Fri.
Lunch served noon-2pm, **dinner served** 5-
7pm, Mon-Fri. **Average** fl7.50. **No credit
cards.**
See picture and caption.

Het Trefcentrum De Weesper
*Weesperstraat 5, IE (622 4036). Tram 9,
14/Metro Waterlooplein.* **Open** 5-7pm Mon-
Fri. **Average** fl7.50. **No credit cards.**
A bargain fl7.50 for the main dish buys a
choice of meat, fish, vegetarian and salad
dishes. If you're still hungry you can have
second helpings. The Weesperstraat student flats complex (*see p68* **Post-war**)
didn't prove as practical as was hoped, and
is due to close sometime between
September 1991 and January 1992, when
the replacement is completed. The new
complex in nearby Roeterstraat will be an
unmissable triangular blue structure and
its mensa will be open for breakfast, lunch
and dinner.

Joodse Studenten Mensa
*de Lairessestraat 13 (676 7622) Tram 3, 5,
12, 16.* **Open** 5.45-7.15pm. **Average** fl13. **No
credit cards.**
The Jewish students' mensa has a kosher
menu, and while the food is about twice as
expensive as in the other mensae, it's still
reasonable.

Mensa VU
De Boelelaan 1105, OS (548 9222). **Bus** 8,
23, 26, 48, 49, 64, 65, 67, 173. **Open**
10am-7pm Mon-Fri. **Average** fl6.50. **No credit
cards.**
Mensa VU is large, modern and spacious.
Visitors get their meals in the cellar, but can
choose a table on one of the three floors.

STUDENT SHOPPING

Fortunately for impecunious
students, Amsterdam has plenty
of outlets selling cheap clothes,
food, records and books. For
markets, *see page 153* **Shopping
Around**; for cheap and **second-
hand shops**, head for the Jordaan,
Damstraat, Kalverstraat and
Nieuwendijk.

For cheap, second-hand scientific
and academic books, often in
English, peruse the stalls in
Oudemanhuispoort. For new academic volumes, the principal outlets
are **Athenaeum** (for both of these,
see page 153 **Shopping Around**)
and the following:

Scheltema, Holkema en Vermeulen
*Koningsplein 20, IS (626 7212). Tram 1, 2,
5.* **Open** 1-6pm Mon; 9am-6pm Tue, Wed,
Fri; 9am-9pm Thur; 10am-5pm Sat. **Credit**
(minimum fl00) AmEx, MC, V.
Specialists in books on medicine, law, economics and science.

Allert de Lange
*Damrak 62, C (624 6744). Tram 4, 9, 16,
24, 25.* **Open** 1-6pm Mon; 9am-6pm Tue-Fri;
9am-5pm Sat. **Credit** MC, V.
Books on the language, literature and culture of France, Germany and England are
the speciality of Allert de Lange. You'll also
find sections on philosophy, history, history
of art, film and photography.

Pegasus
Leidsestraat 25, IS (623 1138). Tram 1, 2, 5.
Open 1-6pm Mon; 9am-6pm Tue, Wed, Fri;

9am-9pm Thur; 9am-5pm Sat. **Credit** AmEx, MC, V.
A small shop, specializing in political science, politics, social economics, and the culture and art of Russia, Eastern Europe, Asia and South America.

VU Academic Bookshop
De Boelelaan 1105, OS (548 9111). Bus 8, 23, 26, 48, 49, 64, 65, 67, 173. **Open** 9am-5.30pm Mon-Fri. **Credit** AmEx, DC, MC, V.
The VU Bookshop (VU Boekhandel) has a large selection of books relating to all sciences, and a good collection of novels, tourist guides and children's books.

STUDY

For people wishing to study in Amsterdam, a number of UVA departments offer international English-language courses and programmes for postgraduates, graduates and undergraduates. Details are available from the Maagdenhuis administrative department (*see above*). Most postgraduate institutes of the UVA also take in foreign students. A relatively new initiative is the Erasmus Programme, developed by the European Community to encourage co-operation and exchange between a number of universities throughout Europe, including UVA and VU. The

programme allows students from EEC universities to study in equivalent faculties of other European universities; to find out more enquire at your college.

Amsterdam Summer University
Felix Meritis Building, Keizersgracht 324, IW (620 0225). Tram 1, 2, 5. **Courses** last week of July-end of first week of Sept.
Housed along with the Shaffy Theatre (*see p126* **Theatre**) in the Felix Meritis Building, ASU offers an extensive, annual summer programme of courses, workshops, training and seminars in the arts and sciences to international classes. All classes are in English. Courses last between three days and six weeks and are for postgraduates, graduates and undergraduates. During the summer courses a cultural programme, including dance, theatre and music, is held in the theatre.

Foreign Student Service
Oranje Nassaulaan 5, 1075 AH; OS (671 5915). Tram 2. **Open** 9am-5pm Mon-Fri.
The Foreign Student Service (FSS) promotes the well-being of foreigners who come to The Netherlands for study or training. FSS provides personal assistance and general information on studying in The Netherlands and runs the International Student Insurance Service (ISIS), in addition to organizing a number of social and cultural activities.

Student Information
(525 4307).
A information line for Dutch and foreign stu-

dents. Callers are referred to relevant organizations if Student Information can't help.

UVA Main Library
Singel 425, C (525 2301). Tram 1, 2, 5. **Open** *for study* 9.30am-midnight Mon-Fri; *for book lending* 10.30am-5pm Mon-Fri.
Anyone can use this library for study. For reference you need a consulting card (obtainable free of charge on production of passport). To get a book you must phone in advance with details of the volume you require, since you can't look for books yourself. Only students of Dutch universities and holders of Dutch degrees can borrow books. No charges are made for study, reference or the borrowing of books. For details of the British Council and American Institute libraries, *see p221* **Survival**.

VU Main Library
De Boelelaan 1105, OS (548 2613). Bus 8, 23, 26, 48, 49, 64, 65, 67, 173. **Open** 10am-4pm Mon-Fri. **Membership** f30 per year. No credit cards.
Anyone can apply for membership, which entitles you to study, borrow and use books for reference.

DUTCH-LANGUAGE COURSES

If you're feeling guilty about the superb English spoken by Amsterdammers, you can tackle the Dutch language at several institutions. Below we've listed a reputable selection.

VU Department of Applied Linguistics
De Boelelaan 1105, Room 9A21, 1081 HV; OS (548 4968). Bus 8, 23, 26, 48, 49, 64, 65, 67, 173. **Open** *information* 10am-4pm Mon-Fri. **Credit** AmEx, MC, V.
Anyone can enrol on the VU self-study programme *Nederlands Tweede Taal* (Dutch Second Language) and use the language laboratory facilities. The fee is f1,150 for 12 hours of instruction. *Beginner's Dutch*, a three week intensive course in September and October runs for five hours a day, five days a week and costs f200. Levels II, III and IV are eight-week courses with three-hour lessons three times a week and cost f200 for each course. Level I and III courses start in October, November and December; Level III in February; and Level IV in February and April.

British Language Training Centre
Keizersgracht 389, 1016 EJ; IW (622 3634). Tram 1, 2, 5. **Open** *information* 9am-5pm Mon-Fri. No credit cards.
See picture and caption.

The British Language Training Centre (see under **Study: Dutch-Language Courses**) *runs various courses in Dutch language. The intensive course* Nederlands 1 *runs from 9.30am to 3.30pm Monday to Friday for two weeks and costs f875. The* Nederlands 2 *course runs for one week from 9.30am to 4.30pm and costs f595. There are five levels of evening courses running for approximately three months. The foundation course costs f790 and there are two-hour lessons twice weekly. Higher level courses have two hours of lessons per week and cost f490. There are a maximum of 12 students per class. The centre can arrange tailor-made courses at an approximate group rate of f180 per hour.*

Volksuniversieit Amsterdam
Herenmarkt 93, 1013 EC; IW (626 1626). Tram 1, 2, 4, 5, 9, 13, 16, 17, 24, 25. **Open** *information* 10am-4pm Mon-Fri. No credit cards.
There are three levels of day and evening courses at the Volksuniversiteit. Twelve weekly lessons of 2½ hours each cost f175, with a maximum of 15 students in a class. An intensive course of 24 lessons costs f325

Trips Out of Town

Take a trip out of Amsterdam and you'll see how unlike the rest of The Netherlands the capital city is. All the entertaining Dutch clichés, from cheese and flower auctions to costumed locals posing in front of windmills, are within an hour's travel.

Also in the Holland region are the famous Randstad towns of Haarlem, Delft, Rotterdam, The Hague, Leiden and Utrecht. Individual in character, each city possesses beautiful art and architecture.

Beyond North and South Holland are ten other provinces with diverse landscapes and character. They can all be reached in a day and can be explored by boat or bicycle. Go provincial and you'll discover prehistoric tombs, water villages, carnivals and thriving traditions.

CONTENTS:

Beyond Amsterdam

Ann Campbell-Lord takes a look at The Netherlands and its people, while Ailsa Camm gives a taste of what's over the Dutch border.

Amsterdam is not typical of The Netherlands. The essence of the country and its people lies in its 12 distinctive provinces. The national borders enclose just 41,864 square kilometres (16,000 square miles), so all but the remotest corners are within a day's drive or train ride; many attractions are less than an hour from Amsterdam. It's particularly pleasant to cycle across the flat landscape or to cruise its many waterways by boat.

COMMON GROUND

This country, more than almost any other, has been shaped by its inhabitants. Over half of the land is below sea level, much of it laboriously reclaimed from the sea (*see page 213* **The Provinces: Fighting the Sea**). In turn, the often hostile elements have moulded the attitudes and lifestyles of the 14.9 million population, contributing to their stoicism and pragmatism.

The vulnerability of their land explains the Dutch sympathy for the environment (*see page 75* **Green Issues**) and has forced them to work together for the common good. In the past, one person's failure to maintain his part of the dike could imperil an entire town. This obligation was enforced by medieval polder boards and may explain the early arrival of democracy in the country. A sense of community has become ingrained in the Dutch nature. In the 1980s, workers agreed to forego pay rises for five years until the economy could be revived. Social provision has also been generous, from medieval *hofjes* (almshouses) to today's welfare state.

Other Dutch traits can be traced to religion. The humanism of Erasmus has combined with Calvinist beliefs in social responsibility and the liberty of conscience to produce a mixture of tolerance and conformity. Generally, it's considered good to be *gewoon* (plain

and ordinary); ostentation is shunned. The former Queen (now Princess) Juliana was admired for travelling by bicycle and prime minister Ruud Lubbers is respected for taking sandwiches to work. Living at close quarters has resulted in formalities to create distance. In rural areas, neighbours often wear hats and gloves when going next door for coffee, every greeting and departure involves a handshake, and first names are seldom used without an invitation to do so.

WHERE IS HOLLAND?

The region of Holland has been so dominant in Dutch history that the entire country has confusingly become widely known by that name. In fact, the region accounts for just two of the 12 provinces: Noord (North) and Zuid (South) Holland. Amsterdam lies in the south of Noord Holland, and is thus an easy day trip away from most of the classic Dutch attractions: windmills, cheese towns, costumes, tulips and clogs. However, many of these traditional sights (*see page 203* **Excursions in Holland**) have been preserved artificially.

The contemporary face of Holland is represented by its ring of major cities called the Randstad (*see page 208*), which also encompasses the province of **Utrecht**, focus of the public transport network and home of the stockbroker belt. Provincial Dutch sometimes see the cosmopolitan Randstad as a rather self-obsessed state-within-a-state, yet it's not homogeneous. People from The Hague are portrayed as gracious; those in Utrecht as proper; and citizens of Rotterdam as industrious. Amsterdammers are considered to be an anarchic, permissive lot, and their city to be a magnet for those who don't give up their *gewoon*. It's been like that since before 1608, when the Pilgrim Fathers fled that 'sinful city' for the

calm of Leiden (*see page 208* **The Randstad**).

The Netherlands, particularly Holland, has for centuries been a hub of transport and maritime trade. Now improved road and high-speed rail links are unifying the country ever more tightly and binding it into Europe. Regional customs and accents are being eroded in the process, but the provinces are fighting to preserve their identity.

PROVINCIAL CHARM

The hardy people of the predominantly Protestant northern provinces – **Friesland**, **Groningen** and **Drenthe** – are renowned for loyalty and hard work. Friesland was once an independent tribal nation that ranged along the coast from North Holland to eastern Germany, and whose people were called 'unconquerable' by the Roman writer Pliny the Elder. Theirs is still the most individualistic province. Famous for costumes (now seldom worn) and breeds of cattle and dog, they still stick to their own distinct language and literature; even the road signs are bi-lingual. Folklore attributes the Frisians' greater than average height to constant flooding, which only the tall survived.

Neighbouring Groningen, a staid, rural and conservative province, has a surprisingly liberal university, although graduates don't usually stay around long. Despite state efforts to attract people there, it's the only province with net outward migration. A world apart are the fens, moors and forests of Drenthe, inhabited (sparsely) since the Palaeolithic age. Saxons initially occupied slightly hillier **Overijssel**, due east of Amsterdam. Many traditions in this ultra-conservative area have survived tourism and the arrival of new industries.

The largest province, **Gelderland**, borders Germany and is sandwiched between north and south. Its terrain of wild countryside, orchards and commercial rivers has been continually fought over. That probably explains the good neighbourliness of its quiet, self-assured people. Gelderland's coastline became landlocked when part of the Zuider Zee was drained to form **Flevoland**. That flat, agricultural province is so new that its chief characteristic is its very existence.

Another victory over the sea was

the building of the Delta Works flood barrier to protect the islands of **Zeeland**, once isolated in the river delta bordering Belgium. Increased tourism and industry is transforming the province's traditional way of life.

Caricatures of the Dutch come unstuck in the Catholic south, where there are even a few hills. Pleasure-seeking and light-hearted, the people of **Noord Brabant** and **Limburg** celebrate carnival in the streets. The entire Noord Brabant village of Eersel sometimes gathers for weddings in a large tent on the marketplace, savouring milk and brandy with sugar. Wedged between Belgium and Germany, the rolling landscape of Limburg is also home to bon vivants, who thrive on its famed cuisine. Ultimately, though, all Dutch provinces share *gezelligheid* – cosiness, friendliness and conviviality.

TRAVEL INFORMATION

The **Netherlands Board of Tourism**, *Vlietweg 15, 2266 KA,*

Leidschendam (070 3705 705) and branches abroad, can help with general information. For each centre of interest, we've listed the VVV tourist office, which can also find and reserve accommodation, as can National Reservings Centrum (*see page 3* **Essential Information**).

ROADS

The Netherlands' extensive network of motorways and roads is well-maintained, and clearly signposted. *See page 221* **Survival** for advice on driving and for the motoring organization ANWB, which offers a broad selection of maps and suggested excursions.

BUSES & COACHES

The national bus service is reasonably priced, but arguably not as punctual, comprehensive nor easy to negotiate as the railway (*see below*). For bus information and timetables, contact **GWB** (*see p3* **Essential Information**). Private coach companies offering good value half- and full-day excursions (from f30 per person for local trips to f60 per person to Belgium) are listed in **Sightseeing** *p13*.

CYCLING

The Netherlands is flat (but windy) and cycle paths are plentiful; the VVV and ANWB sell cycle tour maps. Most major rail-

way stations have bike hire depots. You'll need proof of identity and a deposit; rail ticket holders get a discount and you can reserve a cycle until 11am. Bikes can only be taken on Dutch trains outside peak periods (Mon-Fri 6.30-9am, 4.30-6pm), and cost extra.

NETHERLANDS RAILWAY (NS)

The extensive NS rail network is efficient, clean, punctual and quite cheap. Services are frequent, so reservations are unnecessary, unless heading abroad. Departure times are displayed on yellow station posters. Holders of Rail Europe Senior Cards are eligible for 40% discounts. **Tickets** are valid for 2 months. Children under 4 travel free; 4 to 11-year-olds pay 60% of full fare, or a flat rate of f1 if on a Railrunner ticket or with an adult holding a Holland Rail Pass. **Passes** offer unlimited rail travel for f53 (1 day) or f108 (1 week); a supplement to include trams, Metros and buses costs f5.35 (1 day) or f20.15 (1 week). Other passes include the 3-day Holland Rail Pass and ones for teenagers, families and groups of two to six; another covers all of Benelux. InterRail tickets are valid.

Day Excursions

NS offers 75 all-inclusive excursions (discount rail and other travel, admission to sights and occasional extras) to destinations all over The Netherlands and also to Brugge (Bruges) and Antwerp in Belgium. Most of those we mention in the following chapters cost f30-f50 from Centraal Station.

CROSSING THE BORDER

Because The Netherlands is so small and its transport links so good, the Dutch have become a nation of border-hoppers. Relations with their neighbours, Germany to the east and Belgium to the south, eased by almost non-existent border formalities, have always been close. The Low Countries had a common history up to Belgian independence in 1830 and Northern Belgium still shares the Dutch language, although they call it 'Flemish' and speak it, claim the Dutch, with a French accent.

Germany is the main hinterland of Rotterdam's port. Alongside commercial barges, pleasure boats cruise up the Rhine, passing **Köln** (Cologne), then the former West German capital of **Bonn**, and meander on through the **Rhineland** rift valley, lined with vineyards, castles and towns straight out of *Grimm's Fairy Tales*.

Hugging the border with Limburg is the German city of **Aachen**, former capital of Charlemagne, whose bones are contained in the crown-shaped Palatine Chapel (792-805).

Aachen's also known as Aix-la-Chapelle in this linguistically mixed region, which is bounded on the west by the valleys of the Geul and Gulpen, on the south by the Belgian Ardennes' rocky outcrops and on the east by the volcanic Eifel hills.

The Dutch habitually visit Germany for shopping sprees, particularly at Christmas, to buy goods such as high-quality clothes. Dutch relations with **Belgium** are more complex. Age-old rivalries are epitomized by the continued existence of **Baarle-Nassau-Hertog**, a Belgian enclave just inside Dutch Noord Brabant, within which there are Dutch areas. Unsurprisingly, administration of the municipality is absurd, with two town halls, two police forces, and a house which has two addresses – 2 and 19 Loveren – because its front door straddles the border.

The Dutch descend on Belgium in droves mainly to shop and eat out. The European Community capital of **Bruxelles** (Brussels), with its English shops, handmade choco-

lates and superior cuisine is different enough to be exotic (they speak French there), but is only three hours by car or train from Amsterdam. Belgium's main gastronomic region is around **Antwerp**, a city full of tiny shopping streets, small museums and pavement cafés. **Gent** and canal-lined **Brugge** (Bruges) are two of the most important centres of medieval Flemish art and architecture.

Belgium

Belgium Tourist Bureau, Amsterdam
Herengracht 435-437, IS (624 5953). Tram 1, 2, 5. Open 9am-6pm Mon-Fri, 9am-1pm Sat. **Antwerp tourist office** *Grote Markt 15, 2000 (32 3 232 0103).* **Brugge tourist office** *Burg 11, 8000 (32 50 448 686).* **Brussels tourist office** *Graf Markt 63, 1000 (32 2 512 3030).* **Gent tourist office** *Belfortstraat 9, 9000 (32 91 253 641).*

Germany

German Tourist Bureau, Amsterdam
Hoogoorddreef 76, OE (697 8066). Bijlmer train station/bus 62, 137. **Open** *10am-4.45pm Mon-Fri.* **Aachen tourist office** *Haus Löwenstein, Markt 39, 5100 (49 214 180 2960).* **Köln tourist office** *Unter Fettenhennen 19, 5000 (49 221 221 3345).*

TOER-IN-TIP

NOORD-HOLLAND
THE PROVINCE AROUND AMSTERDAM

TOER-IN the tourist-cultural summer event in Noord-Holland. From mid-May until the end of September almost 2,000 events: from exhibitions with visual and painting arts, theatre performances, concerts and organ journeys to walking, cycling and motor car routes as wel as sports activities. This TOER-IN-TIP is a foretaste of the routes past lively evidences of olden days.

1. **Amsterdam:** canals, decorative facades and spectacular museums.
2. **Broek in Waterland:** picturesque wooden houses with umbrageous gardens and an imposing 17th century church.
3. **Marken, 4. Monnickendam,**
5. **Volendam, 6. Edam.**
7. **Purmerend:** cattle market on Tu., summertime cheese market on Th.
8. **Middenbeemster**
9. **De Rijp:** facades, Weighouse, town hall.
10. **Hoorn:** Main tower, VOC warehouses, gates and churches.
11. **Enkhuizen:** Zuiderzee Museum, 'Dromedary', yacht basin.
12. **Medemblik:** Radboud castle (1288).
13. **Twisk:** lovely farmhouses with decorated doors, windows, fences and roofs. One great monument.
14. **Broek op Langedijk:** oldest sailing vegetable market.
15. **Schagen:** West-Frisian folklore with ancient gigs, coaches, horses, traditional costumes.
16. **Den Helder:** fortifications built by order of Napoleon; lighthouse De Lange Jaap (Long JIM); Salvage museum.
17. **Texel:** Oosterend and Den Hoorn: two idyllic villages, wholly protected village landscape.
18. **Bergen:** artists' village, intimate village centre with church ruins; many pleasant pavement cafés.
19. **Alkmaar:** cheese market, Hans Brinker museum, courts of almshouses, Biermuseum.

20. **Egmond:** remnants of castle op Den Hoef; abbeys, lighthouse.
21. **Zaanse Schans:** open-air museum with wind mills, green-white houses, wooden shoe and cheesemaking shops, tin dome.
22. **Haarlem:** city of Frans Hals, Teylers museum, Great Church.
23. **Cruquius:** polder pumping-station of the Haarlemmermeer, with slides presentation and scalemodel of Holland in storm tide.
24. **Aalsmeer:** world-famous Flower auction hall.
25. **Ouderkerk aan de Amstel:** 17th century country estates in idyllic setting.
26. **Hilversum:** broadcasting city of Holland, architecture of Dudok and in the surroundings of the Amsterdam School.
27. **'s-Graveland:** 17th century country estates after French example; Trompenburgh equals a Loire castle in miniature.
28. **Naarden:** Fortified city (museum), shooting festivities.
29. **Muiden:** Muiderslot (castle), traditional sailing ships in attractive entourage around the big lock.

The Tour Tips and various routes are specified in the free TOER-IN-paper to be obtained as from early May at the Tourist Information and ANWB offices, and in Noord-Holland also at museums, camping sites, hotels, restaurants and cafes.

More information: VVV NOORD-HOLLAND, Florapark 6, 2012 HK Haarlem, Holland. Tel: 31.23.319413. Fax: 31.23.340093.

Excursions in Holland

Cheese markets, bulb fields, traditional towns and castles are all close to Amsterdam. Ann Campbell-Lord and Lyn Ritchie take some day trips.

Most of The Netherlands' stereotypical sights are concentrated in the area around Amsterdam: Noord and Zuid Holland. Both these provinces are small, and many of the places we've reviewed by theme are close to each other and well linked by public transport or special tours (*see page 200* **Beyond Amsterdam**). Amsterdam, Haarlem, Leiden and Utrecht (*see page 208* **The Randstad**) are excellent bases from which to make excursions.

CHEESE

The Dutch eat cheese (*kaas*) for breakfast, lunch, dinner and snacks – and still have enough to export some 420,000 tonnes per year (in 1989). For the many varieties of cheese, *see page 149* **Shopping: Food & Drink**. The summer cheese markets, museums and traditional farms show how this commodity used to be made and sold. The most famous – and best – is at **Alkmaar**. Little-known but authentic farmers' cheese markets are held year-round in the villages of Bodegraven (Tuesdays) and Woerden (Wednesdays), both between Gouda and Utrecht.

There are more thatched-roof **cheese farms** (*kaasboderijen*) near Gouda, several of which are along the picturesque Vlist River. Look out for the sign '*kaas te koop*' (cheese for sale), indicating a farm shop where you can buy freshly-made Gouda, often laced with herbs, and perhaps look behind the scenes. De Driesprong, at Bergambacht near Schoonhoven (*listed under* **Traditions**), offers a tour (Monday to Saturday from mid-February to 1 December). Ticket prices include 2kg/4lb of cheese, and, by appointment, a typical Dutch *koffietafel* lunch. Phone *01826 314* for details.

Alkmaar
Getting there 37km (22 miles) north-west; *by train* direct from Centraal Station.

VVV *Waagplein 2 (072 114 284)*. Open *mid Apr-Sept* 9am-5.30pm Mon-Wed; 9am-7pm Thur; 9am-6pm Fri; 9am-5pm Sat; *Oct-mid Apr* 9am-5.30pm Mon-Wed; 9am-6pm Thur, Fri; 9am-5pm Sat.
After seeing the **cheese market** (mid April-mid Sept, 10am-noon Fri) and **Cheese Museum** (for both, *see p204* picture and caption), you can peruse the craft stalls. The VVV runs a walking tour of the medieval centre, dating from 935 AD, which often resounds to the sound of a carillon concert. Then head for the **Hans Brinker Museum**, dedicated to the fictitious boy who stuck his finger in a dike to save Haarlem; the **Biermuseum**, which has a beer-tasting cellar; or the art and toy collection at the **Stedelijk Museum**. There are boat tours through the drawbridged canals, or to **Broeker Veiling** auction (*listed under* **Flowers**) on Fridays at 12.30pm.

Edam
Getting there 10km (5 miles) north; *by train* NS Excursion ticket (including Volendam and Marken); *by bus* 110, 112, 114 from Centraal Station.
VVV *Stadhuis, Damplein (02993 71727)*. Open *Oct-March* 10am-1pm Mon-Sat; *Apr-Sept* 10am-5pm Mon-Sat.
This tiny town was a prosperous Golden Age port and it has some exquisite façades and drawbridges. It suffers fewer tourist hordes than Volendam (*see under* **Traditions: Waterland**), a 101 bus-ride away. At the **cheese market** (July, Aug, 9.30am-1.30pm Wed), the famous red-skinned cheese arrives by boat. **Grote Kerk**, rebuilt in 1602, has remarkable stained glass, and the *speeltoren* of **Kleine Kerk** has one of the country's oldest carillons (1561). The 1737 **Raadhuis** (town hall) has an elaborate stucco interior. The town has two oddities: the municipal **museum** on Damplein has a floating cellar and in a former **Captain's House** are portraits of a 202kg (445lb) man and 2.75m (9ft) tall woman.

Gouda
Getting there 29km (18 miles) south-west; *by train* direct from Centraal Station.
VVV *Markt 27 (01820 13666)*. Open 9am-5pm Mon-Fri; 10am-4pm Sat.
Golden wheels of *kaas* are traded at the Thursday **cheese market** (July-Aug, 9am-1pm) in front of the 1668 Weigh House – which has a gablestone depicting cheese-weighing – and the Gothic City Hall of 1450. Handicrafts, such as wooden shoes, are also sold then; a **general market** (9am-1pm Sat) runs all year. Gouda's other famous products include clay pipes and pottery, which are displayed in the De Moriaan Museum, and candles, some 20,000 of which illuminate the square during the Christmas tree

ceremony. Adrie Moerings gives ceramic and pipe-making demonstrations at Peperstraat 76 (9am-5pm Mon-Fri). **St Jans Kerk** boasts over half of Holland's antique stained-glass windows, 70 in all, and holds carillon concerts from 10am to 11.30am Wed (f5) and 11.30am to 12.30pm Thur (free). **Caterina Gasthuis Museum**, a hospice and hospital from 1320 to 1910, has an eclectic collection of ancient surgeons' rooms, Golden Age silver and modern art. You can also see a corn grinding windmill, **Molen De Roode Leeuw**. The VVV runs a guided walking tour on Thursdays at 11am, but you could take a cruise on the Reeuwijk lakes. And do sample the local *stroopwafels* – two thin waffles glued together with syrup.

Purmerend
Getting there 26km (15 miles) north-east; *by train* direct from Centraal Station; *by bus* 100 from Centraal Station.
VVV *Kaasmarkt 20 (02990 52525)*. Open 9am-5pm Mon-Fri; 10am-4pm Sat.
Purmerend has become an Amsterdam dormitory town. Its population explosion – from 10,000 to 56,000 since 1960 – has changed its character, but not the Thursday cheese market outside the Renaissance Town Hall (July, Aug, 11am-1pm). The costumed women and dancers, although strictly for tourists, are colourful and convivial. More authentic is the Tuesday morning cattle and general market, where deals are sealed by a handclap. There are art exhibitions in **Museum Waterland** and local history in **Purmerend Museum**. The most rewarding return route to Amsterdam is on the country roads through Den Ilp and Landsmeer.

FLOWERS

The tulip is Holland's hallmark, and when it blooms (March to May) thousands of tourists head off to the **Keukenhof Bulb Gardens** in Lisse, on the Noord/Zuid Holland border. But all year round Dutch blooms can be seen in markets, botanical gardens, auctions and flower parades. For export rules on bulbs and flowers, *see page 161* **Specialist Shops**.

Floral calendar
Spring: The flower trade's year kicks off in mid to late February with the indoor **Westfriese Flora** *(02285 11644)* at Bovenkarspel, near Enkhuizen (*see below* **Traditions: West Friesland**). From late March to late May, the **bulb district** (*bloembollenstreek*), from Den Helder to The Hague, is carpeted with blooms of the principal crops: daffodils, crocuses, gladioli, hyacinths, narcissi – and tulips. Between late April and early May, residents of Lisse and the Noord Holland towns of Anna Paulowna and Limmen vie to create the season's best **flower mosaics** on their front lawns.
Summer: In mid to late May, golden fields of rapeseed brighten Flevoland, Friesland and Groningen (*see p213* **The Provinces**). In The Hague (*see p208* **The Randstad**), the Japanese Garden at **Clingendael Gardens** is in flower from early May to mid June, and in **Westbroek Park** the rose garden (which contains 350 varieties) flowers in

Alkmaar cheese market (see under **Cheese**) *is as much a ritual for tourists as for members of the cheese porters' guild. Garbed in pristine white uniforms and straw hats with coloured ribbons denoting the competing guild companies, they weigh the cheeses and carry them in wooden barrows hung from their shoulders. Arrive by 9.30am to see the buyers smelling, tasting and testing a core of cheese from each lot. The ceremony, explained in English in a VVV brochure, takes place at the Weigh House, converted in 1582 from a 1431 chapel. There's a Kaasmuseum (Cheese Museum) upstairs.*

July and August. In late June there's the **Floralia** exhibition at the Zuider Zee Museum, Enkhuizen (*see below* **Traditions: West Friesland**). The **Deltaflora** show is held in early August at Stellendam (*01870 3002*), part of the giant Delta Works (*see p213* **The Provinces: Zeeland**).
Autumn: Heather purples the landscape (especially in Gelderland's Veluwe; *see p213* **The Provinces**) during August and September, when greenhouse flowers also emerge. This is the season of most flower parades (*see below*). The autumn colours are captured at **Herstflora**, held in early October (4-13 Oct 1991) at the Singer Museum in Laren, Noord Holland (*02153 15656*).
Winter: In November, the public and florists from all over the world view new varieties at the **Professional Flower Exhibition** at Aalsmeer Flower Auction (*listed under* **Flower Auctions**). At Christmas time there's the **Kerstflora** show at Hillegom, near Lisse in Noord Holland.

Floriade 1992
At Zoetermeer, near The Hague (079 681992). **Dates** April-Oct 1992.
Acres of waste ground at Zoetermeer will be landscaped for this third decennial garden festival. After the crowds and displays have gone, it will become a new park, following Amsterdam's Amstelpark (1972) and Gaasperplas Park (1982).

Flower parades
Haarlem-Noordwijk Parade *Via Bennebroek, Hillegom and Lisse.* **Date** last Sat in April. Floats on show at Lisse and Hobahohallen (Fri, Sat evenings).
Rijnsburg Parade *Rijnsburg (11am) via Leiden (1pm) to Noordwijk (4pm).* **Date** first Sat in Aug. Floats on show at Flora Auction Hall, Rijnsburg (Fri evening) and Boulevard, Noordwijk (Sat evening).
Aalsmeer-Amsterdam Parade *Aalsmeer (9.30am) to Amsterdam (4pm).* **Date** first Sat in Sept.
The Aalsmeer-Amsterdam Parade is Europe's largest flower procession and floats can be viewed (3-10pm Fri; 11am-6pm Sun) in Aalsmeer Auction Hall (*see below* **Flower Auctions**). Highlights are the parade down Amstelveenseweg prior to lunch break, the 4pm reception at Dam Square, Amsterdam (*see p36* **Amsterdam by Season**), and the illuminated cavalcade through Aalsmeer (9-10pm). Be on site early.

Keukenhof Bulb Gardens
Keukenhof, near Lisse. **Getting there** 27km (17 miles) south-west; *by train* discount train-bus-admission packages for Keukenhof and surroundings from rail stations. **Open** *28 Mar-20 May 1991* 8am-6pm daily; similar in 1992/93. **Admission** f13; 4-12s f6.50.
See p205 picture and caption.
Café. Wheelchairs and pushchairs for hire.

FLOWER AUCTIONS

Aalsmeer Flower Auction
Legmeerdijk 313 (02977 32185/34567). **Getting there** 15km (9 miles) south-west; *by bus* 172 from Centraal Station to Aalsmeer, then bus 140. **Open** 7.30am-noon Mon-Fri. **Admission** f4; under-12s free.
More than 3.5 billion cut flowers and 400 million pot plants are handled annually, mostly for export, at the Verenigde Bloemenveilingen Aalsmeer, the world's biggest flower auction. Try to arrive at the visitors' gallery, which overlooks an auction floor

the size of 100 football fields, before 9am. To bid, dealers push a button to stop a 'clock' which counts from 100 down to 1 – bidders risk either overpaying or not getting the goods. This procedure, explained in an English-language brochure, gave rise to the English phrase 'Dutch auction'. Of growing importance is **Westland Flower Auction** at Naaldwijk, south of The Hague; phone *01740 32158* for details. It stands amid the world's greatest concentration of glass houses (open by appointment, phone *01740 27101*).

Broeker Veiling Auction
Voorburggracht 1, Broek-op-Langerdijk (02260 13807). **Getting there** 36km (22 miles) north; *by train* to Alkmaar, then bus 155; NS Excursion ticket (includes admission and boat tour). **Open** *Easter-end Sept* 10am-5pm Mon-Fri. **Admission** *auction and museum* f3.50; f2 under-12s; *incl boat trip* f7; f4 under-12s.
This market is now strictly for tourists, who can buy small lots of flowers, fruit and vegetables. Bidding is done as at a professional auction, by pressing a button to stop a 'clock' that is reducing the price. Admission includes a museum of old farming artefacts and (for a small amount extra) a boat trip around the area. A visit is easily combined with a trip to Alkmaar (*see under* **Cheese**), a cruise away through the polderland.

NURSERIES & GARDENS

Over a hundred botanical gardens serve as research centres for the industry, notably Hortus Botanicus, Leiden (*see page 208* **The Randstad**) and Hortus Bulborum, Heiloo (*02205 1214*), which from 15 April to 15 May displays offshoots of the original tulips introduced from Turkey. For Flevohof farm, *see page 213* **The Provinces: Flevoland**.

Frans Rozen Nursery
Vogelenzangsweg 49, Vogelenzang (02502 47245). **Getting there** 25km (16 miles) west; *by train* to Heemstede, then bus 90 to Café Rusthoek, opposite nursery. **Open** *Apr-May* 8am-6pm daily; *July-Sept* 9am-5pm daily. **Admission** f2; under-14s free.
The huge greenhouse and extensive fields of this 200-year-old nursery are open to the public. Here you can gain an insight into commercial cultivation and the meticulous development of new hybrids – and also purchase bulbs for export. There's a tulip show (Apr-May) and a summer show (July-Sept).

TRADITIONS

A few Dutch diehards still wear local costume or keep to their old ways. Some make a genuine effort to preserve traditions, as at Staphorst (*see page 213* **The Provinces: Overijssel**), while others entertain tourists looking for authentic Holland by hauling out their lace caps and turning on windmills (*windmolens*) for special days.

Kinderdijk windmills

Molenkade, Alblasserdam. **Getting there** 60km (37 miles) south-west; *by train* from Centraal Station via Rotterdam to Dordrecht, then bus 52 from station to Alblasserdam, then bus 154. **Open** *Apr-Sept* 9.30am-5.30pm Mon-Sat. **Admission** f2.50; f1.50 6-16s; under-6s free.

The sight of these 19 windmills under sail is spectacular, particularly when they're illuminated in the second week of September. To drain water from reclaimed land, windmills were usually clustered in a co-ordinated group called a *gang* (a term adopted in English). This *gang* now operates just for tourists (July, Aug, 2.30-5.30pm Sat); you can look around inside Nederwaarde mill. The name Kinderdijk (Child's Dike) came when a baby in a cradle was apparently stranded here during the St Elizabeth Flood of 1421.

Schoonhoven

Getting there 48km (30 miles) south; *by train* from Centraal Station to Gouda, then bus 197 from station.

VVV *Stadhuisstraat 1, (01823 5009)*. **Open** *May-Sept* 10am-12.30pm, 1.30-4pm, Tue-Fri; noon-4pm Sat; 2-4pm Sun.

Schoonhoven has been famous since the Middle Ages for its silver artisans, who crafted such items as filigree jewellery, miniatures and ornaments for traditional costume. You can see antique pieces in **The Netherlands Goud-Zilver-en Klokkenmuseum** (Gold, Silver and Clock Museum) and the **Edelambachthuis** (Museum of Antique Silverware). Since 1900, students of many countries have trained at the special school to be gold- and silversmiths and engravers. There's an annual **silver market** (Easter Mon 11am-5pm), but silver shops are open all year. Starting at *Silverhuys* (Silver House), Haven 1-3, is a row of buildings full of silver and pewter collectables, many of traditional design. *Klokkenhuys* (Clock House), Haven 9, stocks barometers and 500 timepieces including Frisian clocks. At *Sint-Andries Huis*, Haven 30, master silversmith Kuijf specializes in filigree jewellery and buttons. This attractive town (close to Oudewater, *see below*) retains large sections of its ramparts. Olivier van Noort, the first Dutchman to sail around the world (1598-1601), and Claes Louwerenz Blom, who in 1549 first introduced the windmill to Spain, are buried in **St Bartolomaeus Kerk** (1354); there are great views from its tower, which leans 1.56m (5 ft) off centre. The carillon of the 1452 **Stadhuis** has 50 bells made from the guns of Van Noort's ship.

Traditional costume

Bunschoten-Spakenburg 40km (25 miles) south-east; *by train* from Centraal Station to Amersfoort, then bus 116 from station. **Dates** last two Wed of July, first two Wed of Aug. **Schagen** 48km (30 miles) north; *by train* direct from Centraal Station. **VVV** *Markt 22 (02240 98311)*. **Dates** *July, Aug* Thur.

About a fifth of Bunschoten-Spakenburg residents still wear traditional dress on special market days. At Schagen, which has two medieval castle towers, costumed dancers entertain tourists (not too many), who also enjoy the cattle and craft markets and parades of horse-drawn carriages. Costumes are also worn at the markets in Hoorn and Medemblik (for both *see below* **West Friesland**), and sometimes on Sundays in Urk, Flevoland and on market day (July,

Aug 10am-4pm Thur) in Middelburg, Zeeland (for both, *see p213* **The Provinces**). The **National Costume Museum** is in The Hague (*see p208* **The Randstad**).

Witches' Weigh House, Oudewater

Getting there 29km (18 miles) south; *by train* from Centraal Station to Gouda, then bus 180 from station.

VVV *Markt 8 (03486 4636)*. **Open** *Apr-Sept* 10.30am-12.30pm, 1.30-4pm, Tue-Sat; 1-4pm Sun; *Oct* 10am-noon Tue; 11am-3pm Sat; 1-4pm Sun; *Nov-Mar* closed. **Witches' Weigh House** *Leeuweringerstraat 2 (03486 3400)*. **Open** *Apr -Oct* 10am-5pm Tue-Sat; noon-5pm Sun, public holidays; *Nov-Mar* closed. **Admission** f2; f1.25 under-12s.

Dating from AD 1000, Oudewater (just north of Schoonhoven, *see above*) was known for cheese, rope making and its particularly honest merchants. Then in 1487 an epidemic of witch hunting broke out. Oudewater achieved fame for weighing suspected witches and warlocks in the *Hexenwaag* (Witches' Weigh House). Each of the accused received a document, recognized throughout Europe, verifying that he or (usually) she was too heavy to travel by broom. Thus thousands were saved from being burnt at the stake. Today's (free) certificate comes in six languages for the thousands of tourists who step on the scales. The Weigh House also has a museum of witchcraft.

WATERLAND

Until the IJ tunnel was built in 1956, the Waterland district north of

Amsterdam was accessible mainly by ferry and steam tram to Volendam. That isolation preserved much of the area's heritage. For nearby Edam and the Museum Waterland in Purmerend, *see above* **Cheese**.

Broek-in-Waterland

Getting there 10km (6 miles) north-east; *by bus* 111 from Centraal Station. For VVV, *see under* **Monickendam**.

Full of eighteenth-century charm, this town has Waterland's greatest collection of old wooden buildings. Even rich Amsterdam merchants declined to build their country homes here in stone, for fear of them sinking. You can still see a wooden shoe-maker carving *klompen* (clogs), at Havenrak 21, 8am-2pm daily, and buy a souvenir pair.

Marken

Getting there 15km (9 miles) north-east; *by train* NS Excursion ticket (including Edam and Volendam); *by bus* 110 from Centraal Station to Volendam and then boat to Marken; or bus 111 from Centraal Station to Marken. For VVV, *see under* **Monickendam** or **Volendam**.

Now accessed by a causeway, this island was once full of fishermen, but is now bursting with costumes, souvenir shops and tourists. However, it's bearable out of season and is far more attractive and authentic than Volendam (*see below*), a boat ride away. The pristine wooden houses are painted green

Keukenhof Bulb Gardens (see under **Flowers**) *contains over 500 varieties of tulip, a plant first imported from Turkey during the Golden Age amid a wave of 'tulipmania' speculation. Altogether over seven million bulbs bloom in the 28 hectares (70 acres) of this former royal 'kitchen garden', some under glass. The gardens and café get overrun, so arrive early with a picnic lunch. With the help of a VVV map, you can tour the bulb district (in bloom from March to late May), from which over half of the world's cut flowers and pot plants originate. The bulb district's history is covered at the* Museum voor de Bloembollenstreek *(02521 17900), also in Lisse; and at the* Bloembollen Museum *(02205 1214) in Limmen.*

with white stripes and stand on stone piles to escape flooding. The **Marker Museum** explains the island's history.

Monickendam

Getting there 12km (7½ miles) north-east; *by bus* 111 from Centraal Station.
VVV *De Zarken 2 (02995 1998)*. **Open** *Oct-Mar* 10am-noon, 2-4pm, Mon-Sat; *Apr-June, Sept* 10am-5pm Mon-Sat; *July, Aug* 10am-6pm daily.
A remarkable proportion of Monickendam's ancient buildings have been preserved, from the homes of its wealthy Golden Age merchants to herring smokehouses by the harbour. The good harbour fish restaurant Stuttenburgh, Haringburgwal 2-5 (02995 1896), displays a collection of music boxes. On the *speeltoren* of the old town hall, now a museum, there's a delightful antique carillon, with two mechanical white knights parading as it plays.

Volendam

Getting there 18km (11 miles) north-east; *by train* NS Excursion ticket (includes Edam and Marken); *by bus* 110 from Centraal Station.
VVV *Zeestraat 21 (02993 63747)*. **Open** *Apr-Sept* 9.30am-5pm daily; *Oct-Mar* 10.30am-noon, 1.30-4pm, Mon-Fri.
Volendam was such a successful fishing village that its flag flew at half-mast when the Zuider Zee was enclosed in 1932, cutting off access to the sea. Their enterprise was soon applied to creating a theme park out of the historic features, which are modest compared to Marken (*above*) and Edam (*see under* Cheese). The gaily garbed locals can barely be seen for the crowds of tourists and the coaches that dump them there. Avoid it – unless you want to be photographed in a cardboard costume.

De Zaanse Schans

near Zaandijk (information Zaandam VVV *075 162221)*.
Getting there 14km (9 miles) north; *by train* NS Excursion ticket (includes cruise on River Zaan, admission to windmill museum and a pancake); *by bus* 97 from Marnixstraat.
See **picture and caption**.

WEST FRIESLAND

Facing Friesland across the northern IJsselmeer is **West Friesland**. Although part of Noord Holland for centuries, it has its own customs and slightly fewer visitors. One way to visit is to take a train via **Hoorn** to **Enkhuizen**, then a boat to **Medemblik**, returning to Hoorn via the **Museum Stoomstram** (steam railway); there's an all-inclusive NS Excursion ticket for this route.

De Zaanse Schans (see under **Traditions: Waterland**) *is a reconstructed museum village with a difference – people actually live in it. It's done well, but is becoming more commercialized, with 800,000 visitors a year. The Zaan district was noted for industrial windmills (making paint, flour and lumber), and you can buy mustard produced in one of the five working mills here. Amid the gabled homes, green with white trim, are an old-fashioned Albert Heijn grocery store (forerunner of Holland's biggest supermarket chain), a former merchant's home and a cheese house that's more commercial than authentic. Boat trips on the adjacent Zaan River provide another perspective.*

Enkhuizen

Getting there 45km (28 miles) north-east; *by train* direct from Centraal Station, NS Excursion ticket (includes admission to Zuider Zee Museum).
VVV *Stationsplein 1 (02280 13164)*. **Open** 10am-5pm Tue-Sat.
Zuider Zee Museum *Westerstraat 122 (02280 17903)*. **Open** *Apr-21 Oct* 10am-5pm daily. **Admission** f9; under-18s, over-65s f7.
This once-powerful fishing and whaling port has many relics of its past, but most people come to visit the remarkable **Zuider Zee Museum** (opened 1983). It comprises two separate sites: the indoor Binnenmuseum with its section on seafaring life and crafts, and an open-air reconstructed village, Buitenmuseum. To make good use of the one-way crowd control system, start with the Buitenmuseum; it is reached by boat from the main entry near the station jetty. Take a guided tour, or just wander around the hundred or so homes, shops, and other buildings transplanted from towns around the Zuider Zee and authentically arranged.

Hoorn

Getting there 33km (20 miles) north-east; *by train* direct from Centraal Station.
VVV *Nieuwstraat 23 (02290 13586)*. **Open** 1.30-5pm Mon; 10am-12.30pm, 1.30-5pm, Tue-Fri; 10am-2pm Sat.
Museum Stoomstram Hoorn-Medemblik *Tickets from Postbus 137, 1620 AC Hoorn (02290 14862), or any rail station; NS Excursion ticket*. Trains run *May-June, Sept* 11.30am Tue-Sat; *July, Aug* 11.30am daily.
One of Holland's prettiest towns, this port dates from 1311 and grew rich on the Dutch East Indies trade; its success is reflected in the grand architecture. Local costume and crafts can be seen in the weekly folklore celebrations called **Haartje Hoorn** (Jul, Aug 10am-5pm Wed). The baroque former Staten-College (council building) of 1632 now houses the **Westfries Museum**, which is better on art and décor than explanation of the region's past. A half-hour slide show at **Noorder Kerk** recounts the city's history in English. The **Bossuhuizen** buildings are noted for Frisian sculptures and the visit by Spanish Admiral Bossy after his 1573 defeat in the harbour. Even older are the **hoofdtoren** (harbour towers) and **St Jansgasthuis**, a hospital from 1563 to 1922 and now an exhibition centre.

Medemblik

Getting there 45km (28 miles) north; *by train* from Centraal Station to Hoorn, then steam train (*see above* Hoorn) to Medemblik.
VVV *Dam 2 (02274 2852)*. **Open** *May-Sept* 10am-4pm Mon-Fri; 10.30am-3pm Sat; *Oct-Apr* irregular hours, phone first.
This ancient port dates from AD 334 and is dominated by the Gothic St Bonifacius Kerk and **Radboud Kasteel**. Built in 1289, the castle's smaller than when it defended Floris V's realm, but retains its knights' hall, towers and prison, and has a cellar tavern. Costume is worn at the Saturday market (July, Aug), when goods are brought in by barges. Nearby is the circular village of **Opperdoes**, built on a *terp* mound (see *p213* **The Provinces: Fighting the Sea**), and the 'long-village' of **Twisk**, with pyramid-roofed farm buildings.

CASTLES

The Netherlands is studded with 400 castles (*kastelen*) and many fortress (*vesting*) towns retain large parts of their defences. Some of the best examples are within half an hour from Amsterdam; for those further afield, *see page 213* **The Provinces**. Eighty of the castles are open for tourists, business conferences or hotel guests; the late fifteenth-century Kasteel Assumberg at Heemskerk, between Haarlem and Alkmaar, is now a youth hostel (*02510 32288*). Alternatively, you can indulge in the ultimate power lunch by taking the NLM CityHopper package, including a return flight from Schiphol to Beek airport in Limburg, and a four-course lunch at either Château Neercanne in Maastricht (*043 251359*) or Kasteel Erenstein in Kerkrade (*045 461333*). Far closer and cheaper is the castle tour you can do simply by driving, cycling or boating down the River Vecht.

De Haar

Kasteellaan 1, Haarzuilens, Utrecht (03407 1275). **Getting there** 30km (19 miles) south; *by train* NS Excursion ticket (includes admission, coffee and apple pie). **Open** *Mar-2nd Sun in Aug, and 2nd Sun in Oct-mid Nov* (tours every hour) 11am-4pm Mon-Fri; 1-4pm Sat, Sun. **Admission** *castle and grounds* f7.50 adults; f5 over-65s; f3 under-13s; *grounds only* f1. *See* **picture and caption**. *Car park (f1).*

Muiden (Rijksmuseum Muiderslot)

Herengracht 1, Muiden (02942 1325). **Getting there** 12km (7½ miles) south-east; *by bus* 136 from Amstel Station. **Open** *Apr-Sept* 10am-5pm Mon-Fri; 1-5pm Sun (tours hourly 10am-4pm); *Oct-Mar* 10am-4pm Mon-Fri; 1-4pm Sun (tours hourly 10am-3pm). **Admission** f4 adults; f2.50 under-18s, CJP holders, over-65s; free under-3s, Museum Card holders; group discounts by arrangement. **No credit cards.**
Muiden is a moated rectangular castle strategically situated at the mouth of the River Vecht to repel attacks from land or water. It was originally built in 1280 for Count Floris V, who was murdered here in 1296 (*see p52* **Early History**). Devastated and rebuilt in the fourteenth century, the fortress has been through many sieges and frequent renovations. It now contains seventeenth-century furnishings from the period of its most illustrious occupant, the Dutch poet and historian P C Hooft, who entertained the Muiden Circle of writers, musicians and scholars in the splendid halls. You can look round only on a guided tour (in English by arrangement). The grounds contain a herb garden.
Café (Apr-Oct).

De Haar (see under **Castles**) *looks just like a medieval castle should. However, its romantic embellishments are a relatively recent neo-Gothic re-creation. In 1887, the baron who inherited the ruin of De Haar married a Rothschild and together they re-created it on a majestic scale, commissioning the Rijksmuseum's architect, PJH Cuypers and moving the entire village of Haarzuilens 2km (¾ mile) to make room for the outstanding 100 hectare (250 acre) formal grounds. The whole process took over 20 years. The castle (the largest in The Netherlands) had previously been completed in 1391, destroyed in 1482, rebuilt in 1505 and damaged again, by the French, between 1672 and 1673. The lavish interior boasts tapestries, Louis XIV-XVI furniture and Far Eastern art, with spectacular stone carvings and stained glass in the hall.*

Naarden

Getting there 20km (12 miles) south-east; *by train* direct from Centraal Station; *by bus* 136 from Centraal Station.
Naarden VVV *Adriaan Dortsmanplein 1B (02159 42836).* **Open** *May-Sept* 9am-5pm Mon-Fri; 1-4pm Sun; *Oct* 10am-3pm Mon-Fri; 10am-2pm Sat; *Nov-Apr* 10am-1pm Mon-Fri.
Vestingmuseum *Turfpoortbastion (02159 45459).* **Open** *Easter-Oct* 10am-4.30pm Mon-Fri; noon-5pm Sat, Sun, public holidays. **Admission** f3; over-65s f2.50; 5-12s f2; free under-5s, Museum Card holders.
This double-moated, star-shaped stronghold with arrowhead-shaped bastions, is one of Europe's most perfectly preserved fortified towns. It was in active service until 1926 and is still being reconstructed. The defences are explained in the **Vestingmuseum**, located partly underground in the Turfpoort (Peat Gateway) bastion; admission includes a boat trip around the *vesting* (fortress). Cannons are fired by men in sixteenth-century soldiers' uniforms (2-4pm third Sun of month, May-Aug). The fortifications date from 1675, after the inhabitants were massacred by the Duke of Alva's son in 1572, the slaughter being depicted on the wall of **Spaansehuis** (Spanish House), now a museum. Bach's *St Matthew Passion* is presented in the **Grote Kerk**, noted for its fine acoustics, on the Thursday (7pm), Friday and Saturday (both 11.30am) before Easter.

River Vecht tour

Getting there 12-35km (7½-22 miles) south-east; *by train* NS Excursion ticket (includes train to Utrecht, return cruise to Loenen, admission to Terra Nova gardens and refreshment).

Cruise Utrecht Canal Touring Co *(030 319 377/03402 41376).* **Times** *18 Jun-1 Sept* leaves Utrecht 9.30am to Loenen for lunch, returns to Utrecht 6pm. **Tickets** (excluding lunch) f25 adults; f15 under-13s.
Meandering upstream from Muiden (*see above*) into Utrecht province (*see p213* **The Provinces**), you reach **Loenen**, a charming town of cobbled streets, a leaning church spire and the restored castle of **Loenersloot**, with a thirteenth-century keep. Gracing the river banks are seventeenth- and eighteenth-century mansions, built as retreats by Amsterdam merchants. At Breukelen, which gave its name to **Brooklyn**, New York, is the elegant, classical house of **Gunterstein** (rebuilt in 1681). Beyond it on the other bank is **Nijenrode**, a medieval castle destroyed in 1672 and rebuilt, which fell into disrepair and was restored in 1907 in seventeenth-century style. It's now a business school. Across the river is **Oudaen**, a country house partly dating from 1303. A detour east around Loosdrechtse Plassen lake leads to **Sypesteyn**. Built on the foundations of a manor house destroyed in about 1580, this castle was rebuilt at the turn of the century in medieval style; its art and museum collection includes Loosdrechtse porcelain. Phone *02158 3208* for tours (*Easter-mid Sept* Tue-Sun; f5 adults; f2.50 5-14s). Back on the Vecht, between De Haar castle (*see above*) and the city of Utrecht (*see page 208* **The Randstad**) is **Slot Zuylen** at Maarsen; phone *030 440 255* for tours (*mid Mar-mid May* Sat, Sun; *mid May-mid Sept* Tue-Sun; f5 adults, f3 3-15s, f3.75 over-65s). Surrounded by woods and a moat, it dates from about 1300, but has an eighteenth-century façade.

The Randstad

The ring of cities encompassing The Hague, Rotterdam, Utrecht and Amsterdam, is known as The Randstad. As *Ailsa Camm* explains, it's the heart of The Netherlands.

You'll never see a sign to it, but the Randstad is the cultural, political and economic powerhouse of The Netherlands. It's the vast, almost circular conurbation bounded (in anti-clockwise order) by Amsterdam, Haarlem, Leiden, The Hague, Delft, Rotterdam and Utrecht; the town of Gouda (see *page 203* **Excursions in Holland: Cheese**) and increasingly the city of Dordrecht (see below) could be counted in the clique. Regarded by many as a masterpiece of planning, it manages to house six million of The Netherlands' 15 million population in under 20 per cent of the country's land area, as well as enclosing a sanctuary of green space and lakes the size of Greater London. The towns are separately administered and fiercely independent, yet they work together by choice for their common good.

The Randstad's influence on Dutch life is huge: it has an impressive road, rail and waterway system and a strong economy accounting for half of the national turnover. It contains the world's largest port (Rotterdam), a major international airport (Schiphol, Amsterdam), a huge agricultural belt (see *page 203* **Excursions in Holland: Flowers**), a major European banking and finance centre (Amsterdam, the country's capital) and the seats of government and royalty (The Hague).

Regarded with awe and sometimes resentment by the outlying provinces, the Randstad is often accused of monopolizing government attention and funds, although it has no formally defined status and is still prone to bitter rivalries between cities and municipalities.

PROMOTING DORDRECHT

'One ought to stay in Dordrecht...', wrote Marcel Proust, and the oldest of Dutch cities (given city rights in 1220) has now been targeted for development to make it the southern outpost of the Randstad. The aim is to attract people to live in converted warehouse apartments and new housing estates. Known locally as 'Dort', the city still has an active waterfront at the confluence of three rivers, the sunsets over which have inspired painters from the Cuyps to Van Gogh, who worked here as a bookseller. The centre, dominated by the distinctive slanting tower of the enormous **Grote Kerk**, is full of character, and there's a great art collection in **Dordrechts Museum**. As is the fashion in nearby Rotterdam, delapidated buildings are to be refurbished, not demolished.

Dordrecht's VVV office is at *Stationsweg 1 (078 132800)*.

DELFT

The best thing about Delft is its compactness. Almost everything you need to see is located along the Oude Delft, as are the best views of the old city. Position yourself in the middle of the canal, either on the Boterbrug bridge or on one of the floating cafés, for a spectacular view of one of Holland's most photogenic waterways. Delft was built largely from trade generated through a four-teenth-century canal link to the Maas at Delfshaven (now swallowed up by Rotterdam) The decline in trade has enabled the city's centuries-old gables, hump-backed bridges and shaded canals to remain unchanged. To get an idea of how little it's altered, stand on the Hooikade, where Vermeer, whose home town this was, painted his *View of Delft* now hanging in Mauritshuis (see *below* **The Hague**).

Delft invariably means blue and white Delftware pottery (see *page 161* **Specialist Shops**). The **Lambert van Meerten Museum**, Oude Delft 199 (open daily June-Aug; otherwise closed Mon), is a nineteenth-century mansion housing fine pieces of tin-glazed earthenware from the city's Golden Age pottery boom, and a vast collection of magnificent ebony-veneered furniture.

The enormous range of tiles – depicting everything from battling warships to copulating hares – compares startlingly with today's mass-produced 'New Delft' (post-1876) trinkets. If you must buy, avoid tourist shops around the Markt and head for a pottery such as De Porceleyn Fles (see *page 161* **Specialist Shops**).

Museums in Delft have the air of private residences, and perhaps for this reason are happily devoid of crowds, even in high summer. **Het Prinsenhof** on Sint Agathaplein (open daily June-Aug; otherwise closed Mon) has permanent exhibitions on William the Silent, who was assassinated here in 1584, and on the building's role until 1572 as St Agatha Convent. Opposite, another wing of the Convent houses the ethnographic collection and exhibitions of the **Nustantra Museum** (open daily June-Aug; otherwise closed Mon).

The city also has two spectacular churches, whose soaring spires can be seen for miles across the Schieland polders (reclaimed land, see *page 213* **The Provinces: The Fight Against the Sea**). The **Nieuwe Kerk**, in the Markt opposite De Keyser's 1618 Town Hall, contains the mausoleums of William the Silent and lawyer-philosopher Hugo de Groot. Not to be outdone, the Gothic **Oude Kerk**, with its picturesque tilting tower, is the last resting place of Vermeer (1632-75). A delightful contrast is the tiny, late-Gothic **Hippolytus Chapel** nearby, a vestige of one of Delft's many vanished convents.

Transport & Information
Getting there 60km (37 miles) south-west on A4, then A13; *train* 53 mins direct; 1 hour change at The Hague.
VVV Office *Markt 85 (015 126 100)*. **Open** 9am-6pm Mon-Fri, 9am-5pm Sat; *Apr-Oct* also 11am-3pm Sun.

Eating & Sleeping
Restaurants Just out of Delft in the village of De Zweth on the River Vecht is Zwethheul *Rotterdamweg 480 (010 470 4166)*; quiet and expensive, it's in a former farmhouse. In summer, delicious sandwiches are served on a canal barge, Klijwegs Koffiehuis *Oude Delft 133 (015 124 625)*.
Hotels De Ark *Koommarkt 59-65 (015 140552/157999)* is up-market with f185 singles and f215 doubles; Dish *Kanaalweg 3 (015 569258)* is reasonably priced with singles at f85-f100 and doubles f110-f130; the cheapest is De Kok *Houttuinen 15 (015 122125)* where singles cost f45-f85 and doubles f75-f120.

THE HAGUE

The quiet boulevards and patrician houses of The Hague (Den Haag in Dutch, or s' Gravenhage, to use its correct name) have always given Amsterdammers (whose city is the capital) a reason for dismissing it as stuffy, particularly as it's the seat of government, the royal residence and the diplomatic centre all in one. But the air of restrained *hauteur* which pervades its public buildings and old shops – try the area around Noordeinde for a taster – is precisely what gives the city its charm.

The Hague, once the centre of a vast forest, was founded in 1250 by Count Willem II of Holland, who started a palace craze by building a castle – *Die Haghe* – on the site of the present **Binnenhof** parliament buildings (*see* **picture and caption**). The Dutch respect rather than revere their monarchs, and expect them, if not to live, then at least to work like ordinary citizens. Sadly, today you cannot visit the palaces: Voorhout Paleis and Paleis Noordeinde at each end of the fashionable Lange Voorhout avenue, and Queen Beatrix's residence, Huis ten Bosch, at the far end of Haagse Bos. One former regal home which can and must be seen, however, is Mauritshuis (*see page 100* **Museums: Further Afield**). Located in the Binnenhof, it houses a breathtaking art collection.

The Hague is one of the greenest cities in Europe, and is peppered with parks and woods: Clingendael has a Japanese garden and Meijendel, out of town, is part of the ancient forest. The Scheveningse Bosjes, big enough to get lost in, is flanked by the Madurodam miniature city (*see page 180* **Children & Parents**), and the **Haags Gemeentemuseum**, Stadhouderslaan 41 (closed Mon). Notable for works by Mondrian and other modern masters, the museum incorporates the Dutch costumes, clogs and caps of **Kostuum Museum**, and is linked to the **Museon**, a hi-tech display on how mankind lives, and the **Omniversum**, a planetarium with state-of-the-art projections. Between the Scheveningse Bosjes and the city is **Vredes Paleis**, the Peace Palace, built in 1907 to host peace conferences, a role it still has as the UN's Court of International Justice. More cultural diversions are

The Hague *is The Netherlands' other capital, the home of one of Europe's smoothest-running democracies. The elegant parliament buildings, the* **Binnenhof** *(inner courtyard), are pure Golden Age design, but retain a bastion-like appearance, complete with water-lilied moat and medieval* Ridderzaal *(Knights' Hall). This is where, every third Tuesday in September, the Queen arrives in a golden coach for the State Opening of Parliament. You can see proceedings in the First and Second Chambers, although because Dutch politicians are often willing to compromise, debates are less than dynamic. For a hint of more visceral politics, pop across Hofweg to the* Gevangenpoort, *the only surviving town gate, a former state prison outside which the brothers De Witt were lynched.*

the Anton Philipszaal concert hall (*see page 130* **Music: Classical & Opera**) and the North Sea Jazz Festival in early July (*see page 135* **Music: Rock, Folk & Jazz**).

Just beyond the parks is **Scheveningen**, a former fishing village once linked to The Hague only by canal, but now a huge resort with high-rise hotels and, in summer, an impossible choice of beach cafés where topless sunbathing is *de rigueur*. Presiding over the beach is the 1887 Kurhaus (spa hotel), a legacy of Scheveningen's days as a bathing place for Europe's jet-set. The main salon, with its monstrous chandeliers and awesome glass cupola, is a wonderfully intimidating place to take tea. To stand any chance of recapturing the past, avoid the pier, which is over-priced and could be anywhere, and head back towards The Hague to visit **Mesdag Museum**, Laan van Meerdervoort (closed Mon), which contains paintings by members of the Hague School. Displayed round the corner at Zeestraat 65 is the remarkable 360° painting, **H W Mesdag's Panorama** (open daily), depicting Scheveningen village in 1880. You can still visit the dune-top from which it was painted.

Transport & Information

Getting there 50km (31 miles) south-west on A4, then A44; *train* 50 mins direct.
VVV Office *Koningin Julianaplein*, at *Centraal Station* (070 364 6200). **Open** *Easter-Sept* 9am-9pm Mon-Sat; 10am-5pm Sun; *Oct-Easter* 9am-8pm Mon-Sat; 10am-5pm Sun.

Eating & Sleeping

Restaurants So popular with locals that you must book, Luden *Frederikstraat 36 (070 360 1733)* serves expensive Dutch food with a French gloss. Schlemmer *Lange Houtstraat 17 (070 360 8580)* has a medium-priced restaurant frequented by politicians and a trendy upstairs café. At Salvatore *Deltaplein 605-606 (070 325 9635)* an Italian meal averages f12.50.
Hotels Lange Voorhout 54 *(070 363 2932)* is the most luxurious hotel in town, with a restaurant – and prices – to match. City Hotel *Renbaanstraat 1-3 (070 355 7966)* has singles for f45-f60 and doubles at f80-f135; the youth hostel, NJHC Hostel Ockenburg, is at *Monsterweg 4 (070 397 0011); see p39* **Accommodation** for rates.

HAARLEM

All trace of Haarlem's origins as a tenth-century settlement on a choppy inland sea disappeared with the draining in the mid nineteenth century of the Haarlemmermeer, a massive lake which is now the site of Schiphol airport. Today the city somehow lacks a sense of purpose

319091) is as pricey as it sounds (single
f170-f225; double f195-f250); Waldor *Jansweg
40 (023 312622)* is reasonably priced at f65-
f120 for singles and f75-f135 for a double;
NJHC Hostel Jan Gijzen *Jan Gijzenpad 3
(023 373 793)* is a youth hostel; see p39
Accommodation for rates.

LEIDEN

Leiden bravely stood up to the
Spanish during the Dutch Revolt in
1574 (*see page 53* **War &
Reformation**), and was almost
starved out under siege. The city
was rescued when Willem I of
Orange had dikes opened to flood
central Holland, enabling his ships to
sail to the town walls. The townsfolk
noticed the enemy had abandoned a
large pot of beef stew at the foot of
the ramparts, and *Leidens Ontzet*
(Relief of Leiden) is an excuse
for a carnival-like binge every 3
October, when stew, herring and
white bread are consumed in vast
quantities (and museums are
closed). Festivities centre on the
ninth-century Burcht, a fortress built
on an artificial mound. Its walls command a good view of the city.

Willem rewarded Leiden's courage
in 1581 by founding its famous university, the residents having declined
the alternative – exemption from
taxes. The oldest university in The
Netherlands, it attracted Descartes
and American president John
Quincy Adams. The university itself
isn't easy to spot; much of it's hidden
behind former merchants' houses
and a nunnery that was requisitioned. Better than the buildings,
though, is the university's Hortus
Botanicus behind it (*see page 203*
Excursions in Holland: Flowers).
The main student quarter is around
Pieterskerk; young people use the
former cemetery as a place to relax,
and the church has a wall chart
showing President Bush's descent
from two Leiden-based pilgrims. As a
VVV leaflet explains, the Pilgrim
Fathers fled England to Amsterdam
in 1608 and then to Leiden, where
they held services in the home of
their leader John Robinson on the
site of Jean Pesijnhofje. In 1620, 30
pilgrims left for Delfshaven (*see
under* **Rotterdam**) without
Robinson, who is buried in
Pieterskerk. They later sailed on the
Mayflower to America from
Plymouth, England. The **Pilgrims'
Documentation Centre**, Vliet 45, is
due to be renovated in 1991-92.

Haarlem *produced almost all of the major Golden Age landscape painters,
and was a favourite subject for Jacob van Ruisdael, perhaps because its main
industry, linen, offered the sight of people bleaching huge lengths of the cloth in the
fields. If its* **Church of St Bavo** *looks familiar, that's probably because you've
seen it countless times before in paintings, such as the* (above) *view by Gerrit
Berckheyde (1696), that hangs in Haarlem's* **Frans Hals Museum** *(see page
100* **Museums**). *St Bavo's is among the loveliest Dutch churches, with
cavernous, whitewashed transepts as high as nave and choir. The biennial
International Organ Competition is held here in the first week of July 1992.*

and has spilled indiscriminately over
its outer canal, as more people abandon Amsterdam to set up home in
the increasingly bustling provincial
capital of Noord Holland. However, it
isn't difficult to locate the **Church of
St Bavo**, rising majestically at the
confluence of eight roads (*see* **picture and caption**). At its foot lies
the Grote Markt, with the Vleeshal, a
former meat market built in 1602,
now full of tiny gift shops.

The Netherlands' highest concentration of **almshouses** or *hofjes* (*see
page 13* **Sightseeing: Hofjes**) is in
Haarlem. Prime examples are: the
town's largest, Proveniershuis,
reached by a portal on Grote
Houtstraat; Brouwershofje, on
Tuchthuisstraat, one of the oldest
(1472); and Hofje van Loo,
Barrevoetestraat. Frans Hals is
famous for his group portraits of
almshouse regents, including those
of the **Oudmanhuis**, a former shelter for elderly men at the foot of
Groot Heiligland which now houses
the **Frans Hals Museum** (*see page
100* **Museums**). At Sparne 16 is
Holland's oldest museum (1778), the
Teylers Museum, (open 10am-5pm
Tue-Sat; 1-5pm Sun), where fossils
and minerals sit uncomfortably alongside antique scientific instruments in

passable imitation of an alchemist's
workshop. Unexpectedly, it also has a
superb set of 4,000 drawings from the
sixteenth to the nineteenth centuries.

Although polders have made the
sea further away than it used to be, it's
still only 11km (7 miles) from the
town centre. Nearby **Zandvoort**, one
of the busiest Dutch resorts, has been
transformed from a sleepy village by
Amsterdammers who flock there in
droves whenever the sun peeps out.
For watersports and Zandvoort
motor-racing circuit, *see page 183*
Sport & Fitness. Just to the north
are the rugged dunes and woods of
the Kennemer Duinen National Park;
take the 81 bus from Haarlem's
Stationsplein, having acquired a ram-
bler's pass from the VVV.

Transport & Information

Getting there 20km (12 miles) west on A5;
train 17 mins direct to Haarlem, carrying on
to Zandvoort.
VVV Office *Stationsplein 1 (023 319 059)*.
Open 9am-6pm Mon-Sat.

Eating & Sleeping

Restaurants Mooi Java *Kruisweg 32 (023
323121)* serves Indonesian meals from f48;
French food at Jack House *Gen Cronjéstraat
14 (023 276476)* is mid-priced, dinner from
f22; Coach House Inn, *Oude Gracht 34 (023
312760)* has basic snacks and grills from f5.
Hotels Carlton Square Hotel *Baan 7 (023

Leiden is rich in museums, the most comprehensive being the former cloth hall, De Lakenhal (*see page 100* **Museums**). It includes paintings by Jan Steen, who's buried in Pieterskerk, and Rembrandt, who was born in Weddesteeg, a site since lost under a housing development. Nearby on Binnenvestgracht are both the superb ethnographic collection of the **Rijksmuseum voor Volkenkunde** (closed Mon) and **Molenmuseum Valk** (closed Mon), a restored corn-ginding, stage windmill of 1743, with one resident miller and six hazardous storeys to climb. On the Rapenburg, the **Museum van Oudheden** (Antiquities Museum; closed Mon) is huge, and is especially strong on grisly Egyptian mummies and local archaeological finds.

Transport & Information

Getting there 40km (24 miles) south-west on A4; *train* 30 min direct.
VVV Office *Stationsplein 210 (071 146 846)*. **Open** 9am-5.30pm Mon-Fri; 9am-4pm Sat.

Eating & Sleeping

Restaurants Try Le Grand *Herengracht 100 (071 140876*; closed Mon); the vegetarian De Zaarling *Hooigracht 41 (071 146917*; closed Sun, Mon); or the café De Oude Harmonie *Breestraat 16 (071 122153)*.
Hotels Mayflower *St Aagtenstraat 5-7 (071 142641)* has singles at f100-f125 and doubles at f150-f175; Nieuw Minerva *Bookmarkt 23 (071 126358)* has singles at f65-f100 and doubles at f90-f150; Bik Hotel *Witte Singel 92 (071 122602*; closed Oct) is cheaper at f33-f40 for singles and f63-f70 for a double.

ROTTERDAM

Practically the whole of Rotterdam's old city centre was destroyed by bombs in May 1940 and, with commendable daring, the authorities decided to start afresh rather than try to reconstruct its former maze of old canals. Modern boulevards such as Coolsingel and Meent were once navigable waterways, and the sites of once-great buildings and squares are remembered in name only. Perch on the busy Willemsbrug bridge for a magnificent view of the futuristic skyline, or, if you can stomach the expense and the height, go up the **Euromast** at Het Park for an overview of the immense Rhine-Maas delta.

Not every bombsite was developed immediately, because the city first wanted to plan its future function.

One success of this policy is the redeveloped **Old Harbour** (*see picture and caption*).

The few original buildings left have been raised to the level of icons. **St Lawrence Church**, built in 1646, has been heavily restored; a solitary row of merchants' houses survives on Wijnhaven; but best of all is **Schielandshuis**, Korte Hoogstraat, off Beursplein (closed Mon), a seventeenth-century mansion which doubles as an excellent city museum. Its displays recreate life in Rotterdam from late medieval times, when it was a village on a dike where Renaissance scholar Erasmus was born in the fifteenth century, to the construction of the Nieuwe Waterweg.

This deep-water channel to the sea facilitated the creation of the world's biggest harbour, **Europoort**. Go and see it if you can; take one of the various SPIDO boat tours from Willemskade (*010 413 5400* Easter-September), or follow the *Havenroute* map (from the ANWB motoring organization; *see page 221* **Survival**). Just downstream is **Delfshaven**, where genuinely old buildings are being restored. These include the former warehouses containing **Museum de Dubbelde Palmboom** (closed Mon), which explains working life in the Meuse estuary. A plaque on the quay marks where in 1620 the Pilgrim Fathers (from Leiden, *see above*) left for America, via Plymouth, having held a final service at nearby **Oude Kerk**, where they are also commemorated.

Rotterdammers have a serious, workmanlike reputation, exemplified by prime minister Ruud Lubbers, who sobered up the country during the eighties. Unsurprisingly, the best shops here are major, modern stores, although Europe's first pedestrian precinct, the Lijnbaan, isn't one of the city's better constructions.

Without doubt the best museum in Rotterdam is the Boymans-Van-Beuningen (*see page 100* **Museums**), but look out for the **Prins Hendrik Maritime Museum**, Leuvehaven 1 (closed Mon). A startling piece of architecture with stunning river views, it has comprehensive if slightly exhausting displays on seafaring, plus interesting ships docked outside.

Transport & Information

Getting there 73km (45 miles) south on A4, then A13; *train* 1 hour direct.
VVV Offices: Coolsingel 67 *(010 402 3200)*. **Open** 9am-6.30pm Mon-Thur, 9am-9pm Fri, 9am-5pm Sat; *Easter-Sept* also 9am-5pm Sun. **Centraal Station** *(010 413 6006)*. **Open** 9am-10pm daily.

Eating & Sleeping

Restaurants Tropicana *Maasboulevard 100 (010 402 0720)*, is an expensive revolving

Rotterdam *lost its old centre to bombs in 1940, but its charm lies in the shock of the new. The redeveloped* **Old Harbour** *is a lesson in imaginative modernism and has given the world Piet Blom's witty Kijk-Kubus. These tilted, cubic houses on stilts are nicknamed 'the bleak woods', but are popular with tourists, who can visit number 70 (010 4142285). In an attempt to revive links with the inner city, this area is promoted as 'Waterstad' (water city), and there is a sign-posted walk for visitors.*

restaurant with great river views. The fine food at Zocher's *Baden Powellaan 12 (436 4249)* averages f35. Café de Unie *Mauritsweg 34 (010 411 7394)* is a reconstruction of a famous pre-war café; the well-presented (usually fish) dishes are medium-priced.

Hotels King's Garden*Westersnglaan 1 (010 4366633)* has singles for f75 and doubles for f135; the NJHC youth hostel is at *Rochussenstraat 107-109 (010 436 5763)*; see p39 **Accommodation** for rates.

UTRECHT

St Willibrord, patron saint of The Netherlands, chose Utrecht as a base from which to convert the country to Christianity in about AD700. It obviously worked, because eight centuries later the city produced Adrian VI, the only Dutch pope, who, if he'd lived longer, would have inhabited the **Paushuize** on the peaceful Pausdam square. Yet the city was firmly committed to the Dutch Revolt (*see page 53* **War & Reformation**); indeed the Union of Utrecht in 1579 authorized Protestantism as the United Provinces' official religion.

Taking its name from *Oude Trecht* (old ford), Utrecht was founded in AD47 as a strategic Roman ford over the Rhine. Still The Netherlands' transport focus, it's the appropriate site of the **National Railway (Spoorweg) Museum**, at Maliebaan Station (closed Mon). But it's the medieval past that dominates the city, in the shape of the Domtoren (cathedral tower) looming over **Oudegracht** (*see picture and caption*).

Utrecht's a Mecca for music lovers. All year round choirs give free concerts in the cathedral, usually at lunch-time, and the city hosts classical events such as the Festival of Early Music in early September every year, and, during May 1991, the Liszt Piano Competition at Vredenburg Muziek Centrum. For both, *see page 130* **Music: Classical & Opera**. Whether or not you're with children, you should see the **Rijksmuseum van Spielklok tot Pierement** (from music box to street organ), where the guides will gladly demonstrate the exhibits. There's also a **Phonographic Museum** (closed Mon) in the maze-like Hoog Catharijne shopping complex. Ignore the ubiquitous signs to it, and head instead for the book and antique shops, on a bend in the Oudegracht and on Nieuwegracht parallel to it. In the teashops nearby, apples baked in sweet dough are a speciality.

Among the many museums, try **Central Museum**, Agnietenstraat 1 (closed Mon), although it takes some getting round because of its sheer diversity. Exhibits cover decorative arts, paintings and archaeological finds, and the complex also incorporates a school for orphans and two almshouses. By contrast, the **Catharijneconvent**, Nieuwegracht 63 (closed Mon), has won awards for presentation of its important medieval art collection. Alternatively, join the trail of architecture pilgrims for a guided tour of the **Rietveld-Schröder House**, Prins Hendriklaan 50A (tours Tue-Sun; book at least a day ahead on *030 333370*). Designed in 1924 by Gerrit Rietveld, whose famous red-blue chair is displayed inside, it looks like a three-dimensional projection of a Mondrian painting. As a masterpiece of the *De Stijl* movement (*see page 61* **Between the Occupations**), the house is on the World List of Protected Buildings.

Transport & Information
Getting there 40 km (25 miles) south-east on A5; *train* 28 mins direct.
VVV Office *Vredenburg 90 (06 34034085)*.
Open 9am-6pm Mon-Fri, 9am-4pm Sat.

Eating & Sleeping
Restaurants De Oude Muntkelder *Oudegracht a/d Werf, under Post Office (030 315126)* is a pancake house, with meals from f7; Auberge het Oude Tolhuis *Weg naar Rhijnauwen 13-15* has food from f16; Surinams-Java restaurant *Wittevrouwenstraat 22 (030 319272)* has food of those countries from f12.
Hotels Malie Hotel *Maliestraat 2-4 (030 340661)* has singles at f100-f115, doubles at f120-f140; Hotel Ouwi *FC Donderstraat 12 (030 716303)* charges f50-f71 for singles, f71-f91 for doubles; Pension Hensen *AHG Fokkerstraat 59 (030 444185)* is cheaper at f35 for a single, f70 for a double.

Utrecht *combines the attractions of a city with a delightful provincial charm. Stroll along the 'sunken' quays of* **Oude Gracht** *(old canal), where the damp and smelly storerooms have now been turned into inviting, but damp and smelly, restaurants and shops. By Vriebrug, where boat tours embark, glance upward past patrician houses – such as the fourteenth-century Het Oudaen (number 99) and Huis Drankenborch, opposite – to the* **Domtoren**, *the highest steeple in the country, which you can climb. Only on closer inspection do you realize there's no nave connecting the beautifully proportioned Gothic spire to the dignified but rather forlorn-looking chancel.*

The Provinces

Escape Holland's urban sprawl and explore the other ten Dutch provinces. *Ailsa Camm* guides you round the country and *Eric Nicholls* reports on Overijssel, his adopted home.

Many visitors to The Netherlands see only North and South Holland, and miss out the other ten provinces. But if you take the trouble to explore further, you'll find that not all of the country is one big urban sprawl and that each region has its own subtly distinctive character. We have listed the VVV tourist offices for each province (most accept only postal and phone enquiries), and for important regional centres; unless otherwise stated, they're open from 9am to 6pm Monday to Saturday. We've also stated if there's an appropriate NS rail excursion ticket (*see page 200* **Beyond Amsterdam**). For a sketch map of the country, *see page 235*, although you will require a scale map; the *Falk Plan* tourist map has a useful place index.

DRENTHE

Drenthe's affectionate nickname – *De Olde Landschap* (the old landscape) – goes back centuries, but human habitation dates back even further, about 50,000 years. Located in the north-east of the country, the province has tended to be neglected by the more vibrant west, which could explain why it has the reputation of being a dark, mysterious landscape haunted by its pagan past. It's certainly why the population took so long to abandon Catholicism and also partly why the area was, until recently, relatively backward economically. Even today, Drenthe is unashamedly rural. The best place to appreciate what much of the countryside looked like even as little as 20 years ago is in **Orvelte** at the Oud Saksisch Kijkdorp (Old Saxon Village). This preserved village-cum-museum presents traditional activities and has typical 'hall' farmhouses with thatched roofs gracefully sloping to within a whisker of the ground.

To find out more about the province's prehistoric, Roman and Merovingian past, start at the magnificent Drents Museum (open daily) in **Assen**. The area's full of peculiar ancient sites. Just outside Assen is the **Balloërkuil**, an enormous terrace dug into the ground, where the provincial assembly met until 1602. But the most impressive monuments are the **hunebedden** (*see page 214* **picture and caption**), towards the German border.

The Drenthe countryside is the perfect backdrop to the *hunebed* tombs. Rivulets run through peat cuttings (look out for villages ending in *veen*, meaning 'peat bog') on huge silent heaths such as the Fochtelooer Veen near Assen and the Dwingeloose Heide and Uffelter Veen, either side of Uffelte. There's also a great forest near Uffelte, the Drentse Wold, and another, Ellertsveld, west of the hunebedden. Near Ellertsveld is a more chilling reminder of the past, the Nazi transit camp at Westerbork (*see page 64* **World War II**).

Further information
Drenthe province VVV *PO Box 10012, 9400 CA Assen (05920 51777)*. Open 8.30am-5pm Mon-Fri.
Assen VVV *Brink 42, 9401 HV (05920 14324)*.
Emmen VVV *Raadhuisplein 2, 7811 AP (05910 13000)*.
Nationaal Hunebedden Informatie Centrum *Bronnegerstraat 12, Borger (05998 36374)*. Open Feb-Oct 10am-5pm Mon-Fri; 1-5pm Sat, Sun.
Orvelte Saxon Village *Dorpstraat 3 (05934 335)*. Open Apr-mid Oct 9.30am-5pm Mon-Fri; 11am-5pm Sat, Sun, public holidays. **Admission** f7; 5-15s, over-65s f5; under-4s free. **No credit cards.**

FLEVOLAND

Stay in Flevoland long enough, and someone's bound to point out that the land you're standing on was under water as little as 40 years ago. Just north-east of Amsterdam, it only became a province in its own right in 1986, when the polders of South Flevoland and East Flevoland were combined with the North-east Polder (formerly in Overijssel, *see below*). It's the most recent stage in The Netherlands' massive, historic land reclamation process (*see page 220* **Fighting the Sea**). If you're wondering why the Dutch bothered, you might have a point. Drained in 1950-57 to create more room for the burgeoning population, Flevoland, when finished, offered little to entice new residents. The authorities are still worrying about how to create new jobs and attractions.

Flevoland's capital, **Lelystad**, named after Dr C Lely who championed the Zuider Zee Reclamation Act of 1918, should have been a planner's dream. Development there is refreshingly low-level and it has an interesting community centre, the Agora, but it's tiresome to get to and sits symbolically hunched on the windy outer edge of the province. By contrast, the beautiful space-age city of **Almere**, intended as a satellite to Lelystad, is almost embarrassingly successful. Now an outpost of Amsterdam, with low-cost, low-energy housing, it attracts thousands of the capital's commuters. The country's first solar-powered home was built here, and the all-white marina looks spectacular from across the Gooimeer lake.

The low human population is emphasized by the presence of a large bird sanctuary at the **Oostvaardersplassen** lake, southwest of Lelystad, and an enormous working farm museum at **Flevohof**. Although in danger of going the way of all theme parks, Flevohof has stuck to its original aim of demonstrating the importance to the province of the agriculture which covers 75 per cent of its land. An extraordinary number of 'live' exhibits explain it all, from intensive production methods and stock breeding to horticulture.

Reminders of Flevoland's recent past as a sea bed are periodically unearthed by archaeologists. Centuries-old remains, some Roman, of vessels, anchors and cannon balls are now displayed in the Schokland Museum and Scheepsarcheologiemuseum (Museum of Maritime Archaeology) in **Ketelhaven**. Schokland, like nearby **Urk**, a town famous for its regional costumes (best seen on Sundays), is a former island now land-locked by the North-east Polder.

Further information

Provincial VVV *Postbus 548, 8200 AM Lelystad (03200 30500)*. **Open** 9am-5pm Mon-Fri.
Almere-Stad VVV *Spoordreef 20, 1315 GP (03240 34600)*.
Lelystad VVV *Agorahof 4, 8224 BZ (03200 43444)*.
Urk VVV *Postbus 9, 8321 AA (05277 4040)*. **Open** *Apr-mid Oct* 10am-1pm, 2-5pm, Mon-Fri; *mid Oct-Mar* 10am-1pm Mon-Fri. *NS rail excursion.*
Flevohof *Spijkweg 30, Biddinghuizen (03211 1514)*. *NS rail excursion.* **Open** *Apr-Oct* 10am-6pm daily.
Scheepsarcheologiemuseum *Vossemeerdijk 21, Ketelhaven (03210 13287)*. **Open** 10am-5pm daily. **Admission** fl.50; 75c under-14s.

FRIESLAND

Friesland, in the far north, has always been regarded by southerners as a kind of windswept barbarian outpost. It has its own dialect, a highly unusual landscape and the nearest thing to provincial nationalism you're likely to find in The Netherlands. The region used to be literally cut off because of its vast network of lakes and canals.

In summer, the lakes are packed with private yachts and motor cruisers, partly because many Dutch people opt for a boat instead of a second house. The town of **Sneek** is the boating focus (*see page 215* **picture and caption**) and has a *scheepvaart* (maritime) museum (closed Sun). The best way of exploring the waterways and their towns is to go on an excursion or rent a boat and stop off at the lovely little fishing towns of **Grouw**, **Terhorne**, **Heeg** and **Sloten** or, towards the northern coast, **Dokkum**. Sloten's narrow cobbled streets, illuminated bridges and high-water warning cannon make it one of the most attractive villages in Friesland. Although tiny, it's officially designated a 'city' for the purposes of the Elfstedentocht, an 11-city skating race held when it's cold enough for the waterways to freeze (*see page 183* **Sport & Fitness: Skating**). On the IJsselmeer coast is tranquil **Hindeloopen**, known for its traditional, hand-painted red and green furniture, still sold locally.

The best feature of the province is its landscape, but the capital, **Leeuwarden**, has a picturesque centre within a star-shaped moat. Among its attractions is the Fries Museum, about the province's history, and the Fries Letterkundig Museum, where exhibitions on Frisian writers are held in the former home of the World War I spy Mata Hari. Like Groningen (*see below*), Friesland is dotted with beautiful brick churches, built on *terpen* mounds to escape flooding. The best examples, such as that at **Hogebeintum**, west of Dokkum, are at the far north of the province, huddled against the winds which blow off the Wadden Sea.

The five **Frisian Islands** (or Wadden Islands), and the sea around them, have become the symbol of the Dutch conservation movement. Even today they are reserved more for migrant birds and a diminishing grey seal colony than for human visitors. But they're appealing precisely because they are so remote, peaceful and sparsely populated. Although they are somewhat bleak in winter and occasionally prone to overcrowding during holiday weekends, the sound of the wind in the dunes and the cry of oystercatchers make a wonderful experience. Sadly you can't island-hop, since each island's ferry only shuttles to and from the coast (two to five times per day). Between May and September, when the tide is out you can cross to the nearer islands by foot, provided you're with a local guide and don't mind *wadlopen* – wading up to your ankles in mud.

Terschelling, with its sixteenth-century lighthouse and old fishing villages, is the most picturesque island. **Ameland** is good for walking and cycling tours, and has a nature reserve. The biggest island, **Texel**, is in fact administered by Noord Holland and reached via Den Helder. It has two bird reserves (De Slufter and De Muy) and a seal sanctuary at the resort of De Koog. On more remote **Schiermonnikoog**, further east, local accents are thicker and cars are banned. **Vlieland**, also car-free, is the most deserted island, which is not surprising since some of its beaches are reserved for bombing practice by the Dutch Air Force. The archipelago continues east as Germany's Ostfriesische Inseln; the resorts on **Borkum** island can be reached from Delfzijl in Groningen, *see below*.

Further information

Provincial & Leeuwarden VVV *Stationsplein 1, 8911 AC (058 132224)*.
Dokkum VVV *Grote Breedstraat 1, 9100*

Drenthe *is a mystical, rural backwater in which you can escape the tourist hordes. In the silence, you might even sense the spirits of the province's oldest residents, buried between 3400BC and 2300BC in the* **hunebedden** *(above). This string of 53 megalithic stone burial sites was constructed from boulders shed by the nearby Hondsrug (Dog's Back), a glacial moraine on which most of Drenthe is built. Almost all are located off the N34 road between Emmen and Noordlaren. The best are at Emmerdennen, Exloo, Noordsleen, Eexterhalte and Borger, where their history is explained at the* **National Hunebedden Information Centre**.

KH (05190 3800). **Open** 1-6pm Mon; 9am-noon, 1-6pm, Tue-Thur; 9am-noon, 1-6pm, 7-9pm, Fri; 9am-noon, 1-5pm, Sat.
Hindeloopen VVV *Postbus 4, 8713 ZG (05142 2550).*
Sneek VVV *Marktstraat 18, 8601 CV (05150 14096).*

Frisian Islands

Ameland VVV *Rext van Donerwecht 2, 9163 TR (05191 2020).* **Open** *Apr-Sept* 8.30am-8.30pm Mon-Fri; 8.30am-4pm Sat; *Oct-Mar* 8.30am-noon, 1.30-6.30pm, Mon-Fri; 8.30am-4pm Sat.
Schiermonnikoog VVV *Reeweg 5, 9166 PW (05195 1233).* **Open** 9am-1pm, 2.30-6.30pm, Mon-Sat.
Terschelling VVV *Postbus 20, 8880 AA West Terschelling (05620 3000).*
Texel VVV *Groenplaats 9, 1791 CC Den Burg (02220 14741).* **Open** 9am-6pm Mon-Fri; 9am-5pm Sat. *NS rail excursion.*
Vlieland VVV *Hafenweg 10, 8899 ZN (05621 1111).* **Open** 9am-12.30pm, 1.30-5pm, Mon-Fri; when ferry arrives Sat, Sun.

GELDERLAND

Gelderland, in the east, is the largest province. Nearly a third of it is covered by the **Veluwe** (Bad Land), a 4,600 hectare (11,400 acre) stretch of forest and moorland. In the south of the Veluwe, near Arnhem, is The Netherlands' biggest national park, the **Hoge Veluwe**. Hidden among the trees, near the park's Otterlo entrance, is the fascinating **Kröller-Müller Museum**. Principally housing a bequest by the art lover Hélène Kröller-Müller, it has an impressive number of well-known paintings, including the most important collection of Van Goghs outside Amsterdam and works by Mondrian and the Dutch symbolists. Outside, the woods have been transformed into a sculpture garden dotted with over 90 works including pieces by Rodin, Moore, Hepworth and Giacometti.

The Dutch come to the Veluwe to walk, cycle, go camping or to stay in rented chalets in the woods, but on a slightly less grand scale than their forebears, who used to hunt deer and wild boar here. The biggest chalet in the area is undoubtedly **Paleis Het Loo**, built originally as a hunting lodge by *stadhouder* Willem III, and the country's nearest approximation to the Palace of Versailles. Added to constantly since 1685, it's the last word in Dutch seventeenth-century fine and decorative art. You'll need to psych up for the tour, though; choose a bright day, as many of the rooms are dimly lit, and try to avoid

Friesland *is the most idiosyncratic of all the provinces. One of its characteristics is the peculiar sight of a huge, brown-sailed, flat-bottomed* skûtsje (above) *moving slowly between the polders, as if sailing on land. During two weeks in July or August they're raced in the* skûtsjesilen *competitions on Sneekermeer and Heegermeer. In early August, regattas are held at* **Sneek**. *Another ubiquitous Friesland trait is the cavernous, pyramidal* stolp *farmhouse. You can identify them by their swan-shaped* uleborden – *gable panels designed to allow access to owls.*

busy days, when unceremonious tides of humanity spoil the mood. As with most big houses, there's too much to see, but afterwards you can recuperate in the grounds, which have fountains and show-piece gardens.

The **Betuwe** (Good Land) is the south-west region of fertile land sandwiched between the River Waal, the River Maas (Meuse) and the River Lek further north. It makes perfect cycling country; go east from **Zaltbommel** or try the orchard region along the banks of the Linge stream, which is a riot of colour during blossom and harvest times. The countryside east and towards Germany, dubbed *Achterhoek* (Black Corner), is dominated by commercial waterways.

The number of times you'll need to cross rivers will make it obvious why Allied divisions found it so difficult to stage a surprise attack on **Arnhem**, the provincial capital, in 1944. Known as Operation Market Garden, the campaign ultimately failed, and was later recorded in the film *A Bridge Too Far*. The actual 'bridge too far' is not the original, but there are other reminders near Arnhem. The war cemetery and

Hartenstein Villa, once General Urquhart's headquarters and now the Airborne Museum, are in **Oosterbeek**, while the Bevrijdingmuseum (Liberation Museum) is in **Nijmegen**. Arnhem and the province's biggest city, Nijmegen, both have several good museums, notably Arnhem's excellent **Nederlands Openlucht Museum**, an open-air collection on folklore (NS rail excursion available). The history of Nijmegen, which rises in steps up from the River Waal, is explained at the Stedelijk Museum, housed in the Commanderie van St Jan, a medieval former hospital. The best thing about both cities are their imposing Gothic churches and riverside views. Nijmegen's survived the city's almost total destruction by Allied bombs in World War II.

Further information

Provincial VVV *Postbus 142, 6860 AC Oosterbeek (085 332033).* **Open** 8.30am-5pm Mon-Fri.
Arnhem & Zuid Veluwe VVV *Stationsplein 45, 6811 KL (085 420330).*
Nijmegen VVV *St Jorisstraat 72, 6511 TD (080 225440).*
Hoge Veluwe National Park *entrances at Schaarsbergen, Otterlo and Hoenderloo*

(Visitor Centre 08382 1627). NS rail excursion/bus from Arnhem (late Jun-early Aug). Open park 8am-dusk daily; Visitor Centre 10am-5pm daily. Admission f6.25 per person; f6 per car.
Kröller-Müller Museum Hoenderloo, Hoge Veluwe (08382 1041). NS rail excursion. Open 10am-5pm Tue-Sat; 11am-5pm Sun. Admission f6.25.
Paleis Het Loo Amersfoortseweg, Apeldoorn (055 212244). NS rail excursion. Open 10am-5pm Tue-Sun.

GRONINGEN

All roads lead to the city of **Groningen**, the far north-eastern province's capital and namesake. This isn't surprising when you discover that it has generated six centuries of local wealth, first as a member of the Hanseatic League and then as the only grain market for miles around. The province's history is explained in the **Groninger Museum** (open daily), also noted for its exhibitions of modern art. Despite being a former inland harbour, Groningen city managed to escape being spoiled by heavy industry, which has been pushed further up the Eemskanaal to the port of Delfzijl. Some of the world's biggest deposits of natural gas were found at Slochteren, east of Groningen.

In the capital, give the old harbour a miss and bone up on the history of inland shipping at the Noordlijke Scheepvart (Northern Shipping) Museum. The scope of the exhibits is surprisingly wide, covering everything from the local transportation of bricks to the world-wide wanderings of the Dutch East India Company (see page 55 **The Golden Age**). It's housed in the thirteenth-century Gottischhuis; next door, in the equally old Canterhuis, is the Tabacologisch (Tobacco) Museum.

The symbol of Groningen's good fortune is the capital's fifteenth-century Martinikerk. Its six-tiered church tower has a carillon and can be climbed for fine views. Get your breath back in the Martinikerkhof, behind the church. This small square has a rose garden and is lined with restored Renaissance houses. It opens onto the Turfsingel, a canal through which peat was once transported. At the foot of the Martini tower, off the Grote Markt, is a warren of small streets full of interesting, ramshackle craft shops.

The lush agricultural landscape that you can see from the Martini

Tower is sprinkled with peaceable, eighteenth century *kop-romp* ('head-trunk') farmhouses. These rural landmarks are a combination of tall, stuccoed villas and wide barns built for heavy harvests. They can best be seen in the Westerwolde district bordering Germany, particularly lining a 5-kilometre (3-mile) street at **Bellingwolde**, near **Winschoten**.

However, the real glory of the province is its rural churches. Unusual, beautifully proportioned and generally with high, saddleback towers peeping over a ring of trees, they're seen to best effect in the morning mist or under a thick blanket of snow. Many are to be found in tiny villages, whose circular shape betrays their origins as *terpen* mounds (*see above* **Friesland** and *page 220* **Fighting the Sea**). You can see some wonderful examples in a 70-kilometre (44-mile) loop northeast of Groningen city. Begin the tour with the church at **Garmerwold**, a typical *tour de force* in brick, with geometric designs outside and sixteenth-century frescos inside. Move on past the chapel of a former Benedictine monastery at **Ten Boer** to **Stedum**, where the church sits astride a mound, surrounded by a moat. The church at **Loppersum** has well-preserved frescos and the one at **Appingedam** sits in the marketplace of the attractive town centre, next to an arcaded town hall of 1630. Skirt north up the coast, passing the churches at **Bierum**, **Spijk** (mounted on a *terp*) and **Uithuizermeeden**, to **Uithuizen**. This town has a church with a twelfth-century tower and one of the loveliest, but least visited, country houses in The Netherlands, the fortified fifteenth-century **Menkemaborg** (closed January and Mondays October to March). Return to Groningen via **Het Hogeland** open-air museum at **Warffum** (March to October, Tuesday to Saturday) or the circular villages of **Kantens** and **Middelstum**, each built round a *terp*.

Further information

Provincial & Groningen VVV Naberpassage 3, 9712 JV (050 139700).
Appingedam VVV Blankenstein 2, 9901 AX (05960 24488). **Open** 1-5pm Tue-Fri; 2-5pm Sat, Sun.
Uithuizen VVV Hooftstraat 1, 9981 AA (05953 1555). **Open** 9am-noon, 1-4pm, Mon-Fri.
Winschoten VVV Stationweg 21A, 9671 AL (05970 12255).

LIMBURG

This undulating southern spur of Dutch territory, wedged between Belgium and Germany, is the antidote to all those clichés about The Netherlands being a flat country. For a taste of its countryside, aim for the valley of the **Geul**, a small stream which drives water-wheels and clatters past black and white half-timbered farmsteads. The valley is dominated by **Valkenburg** (*see page 217* **picture and caption**), and is dotted with picturesque villages such as **Schin op Geul**. Nearby **Heerlen** has remarkably complete Roman baths in its Thermen Museum (closed Mon). Try not to miss the strangely peaceful, pink and white town of **Thorn** close to the Belgian border.

Maastricht, the provincial capital, is notably un-Dutch in character. Its eleventh-century, Romanesque Basilica of St Servatius is built of stone, a material found nowhere else in the country, and is most reminiscent of Rhineland churches, with its vividly painted and gilded north portal. Dubbed *Mosae Trajectum* by the Romans because they crossed the Maas (Meuse) river here, the city was later part of the Frankish kingdom of Charlemagne, whose capital was **Aachen**, just over the border in Germany (*see page 200* **Beyond Amsterdam: Crossing the Border**). Maastricht was jealously guarded and was heavily fortified from 1129. Walk the length of the remaining southern ramparts for a breathtaking view of the river and the city's oldest building, the Romanesque Basilica of Our Lady.

Maastricht is a wonderful town to wander about in; make for the tiny streets jostling around the Markt, many of whose shops sell *Limburgs vlaai*, a fruit tart often eaten around **carnival** time as a special treat before Lent (*see also below* **Noord Brabant**). The French influence has turned Maastricht into the gastronomic capital of The Netherlands, a fact celebrated in the last week of August, when restaurateurs fling open their doors for public tastings, the so-called *preuvenement*.

Almost as rewarding, both gastronomically and culturally, is **Roermond**. The part-Romanesque, part-Gothic Munsterkerk was built in 1220; nine years later the impressive tombs of the Count of

Gelderland and his wife were installed. Local antiquities and works by artists from the town are exhibited in the Gemeentemuseum, alongside displays on PJH Cuypers, architect of Amsterdam's Rijksmuseum, whose house this was.

Further information
Provincial VVV *Postbus 811, 6300 AV, Valkenburg (04406 13993)*. **Open** 8.30am-5pm Mon-Fri; 10am-noon Sat.
Heerlen VVV *Stationsplein 4, 6411 NE (045 716200)*.
Maastricht VVV *Kleine Straat 1, 6211 ED (043 252121). NS rail excursions.*
Roermond VVV *Markt 24, 6041 EN (04750 33205).*
Valkenburg VVV *Th Dorrenplein 5, 6301 DV (04406 13364). NS rail excursion.*

NOORD BRABANT

Noord Brabant, bordering Belgium in the south, was one of the last provinces to renounce support of Spain during the Dutch Revolt at the turn of the seventeenth century (*see page 53* **War & Reformation**) and one of the most reluctant to forget its Burgundian past. Consequently, its character has been shaped to a large extent by its Catholic population, who in 1867 had PJH Cuypers and G van Swaay build a replica of Rome's St Peter's Basilica in **Oudenbosch**, east of Breda. Five centuries earlier, and with a better result, the **Cathedral of St Jan** was built at **'s-Hertogenbosch**. It is the only real example of pure Gothic architecture in the country.

Den Bosch, as the provincial capital is called in practice, was the birthplace of Hieronymous Bosch and there's a statue of the painter in the market-place. Den Bosch is one of the two main Dutch centres of **carnival** (the other is Maastricht). Each February or March before Lent, residents spend a fortune in beer, bands and false noses and career around town holding up traffic. The carnival atmosphere can be sampled all year round at fantasy park **De Efteling** (*see page 180* **Children & Parents**). It is just north of **Tilburg**, a dull textile town you would visit only for the Nederlands Textiel Museum (closed Mon).

The city of **Eindhoven** is dominated by the industrial multi-national Philips, whose football club, PSV Eindhoven, has come a long way

since it was the factory team (*see page 183* **Sport & Fitness**). An electric bulb works was founded here in 1891 by Dr AF Philips, whose statue is on Stationsplein, but plans to celebrate the ailing company's centenary are low key and its Evoluon science museum has been closed down. However, one extraordinary attraction does remain, the **Van Abbe Museum** (closed Mon). Few people have ever heard of it, yet the permanent collection of major modern art is of such size it can't all be exhibited at once. Art lovers also head a few miles north to **Nuenen**. Van Gogh's family lived in the vicarage there and displays of memorabilia have made it something of a pilgrimage centre; a memorial to the painter stands in Op den Bergh Park. Towards the German border are the nature reserve of **De Groote Peel**, where duckboards get you over the reeds, and the National War and Resistance Museum at Overloon (*see page 64* **World War II**).

If you prefer to be out of doors, head west to the wilderness of the **Biesbosch** tidal estuary, north of **Breda**, a shopping town whose main sight is the Grote Kerk. You can take boat excursions through the *Biesbos* (reed forest) from the fortress town

of **Geertruidenberg**. Vintage car enthusiasts would also enjoy the nearby **Nationaal Automobiel Museum** (*01621 85400*), open April to September. Downstream is another fortified city, **Willemstad**, built (1565-83) by *stadhouder* Willem the Silent of Orange to safeguard the choppy Hollandsch Diep waters. South towards Antwerp in Belgium (*see page 200* **Beyond Amsterdam: Crossing the Border**) is the ancient town of **Bergen Op Zoom**, once the most fortified of Dutch cities, now a characterful market town.

Further information
Provincial VVV *Postbus 3259, 5000 DG Tilburg (013 434060).*
Bergen Op Zoom VVV *Hoogstraat 2, 4611 MT (01640 66000).*
Breda VVV *Willemstraat 17-19, 4811 AJ (076 222444).*
Eindhoven VVV *Stationsplein 17, 5611 AC (040 449231).*
's Hertogenbosch VVV *Markt 77, 5211 JX (073 123071).*

OVERIJSSEL

Randstad residents might look upon Overijssel, due east of Amsterdam, as being in *tukkerland* – out in the sticks – but they're happy to holiday in the province over the IJssel river

Limburg *is as far removed from the Randstad's flat polders as it's possible to be without leaving the country. It even has hills. You can get dramatic views of the Geul valley slopes from the castle ruins in* **Valkenburg** *(above), a fortified town with prehistoric caves and Roman catacombs. Southwest at Vaals is* **Drielandenpunt**, *where The Netherlands meets both Belgium and Germany (NS rail excursion available). At 321 metres (1,050 feet), it's the highest point in The Netherlands. Limburgers don't like to think of themselves as Dutch; they speak a dialect akin to German, hold carnivals and eat a French-style cuisine.*

(hence its name). Criss-crossed by long, winding rivers and 400 kilometres (249 miles) of canoe routes, the province is superb for watersports and is dotted with holiday homes and hikers' cabins; the VVV even provides self-drive, horse-drawn carts, which you can sleep in.

Most visitors head for the **Lake District**, comprising the **Weerribben** and **Wieden** districts. Between the two runs the road linking **Steenwijk** and **Blokzijl**, both fortified towns, the latter with a marina in its old harbour. Dominating Wieden is the huge **Beulaker Wijde/Belter Wijde** lake, bordered by **Vollenhove**, a Zuider Zee port until the North-east Polder was drained; **Zwartsluis**, where paintings dating from the seventeenth century, when it was Fortress Zwartsluis, still hang in the town hall; and the watersports centre of **Wanneperveen**, with its splendid thatch-roofed farmsteads. Almost completely hidden among the reedlands are the 'water villages' of **Belt Schutsloot** and **Giethoorn**, where the residents get around mostly by boat (*see* **picture and caption**).

Tracing the boundary of the province up the IJssel you reach **Kampen**, which has a wealth of historic buildings and a particularly beautiful waterfront. Upriver is

Zwolle, which like Kampen was a Hanse town and retains its star-shaped moat and bastions. In the town hall, parts of which date from 1448, is an imposing *schepenzaal* (elders' meeting chamber), a feature found only in Overijssel. The rococo former *stadhouder's* palace now houses the Provinciaal Overijssels Museum. Boats leave for the lakes from Zwarte Water. Where the IJssel enters the province is the major city of **Deventer**. Known for *Deventer koek* honey gingerbread and the domed tower of St Lebuinuskerk, it has attractive façades on Brink square and in the old Berg Quarter.

Almost every town in Overijssel has a summer **carnival**. **Raalte** holds its harvest festival in the third week of August (Wed-Sat); people parade through **Lemelerveld** covered in flowers during *Bloemen Corso* on the first Saturday in August; and sheepdogs herd sheep around **Hellendoorn** during its sheep market around 14 and 15 August. It's on special market days (Wednesdays, late July to early August) and on Sundays that you're most likely to see people in traditional costume at **Staphorst**, just north of Zwolle. Many of these severely Protestant locals also inter-marry and shun the modern world, banning vaccinations, cars on Sundays – and cameras. This *lintdorp* (ribbon village) – or *ween-*

dorp (peat village) – is nearly 12 kilometres (7.5 miles) long; it swallowed up settlements along canals dug in peat, and incorporates farmhouses decorated in unique colour schemes. The community has retained a rigidly religious lifestyle centred on its countless Dutch Reformed Churches.

East along the River Vecht from Zwolle and surrounded by woods is the superb fishing centre of **Ommen**. One British angler recently landed 48 kilos (88 pounds) of bream in four hours. Collect a fishing licence from the post office and ask about the best baits and fishing spots in the first-class tackle shop, Beste Stek (*Vrijthof 3; 5291 54972*). Hotel de Zon, on the river bank, is favoured by fishermen swapping angling stories. Stretching south are the **Salland Hills**, which rise to 81m (266ft) at Holterberg, south of Nijverdal, where there's fun to be had at **Hellendoorn Adventure Park**.

The district stretching up to Germany is **Twente**, dominated by the province's biggest city, **Enschede**. Rebuilt after a fire in 1862, its main draws are Los Hoes, a textile industry museum, and the Rijksmuseum Twente, which displays modern art and an authentic farmhouse. Some of Twente's surviving Saxon farms (*Saksische boerderijen*) can be seen on an NS day excursion (which includes travel in a horse-drawn covered waggon or *huifkar*), or on a six-day cycle tour (April to September) organized by the provincial VVV, who can forward luggage from hotel to hotel. Some of the finest farms are concentrated around **Ootmarsum**, a knot of narrow streets lined with timber buildings, and **Denekamp**, with its thirteenth-century sandstone church and Natura Docet natural history museum. These two Catholic towns celebrate Easter with tree felling, street processions, ritual chanting and bonfires. If in Twente around Christmas, you're likely to hear a mysterious horn sounding through the countryside or emanating from church services. Don't be too alarmed; it's local men signalling to each other by playing a long *midwinterhorn* in a pagan fertility ritual.

Further information

Provincial VVV *Postbus 500, 7600 AM Almelo (05490 18767)*. **Open** 9am-5pm Mon-Fri.

Overijssel *is famous for its lake district, where visitors go for watersports and to explore its 'water villages'. The most peculiar of these is* **Giethoorn***, the curious result of improvident peat digging in about 1280 by a sect of flagellants, who named their settlement after the goat horns they unearthed. Where the peat once was, water found its level and left the buildings individually marooned, with only boats and foot bridges to connect them. On the second and third weekends of August the Jazz Inn and Blues Inn music festivals are staged on a platform in the lake, and a procession of flower-decked boats takes place the following Saturday.*

Enschede VVV *Oude Markt 31, 7511 GB (053 323200).*
Giethoorn VVV *on a boat, Beulakerweg, 8355 AM (05216 1248). NS rail excursions.*
Ommen VVV *Markt 1, 7731 DB (05291 51638).* Open 9.30am-5pm Mon-Fri; 10am-5pm Sat; 2-5pm Sun.
Zwartsluis VVV *Stationsweg 32, 8064 DG (05208 67453).* Open 8am-6pm Tue-Sat.
Zwolle VVV *Grote Kerkplein 14, 8011 PK (038 213900).*

UTRECHT

If you go anywhere in The Netherlands by land, the chances are you'll go through the city of Utrecht, the country's main rail and road junction (*see page 208 The Randstad*), just south of Amsterdam. Earlier travellers, who came down the Lek river, chose the province in 863 as the location for Europe's largest trading post, Dorestad. It is the site of present-day **Wijk-bij-Duurstede**, which still has many ancient buildings. In either direction along the Lek, old towns such as **Rhenen**, where the graceful, silvery Cunera tower is mirrored in the river, **Amerongen** and **Culemborg** remain virtually unchanged.

Water is Utrecht's chief asset. Between Amsterdam and Utrecht are the 2,500 hectare (6,200 acre) **Loosdrechtse Plassen**, and smaller **Vinkeveense Plassen**. These fan-shaped lakes have narrow strips of land radiating into them and are now used mainly for fishing and watersports. The area groans with private wealth, as the many villas dotted around the picturesque old villages of **Oud-Loosdrecht**, **Westbroek** and **Breukeleveen** testify. A few kilometres away in Noord Holland are **Hilversum**, home of Dutch television, and the mini-Hollywood at **Laren**. For a taste of more ancient privilege, wander down the Vecht, which flows north between the *plassen*. It's The Netherlands' prettiest navigable river, overshadowed by iron bridges, grand, decaying estates at **Loenen**, **Vreeland** and **Breukelen**, and the province's ubiquitous castles (*see page 203 Excursions in Holland: Castles*). Compare it with the willow-lined Hollandse IJssel further west, famous for the witches' scales at Oudewater (*see page 203 Excursions in Holland: Traditions*).

In the eastern half of the province,

Zeeland *has been transformed by the world's biggest flood barrier, the* **Delta Works** *(above). Built in response to the 1953 flood, it keeps the sea under control and reduces the cost of coastline maintenance (see also page 220* **Fighting the Sea***). Environmental protests ensured that this curtain across the mouths of the major rivers – Lower Rhine, Maas, Waal and Schelde – would not be a fixed dike, but a series of moveable storm surge barriers. It was completed in 1986, after 30 years of construction costing f14 billion. The revolutionary technology is explained at* **Delta Expo** *on Neeltje Jans, an island halfway along the Ooster Schelde Dam.*

water makes way for a large wooded area, ostensibly for recreational purposes but dominated by danger signs as walkers constantly risk stumbling onto military firing ranges. The wood has other interesting features, though. **Soestdijk** is home to the country's former queen, now Princess Juliana, and at **Austerlitz**, Napoleon's army built a huge sand pyramid purely because they had nothing else to do at the time. Best of all, though, is **Amersfoort**, a beautifully-preserved medieval town set in a ring of canals on the edge of the Leusder Heide heath.

Further information
Provincial VVV *Postal enquiries only to Maliesingel 38, 3581 BK Utrecht (030 310701).*
Amersfoort VVV *Stationsplein 27, 3818 LE (033 635151).*
Utrecht VVV *Vredenburg 90, 3511 BD (063 4034085). NS rail excursions.*
Wijk-bij-Duurstede VVV *Markt 24, 3961 BC (03435 75995).* Open *Apr-Oct* 1-4.30pm Mon; 10am-noon, 1-4.30pm, Tue-Fri; 10am-4pm Sat; *Nov-Mar* 10am-noon, 1-4.30pm, Tue-Fri; 10am-4pm Sat.

ZEELAND

This collection of islands in the river delta bordering Belgium has a famous maritime past and the distinctive Zeeland traditions were preserved by its isolation. Then in January 1953 massive storm floods swept away many old buildings and farms, brutally launching the province into the twentieth century. Salt water damage and tide-marks, seen halfway up columns in the medieval churches of **Kruiningen** (on the isthmus to Beveland Island) and **Brouwershaven** (on Schouwen Island), are the only reminders of the perennial threat of flooding which was hopefully eliminated by the **Delta Works** (*see* **picture and caption** *and page 220* **Fighting the Sea**).

Changes in tide movements have not affected the main activity of oyster and mussel catching. Seafood is available all over Zeeland, but the best hauls of the day usually find their way to restaurants in **Yerseke** (a town near Kruiningen named after the Dutch for oyster). In season (September to April) you can take a tour of the oyster beds.

In the Middle Ages, Zeeland grew fat on the cloth and wool trade with England and France. Indeed the English still know the port of **Vlissingen** as Flushing. It's the birthplace of the heroic Admiral de Ruyter (*see page 59* **Decline &**

Fall), whose statue in the Rotunda surveys the dramatic seascape. Among the local artefacts in the Stedelijk Museum is a copy of De Ruyter's portrait by Ferdinand Bol; the original is in Zeeuws Museum in the provincial capital, **Middelburg**, alongside tapestries depicting local sea battles and examples of Zeeland costume. Elderly Middelburgers sometimes wear traditional dress at the Thursday market or at church on Sunday. Although bombed in 1940, Middelburg has a charming circular centre parcelled within star-shaped fortifications, now landscaped. Like **Goes**, it owed its prosperity to medieval trade with England. That wealth was reflected in the towns' hall churches, which are of a size and splendour normally reserved for the Grote Kerk of a major city.

Over the Westerschelde estuary is **Zeeland Vlaanderen** (Flanders). From there it's a short hop over the Belgian border to the beautiful cities of Antwerp, Gent and Bruges (*see page 200* **Beyond Amsterdam: Crossing the Border**).

Just north of Middelburg is the most beautiful town in Zeeland, **Veere**, where elegant flèche spires and the towering Church of Our Lady can be seen across the flats for miles. The churches in the province are worth a tour in themselves. Many were used as lighthouses for ships at sea. The churches at **Kapelle, Zoutelande** and **'s-Heer Arendskerke** are among the biggest and best.

Further information

Provincial & Middelburg VVV *Markt 65, 4330 AC (01180 33000)*. Open 8.30am-12.30pm, 1.15-5pm, Mon-Fri. *NS rail excursion (includes Walcheren miniature town)*.
Goes VVV *Stationsplein 3, 4461 HP (01100 20577)*. Open 1.30-5pm Mon; 10am-12.30pm, 1.30-5pm Tue-Fri; 10am-noon Sat.
Veere VVV *Noordstraat 50, 4331 CE (01181 1365)*. Open 8.30am-noon, 1-5pm, Mon-Fri.
Vlissingen VVV *Nieuwendijk 15, 4381 BV (01184 12345)*.
Yerseke VVV *Kerkplein 1, 4401 ED (01131 1864)*. Open 2-4pm Mon; 10am-4pm Tue-Fri; 10am-noon Sat.
Delta Expo *Oosterschelde Dam, on Route N57 (01115 2702)*. Open 10am-5pm daily. Admission f10; under-12s, over-65s f7.50.

FIGHTING THE SEA

Everything you see in the Dutch landscape is affected by its relationship with the sea. Over half the country is below sea level, so without flood defences, at high tide most of the the major towns and cities and two thirds of the population would be underwater: all of Holland, Zeeland and Flevoland; most of Friesland, Groningen and Utrecht; and parts of Gelderland and Overijssel. The Zeeland flood of 1953 (*see under Zeeland*) illustrated the threat, and the Dutch are willing to spend upwards of f50 billion per year just to maintain the 450 kilometres (280 miles) of sea defences. There are many more barriers against river flooding.

Man-made alterations to the countryside began in around AD 1000 with Friesland's *terpen* (mounds), on to which the population would scramble during floods (for examples, *see under* **Friesland** and **Groningen**). Early settlers devised ways of 'winning' land by linking *terpen* via raised walls (dikes). The enclosed land was drained to make a *polder*, the excavated ditch inside the dike became a canal (*gracht* in town, *sloot* in the country) and freshwater rivers were used to flush salt out of the soil. All rural landscape matches this pattern, and street plans of towns (Amsterdam, Rotterdam) follow original polder divisions. Windmills, such as those at Kinderdijk (*see page 203* **Excursions in Holland:**

Traditions), were built to speed up the continuous draining required, later to be replaced by steam, then electric pumping stations (for example, **De Blocq van Kuffeler**, Flevoland).

The first large-scale draining scheme (1848-52) was the Haarlemmermeer, an 180 square kilometre (70 square mile) lake, now the site of Schiphol Airport. The polder system literally 'made' The Netherlands; it increased the size of the country (almost doubling it over the past millennium); formed freshwater basins; improved drainage; reduced the length of the coastline to make it more manageable against flooding; and made direct road links possible. The A7 links Noord Holland and Friesland, via the **Afsluitdijk**, which enclosed the former Zuider Zee in the most ambitious reclamation project of all (1927-1968).

Land for agriculture and new towns was created on first the Wieringermeer polder (1932), then the North-east Polder (1942) and Flevoland (1968), a total of 1,650 square kilometres (637 square miles). In the process it formed the freshwater IJsselmeer and the recreational *Randmeren* (ring of lakes) between Flevoland and the mainland. The battle against the sea had seemed all but won following the completion of the **Delta Works** in 1986 (*see page 219* **picture and cap-**

tion) and the storm surge barrier at **Krimpen a/d IJssel**, near Rotterdam.

The sense of common purpose in fighting the sea has had profound social effects; *see page 200* **Beyond Amsterdam**. Yet the Dutch are now resisting this perpetual driving force of their history and national psyche. The last planned Zuider Zee polder, the 600 square kilometre (232 square mile) **Markerwaard**, has been suspended. There are fears that it threatens ecology, poses unacceptable financial risks to the state, and that it may not even be needed. However, Amsterdam still plans to drain part of IJ Meer to create a new eastern suburb.

But the fight against the sea isn't over. The Dutch are now having to contemplate a threat to the entire future of the country they've handbuilt: the greenhouse effect. The sea level is already rising at the rate of 12-20cm (5-8 inches) a century and dikes are being raised. But scientists and the government admit this will not compensate for any effects of global warming and are studying contingency plans to find a permanent solution. The most bizarre idea is to inject sulphuric acid (a plentiful waste product of Dutch industry) into the limestone layer deep below the surface. A chemical reaction would then form expanding gypsum and raise the country slightly. Apparently, it's not as crazy as it sounds.

Survival

In a foreign city apparently simple tasks, such as using the phone, can be initially baffling, and emergencies can be especially traumatic. The ability of many Dutch to speak English can be very helpful, but detailed and practical information is nonetheless essential.

CONTENTS:

Survival

Coping with a crisis is hard enough at home; but where on holiday can you find a locksmith, a 24-hour chemist or an ambulance for your dog? *Julie Sinclair-Day* **has the answers.**

COMMUNICATIONS

TELEPHONES/ PTT TELECOM

Public phone boxes are scattered throughout the city. The kiosks are mainly glass with green trim and have a green and white *ptt telecom* logo. There are both coin-operated and card phones. The coin boxes take 25c, f1 and f2.50 coins. Phonecards are available from post offices and phone centres (*see below*), priced f5, f10 or f25.

The procedure for **making a call** is as follows:
Listen for the dialling tone (a low-pitched hum), insert money – a minimum of 25c for about 3 minutes' local connection – dial the appropriate code (none required for calls within Amsterdam), listen for the dialling tone to return (usually with a higher pitched hum), then dial the required number. A digital display on public phones shows the credit remaining, but only wholly unused coins are returned. Phoning from a hotel room is more expensive.

International phone calls:
The code is 09 (remember to wait for a new dialling tone before dialling the country code). International calls can be made from all phone boxes. The time for **off-peak rates** for international calls is generally 6pm-8am Monday to Friday (the USA get an hour less, 7pm-8am), and all day on Saturday and Sunday. **European countries** are not counted as international by the Dutch phone system and so there are no off-peak rates for them. For more information on off-peak rates, phone international directory enquiries (*below*).

Telephone directories can be found in post offices and phone centres, *see below*. When phoning information services, taxis or train stations you may hear the recorded message, '*Er zijn nog drie (three)/twee (two)/een (one) wachtenden voor u.*' This tells you how many people are ahead of you in the telephone queuing system.

Many **Amsterdam phone numbers** **were** **changed** in February-April 1991. By 1 March 1991 all six-digit numbers will have '6' added in front of the number; all

seven-digit numbers will remain the same. Throughout the Guide, we have printed the full seven-digit number; if, in Spring 1991, you dial a seven-digit number and do not get through, try redialling, omitting the first '6'.

Emergency phonelines are listed under **Emergencies** *page 223*; help phonelines are listed under **Help & Information** (*below*). The following operator services are open 8am-10pm daily.

Directory Enquiries *008*
International Operator *06 0410*
International Directory Enquiries *06 0418*

PHONE CENTRES

If you have a number of phone calls to make, and little change, use a phone centre.

Telehouse
Raadhuisstraat 46-50, C (673 3654). Tram 1, 2, 5, 13, 14, 17, 21. **Open** 24 hours daily. **Credit** AmEx, DC, MC, TC, V.
As well as being a convenient place to make international phone calls (*see p225* **picture and caption**), Telehouse offers fax, Telex and telegram services. The cost of sending a **fax** ranges from f6 for one page (f3 per additional page) to f12 for one page (f7.20 per additional page). You can arrange to have a fax sent to you at Telehouse on 626 3871 or 626 5326, at a cost of f9.50. The sender must include your name and telephone number with their fax, and Telehouse will phone to inform you of its arrival. The **Telex** service costs f9.50 per minute to send, f7 to receive, on the numbers 11101 TELEH NL or 15470 TELEH NL. For **telegrams**, *see below*.

Teletalk Center
Leidsestraat 101, IS (620 8599/fax 620 8559). Tram 1, 2, 5. **Open** 10am-midnight daily. **Credit** AmEx, DC, MC, V.
The cost of sending a **fax** from here is f5 plus standard telephone charge, which drops in off-peak hours. It costs f3.50 to receive a fax here, however long the document, and photocopying costs 25c per page of A4 paper.

TELEGRAMS, TELEX & FAX

Telegrams can be sent from phone centres or post offices for a basic

charge of f15, plus 45c-f1.10 per word (including address and signature). For **Telex** and **fax** facilities, *see above* **Phone Centres** and *p188* **Business**.

POST/PTT POST

Post offices and letterboxes are spread throughout Amsterdam. The logo for the national postal service is *ptt post* (white letters on a red oblong). **Post offices** are generally open from 9am to 5pm Monday to Friday. Here you can weigh letters, buy stamps and postal orders, send telegrams and send letters by express post. For post destined outside Amsterdam, use the *overige* slot. The **postal information phoneline** is *0017*.

Stamps
At time of writing, it costs 55c to send a postcard from Amsterdam to anywhere in Europe (75c to the USA) and 75c for letters weighing less than 20 grammes. To send post elsewhere prices vary according to weight and destination. Stamps (*postzegeten*) can also be bought with postcards from many tobacconists and souvenir shops.

Main Post Office
Singel 250, C (655 6331). Tram 1, 2, 5, 13, 14, 17, 21. **Open** 8.30am-6pm Mon-Wed, Fri; 8.30am-8.30pm Thur; 9am-noon Sat. **No credit cards.**
In addition to usual services, facilities here include: phones; directories; photo-booths; a wall-map of Amsterdam; stamp machines; counters where you can buy packaging for parcels; and a counter for collectors' stamps and commemorative stationery.

Post Restante
Post Restante, Hoofdpostkantoor ptt, Singel 250, 1012 SJ, Amsterdam, Netherlands.
If you're not sure where you'll be staying in Amsterdam, people can send your post to the above address. You'll be able to collect it from the main post office (*above*) if you produce ID such as a passport or driving licence with photo.

Centraal Station Post Office
Oosterdokskade 3, C (555 8911). Tram 1, 2, 4, 5, 9, 13, 16, 17, 24, 25. **Open** 8.30am-9pm Mon-Fri; 9am-noon Sat. **No credit cards.**
This is the parcels post office. Only this and the main post office (*above*) deal with parcels. Despite its name it is in fact a five-minute walk east of Centraal Station.

FOREIGN NEWSPAPERS

If you can't bear not to know what's happening back home try one of these newsagents. For the American Discount Book Centre and Athenaeum Nieuwscentrum, *see page 153* **Shopping Around.**

AKO

Rozengracht 21, IW (624 5369). Tram 13, 14, 17. **Open** *8am-8pm Mon-Fri; 9am-6pm Sat; 10am-6pm Sun.* **No credit cards.**
Kiosk *Centraal Station, Stationsplein 13, C (627 4320). Tram 1, 2, 4, 5, 9, 13, 16, 17, 24, 25.* **Open** *6.30am-10.45pm daily.* **No credit cards.**
Two of the best-stocked branches of this large chain. Others are dotted around the city.

Bruna

Leidsestraat 89-93, IS (622 0578). Tram 1, 2, 5. **Open** *9am-9.30pm daily.* **No credit cards.**

DISABLED

The most obvious difficulty people with mobility problems face in The Netherlands is in negotiating the winding cobbled streets of the older towns. Poorly maintained and broken pavements are also widespread and the canal houses, with their narrow doorways and steep stairs, can also present access problems.

On the positive side, the pragmatic Dutch don't have preconceptions about people with disablties and any problems are generally solved quickly and without fuss.

Most of the large museums have reasonable facilities for wheelchair users but little for the blind and hard of hearing. Most cinemas and theatres, too, have an enlightened attitude and are accessible, some with help. Throughout the Guide, we list establishments that claim to have wheelchair access. It's advisable to check in advance and always be specific about your needs.

The **Metro** is accessible to wheelchair users who 'have normal arm function', except for the Waterlooplein station which has no lifts. There is a **taxi service** for wheelchair users (*see page 3*

Essential Information). Trams are in no way accessible to wheelchair users and the high steps may also pose problems for those with limited mobility.

NS (Nederlandse Spoorwegen), the national railway network, produces a booklet called *Rail Travel for the Disabled*, plus timetables in braille, available from all main stations. There is wheelchair access to refreshment rooms and toilets at all stations. If you need assistance to board a train, phone *030 331 253* between 8am and 4pm Monday to Friday, at least a day in advance.

The Netherlands' Board of Tourism and the VVV (*see page 3* **Essential Information**) produce brochures listing accommodation, restaurants, museums, tourist attractions and boat excursions with facilities for the disabled.

Gehandicaptenoverleg Amsterdam

Keizersgracht 523, 1016 DP, IS (638 3838). Tram 1, 2, 5, 16, 24, 25. **Open** *9am-5pm Mon-Fri.*
This organization campaigns to improve facilities for the disabled. The information literature is in Dutch, but the staff speak English. Phone for local information and advice.

DRUGS

It's widely known that the Amsterdam authorities have a relaxed attitude towards **soft drugs** such as cannabis. Possession of up to 28g (1oz) of cannabis, though technically still an offence, is generally regarded as a misdemeanour for which you're unlikely to be prosecuted. Of course, official attitudes can change at any time.

There exist numerous coffee shops and **smokers' bars** (*see page 91*

Cafés & Bars) where the drug is openly sold over the counter. It's extremely unwise to buy drugs on the street, although there's ample opportunity to do so. Dealers here are as unscrupulous as anywhere else in the world. At best you'll be ripped off; at worst, made ill or poisoned.

It's not acceptable to smoke everywhere in Amsterdam; a certain amount of discretion is required. Many bars and all tea houses will not tolerate the practice and eject any offenders. Similarly, outside Amsterdam, public consumption of cannabis is highly unacceptable.

Foreigners found with any amount of hard drugs, especially heroin, should expect prosecution. Organizations offering help and advice to users have become increasingly restricted in their ability to help foreigners with drug-related problems – government subsidies are generally aimed at helping nationals. Visitors caught dealing in drugs are likely to be prosecuted and repatriated pretty swiftly.

There are no helplines for drug abusers. General hospitals and doctors should be the first port of call for sufferers. If you are suffering from the ill effects of too much cannabis, for example, go to a hospital outpatients' department or see a doctor, who will be well-used to dealing with the problem.

EMBASSIES & CONSULATES

The VVV offices (*see page 3* **Essential Information**) have comprehensive lists of embassies and consulates. Most countries have their embassies in The Hague (*Den*

EMERGENCIES

Emergency Switchboard

(0611)
This 24-hour switchboard deals with ambulance, fire and police emergencies.

Central Medical Service

(664 2111/679 1821)
A 24-hour medical and dental service, referring callers to a duty doctor or dentist. Operators can also give details of chemists open outside normal hours.

Tourist Medical Service

(673 7567)
Another 24-hour medical referral service, geared to foreign visitors.

Lost credit cards

Report lost or stolen credit cards on the following 24-hour numbers:
American Express *(642 4488)*
Diner's Club *(627 9310)*
Mastercard *(01 04 57 0887)*
Visa *(520 5534)*

Rape & sexual abuse

Tegen Haar Wil (Against Her Will) *(625 3473)*
A 24-hour helpline for women who are victims of rape, attack, sexual harassment or threats.

Blijf-van-m'n-lijf-huis (Don't Touch My Body House) *(694 2758)*
Women being abused by their husband or friend will be referred to a safe house.

Haag), but, unless otherwise stated, if only a consulate is listed then it will deal with all visa enquiries and other problems.

American Consulate General
Museumplein 19, OS (664 5661/679 0321). Tram 3, 5, 12, 16. **Open** 8.30am-noon Mon-Fri.

Australian Embassy
Koninginnegracht 23, 2514 AB Den Haag (070 363 0983). **Open** 9am-12.30pm, 1.15-5.15pm, Mon-Thur; 9am-12.30pm Fri.

Belgian Consulate
Drentestraat 11, OS (642 9763). Bus 40, 60 158, 173. **Open** 9am-2pm Mon-Fri.
Deals with visa enquiries and documentation for Belgians in Utrecht and North Holland.

Belgian Embassy
Lange Vigversberg 12, 2513 AC, Den Haag (070 36 44 910). **Open** 9am-noon, 2-4pm, Mon-Fri.
Deals with all other visa enquiries.

British Consulate General
Koningslaan 44, OS (676 4343); visa enquiries 675 8121). Tram 2, 6. **Open** 9am-noon, 2-4pm, Mon-Fri.

British Embassy
Langvoorhout 10, 2514 ED, Den Haag (070 36 45 800). **Open** 9am-1pm, 2.15-5.30pm, Mon-Fri.

Canadian Embassy
Sophialaan 7, 2514 JP Den Haag (070 361 4111). **Open** 10am-noon, 2.30-4.30pm, Mon-Fri.

Eire Embassy
Dr Kuyperstraat 9, 2514 BA, Den Haag (070 363 0993). **Open** 10am-12.30pm, 3-5pm, Mon-Fri.

Federal Republic of Germany Consulate
De Lairessestraat 172, OS (673 6245). Tram 16. **Open** 9am-noon Mon-Fri.

French Consulate
Vijzelgracht 2, IS (624 8346). Tram 6, 7, 10, 16, 24, 25. **Open** 9-11.30am Mon-Fri.

Italian Consulate
Herengracht 609, IS (624 0043). Tram 4. **Open** 9am-12.30pm Mon-Fri.

New Zealand Embassy
Mauritskade 25, 2514 HD Den Haag (070 46 9324). **Open** 9am-12.30pm, 1.30-5.30pm, Mon-Thur; 9am-12.30pm, 1.30-5pm, Fri; *visa enquiries* 9am-12.30pm Mon-Fri.

Portuguese Consulate
Willenskade 18, 3016 TL, Rotterdam (010 411 1540). **Open** 9am-3.30pm Mon, Wed-Fri; 1-8pm Tue.

Spanish Consulate
Frederiksplein 34, OS (620 3811). Tram 3, 4, 6, 7, 10. **Open** 9am-2pm Mon-Fri.

Swiss Consulate
Johannes Vermeerstraat 16, OS (664 4231). Tram 16. **Open** 10am-noon Mon-Fri.

HEALTH

For **emergency services and medical or dental referral agencies** *see page 223* **Emergencies**.

In the case of minor accidents, try the outpatients' departments at the following hospitals (*ziekenhuis*), all of which are open 24 hours daily and offer first aid facilities.

Academisch Medisch Centrum
Meibergdreef 9, OE (566 9111; 566 3333). Bus 59, 60, 61, 62, 120, 126, 158.

Boven Ij Ziekenhuis
Statenjachtstraat 1, OE (634 6343). Bus 36, 37, 39.

VU Ziekenhuis
De Boelelaan 1117, OE (548 9111). Bus 23, 48, 64, 65, 173.

Lucas Ziekenhuis
Jan Tooropstraat 164, OW (510 8911). Bus 19, 47, 80, 82, 97.

Onze Lieve Vrouwe Gasthuis
1E Oosterparkstraat 179, OE (599 9111). Tram 3.
The most central outpatient department.

DENTISTS

For a dentist (*tandarts*), phone the Central Medical Service (*see page 223* **Emergencies**).

AOC
Wilhelmina Gasthuisplein 167, OW (616 1234). Tram 1, 2, 3, 5, 6, 12. **Open** 8am-midnight Mon-Fri; 8am-9pm Sat; 1-5pm Sun. **Credit** (minimum f50) AmEx, DC, MC, V.
Emergency dental treatment is unlikely to cost more than f100.

OPTICIANS

To save time it is wise to phone and make an appointment before visiting an optician (*opticien*). Three of the central clinics are listed below; for more consult the Yellow Pages (*Gouden Gids*).

Azijnman Optiek
Kinkerstraat 317, OW (618 2102). Tram 7, 17. **Open** 9am-6pm Tue, Wed, Fri; 9am-5.30pm, 7-9pm, Thur; 9am-5pm Sat. **Credit** AmEx, DC, MC, V.
No charge for eye examinations.

Schmidt Optiek
Rokin 72, C (623 1981). Tram 4, 9, 14, 16, 24, 25. **Open** 1-5.30pm Mon; 8.30am-5.30pm Tue-Fri; 9am-5pm Sat. **Credit** AmEx, DC, MC, V.

Eye examinations cost f17.50, which is deducted if you buy new frames.

York International Optical
Leidsestraat 32, IS (618 2102). Tram 1, 2, 5. **Open** 9.30am-6pm Mon-Fri; 9.30am-5pm Sat. **Credit** AmEx, DC, MC, V.
Eye examinations are f17.50, which is deducted if you buy new frames.

PRESCRIPTIONS

Chemists (*drogisterij*) sell toiletries and non-prescription drugs such as aspirin and cold remedies, as well as tampons and condoms. They are usually open between 9.30am and 5.30pm Monday to Saturday. For prescription drugs you will have to go to a pharmacy (*apotheek*), usually open 9.30am to 5.30pm Monday to Friday.

If you need a chemist or pharmacist outside these hours phone the **Central Medical Service** (*Centraal Dokters Dienst*) on 664 2111 or 679 1821 (24 hours daily) or consult the daily newspaper *Het Parool* which publishes details of which *apotheek* are open late that week. Details are also posted at local *apotheeks*.

SPECIAL CLINICS

AIDS Helpline
(06 022 2220). **Open** 2-10pm Mon-Fri.
This is a free national helpline with English-language advice, information and counselling for those concerned about AIDS and related problems. AIDS is not a notifiable disease in The Netherlands and no one is repatriated for being HIV positive.

GG and GD VD Clinics
Groenburgwal 44, C (625 4127). Tram 9, 14. **Open** 8.30am-5pm Mon-Fri.
Van Oldenbarneveldtstraat 42, IW (625 4127). Tram 3, 12. **Open** 1-3pm Mon-Fri.
These clinics offer free and confidential advice and treatment on sex-related problems and sexually transmitted diseases. Phone first as there are various walk-in clinics with changing times and an appointments system. There are also men-and women-only clinics.

CONTRACEPTION & ABORTION

Condomerie Het Gulden Vlies
Warmoesstraat 141, C (627 4174). Tram 1,

2, 4, 5, 9, 13, 16, 17, 24, 25. **Open** 1-6pm Mon-Fri; noon-5pm Sat. **No credit cards.** Condoms for all occasions. There is a multitude of colours, flavours and shapes to choose from. *See p161* **Specialist Shops.**

Polikliniek Oosterpark
Oosterpark 59, OE (693 2151). Tram 3, 6. **Open** 9am-5pm Mon, Wed, Fri. Information and advice on contraception and abortion. Abortions are carried out although non-residents without appropriate insurance will be charged from f480 for the operation. The process is prompt and backed up by sympathetic counselling.

Rutgersstichting
Aletta Jacobshuis, Overtoom 323, IW (616 6222). Tram 16. **Open** by appointment 9am-4pm Mon-Fri. **Consultation** fee f27.50. **No credit cards.** Staff at this family planning centre can help non-Dutch visitors with prescriptions for contraceptive pills, morning-after pills and condoms, IUD fitting and cervical smear tests (with prompt results). Prescription costs vary; none are free.

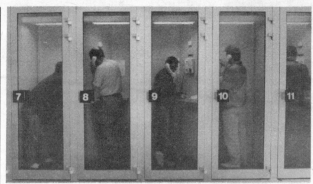

There are 21 phone booths at **Telehouse** *(see under* **Communications: Phone Centres***), one of which has wheelchair access. On completion of calls, payment can be made with cash, credit card or cheque. There are also a number of coin-operated and card phones. International dialling codes are clearly displayed and national and international directories are available. English-speaking staff will help with any problems. Telehouse is open 24 hours daily, and also offers fax and Telex services.*

HELP & INFORMATION

VVV (tourist office) *(626 6444).* **Open** 9am-5pm Mon-Sat. *See also p3* **Essential Information.**

Transport information: GVB *(627 2727).* **Open** 8am-11pm daily. *See also p3* **Essential Information.**

Time *(002; recorded in Dutch).*

Weather *(003; recorded in Dutch).*

HELP PHONELINES

Alcoholics Anonymous
(686 5142). **Open** 24-hour answerphone. Phone and leave a message on the answerphone and a counsellor will ring you back.

Crisis Helpline
(616 1666). **Open** 9am-3am Mon-Thur; 24 hours Fri-Sun.
A counselling service, comparable to the Samaritans in the UK and Lifeline in the USA, for anyone with emotional problems, run by volunteers. Occasionally they cannot understand much English, but keep trying as inevitably someone will be able to help you.

LEGAL & IMMIGRATION

Legal Advice Centre/Bureau Voor Rechtshulp
Spuistraat 10, C (626 4477). Tram 1, 2, 5. **Open** 9am-5.30pm Mon-Fri.
Funded by the Ministry of Justice, this centre has qualified lawyers who give free legal advice on matters of tenancy, social security, immigration (residence permits), insurance, consumer complaints and disputes with employers. Staff will assess whether they can help you and then refer you to the nearest of their four offices.

Legal Advice Line
(548 2611). **Open** 9am-5pm Mon-Thur; 9am-1pm Fri.
You can get free advice on this phoneline from student lawyers, who offer a relaxed, friendly service. They deal mainly with civil law queries and problems, but will occasionally be able to help with minor criminal law matters. Most speak excellent English.

MAIC
Hartenstraat 14, IW (624 0977). Tram 13, 14, 17. **Open** noon-5pm Mon-Fri.
A very central information service, offering legal advice and general information on things such as accommodation rights, permits and social benefits.

LIBRARIES

You'll need to present proof of residence in Amsterdam if you want to join a library (*bibliotheek*) and borrow books. However, in the public libraries (*openbare bibliotheek*) you can read books, newspapers and magazines, without membership or charge. For university libraries, *see page 196* **Students.**

American Institute
Jodenbreestraat 9, C (525 4380). Metro Nieuwmarkt. **Open** 10am-5.45pm Mon-Fri.

British Council Library
Keizersgracht 343, IW (622 3644). Tram 1, 2, 5, 7, 10. **Open** 10am-4.30pm Mon-Fri.

Centrale Bibliotheek
Prinsengracht 587, IW (623 5065). Tram 1, 2, 5, 7, 10. **Open** 1-9pm Mon; 10am-9pm Tue-Fri; 10am-5pm Sat.
Anyone is welcome to use this, the main public library, for reference purposes. There is a variety of English-language books and newspapers and a small coffee bar.
Wheelchair access with assistance.

LEFT LUGGAGE

There is a manned left-luggage counter at Schiphol Airport, open 7am-10.45pm daily. The charge is f3 per item per day. There are also lockers in the arrival and departure halls, costing f3 (small), f5 (large) per day. Inside Amsterdam, there are lockers at Centraal Station.

LOST PROPERTY

For the sake of insurance, it's wise to report **lost property** (*gevonden voorwerpen*) to the police as quickly as possible; for the central police phone number, *see below* **Police & Security.** Should you lose your passport, inform your embassy or consulate as well. If you lose anything at the Hoek van Holland ferry terminal or Schiphol Airport contact the company you're travelling with, as there are no central lost property depots at either of these points. To report lost credit cards, *see page 223* **Emergencies.**

Centraal Station
NS Lost Property Information, Stationsplein 15, C (557 8544). Tram 1, 2, 4, 5, 9, 13, 16, 17, 24, 25. **Open** 24 hours Mon-Sat; 7am-10pm Sun.
Items found on trains are kept here for ten days and then sent to *NS Afdeling Verloren Voorverpen, Concordiastraat 70, 3551 Utrecht.*

GVB Head Office
Prins Hendrikkade 108-114, C (551 4911).

Tram 1, 2, 4, 5, 9, 13, 16, 17, 24, 25. **Open** 9am-4pm Mon-Fri.
Report here for any item lost on a bus, Metro or tram. If reporting a loss from the previous day, phone after 2pm to allow time for the property to be sorted.

Police Lost Property
Waterlooplein 11, C (559 8005). Tram 9, 14. **Open** 11am-3.30pm Mon-Fri.
Try here for any items lost in the streets or parks. It's always advisable to report any loss to the police station in the same district as they generally hold items for a day or so before sending them on here.

PETS

To bring cats and dogs over the border into The Netherlands you must have rabies vaccination certificates. There are no restrictions for other common domestic pets, but it is wise to check before bringing them over. Protected animals and livestock cannot be brought into The Netherlands without clearance. Remember that you'll face your own country's regulations if returning with an animal.

Although rabies is mostly restricted to rural areas and wild animals, contracting the disease from a stray dog or cat is always possible. If you are bitten by an animal, it's always wise to check with a doctor.

If your animal gets sick while here, consult one of the numerous **veterinary surgeries** (*dierenartsen*) listed in the Yellow Pages (*Gouden Gids*), where you can also find details of cat and dog **kennels** (*dierenpensions*). In an emergency, you could even call out an **animal ambulance**.

De Poezenboot (The Cat Boat)
Moored outside Singel 40, C (625 8794/624 9160). Tram 1, 2, 4, 5, 9, 13, 16, 17, 24, 25. **Open** 1-2pm daily. **Admission** free, but donations encouraged.
On this craft around 40 stray or unwanted cats have found a home, and another 90 are kept on a farm outside the city. Despite unfair rumours to the contrary, the boat is perfectly clean and its inhabitants content. It can often be glimpsed from a canal cruise, but cat-lovers can take advantage of its central location and have a closer look. Cats cannot be purchased from the boat, nor can strays be dropped off without a contribution for upkeep and treatment. By neutering animals (funded by public contributions) the foundation strives to keep the numbers under control.

Dierenambulance Stichting Centrale
Hoogte Kadijk 61, IE (626 1058/24-hour emergency line 626 2121). **Open** for emergencies 24 hours daily.
If you take pity on an injured animal in the street, for f25 this unique ambulance service

will collect and treat it. Staff also attempt to find the owner or a new home. If it's your own animal, you must pay both the f25 plus the cost of treatment and boarding.

Dierenopvancentrum
Polderweg 12, OE (665 1888/93 5494). Tram 9. **Open** 10am-1pm, 2-4pm, Mon-Fri.
This particularly good animal hospital and sanctuary offers comprehensive veterinary services. You can also board cats and dogs here for between f8 and f18 per day.

POLICE & SECURITY

The low profile and 'hands-off' approach of Amsterdam's police force doubtless add to the city's relaxed atmosphere and reputation for tolerance. But don't be misled. Although the sight of officers on the beat is unusual, the police keep a keen eye on events, and can often be seen cruising in their cars.

The Dutch police are under no obligation to grant a phone call to those they detain (they are entitled to hold people for up to 6 hours for questioning if the alleged crime is not too serious, 24 hours for serious matters), but they will usually allow well-behaved foreigners to phone their consulate.

If you are a victim of theft or assault, report to the nearest police station. In the case of a serious incident or an emergency, phone the emergency switchboard on *0611* and ask for the police.

Hoofdbureau Van Politie (Police Headquarters)
Elandsgracht 117, IW (559 9111). Tram 7, 10. **Open** 24 hours daily.

Mugging (robbery with violence) and crimes against the person are rare in Amsterdam, but petty thievery is rife, especially in the red light district (*see page 26* **Amsterdam by Area**). Tourists are particularly vulnerable to pickpocketing, handbag snatching, bike theft and theft from cars. Be aware of these dangers and adopt as many of the following **basic precautions** as possible:

Don't wear valuable watches and jewellery, and don't leave them in your car. Deposit valuables in your hotel's safe or in a locker in dormitories and campsites.
Don't flash your money or credit cards around. Don't leave your purse on a restaurant or shop counter while paying.
Keep your wallet or purse out of sight and never in your back pocket. Ensure handbags are securely closed, with your purse at the bottom of the bag.

Keep traveller's cheques in a separate place to their counterfoils and your passport.
Don't wear your bag on one shoulder, or leave it or your coat unattended, nor beside, under or on the back of your chair; hook the bag's handle round the chairleg.
Avoid wandering aimlessly on your own in parks, the red light district, particularly around Zeedijk, or the side streets off Albert Cuypstraat, especially after dark.

LOCKSMITHS

Amsterdam Security Center
Prinsengracht 1097, IS (626 9143). Tram 4. **Open** for emergencies 24 hours daily. **Credit** AmEx.
The cost of calling a locksmith varies depending on area. To get into a car will between f65 and f85; into a house f85 to f125. After midnight prices rise and you can expect to pay a minimum of f135. Someone will be with you within the hour.

RELIGION

Catholic
St John and St Ursula *Begijnhof 30, C (622 1918). Tram 1, 2, 5, 4, 16, 24, 25.* **Open** 10am-6pm Mon-Sat. **Services** Dutch 8am, 9am, Mon-Fri; 9am Sat; *English* 12.15pm Sun; *French* 11.15am Sun; *German* 6pm Sun.
A small and serene chapel in the peaceful Begijnhof.

Papegaai *Kalverstraat 220, C (623 1889). Tram 4, 9, 14, 16, 24, 25.* **Open** 10am-6pm Mon-Sat. **Service** Latin 10.30am Sun.
The church is open during the week for *een kwatier voor God*, fifteen minutes with God. Many escape the bustle of Kalverstraat for a moment of private prayer in what was once, following the Reformation, a clandestine church.

Christian Scientist
First Church of Christ Scientist *Richard Wagnerstraat 32, OS (662 7438). Tram 5, 24.* **Services** Dutch 10am Sun; *English* 8pm Wed; 11.15am Sun.

Dutch Reformed Church
Oudekerk *Oudekerksplein 23, C (625 8284). Tram 4, 9, 16, 24, 25.* **Open** 15 Apr-15 Sept 11am-5pm Mon-Sat; 16 Sept-14 Apr 1-5pm Mon-Sat. **Services** Dutch 11am Sun.
This medieval church is the oldest monument in Amsterdam (*see p13* **Sightseeing**).

Westerkerk *Prinsengracht 281, IW (624 7783). Tram 13, 14, 17.* **Open** 10am-4pm Mon-Sat. **Services** Dutch 11am Sun.
A notable feature here is the ornate organ, installed in 1680 and still in use today. *See also p13* **Sightseeing**.

Episcopal Church
English Episcopal Church *Groenburgwal 42, C (624 8877). Tram 9, 14.* **Open** for services only. **Services** English 10.30am, 7.30pm, Sun.

Jewish
Liberal Jewish Community Amsterdam *Jacob Soetendorpstraat 8, OS (642 3562).*

Tram 4. **Open** *office* 9am-5pm Mon-Thur;
9am-3pm Fri. **Services** 8pm Fri; 10am Sat.
Times may vary so phone first to check.

Orthodox Jewish Community
Amsterdam *PO Box 7967, Van der
Boechorstraat 26, 1008 AD; OS (646 0046).
Bus 23, 65, 173*. **Open** 9am-5pm Mon-Sat;
9am-3pm Fri.
Information on orthodox synagogues and
Jewish facilities in Amsterdam. Phone first
for an appointment.

Moslem
THAIBA Islamic Cultural Centre
*Kraaiennest 125, OS (698 2526). Bus 120,
126, 137/Metro Gaasperplas*. **Prayer**
1.30pm, 2.30pm, daily.
Times vary, so phone for details of prayer
times and cultural activities.

Quaker
Religious Genootsch der Vrienden
*Vossiusstraat 20, OS (679 4238). Tram 1, 2,
5, 6, 7, 10*. **Open** for services only. **Service**
10.30am Sun.

Reformed Church
English Reformed Church *Begijnhof 48,
C (624 9665). Tram 1, 2, 5*. **Open** *May-Sept*
2-4pm Mon-Fri. **Services** *English* 10.30am
Sun; *Dutch* 7pm Sun.
The main place of worship for the English
speaking community in Amsterdam. The
church is believed to have been built in
1392, and was handed over to English-
speaking Presbyterians in 1607. *See also*
p130 **Music: Classical & Opera.**

Russian Orthodox
St Nicolaas *Utrechtsedwarstraat 5, OS
(622 5385). Tram 4*. **Open** for services
only. **Services** 5.30pm Sat, 10.30am Sun.
Services on the first and third weekends of
the month are mainly in Slavonic languages, mainly Dutch on the other
weekends. There is a mixed nationality
congregation.

Salvation Army
National Headquarters *Damstraat 15, C
(624 1703). Tram 4, 9, 16, 24, 25*. **Open**
9am-5.30pm Mon-Fri.
Phone or drop in for information on
Salvation Army Citadels in Amsterdam. The
office is due to move in October 1991; at
time of writing no new address was available.

WASHING & CLEANING

BATHS & SHOWERS

Opening times for the showers and
baths (*badhuis*) listed below tend to
fluctuate, so phone before setting
out.

Fronemanstraat 3
OE (665 0811). Tram 9. **Open** 12.30pm-
7am Mon; 10am-1.30pm, 4-7pm, Tue;
10am-4.30pm Wed, Thur; 12.30-6pm Fri.
Cost f2.50 per shower.
Bring your own towel.

Marnixbad
*Marnixplein 5-9, OS (625 4843). Tram 3,
10*. **Open** 5-7.30pm Mon; 10am-5.30pm Tue,
Thur, Sat; 12.30-7.30pm Wed, Fri. **Cost** f2
per shower; f2.50 per bath.
This is the best place in town for a wash;
there's a bar to relax in afterwards, and towels can be hired.

De Warme Waterstaal Sticht
*Da Costakade 200, OW (612 5946). Tram 3,
7, 12, 17*. **Open** 9am-9pm Tue; 10am-5pm
Sat. **Cost** f2.50 per shower; f4.50 per bath.
Take your towel with you.

LAUNDERETTES

A comprehensive list of launderettes
(*wassalons*) can be found in the
Yellow Pages (*Gouden Gids*). The
reliable Clean Brothers chain is
listed in **Services** (*page 165*), as are
dry-cleaners.

TRAVEL & DRIVING

For details of rail travel, *see page 200*
Beyond Amsterdam.

DRIVING & BREAKDOWN

It's advisable to join a **national**
motoring organization before arriving in The Netherlands. These provide international assistance
booklets, which not only explain
what to do in the event of a break-
down in Europe, but also offer
general information on continental
motoring. To drive in The
Netherlands you'll need a valid
national driving licence, although the
Dutch motoring club, **ANWB** (*see
below*) and many car hire firms
favour an **international driving**
licence, available from branches of
national motoring organizations. In
Britain, take your full licence, £3 and
a passport photo to a branch of the
AA or RAC and they will process it in
minutes.

Major roads are usually well-maintained and clearly sign-posted.
Motorways (which have traffic
lights) are labelled 'A'; major roads
'N'; and European routes 'E'.

Some points to note: the Dutch
drive on the right; drivers and front-
seat passengers must always wear
seatbelts; speed limits are 50kmh
(31mph) within cities, 80kmh
(50mph) outside, and 120kmh
(75mph) on motorways; be wary of
cyclists; trams will not give way to
cars in most circumstances.

Amsterdam's **wheel-clamp** *(wielklem) teams are swift to act and show little
mercy. If you outstay your allotted time at a meter (usually about f3 per hour)
you'll be clamped, and while the charge for removal is relatively low, there's a
high price to pay in terms of wasted time and inconvenience. A yellow sticker on
the windscreen informs you where to go to pay the fine – about f3 for every hour
in excess. Once you've paid the fine you must return to the car and wait for the
Traffic Police – information on 627 5866 or 523 3115 – to remove the clamp.
Happily, this service is also prompt. If you park illegally (double-parking, for
instance), your car will almost certainly be towed away. It'll cost at least f200 to
reclaim it from the pound (Oostelijke Handelskade 2, east of Centraal Station;
open 24 hours daily). Take your passport and enough cash or personal cheques to
pay the hefty fine. Credit cards are not accepted. For details of car parks in
central Amsterdam, see under* **Travel & Driving: Parking & Petrol.**

To bring your car into The Netherlands you'll need an international identification disk; a registration certificate; proof of the vehicle having passed a road safety test in its country of origin; and insurance documents.

Royal Dutch Touring Club (ANWB)

Museumplein 5, OS (673 0844; 24-hour emergency line 06 0888). Tram 2, 3, 5, 12, 16. **Open** 8.45am-4.45pm Mon-Fri; 8.45am-noon Sat. **Credit** AmEx, DC, foreign currency, MC, TC, V.

If you haven't already joined a motoring organization, you can enrol here for f86.25, which covers the cost of assistance should your vehicle break down. It will cost you more if you wait until you need the emergency services. If you're a member of a foreign motoring organization, you're entitled to free help providing you can present membership documents. You may find emergency crews don't accept credit cards or cheques at the scene; be sure to ascertain the method of payment when you phone.

Spare parts

Bergam Automaterialen *Kalfjeslaan 25, Amstelveen, OS (643 0321). Bus 49, 64, 66, 67, 149.* **Open** 8.30am-6pm Mon-Fri; 9am-4pm Sat. **No credit cards.**

Brezan Automaterialen *Lutmastraat 113, OS (679 4750). Tram 12, 25.* **Open** 8.30am-5.30pm Mon-Fri; 9am-4pm Sat. **No credit cards.**

Dick's Car Clinic *Groenmarktkade 5, OW (626 3217). Tram 3.* **Open** 8am-5.30pm Mon-Fri. **No credit cards.**

If you think you can fix it yourself, try one of these. Phone first to check they've got the part you need.

PARKING & PETROL

Parking space is at a premium in central Amsterdam – you're unlikely to find space on the streets. Illegally parked cars get clamped or towed away (*see page 227* **picture and caption**). There are no 24-hour car parks (*parkeren*, indicated by a white 'P' on a blue square), but after 7pm you can park at meters for free, and after midnight parking in uncovered car parks is also free. Below we list a selection of central car parks where you're more likely to find a space during peak times.

De Bijenkoorf *Beursplein, Damrak, C.* **Open** 9am-midnight daily. **Admission** f1.25 first half hour; f2.25 per half hour following.

Europarking *Marnixstraat 250, IW (623 6664).* **Open** 6.30am-12.30am Mon-Thur; 6.30am-1.30am Fri, Sat; 7am-12.30am Sun. **Admission** f1.75 per hour; f15 for 24 hours.

Museumplein (uncovered), *OS (671 6418).* **Open** 8am-midnight daily.

Admission f3 per hour Mon-Sat; free Sun.

Prinsengracht 540-542 *IS (625 9852).* **Open** 7.30am-4pm Mon-Wed; 7.30am-5pm Thur; 7.30am-6pm Fri, Sat. **Admission** f2.50 per hour.

In the city limits the main **24-hour petrol stations** (*benzinestation*) are at:

Gooiseweg 10, 11, *OE*
Sarphatistraat 225, *IE*
Marnixstraat 250, *IW*
Spaarndammerdijk 218, *OW*

CAR HIRE

Dutch car hire (*auto-verhuur*) companies generally expect at least one year's driving experience and will want to see a valid national driving licence and passport. Unless stated otherwise, each company will require a deposit through an international credit card, and you'll need to be over 21. International companies are considerably more expensive than local ones. Other firms are listed in the Yellow Pages (*Gouden Gids*). Prices given below are for the hire of the cheapest car available at the company office at time of writing, not including insurance.

Adam's Rent-a-Car

Nassaukade 344-347, OW (685 0111). Tram 7, 10, 17. **Open** 8am-9pm Mon-Sat. **Credit** AmEx, DC, MC, V.

If you're over 18, you can hire a car from Adam's with unlimited mileage from f50 per day.

Avis

Nassaukade 380, OW (683 6061). Tram 10. **Open** 7.30am-9pm Mon-Sat; 7.30am-6pm Sun. **Credit** AmEx, DC, MC, TC, V.

Prices start at f219 per day, including unlimited mileage and insurance.

Budget

Overtoom 121, OW (612 6066). Tram 1, 6. **Open** 7.30am-7pm Mon-Fri; 8am-4pm Sat; 9am-1pm Sun. **Credit** AmEx, DC, MC, V.

Hire costs start at f150 per day, unlimited mileage and insurance included. You'll need a credit card to pay the deposit plus passport as ID, and you must be over 23.

Diks

Van Ostadestraat 278-280, OS (662 3366). Tram 3, 4. **Open** 8am-7.30pm Mon-Sat; 9am-12.30pm, 8-10pm, Sun. **Credit** AmEx, DC, MC, V.

There's no minimum age restriction to hire a car here; prices start at f37 per day plus 37c per km.

Europcar

Overtoom 51-53, OW (618 4595). Tram 1, 6. **Open** 7.30am-6pm Mon-Thur; 7.30am-6.30pm Fri; 8am-4pm Sat; 8am-noon Sun. **Credit** AmEx, DC, MC, V.

Hire charges rise from f83 per day, inclusive of unlimited mileage.

Hertz

Overtoom 85 OW (612 2441). Tram 1, 6. **Open** 8am-6pm Mon-Fri; 8am-4pm Sat; 9am-2pm Sun. **Credit** AmEx, DC, MC, £$TC, V.

Prices start at f271 per day, including unlimited mileage and insurance.

Kasper and Lotte

Van Ostadestraat 234-236, OS (671 0733). Tram 3, 4. **Open** 8am-8pm Mon-Sat; 9am-1pm, 9-11pm, Sun. **Credit** AmEx, DC, MC, V.

Including unlimited mileage and insurance, prices start at f119 per day.

DISCOUNT TRAVEL

Budget Air

Rokin 34, C (627 1251). Tram 4, 9, 16, 24, 25. **Open** 9.30am-5.30pm Mon-Fri; 10am-4pm Sat. **Credit** AmEx, DC, MC, V.

Low-cost fares to world-wide destinations with discounts for students, young people and senior citizens.

Budget Bus

Rokin 10, C (627 5151). Tram 4, 9, 14, 16, 24, 25. **Open** 9.30am-5.30pm Mon-Fri; 10am-4pm Sat. **Credit** MC, V.

This agency sells bus tickets for Europe and Morocco, with discounts for students.

NBBS

Dam 17, C (620 5071). Tram 1, 2, 4, 5, 13, 14, 16, 17, 24, 25/Leidsestraat 53, IS (638 1736). Tram 1, 2, 5. **Both open** 9am-6pm Mon-Fri; 9am-5pm Sat. **Credit** AmEx, DC, MC, V.

Low cost flights to world-wide destinations, with discount travel for students and young people, and a Eurotrain discount for under-26s.

Travel Express

Rokin 38, C (626 4434). Tram 4, 9, 14, 16, 24, 25. **Open** 9.30am-5.30pm Mon-Fri; 9.30am-4pm Sat. **Credit** AmEx, MC, V.

Travel Express arrange bus travel to European destinations. There are also 'bike' buses – buses with space allocated for bicycles – to some locations, package trips to London by air and flights to Paris.

HITCH-HIKING

There is no central co-ordinating agency to put hitch-hikers in touch with drivers – just stick out your thumb and wait. Dutch drivers are fairly good about picking people up. Certain spots are well known as good places to start a journey out of Amsterdam:

Direction The Hague and Rotterdam: at the access to the motorway, between RAI rail station (terminus of tram 4) and the RAI congress building on Europa Boulevard.
Direction Utrecht: by the corner of Rijnstraat and President Kennedylaan (terminus of tram 25).
Direction Arnhem and Germany: Gooise Weg, close to Amstel rail station.

Index

If page numbers after an entry are not in numerical order, the first number given is the principal entry.

Written, edited and designed by Time Out Publications Limited,
Curtain House, 134-146 Curtain Road, London EC2A 3AR (Tel 071
729 5959/Fax 071 729 7266).

Editorial
Senior Managing Editor Peter Fiennes
Managing Editor Marion Moisy
Editor Ruth Jarvis
Consultant Editor Ann Campbell-Lord
Assistant Editor Philip Cornwel-Smith
Listings Editor Edoardo Albert
Researcher/Writer Julie Sinclair-Day
Copy Editor Philip Harriss

Design
Art Director Kirk Teasdale
Art Editor Iain Murray
Camera Work Joseph Roberts
Artwork Warren Beeby
Picture Editor Tricia de Courcy Ling

Advertising
Sales Director Mark Phillips
Group Advertising Sales Director Lesley Gill
Sales Executives Nana Ocran, Jonathan Cash, Kim Vernon
Advertising Sales in Amsterdam were handled by VVV (Amsterdam
Tourist Office), Hans Dominicus, Louis Zwaan

Administration
Publisher Tony Elliott
Managing Director Adele Carmichael
Financial Director Kevin Ellis
Company Accountant Suzanne Doyle
Accounts Assistants Sonia Jackson, Dawn Hickey

Production Manager Su Small

Features in this guide were written and researched by: Introduction
Ailsa Camm. Essential Information Julie Sinclair-Day. Sightseeing Abi
Daruvalla; additional research Julie Sinclair-Day; Collapsing Houses, Hofjes and
Houseboats Jon and Sara Henley. Amsterdam by Area Leidseplein Michael
Cooper; The Museum Quarter Bambi Bogert; The Red Light District Robin
Pascoe; The Jordaan Jonette Stabbert; Waterlooplein & The Plantage Robin
Pascoe; De Pijp Michael Cooper; The Port David Post. Canals Jon Henley.
Amsterdam by Season Abi Daruvalla. Accommodation Julie Sinclair-Day.
Early History Sophie Marshall. War & Reformation Sophie Marshall. The
Golden Age Sophie Marshall. Decline & Fall Sophie Marshall. Between
the Occupations Sophie Marshall; The Amsterdam School Philip Cornwel-
Smith. World War II Kees Neefjes. Post-war Mark Fuller. Amsterdam
Today Sara and Jon Henley. Green Issues Sara Henley. Cafés & Bars Jon
Henley. Museums Judi Seebus. Galleries Mari Shields. Dance Ariejan
Korteweg. Film Chris Fuller. Theatre Bert Verheij. Music: Classical &
Opera Rose Anne Hamilton; Carillons Robert Perry. Music: Rock, Folk &
Jazz Maz Weston. Night-clubs Paul Jay. Media Sara Henley. Shopping:
Food & Drink Jonette Stabbert. Shopping Around Jonette Stabbert.
Specialist Shops Lyn Ritchie. Services Jonette Stabbert. Gay Amsterdam
Kees Neefjes. Women's Amsterdam Marieke Sjerps. Children & Parents
Marieke Sjerps. Business Jon Henley; additional research Julie Sinclair-Day.
Students Kees Neefjes. Sport & Fitness Jeroen van den Berg. Beyond
Amsterdam Ann Campbell-Lord; Crossing the Border Ailsa Camm.
Excursions in Holland Ann Campbell-Lord and Lyn Ritchie. The Randstad
Ailsa Camm. The Provinces Ailsa Camm; Overijssel Eric Nicholls. Survival
Julie Sinclair-Day.

The Editors would like to thank the following people and organizations for
help and information:
Amsterdam VVV (with special thanks to Jane Kat-Honcoop, Documentation
Department); Netherlands Board of Tourism, London Branch; Penguin
Books (with special thanks to Peter van Gorsel, Penguin Netherlands).

Photographs by Mark Kohn except for:

pages v & 1 Collections/Brian Shuel; page 37 Kippa International Press &
Photo Agency; page 57 courtesy of The Amstelkring Museum; page 65
courtesy of The Verzetsmuseum Amsterdam; page 76 courtesy of
Provinciaal Electriciteitsbedrijf Van Noord-Holland; page 105 courtesy of
The Amsterdams Historisch Museum; page 120 Hans Gerritsen; page 127
courtesy of The Stalhouderij Theatre Company; page 128 courtesy of The
Netherlands Theatre Institute; page 177 Fotobureau't Sticht B.V/Jaap J
Herschel; pages 199, 204, 205, 207, 209, 211, 212, 214, 215, 217-
219 courtesy of The Netherlands Board of Tourism, London; page 210
courtesy of Frans Halsmuseum.